The Cambridge Illustrated History of

THE MIDDLE AGES

This volume forms the third part of one of the finest general introductions to the medieval world of recent times. Lavishly illustrated, with numerous accompanying maps and charts, each of the three volumes presents a synthesis of scholarly research and interpretation, translated from the original French and revised thoroughly for an English speaking readership.

Volume III covers the close of the Middle Ages, an era of crisis, plague, famine and civil strife, and yet also – towards its end – of vigorous economic and colonial expansion, intellectual renewal and religious reformation. Full coverage is given not only to Western Europe, but also to the Byzantine and Islamic worlds, whose artistic heritage is displayed in several of the colour plates. A bibliography is appended as an aid to further study, whether by the general reader or by teachers and students of the period.

The two further volumes, on 350–950 and on 950–1250, are also available. *The Cambridge Illustrated History of the Middle Ages* is also sold as a three-volume boxed set.

The Cambridge Illustrated History of

THE MIDDLE AGES

III   1250–1520

Edited by
ROBERT FOSSIER

Translated by
SARAH HANBURY TENISON

PUBLISHED BY THE PRESS SYNDICATE OF THE UNIVERSITY OF CAMBRIDGE
The Pitt Building, Trumpington Street, Cambridge CB2 1RP, United Kingdom
40 West 20th Street, New York, NY 10011–4211, USA
10 Stamford Road, Oakleigh, Melbourne 3166, Australia

Originally published in French as *Le Moyen Age. 3. Le Temps
des Crises 1250–1520* by Armand Colin, 103, boulevard Saint-
Michel, Paris, 1983 and © Armand Colin Editeur, Paris, 1983

First published in English by Cambridge University Press, 1986, as
The Middle Ages III. An Illustrated History, 1250–1520.

Reprinted 1987, 1997

English translation © Cambridge University Press 1986

Printed in Great Britain at the University Press, Cambridge

British Library cataloguing in publication data

The Cambridge Illustrated History of the Middle Ages
III: 1250–1520
1. Europe–History–476–1492   2. Europe–
History–1492–1517
I. Fossier, Robert   II. Le Moyen Age, English
940.1'7   D202

Library of Congress cataloguing in publication data

Moyen Age (Armand Colin Firm). English.
The Cambridge Illustrated History of the Middle Ages.
Translation of: Le Moyen Age.
Bibliography: v. 3. p.
Includes index.
Contents:–3. 1250–1520.
I. Civilization, Medieval. I. Fossier, Robert,
II. Title.

CB351.M7813 1986   909.07   85-21268

ISBN 0 521 26644 0 (v. I)
ISBN 0 521 26645 9 (v. II)
ISBN 0 521 26646 7 (v. III)
ISBN 0 521 59078 7 (3-volume boxed set)

SE

Contents

Contents

Colour Plates

Acknowledgements

a) Photographic Agencies

Atlas Photo pp. 108, 180, 267, 439

Bulloz pp. 9, 32, 82, 415, 501, 517 (upper right)

Michel Cabaud pp. 183, 427, 450

Serge Chirol pp. 13, 121, 128

Gérard Degeorge pp. 217, 275

A. Dufau/Anne Leclerc pp. 271, 377, 378

Gérard Dufresne p. 255

Edimedia 'Archives Snark' pp. 57, 431

Foto Enit pp. 23, 174

Giraudon pp. 10, 19, 54, 72, 79, 86, 92, 110, 143, 152, 155, 175, 396, 404, 407, 411 left, 418 left, 420, 434 right, 444, 456 right, 460, 464, 467, 505, 508 right, 517 lower and upper left, 519

Alinari–Giraudon p. 135

Anderson Giraudon p. 223

Lauros–Giraudon pp. 6, 30, 114, 187 lower, 263, 475 right, 508 left, 513

Ampliaciones Reproducciones Mas Freneria pp. 12, 20 right, 142, 368, 369, 492

Nicolaidis pp. 209, 229, 245, 249, 253

Office du Livre S.A., Fribourg pp. 280, 296

Photo Archives–Editions Arthaud pp. 235

Phototheque Armand–Colin pp. 9, 20 left, 26 left and right, 27, 41, 43, 47, 72 upper left, 83 left, 94 left, 103, 106, 124, 140, 148, 154, 161, 165, 177, 181, 190, 199, 211, 269, 331, 345, 350, 377 left, 381, 384, 401, 410, 418, 423, 424, 427 right, 447, 448, 475 left, 479, 489, 496 right, 498, 503

Rapho pp. 75, 186, 364

Roger–Viollet pp. 64, 151, 192, 202, 259, 261, 289, 299, 309, 339, 353, 358, 366, 390, 463

Scala pp. 171, 316, 511, 512

Turkish Tourist Information Office pp. 239, 285, 293, 319, 322, 326, 335, 341

Jean Dieuzaide Photographe (photos Yan) pp. 25, 67

b) Scholarly Institutions

Athens, Naval Museum of Greece p. 197
Berlin, Archiv für Kunst und Geschichte p. 65
Besançon, Bibliothèque Municipale pp. 61, 126
Brussels, Bibliothèque Royale p. 94
Cambridge, University of Cambridge Committee for Aerial Photography p. 77
Chambéry, Musée Municipale p. 3
Konstanz, Rosgartenmuseum pp. 133, 147
London, The British Library pp. 83 lower, 94 lower, 101 lower, 138, 167, 407 left, 416, 419, 451
London, The Mansell Collection p. 58
Munich, Bayerische Staatsgemäldesammlungen p. 7
New York, The Metropolitan Museum of Art p. 522
Oxford, The Bodleian Library p. 83 left
Oxford, New College Library, p. 159
Paris, Bibliothèque Municipale pp. 88, 214, 226, 227, 406, 496
Paris, Collection de l'Ecole des Hautes Etudes en Sciences Sociales p. 218
Paris, Réunion des Musées Nationaux pp. 33, 45, 60, 118, 130, 149, 187, 440
Rome, Biblioteca Apostolica Vaticana p. 411 right
Rouen, Bibliothèque Municipale p. 434 left
Vienna, Bildarchiv Österreichische Nationalbibliothek p. 83 right
Vienna, Kunsthistorisches Museum p. 45

COLOUR PLATES (between pages 174 and 175 and 342 and 343)

Atlas Photo
Edimedia 'Archives Snark'
Explorer
Giraudon
Photothèque André Held/J. Ziolo
Office du Livre S.A., Fribourg
Metropolitan Museum of Art, New York
Oronoz/J. Ziolo
Rapho
Réunion des Musées Nationaux
Scala Istituto Fotografico Editoriale plates

Glossary

Only those terms have been retained in the glossary which have appeared several times without being explained. Familiar terms or those easily found in a dictionary have been eliminated.

ACADEMY: from the name of the Athenian gardens where first Socrates and then Plato held their discussions; in *Quattrocento* Italy the word Academy designated a literary circle.

ACT OF HABITATION: when a lord grants immigrants or returning peasants lands exempted from certain impositions and tied houses.

AKHI: a pious group in Turkish society whose members were often engaged in the same profession.

AKRITES: garrison soldiers on the frontiers of Byzantium.

AMT: a guild organisation in the Empire; by extension, the quarter in which it was exercised.

ANNATES: annual payments to the Holy See incumbent on the holder of an ecclesiastical benefice on taking possession of it.

APPANAGE: the concession by a king or a prince to a member of his family, his son or brother, of a land and its attached military ban; in principle, this land reverted to the patrimony when there was no heir. It was often implemented to allow a territory to be taken in hand prior to its definite attachment to the patrimony, for instance to the royal domain.

ARBALEST: a weapon designed to project a bolt by releasing a metal spring. Its precision and impact (killing at 200 metres) were redoubted and it was considered ignoble by the cavalry. Its weight and unwieldiness meant that each weapon had to be manned by two specialists.

ARTS, LIBERAL: the elements of the academic programme of Antiquity and the Middle Ages: rhetoric, grammar, dialectics (*trivium*), and geometry, arithmetic, astronomy and music (*quadrivium*).

AVARITIA: the lack of moral charity (rather than avarice in its more limited sense). It competes with SUPERBIA for first place in the list of mortal sins.

BAIL, BAILEY: an adult who takes charge of a minor, and the function itself. By extension it was used in the South of France to designate the guild representatives in a town corporation. Another meaning: a castle courtyard.

BEGARDS: Christians who adopted mysticism, living in lay and sometimes itinerant communities, and who succoured the poor. They were suspected by the Church because they did not have a recognised Rule.

BENEFICE: (ecclesiastical): every office, parochial or otherwise, assigned to a cleric in the body of the Church.

BEY; BEYLIK; BEYLERBEY: a Turkish tribal chieftain, and later a local representative of the Ottoman Sultan's authority; the territory he commanded; a top-ranking Bey commanding several Beyliks.

BILL: a regulation, and even a law, issued by the English sovereign.

BOGOMILS: a Bulgarian sect which repudiated the doctrine of Transubstantiation.

BOIARS: see BOYARDS

BOOK OF COPYHOLDERS: a book in which the names of those who held land by charter (copy) in English manors, were written; a depressed social statute.

BOSC: the wood, in fact all the land which was not ploughed or lying fallow.

BOURSE: originally a trading entrepot in western Europe; by extension the place for drawing up commercial transactions over samples, and then for changing money, and finally a bank.

BOUVEROT: found among the Cistercians, and later outside their Order, meaning all the land, cultivated or planted with fruit trees, surrounding one of their granges or farms.

BOYARDS, BOIARS: the Hungarian or Bulgarian landed nobility.

BRASSIERS: those whose only resource is their hands; a depressed legal status; found mostly in the countryside.

BREUIL: the enclosed part of the BOSC, reserved for the lord's hunting.

BULL: a lead or gold seal (chrysobull) used to authenticate certain pontifical and imperial acts; the term has been extended to include the act.

CADASTER, CATASTO: an estate book comprising in principle a list of the parts of a real estate, their location, the expenses bearing on them, and the list of individuals living in them; used for assessing ground rents.

CALIMALA: a road in Florence in the Roman town level with the Palazzo della Signoria, where the merchants and money changers used to gather; the 'art' they practised (long distance sales and transport) and then their accounting methods, were given the name of the road; known as the *arte di Calimala*.

CANTONING: in a forest, the enclosure of one or several parts for restocking.

CANZONE: an Italian literary form, lyrical in style, and often accompanied by polyphonic music.

CARRAQUE: a cargo ship, generally Genoese, capable of carrying freights of 1,000 tonnes.

CASANE: Piedmontese and Lombard houses specialising in loans and money changing.

CATASTO: see CADASTER

CENSES: a big farm in northern France.

CEPHALE: a rural district in Byzantium.

CHRYSOBULL: a legal act or privilege in Byzantium, with a golden bull.

CLOTHIER: an English businessman, and eventual owner of flocks, who dealt in wool, either selling it or getting it spun and woven.

COLLOQUIA: gatherings, often clandestine, of both workers in the guilds and those not inscribed in any trade.

CONCORDAT: a term generally used to mean an agreement between the Papacy and a State over the problems of ecclesiastical discipline and hierarchy.

CONDOTTIERE: a military leader who has contracted (*condotta*) mercenaries under his command.

COQ: a sixteenth-century term for a village notable.

CORPO: the capital deposited in an Italian company (generally family funds).

COTTAGER, COTTAR: an English peasant driven onto a patch of poor land, often on the fringes of the manor, and obliged to render frequent and heavy labour services.

CUEILLOIR: a booklet or roll, in which a tallage receiver records the names of those liable and their payments.

CURIA: any State court anywhere, but has come to mean the Papal Court.

DANSE MACABRE: a very popular iconographical theme from the end of the fifteenth century, representing Death dragging all the states of the world in an endless round dance. The origin of the word macabre is uncertain; either Macabré, the name of a painter of the time, or the Biblical Maccabeus.

DAUPHIN: title borne by certain princes of the Franco–Provençal region, especially by the prince of the 'Dauphiné'; when this region was annexed to the French crown, the local representatives were promised that the heir to the throne would carry this title until his accession to power.

DECIMA: one tenth of the income of a church raised by the king, with the authorisation of the Pope, to contribute in principle towards the expense of his religious commitments; crusades, pilgrimages etc. It gradually became a regular tax on the clergy.

DEME: a rural or urban area in Byzantium.

DISPUTATIO: a favourite scholastic exercise, in which Master and students, and Masters among themselves, engage in public and erudite discussions on a text or a theme generally selected beforehand.

DISTRAINTS: when the Pope reserves the right to appoint a beneficiary to certain vacant benefices and takes a cut of part of their revenues.

DIWAN: a Persian term adopted by the Arabs, and then the Turks, to designate the tax registers, which came to mean the offices of public administration and finally the ruler's council.

DOMINANTE: the metropolis; in Venice, this designated both the town when she intervened in her overseas possessions, and her rights over them.

ÉCHELLE: anchoring point along a commercial sea route; these were basically fixed in the ports of Syria and Palestine; *échelles du Levant*.

EMPHYTEOSIS: a long-term lease (generally 99 years) conferring important rights over the land on the lessee, on condition that he improved the property.

ENCLOSURES: the phenomenon by which arable land is enclosed, generally in order to turn it into pasture.

ENTRÉES, ROYAL: the feasts accompanying the first *entrée* of a newly crowned king into a town; in fact this event could recur several times, involving the town in very heavy expenses, as well as being the occasion for lavish and lengthy performances (see MYSTERY PLAYS).

FARM: a short-term, renewable lease, in which the lessee contracts to pay a fixed lump sum to cover all his obligations. In the case of an office, public or otherwise, the farmer pays the anticipated revenues of the office and recoups his losses from his administration of the farm.

FIQH: Jurisprudence in Islamic Law.

FISCUS: at the end of the Middle Ages, this term assumed its present meaning of the sum of financial exactions, as opposed to its old meaning of the public property.

FONDACO: see FUNDUQ

FOREST: in England, this designated royal land regardless of its vegetation.

'FOUAGE': HEARTHTAX, supposed in principle to be an extraordinary levy.

FRANC ARCHER: a foot soldier trained in the use of the bow; he formed a sort of territorial force, exempt when called up from paying the *taille*, hence the name *franc* (free).

FRÉRÈCHES: administration and management of a property by brothers.

FULLER: a worker who treads woolen cloths in a bath of dye; this was exhausting and underpaid work, needing no qualifications.

FUNDUQ, FONDACO: a covered market, in principle reserved for a group of merchants foreign to the country or the town; used in the East as well as in Italy.

FUSTIAN: a weaving technique, possibly from the East, which involves mingling cotton with silk, or with woollen threads.

FUTUWWA: an urban initiation society in Islam; a political power, often inspired by Shiite thought and liable to be involved with religious disturbances in the towns.

FYRD: the militia of free men in Saxon England.

GABELLE: a tax raised on the sale of salt, controlled by royal officials in charge of *greniers* in which the salt was stored.

GALLICANISM: the attitude of French rulers and prelates towards the Holy See, illustrating their tendency to distance themselves from disciplinary regulations emanating from Rome. Not a medieval term.

GÄRTNER: a German peasant of low degree, similar to the English cottar.

GASAILLE: a lease for a flock of sheep or a contract between a sheep farmer and a burgher, by which the farmer rents his animals back after selling them to the latter, splitting the profits along very variable lines. A form of agricultural loan.

GASTE: deserted land.

GENTILEZZA: meaning *courtoisie* in Italy, where it tended to acquire a more urban and 'bourgeois' meaning.

GESTA DEI PER FRANCOS: an expression employed in accounts of the Crusades, meaning that by their deeds in the Holy Land the Europeans were performing the will of God.

GEWERKE: a trade or guild in Germany.

GHAZI: a pious confraternity among the Turks.

GHIBELLINES: in the Italian towns, they were the partisans of foreign interventions to restore order; they gradually fell from power because they were suspected of being Imperial agents.

GÎTE: a tax levied to pay for the accommodation of the ruler's followers or agents.

GLEANING: when the pigs are sent into the forest to forage; a tax was levied on this occasion.

GOTHIC: a term of disparagement thought up in fifteenth-century Italy to designate Medieval architecture and script.

GRANDEES: the very great landed proprietors of the Castillian Mesta.

GRIOTS: the poets, genealogists, chronologists of black African society who were both consulted and despised; they did not possess magic powers.

GUELFS: in the Italian towns, they were the partisans of urban autonomy, with the Whites in favour of Papal control and the Blacks wanting more independence from Rome.

HABEAS CORPUS: the famous English Bill of 1679, which granted every man the right to a legal trial before being imprisoned.

HALLIER: a merchant who lends tools or livestock to a peasant in financial difficulty, in exhange for buying part of the produce in advance at a low price; a form of credit.

HANBALITES: the partisans of Ibn Hanbal, a Persian intellectual with Isma'ili leanings.

HEARTH: the family group. Its size is problematic and must have varied. It became the unit of taxation (taxable hearth) independent of the real number of individuals living around it (real hearth).

HERM: wasteland; abandoned lands.

HESYCHASM: a belief often maintained by Greek hermits, according to which the faithful worshipper is allowed to contemplate the light emanating from God before the Last Judgement.

HIDALGO: 'The son of something' in Spain; the lowest degree of nobility.

INDULGENCES: the partial remission of the punishment supposed to devolve on the sinner in Purgatory, following a particularly meritorious act of piety. In the fifteenth century, concessions of this kind were greatly expanded, and even sold.

IQTA: the (supposedly short-term) concession of a taxable territory by the ruler to a servant, a warrior or a landed proprietor in Islam.

ITALIC: a printing type used in Italy since 1465, as opposed to the types cast further north, called 'Gothic'; it was what we now call 'Roman' type, since our 'italic' came later.

JIZYE: capitation tax incumbent on non-Muslims.

JUNKER: a German landed proprietor of noble birth; generally found to the east.

KABBALA: all the holy texts of the Jews prior to the Christian era, in which are contained ideas explaining and measuring the world, and which have been described as a sort of encyclopaedia of Judaism.

KARAJ: all taxes on property in Islam at the end of the Middle Ages.

KARIMI: Egyptian merchants, sometimes Jews, operating in the Red Sea and towards Asia.

KASHIF: inspector, and then collector of taxes in Mameluke Egypt.

KHAN: title of the Mongol rulers, but also a sort of market-place outside the towns in Islam.

KHUTBA: the Friday sermon in Islam, which includes a prayer for the ruler.

KOINÉ: a gathering, a community, a cultural and religious trend.

KOSSÄTEN: very lowly German peasants; see GÄRTNER.

KULAK: a term from nineteenth-century Russia, meaning well-off peasants, owning their tools and generally free from serfdom; this term is also applied to Medieval peasants.

LANCE: a group of six men or more, two of whom were mounted, forming a new unit of combat of the *gendarmerie* in the French army.

LARGHEZZA: a term meaning there is plenty of money available in the market and on the exchange.

LATIFUNDIA: the huge domains of late Antiquity, often used for stock farming; the term is also used for later periods.

LECTIO: a Scholastic exercise, which involves the master or a pupil reading a text and explaining it in literal terms.

LIMES: the frontier of the Roman Empire.

LLANOS: the great steppe-like plains of Mediterranean Europe, notably in Spain.

LOGOTHETE: a Byzantine palace official with fiscal powers.

MADRASAS: establishments for training and instruction in Islam.

MALOS USOS: seignorial innovations (bad customs) which the peasants considered to controvert the established order.

MANSA: in black Africa, a tribal council; by extension the King himself who incarnates the collective wisdom of the council Elders.

MECHANICS: in the West this meant workmen.

MELLAH: the Jewish quarter in Islam.

MESNIE: all the servants, relations and clients accompanying the master or the prince, who make up his household.

MESTA: the association of sheepbreeders in Castile; has come to mean everything to do with transhumance in Spain.

MEZZADRIA: short-term and renewable fruit-farming lease. In Italy the rent generally amounted to half the harvest.

MILLENARISM: an eschatological conviction which induces its adepts, while waiting for the end of the world, to make various public (preaching, processing, public repentance) or private demonstrations (retreat, flagellation, etc.).

MINISTERS: those who hold a function, a ministerium; in the fifteenth century the term tended to be restricted to those officers around a ruler who exercised a particular function; its present-day meaning only came later.

MIRACLE PLAYS: theatrical performances much enjoyed by town crowds, dealing as much with profane themes as with religious ones; they were generally performed by locals in the public square or in front of a church, for instance on the occasion of a ROYAL ENTRÉE.

MONTRE: when a condottiere presents the officers of the ruler employing him with a list of his men and their weaponry.

MUDA: the Venetian commercial fleet escorted by war galleys.

MUEZZIN: the call to prayer in Islam.

MUFTI: a pious man reputed for his religious knowledge; he may exercise a sort of public function by assisting at acts of everyday life, for instance weddings.

MULK: a personal landed property among the Ottomans.

MYSTERY PLAYS: see MIRACLE PLAYS above, but in this case, the theme was exclusively religious.

NOLIS: a contract chartering a ship, which does not necessarily include insurance.

NOMINALISM: a traditional philosophical attitude in Christian circles from the thirteenth century onwards, which favoured reason and dialectic over ontological thought.

NOURKIAGE: a contract between a stock raiser and a townsman (in northern Europe) similar to GASAILLE.

OBIT: the day of a person's death, and by extension, the anniversary of his death and the offices requested by the dying person or his heirs to be performed on it.

ÖSTERLINGEN: German merchants belonging to the Hanse.

PARFAIT: a term used by the Cathars to mean a believer who observes all the demands of the faith (complete abstinence) and is able to administer the sacrament of *Consolamentum* to the dying.

PATRICIANS: town notables; an unsatisfactory term which leads to a lot of ambiguity.

PEONES: the footsoldiers of Spain; both infantry and small peasants without horses.

PLAIN: cultivated land, as opposed to BOSC.

POLLEN: measuring pollen deposits in the ground tells us how many different plants were growing in the area at a given period, and their proportion to one another.

POORTER: a merchant (mainly in draperies) of the Flemish towns; also means town notable.

PORTULANS: maps providing lists of anchoring points; map-like drawings of Mediterranean origin.

PREDESTINATION: elaborated by Saint Augustine, a part of Christian dogma which considers that God has destined each human creature to be saved or damned according to God's mercy.

PRESIDIOS: Portuguese counters in Africa.

PRONOIA: the concession in Byzantium of a land (public or otherwise) in return for a number of favours to the Emperor.

QAISARIYIA: a public hall in Islamic towns.

QUAESTIO: the scholastic exercise which comes after the LECTIO, namely the discussion of terms and ideas found in a prepared text.

QUIETISM: a mystical Christian attitude which considers that a person does not need to perform external works of mercy or to engage in a constant process of self-improvement in order to achieve perfection and to draw near to God. BEGARDS and HESYCHASTS were susceptible to this attitude.

QUINT and REQUINT: inheritance tax on lands, feudal or otherwise, corresponding to a fifth or two fifths of a year's revenues.

RAT: a German town council.

REALISTS: they differed from the NOMINALISTS in believing in the reality of ontological concepts; their adherents dwindled towards the end of the Middle Ages.

REGALIA: the sum of public rights pertaining to the King, which could eventually be delegated by him.

RITTER: a knight in Germany: the word came to imply 'mercenary' in the 15th century.

SANJAK: an Ottoman term, meaning a territory under the military command of a member of the Sultan's family.

SAYETTERIE–WEAVING: a form of cloth manufacture in the country, which missed out some of the processing required for woollen cloth (*gros draps*) and produced cloth similar to light serges. A cheap and simple method.

SCHOLASTICISM: the pedagogical method of Medieval universities, which was eventually reduced to simple formulae for instruction, whence the pejorative meaning of the term nowadays.

SEQUIN: the Venetian ducat; it got its name from the *Zecca*, where it was minted.

SHARI'A: the revealed Holy Law of Islam; also includes the customary practices of religious and legal life.

SHURFA: a group of Arab shepherds in southern Morocco, who claimed to descend from the tribe of Idris I and hence from the Prophet, and who tried to create a local state, independent of the Almohads and their successors.

SOCCIDA: a stock-raising contract similar to GASAILLE.

SOTTOPOSTI: underemployed or unemployed persons in Italy.

SOUK: an Islamic market.

SPOLIA: the revenues and inheritance of a churchman who died in Rome or Avignon, reverted to the Pope, who tended to demand this inheritance in a wider range of cases.

SQUIRE: a term which began by meaning a knight's aide and came to mean a petty land-owner.

STÄMME: ethnic or cultural groups in Germany which formed the basis of large territorial principalities.

STAPLE: a disembarkation point for merchandise, above all for unloading English wool on the Continent.

STRETEZZA: a term meaning that the amount of money circulating in the market places has contracted.

STYLE: legal formula supposed to make it easier to formulate legal judgements and regulations.

SUFISM: a form of Islamic mysticism which invited the believer to live in a manner conducive to ecstasy and solitary meditation.

SUPERBIA: along with AVARITIA, this is the worst sin in the Christian tradition.

TAKEHAN: stopping work and striking, generally accompanied by rioting and disturbance.

THEMES: the boundaries of a province in Byzantium.

THIRD ORDER: groups of pious Christians who apply the rules of certain orders, especially the Franciscan Order, to their lives without actually leaving the lay world.

TIMAR; TIMARIOT: an Ottoman term, meaning tax-paying lands which have been ceded to an individual who is entitled to draw an income from them; the beneficiary.

TIMURID: a descendant or successor of Timur-Lenk (Tamerlane).

TRANSSUBSTANTIATION: part of Christian dogma which states that the Eucharist is the real transformation of the bread and wine into the Body and Blood of Christ.

UJ: a frontier territory in a state of war, among the Ottomans.

ULAMAS: doctors of the faith in Islamic countries, who act as judges and counsellors.

ULUS: a part of Mongol domination generally allotted by the Great Khan to a member of the Ghenghis Khan clan.

USAGES: the rights of the peasantry, recognised in custom by the lord, to use the produce of the forest, the waters and the fenland for their own purposes.

USANCE: the permitted delay between the issue of a bill of exchange and its eventual settlement.

VAKIF: an Ottoman term (Arabic, *Waqf*); land consisting of the property of religious establishments, although it might have been confiscated and given to a lay person.

VILLEIN: the average English peasant; the term came to mean more precisely peasants of low legal status, superior to the COTTARS but inferior to the YEOMEN.

WOOLMAN: an English businessman who bought wool while still on the sheep's backs and sold it later at a profit. A form of speculation and of cash advance.

WÜSTUNGEN: former farming land which had reverted to woodland or scrub in Germany.

XYLOGRAPHY: wood engraving; for a long time this involved engraving a picture, but then characters were introduced.

YEOMEN: free English peasants who generally owned their land.

ZAKAT: a legal fine imposed on the Muslim population in Islam.

ZEALOTS: a pious Byzantine association, whose members favoured a mystical, even puritanical, attitude to life and who generally embraced the beliefs of HESYCHASM.

ZUPAN: originally a Serb tribal chieftain, and later a territorial ruler.

Introduction

Faith, love for all creation, and a philosophy that touched the poetry and reason within him, guided the Christian from Hell to Heaven much as Bernard, Beatrice and Virgil guided Dante Alighieri through the circles of damnation, penitence and beatitude in a Comedy made Divine by its inspiration. Dante's poignant cry at the beginning of the fourteenth century symbolises better than any subsequent poem the anguish of a world that had reached the limit of its potential and was suddenly confronted with the very shadows, fears and disasters it thought it had escaped forever. Our own age has much in common with theirs; we too are faced with the terrors of annihilation, famine and death, which our technology and ideologies fail to avert.

The three centuries from Saint Louis to the Reformation were no more a period of transition than any other period in history: although the late Middle Ages are considered decadent, we know what followed them and prefer to call the period 'difficult', subjected as it was to crises of development. Such terms are necessarily vague, and the period remains hard to define. When did the Middle Ages end? With a political event like the fall of Constantinople in 1453, which brought down with it the last vestiges of Antiquity? Or a symbolic action with portentous overtones like Columbus' voyage into the uncharted Atlantic in 1492, or Luther's provocative outburst in 1517, which publicly affronted the wormeaten edifice of traditional Christianity? Or was it even, as researchers nowadays prefer, as late as 1540 or 1560, when the social and economic effects of the newly discovered lands were apparent? Historians have asked questions like these for a long time without finding convincing answers. We too should tread carefully; Henry V was medieval, Henry VIII was not: these are our limits. Few periods in the history of Europe, apart from the maligned tenth and eleventh centuries, have revealed so much latent energy, so much wealth on the point of expansion and so many forces of the future gathering to project the next period of growth. Here was the turning point, not in the history of Europe (that happened around 1000) but in the history of the world, from which Dante's heirs went out to conquer new continents over the next four centuries. The spotlight must be shone on Europe, where the sword of conquest was being forged during fitful processes of adjustment which discarded some of the legacy of earlier centuries. The Alhambra, Ibn Khaldun, Suleiman and other names of the East and South will not be forgotten, but during this

The evils of the age and the horrors of war. The massacre of the Innocents, a fragment from the Chapelle des Princes at Hautecombe Abbey. (*c.* 1335; Musée de Chambéry.)

period significant names and events tend to concentrate around the European world.

After the mid thirteenth century, those internal struggles and structural changes, whose shattering effects Dante deplored, accelerated and appeared in all sectors of society. Surprisingly, no external repercussions have been observed; Christendom's turmoil in casting her slough affected herself alone. It is tempting to ascribe the disruption to localised climatic changes, especially since there is now more evidence for a perceptibly warmer northern hemisphere, for a rising sea-level, a retreating ice-zone, torrential downpours and sudden temperature fluctuations. These factors contributed towards rotting grain crops, spreading disease, driving the nobility to war and forcing the peasantry to starve. Nonetheless, when we try to ascribe phenomena of this nature to the tenth and eleventh centuries, we are thwarted by contradictory evidence for bouts of cold weather in northern Europe and for climatic conditions which should theoretically have favoured the Islamic world. A further problem lies in the relative brevity of these phenomena, ending around 1520–50, while the trend they initiated carried on evolving. Leaving this issue open, let us move on to others.

Christianity, a sensitive and fragile colossus

The triumphant Europe of Saint Thomas Aquinas and Saint Louis was a splendid edifice, secure once more in her territory, her freedom and her age, which presented the traveller from Africa with a countenance as serene as that of the *Beau Dieu* of Amiens. She had achieved a common unity of expression, of thought and speech in a dogmatic and moral consensus guaranteed by the Church. There were of course, a few pessimists who grieved over the real wars engaged in by Pope Innocent IV, his demands on the faithful and his efforts to suppress new movements such as the Spiritual Franciscans. People like Jacques de Vitry were worried by growing moral laxity, others like Jean de Meung stigmatised the decline of a corrupt society. In Spain, Islam survived like an open sore, while the loss of Jerusalem was mourned in the East. There were still large areas of deprivation and even some unconverted countries like Lithuania, but these were minor lapses in an ordered world.

Christian order rested on a number of preconditions established in the twelfth century which had allowed three or four generations to attain a certain level of social, economic and moral stability. Some of these preconditions involved the mechanisms of production and exchange; man, whose labour had been made more effective by improved equipment and the expansion of accessible resources, was still the mainspring of the economy. Both in town and country, machines could still only relieve him of time-consuming work without reducing his out-lay. The inadequate circulation of money restricted him to renewing his personal assets, which meant that the equilibrium of the manorial enclave was extremely fragile. In social terms, the rents and dues paid to the lord of the manor were only requited if he in his turn could ensure justice and protection for his peasants and guarantee them an essential minimal return. In economic terms, the system demanded that unprofitable land and labour dues be rigidly maintained, creating a delicate balance, which could easily be

3

Gothic serenity, as expressed by *le Beau Dieu*, the Christ figure in Amiens Cathedral (*c.* 1230), would give way to anxiety.

upset by any major move towards stock-raising or by pressing demands for cereal crops. Disruptions to climate and population became acute around 1220–60, when agriculture reached the maximum level of production available to the technology of the age. The lord's need for cash to arm himself and serve his ruler could well drive him to add to his machinery, to invest in speculative crops or in stock-raising, to enclose his lands or raise his rents, thereby putting intolerable pressure on his peasants and breaking their mutual contract. At a time too, when the lord's role was diminishing, and when the influence of the king, along with his military and legal henchmen, was increasing.

In places like Germany and Spain, where land was still available, the colonising drive of the thirteenth century could still be pursued. Everywhere else, there were too many people on inadequate holdings to resist change. Worse still, a peasant elite was emerging, made up of the agents of rich lords exempted from paying tolls, of parish wardens who had seized the local fraternities' tools, of former members of the minor nobility and successful farmers. People like these stood between the lord and the common people; they extorted high rents, were able to advance loans against future wages and buy up abandoned holdings. The village community was being split into two separate rural groups. In towns the same fragile equilibrium existed between the workers and guilds, the masters and the authorities established in the cities. Such were the material preconditions heralding an inevitable collapse, of both production and the manorial system. Further rumblings were heard by the perceptive author of the *Roman de la Rose*, this time in universities and schools, whose Latin and Law formulated the prevailing consensus – an imposing gothic front constructed on the principle of divine order.

The authority of God's ministers had been undermined in spite of the reconciliation with the Orthodox Church in 1254 which crushed heresy and restored the unity of the Christian fabric. The Roman Pontiff's waning authority was a consequence of his interminable wranglings with the German emperor. The lucidity and progressiveness of the established Church came under increasing question, inspired by her excessive reserve and uncompromising rejection of any form of Aristotelian thought on the one hand, and her indulgence in clouds of mysticism on the other.

It could be argued that a greater danger lay in the general disregard for the ideal of the Common Good, which upheld both those who toiled and those who did not in an angelic vision of society built around helping one another. A society where everybody played their part and performed their duties, but always in the service of the community. This ideal had been so diminished by scribes, merchants, labourers and even kings by the mid-thirteenth century that it had become mere legal and canonical theory. Most of the social categories were in no position to substitute an alternative moral system; their philosophical immaturity meant that when the ideal of unity was removed, Christianity would collapse.

The metamorphosis of the west

During the later Middle Ages, the Christian world exploded into different elements. This fragmentation was structural rather than geographical and was characterised more by an

5

Never-ending war. A miniature from Vincent de Beauvais' *Miroir historial*. (Ms. 722; Chantilly, Musée Condé.)

utter neglect for the rules of life constraining the Christian world than by any diffusion of energy. Those elements which grew out of the medieval community, however, retained its dynamism and vigour in spite of the surface disasters and calamities which have given the times their unfavourable reputation – provoked as they were by the shock of transformation. Contemporaries contributed to the bad press by recognising the escalating wars and recurrent pandemics, successive famines, collapsing fortunes, bankruptcy, flight and death, as manifestations of divine wrath. They were watching immediate events and may well be forgiven, unlike those historians of today who still look no further.

Within the chaos, changes were developing even before Saint Louis' death. They spread rapidly from the beginning of the fourteenth century and reached their main phase between the Black Death (1348) and the mid-fifteenth century before stabilising over the next hundred years. The principal factors may be summarised by two particular series of events.

The grand, unified concept of Christianity was no more, though not from any lack of faith or good works, for missions were springing up, 'official' piety was flourishing and thousands of signs witnessed to the fervour of the faithful. The spirit of unity, however, had been replaced by national Churches, which restricted university teaching to local communities. Latin, the vehicle of learning and common thought, faded before the onslaught of regional languages. Bishops were no longer appointed to dioceses in distant

The Plague, a sign of Divine Anger. The scourge, which could strike down more than the third of a town's population in a few months, is represented by arrows. (German school, *c.* 1510; Munich, Bayerische Staatsgemäldesammlungen.)

countries; preachers and lecturers could reach only home-grown listeners. Even books circulated increasingly among territorial audiences, a regression accelerated rather than impeded by printing, a fact not always recognised. This fragmentation was certainly closely connected with the emergence of national interests.

The last indeterminate Frankish plans for a general crusade gave way to local preoccupations after the setback at Nicopolis in 1396. The interests of a dynasty, a town or a company or even of a political faction took precedence over the interests of Christendom, and destroyed it. The 'birth of nations' is applauded by nineteenth century and contemporary historians who search for its first stirrings in the wake of Joan of Arc, Wat Tyler or Huss. As their successors, we have tasted the bitter fruits of this development and nowadays medievalists are unlikely to consider any form of 'national' dynamism, whether it be modern England's colonial expansion, pan-German imperialism or Russia's advance into Asia, superior to the *Gesta Dei per Francos* of the eleventh and twelfth centuries.

This movement was able to accelerate out of all control only because Christendom was suddenly deprived of its head. Two translations to Avignon, three concurrent popes, papal humiliation before Councils and abuse of the Church's temporal possessions in Italy – all impaired religious belief rather than the Church's unity. This was worst affected by the obvious resignation by the Pope and Church hierarchy of their role as guardians of the

7

flock. When Pope Clement VI threw the new and profound movement of Spiritual Franciscans out of the Church at the Council of Vienne in 1311, it was the first time a Pope and his bishops had failed to channel a powerful current of orthodox piety. No effort was made to win the Spirituals back, as would have been attempted previously, and they were condemned without chance of appeal. This meant that the Church had lost its lead in clearing the way of Salvation, leaving Christians to seek it on their own, possibly in quite a new place. The door to secular thought was open and was to swallow up the best and worst of men.

A series of events at grass-roots level revealed another world, where the interests of landowners and peasants were diverging with the disruption of the fragile equilibrium between uncertain production and pressing demands. This development was uneven due to population fluctuations leading to delays in recovery and giving speculators their opportunity. Areas with few resources were given over to speculative crops, a process which encouraged the circulation of money and boosted reconstruction and expansion. In other areas the disruption was aggravated by extortion and processes such as enclosure, stock-raising and planting new vineyards, all of which destroyed traditional systems of production. Cheated in the economic sector, men were driven to compete with one another; lords urged their princes to war hoping for a profitable outcome. Once defeated and put to ransom, or with their lands ravaged, they would raise their demands, trying also to keep pace with royal taxation, and their men, whether wealthy or ruined, could only resist and rise up or flee. It was clear that the nobility, in spite of its political preponderance, was becoming economically fragile and socially parasitic. This did not mean that the condition of the peasantry was improving; the system's collapse profited only farmers, manorial agents and wage-labourers; the rest were reduced to destitution.

In towns, this process had an extra dimension, possibly explaining the more frequent and acute nature of urban risings: unemployment, and its companion famine, which in open country could be alleviated by turning to the woods for subsistence. In spite of this, it was precisely during times of famine or plague that refugees from the countryside poured into the towns and swelled the mass of unskilled and unemployed workers. At a time too, when technical advances demanded a further division of labour and manufacturers tended to use cheap labour in the outlying villages to carry out preliminary unskilled work. Practices like these only aggravated hostility between town and country.

Both the disintegration of the manorial system and the docility of the mass of underemployed urban workers contributed a final feature to the structural changes: the principality, which emerged between collapsing Christianity, the beginnings of the State, and the expiring manorial system. Principalities were the result of realigning villages and estates over an area of several thousand acres around a dominant town, as in Italy or Germany, or around some great noble or rich merchant family. They were mini-states whose workings imitated those of greater kingdoms, but which ensured a wider diffusion of the surplus obtained from the workers. Only where huge territories, autonomous states like the Milanese campagna, Burgundy and Frisia, were concerned, did this process involve a dislocation of central authority comparable to that of the tenth century. The new rulers'

The Peasants' revolt in Germany; this mercilessly realistic drawing was executed at the end of the fifteenth century (Berlin, Prints Cabinet).

authority had an economic rather than a political dimension, and it acted as an intermediary between the royal state and a disintegrated peasantry.

New masters

Now that men could claim the right to work, admit a plurality of truths, of worlds and of ways leading to God or happiness, very few of the constraints which maintained the unity and stability of ordered Christian society were left in place. Conservatism, the golden rule of the Church Triumphant, was giving way to the spirit of progress; henceforth the spirit of profit, a feature of human cupidity, was unleashed. On the official scale of sins, *avaritia* would take precedence over *superbia*; cupidity before pride. Furthermore, the confusion of men and ideas and the greater contact with other ways of believing and seeing things could only explode the concept of an immutable earthly Jerusalem.

There were plenty of optimists, beginning with William of Ockham and Duns Scotus in the mid-fourteenth century, who had the presence of mind to show men a new way of behaving, a *via moderna*. This was the path leading from *homo faber* of the Romanesque and Gothic periods, the artisan of a world still ruled by God, to *homo sapiens* of the 'Pre-Renaissance', who deemed himself worthy of an individual destiny and took up arms to achieve this. The end of the road would allow humanism to unfold in all its egoism; as the object of his own curiosity and attention, man would gain the centre of the universe and aim at dominating it – he would put God on trial. On a more limited and everyday scale as well, individual energies and ambitions were released from the constraints of Christian order to move upwards into the company of 'new men' and new masters. New social types and relationships evolved which still feature in our environment.

The most enduring phenomenon was the triumph of money and its masters. This phenomenon dated back to antiquity, but had now acquired the importance of a major social catalyst, driving a society whose wealth and power were based on land into a phase

9

Stews and bathhouses catered for all fleshly pleasures; hygiene was often closely associated with debauchery. (Miniature from the *Memorable deeds and sayings of Valerius Maximus*. Fifteenth century, Leipzig, City Library.)

where the possession of liquid assets predominated. Was this mainly the result of a tightening of fiscal control and the first sign of the State's awakening as a great financier, or a result of the shortage of precious metals? The gold and silver famine, which motivated subsequent colonial expansion, was merely aggravated by enormous expenditure and new technology for exploiting the deepest mines. The demand for money created a hierarchy of moneyed wealth able to realise immediate and future revenues with meticulous skill and transferred power from the landed aristocracy into the hands of businessmen, merchants, 'bankers', farmers hiring wage-labour and burgesses who invested in profitable vineyards and bought wool still on the sheeps' backs and oak groves that were replaced by fast-growing conifers. The immediate effect of this transfer of power was only a new preponderance of moneylenders around princes, kings and the governing bodies of towns, and this continued until the fifteenth century when a frankly oligarchic role devolved upon them, the Medici being one example among hundreds. Essentially, the effect was to introduce the idea that the *Respublica* was only a *res privata*; that its government, upon which the fate of thousands depended, should serve the interest of a mere handful, that private interest should dominate public, that 'what profits the Medici Bank profits Florence'.

10   The image of the horrible Boine Broke of Douai, exploiting his workforce as no factory owner in the nineteenth century would have dared is surely a caricature and an exception.

Paternalism as it evolved would remedy many ills. Nevertheless, the employer owned the tools, hired the workforce, rented out their lodgings and sometimes also administered the law. He moved into the foreground as soon as wage labour spread among the workers. The very principle of this social and economic relationship was the source of alienation and revolt, since the reciprocal services no longer justified the exploitation of the manorial system. Successive urban disturbances and peasant uprisings running through Europe from 1285–90 to the German explosion of 1525 pointed to the extent and gravity of the problem.

All the features of a labour movement in its infancy could be distinguished in the upsets of the fifteenth century: a growing division of labour polarised the workforce at its extremes, technical advances boosted unemployment in a period of stagnation or depression and rivalries developed between guilds and masters in the towns and between the underemployed urban workforce and the 'illicit' workers of the surrounding countryside. Finally, wages were not linked to their currencies, which fluctuated beyond hope of any immediate control.

The emergent labour movement was not yet matched by a peasant movement, in spite of the concentration of land ownership and legal degradation mentioned earlier. The town had become the centre of social and economic power, drawing the people and the produce of its territory within its walls, pursued by wars and the plague. The millenary trend, which since the fall of Rome had robbed towns of their prestige and dominance, was being upturned, perhaps as decisively as we see it happening in our day. Even if the princes, in middle and northern Europe at least, continued to prefer their semi-rural residences at Melun, Plessis or Chinon, how many of the nobles gathered around them still relied on harvests and ploughs for their living?

Among the money changers, contractors and court officials installed at the top of the heap, there were those characters culled from palaces and towns whom Chaucer, Alain Chartier and Villon found so irritating; the lawyer growing fat on his cases, not the busy and devoted notary or the former legal assistant, but the attorney, the solicitor, the bailiff. The professional soldier was depicted too, 'to be hired for everyman's money to do any mischief' – at worst a salaried vagabond, a best a soldier of fortune, a Sforza, a Chandos, a La Hire; men who drove the memory of Lancelot, Richard Lionheart and William the Marshall into a semi-mythical past. Finally, there was the intellectual, who made it his business to think for others and to expound his own thoughts in their name. After the mid-fifteenth century, the university teacher, bastard descendant of Saint Thomas Aquinas and petrified in an outdated scholasticism, was forgotten in favour of the men of letters who were cherished by courts and 'academies' and freed by their adulation from vulgar preoccupations. All over Europe, from Petrarch to the humanism of the waning fifteenth century, the flowers of criticism, lyricism and correct speech were flourishing alongside those of egoism, self-absorbtion and verbosity.

The backdrop to all this was the State as it finally emerged from successive convulsions, hung about with regulations and salaried officials, beginning its development towards bureaucratic absolutism. The functionary was evolving (the official and agent were already there) imbued with the sentiment that they were the repository of part at least of

The anguish of Death. Collective sorrow was expressed at funerals by mourning dress, lamentations and ritual gestures. A wooden panel from the tomb of a Spanish nobleman in Mahamid (Burgos). (Barcelona, Museum of Catalan Art).

the *Respublica*. There was still plenty of dross cluttering up the career they would pursue: seignorial justice, feudal aid, local communities, Church immunities, princely holders of royal privileges – but these obstacles were eroded witnesses to a vanished age. The idea that a ruler owed a real responsibility to his subjects was rooting itself in mens' minds; a hundred years later, the king and his subjects confronted one another on this issue.

The violent tenor of life

This famous chapter of Huizinga's epitomises the astonishing psychological climate of the three centuries ending the Middle Ages in Europe. It also explains the attraction they have for researchers and inquiring people, even more so now that twentieth century Europe has rediscovered the agonies and conditions experienced by men in those times. Their mental and psychological landscape enthralls us now as it did then and has provoked wails and sarcasm rather than praise and understanding. The decline of established morality, the disregard for traditional behaviour and the triumph of wilfulness and violence have been stressed; 'all experience had yet to the minds of men the directness and absoluteness of the pleasure and pain of child-life'. Indeed, the juvenile character of the age is striking; following the catastrophic losses of the Black Death, the average age of the population fell without any change in the prevailing custom of marrying very young girls to thirty year old men. This only increased the numbers of single men in their twenties who formed the cores of armies, mobs, feastdays and jacqueries; the tenor of emotions, conflicts and enterprises became generally more violent. Few periods have seen the juxtaposition of so many emotions; irrational pardons following on chilling injustice, demented anger taking over from total prostration, luxurious appetites and pleasures, sexual excesses, immeasurable greed and outrageous clothing. Moodiness, extravagance, exhibitionism and frivolity went hand in hand; sensitivity and coarseness, total renunciation and the spirit of profit. Princes lived among astrologers, charlatans and incorruptible preachers; the common

The façade of Josselin castle (Morbihan) rises up proudly from a rocky escarpment alongside the river. This fortress was rebuilt by the Constable Olivier de Clisson at the end of the fourteenth century and became one of the surest bases of French power in the Duchy of Brittany. The inner façade and living quarters were rebuilt by Jean de Rohan at the end of the fifteenth century, and their flamboyant ornamentation contrasts with the military austerity of the older façade.

13

people swung from devotions to debaucheries, from religious feasts to violence. All these offensive convulsions were evidence of a very great affective wealth and of psychological and nervous tensions which are sufficiently explained by the dangers of the age and millenary fears. They are the signs of a painful fermentation which would explode into the modern world.

At first glance, fear predominated. The way to incredulity and mysticism was opened by the collapse of the Church's authority and the glaring evidence that she no longer responded to the cries of the faithful. Already one and a half centuries before the Reformation, men were uncertain of their faith and agonised about death in a way unknown to their ancestors of the eleventh and twelfth centuries. Death was present everywhere, its manifestations were hideous. War, plague, epidemics and death were inevitable and accepted. They haunted artists, preachers and poets alike. Villon's hanged men, 'translations' of noble corpses, *danses macabres* . . . both vice and virtue lay closer at hand when life was shorter and the way to Salvation was obscure, especially when the real head of the Church and the validity of the baptisms and the viaticums administered was not known. Doubt reduced men to first priorities; the poor were no longer sent by God but were idlers, the sick were not suffering brothers but useless mouths, men of good will were allowed no peace on this earth – they were weaklings or even traitors. In spite of the din of useless feasts, constant groans and excesses of body and soul, hope of renewal still glowed in prophets and apostles such as Catherine of Siena and Vincent Ferrer, in earnest revolutionaries like John Huss and even Luther, and more simply still in the untiring perseverance of successive rebuilding, the irrepressible advance of knowledge and the spirit of enterprise, spurred on by difficulties. All these merged after 1500 in a powerful wave of conquest.

PART 1

Crisis of growth in Europe 1250–1430

Clouds gather in the West   1

Those historians of the late Middle Ages who are sensitive either to political and military events or to religious trends, or keep their ears attuned to the complaints of the lowest ranks of society, long ago pinpointed the most obvious features of the crisis: the chivalry of France floundering in the mud under a hail of English arrows; plague-blackened bodies littering town streets; ragged and famished peasants running amok, brandishing their pitchforks against the nobility. These images of death predominate, flanked by images of two or three Popes locked in combat, of Joan of Arc and Jan Huss at the stake. There is nothing wrong with all this, and those historians who see them in general economic terms, as features of a phase of depression, simply add to the overall picture. All these events, so portentous for the destiny of Europe, took place in the crucial years from 1330–50 to 1440–60. This has led historians, in France and England more than elsewhere, traditionally to interpret the outbreak of wars, epidemics and famines in the mid fourteenth century as the marks of a major change of course in history. However, this interpretation neglects their chief cause – even contemporaries cast their eyes heavenwards and asked themselves what could have aroused God's anger against them. For the last twenty years, historians too have considered that the escalating wars were not due merely to the arbitrary decisions of rulers, that famine could not occur without a reason, and that even the plague bacillus needed a receptive environment in which to proliferate. Studying the causes of the 'crisis' involves a large part of the thirteenth century and means ripping the saintly mask from the age of cathedrals and universities in order to see its features more clearly and to reveal the lines of strain and ageing in a once radiant Christianity.

In good King Louis' time

In troubled times, intellectuals, like everyone else, tend to recall the past with nostalgia, investing it with imaginary virtues. History is full of golden ages with their misleading appearance of stability and brilliance, belying their creative dynamism and scepticism. It does not take much probing to show what lay beneath the surface of *fin de siècle* Paris; a deprived working class, a regressive economy, with wholesale bloodshed remorselessly closing in on them. The Middle Ages did not escape this particular form of self-delusion;

even outside France, the men of the fourteenth century recalled the days of good King Louis, when royal justice and the rule of order flourished, when cathedrals rose up, when Thomas Aquinas was teaching and when ships were ploughing the seas. They forgot the Jew-brandings, the failed crusades, the hounding of the Cathars and the throttled communal movement. Historians must not let themselves be duped by this partiality.

Fair seeming . . .

Like this character in the *Roman de la Rose*, Europe in the 1260s and 1280s seemed attractive. Areas like Catalonia, Flanders and the plains around Padua and Bologna, the Fens, Kent and Andalusia, which had been developed very early on, continued to be settled – a process which was pursued with greater reason on the fringes of the western world; on the far side of the Elbe and in Sweden and Moravia. Cultivation made advances, even in the mountainous Dauphiné and in the Piedmont, accompanied by new attempts to adapt crops to particular soils. New or previously unknown varieties were included in the agricultural treatises, in which rulers took such an interest. Hops were planted on the banks of the Rhine, rice in Lombardy, spinach flourished in Italy and buckwheat began its long career on the Atlantic side of Europe. The diversification of demand (which I will discuss later) explains the new attention being paid to kitchen gardens and orchards. We know from accounts drawn up for the Countess of Artois and for various burgesses and administrators in Milan, Poitiers and Pisa, that strawberries, apricots, lettuces and vegetables were grown as well as plants used in the dyeing process – woad of Toulouse and madder of Spire were increasingly sought after. A more enlightened and, for once, unspeculative approach to wine growing led to the gradual disappearance of the vine from England, and to its triumphant emergence in Limogne, Burgundy and the Languedoc a few decades later. Both princes and burgesses developed more discriminating palates; in the *Disputoison du vin et de l'eau* the relative merits of Beaune, Auxerre, Angers and Bordeaux vintages were assessed, demoting the mediocre Parisian and Laon wines, which had been highly valued in Philip Augustus' time.

In other places too, the countryside was being reorganised as crop rotation and strip ploughing were adopted. Between 1250 and 1290, the three field rotation system seems to have been established in all the rich corn-growing country around London and in the Paris basin. During 1320–28, Normandy and even Tuscany were won over to it. Germany had to wait until 1325 for the three *Zeigen*, the three *Felder*, to take over from individual or partial rotation systems. There were however, still some regions where cultivation did not reach this level; wintery, cold and humid lands continued to grow short-lived and meagre crops on the *outfield*, limiting their use of fertiliser and rotation to fields lying close to the villages. These restrictions also applied to their tools; although ploughs equipped with coulters were taking over in the South, the peasants' awareness of what their local terrain required limited their reception elsewhere. It was not custom or ignorance but the landscape itself that dictated that vast areas of rich soil were still worked by ox-drawn ploughs; dangerous slopes, stony ground and the expense of keeping delicate horses were all factors. Around 1290, oxen were still being used for ploughing in England, Brie and

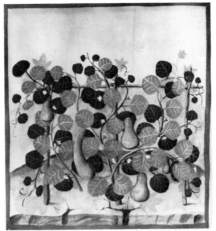

The new vegetables: spinach, cucumber, lettuce. (Miniatures from the *Tacuinum Sanitatis*; fifteenth century, Rouen, Bibliothèque Municipale.)

northern Burgundy. In consequence, oats, which working horses require, were very little grown in these places.

The country fairs were multiplying and specialising, showing that the economy was progressing beyond what economists call the primary sector and that rural crafts were developing. Livestock fairs were held in Cornwall, Ireland and Sologne. In other places as well, peasant produce was improving in quality and in volume; for instance, the pedal-driven spinning wheel is supposed to have been introduced into country homes around 1300. It was a great time-saver and promoted women's work to equal status with men's work, though it also involved their isolation inside their cottages. By then, the rural sector was producing a sufficient surplus to make it worth while taking it to town, even before the urban sector started demanding it. Lorenzetti's famous fresco in the communal palace in Siena shows how the countryfolk came to town, bearing wheat, skeins and wood.

19

a) Wine growing was being adjusted to climate and soil conditions. The *vendanges*, a miniature from Ububchasym of Baldach's *Theatrum Sanitatis*; Cod. 4182. (Rome, Biblioteca Casanatense.)

b) Watched over by his father, the farmer's son ploughs a furrow with an ox-drawn plough. The picture does not allow us to see if there was a coulter on the right hand side of the plough. (Alfonso X's *Cantigas*, end of the thirteenth century; Madrid, Escorial.)

. . . And its reverse

'Good governance' was Lorenzetti's comment on the poignant harmony he illustrated, but it should not deceive us; beneath the surface the virus of destruction was spreading. This was felt by only a few churchmen in their capacity of professionally scathing moralists, leaving historians to find out just where the system was creaking. We have discussed the medieval ecosystem, according to which the countryside was divided into woodland and ploughland, vulnerable to periods of low productivity and to unexpected increases in demand. Prior to 1200, while the phase of expansion was in full swing, there had still been enough empty space around to mitigate the effects of a crisis. But after 1250, the world was full up, in terms of the resources then available, although this began to be felt very unevenly. The medieval economy had always been compartmentalised without any reserves of energy or regulations for production and distribution of food and although production was increasing, this did not happen everywhere at the same rate. In the Île-de-France, in Champagne and the Saône valley, and in many other areas, poor lands lay alongside others saturated with harvests and inhabitants. What we know about the population of Warwickshire in relation to the area of arable land seems to indicate that the level of production in the South of England had remained unchanged since the Norman Conquest, whereas in the North, it had risen by 100 per cent, or even by 750 per cent, in some cases. Such strains loosened the fabric of society and made it extremely vulnerable. Even on the level of a province, there was no authority capable of containing a food shortage or an uprising.

20   Another factor was the spread of woodland or at least of uncultivated land. Although the

plough was not losing its vigour, in many regions assarting had had to stop. This was the case around Paris in the 1230s, in Poitou, Picardy, Normandy and Provence by 1250, in England, Sologne and Lombardy by 1270, in southern France as far as the Pyrenees by 1290 and in Scotland, Forez and the Dauphiné by 1320. By then, there was no longer enough woodland both for the peasant to pasture his pigs and meet his other needs and for the lord to hunt and carry out his military exercises. What was left was more scrupulously exploited. The first regulations about culling trees and re-planting were formulated by the Cistercians around 1200. Later, everybody was implementing them, including kings, like the Capetians who appointed river and forest wardens in 1317, prosecuted poachers and doubled their customary forest rights. The Plantagenets were responsible for extending the royal forest after 1275, which stretched unrestrained around Windsor, over the Chilterns, Sherwood, Dartmoor and over Devon and Lancaster. Even emperors were involved, like Henry VII who took over large stretches of forest around Nuremberg and Frankfurt in 1309. This policy is easily associated with the growing demand for royal building sites, ship-yards, mines and urban development. Finally, revenues from woods were actually greater than rents from land; in 1332, the income from the Gatinais alone furnished a queen of France with her dowry.

In spite of new forestry regulations and increased restrictions on the peasants' use of the forests, the agricultural equilibrium was seriously affected by the shortage of woodland. At the same time, thanks to new farming techniques, fallow land was being planted with snatch crops such as peas, lentils and vetches, which had been known in Flanders since 1270. They were grown in many other regions too, thus seriously reducing the land available for pasture – at a time when local towns were demanding more meat. The only solution was to convert wild life areas into pasture, enclosing them to prevent theft or cattle raids. Cattle were farmed around Albi, in the Cantal, in Ponthieu and the Midlands from the 1290s and around Toulouse by 1320, where the herds were large enough to keep more than a hundred town butchers supplied. Before 1320, in Flanders, flocks belonging to the Count or to others grazed on former wheat fields. In England, Picardy and southern Champagne, wealthy princes, lords and even burgesses laid out parks over several hundred acres of land, and surrounded them with hedges.

For the modest villager, the situation was even more dramatic, since the abolition of his customary rights (Philip VI issued an *Ordonnance* on this subject) involved the loss of former fallow land to pasture and the forfeiture of common lands which the emergent local communities had painstakingly acquired in the thirteenth century. Even though we know very little about this, it appears that common land was systematically subdivided, in northern and eastern France at least, no doubt as a result of the shortage of arable land due to the growth of the population.

Upper and lower classes

Although these terms have been borrowed from the urban sector, they apply perfectly well to the peasantry of Europe around 1320–25. All the features I have just discussed began as

21

logical and positive consequences of earlier developments and between 1260 and 1280 they contributed towards breaking the peasants' world, first economically and then socially; a world, which had hitherto been more aware of its legal constraints. In the first place, the practice of enclosing woods and even tillage at a time when there was still a strong demand for workable land, raised the value of such landholdings as remained, by about 100 per cent in the Chartrain between 1240 and 1280, and by rather less in the Meuse valley where there was doubtless more available land. It was not only the price of parcels of land that rose but also their rents; landowners tried to increase their rents, whenever they could, for instance on renewing leases, or to raise polltaxes. In Normandy, the overall increase was around 500 per cent between 1260 and 1300. The lord was especially keen on exercising his rights to reliefs, succession taxes, and to the profits of justice. This explains the landed nobility's bitter struggle to defend its various sources of income against encroachment by royal taxation with its claims to an authority higher than theirs. This was happening in England in Edward III's time and in France at the end of Philip the Fair's reign.

Land was also being redistributed, either among the old-established landed gentry at all levels of society or to newcomers from the towns, a phenomenon which took on two strongly contrasting aspects. Landowners were sometimes tempted by their need for a direct income to take the land in hand, as was being done in Germany and England, where their first concern was to produce enough to supply the local markets without the uncertainties of collecting rents and exacting services and without losing their profits from the administration of justice. The Bishop of Winchester, for instance, managed to raise the proportion of corn grown and sold on his land from 31 per cent to 46 per cent between 1208 and 1299. Such an arrangement required salaried staff, since forced labour dues had become archaic and unreliable. However, both salaries and employees varied according to the density of the local population, and neither was entirely reliable. The solution was to farm out. Since landowners were either frequently absent or soon replaced, the previous close relationship between them and their peasants was attenuated; the practice of leaving agents in charge or of relying on the traditional and uneconomic manorial system invited fraud and negligence. Accordingly, even the most tenacious exponents of farming their own land, the Cistercians, were already leasing their land by 1325. Church lands provide many examples of this; the Premonstratensians in Auvergne, the Hospitallers in Provence, the Abbot of Ramsey and the bishops of Ely, Saint-Denis and Saint-Martin de Tournai – all farmed out their lands between 1270 and 1350. It is certain that the lay world resorted to this as well. In Germany, in Baden or Wurtemberg, in Switzerland or in the Bordelais, we have lay examples scarcely later in date, as in the Liège countryside and the Île-de-France after 1350.

To start off with, short leases were granted on farms which tended to be peripheral to, or far from, the main estate. Soon, however, the system was employed right up to the feudal heart-lands and in some cases it took over as much as two-thirds of the estates without impinging on the lord's hunting, fishing and forestry rights. Life tenure however, was achieved with difficulty and only came into use after the onset of the crises. The advantages

A domain of the landed nobility: the Castello delle Quattro Torri, east of Siena, dominates a typically hilly Tuscan landscape. Fourteenth to fifteenth centuries.

of the practice were obvious; it assured the landowner a regular income from his property and allowed his most prosperous peasants, the *labourers* of the thirteenth century, to exploit their fifty to sixty acre holdings at their own convenience. On the other hand, the form of share cropping known as *facherie* and *megerie* from Toulouse to the Alps, and as *mezzadria* in Italy, was employed in areas where the harvests were more uncertain and where the tenant ran disastrous risks in bad years. Where fruit farming was involved, the practice of granting short-term share-cropping leases in which seed and tools were provided by the landowner, involved the combination of capital and labour (an association already well understood in the towns) in areas strongly influenced by urbanisation. This system was also employed in other less urbanised regions, such as the Limousin and in Poitou, no doubt because it broke up leaseholds into units small enough for cultivators who would not have taken on big farming leases.

So it was among the peasantry that the first signs of economic collapse appeared. The lower classes were forced to pile up on their tenures, and they found it practically impossible to save up the minimum necessary for squeezing into the developing market economy. Even worse, either local inheritance practices or the progressive subdivision of the family allotment resulted in its fragmentation into mockeries of smallholdings. Along

23

the Escaut and the Meuse around 1300–10, 70–80 per cent of tenancies consisted of strips of land a few metres wide amounting to less than three acres per *hearth*, just enough to stave off starvation. Seasonal wages were just as negligible; shepherds were alone in earning up to four pounds per annum as a result of the growth of sheep farming around 1335. The peasant, however, could hope for only a few meagre pence a day, a shilling at best. This was about half the going wages in towns, where labour was not as plentiful as in the country.

The menacing shadow of the town

Towns were indeed a major feature of this period, whether during lean years in the 1250s, when Italian towns like Siena engaged in military operations against their contados with the aim of seizing their food stores, or whether in the Toulousain when, before 1300, local merchants controlled all business within a radius from Bayonne to the Puy and from Agen to Béziers. As was to be expected in zones of growing urbanisation and declining village prosperity, the foundations for the control of all Europe by her towns were laid well before 1350.

Urban expansion began rather later and did not level off like agricultural production during the last decade of the thirteenth century. Christian Europe had almost reached maturity by 1300: according to the most conservative estimates, six towns had populations of over 50,000, more than thirty had over 20,000 and almost eighty claimed more than 10,000 souls. With very few exceptions, this level of population did not alter until the new expansion of the seventeenth century. Towns as large as these could no longer consider themselves separate and distinct from their rural surroundings. But although people were moving from the country in such numbers as to necessitate the rebuilding and extension of city walls, it was rather by direct action, by their growing demands on the countryside, that the cities came to dominate a landscape to which they had previously been extraneous.

Historians tend to dwell on merchants, banks and ships as I will, but these were only some features of urban influence, in the same way as the brilliance of an intellectual school or of a ruler's sojourn are not attributed major historical significance. What does appear of prime importance is the draining effect towns had on rural populations and food supplies. From the mid thirteenth century, a demanding and voracious consumer class was growing in towns whose needs could only be met by exercising strict control over their surrounding countryside. Of course there had always been such people in towns, a bishop here and a count there and their followers, more so in the South, not to mention the well-established noble houses of Italy and Provence. This class grew energetically in the thirteenth century, even rising up *de novo* in the Low Countries, the Rhine valley and in England, where many lords chose to live in town rather than in their country residences. They were able to satisfy their desire for comfort by successful farming out; the nobility in Ghent, Strasbourg, Paris and London could thus afford ostentation and profligate waste on a par with their peers in Genoa and Florence.

Philip *le Hardi*'s keep, built at Domme in the Périgord in 1280, is defended by walls, with towers flanking its gate.

When princes, accompanied by their courts, armed men and flocks of clerks, chose to reside in Milan, Avignon or Frankfurt, consumption necessarily multiplied. The great men, the *magnati* of Italy and the *rikes hommes* of France attracted merchants and fashionable craftsmen to them. Although these high-born citizens were not important numerically (around one hundred of their families were expelled from Florence and they were surely fewer elsewhere) their demand for wine, clothes, mounts, meat, weapons, dinner-services and all sorts of servants was prodigious. A town of 10,000 inhabitants for instance, consumed the produce of twenty square kilometers, but its wealthy class consumed the produce of fifty. This meant that the countryside was increasingly partitioned off, and although it was still only the aristocracy who could own estates as well as town and country residences, the day was dawning when the burghers would be allowed to buy land.

For the moment, towns drew their workforce from those countrymen who had been driven from their villages by the problems of rural existence. A large proportion of 'craftsmen' in town workshops were in fact unskilled newly arrived rustics with a low standard of living. Around 1322 in Aix, the carpenters, tanners, bakers and other trades which had close ties with the farming community, made up three-fifths of the urban workforce. At the same time, non-productive industries like carpentry, tiling, milling and cobbling tended to concentrate in towns, to the great loss of country trades. In most cases studied, the proportion of such trades rose from 15–20 per cent to 40–60 per cent of all urban activities.

These were men who had been enrolled into a trade or included in one of the

a) The baker's oven is operated by women. The bread was made of wheat, barley or rye flour and one batch was supposed to last a week, sometimes even a fortnight. Bread remained the basic food of poor families. (*Theatrum Sanitatis* of Ububchasym of Baldach.)

b) A town workshop, showing a fourteenth-century forge and the iron-workers' tools (bellows, hammers and pincers). A drawing from a treatise on astronomy. (Ms. Sloane 3983, London, British Museum.)

neighbourhood or devotional associations mentioned earlier, variously known as guilds, fraternities, *consorterie* or *vicini*. Many others though, were kept in dependence and excluded from admission to a trade until a long probation period had been served, as was required in Pisa, or else were relegated to special quarters, sometimes even to the town moats, as at Liège or Montpellier around 1330. This seasonal, short-term workforce consisted of an indeterminate marginal mass, easily swayed and exploited, which employers conspired against to pay minimal wages in order to prevent their seeking better terms elsewhere. This sort of cartel was drawn up, for instance, between Liège and Huys in 1348.

The craftmasters hoped to control the countryside by these means, and their control grew and hardened until they were able to exercise a regulated political pressure over the peasantry.

Their power extended not only over established *contados* along traditional lines, where urban law was enforced, but much further afield in a variety of ways. Firstly, because a town could impose its own law over its countryside, as Cologne, Magdeburg and Lübeck did in East Germany and the Low Countries, secondly because the towns could also impose their own systems of weights and measures on their surrounding lands. For instance, all corn prices were fixed by the *amandellerie* of Metz and the *capitouls* of Toulouse and were imposed on local markets. Rural crafts within a certain radius were also forbidden to compete with urban crafts, as was the case in Ghent, whose inhabitants did not shrink from sacking rebellious workshops in little neighbouring villages in 1314. Since the nobility shared the power with the craftmasters, who was to prevent them from exercising it?

Travellers recognised a hospice or hostelry by its sign.
Travellers on foot and horseback were put up in
dormitories and their horses fed and stabled.

The glitter of merchandise

In spite of the allure their fascinating accounts and lives hold for historians, merchants
were only marginal figures. There is no doubt that the spirit of enterprise, a taste for danger
and the dynamism of those men who travelled from London to Novgorod, from Lisbon to
Alexandria on ships of three hundred tons, or at the head of a train of twenty mules, is most
appealing. For ages now, Italians, and after them, men of Aquitaine, Germans, Catalans
and Englishmen had braved the terrors of long-distance travel. Although navigational
skills had improved and roads were better maintained and a system of safe conducts and
hospices reduced the element of risk, the perils of the sea remained as real as ever. Greater
even than these were the dangers the Pisans incurred from the Genoese, the Genoese from
the Venetians, the Venetians from the Turks, the Catalans from the Barbary pirates and the
men of Marseilles from the Catalans, not to mention the men of Bayonne or the Bretons. To
guard against these dangers, insurance was developed before 1250 in Genoa where
premiums were calculated at as much as 30 per cent of the value of the ship and 10 per cent
of its cargo. The annual totals were staggering; 100,000 to 200,000 florins – amounting to
three or four times the resources of a consular town. Insurance made it possible for
merchants to establish a trading network linking the furthest points of the Christian world;
the arrival of the first Italian ships in Bruges after 1270 demonstrated the strength of these
links and the breadth of their business concerns.

Merchants also had to take measures against bankruptcy. They, who had long been held
in suspicion or at least in contempt by others, had at last penetrated the fabric of urban
society. In Florence, they had infiltrated all the *arti maggiore* – the richest guilds for wool,
silks, spices, medicines and groceries – and of course the trade in money changing and

'business' engaged in by the Calimala. Since 1308 they had enjoyed their own jurisdiction, the *mercanzia*. In France, the Capetian King Philip the Fair took merchants under his protection and in general, they had no difficulty in getting their hands on manors, lordships and even on the magistracies and consularships of the German *Rat*. It was especially important to them to secure positions in bodies which set tariffs and taxes. It is not surprising that the watchful public was so keen on detecting and denouncing fiscal fraud and bribery when so many took a dubious pride in it; Jehan Boine Broke in Douai, Crépin in Arras and the Acciajuoli in Florence. Merchants controlled money as firmly as they did trade and they lent fantastic sums: Edward III was advanced 900,000 florins by the Bardi and 600,000 by the Peruzzi against mortgaged royal revenues. This was six times the price the Pope paid Queen Joanna of Naples for Avignon.

When they rattled the spurs they had the effrontery to wear, the Peruzzi did indeed seem to open the way to lordship for a whole class of new men, but this was mere show. The companies of the thirteenth and early fourteenth centuries were in fact only provisional associations which lasted between two and twelve years and were easily dissolved. Exceptions to this included the Scali, who lasted one hundred years, and the Peruzzi who disappeared after sixty, even though eleven of their associates (half of them) were members of the family. The Bardi employed up to 380 persons and opened twenty branches with a deposited capital of 700,000 florins, but disagreement was prone to grow within these enterprises which lacked any rational organisation and proper capital flow. Profits of 20–30 per cent per annum were followed unexpectedly by disasters and when debtors refused to pay up, the whole enterprise collapsed because everybody in it was liable. When Edward III refused to honour his debts between 1340 and 1345, the whole Florentine economy suffered. The time when town bankers would dictate to princes had certainly not arrived.

The birth of 'states'

Another aspect of Christianity was also changing; it seemed by now that the king's God-given power no longer depended on the sanctity of his office but on politics. The latter half of the thirteenth century was the period when the Christian king's power was at its greatest, when he succeeded in combining the charisma of the Jewish king with that of the barbarian chieftain, and in controlling his followers and family on whose support he depended. He had inherited supreme justice and fiscal powers from the Romans. His income was based on lands, windmills, castles and customs duties, which were good substitutes for an unreliable system of taxation. There were also degrees of princely authority and of establishments; the Polish king was not on a par with the Capetian and a town corporation in Italy was not on the same level as an English royal palace. Everywhere, however, the Christian State had reached its apogee, even without laying special claims to adulation like Saint Louis. Tracing its foundations is all the more important since close inspection reveals weaknesses which precipitated its collapse.

The power of the king or urban patriciate was unlimited. It was saturated with the old Roman idea of the *respublica*, the common good, henceforth incarnate in the royal person or entity. The lawyers who surrounded the Capetian and German sovereigns repeated this unceasingly. Jacques de Révigny, Pierre Dubois, Marsilius of Padua, all affirmed that the king is emperor in his kingdom. Since the German claims were substantially impaired by the suppression of the Hohenstaufen line, and since the Papacy, in spite of its triumph, was morally discredited by its stratagems and ambitions, neither had the power to restrain monarchs and city states. Universalism was concentrated in the hands of a single person or team; the State became a state. This was the surprising result of political evolution; by virtue of his coronation oath, his annointing, the king was God's right hand, and as such was able to arrest the Pope, deny imperial authority, tax his subjects and sap the power of the nobility. More significant still was the concentration of increasingly efficient powers in the hands of a single person that characterises the end of the thirteenth century. In the eleventh or twelfth centuries, if a prince was inadequate, it didn't matter because his bishops could hold his hand and his nobles clustered around him. His royal aura bathed his advisors and relations. But in the thirteenth century, if he was inadequate, there was no way of preventing cliques and pressure groups from forming – or deserting. The risk was all the greater because kings, especially in France, maintained the tradition of appanage, by which their younger brothers were provided with a share of the inheritance. It was also a way of subduing a region and attaching it directly to the central administration, and was applied to difficult or intractable regions such as Languedoc, Toulousain, the French marches etc. The risk of a princely dynasty rising up, supported on a local base with its royal roots well dug in, was equally obvious.

Once a ruler had been handed one of these 'states', he was not content to remain a nonentity. He established or consolidated governmental mechanisms, for instance the council chambers and magistracies of Burgundy and Aquitaine between 1290 and 1335. The example was set by such as remained of the great fiefs; Flanders had her 'audience' from 1309 and Brittany her seneschals, and local dynasties too could play at autonomy or even greater things. The concentration of power in the hands of individuals was accompanied by the emergence of capital cities with their royal and noble palaces: London, Paris, Seville, Avignon, Milan and even Lübeck and Florence. Crowds of suppliants and servitors flocked to them because the king had given up visiting his subjects as he had done formerly. Indeed, the king could no longer deal with all the business that came to him and he relied increasingly on his royal entourage whose numbers increased rapidly. When historians nowadays discuss the growth of royal administration they do not dwell enough on the blind routine and cold cruelty implicit in the term. The administration that evolved was worse than that of late Antiquity because it was efficient and specialised, as we shall see.

From now on, the king's personal demesne was no longer of primary concern, although it remained indisputably the basis of, for instance, Capetian and Plantagenet power. One has only to look at the irreversible decline of the prestige of the Empire following the loss of its land in Germany to see how important land was. No less important were the other two pillars of royal renown; firstly, the Church; the ruler was a member of it and he protected it as much as he was governed by it. He could appropriate the revenues of vacant

The Christian ideal of the knightly king. Bamberg Cathedral's rider (1240) probably portrays Saint Stephen, King of Hungary, since the Cathedral used to own his relics.

ecclesiastical offices and levy tithes autocratically from the clergy – substantial trumps, but the ruler's aura of spirituality was now due much more to the emergence of a cult of royalty. Subjects felt at one with their king, as Christians did with Christ. What did the terrestrial Church matter, when Kings Edward I and II pillaged Church lands and property with impunity, and when Philip the Fair summoned the Pope to justice? As for the feudal nobility, faithful guardian of bygone virtues, it was slipping gradually towards its secondary political and military role of modern times. Its fidelity towards its natural head remained certain, but its powers of action were limited by its economic weakness. Any reaction by the 'barons' against this trend was motivated more by anguish than by ambition. From 1281, the French king pursued a deliberate policy of ennobling newcomers and the old nobility was compensated with the creation of new orders of chivalry which it alone could aspire to, and in which it could drown its sorrows.

The scribes and courtiers stayed on; after all, in spite of his aura, the ruler was still a man who needed to eat, sleep, move about and meditate. Whether a Doge or a Capetian, he needed his town *hôtel* or his residence, which may have still been peripatetic, but was always *familial* in the wider and ancient sense of the word. The old offices of the Chamber and the Table did not mean much any more, but the Plantagenet 'wardrobe' and the Capetian *chambre à deniers* which emerged around 1280–1303 were not just concerned with providing clothes or private expenses. The flow of royal writs swelled according to the rate of princely interventions and the spate of supplicants, amounting to 35,000 letters in 1332 in Paris (but only twelve per annum in Sweden!). Chancellors were no longer the redoubtable men Philip Agustus had seen fit to eliminate, but lawyers, burghers, loyal men like Guillaume Flotte and Pierre D'Orgemont, who were capable of giving legal form to royal ordinances in which the king now sought to deal, no longer with domestic matters, but with very general concerns such as prices, duelling, security and the coinage. Clerks, *chevaliers de l'Hôtel* (Knights of the Household) like the famous Marigny, formed a mobile nucleus of councillors and executors with whom the ruler's cousins and nephews and their coteries mingled – it is fascinating to watch the different clans (Burgundian, Poitevin, Provençal) rising to power one after another. Altogether, several hundred individuals, among whom the *'enquêteurs de justice'* (similar to *Justices in Eyre*) distinguished themselves. In 1314 there were four master-scribes handling petitions in Paris; by 1343 there were twenty-nine.

As for the Court, the *curia regis*, the nobility had not been seen there for some time. Instead, local agents were met there, handing over their accounts, and growing numbers of clerks specialising in some business or other, which would then be discussed *in parlemento*. Even in England, where the baronage insisted in 1260 on a regular assembly, the *Parlement* was only a meeting of bureaucrats; the King's and the Exchequer Benches for the Appeal Court and for rendering accounts were set up in the mid thirteenth century, the *Grand'chambre* and the *Chambre des comptes* in France in 1315–20. These men were salaried, hierarchised, blindly devoted and they are today's civil servants.

The Île de la Cité, in Paris, showing the King's Palace and the Sainte-Chapelle, which was consecrated in 1248. At the foot of the walls, a haymaking scene. From the *Très Riches Heures du Duc de Berry* (June), beginning of the fifteenth century (Chantilly, Musée Condé).

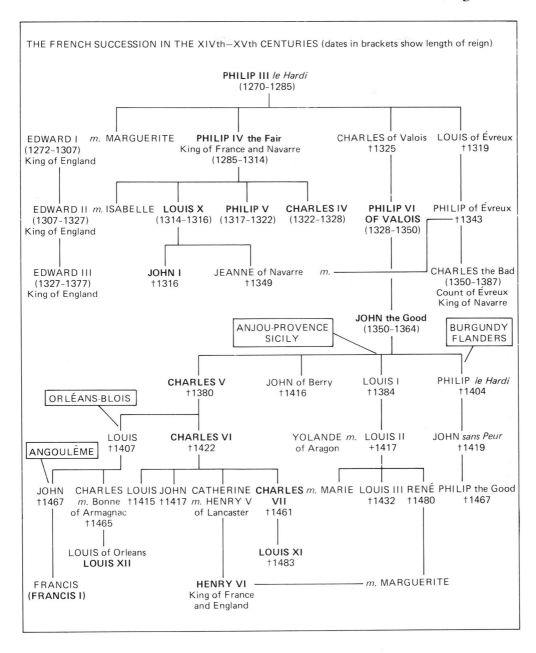

THE FRENCH SUCCESSION IN THE XIVth—XVth CENTURIES (dates in brackets show length of reign)

PHILIP III *le Hardi*
(1270–1285)

EDWARD I *m.* MARGUERITE **PHILIP IV the Fair** CHARLES of Valois LOUIS of Évreux
(1272–1307) King of France and Navarre †1325 †1319
King of England (1285–1314)

EDWARD II *m.* ISABELLE **LOUIS X** **PHILIP V** **CHARLES IV** **PHILIP VI** PHILIP of Évreux
(1307–1327) (1314–1316) (1317–1322) (1322–1328) **OF VALOIS** †1343
King of England (1328–1350)

EDWARD III **JOHN I** JEANNE of Navarre *m.* ———— CHARLES the Bad
(1327–1377) †1316 †1349 (1350–1387)
King of England Count of Évreux
King of Navarre

ANJOU-PROVENCE **JOHN the Good** BURGUNDY
SICILY (1350–1364) FLANDERS

CHARLES V JOHN of Berry LOUIS I PHILIP *le Hardi*
†1380 †1416 †1384 †1404

ORLÉANS-BLOIS

LOUIS **CHARLES VI** YOLANDE *m.* LOUIS II JOHN *sans Peur*
†1407 †1422 of Aragon +1417 †1419

ANGOULÊME

JOHN CHARLES LOUIS JOHN CATHERINE **CHARLES** *m.* MARIE LOUIS III RENÉ PHILIP the Good
†1467 *m.* Bonne †1415 †1417 *m.* HENRY V **VII** †1432 †1480 †1467
of Armagnac of Lancaster †1461
†1465

LOUIS of Orleans **LOUIS XI**
LOUIS XII †1483

FRANCIS **HENRY VI** ———————————— *m.* MARGUERITE
(FRANCIS I) King of France
and England

Crowns in shadows

The picture I have just sketched, filling in the English and French details, because these two represent the main poles of authority in the Christian states of 1300, is not without its darker patches. To start off with, although in principle everything depended on the king, it was vitally important that he should be up to such a crushing territorial responsibility. Heredity is unpredictable; Edward I, with his exceptional valour, was succeeded by his weak and clumsy son. Philip the Fair has puzzled both his contemporaries and present-day historians; did he instigate his ambitious policy or was he a weakling manipulated by rascals? The elective principle, on the other hand, which was employed in the Empire and in Venice, tended to establish a dynastic faction rather than select the fittest. If the line of succession was broken, what might otherwise have been just an accident, could become a major problem. We know that the Capetian dynasty, regularly blessed by fortune as it was for three and a half centuries, was as abruptly forsaken by it in 1328 after a series of short reigns which left the crown to girls. Nowadays, no one believes that the Hundred Years' War began from the opposition of the Valois dynasty, cousins through the male line, to the English king's succession through the female line, a pretext which was invoked later on. However, this did not mean that any *roi trouvé* could claim to be a successor of Saint Louis. It was under these conditions that court intrigues and the pressure of provincial interests revolved slowly around Philip VI of Valois and the aged Edward III. Understandably, the gerontocracy tried to defend its position against the avidity of the 'young wolves' by mustering a barrage of tested loyal followers against them. This situation did not last.

Matters were in fact much worse. The growing volume of business handled in the palace, even without the final touches added by the deteriorating economic situation, created a crushing burden of public expenditure. Paying and maintaining an army over and beyond the short campaigns which feudal military service provided for, building castles, taking the failing urban finances in hand again after 1256–60, employing masses of officers and agents, all these things could no longer be covered by the king's ordinary income alone, drawn from the royal demesne and royal rights. This was just enough to pay the expenses of the royal household. As a result, the clerks of the accounts became – and were to remain – immensely important; their solution was firstly to tax the merchants, following the example set by Genoa and other towns since 1274, which is what Philip III did in 1277 and Edward I in 1275. Then they raised a value tax on all produce, which was called *maltote* in France, where it was deeply suspected. It was adopted first by Philip the Fair and then by Edward II around 1305 and 1320, again on the lines of the Italian city states. Otherwise, a monopoly on an essential commodity like salt could be established; the kings of Naples had controlled its sale since 1259 and they were imitated everywhere, in France in 1341, in Castile in 1338 and in Venice at the same time. The *gabelle* has not got a good reputation, but in fact it never amounted to more than 2 per cent, like the *maltote* for that matter, which is a great deal less than our present-day Value Added Tax. And of course, it wasn't always enough. The Church tithes were inadequate sources of income and robbing Jews and Lombards was only a short-term resource. What was required was an extraordinary

A corn measure for the tithe; a parish priest would collect around one tenth of his parishioners' agricultural produce (Paris, Musée de Cluny).

source of income, such as would be provided by reintroducing direct taxation. The times were, however, not ready for this; instead Edward I and Philip IV were reduced after 1295 to debasing the coinage. Their devaluations were only slight and indeed were inadequate palliatives; even kings were chary of tampering with their currencies. Contemporaries nonetheless reacted violently and from Dante to our times, the accusation of *faux monnayeur* has been levelled against those kings whose debasements were only a result of the unstoppable rise in the price of silver.

There remained the extraordinary 'aid'; it was supposed to be exceptional and could not be raised by force but required the assent of the subjects of the realm. Public consultation was the direct result of the growing precariousness of royal finances, involving as it did a violation of the principles investing kingship. A convocation of bishops and nobles could pass as normal, but an assembly of the third estate, of the workers or rather of the moneyed burgesses, scandalised the theorists of royal authority. It had to be done, and indeed the example of the Iberian *brazos*, the embryos of the later *cortes* was reassuring; from 1240 or earlier they had obediently granted subsidies to the king. But the infidel was still at their gates, providing a specific reason for raising money, although Charles of Anjou in Naples and his nephew Philip III used it as a pretext for disguising their Catalan ambitions as a Crusade and to raise some cash. The Aragonese king used the same pretext against them in 1283.

The two determining events, however, happened firstly in 1265 when the English barons and town representatives forced Henry III to agree to a prior consultation with them before he ever raised an aid, and secondly in 1302 when Philip the Fair was embroiled in war with Flanders and in a bitter conflict with the Pope, obliging him to call an assembly of the three estates; initially to discuss matters of general import, but in 1308 and 1321 to discuss the question of money.

These consultations were clearly in response to the stirring of popular demands, flying in the face of the concept of an administrative and victorious kingship. For the moment these demands were restricted to immediate problems, but they produced their first fruits in the period from 1280 to 1330.

The first rumblings

When the Jacquerie flared up in 1358, the aristocracy was taken completely unawares. This at least is the impression one gets from the chroniclers. For all that, there was no shortage of warnings, which were perhaps mistaken for eschatological ravings or confused with urban riots. Historians are in business to see things more clearly, in spite of producing occasional blunders, to wit that there was no class conflict in the Middle Ages. Although the sensitive points of peasant life can be identified fairly easily, it is not clear which particular irritations provoked the explosion. It is absolutely certain that the rural troubles prior to the risings of the fourteenth and fifteenth centuries had a religious dimension, but it would be obtuse to interpret this aspect of peasant grievances as a simple manifestation of spiritual discontent. The first fundamental requirement of rural production was *necessitas*, the minimum essential to the survival of the peasant household. What fraction of its total production this represented depended on the fertility of the soil, the tools available and the level of the lord's exactions. Threatening factors were for instance the lord's refusal to accept money payment in lieu of forced labour dues, or when he restricted their forest rights. Such measures invited protest, especially from the most deprived, and the occasions for such conflict within the limits dictated by the tacit contract between lord and village were many, in a period when the lordly class was growing. When the *necessitas* was reduced, the problem of subsistence became acute, the more so since holdings were being divided up to an abusive degree. The average peasant household in England and France around 1330 paid 15 to 20 per cent of its crops in seignorial dues of all kinds, 10 per cent went as the tithe, rather less for the polltax, reserving around 20 per cent as seed for the next sowing season. At the current price of wheat, and where adequate tools were available, this meant that more than half the peasant's produce slipped out of his grasp, and if his family could not survive on the remainder, he had to borrow. Peasant debt is a very complex problem. To begin with, the interest demanded by the money-lender, who could be a neighbour, the parish priest, a passing Jew or a townsman, was a twentieth or more often, a twelfth (5 to 8.33 per cent) of the loan. If one considers that a sou or a shilling represented two full day's work, or a day's rent for a horse, it is clear that the poor were trapped in a vicious circle. They tried to escape from this by paying their debts in free labour services, which put them at the mercy of richer men and gradually forced them to become unfree.

There were many other sources of friction, for example, salaries varied according to age and sex; around 1300 in Provence women and young men were paid half the going rate for men. Since the land shortage forced many people to live together under the same roof, they tended to covet the underpopulated Church lands and to demand an end to inequities. These hopes were at the root of the eschatological longings for a golden age with no

Church, no feudal estates, no rich or poor – an evangelical idea which springs up in the mental hinterland in all periods of hardship, like the promise to raise up the poor at the end of time. In 1249, during Saint Louis' captivity in Egypt, shepherds, artisans, and swineherds in the French Midi gathered to bands of *Pastoureux* led by an *illuminato*, the Master of Hungary. Likewise Lombard peasants followed an apostle, Segarelli of Parma, around 1270, and a radical Franciscan, Fra Dulcino, around 1305, who ended up burnt at the stake.

In other places changes were more substantial; in Sicily, near Naples and in Provence along the Rhine, the boundaries of Church lands were ripped up in the 1310s. In 1318, rural communities – the *università* of the Appenines – revolted against seignorial taxation and refused to pay up. These movements were generally broken by force. The established Church was also suspicious of prophets and egalitarians; in June 1323, Pope John XXII tried to remove the prestige of the most rigorous Franciscans, the Spirituals, by denying the poverty of Jesus. When Flemish peasants formed bands to attack the chateaux in 1322–3, anticipating the Jacquerie, the affair was all the more worrying because their leaders included wealthy labourers, like Nicholas Zannequin, not famished peasants or false prophets. In Flanders, nothing much could be achieved without the townsmen and the movement merged into a vast protest within the whole county. It included princely intrigues, a few royal ambitions and some anti-French opposition, and the historian loses sight of the rural movement as contemporaries also did. It was crushed at Cassel in 1328 by Philip VI's army, thus inaugurating his repressive rule.

The age of the communes had trained chroniclers to see the influence of the towns in these rural movements, because they were more used to town uprisings and their understanding was more subtle when the urban milieu was seething with resentment, as it had periodically done since the communal movement and even before. Their analysis was nonetheless brief. They confused two types of troubles; the internal struggles of factions for the town government and the social repercussions. As with the religious dimension to rural revolt, urban factions gave rise to deep movements which they first caught up and then abandoned. In the history of urban troubles, the only obvious elements are the rivalries between clans, and some historians claim that only these existed. Inside the towns, in Italy more than elsewhere, there were whole groups of dependants from needy relatives to salaried renegades who were ready to carry any particular movement through. It has been shown that in Genoa, Metz and Barcelona, the control of a particular family over a certain quarter of their town included certain guilds or social groupings, which rose to the forefront of affairs when accounts were settled between *case* or between *Junkers*. Events like the disturbances in Florence in 1293 or Venice in 1297, which ended by replacing the great men at the head of city affairs with less great men, are not our concern. We may examine the three levels at which urban discontent festered and swelled; the first, where town land was confiscated, within and sometimes without the walls, to a distance of several leagues away, as happened in France around Toulouse, Reims, Metz and Lyon; the second, where the houses, booths, market stalls, gardens and quays all belonged to someone, the Church or others; the third, where town lodgings and jobs were controlled by the *magnati*, who even held the offices of town magistrate and consul. Wherever it has been uncovered, the evidence is glaring; in 1335 in Toulouse, 7 per cent of the inhabitants held 65 per cent of the land. In Reims it was higher at 18 per cent. The situation paralleled that of the fragmented smallholdings in the countryside.

In the second place, the liquidity problem inherent to the poor performance of the economy after 1310–20 forced businesses to merge either by buying out workshops in financial difficulties, or by forming coalitions of masters who arranged to keep their apprentices' salaries very low. The first example of this was in Florence, where the number of cloth manufacturers shrank from 325 in 1235 to 50 by 1300; the second was that of the master ironmongers in Speier and Worms. As a result, the main body of the workforce began to show signs of economic collapse; it was possible for an employer to offer wages varying from 7 to 300 florins per annum. Work contracts were tacitly renewed for some, whilst others were hired by the day. The pool of unemployed, school-leavers, marginals, swelled, while they watched for their every opportunity to grab.

Taxation, royal or otherwise, was the pressure which generally unleashed riots. The picture was similar everywhere; an obscure Franciscan friar would preach and then disappear; an employer would incite with intent; a public official would insult someone and people would draw in their shutters, grab a spear and run to the town square. As soon as famine threatened, violence was near at hand. In 1267 the Mayor of Pontoise was assassinated, as was the Mayor of Provins in 1279. 1280–92 were years of constant arson in Languedoc, Lombardy, Normandy and Tuscany. In Catalonia, a leader named Berenguer Oller managed to hold Barcelona for one year in 1285 against royal troops before dying alongside several hundred others. Paris in 1306, Toulouse in 1335 and Lyon in 1347 all rioted. The Low Countries were always half-way between political reprisals and social demands and in Bruges in 1347, when it was a question of massacring the French, Peter Deconinck raised the cry 'all should have as much as one another'. In Liège in 1253–6, the *conductor populi* Henry of Dinant who led his men to the cry of 'work and liberty' was as hostile to the bishop as he was to the rich.

There have been few agonies as protracted as the Hundred Years' War, which have been preceded by so many warnings. But in terms of 200 years of almost continuous expansion, contemporary observers could not understand many of them and indeed, we are still unsure about them.

One or several crises?

We may start by eliminating two hypotheses, which, though they have become articles of faith, do not stand up to serious investigation. The first is psychological; the 'betrayal of the clergy', which deals with the phenomenon of the rejection of Christianity, which had reached its apogee and was doomed from then on to 'decadence'. The responsibility for this *accidia*, the prostration that accompanies violence, laziness and disorder, was laid at the door of the spiritual leaders; a facile excuse for the economic factors really responsible, and a stale concoction that has frequently been served up to account for the fall of Athens and

Rome as well as for more recent disasters in France. It is easy to point the finger at intellectuals, people who lack the energy of military men and the practicality of businessmen. Such views are nonsensical in the context of the period under discussion: I would like to point out that although the Church hierarchy may have been rocking on its pedestal, there have been few periods richer in new enterprises, daring speculation and admirable achievements than the fourteenth century. Let us proceed, without pausing to explore the awakening of national consciousness which Jan Huss and Joan of Arc came to symbolise, and to be claimed as such by men of conflicting convictions.

The flotsam of politics and war rises to the surface and emerges in history books. The two kingdoms, England and France, were so closely related that they spoke the same language and possessed the same institutions or nearly so, thus making coexistence impossible. Their long rivalry (from 1152 to 1259) over the formation of the Plantagenet 'empire' was not settled by the peace drawn up between Henry III and his brother-in-law Saint Louis. War was resumed in Aquitaine and Flanders in the reign of Philip the Fair and matters were further aggravated by the bungled succession of 1328. In 1338 – after mature reflection – Edward III laid claim to the French crown. These facts certainly provided an essential weft to daily life, in France at any rate, but nothing explains the recurring outbreaks of war between one truce and the next. And why stop at the end of one hundred years, when only in our century have English rulers forgone assuming their traditional style and title of 'King of France' at their coronation? In any case, what did the French succession matter to Castile, Florence or the Empire? Further, could it not be maintained that war was, alas, a good and profitable thing, a mental discipline for many people and not a negative occurrence?

Beyond mens' reach

Evaluating human causality is so unsatisfactory that nowadays historians tend to look for explanations that transcend human ambitions and mistakes. This is a very old tendency; when men in the fourteenth century interpreted the evils of their age as manifestations of divine wrath, they were thinking along the same lines. Historians nowadays are more likely to substitute grains of pollen for the Will of God and to seek for signs of major climatic deterioration in peat bogs and glaciers. If it is true that European harvests between 1000 and 1250 were the result of optimal hydrological and thermal conditions, the termination of these conditions may explain many of the phenomena we have such difficulty accounting for. That there was change cannot be denied; the Channel was encroaching on the coast of Flanders, the ice zone was expanding and in consequence the highest altitude at which beech trees could grow was reduced; the advance of willow pollen and the withdrawal of wheat pollen are facts which can be quantified and we do not need to look outside western Europe for further evidence. What is more, the texts themselves confirm these observations; Greenland's Danish colonies were evacuated between 1345 and 1380, giving way to Eskimos and polar bears, and icebergs regularly cut off the route to Iceland. Froissart describes endless summer rains bogging down armies; a Parliamentary scribe blamed his clumsiness on the paralysing cold and the Paris burgher's story of how wine was dealt out in the Place de la Grève with an axe, so that everyone could take a bit home in their hat, is well-known. Manorial accounts are not lacking in comparable evidence; Winchester and Regensburg and a few other places carefully noted when the wine harvest began. The clearest sign of all was the unpredictability of the climate; winters were humid and overcast or glacial.

It is clear that these changes in the ecology, mysterious as they were, soon had their effect on human beings. To start with, they seem to have disrupted cereal production and, given the compartmentalised nature of the economy of medieval Europe, this inevitably led to serious food shortages and price rises. These effects were recorded in the Île-de-France from 1305 onwards and in Germany in 1309 and 1311, and the spectre of famine, which had been almost banished for more than a century, reappeared once more on the horizon. We can now understand that the serious food crisis of 1315–17, which apparently affected the whole of North West Europe, was an urgent warning sign. A series of rotten summers forced the French armies to abandon their campaigns and were followed by such poor harvests that the sowing seed had to be eaten. This introduced a vicious cycle of poor harvests leading to inevitable disaster. The Winchester manorial accounts reveal a two-thirds fall in production. In Ramsey, almost all the cattle died. By the time the price of grain in Paris had quadrupled – with the help of speculation – in 1315 and had risen eightfold in 1316, it is clear that hunger had reached catastrophic proportions. Towns were especially vulnerable because of the greater instability of wheat prices compared with the prices of products less vital to survival, such as meat and wine. If the Ypres town registers are to be believed, 2,800 persons (10 or 15 per cent of the population; almost 6 per cent at Bruges) died of starvation during those two years. The local authorities, which were anyway badly policed, appear to have let it happen and limited themselves to requisitioning speculators' stocks. In Scandinavia, fish and butter exports were blocked and could only be exchanged for imported grain.

Of course, these and all subsequent failures in the food supply (1332–3 in Spain; 1340 in Provence; 1348 in the region of Lyon) affected contemporaries especially harshly both because these generations were not used to them and because they were accompanied by wars and were soon followed by epidemics. These should not be exaggerated. Later on, in the fourteenth century and the mid fifteenth century, chroniclers grew less and less concerned about them; one can get used to anything, and country people probably adapted to the intermittent food shortages by retreating into the forests and the townsfolk did so by setting up public granaries.

One fundamental problem could not be dealt with, even if humans themselves were responsible for it; that of the spontaneous decline in the population growth-rate, which had harmed productivity at all levels. Between 1310 and 1320 (in some areas earlier, from 1280 to 1290) the population of Christian Europe seemed to have reached its peak, which meant relative overpopulation as far as the food supply was concerned. This surplus accounts for such practices as subdividing farmholdings and urban sprawl, which were unevenly distributed among the different regions. From this time on, we begin to be well

A woman sits on her doorstep suckling her child, who is tightly swaddled with its head bound in a cloth. Her husband holds another baby. A miniature illustrating the *Book of the stories of the beginning of the world*, a fourteenth-century manuscript. (Paris, Bibliothèque nationale).

informed about the population of Europe. Apart from erudite discussions about the exact significance of terms like 'hearth' or 'household', our information about Lombard, Provençal, Tuscan, Neapolitan and English populations tends to be fairly precise.

There were on average 13 to 14 hearths – around 70 inhabitants – per square kilometre in central Italy; this was double the population in Picardy or around Béziers or along the Po valley and half that of southern Italy. The famous *État des feux* (inventory of hearths) which was drawn up for the King of France in 1328 covers some 24,000 parishes over more than 300,000 sq km, and gives average densities of 8 to 15 hearths, with as many as 30 hearths per sq km in the Île-de-France; considerably more people than in today's countryside or even that of 1900. The population of the Capetian kingdom has been estimated at twenty million souls – quite a lot more than in Louis XIV's France – that of Italy and Germany at ten million, with four million in England.

Nonetheless, there were already signs before 1320 that the population was shrinking. Although more people died during the food shortages and epidemics, these were only occasional disasters; there seems to have been typhus in Thuringia and Hesse around 1322–3. Research into the rate of population growth in Picardy and Winchester over a long period between 1290 and 1340, however, reveals an over-all decrease in the number of children per fertile household. The death-rate, on the other hand, seems to have risen, according to some accounts, by almost 50 per cent of all infants up to five years old. The only baptismal and death register for that period to have survived in France, is that of the little village of Givry in Burgundy. It reveals that, ten to fifteen years before the onset of the Plague, the number of deaths rose regularly. It is difficult to know how to interpret these facts; a high proportion of deaths is scarcely a voluntary phenomenon and must be linked

41

with some biological weakness. Assuming that famine, massacres and epidemics accelerated a process that had already begun, the hypothesis follows that human resistance to climatic changes and to infectious diseases was weakened. It has also been suggested that the disruption of medieval dietary patterns, leading to abusive consumption of carbohydrates and fatty foods could give rise to a variety of chronic diabetic conditions. It is of course also possible that the fall in population, especially in the birth-rate, was the result of a deliberate form of population control in the Malthusian sense, effected by a society which did not have enough food to go around. Alternatively, it could have been due to the gradual (and surely more voluntary) rejection of the fecund matrimonial model of previous generations, with girls being married off older. Unfortunately, we are as yet ill-equipped to decide the issue. In any case the fall in population, whether voluntary or otherwise, definitely contributed to the general decline.

What started off the decline?

Many historians prefer economic explanations, and, after giving the preceding hypotheses a passing nod, turn to the context of production. It seems natural to look there for the explanation, since productivity suffered definite set-backs, as we will see, and indeed the technical backwardness of Europe has long been held responsible for this. Once the technology of Antiquity and the Orient had been assimilated, on the levels of production, manufacture and transport, Christendom is supposed to have been stuck with the same equipment, as far as technology and its application were concerned, until the age of steam four centuries later. The inability to supply a demand, which by 1300 had become excessive and increasingly diversified, is supposed to have induced the phenomenon of an 'overheated' economy. The machinery of production and its distribution seized up, which ended with less food being grown, and, paradoxically, with food prices slumping after 1350 when the population collapsed.

This 'mechanistic' explanation is typical of a 'B-phase' in economists' jargon, a phase of depression, and depends on a variety of certainties which I will discuss later, but it is not enough to explain the complexity of the phenomena. Several contradictions have to be accounted for: if the revival of technical invention dates from Newton and Denis Papin, [1647–1714, a French physicist, the first to recognise the elastic power of steam – Transl. n.], how are the phases of undeniable 'reconstruction', which proliferated between 1450 and 1550, to be explained? If the machinery of production failed as a result of trying to meet the increased demand and for lack of inventiveness, the abrupt fall in population after 1350 should have relieved the situation completely. This did not happen. As for the reduced volume of food production, which is mathematically undeniable, it should have led to a drastic rise in cereal prices, due to scarcity. But quite the opposite happened; historians have observed only persistent stagnation. Much more striking however, is the lack of evidence that men of the time were technically incompetent and we even have evidence to the contrary. Take cereal production, for instance; enough fragments of manorial accounts survive for England, northern and southern France and the Low Countries, for us to realise

Although sales of corn were falling off, harvests showed an increased yield. In this miniature from the *Theatrum Sanitatis* of Ububchasym of Baldach, a peasant couple is threshing wheat in front of their barn.

that yields were high, often clearly higher than before; ratios of four, five or six to one were rare before 1300, but common during the fourteenth century, even high up in Lorraine, in Périgord or on the poor farmland of Provence and Languedoc. A ratio of eight or ten to one was the average on the farmlands of Saint-Denis, in 'France' in Flanders, Forez, or the properties of Merton College, Winchester or Ramsey Abbey. In Artois in a good year, yields could even reach thirteen or fifteen to one, giving an average of fourteen quintals to the hectare – a ratio seldom achieved in France around 1900. I have already mentioned snatch crops and market gardens and will discuss the great progress made with plants used in industry. We know too that the introduction of closer furrows and three-year crop rotation together with a more widespread use of fertiliser helped improve the quality of the soil. Such practices show that men were not betraying their birthright; if the price of wheat fell, it was due to lack of demand, and if land prices stagnated or fell, it was for the same reason. The difficulties did not arise from lack of production but from a distortion between the marketable volume, which was worth more or less the same as before, and the overall rise in the cost of wages and taxes, due to the reduced workforce.

Having said this, two features of the regression which certainly had an effect on the overall situation should not be neglected. The first concerned the craftsmen and several of its social aspects have already been discussed. Processing raw materials, both in town and in the country was the prerogative of particular groups who were grimly determined to keep production within the family, to preserve the non-division of labour and the exclusivity, not to mention monopoly, of their branch of business. The wool industry was the only one to escape this, if only partially, since the agreements drawn up between

43

masters conspired with urban regulations to proscribe competition, and these were generally enforced fairly strongly.

This attitude can of course be embellished with noble motives such as the rejection of abusive profits, concern for quality, protection for the buyer, fear of ruining the market by over-production and suchlike. But it tended to damp the spirit of enterprise and restrict the volume of production; it has for instance been reckoned that 600 textile workers in Prato, Tuscany (one of the major industries) could put on the market only 20,000 pieces of cloth per annum, each around 4 square metres, which works out at an average production of thirty pieces of cloth, that is, scarcely more than 100 square metres per worker per year. This slow rate of production together with strict supervision of the manufacturing process guaranteed the quality of the goods. In a period of growth and regular demand, the evil was not too great. But if the supply of raw materials failed, if the ratio of supply to demand fluctuated without adequate stocks to fall back on, if the dwindling number of workers forced wages up, the system fell into chaos. This is precisely what happened after 1270 and 1290, whether iron ore extraction or the sale of woollen cloth was involved; rivalries between rulers in Germany and hostilities between France and England and in the Iberian peninsula, all interrupted the flow of commerce. During the 'Aragonese Crusade', iron production in Catalonia was suspended; troubles in Tuscany blocked Porto Pisano where iron from the island of Elba was unloaded. The 'grand interregnum' in the German Empire (1254–73) paralysed the convoys from the Harz mountains. Matters were further complicated by the kings' galloping taxation; for instance, when the Plantagenets decided to raise heavy duties on the export of woollen cloth or to set up staples – obligatory unloading points – in Flanders, they slowed down the movement of woollen goods and in doing so, forced an autonomous English cloth industry to emerge. In Flanders, ceaseless fighting from 1292 to 1295 scarcely helped improve matters.

It should not be forgotten that sea transport, while it managed to avoid some of these hazards, remained distressingly precarious. Nowadays, the volume of the cargoes seems ridiculous; its organisation, which could not guarantee return cargoes, was the dubious monopoly of certain entrepreneurs in certain products, who relied on official piracy. Such were the Zaccaria of Genoa, who controlled the export of alum from Phocea in Asia Minor. In the Mediterranean too, the freedom of the sea was deteriorating. Venice and Genoa fought their duel in the Black Sea right up to the Tyrrhennian Sea between 1204 and 1284, and Aragonese fought Angevins for control of Sicily until she was forcibly divided up in 1282–5. In 1291 the last stepping-stones to the Levant were lost, and the gradual isolation of Constantinople suffocated by the Turks together with Mameluke aggression in Alexandria contributed to the unreliability of commerce. The repercussions were soon felt; the gradual disappearance of the Champagne Fairs has traditionally been attributed to war and to the rival attractions of Paris, but the Fairs were abandoned after 1285 or 1290 because the wheels of commerce were already turning towards the Atlantic and the Empire and away from the traditional merchant routes. Further, although production was impeded, times were changing and a new dominant class was replacing the old, made up of ostentatious rich parvenus. True to type, they were demanding, extravagant and

The war horse, or charger, was protected like the knight by armour: the head was covered by a helmet and the rest of the body by a caparison made up of articulated metal plates. A knight's and his horse's armour would together weigh between 50 and 60 kilograms. (Vienna, Kunsthistorisches Museum.)

An iron chest, made in France in the fourteenth century. (Paris, Musée de Cluny.) Chests were essential furnishings in the Middle Ages and were only replaced by cupboards in the sixteenth century. They were used for storing clothes, crockery, jewels and armour.

exhibitionist and the price of their clothes, furniture, jewels and even armour rocketed accordingly. Highly skilled craftsmen were paid inflated wages, the most ambitious controlled all the local workshops, with obvious results. Certain rulers were aware of these developments; Philip the Fair envisaged lengthening the working day or fixing prices according to quality, in order to diversify production and support the market. Such measures could only be theoretical because in general they were opposed by the guild masters, who were imbued with the spirit of profit, and by the town magistrates, who were afraid of over-production, and their opposition tended to counter and nullify such attempts at reform.

The treachery of gold and silver

Where minting gold and silver was concerned, any change was definitely for the worse. When gold started coming to the West again via the Maghrib and Sicily, or from the Byzantine and Egyptian East, it was minted into coins of good title, such as the florin of Florence, the *écu* of France, the ducats of Venice and the English nobles. At the same time, more or less standardised silver coins, worth twelve of the old *denarii*, were being issued all over Europe, known variously as *gros*, *groschen*, groats, etc. The bimetallic system was essential to the expansion of trade and for meeting the needs of the triumphantly growing administrations. It rested on two assumptions: that the supply of gold and silver would continue to increase, and that the ratio of gold to silver, which was fixed at 1:9.65 between 1270 and 1289 from England to Sicily, was immutable.

In reality, an economy incapable of regulating its means of exchange, even when the ruler monopolised the minting of money, was controlled by the market mechanism. The gold supply was extremely vulnerable; from 1275–80 profound political ructions, about which westerners had no inkling or information, shook the empires of Niger and Senegal. As Africa was progressively Islamised from Dakar to Chad, her links with the Maghrib grew weaker, itself torn by the painful suppression of the Almohad dynasty. From then on, the Emperors of Mali, the rulers of Bambuk and even of Gao, turned their gaze and soon their caravans towards the Nile. Here too, the destruction of the Shiite Fatimids, who had previously formed a difficult obstacle on the way from Timbuktu to Mecca, played a major role around 1160. Then the orthodox Mamelukes, who were fairly interested in trading directly with the African Sahel, drew pilgrims and tradesmen to them. After 1275, the supply of gold to Morocco and Algeria dwindled and instead very many Africans came to Cairo. The Emperor of Mali made a sumptuous pilgrimage to the Kaaba in 1325, which set the seal on this fundamental change in direction. For a while, the failures in the gold supply seem to have been repaired in other ways; in Spain, for instance, during the final stages of the *Reconquistà* up to 1270, when *razzias* on captured Andalusian towns and Catalan attacks on Ceuta and Bone proved very profitable.

In the East, the European position remained excellent up to 1280. Unfortunately, the growing demand for gold made the shortage appear greater than it was: periods of *strettezza* (when the gold market in Italy contracted) increased, and the price of ingots rose; it had been fixed in 1253 when the florin was first minted at 45 *grossi* the *oncia* (ounce). By 1271, gold cost 50 *grossi* in Naples: between then and 1290 the ratio of gold to silver rose from 1:9.65 to 1:10.5 and even to 1:11.4 at the Roman Curia. The distortion would doubtless have been even greater if silver had not simultaneously been subjected, albeit to a lesser degree, to a considerable price rise. In 1266, the mark cost 54 *sous tournois*; in 1285, it cost 58. This was partly due to the exhaustion of silver mines, particularly those at Melle in Poitou, and partly to speculation, which gave rise to many law suits, as well as to the problems involved in the extraction of German silver. Towards 1290, the official gold–silver ratio in France and England had to be readjusted to 1:10.15, which was way below the commercial rate. It is not too clear, given the general level of economic awareness, what the money masters were hoping for. Nicholas Oresme, a member of Charles V's entourage, tried to demonstrate the various elements of a monetary crisis, but he and others like him concentrated on the rights of the ruler and its social repercussions. They were not to understand its economic workings for a long time to come.

In our age, when we are no longer subjected to the economic disruptions which our grandparents blamed on the rapacity of rulers, the working of the economy seems very straightforward. In the absence of proper stocks of gold and silver, money was obliged to rely on the market for its circulation and while this system could flag, it never did so to such a degree as to justify the abruptness or the range of the monetary devaluations. Although the thirst for precious metals began to be felt, it was not yet strong enough to drive Europeans over the seas in search of African or Asian mines to conquer. It was rather the anarchic nature of demand that induced panic: anarchy too in the waves of taxation; in the payment of the wages; in the assessment of military aids, and in the coinage, since so many

a) On the left the Venetian ducat, or sequin, a gold coin first minted in 1284, which remained unaltered until 1797. It was used during the fourteenth and fifteenth centuries in the East as an international coinage.
b) The Florentine florin on the right dominated the West in the same period.

New coins:
a) Edward III's gold noble on the left and
b) John the Good's franc on the right.

different coins circulated simultaneously. Of course, this operated in favour of the less good coins, since the better ones were hoarded in treasure troves, giving rise later on, in 1558, to Sir Thomas Gresham's famous dictum; 'bad money drives out good'.

Like lots of government ministers nowadays, rulers began by running through the whole gamut of economic sanctions available to them; regulations, inventories declaring precious metals, closing frontiers, condemning speculation. The slight effect of such sanctions in the twentieth century is a measure of their ineffectuality in the fourteenth. They were next driven to adjusting their coinage to the rate at which its users bought and sold it. Nothing clears rulers of the accusation of monetary malpractice better than the simple observation that when a mediocre coinage replaced a better one, prices went up, so that sellers received the same quantity of precious metal in payment for their wares. Those who benefited from this system were those whose incomes grew in line with the inflation of prices: merchants, guild masters and the wealthiest peasants. Those whose incomes were fixed by custom or contract lost out, because their incomes could not be increased by a single penny, such as workers in towns and in the countryside as well as *rentiers*, that is, nobles with the king at their head.

Mint masters were thus obliged to debase their coinage to bring it in line with the going rate for gold and silver, a rate which was strongly influenced by the social classes which benefited from the debasements. Although rulers tried to put a stop to these alterations whenever a favourable factor turned up, they ended by disorganising the administration and in upsetting prices and wages far beyond what would normally have happened. It would be pointless and pedantic to follow this process step by step as it gradually got completely out of control, but since it began well before the crisis which text books set at 1350 occurred, we should recall the basic facts about it. Forced to pay more for the mark of silver and gold than in the previous year, the money masters could resort to three expedients to cover their outlay and costs. They could reduce the overall weight of the coins; they could alter the gold and silver content, and they could increase the rate of

47

exchange. Finally, all three measures could be combined. Silver obviously had the wider circulation and was more suited to clipping and to alloys. In 1289, silver was sold at 58 *sous tournois* the mark; in 1295 at 61 *sous*; in 1295 at 68 *sous*, in 1298 at 75 *sous*, in 1299 at 85 *sous*, in 1303 at 104 *sous*, in 1304 at 120 *sous* and at 145 *sous* in 1305. Its price fell in 1306 and 1313 to 66 *sous* before rising again and stabilising around 1330. At the same time, the price of gold underwent great and sudden alterations, so that a graph of the gold–silver ratio would describe a curve with jagged teeth climbing from 1:11 to 1:18.95, stabilising at 1:13.90 in 1330.

The mint masters even attempted to anticipate a phenomenon which they did not understand, and resorted to reducing the intrinsic gold content of their coins by as much as 25 per cent (coins of 18 carat gold instead of 24 carat). Most devaluations involved putting new coins into circulation; *chaises*, *agnels*, *francs d'or* for the Capetians, the English *noble*, and various types of *florin* at the Curia in Avignon, in Brabant, Holland and Lübeck. As for silver coins, apart from the smaller very poor quality coins known as 'black money' which had a free rate of exchange, their value was adjusted according to the official rates announced whenever new coins were issued (the *gros*, theoretically worth 12 *deniers*, could climb to 39 *deniers*), or according to its weight (the same coin could start off weighing 4.22 grams and be reduced to 3.50 grams) and above all its title, which was reduced by 30 per cent. French coins were subjected to a series of devaluations in 1295, 1303, 1311, 1318 and 1322, which were punctuated by attempts to return to the original coin, *la bonne monnaie de monseigneur Saint Louis*, in 1306, 1313 and 1329–30, by which date a level had been reached which rulers and towns considered stable. However, since none of the conditions which caused the money supply to contract had been removed, this respite was clearly due to a brief hiatus in the demand for money. As with our discussion of the demographic situation above, any examination of the economic situation ends in uncertainty; was it cause or effect of the disruption? Modern historians are forced to turn to the structures of production for their answer.

The crisis of feudalism

I have already pointed out that I dislike this term and prefer to speak of the disintegration of the manorial system, but it does have the merit of pinpointing how the production mechanism actually functioned in the period immediately preceding the crisis.

The overall scheme has already been sketched in. The basis of production was the family unit, without any diversification of labour or specialisation, which combined with other units to form a vast entity supporting one master, a lord. All those about him, who served him and lived off him and in principle contributed to his prestige, were maintained in part by the labour and produce he could obtain on his own property and from his relations and his servants, but much the greater part came from the primary sector, paid in labour services, in money and in kind. Manorial dues, or 'rentes', were justified in principle by the necessary and expensive functions of defence and justice administered by the lord, a system which offered both parties obvious advantages and which worked, interspersed with readjustments – along with some written guarantees and the occasional confrontation – for two centuries. Between 1050 and 1250, the two social classes resorted only very seldom to violent confrontation, which is why it is difficult for us to trace the origins of such practices as sabotaging labour services or withholding rents. In any case, this system rested on a sort of challenge; on the one side, the lord had to fulfil the task tacitly left to him by his men at the price he demanded, and on the other, the workers had to supply enough to satisfy the master and maintain their own *necessitas* without forgoing either their freedom or their tools. Even in its purest form, such a system contained obvious structural weaknesses, irrespective of different regions' suitability for supplying the corn or linen required of them, since masters varied considerably; the Church, for instance, could not guarantee military protection, but did not for all that reduce its demands on its tenants. Surviving documents show that the Church had the naivety (true or simulated) to attribute the unpleasant shocks she suffered as a result of her churchmen's demands, both in towns and elsewhere, to mens' wicked natures. Equally striking is how, in a period when workers were progressively better equipped and could hope to profit from their surplus produce, the system by which they were forced to pay their lord in day-labour dues, to the detriment of their own farms, irritated the better-off workers most of all. As for the less well-off, they obviously suffered as the lords were obliged by their higher standard of living to increase their demands on them. Finally, the introduction of money into such a system vitiated its principle and disrupted its mechanism, since money implies contact with a market, and hence transactions and then social relationships far removed from the quasi-physical contract between lord and man.

Before 1250, the weaknesses inherent to the system of production were invisible or minor, due to the regular growth in production and the availability of land; the food supply was also in proportion to the work force. But things changed in the last third of the thirteenth century and the weaknesses began to emerge as a consequence of the preceding boom. Small peasant holdings had managed to achieve a higher level of equipment and skills than that available on the lord's demesne, and the peasants began sending an important part of their produce to market, thus undermining the lord's monopoly and control of the sale of produce. A 'kulak' class was emerging and is supposed to have led the struggle for rights of tenure, fixed rents and for limiting tallages and various taxes. The lord was ill-equipped to withstand this onslaught; he organised his own lands along the lines of his peasant neighbours' holdings. He managed to increase an inadequate work force by resorting to wage labour, which emptied his coffers, and to imposing the *corvée* on his peasants, who were increasingly loath to perform it. His basic problem was that of keeping up his manorial 'rentes'.

To start off with, a great number of landlords tried to keep to the old practices; in England around 1340, the Bishop of Ely insisted on *corvées* on 43 per cent of his lands, which secured him a total of 3,700 workers, whom he could not in actual fact employ. The Abbot of Ramsey was even more hide-bound; 44 of his domains were worked entirely by labour service, 15 were contracted out and 22 retained a few services. Cases like these were fairly archaic, and on the continent, where instances of peasants buying their freedom were

49

fairly frequent, the growing shortage of labour soon made it difficult to recruit wage labourers. Consequently, domains had to be leased out; the success of 'farming out' was largely due to these difficulties. If, in the teeth of the peasants' intransigence, a lord did want to keep enough land in hand to maintain his entourage, he could put heavier pressure on his tenants, but was quite unable to increase their polltax or dues in kind and services, such as delivering hay and wood. The bulk of these traditional forms of payment no longer featured in the country gentleman's budget, and by allowing his tenants slowly to form the notion that they had a fundamental right to their holdings, he further sapped his other claims on them. In Normandy, about half the total allotments either refused to pay their dues or allowed arrears to mount up, evidence both of the lord's disdain and the peasants' ill-will. This led the lords to put pressure on reliefs, or succession taxes – the *lods* of northern France or the *vendas* of the South; they also put an end to the practice of waiving such tithes (or thirteenths) they still retained; and, above all, they imposed hearth taxes as substitutes for tallages which had often been rescinded, and non-payers would be pursued through the law-courts until they were ruined. Finally, the alienating nature of certain personal obligations concerning marriage or inheritance, as in the Pyrenees, was stepped up to enable the lord to sell exemption from them at a high price.

Given the lord's increasingly aggressive attitude when his 'rentes' were threatened, as the crisis continued, the peasantry reacted on two levels: for those who were already unable to produce more than their *necessitas*, servitude ensued, a new serfdom, which began for exclusively economic reasons and as it developed, enfolded those who could not acquit their dues, pay the *molitura* (mill-tax) or face up to the pressure of taxation. Gradually rejected from the community, they were the only people still constrained to render the remaining labour services. They passed as unfree and consequently saw new constraints fall on them: succession taxes, restrictions on their freedom of movement, seizure of their tools. Their attempts at getting fair wages from their master or neighbouring employer only chained them down still further. Pressure could also be put on labourers, who reacted violently; the lord's inability to extend his property, his often prolonged absences and his virtual disappearance when he farmed out his land, left the field open to peasant cultivation. Since the very reason for the old system of payment in return for being judged and defended had crumbled at the same time as public justice and the royal army were taking over, the lord's demands did not appear to be justified any more. He was now a parasite, a profiteer, and useless. The fragmentation of the peasant world, which was already implicit in the uneven distribution of equipment and variations in living standards, was aggravated when confronted with the extortions of a seigneurial class, whose very principle of existence was at stake. Among the empty bellies piled up in inadequate holdings, the labourers, farmers or otherwise, held out the best they could; the peasant world of 1300, hemmed in on one side by resentful and money hungry *hobereaux* (squires), and on the other by absentee lords, who preferred court life to the country, slid into serious difficulties.

It was clear that storm clouds were also gathering over the towns. In this corner of society, the same phenomena could be glimpsed; the town was an oligarchy ruled by merchants and the masters of the leading guilds and the nobles who resided there. There too, the bulk of the workforce was divided into apprentices, who were learning a specialised skill, and into the growing ranks of the unskilled. There too, the problem of an alienating wage had existed for longer than the last ten years. There too, the taxation imposed by the rich or by the ruler was inequitably applied. The difference, which was not slight, lay at the root of the acute problems facing the poor, which doubtless explains the violence of subsequent urban protests.

The foregoing pages are gloomy; with so many weaknesses, distortions, alarm signals and alarming prophecies, did nobody realise anything? Almost nobody, since the prating of a few Dominican friars cannot be taken for visionary analysis. As for those men in the swing of things, as good lawyers, they had eyes only for appearances, words and principles. They are not to be blamed for their lack of clairvoyance. Generally speaking, all major economic, social, and in this case cultural changes determining the course of history are obvious only to people living five centuries afterwards. At the time men noticed only immediate events. That was how there were 'Romans' living under the rule of Dagobert, who believed that they were living still in the age of the Caesars. This time, however, there was a new element: the Church's teaching had accustomed the men of the fourteenth century to consider events as manifestations of Divine Will and they were duly petrified by the deluge of inexplicable and entwined disasters which overtook them from 1340 onwards. They confused economic and spiritual, social and political factors. How could the undermining of Gods's creation be explained as His Will? They could not see the causes of the whole brutal process, which plunged them into desolation and despair for a long time to come.

2 The great trial

The ninety years from 1340 to 1430 share with the tenth and twentieth centuries the dubious honour of being one of the most violent periods in the history of Europe. Violent not so much due to the bloodshed, the blind cruelty, the reigning injustice, which were indeed present, but to the harshness of daily existence, the complete uncertainty about the future. 'I never knew a single year in my village without troubles, war or death,' an old man would say on his deathbed in Charles VII's reign. These periods are often the most fruitful ones in the human adventure, as will be seen below. For the peasant or the townsman huddled between wars and plagues, princes and popes, cut back by rising prices, life had not been harsher since the Dark Ages in the tenth century.

No doubt this accounts for historians' interest in these years, over and above even the statistics they track down so passionately in our archives, and which are finally emerging. Historians and other people in France, England, Germany, Belgium and even the brilliant Italy of Florence and Venice, all find that their collective memories of the Middle Ages stem almost entirely from this period: the Plague, the English, Joan of Arc at the stake or Étienne Marcel – events which in France almost efface memories of Saint Louis, Charlemagne and Bouvines.

Pestilence and great sorrow

Into a world of undernourished and, in towns certainly, overcrowded people, where the pattern of production was deteriorating without anyone benefiting, where the economy was slowly contracting, and the rulers lacked the foresight to avert great hardships, came ever more sinister evils, not least of which the Plague.

The Black Death

In the early Middle Ages, there had been no shortage of attacks of the plague in the West. The Justinian Plague appears to have struck very severely if very unevenly; the scourge was endemic in the Middle East and even further to the East, and the Mongols may even have deliberately catapulted corpses of plague victims over the walls of Caffa, the Genoese depot in the Crimea, which they besieged in 1344. A minor detail. In early October 1347, Genoese ships unloaded their cargoes and their sick at Messina; the following weeks were blasted by the contagion which spread all over Italy. In December another ship landed the virus in Marseille. From then on its implacable advance can be followed, abetted by the summer months. In June 1348, it reached Paris, in December, the Channel and the Low Countries and southern England. In 1349 it ravaged Britain and passed into Germany and Austria. In December that year it was in Scotland and Scandinavia and also reached the Atlantic shores of Europe; the Pyrenees and Spain. This blow had scarcely been effected, when it reappeared in 1360 to strike down the youngest children and, possibly complicated by influenza, it lasted two years before fading and reappearing brutally in 1368, 1369, 1370, and again from 1375 to 1378, 1380 to 1383, 1399 and 1400. In 1418 a new onslaught was all the fiercer because resistance to the bacterium was lower, due to an epidemic of typhus fever and a great wave of whooping cough in 1408. The burghers of Paris found this particular complaint distressing because the coughing made sermons inaudible. 1420, 1421, 1433, 1438 to 1441 – the pitiful litany runs on for almost a century.

One hundred years of plague! And what a plague; bubonic plague with pneumonic complications which covered the victim in buboes and, as described by all the chroniclers of the age, his limbs would blacken, his body would be shaken by convulsions, he would vomit blood and die without hope of recovery in three days clear. Whoever survived this peak got better, but it was impossible to avoid contagion. Breath from several metres distance was more dangerous than touch; clothes spread the scourge and the blackened corpses lying in the streets were infectious for at least twenty-four hours after death. Prophylactic measures, even those based on experience, were derisory; masks for doctors, nurses and grave-diggers; burning the clothes of the dead; piling lime on the bodies; massacring a few Jews – none of these were notably effective. After 1440, when the epidemic began to fade (it stayed around until 1510) this seems to have been due more to competition from tuberculosis and cholera than to any increase in immunity.

The reasons for the success of the Black Death are still not understood today. The climatic conditions may have favoured it; sanitary conditions had deteriorated over the last twenty years. At Givry the annual death rate rose from 10 to 18 between 1334 and 1340, although this was nowhere near the 750 deaths in 1348. In the Lyon region, the number of last wills registered increased greatly after 1343, but reached enormous numbers in 1392, when the scourge returned. One has the feeling that the occasions when the plague failed to devastate rather than when it succeeded would explain its progress better. Clearly, the growth in the population, of urban overcrowding especially, is the reason for the huge numbers involved in the catastrophe, which would not have been the case earlier on in the Middle Ages. In Carcassonne, all the Franciscans were struck down in their monastery; in Toulouse twelve out of twenty of the Canons of Saint-Sernin died and one quarter of all the Curial officials at Avignon. Towns paid even more dearly, as will be seen. In other places, the plague was more selective; adults were infected first, but afterwards and to a greater degree, the children, who were probably less resistant to infection than their predecessors

53

The Pope leads a procession in Rome against the Plague during which a monk collapses. From the *Très Riches Heures du Duc de Berry* (Chantilly, Musée Condé).

of 1348 or 1350. The poor, undernourished and overcrowded, suffered worst, but indeed, apart from high-ranking victims like the Duke of Burgundy, many wealthy burghers, notaries, sheriffs and of course doctors succumbed, tied as they were to town by their offices. Perhaps most interesting are the white areas in the ocean of blackened bodies: Béarne, Rouergue, Hungary, part of Hainaut and Brabant and a town here and there were unaccountably spared. Modern science will perhaps provide a solution for this by establishing that people with blood type O are immune to the plague. If it is a fact that this blood type predominated in Hungary and had but recently taken root in the heartlands of Europe, this hypothesis has serious implications and suggests that the distribution of blood typings coincided precisely with those places where death did not strike.

What sort of overall assessment is possible? Our information is spotty, seldom illustrative and almost exclusively urban. Further, the general terror meant that many accounts were exaggerated. The only complete estimate we possess is for England; according to the records of attempts at taxing the entire population between 1338 and 1415 and later, the population numbered c. 3,125,000 souls on the eve of the epidemic, which was certainly already less than two generations earlier. In 1358, it fell to c. 2,750,000 and, according to the poll tax of 1377, the major source of population data for the period, to c. 2,250,000. By the beginning of the fifteenth century, when the House of Lancaster was coming to the fore, the population was only just above two million. A total loss of more than one third of the urban and rural population, which can be attributed not only to the Plague but also to starvation or to the Malthusian consequences of overpopulation. Here and there, horrific death rates were reported; in the village of Givry, 750 out of a total population of 1,800 were buried in 1348; at the royal Court in Westminster, the death count leapt from 25 to more than 700; at Périgueux, Lyon, Reims, Ypres and Florence, it seems plausible that an average of 25 to 35 per cent of their populations died. In Aix, Apt, Toulouse and Bourges, it was half and in Brême it was said to be 70 per cent. Jean Thevenel counted 20,000 dead at Rouen and Gilles li Muisis 25,000 at Tournai, although these figures appear to have exceeded the total number of inhabitants. Over a longer period, thanks to the increasing number of hearth-tax surveys implemented by the agents of royal or municipal taxation after 1380, huge population losses can be observed. In Languedoc 210,000 hearths were counted in 1328 but only 90,000 were left in 1370 and 75,000 in 1382. The Dauphiné lost 60,000 hearths, Provence lost 60 per cent and Burgundy 40 per cent. It does seem true that France and England were worse affected than other areas; in Catalonia, for instance, the number of hearths remained more or less constant between 1350 and 1378, after which it fell. In the Empire, it seems plausible that the average mortality rates varied from 20 to 35 per cent. In any case, although the recurring epidemic struck again very fiercely in 1360 and 1418, it tended to spare more and more regions. After 1390, Southern Germany, the Low Countries and Spain appear to have escaped altogether. Altogether the exceptionally high death rate probably claimed one out of every three or four people, that is to say six times more than was achieved in a few years during the bloodiest military conflicts of this century.

At this point the impervious historian will observe that the result was to remove the population surplus. The economic consequences were equally evident. First, as with all changes in population, the effects on the workforce and the birthrate were felt only in the next generations. This is the phenomenon of the 'empty classrooms' which the last two world wars have taught historians to look for. Even after the pandemic had retreated, attempts at reconstruction lacked energy and were quickly exhausted, allowing the bacillus to return. One form of instinctive human resilience was in evidence; at Givry, on average ten to twelve marriages took place each year, before the Plague and in 1348 the *curé* did not officiate at any, but in the following year, eighty-six weddings took place. In spite of this, the number of celibate men remained high and on top of this, the family unit, already weakened, declined more rapidly. People married later; in Champagne in the South the average age for brides rose from 18 to 22 and to 24 around 1430. Prostitution and premarital sex became firmly anchored in the customs and there were so many bastards that laws were changed to allow them, who had previously been excluded from society, to inherit property and adopt professions. Many bastard sons of rulers were now able to play political and military roles of the first importance. The number of children born within families fell drastically. In Champagne 48 per cent of peasant couples were childless, or at any rate lacked living children to show the census takers. The birth rate was also slowed down by the shortage of wet nurses, which forced mothers to nurse their own babies. It has even been suspected that in Italy and around Paris, for instance, the practice of exposing babies, especially girls, was resumed.

One of the most notable effects of the impact of the Plague was to have highlighted the inequitable distribution of the population between the towns as places of refuge and the protective forests on the one side and the ravaged lands on the other. In France, disparities which had already been reported on a state level in 1328 became more obvious; certain mediocre or devastated areas were being abandoned. This population shift fundamentally altered the economy of Europe and I will discuss this later. People had to know where to flee to. As they escaped from the Black Death, the refugees succumbed to war, its pander and accomplice.

The tug of war

When Edward III decided to assume the title of King of France on 7 October 1337 (one which he had previously renounced without too much bother) he is traditionally supposed to have started the Hundred Years' War. That war never ended, not even in 1475 at Picquigny when a distant successor of the Plantagenet's, Edward IV of York, was prepared to concede the title to Louis XI. Over this long period, war was really only fought, king against king or through the mediation of captains or princes, for about thirty years; one in five. Moreover, these two countries had waged war intermittently from 1292 to 1327. On the other hand, although the Scottish and Castilian wars, the wars between Italian towns and those fought in the Baltic by the Hanse, occurred simultaneously, they often had only slight connections with the great French and English rivalry. Although its name has little logical or universal meaning, we must retain it.

This is because, during these hundred years and more, war everywhere loomed over

The effects of war: soldiers pillage a house. (Fourteenth century; Ms. C VII London, British Museum.)

everyday life. Thomas Basin has described the watchmen posted at the tops of bell towers or on the outlets of forest settlements, to alert the harvesters or the ploughmen by blowing their horns as soon as they saw an armed band, warning them to gather their beasts and families into fortified churches or within castle walls or else to flee into the woods and watch the soldiers looting and burning from a distance. Towns held out better, if there was no conspiracy to open the gates, but once inside there was no escape at all and every life could be sacrificed in a tragic gamble. It is not certain that this continuous war actually caused many deaths, apart from a few town sackings so savage (as when the Black Prince reduced Limoges in 1370) that even blasé contemporaries were shocked. But its secondary effects were devastating; food stores were emptied and the population starved, unable to withstand the Plague which committed ravages whose effects would last for years. It was already a grievous loss when crops or hay were stolen from granaries or burnt on the stalk, but in the following year the land would restore what had been lost, yielding perhaps more if it had been fertilised by the ashes. Burning cottages or destroying machinery was worse and one year at least was needed to replace them, but the theft or slaughter of cattle, the destruction of vineyards or woods was catastrophic because a herd or a copse needs ten years to grow again, and the soldiers would have returned long before then. At this point it may be pointed out that disaster was much more likely to affect the lord rather than his lowly peasants because it was he who owned the beasts, the forest and the mills. The Church paid even heavier than other lords because she didn't even possess the dubious protection of fortified walls. As for recouping one's losses from the peasantry, it was not to be thought of. Ruined, they could not pay a thing.

In spite of all those truces, hollow peaces and other negotiations which diplomats (who

A naval battle in the fourteenth century: most probably the Battle of Sluys, off Bruges. (London, Mansell Collection.)

were just beginning to emerge) delighted in, war, by its very nature, reigned. Kings or towns could easily have found pretexts for starting a campaign, had they not already been obliged to wage war. As it was, war in the fourteenth century was a class activity, just as it had been in the high Middle Ages. While the aristocracy could still make a living from their rents, they had no need to resort to pillage by open coercion. But as soon as the manorial system began to fail, they had no alternative but to try and re-establish their fortunes by war. The cost of weapons was high, increasingly so as complete coats of armour were being developed, as well as heavier weapons and metal trappings for the horses. The aim was to recoup one's losses from the enemy, and at any rate to live off the particular country that was being overrun and pillaged. War was thus encouraged and engendered more war, and its hazards could involve capture which was ruinous both for the warrior and his followers on whom he would try to impose the burden of paying his ransom. Those in the highest positions could make their ransoms matters of State, as will be seen in the case of John *le Bon*. Their subjects paid if they could, if not, their Lord would stay in prison and for a very long time irrespective of his rank. Charles of Orléans for instance, had only his poetic muse to thank that he was able to bear seventeen years of imprisonment in the Tower of London, which was at least a comfortable stay. So it was the nobility who drove their rulers to war or dragged the towns in with them. A too fleeting or too costly victory entailed its revenge, or yet greater efforts, and so the Hundred Years' War carried on year after year at everyone's expense.

It was no longer enough to carry out short raids, cavalcading from one point to another to impress the adversary, and striking camp in strong positions while royal officials and Churchmen engaged in endless palavers. Nonetheless, this old way of conducting war certainly endured; Edward III and his son the Black Prince behaved in that way between 1350 and 1356, as did the claimants to the Duchy of Brittany or indeed every warrior in the fifteenth century. Negotiations took eleven months at Leulinghem in 1389 and at Arras in 1435, fourteen at London between 1358 and 1360 and even 31 months at Troyes from 1419 to 1420. Nothing was ever settled because it was impossible to implement the peace once it had been sworn to, and those responsible for implementing it, even the most faithful captains, were incapable of ensuring it. The Pope offered his mediation, bankers were involved, but how was the leader of an armed band operating on his own account to be restrained?

Battles were avoided whenever possible, because they were decisive or at any rate murderous, expensive and easily exploited by the winner. It is true that all those fought in France, Castile and Italy which adorn the century, have glitter and prestige. The death of a Breton claimant, the assassination of a King of Castile, the capture of a King of France, the death of a King of Bohemia; events like these had dynastic, financial and psychological consequences. Strategically, however, Najerra, Auray, Poitiers, Crécy and even Agincourt were accidents which solved nothing. There were only two areas where this classic form of warfare was rather less routine; one was the revival of naval warfare, following the Italians' example from the mid-thirteenth century, which unleashed important changes in the lives of coastal populations. Galicians, Basques and Bretons were transformed from fishermen to pirates. At Rouen, Harfleur, Bruges and Southampton shipyards for galleys sprang up to rival those already existing in Genoa, Barcelona or Venice. And certain battles such as the battle of Sluys in 1340 in the Bruges estuary, when the Genoese in the service of Edward III defeated Philip VI's Normans, affected the transport of troops. Of prime importance was the appearance of gunpowder-fired artillery, even if it was still in its infancy. The siege machines inherited from Antiquity and perfected by the Chinese tended to throw stone blocks over the walls, knocking down the houses inside, or pots of Greek fire. But powder-fired artillery claimed to be able to demolish the fortified walls. There is no point in our following the trail of recipes for cannon powder from China to Egypt and thence to Sicily. By 1304 firing pieces were reported in Lombardy and in Florence in 1315. By 1338 they were being cast in Rouen and some were used at the siege of Calais and maybe at Crécy and Hennebont between 1342 and 1346. These bombards threw stone balls, and have for ages been considered rather more lethal for the artillery men than the enemy. But when the town of Saint Sauveur was won after a few bursts of cannon fire in 1374, Rouen in 1418 and Orléans in 1429, no one made fun of artillery any longer. During the second assault on Bordeaux in 1453, it was the French artillery which decided the victory at Castillon, and the old English leader Talbot was killed with his back to his last cannon.

The mercenaries

Although one year of war in every five might be considered tolerable, this would be to forget that in the so-called peace time, men at arms maintained complete freedom of action. The time had passed when these matters concerned only the nobility. Rulers summoned the feudal ban and contingents of free men as in the past; the English *fyrd*, Italian *militias* and the French *arrière ban* were still there, and could supply several thousand knights on horseback, who were well trained for battle charges and were obsessed by an ethos of

Precursors of the grenade: incendiary pots filled with naphtha. (Paris, Louvre.)

individual exploits. These vassals exposed themselves in battle with a sense of duty, courage and chivalry which were no mere show, as the example of King John *le Bon*, who was captured at Poitiers after five hours of battle, demonstrates. Contrary to what their men believed and said, the nobles of those times remained worthy of their ancestors at Bouvines or Las Navas de Tolosa, but the feudal armies were already too divided by rival factions. The infantry was growing in importance and sometimes included arquebusiers, generally Italians, who wielded that deadly weapon which could pierce a breastplate at 100 metres, or at very least slaughter a horse and break the charge. These men were specialists, expensive mercenaries who could not be required to be mobile since their weapon weighed several kilos. Alongside them the numbers of the despised and indispensable footsoldiers multiplied, these were the pikemen and cutlers who for a long time had been allowed only to pillage the enemy tents. By the beginning of the fifteenth century they were developing into quite a different beast; the times of desperate flight before the onslaught of a cavalry charge were over and now the footsoldiers were able to hold their own with their lances bristling in front of them and protected, if they had had the time, by a ditch or hedge of pointed sticks. Already by Barbarossa's time in Italy, the cavalry had to their bitter chagrin found themselves smashed by the footsoldiers; as they were at Lake Piepous by German footsoldiers in 1242 and at Tannenberg in 1410; by the English in 1314 when they were defeated by the Scots at Bannockburn; by the French at Courtrai in 1302 before the Flemish militia, anticipating the archers of Crécy in 1346. Alongside the pike, the bow had become the essential weapon. The Scots and Welsh demonstrated its efficacy to Edward III so well that he equipped his footsoldiers with bows after 1334. Although arrows could not rival the bolts of the Genoese arbalesters in strength and range, they could be effective in disconcerting the horses at less than 50 metres distance. Nor should the nervous tension of the archer, charged by an iron clad monster and sure of being trod underfoot or pierced by a spear if he missed his shot, be dismissed. Squares of pikemen

Pikes, and bows and crossbows, were the footsoldiers' essential weapons. The Battle of Roosebeke, illustrating the *Chronicles* of Froissart at the beginning of the fifteenth century. (Ms. 865, Besançon, Bibliothèque Municipale.)

needed even more courage, with their first line half-kneeling in a hedgehog formation, which only panic could disrupt. This became the Swiss mercenaries' trade mark from around 1420–30 for more than 100 years.

Welshmen, Genoese, Swiss: the new techniques of war gradually and inevitably changed its nature. These men were not all locals; they were trained to the profession of arms and hired out their services; they were peasants fleeing an emptying countryside; marginal people drummed out of town; small noblemen separated from their fiefs or their livelihoods; bastards, adventurers, daredevils. They were often identified as Gascons, men of Navarre, of Brabant, Genoese, Neapolitans, Piedmontese, Bavarians; and maybe these regions did indeed get rid of their surplus manpower as troops. Their appearance in 'companies' (a term which refers both to merchant practice and companionship and explains the two essential aspects of the game) goes back to the thirteenth century and became common in Italy and Catalonia by the very end of the century, either during the troubles which led to the Pope's departure, or during the last attempts at adventure in the East. They would generally agree to a contract, a *condotta*, with a captain, a *condottiere*, who would lead them in the service of an employer on expeditions, which were clearly not inspired by any political or spiritual motive. The war bands mustered between 100 and 400 men and were followed by their doctors and campfollowers as well as more or less

61

defrocked priests, and by munitions men who were responsible for the troops' supply waggons. Whether they served a French King one day and Venice the next, the end of a treaty or a peaceful conclusion meant nothing to the 'company', which just went on with its wandering and looting existence.

They were responsible for the state of permanent war. Mercenaries ignored the truces and obeyed only their Captain. He could be in the service of one particular ruler rather than another, but it was purely an affair of pay. John Chandos, Robert Knowles and John Falstof were on the English side, Du Guesclin, Gressart and Cervolles served the Valois, Hawkwood worked for the Pope in Rome, Colleone for Venice, Campo Basso and Villandrando for anyone and Francesco Sforza for himself alone. This does not account for all the smaller leaders, dug into some stronghold from which they would spill out into the countryside, until they were seized and decapitated. Men like Aymerigot Marchès, whose pitiful exploits were so lengthily recorded by Froissart. Few regions were spared; the richest, Île-de-France, Picardy, Alsace, Lombardy, suffered worst, especially during the truces when the mercenaries had no particular employment and made good their losses off the land, not hesitating to assail towns, as in 1362 when they put the Pope's possessions in Avignon to the sack.

There was little to be done, beyond sending them somewhere else. Du Guesclin, famous for his meteoric career, was sent on a mission to Spain in 1365, and the Dauphin Louis attempted a similar operation against Germany in 1444; a short-term success. It seemed impossible to restrain them and anyway these men had their uses; they could wage up-to-date war, carry out sudden attacks, ambushes and did not shrink from treachery. None excelled better at this than Du Guesclin, who carried out the shameful scorched earth policy literally: 'Burnt soil is worth more than lost land' Charles V would say, for which nineteenth-century historians have praised him enthusiastically, in spite of the condemnation of his scandalised contemporaries. For every decapitated Marchès, there were innumerable successes in the manner of Chandos, the intimate counsellor of the Black Prince, or of constables like Du Guesclin or of Sforza, Duke of Milan.

What about town and countrymen during all this? Despoiled and robbed in great suffering and misery, submitting to pillage by the enemy and by troops whose allegiance was completely uncertain, in their torment they gradually acquired a double attitude, which contemporaries did not immediately grasp. Since the authorities responsible were incapable of protecting them, they protected themselves – notably in places where the communities had long been strong and were well dug in. They drew up treaties between villages and sometimes with the leaders of mercenary bands dominating the country and after 1350, they even got the king to grant them the right to bear arms. Local folklore was gradually swollen by accounts of their individual and ineffectual exploits, telling the deeds of Grand Ferré and William L'Aloue fighting against the English. The Jacquerie came after them, as did Joan of Arc. Their other attitude was also portentous; if the king was not performing his function, the lord was performing his even less. Already suspected of abusing his power, the noble was now considered dangerous. He could be absent, defeated, ransomed; what right had he to claim to be still ruling a community? One must stress the importance of this erosion of the authority of the nobility, not only because of its economic consequences, which I will discuss, but because the screen they had erected between the ruler and his subjects was thereby slowly dissolved. Modern royalty was to pass along this road, but only at a terrible price.

Political turmoil before 1380

The liquidation of Christianity in the thirteenth century was unquestionably the hallmark of a first period, which can be extended from 1320 right up to 1380. What had until then formed the political framework of Europe broke up and disappeared in a series of disasters, about which the chroniclers recorded only their unpredictability. The Papacy was an important determining fact: the Roman magistrature, even after its dubious success against the Empire, could count on a sure audience. At the Council of Lyon in 1274, and later at Vienne in 1311, the Pope spoke out, but who would not contest a pontiff, whose fiscal and domineering policies, whose conservative vision of the world, whose devotion to the ruler who tolerated his presence at his frontier, were so evident? Since its humiliation at Anagni in 1303 in front of the Roman nobility and the agents of Philip the Fair, the much-abused Apostolic See had no longer served as the recourse of the humble. Wandering in France and based in Avignon, however, the Pope was able to remain both an attentive pastor and a wealthy man. Nevertheless, his legates, like Albornoz for instance, wore helmets and tried to retake Rome; once the Papacy had returned to occupy the Holy See in 1378, it split into two, thus precipitating its discredit. Would the Empire be able to rescue the ship of the Church? Since 1273 an end had been made to the comedy of foreign usurpation, but the German sovereign was still not able to tear himself free from the dreams of the Ottonians and of Barbarossa; of conquering Italy and installing himself in Rome, whence the Pope had fled. Louis of Bavaria pursued this chimera for fifteen years before giving up; the new ruling house of Luxemburg would give it a further trial, repeating the ancient ritual, but in fact these lingering ghosts did not worry even the Lombard cities. When Charles IV established his Golden Bull in 1356, he accomplished a gesture of great wisdom and endowed the Empire with what was to remain the rule until Napoleon: the election of the Emperor by the German princes. There were to be seven electors, the Archbishops of the ancient sees of Trêves, Cologne and Mainz, the King of Bohemia, the Duke of Saxony, the Margrave of Brandenburg and the Count Palatine of the Rhine, who ruled Bavaria. It was worth his while giving up his claim to Italy, or indeed to everything, as Wenceslaus the Drunkard, as Robert I, as Albert of Habsburg all did. Among this gallery of ghosts, Sigismund was distinguished by his Christian zeal, which was little enough for the leader of the Holy Roman Empire.

The real explanation for this decline, which already foreshadowed future events, was the fragmentation of Germany; the final consequence of a policy of conceding local franchises, which sovereigns hypnotised by Rome had practised for the last two centuries. This political disruption was perhaps the price Germany had to pay for her powerful economic recovery in the fifteenth century. It would also be unjust not to stress two particular

Bartolommeo Colleone (1400–75) was an Italian *condottiere* who changed sides constantly. He ended his career in the service of the Venetians, who in 1488 raised a bronze statue by Verrocchio to him in the Piazza di SS. Giovanni e Paulo.

William Tell, the Swiss crosbowman, demonstrates his skill by aiming at an apple on his son's head. (Woodcut, Zurich, 1545.)

features of the fragmented land. In the North, the Hanse of the Baltic cities, which controlled the coasts and rivers from Bremen to Riga and even to Cologne, had achieved the status of a political league without stinting on the methods employed. When the King of Denmark, Waldemar Atterdag, tried to shake off the slow immigration of Germans into his country and their control over his customs, and occupied Gotland and advanced into Mecklenburg, he was attacked and Copenhagen was burnt. In 1370 he was obliged to grant the Hanseatic League free passage through the straits at Stralsund. After 1379 the Germans increased their security by uniting under and defending the 'Perpetual Union of Calmar', whereby all Scandinavia and Denmark were controlled by the Hanse's rulers.

In the South the phenomenon was quite different, and it would surely not have deserved to survive had it not endured so triumphantly. What was otherwise so remarkable about the fact that in 1291 the mountain people of the valleys of Uri rebelled, tired of paying the Habsburgs taxes at the entrance to the Saint-Gothard pass, and were followed in this by their neighbours in Schwyz and Unterwalden? It was in one of these cantons that Switzerland was born in 1318. William Tell may never have existed, but his adventure is that of a thousand others from Lucerne, Glaris, Zurich, Berne and later from St Gall, Tessin and Vallais, who in less than fifty years, gathered together in a diet of federated cantons, which recognised no masters. When in 1386 Leopold of Habsburg tried to re-establish order, these bearers of axes and lances with their big leather jerkins routed his vassals and mercenaries. Thus did the Swiss footsoldier make his devastating entry into history.

Europe in the twelfth and thirteenth centuries was used to the sound of Holy War ringing out along her southern flank; the Moor was retreating step by step, and the spectre of an Islam installed within Europe was gradually fading. Here too, the Reconquistà was cut short, ceasing after 1280, when the little kingdom of Murcia fell, and abandoning Granada and Malaga to the Muslims. A strange finale, when the effort required to complete the task would surely only have been slight. It was because the three Iberian powers suddenly got involved in other enterprises; Castile, who should have carried out the final attack since she surrounded Granada, was torn by dynastic struggles at Alfonso X's death in 1284. She seemed to be drawn to the Pyrenees, to the little kingdom of Navarre whose succession was disputed, and to the gulf of Gascony whose sailors were growing increasingly numerous and bold. The reason for this change of policy is not immediately obvious: the silver of Asturia? The commerce of Gascony? The desire to supplant Bayonne and Bordeaux? One of their kings did appear to regain his grasp of the situation; Peter the Cruel (1350–69) installed himself at Seville and surrounded himself with Africans, turning towards Morocco and the future, which was enough to arouse the hatred of the Church and the concern of the great nobility of Castile. A rival was set up against him, his brother Henry of Trastamara. The King of France sent Du Guesclin to support the rebel and the Plantagenet ruler rushed to Peter's defence. After some parries, an inconclusive battle at Montiel was resolved at a meeting in Henry's tent, when he stabbed his brother. This put an end to the dream of an Atlantic-facing Castile for the next hundred years; with Henry, the sheep farmers and the 'grandees' triumphed.

So it was Portugal in the West and Aragon in the East who claimed to lead this sea-borne mission. In actual fact, Lisbon was not that impressive, and in 1386 the English concluded an alliance with the kings of Portugal which is still valid! They were pretty insignificant rulers before the Aviz dynasty was established in 1385, but the Italians were already well aware of the extraordinarily advantageous position of the Tagus estuary. Before 1345–50 the Centurione had opened a trading post there, only 500 km from Morocco and 1,200 km from Madeira. The Catalans had got there first, but Gibraltar closed the ocean to them, so instead they investigated Morea and the Tyrrhenian Sea from 1303 to 1310, where their adventurers did more damage than business. Before then the Catalans had been considered farmers tied to the soil in Languedoc, the Toulouse area and Provence; Barcelona did not count for much compared with Genoa, Naples and Palermo. Now, however, the peasant character was changing, firstly because the rulers had given up their ambitions on the farther side of the Pyrenees, which had been, and could only be, a liability. After 1276, they attacked the Balearic islands, which were theirs by 1343; they launched attacks on Sardinia, and Sicily, where in 1282 they provoked the brutal and bloody revolt of the Vespers against the Angevins, resulting in the long-standing muddle which was solved only by Garibaldi's expedition in the nineteenth century. As masters of the island, the Aragonese kings assumed the title of King of Sicily, which also belonged to Robert of Anjou, who was still in control of Naples. This is the origin of the expression 'the Kingdom of the two Sicilies', which has survived the passage of time.

In Italy too, mother of the arts and of commerce, things were in a state of flux. There was no longer a Pope or an Emperor, but instead excessive numbers of foreigners; the Angevins, who were to requisition Rome and whose family was allied to the ruling house in Hungary, were apparently unable to establish themselves permanently; the French, who came both

At Segovia, the Alcazar was the residence of many Kings of Castile from the thirteenth to the fifteenth centuries.

in 1323 and later to re-establish the rights of the Pope in Avignon; Catalans in Sicily; Greeks in search of support. And all over the place, the towns were increasingly at each others' throats. One might think there was nothing new in all this, but the boundaries of future principalities were already tentatively emerging. Venice, who was being threatened right up to the barriers of her lagoon by the Genoese, began to strengthen her *terra firma* and to extend her lands towards the Po. Florence began by occupying Arezzo and then moved in on Pisa in 1406. Milan, dominated after 1354 by the Visconti brothers, Barnabo and Galeazzo, controlled central Lombardy. The phenomenon whereby the *contado* was transformed into the State was foreseeable, but it was the diminished power of the Papacy and the German Empire which actually allowed it to happen.

67

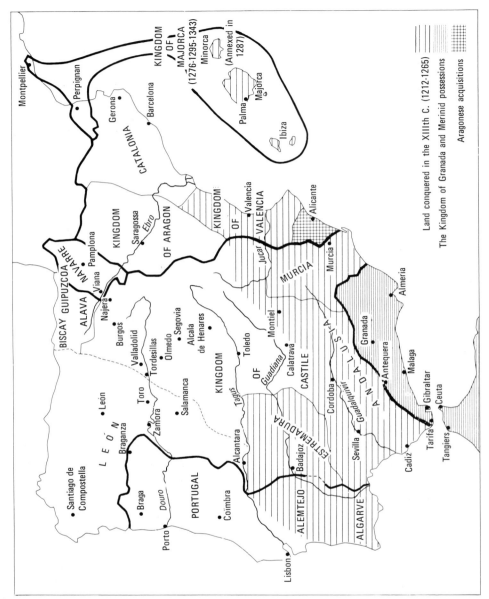

1 The Iberian Peninsula in the XIVth century

The English in the realm of France

Most significant of all was the conflict between the two great monarchies of the West, and this is no mere anachronistic chauvinism. It mattered because it went on for so long, gradually turning from a rivalry between two realms (whose upper classes and kings spoke the same language and shared the same norms of behaviour) into a national affair. It mattered too because of its real purpose; Europe was not big enough for two kingdoms whose concerns and development were so manifestly parallel. It has often been maintained that the French collapse was extraordinary in view of her greater population, developed economy, and the wealth of the Valois; conversely, a perspicacious observer would have given England favourable odds because of the efficient and organised character of her means of action, however modest. But prophecies of this sort are too simplistic to be of interest.

Prior to the outbreak of the continuous hostilities of the fourteenth century, the two powers had clashed without reaching a satisfactory outcome. Capetian agents had stirred up trouble in English Aquitaine, henceforth known as Guyenne, which led to protests and conflict. The French king secured a number of places without too much trouble, but he either would not or could not take Bordeaux, and he mistrusted the barons of South West France and of the Pyrenees, so the matter was suspended. War was resumed in a neighbouring country, because, already around 1300, each kingdom had its own particular problem, which the other strove to worsen. For the Plantagenet, it was Scotland, where Robert the Bruce had set himself up as king in 1306 and had crushed the English army at Bannockburn in 1314. Edward III upheld a pretender called Balliol against him and he defeated King David in 1346, whom Philip VI had supported. Troops had to be garrisoned up there, and worse still, the immensely powerful Marcher lords had to be conciliated, potentates eager to play ruler themselves. For the French king, it was Flanders, a country full of towns, where a foreign language was spoken and which had for centuries rejected the bit. Philip the Fair was trounced at Courtrai by the weavers and cloth workers of Ghent and Bruges (1302), and, although he exacted his revenge two years later, the country, wracked as it was by social unrest and faction, was still not subdued. When he decided on war, Edward III had himself proclaimed king there, with Jacques Van Artevelde at his side, the leader of the rebellious men of Ghent. Fighting also occurred in other places; in Brittany, a country well suited to guerrilla warfare, between 1342 and 1365, following a bungled succession; in Navarre and in Castile, as we have seen; and even in the form of diplomatic skirmishing around Louis of Bavaria, who found this flattering, and the Pope.

Edward III believed in rapid cavalry campaigns. The battle of Sluys convinced him he could cross the Channel easily, and he journeyed around northern France after 1340 while his son, the Black Prince, took care of Languedoc. Philip VI lost his temper and pursued him as he withdrew to Flanders in 1346, but, in spite of their superior numbers, his cavalry was rudely defeated at Crécy, in the county where Edward was in any case already lord (26 August). The important thing was that, once they had got away, the English marched on to Calais, which they took and were from then on able to disembark their soldiers and

69

woolsacks there. In the meantime, Edward had had enough of Artevelde, whose usefulness had expired, and had him assassinated. The second Valois ruler, John II, appeared at first to be more interested in suppressing an inconvenient ruling aristocracy headed by his cousin Charles, King of Navarre, who had an unquestionable claim to the throne. John had him arrested and then rushed off to surprise the Black Prince at Poitou, who fled to Bordeaux with a small following. He caught up with them near Poitiers on 19 September 1356, in the worst possible conditions, and was taken prisoner, although his eldest son Charles was able to escape.

These were crucial events. In itself, the capture of the King, while fighting heroically, turned to his advantage, because Edward III found his position deeply embarrassing. It unleashed a series of problems in France, including attempts to limit the power of the monarchy, which are often forgotten to have begun in 1355. The main sequence of events was as follows; Edward III accepted a limping peace at Brétigny in May 1360, but since the territorial concessions that were granted him in Aquitaine (returning to some extent to the situation in 1250) were practically impossible to implement, the really important condition was the sum of the royal ransom, a fabulous three million *écus*. It was paid, albeit in part, even after war was resumed, as a debt of honour, and thereby laid the foundations of regular taxation in France.

The new Valois king, Charles V, allowed hostilities to be resumed after 1368 because the enforcement of the peace treaty was delayed beyond all measure in the South West, due to assaults, campaigns, the disappearance of the King of Navarre and a war of harassment in the style of Du Guesclin. When Charles died in 1380, the situation had almost reverted to conditions in 1338; Brittany was no longer obedient, but the Dauphiné had been inherited; there were Englishmen at Calais, Cherbourg and Bordeaux, but King Charles's brother had become Count of Flanders. In forty years, nothing had been settled, nothing solved, and the mistakes of the ageing Edward III, as well as Charles V's crushing taxation, had left both kingdoms exhausted, with a dissatisfied aristocracy ready to seize the power which they felt, in economic terms, to be slipping away from them; with tired townspeople, a depreciating coinage, mercenaries and the Plague.

The débâcle

The half century from 1380 to 1430 is considered one of the gloomiest in the history of the French nation, but England and Italy doubtless suffered just as much. It was then that two generations of men foundered in a night without hope.

For twenty years, appearances held good in spite of sporadic revolts. There is something odious about the domination of princes; the princes of the *fleur de lys*, the brothers of Charles V, governed in the name of a young child, and were guided solely by their own interest. Between two shameful pillages of Languedoc, Louis of Anjou left for Naples to relieve the first House of Anjou at bay there; John of Berry, an enlightened Maecenas, played at arbiter and bled the Treasury dry; Philip of Burgundy spun the web in which he would trap the possessions of the Bavarians from Frisia to Luxemburg, dragging the young Charles VI

2 France in the XIVth century

Legend on map:

Boundary of the Kingdom
general fief
fief held as appanage
fief held by the King of England
Aquitaine in 1286

behind him; Louis of Bourbon equipped fleets to fight the Barbary pirates. Italy and the Rhinelands were the privileged theatres of these family and political intrigues, in which one seeks in vain for some grand plan or even some form of economic motive. It is perhaps not entirely fortuitous that the only two French princes capable of a grand conception should founder on those reefs; Philip of Burgundy, master of the two Burgundies, Flanders and Artois, tutor to Albert of Bavaria in Brabant, Hainaut and Holland, who married his

71

To the right of the portrait of Henry V (London, National Portrait Gallery) and that of Charles VII by Fouquet (Paris, the Louvre) is the most moving extant drawing of Joan of Arc. It was sketched in ink by a scribe in the Paris Parlement on a register which referred to the liberation of Orléans. (Paris, National Archives.)

nephew the King to the Bavarian princess Isabeau, was also concerned about Piedmont and Milan. His path crossed that of Louis of Orléans, the younger brother of King Charles, lord of Oise and Marne, where Pierrefonds, La Ferté-Milon and other castles controlling the Paris region were rising up. Louis furthered his interests in Luxemburg, slicing the property, and no doubt the ambitions of his uncle, in two. He was to be found next in Milan, where he married Valentina Visconti, the daughter of Giangaleazzo, 'Duke' of Milan since 1395. He then visited Charles of Durazzo, the Angevin claimant to Naples, before moving to Genoa, which passed under French rule in 1396.

In England too, the princes were growing bolder; John of Gaunt, brother to the Black Prince, was also uncle and regent to the young Richard II. He increased his 'retainers', that is his followers and their lands, to the extent of drawing the revolt of 1381 against himself.

He at least had few ambitions beyond the Channel; he simply aspired to dominate the Treasury and to control the Customs. In France, there was a brief hiatus from 1388 to 1392, when Charles VI shook off his uncles' tutorship and recalled his father's counsellors, the 'Marmosets'; grumpy old men, whose archaic prescriptions aroused unanimous dissent. Richard II also tried to dismiss his princely advisors between 1395 and 1399.

These are the main lines of the *débâcle*. In England, Richard II was eliminated by John of Gaunt's son, Henry Duke of Lancaster, who savagely disposed of all opposition between 1400 and 1413, but at such a price that war was the only option available to his son Henry. In France a further drama was developing: struck by a bout of violent madness while travelling through a stiflingly hot forest, Charles VI left the limelight; but, such was the nature of his tragedy, his affliction was interspersed with increasingly rare remissions, and he could not abdicate. He remained King, but the coteries spoke in his name: the Duke of Burgundy, when he was deranged or dangerous and had to be shut up; and the Duke of Orléans when he was lucid for a few days, and later on only a few hours, at a time. The kingdom was reduced to chaos. When Philip of Burgundy died in 1404, disaster followed.

Firstly, the family war between the two cousins; John of Burgundy, a violent and unscrupulous man, who won his title *sans Peur* (the Fearless) in the East, and the adventurous and challenging Louis, who was further suspected of being the lover of his sister-in-law, Queen Isabeau. In 1407, John had Louis murdered in cold blood in the middle of Paris, and in 1419 was himself no less cynically struck down on the bridge of Montereau by some of Louis' followers. Meanwhile their partisans panicked; Louis' widow obtained the support of Bernard, Constable of Armagnac, and of many nobles and peasants; whereas the 'Bourguignons' were clerks and townspeople. Attacks, town sackings and assassinations succeeded one another and, as might have been feared, the English were appealed to. Henry V took up Edward III's claims. In 1415 he disembarked at Harfleur and in October, in a repetition of Crécy, he was attacked and was victorious at Agincourt. The French disaster was complete on the military level, because in his hurry, Henry V had all but the most exalted of his prisoners massacred, but politically it had no effect at all, because Henry re-embarked immediately afterwards. Further, after the assassination of John of Burgundy, he had in Philip the Good, the new Duke of Burgundy, a sure ally, in whom the desire to avenge his father's death superseded all French sentiment. Queen Isabeau was on bad terms with her third son Charles, who had inherited after the death of his elder brothers, and in May 1420 she agreed to countersign the treaty of Troyes, which has been branded with infamy by traditional French history writing.

The Dauphin Charles, who was at Poitiers with a handful of officials and magistrates, was excluded from the succession; his sister Catherine brought it by marriage to Henry of England with the blessing of Philip of Burgundy. Although recent events might induce us to temper our instinctive indignation at this, we should also remember the spirit of the age; Henry of Lancaster knew and felt himself to be partly French – how could he have imagined reducing fifteen million Frenchmen with two million Englishmen? At the time, many intellectuals enthused about this dual monarchy as a fine attempt to resolve the threefold conflict, to transcend the narrow concept of 'nation', and indeed, France would surely have won at this game. At the risk of further paradox, can it be said that this transaction presented an 'opportunity'?

73

As it was, things turned out otherwise. Charles may have seemed ready to give up all his claims at Poitiers, Bourges and Chinon, but his mother-in-law, Yolande, his cousins of Anjou, one of the Popes, the Emperor Sigismund, the Duke of Brittany and the Spanish rulers encouraged him to rescind. The settlement was resisted and the war did not cease. Henry of France and England was delighted, pointing out that war without fire was as little to his taste as sausage without mustard. In February 1421, his army fought at Baugé and attacked Mont-Saint-Michel. Fortune must have had her eye on him, because the young conqueror was carried off by dysentery at the end of 1422, followed soon after by the unlucky Charles VI, royal jetsam, whose remains were escorted by a weeping crowd all the way to his tomb, weeping for him as symbol of his land's misfortunes. Henry V's son was only a few weeks old, so his uncle, the Duke of Bedford, grabbed the reins of government and hope returned briefly because the Englishman was an excellent administrator and a fine warrior. His victory at Verneuil (1424) procured him all the territory north of the Loire. In the South, Charles dared do nothing; his Treasury had run dry, his counsellors had fled and even his legitimacy was being disputed. Bedford grew bolder; he blockaded Orléans, going against the usages of the time, which proscribed attacking a place whose lord could not defend it – the poet Charles having been made prisoner at Agincourt.

Surely this twist of Fate is known to all: Joan was not the first peasant girl who had been inspired to rescue the *gentil dauphin*, but she was the first to win his confidence, to subjugate the captains and to command the men. Was the fervour which liberated Orléans on 8 May 1429 a sign of God's favour? Did the march to Rheims and Charles VII's consecration in July mark the turning of events? No: Joan faltered, failed at Paris, was surprised at Compiègne and in May 1431, in the most legal manner possible, she was burned alive as a rebel, a relapsed Catholic and a sorceress by an ecclesiastical tribunal, which may have been obtuse and punctilious, but was scrupulously drawn up. Charles VII was prostrated and did not lift a finger to help her, any more than did the Pope, or the Emperor. 1431 was the year of France's deepest abasement and defeat.

In the country, a new aspect and new fears

It is a tradition well established since at least the seventeenth century, that peasants suffered worst from the troubles of the age and were especially exposed to economic problems, to military attack and the whim of politics, and that their revolts were the last resort of the desperately poor. I should like to show that at the time of the Black Death 'the times blest by the Plague' as a husbandman said around 1430, the situation in the country had improved, or at least brightened, and that in the midst of all the suffering, peasants as a whole were less vulnerable than other people. In order to make this clearer, we will have to look beyond misleading appearances, one of them being the deserted villages.

Deserted villages and fortified villages

Fifteen years ago, historians believed as incontrovertible fact that the fourteenth and fifteenth centuries experienced a huge movement away from lands and settlements

Mont-Saint-Michel comprises a castle, a town and an abbey. The Dukes of Normandy decided to build an abbey dedicated to Saint Michael on this rocky island, which was begun in 1023 and was finished in 1080. The blocks of granite were brought by boat from the Chausey Islands and the timbers came from the Abbey's forests. This Romanesque Monastery contained about a hundred monks. In the thirteenth century a new and more enormous abbey was built on the northern flank – the famous Gothic *Merveille* – with the help of Philip Augustus who wanted to turn the Mount into a royal bastion. Pilgrims flocked to it, even during the Hundred Years' War and the English, who controlled the region, sold safe-conducts to them. The town and the abbey built powerful ramparts bristling with keeps and towers (thirteenth to fifteenth centuries) to protect them against the English. The fortified abbey was able to resist all sieges and was never captured.

following the plagues and increased mortality; a belief substantiated by the discovery in England of a surprising number of deserted medieval sites, the lost villages, and by the dramatic rollcall of the *Wüstungen*, deserted lands, established by research in Germany. Nowadays this catastrophic interpretation is no longer valid. To start off with, research in England into texts and stratigraphy has stressed the very belated character of the movement, which occurred with or after the land enclosures, which themselves did not begin until 1420 or 1450, long after the Black Death. In Germany, archaeologists digging in the Rhineland have found evidence for similar massive desertion in periods of full agricultural prosperity, when the countryside was being improved. As for France, the Low Countries and Poland, those deserted villages, which have been enthusiastically excavated (such as Rougiers, in Provence) have revealed a tenacious vitality in the mid fourteenth century, and even signs of growth. In other ways too, the desertions were simply temporary, since villages could be resettled twenty years later. In Artois in the Quercy and in the Île-de-France, there are very few places which have remained empty until today. As for the land itself, once it is overgrown, it is not easy to establish just how long and in what manner it was abandoned, but what was lost was undoubtedly the poorest, the furthest away, the wildest farmland. As for the famous dictum current in the seventeenth century that in France the woods came with the English, in spite of its poignancy, it completely disregards the advantages of good woodland over poor farmland.

What does all this add up to? That villages and fields were deserted by their cultivators, in any case rather later than 1400; in Germany losses have been thought to have amounted to 10–15 per cent of the settlements along the Rhine and in Alsace, along the Weser and in Pomerania, to over 20 per cent in eastern and central Germany, to 40 per cent in the Harz and up to two-thirds in Thuringia; altogether 40,000 places out of 170,000 in the whole Empire; in Great Britain, in Italy an average of 20–25 per cent; but only 10 per cent in Tuscany, Lombardy, Normandy and even less in Languedoc and the Paris basin. In Artois, Champagne, the Entre-deux-mers and south of Paris, with the exception of Hurepoix, the damage was repaired after 1480. Picards, Bretons and Angevins settled in the valley of Bièvre and Chevreuse; Poitevins and other Bretons, known as *gavaches* in Bordeaux, peopled the Dordogne valley. Without doubt, this is the explanation we were looking for; deserted lands and sites were the perks of newly arrived populations, or were redistributed among neighbouring villages, swollen by evacuees. In other words, far from being evidence of flight and failure, the phenomenon is the sign of a felicitous contraction and of rural dynamism: the countryside was being reshaped in response to the realities of the moment.

The process known as *Entsiedlung*, which has been revealed to us by German historians, involved first rejecting lands which the preceding overpopulation had forced settlers to wrest from scrubland. Once this pressure had abated, the price of land fell, which allowed the peasants to stop trying to grow wheat on lands better suited to pasture or hay. It was in this sense a stabilising process, even if it involved substantial changes in farming methods. As for the displaced inhabitants, the general panic and devastations should not be minimised. In the first place, they fled to the towns or at least to their suburbs, not only

An aerial view of Lower Burston (Bucks), a deserted village. Beneath its grass covering, the village's main streets can be distinguished as can traces of its houses on the allotments, separated by ditches.

from approaching mercenaries but also before the Plague, an absurd reaction, but then, not everyone had the wit or the resources of Boccaccio, who sought refuge for his *Decameron* in the pure air of Fiesole above a ravaged Florence. The quarters outside the towns were swollen by the newcomers with inevitable problems of sanitation and provisioning. Urban populations in Reims, Périgueux, Chalon-sur-Saône, Toulouse, Montpellier, Metz, Ypres, to mention but a few case-studies in France, were completely disrupted because the numbers involved were huge: 3,000 peasants crowded in the moats of Montpellier in 1380. But these movements did not last long; more significant were the permanent shifts of population I have mentioned, and even more so the phenomenon associated with the deserted hamlets and villages, which can in some cases be closely examined. In Provence, people came down from the mountains in order to be less isolated and to live on the edges of supply routes. Villages doubled in size; two Rougiers and two Saint-Genis-Jonquières. In southern Champagne around Clairvaux, the villages in forest clearings saw their inhabitants grow in number between 1370 and 1390, and then again between 1425

77

and 1450, whereas the valleys of the Aube, the Marne or the Seine were deserted and left open to attack. People were seen to return to the forest, to new as well as ancient woodlands, in Forez and in Brie; in the Neufbourg country of Normandy around 1400, 25 per cent of the population were said to be *du bosc*; in Alsace, although 150 deserted sites have been found, thirty big market-towns grew in volume and, better still, new settlements were founded, testifying to the vitality of the peasantry. Population charters were issued alongside abandoned bastions and farmsteads in Quercy and Gascony, as also happened in the Burgundian hinterland, mostly after 1420. Even the Cistercians were moved to parcel out their own granges and to fill them with people, in spite of the distance they had previously kept from the peasantry. I have not yet mentioned the *maisons fortes* so typical of the fifteenth century; they rose up just outside the villages, sometimes in places lived in by a specific peasant group, and are evidence, this time, of the vitality of the seigneurial class.

One might well have doubts about the finally positive nature of this reorganisation, but one further aspect of it should suffice to underline the steady vigour of the peasant world; this is the solidity of village communities in the waning fourteenth century. The process of regrouping greater numbers of people within village agglomerations had various consequences, evidence for which is supplied by historical texts and archaeological research. Firstly, the home itself was subdivided in order to allow several families to coexist under the same roof. This has been noted at Rougiers and at Wharram Percy, along with the obvious corollary: less space for each couple. To a certain extent, the instances of overcrowding which have been found in Italy, northern France and Quercy, can be attributed to the desire to be assessed as one taxable hearth, this being the unit of taxation. So of course, crowding together would have been an obvious advantage for tax-payers. However, both municipal and royal authorities cottoned on to the fraudulent nature of this practice and began introducing head counts, in order to establish the real number of hearths at the end of the fourteenth century. Records of these attempts are to be found in our archives, to the intense delight of historians: around 1380–5 in Hainaut, the Low countries and England; around 1412–18 in the Comptat, Provence, Switzerland; and finally, that masterpiece of medieval statistics, the Florentine *Catasto*, of 1427, was achieved.

A second aspect also illustrates peasant vitality: the pious confraternities in the villages gradually hardened into pressure groups such as the *amis* of Rouergue and Switzerland, the Flemish *bloetvrieden*, the *hermandades* of Upper Aragon, the *casaleres* of Béarn, the *escarterons* of Briançonnais, the *fruitières* of the Jura, the *mutuelles* of the Dauphiné, the Frisian *kedde*, the *Gauerberg* of Bavaria, and the *poiles* of Alsace. Although the names varied, they all meant the same thing: forming associations of up to ten villages; owning some of the land as well as having enough tools to rent out; frequently being responsible, as in Hainaut, for keeping accounts both for the association and for the parish church, and of course, defending their ancient rights, usages and privileges. To a certain extent, this sort of organisation gave rise to the *pâtis* which enabled the peasants in France to arm themselves, sometimes with evil intent, but in the larger context, the birth of the Swiss cantons, those valleys which even now consist of ten villages gathered into one commune, was the political outcome of this form of emancipation.

Rustic vitality and village fun: this miniature from the *Heures de Charles d'Angoulême* (1480) shows shepherds dancing. (Paris, Bibliothèque nationale.)

Retreat or progress?

The land presented two contrasting faces to the observer, progress and decay. What part did they play? Of course, the latter has always been stressed, and contemporaries were certainly aware of it. They could not fail to observe that the area under cultivation was shrinking; at Winchester the acreage under plough dwindled by 24 per cent in 1350 as compared with the 1270 acreage, and by another 20 per cent before 1400. The volume of overall production was definitely reduced, and not only due to the population losses. In the Artois, near Douai, the Abbey harvested 300 measures of corn in 1330, but only half this in 1350 after the Plague, and only 175 measures around 1370. Much further away, in Schleswig, the cathedral chapter watched its harvests shrink from 7,600 measures of corn in 1352 to 400 in 1437. Everywhere, assessments reveal overall losses beginning with 35 per cent in Austria, the Île-de-France and Lombardy, and rising to 50 per cent in Normandy, in the Cambresis and even to 63 and 70 per cent in England, along the Main and in northern Germany. Corn was not the only crop affected, and on the whole, every kind of cultivation showed poor yields, especially vines in places where they did not enjoy the best conditions for growth, as in Anjou and in the Île-de-France. In spite of the occasional vineyard being laid out by burghers, the overall volume of wine being produced was considerably reduced, especially in terms of the marketable surplus, as is revealed by the income from taxes like the *forage* on wine in Paris or the *péage* in Mons, which fell by half between 1338 and 1370 before rising slightly between 1375 and 1410 to two-thirds of the 1340 profits. By noting the sums mentioned in farming leases, one can also establish a 'barometer' for the falling income from food production; the big farm of Tremblay, which belonged to Saint-Denis and was leased out for 500 livres in 1335, could only be leased for 250 livres thirty years later, and for scarcely more in 1400.

This regression might lead one to expect the price of wheat to rise, and with the help of speculation prices did indeed reach giddy heights in towns, whenever there was a shortage or they were besieged; they quadrupled if the volume available was half the volume required. Apart from such accidents of circumstance, the general trend was on the contrary towards a continuous fall in prices after 1350, roughly following this pattern: taking the price of wheat in the mid-fourteenth century as our base line of 100, it was 70 in 1380, 76 in 1400, 70 in 1420 and 60 in 1440. This phenomenon, apparently so unusual, was effected by three concurrent factors, the first being the fall in demand following the fall in population, which overtook the fall in production. The second was when local powers, such as the Italian and Flemish towns and the English kings and German princes, started trading in imported Baltic, Polish or eastern cereals, which they bought cheaply in those countries (which were less affected or less grasping) and sold in the West in direct competition with local producers. The third factor was the undeniably greater profit to be made from the sale of other products of the soil, many of which were only grown because less wheat was being sown.

This totally positive aspect of the rural situation is too easily forgotten, or else relegated to the end of the fifteenth century, whereas the movement in fact largely began about 1280. This was the case with plants used in the dyeing process, which were sure of a market, and with market gardens, which were increasingly appreciated by the towns. The vine too must be given its due, because although it retreated from north-western Europe, in the South the search for quality wines imposed new ways of selecting vines, of training specialist workers, and the beginnings of serious wine production. Tradition – in this case accurately – honours the Duke of Burgundy, Philip *le Hardi* (the Bold), with having selected the Beaune plants and broached the development of the Arbois vineyard, and with launching 'Burgundy' at the papal court, by means of successive ordonnances and subsidies around 1395.

The second agrarian resource to prove profitable was stock raising, and we will discuss this at greater length elsewhere. For the moment, it must be said that the consumption of red meat – mostly beef – was increasing in towns to the extent of putting the butchers' trade among the leading trades in Paris, Ghent and Milan. Even in the countryside, the pig, the traditional prop of village civilisation, gave way to the producers of milk. Although pigs continued to be farmed, it was henceforth only in piggeries, where they gradually developed the physical traits by which we know them. From then on, the woods were emptied of the half-wild porcine population, which had been one of their main features. The *panage* is one example among a hundred illustrating this, the tax levied by the lord on the pigs led each September to glean acorns, which fell from 40 livres in Neufbourg around 1360 to 23 in 1397 and 4 in 1440. The consumption of milk products also rose, but nothing in this field equals the irresistible rise of sheep farming.

This benefited from the increased demand for different fleeces and skins and indeed from the beginnings of mutton consumption, which had until then been little indulged in, even along the shores of the Mediterranean, whether by Christians or Muslims. But sheep farming, which involves large herds, irrespective of transhumance, offered big land owners who found the labour involved in growing wheat too expensive, a solution. The *latifundia* of late antiquity, which had been so painfully abolished, were established in the rural landscape of the West; in Spain on the Castilian *meseta*, the Mancha, the Rioja; in Sicily and in Apulia which had reverted slowly to steppeland, and also in Hanover after 1375, in the

Gathering manna, Flemish School, fifteenth century. The Bible story about food falling from the sky spoke to people wracked by fear of famine. (Douai, Musée municipal.)

On the left, the butcher's stall and abattoir (*Theatrum Sanitatis*, of Ububchasym of Baldach). On the right, milk is being preserved and consumed as cheese. (Fourteenth-century miniature, Cod. 2644, Vienna, Österreichische Nationalbibliothek.)

British Isles from Hull to Bristol and further North, around 1380–90. The social and botanical effects of all this were not as yet felt, but their beginnings can certainly be traced to this time.

Crisis or change on the manor?

Our descriptive sources and records of accounts for the fourteenth and fifteenth centuries are mostly derived from the archives of landowners, notably the Church. They provide a steady list of complaints; polltaxes not coming in, retinues being reduced, staff sent home, the sale of parcels of land which, according to the factors' accounts, had rendered *nihil* for ages, largesses being stopped and, finally, the constant struggle against royal taxation. The phases of reconstruction between disasters were only gleams of hope, and were anyway always spaced out between different regions, which only served to emphasise their futility: they occurred in 1360–74 and 1379–1405 in the Bordelais, and in 1365–78 and 1392–1410 in the Île-de-France, but there was no serious recovery until the first thirty years of the fifteenth century (apart from very few areas: Burgundy, Piedmont and the Auvergne). This was not due to lack of interest in farming; Gilles li Muisis, Abbot of Tournai, was a man cast in the same mould as Abbot Suger in the twelfth century; Charles V had several agricultural manuals compiled and circulated, namely the *Art de bergerie* (sheep farming) by Jean de Brie and a rural encyclopedia, the *Ruralium commodorum opus*, the work of the

82

a) Cattle were profitable (above); milking and butter-making. (Ms. Book 764, Oxford, Bodleian Library.)
b) A tavern scene in Italy at the end of the fifteenth century. Good quality wines were sought after and strong wines were taking over. (Ms. add. 27695, London, British Museum.)

Italian Pietro dei Crescenzi. In reality, the manorial structure was too rigid to be able to bear the recurring blows of a runaway economy without showing signs of cracking.

The agricultural crisis of the fourteenth and fifteenth centuries contravened the 'classic' pattern in that salaries stayed level and even increased following the great fall in population, and market products remained competitive, selling better and more profitably in the midst of the falling corn prices, except in cases of sudden and violent penury. While the phenomenon of falling grain prices and rising wages applied in the countryside, it did of course vary in intensity from one country to another.

This pattern was strongly determined by the way different farming units responded in completely different ways to these problems, according to their level of production and their size. In a period of average but falling production, a small farming unit belonging to a poor

83

peasant or to a moneyless *hobereau* (petty landowner), could harvest for instance 250 *quintals* of corn, 200 *quintals* of which he would use for his own purposes and the remaining 50 of which he would sell for perhaps 1,000 livres. Another farmer harvesting 500 *quintals* would retain 300 of them only because at that level, the ratio of produce to *mesnie* was no longer the same, and he would obtain 4,000 livres for the remaining 200 *quintals*. A third farmer, a well-endowed lord or astute burgess or labourer made good, might harvest 1,000 *quintals* and retain only 400, thus obtaining 12,000 livres by selling the other 600 *quintals*. We have already seen how the biggest farming unit was the only one which made enough money to allow the farmer eventually to reinvest it in the land. However, in the event of a sudden shortage, prices were seen to rise by 30 per cent when the volume available fell by 10 per cent; by 80 per cent when there was a 20 per cent shortage and by as much as 450 per cent when only half the necessary volume was available, because in the absence of public granaries, speculators had a free hand. If we apply a 20 per cent fall in production to our three farming units, that is to say, an 80 per cent rise in the market price of corn, the smallest unit would produce 200 *quintals* and would consume the lot, selling nothing. The second unit would produce 500 *quintals*, keep 300 and get 3,600 livres for the remaining 100, a little less than in a normal year. But the third, with 800 *quintals*' production and consuming 400 of them, would get 14,400 livres for the rest, which was more than in a good year. For this sort of farmer, a bad harvest meant big profits; this is what the husbandman meant when he referred to the blessed time of the Plague, and explains why Shakespeare's farmer hung himself because his harvest was good.

The effects of the dual phenomena of contraction and stagnation should now be clear. The small peasant and modest farmer suffered only slightly from the crisis, because they did not have to pay high wages and could live off their 'own'. The biggest farmers, the English landlords, the great burghers of France and Germany, rulers and their agents, had nothing to fear from the crisis, because apart from their profits on corn, they also benefited from their sheep farms and vineyards, which gave profits of 105 per cent. But in the middle, or at the bottom rung of the country hierarchy, disaster closed in. We should pause a moment to consider each of these categories.

Agricultural drive and dynamism (which are too often forgotten) may be seen in the way the big farmers came through the crisis and even benefited from it, profiting from the deserted farmsteads, from other peoples' inability to implement their right to a particular property for lack of the necessary deeds, or more simply, by means of purchase or expulsion. Farming on a large scale had as yet only reached eastern Germany and Spain, where the Haro, the Guzman and the Mendoza flourished after Henry of Trastamara's victory, as well as the military orders at Alcantara, Calatrava and Santiago, which literally confiscated the *llanos* of the *Mesta*. In Brandenburg, the *Landbuch* of 1375 shows the formation of the first concentrations of land by the *Junker*. In Prussia, the Teutonic Order expropriated the Mazovians and the Pomeranians; this form of exploitation was only stopped by the Polish revolt of 1410, in which both nobles and peasants participated. In England too, landed fortunes were being established by the Percys, the Mortimers, the Warwicks and the Leicesters, although the tormented and unpredictable nature of politics here could easily precipitate the ruin of someone who had grown rich in the previous decade. In France, the situation was more blurred; the bourgeois had established enclaves of power not far from the towns. Around Paris, near Josas, fifty-two of the sixty-five seignorial estates passed into the hands of lawyers, wine merchants and royal officers between 1390 and 1430. Among those families studied are the Ysalguier of Toulouse, the Jossard of Lyons; not forgetting those recently ennobled by the king, the Orgemont, the Dormans and others. Around Genoa, the Grimaldi, the Spinola, the Doria and Speroni colonised the mountains; and, albeit rather more discreetly than the others, the Medici, the Pitti and the Strozzi were easing their way into the Florentine *contado* in exactly the same way.

These future 'princes' of the late fifteenth century had few problems. The 'middle class' however, which had gradually emerged between 1200 and 1250, and was made up of the French *hobereaux*, the English *yeomen*, the Castilian *hidalgos* and even those labourers who were closely associated with this class of superior commoners, had many problems. These people had between five and twelve hectares, and some had even less. Around Bar-sur-Seine, in the Lyonnais, more than half of these 'fiefs' made less than 15 livres per annum. These people were losing their safety margin. How indeed did they manage to produce enough for their *mesnie*, however humble? It was impossible to farm land in hand profitably – even the Cistercians had to farm out after 1340 – and in any case, small farmers could not afford to pay the going wages. On top of this, in places where there was no shortage of labour, the towns with their higher wages lured the workforce away. So land had to be farmed out or leased to sharecroppers, which at least provided for the future. I have mentioned the inevitable alienation this involved, which was to the peasant tenant's advantage, because the lord wished above all to farm out ploughland he could not work himself, while his tenant on the contrary wanted meadows and woodland. In this respect, conflict between the Church and her tenant farmers sometimes acquired the air of systematic hostility. On top of this, the polltax was no longer an asset, since it had dwindled to a purely nominal payment. Nor were seigneurial incomes reliable; the accounts show the arrears, or overdue payments, piling up. In Neufbourg around 1435, 60 per cent of these types of returns were no longer assured; delays and rebates had to be allowed and sometimes the master even accepted exceptionally favourable terms for his tenants, in order to see deserted plots cleared and worked again, as for instance in Bordelais, Normandy and Saxony. At Saint-Denis, *champarts* were levied on twelfth instead of sixth parts, in Bordeaux, the *agrière* was reduced from a third to a quarter in 1394 and then to a sixth in 1415, before being frankly given away for practically nothing as a 'perpetual census payment'. There was of course no question of imposing the *corvée*, except perhaps for haymaking, when the workforce would anyway be paid. In England, at the beginning of the fifteenth century, Henvy V proclaimed the general right to buy release from the *corvées* which, as it was, landlords in Essex and around Ely had long ago ceased to demand for fear of making their serfs run away. Here and there, some lords were lucky enough to retain these services, as in Auvergne around 1422, but such instances were the exception.

As the average-sized manorial farms declined in what is known as the 'crisis of feudalism', the farmers and labourers leading the confraternities, the 'cocks' as they were

Farmers profited from lively local markets. These are fruit and corn merchants in fifteenth-century Lombardy. (*De Sphaera*, Ms. lat. 209, Modena, Biblioteca Estense.)

beginning to be called, the *censes* of Cambrésis, the *huis* of Upper Burgundy, the *mas* of Aquitaine and Provence, benefited and gladly took on holdings of up to 60 hectares. The lower farm rents made it easier for the tenants, who were now able to meet rising non-agricultural expenses and pay the wages which the petty squires could not afford. Better still, they were able to control their farming neighbours, who had fewer tools and were unable to save, by renting them belatedly and expensively the implements they lacked and by buying their wheat while still on the stalk and their livestock while still in the field at low prices, in order to furnish them with the cash they needed. This middle class of peasants – whom we shall soon meet again brandishing their pitchforks – thus managed to get through the crisis without suffering too much damage, and were we to ignore this fact, we would fail to understand the nature of the subsequent reconstruction and the liveliness of the local markets, which had maintained regional commerce at a very satisfactory level. In Provence, for instance, very lively country fairs were held in the mid fourteenth century at Pertuis, Riez and Forcalquier, demonstrating the deep resilience of the rural world.

It would, however, be wrong to generalise; in regions where this economically sound class was unable to emerge, because the soil was too poor or local 'liberties' too fragile, the crisis dealt harshly with very many peasants; in Languedoc, Navarre and Aragon and in southern Italy as well as more to the north, the basic units of production were steadily subdivided – a process which inhibited the production of any form of surplus. At Neufbourg around 1380, 43 per cent of the peasantry farmed less than 2 acres. Wages could compensate in some cases, and the *brassiers* of France, the Bavarian *Gärtner*, the *Kossaten* of the Rhineland and the English cottars, could supplement their inadequate resources. But not everyone was able to, as the aggravated harshness of the legal statutes indicates; in England around 1370, a good third of all villeins could not leave their land; in Béarn around 1400, the new serfs were those who could not pay the usual taxes. We saw earlier that the restriction or cessation of rights of usage further served to limit the peasants' use of forest resources.

To sum up, the process by which the masters' class was split into two and the peasant class into three could not be effected without ructions, which were occasionally violent. But it would be too simplistic for us, conditioned as we are by the examples of agrarian crisis and peasant revolt of the 'modern' age, to interpret them simply as the last gasps of the desperate. The Jacquerie was something quite different.

Jacques and Jacquerie

The brief and violent peasant revolt in the Beauvaisis struck contemporaries so sharply that the rebels, given the name of *Jacques*, and their movement, called the *Jacquerie*, came to epitomise rural revolts in general. The origin of the name is not really known; it was possibly the name of a ringleader or the type of jerkin worn by the peasants. None of these movements was interchangeable. We have seen how the peasant mass was split into several classes with contrasting aspirations; the dominant faction, the accomplices of the aristocracy, was not involved, but the middle-ranking farmers, whose progress or the fear they inspired was often behind the advantages and alleviations granted by their lords, were basically keen to maintain their customs. The stronger they grew, the readier they were to defend the 'old law', which meant opposing every requisition, every fiscal levy which they considered illegal, every intervention by individuals representing outside influences, such as towns or the king. During the Flemish revolt of 1325, the insurgents attempted to do away with their count's administration and taxation and to replace them with their own agents, their *keuriers*, or public officials. This desire to preserve the rights they had acquired was matched by the scorn and hostility which the nobility aroused by their obvious inability to fulfil the protective role for which they were paid. They might have been contented with tenacious law suits, like the one fought out between the men of Saint Albans and their Abbot from 1274 to 1381, but in a climate of economic struggle and self-defence, weapons lay to hand.

As for the most disinherited peasants, they reacted more 'naturally' to the ravages of the crisis. But their own weakness forbad the use of weapons or any military-type campaigns. Instead, they ran away, set up ambushes and robbed, to such a degree that the chroniclers, the guardians of the existing order, who could not appreciate the extent to which the *malos usos*, the abuses, weighed on the poorest peasants, saw them simply as bandits.

87

Driven to despair, the peasants formed bands to take revenge on their predators. Here, they are attacking an isolated knight with axes and a dagger. (Jean de Wavrin's *Chronicles of England*, fifteenth century, Ms. fr. 87, Paris, Bibliothèque nationale.)

Nevertheless, these diffuse, elusive and polymorphous movements lasted much longer than the others. In both cases, though, especially in places where family ties or local loyalties were strong, as around the Mediterranean, many of these movements doubled as particular interest groups and vendettas settling old scores, which had nothing to do with the problems of the class concerned. This aspect is typical of the Middle Ages and has misled some purblind historians into saying that these movements had no 'social' significance.

We should appreciate the above remarks better by remembering that the long history of disturbances to the peasant world began in the thirteenth century. On top of this, the general climate of millenarist fears, nourished by the uncertainty of the times, affected most of the rural risings; the *Jacquerie* has rightly been said to have anticipated to some extent the *Grande Peur* of 1789. There is even more reason for dealing separately with the various eschatological and illuminary manifestations, for which there is no shortage of examples from before 1300, and which continued throughout this period, without their social aspect being very clearly delineated. This is particularly the case with the bands of Flagellants, itinerant penitents whose noisy demonstrations involving mystical songs and mutual flagellation accompanied the Plague from Holland to Switzerland between 1349 and

1355. The Lollards too, albeit with more precise social demands borrowed from the disciples of Wycliff, stirred up the area around London between 1408 and 1420, demanding the abolition of all hierarchies, until Henry V and Archbishop Arundel decided to destroy them.

It was after the first onset of the Plague that the middle-ranking peasantry began to express their discontent, along the same lines which had motivated the revolt of the Flemish *karles*, which was broken in 1328 by the King. In England, the protests were provoked by Edward III's *Ordinance of Labourers*, issued in 1349, forbidding or limiting the steep rise in wages as a result of the Plague. This meant that a number of yeomen, who had benefited from the disappearance of many of their neighbours by taking over the empty farmland and were now in a position to pay the going wages, found themselves deprived by royal ordinance of their essential workforce. The countryside was policed by delegations sent out to detect abuses and between 1352 and 1359 they succeeded in provoking serious unrest in Cheshire and Oxfordshire. In France the situation was slightly different, and the general discontent was sparked off by the pressure of royal taxation; the *gabelle*, *fouages*, and especially after 1360 when three million *écus* had to be raised for the royal ransom. As it was, many village communities in the north of the kingdom had been given the right to bear arms in their own defence after 1350, and it is certain that the defeat of the aristocracy at Poitiers, the feeling that royal power was weakening and of the uselessness of war, also played their part in the rebellion of one of the most heavily populated, wealthiest and least ravaged parts of the kingdom.

The episode of the *Jacquerie* lasted fifteen days, the time needed to summon the armed forces to avenge the nobility. It was its sudden appearance and inexplicable character, conducted as it was by men who were supposed to have been partly spared by death, which were behind the indignation and terror felt by Froissard and others; the movement exploded on 23 May 1358 at Saint-Leu d'Esserent and spread in a week over the Valois, Beauvais and Amiens territories. It sprang up around Perthois and Vervins and some echoes of it were heard in Berry and Burgundy. The peasants formed themselves into bands commanded by former soldiers like William Carle. Numbering several thousands, they pillaged and burnt castles and massacred a few nobles, but spared others, demanding instead the confirmation of their customary rights. The towns remained neutral, closing their gates, but they did hand out supplies, as at Compiègne and Soissons. At Paris, where the provost Étienne Marcel was at bay, an agreement with them may have been considered. But nothing was done and events happened rapidly. Charles the Bad, King of Navarre, was frightened for his Norman possessions and had no difficulty mustering 1,500 knights. On 10 June, Carle was treacherously assassinated and his peasant bands were surrounded and slaughtered near Mello and at Meaux, where some had infiltrated themselves. Their defeat was complete. Peasants were strung up in bunches, but among those who escaped this fate by paying a fine were many carters and barrel-makers, sergeants and vintners. It had indeed been a movement of the privileged peasant class. The repression meted out to them reflected the fear they inspired, but there was no question of removing the rights the peasants had acquired when the general amnesty was finally declared. As a result, there were no further such movements in the north; only a few disturbances between 1378 and 1381, well into the period of urban insurrections, in Flanders, near Rouen and in Brie, and later between 1390 and 1393 in the Auxerrois. But the corn-growing areas did not seem capable of rebellion any more, in France at any rate.

It was in England that the most powerful and best coordinated movement exploded, and one of the most notorious in rural history. As with the Jacquerie, the movement began in the most densely populated and wealthy regions, Essex, Kent and in the centre and east of the London basin. Since Henry III and especially since the Edwards, exceptional tallages had been levied and, as in France, taxation does appear to have crystallised discontent, but it was the wage restrictions of 1351–9, together with new taxes, including the 1377–8 polltax, which further served to increase the discontent among the middle-ranking peasantry. In 1381, a polltax of one shilling per hearth, the equivalent of twelve days' wages, was instituted, causing Essex to revolt in May. In June, bands led by Wat Tyler entered London where the rustics were welcomed with cautious sympathy. These loutish petitioners were installed in the Tower of London, where they flouted the conventions of the palace, pulling counsellors' beards and insulting the Queen. They were seen at best as a means of thwarting the favourites of the young Richard II, especially John of Lancaster. Events here developed as rapidly as in France; on 14 June, Wat Tyler had the Archbishop of Canterbury and the Treasurer strung up, but the next day he was himself killed by the Lord Mayor and his bands evacuated London. However, unlike the Jacquerie, this workers' movement endured, possibly because the peasants' situation was more unsettled, or because of the prolonged minority of the king. Surrey, Suffolk and the Midlands were aroused by a priest called John Ball, who started an anti-hierarchical movement, which unleashed attacks on abbeys. The English towns were less afraid of these groups than the French ones had been and although the wool workers were in trouble, the craftsmen in spite of being accomplices, were not actively involved. Bands of peasants entered Chester, York and Worcester in the autumn of 1381, but on the whole, the peasant movement was not supported by other social groups. When the repression took place, those executed were predominantly small folk; very few squires, or members of the gentry like William Coggan had joined the commotion.

This coordinated type of insurrection occurred only in England and France; the Italian movements were immediately capped by the towns and the Spanish ones were related to the disturbances in Languedoc which I will discuss. In Scandinavia, the 'King David' movement of around 1411 seems to have been fairly coherent, but it achieved nothing. We are left with the case of Germany, where there was no shortage of impoverished landlords and dynamic peasants. The absence of violent confrontations points to the harshness of seigneurial control, and the terrible explosion of 1525, in which all ranks of peasants were involved, may have been the result of years of repression. At this point, mention should be made of the Czechoslovak movements, although we will have to return to them. The Czech revolt, which ended with the execution of Jan Huss in 1415, contained much anti-German feeling; the Hussite wars were both nationalist and religious wars, and the only remark I want to make about them is that since 1399–1404, some Franciscan monks like John of Zeliv had launched into a series of egalitarian and millenary sermons, fairly similar to those of John Ball in England. The movement, which was called Taborite after 1420 and which achieved some real military successes, eludes classification as easily as the contemporary Lollard movement does. A few ringleaders like Martin Huska tried, with the support of clergy separated from Rome and of disciples known as Pikarts, to establish an egalitarian society in Bohemia, a primitive communism which the German and Czech aristocracy crushed – not without difficulty.

Tuchins and Maquisards

All these peasants knew what they wanted and felt that they were in a position to get it. Froissard tried hard to turn them into ignorant folk of evil intent, but they on the contrary claimed that there was no longer justification for seigneurial rule and that it was incumbent upon each person to fulfil his duty without imposing on others. Gerson said just this in his fine sermons to Charles VI around 1405. Other peasants were less capable of thought and even less of action; they were the weak elements, the inhabitants of forests, the special victims of hunger and economic disruption. They had no leaders, no doctrine and no aims; they were simply famished and frightened and so they ran away, hid – and killed.

This form of social banditry was almost devoid of real class consciousness: in Catalonia the notion of standing up to the townsfolk may have slowly arisen, but only belatedly and not before 1450. In other places, the urgings of desperate need were obeyed, and it was not especially the seigneur who came under fire. The peasants who took to the *tosca*, the *maquis* or in this case, the *garrigue* (the bush), who pillaged churches, kidnapped merchants and ambushed lost travellers, hardly ever came across the aristocracy. In Languedoc, near Béziers and in the Cévennes the Tuchins had been denounced since 1362–3. Their movement was diffuse and uncertain, but around 1375 it acquired a certain structure. Villages were linked by *sacrementals* by which they engaged to provide mutual assistance; one man out of every three would take to the *maquis*, while the others went on working, awaiting their turn. It was not unusual for nobles to be drawn into these conspiracies, such as Pierre de Brès, Jean de Chalus and Mignot de Cardaillac. Towns for their part were very wary of them; although Saint-Flour and Aubenas were friendly around 1378–9, Montpellier and Pont-Saint-Esprit closed their gates. In areas ravaged by the crushing taxation which Louis of Anjou imposed as the new governor of Languedoc, a certain 'Occitan' state of mind may have animated peasant bands; vagabonds like Friar Roquetaillade sometimes invoked wormeaten memories of Catharism. It was impossible to suppress such a movement; in 1384 the royal army captured several bands at Mentière, but in fact the scrubland of the Cévennes remained cut off from the plain until 1415–20.

The Spanish movements had a more clearly defined legal dimension; the *remensas*, or the price of freedom, had been raised very much beyond the means of a peasantry overburdened with *malos usos* and royal taxation, and many Catalan and Aragonese peasants were forced either to live in narrow dependence or to run away. They did not contest the established social order, but instead demanded that the King, or the Bishop of Gerona, or the Count of Pallars, should ensure their defence and *necessitas*. As well as this, the lands which the Plague had emptied remained uncultivated and unappropriated even

The Jacquerie was mercilessly supressed; the peasants were strung up in bunches. *The hanged men*, drawing by Pisanello (1395–1455). (London, Oppenheimer collection.)

when they were taken in hand. This discontent was also shared by the ruined petty aristocracy; Francisco Verntallat, for instance, a Catalan knight imbued with epic romances, was a precursor of Don Quixote. The *remensas* movement fluctuated, reaching its greatest size between 1350 and 1388, and lasting until the end of the century, interspersed with campaigns of repression. It assumed many forms, varying from nocturnal attacks in town suburbs to escaping from tax-collectors, from refusing to carry out services followed by exodus from the area to mountain ambushes. Linked as it was to an anachronistic and slow-to-change seigneurial structure, the situation did not improve for a long time, not to say never.

Another aspect of the insecurity of the countryside was provided by itinerant bands, the rough *coquillards* of Burgundy, the *chaperons blancs* (white bonnets) of Picardy, the *caïmans* of the Île-de-France, who attacked passers-by from about 1390 and especially in 1410. Paris burghers told terrible stories about little children being eaten, knights being roasted and burghers being robbed of all their clothes. Brigands, vagabonds and runaways, all were known to be involved. Were the outbursts of hatred against the Jews part of the general xenophobia inflaming those troubled times – or were they really due to the urge to massacre the money lenders? Whatever the reason, the number of pogroms multiplied, as early as 1350 in the Rhine valley; 1356 in Gerona, 1380 in the Toulousain, and especially in 1390–1 when the slaughter reached a level unattained for two centuries and the whole of Spain, in spite of being a land of asylum, was bathed in Jewish blood. Was this still another peasant movement? This time however, the towns were involved, a fact which allows us to leave the countryside, where the vilest and the best of human experience were closely associated, and to pass through the jealously guarded gates of the towns.

'Good towns' and 'commotions'

The towns of Europe in the fourteenth century and at the beginning of the fifteenth were not really reluctant to open their gates, but the pendulum-like motion, which soon ensured their dominance over the countryside, is hard to trace. The physiognomy of the towns of the High Middle Ages was extremely unsettled and we have to admit that it would be specious to draw a convincing chronological profile for the urban sector around 1420–40, as we did just now for the rural sector; at the very most, things speeded up, but there was no change of direction. It suffices to say that until around these decades, progress was balanced by problems to such a degree that contemporary observers were in doubt as to which way history was moving, but historians nowadays are better informed and can see more clearly.

Expansion

As the main victims of the Plague, besieged and pillaged and burnt, overrun by soldiers, officials and no less voracious fugitives, and then emptied of their clients precisely when the king raised an aid or hearth-tax, the towns should have presented an even more distressing

Towns were being modernised. Here the roads leading to an imaginary city, or perhaps Brussels, are being paved. (1448 Ms. 9242, Brussels, Bibliothèque royale).

a) Building houses used massive amounts of timber for the beams, floors and the roof, as well as planks for the inner and outer walls. (Ms. 11850, The British Library).

b) One of the last remaining wooden façades, with its arched gable, is to be found in Bruges (right).

picture than the villages. But this was not the case, and their vitality was generally speaking unimpaired and it even increased.

First of all, new towns (really rural boroughs) were created, spurred on by a new activity in the crafts, and their populations grew to number several thousands. It would be absurd to list them all, but one thinks of the centres of rural fairs in southern France (Pézenas, Lunel, Pertuis, Sorgue), or of the seventy trading posts set up by the Hanse. In other places, the increase in population and in built-up areas was striking; definitive rural immigration – passing through the town gates and settling within the walls – has been studied in a number of towns in France and the Low Countries, as well as in Barcelona and Florence. In Paris, the different streams of immigrants were clearly defined; 53 per cent of the newcomers came from the lower Seine and the Oise valley, 26 per cent from the Marne and Morvan. These directions reveal something about the range of the city's political and economic influence; as far as Paris was concerned, this was a period when the English were firmly established in Normandy and Picardy. In thirteenth-century Metz, for instance, the flow of immigration had come mainly from Barre and Champagne, but it now came from the Meurthe and middle Moselle valleys, which formed a very active commercial axis. We are also well informed about the material conditions imposed on the new arrivals; in the Bordelais, after 1370, a probational 'ban' of forty days was imposed before anyone was admitted to a town. In Florence since 1315 all newcomers, even noblemen, had to be inscribed in a guild within a year.

It is difficult to quantify this influx. There were periods when they were welcome and others when they were repulsed. In 1361, around one hundred persons died of the Plague and other causes in the Paris moats because they had not been given shelter. In Bordeaux and Reims it was enough to turn up carrying tools to be accepted. Population figures are still being debated; Paris, Milan, Venice, Florence and very probably Cologne and possibly London, Barcelona and Genoa contained 100,000 inhabitants or more, often at the expense of towns which seemed to be in irreversible decline, such as Bruges, Regensburg, Rome and Bordeaux. The area covered by these growing towns is also a positive indication; Paris expanded from 275 to 450 hectares, Cologne and Louvain from 300 to 500 hectares, Bologna and Milan from 250 to 800 hectares; which in almost every case involved building new town walls, inserting semi-rural areas (for military or fiscal reasons?) within their skimpily built bounds. The great building phase in most western European towns dates from 1350 to 1380; Paris, Ghent, Reims, Metz, Milan, etc. The influx of new men of often low social standing to the towns involved reshuffling their scale of values, as much on the level of professional qualifications as in the matter of housing. In Paris, since the royal household had abandoned the Île de la Cité for the Hôtel Saint-Paul on the north bank of the Seine, moving later to the country and outlying residences, many houses there had begun to fall down, inhabited only by poor immigrants. Around 1420, one-third of the housing blocks looked deserted and ruinous; one house in three on the Notre-Dame bridge was uninhabitable and the others were of ill repute. At the same time, however, house rents were climbing in the quarter of the Innocents and of the Champeaux, where armourers, brocaders and even goldsmiths were moving. The great demand for houses meant that they were built much too rapidly and building standards as a whole deteriorated in this period, evidence for which is found in the wormeaten timbers, in rusty and pitted ironwork, in hastily made tiles which burst in frosty weather, all of which meant that if one of these buildings lasted twelve years, this was seen as a good average.

Nothing demonstrates the powerful vitality of the towns better than the mass exodus of townsfolk into the countryside as a prelude to taming it. Their original motive has frequently been pointed out; they had to eat, and apart from a few small fields, closes, vegetables, pigs and cows of their own, everything else had to be got from the country people. In many areas however, the neighbouring countryside was not in a position to feed the 50,000 mouths within their walls; Genoa could only draw three months' worth of provisions from her Liguria and Venice scarcely more from her Veneto, and even London and Barcelona could not count on more than six months' supply. Once the breaking point came, people panicked. I have mentioned the razzias carried out by citizens on their outlying villages. In the fourteenth and especially the fifteenth centuries, there were so many such incidents that they amount to the first attempts at implementing the policy of urban domination which subsequently flourished. We should at once mention that there was no really firm idea behind the various measures which were applied, no desire for permanence and certainly no theory of economic compensation. John Buridan and Nicholas Oresme, members of the French King Charles V's entourage, limited themselves to repeating Duns Scotus and Thomas Aquinas's theories about the just price and the ruler's right to determine it. A little later in Germany, Henry of Langenstein (died 1397) discovered the idea of profit and automatic reinvestment but was unable to enlarge on it due to the state of the market. They kept faithfully within the narrow margins of immediate urban interest, of a secure subsistance, the guardian of public order. To begin with, purely defensive measures were introduced, such as taxing all foreign products, edible or otherwise, since, for instance, French wines in Milan could bear abusive duties. Or the price of food was fixed, stockpiling denounced and speculators attacked. The Italian towns generally granted themselves the right of preemption on all essential goods trafficked in by individuals, leading towards the idea of aggressive protectionism, which was subsequently to become mercantilism. The first legal enactment inaugurating this concern was the 'Navigation Act' issued by Richard II in England in 1381 (prior to the more far-reaching one of the sixteenth century) which forbade all cargoes which had not arrived in English ships from being unloaded. This was of course an absurd proposal and could not be put into effect for lack of ships and anyway, the Normans and Flemings responded by seizing a fourth or a sixth of all merchandise sailing to England.

For these reasons, it was more important to make sure of the neighbouring countryside than distant trade routes. Many means were introduced to achieve this; since the thirteenth century, rural produce had been sold according to the towns' systems of weights and measures. This form of subjection was imposed on the Bavarian peasants by Ulm and Nuremberg, not to mention all those of the Hanse hinterland, and in Italy, municipal agents from Siena and Florence overran the countryside, assessed the harvest and, with the army behind them, they persuaded the peasants to agree to lion's share contracts, which forced them to sell a proportion of their produce in town. Since there was plenty of resistance in the form of inertia or concealment, the circumference within which the town exercised its requisitioning powers kept on expanding. In northern Germany the cities agreed to divide their surrounding countryside up between them, as did Hamburg and Lübeck, Ulm and Regensburg, Brunswick and Hanover. In other places, the urban demand penetrated very far afield in search for relatively scarce produce, meat and milk by-products. In Provence, Avignon and Aix called on the Massif Central and the Dauphiné to supply them with provisions. In Italy, Venice drained the *terra firma* of its produce up to fifty kilometres inland. Boats from Auxerre, Laon and Rouen flocked to Paris. In this way, relatively important food reserves could be built up; an inventory drawn up for Reims, albeit in February and thus at a fair distance from the inevitable shortage, paints a picture of a town in which two-thirds of its inhabitants stored cereals, hams and wine in their houses, even though half of them would have had to buy in whatever corn they could find at the going price from the few individuals who had much more than they needed in store, before the next harvest.

Another solution, which probably developed independently of the need for food, involved acquiring land. The land of course belonged to the landed aristocracy also living in town, who were to be found not only in the Mediterranean countries, but also in northern France, Lorraine and the Rhineland. The demand for land did not grow at the same rate everywhere; as became increasingly obvious in the seventeenth century, many owners of capital in France and Spain disdained investing it in land or trade, preferring to buy public offices; it was shares in commercial interests which tempted the eventual investor. This meant either that the bourgeois stranglehold on the countryside was still rudimentary by the sixteenth century, or that it had ceased fairly early on. The Ysalguier of Toulouse, who abandoned trade after 1380 and threw themselves into the purchase of land, began by acquiring estates, woods, windmills and manors, and then, after 1420, they started assuming seigneurial rights, fiefs and royal offices. Identical examples could be cited for England, where the La Poles of Hull, having made their fortune in the herring fisheries, pushed out into the countryside around Edward III's time and ended up as Dukes of Lancaster. The Acciaiuoli in Florence owned a slice of the contado and threw themselves into buying up fiefs in the Morea, before controlling the Papal finances, becoming viceroys of the King of Naples and Papal ambassadors. These are but three examples among a hundred similar ones.

Business

Many of the successes achieved by the ruling urban classes along the trade routes or in buying land certainly had their origin in their strengthened links with their customers and family groups within the towns. This phenomenon was very similar to the one concerning the village notables' associations mentioned above. In the towns, the *mesnies* of the wealthy and powerful citizens were strengthened by the influx of immigrants within the town walls. All the *consorterie*, the *alberghi*, the *ostaux* and *paraiges* of Italy, Languedoc and Lorraine which we discussed earlier, far from being swamped by the new men, used them to swell their clientèle. After three out of every four men in the *vicina*, the *connetablie*, the *bannière*, the *quarter*, the *sestier* (among the many names they were called by the different regions of Europe) had agreed to it, the new man would be inscribed in a guild and so became one of the *seguiti*, one of the followers of the clan leader. He could be a stallholder, a handyman, a gyrovague clerk or a *sottoposto* (that is to say unqualified and unemployed), but whatever the case, he would then be integrated into one of those bands in the service of the dominant families and, at the same time, of their own interests. These people were behind the town fights, the raids on the countryside; they toppled economic competition and political rivals and when trouble arose, they were ready to riot and loot. As in the villages, to these already firm links could be added those maintained by the pious associations, which were often established in the churches of the gentry, the necropolises of the ruling families. Such associations included the brotherhoods and caritative associations of the Pays d'Oïl, the *frérèches* and *hermandades* of the south, the *poeles* and *Zunftstube* of the Lorraine and Rhine areas. The ruling powers found the influence exerted by these diffuse groups disturbing, when the authority of their wealthiest members was not preponderant. They were watched very closely in Italy, and in 1387 the English King Richard II launched an inquest into them to discover the size of their membership. We may pause to recall the theatrical productions, which had so long been neglected or reduced to the level of street mime, and which were revived as expressions of flourishing town life. Miracle and Mystery plays rose up in front of the churches and in the market places. These performances, distant echoes of the liturgies of antiquity, were ordered, financed and produced by a town quarter, a family, or one man, for whom these plays provided a dazzling means of publicising the strength of their clientèle or the weight of their purse.

The bourgeoisie thus found that they could count on human assistance in periods of economic depression. They were supported by many other factors; remember how well all those techniques, which had launched the thirteenth century, had held up and even improved. Artisans had started spreading the use of simple mechanisms which had until then been mere prototypes, such as the pedal-driven loom (which was worked by two men) and the spinning-wheel (which, when introduced to Germany, increased the spinners' production by a quarter). Metalworking had attained a reliable stage of perfection even before the mining boom of the fifteenth century; after 1340, the introduction of forge bellows enabled the smelting of pig-iron, or *fer de merde* as it was still called in the fifteenth century. This was an important stage in the development of the metallurgy of modern times with its high-temperature furnaces. As for bronze, since 1290 in Devon and rather later in Italy, its workmanship had reached such a pitch of perfection that armourers could choose between tubes of bronze or cast iron for casting cannon. All along the Mediterranean, paper began to supplant parchment and in the north, more and more paper mills began to be built. They produced rag-paper made from linen scrap, hemp, fustian and felt, which the rag-men brought from cloth-merchants and tailors, surrounded as they were by shreds of slashed material, a by-product of the particularly capricious and excentric fashion in clothes. Finally, although the actual means of land transport do not appear to have

improved any further, sea navigation took a turn for the better, which explains the importance merchants attached to their naval armaments and to the perils of the sea in the fourteenth century. The first improvement was the stern rudder in the ship's axle, which was first used in the Baltic in 1242 and spread to the Mediterranean around 1310, when it came into general use. Next, carvel work was introduced from Spain and the Maghrib to replace the previous clinker work, which allowed ships to move more rapidly through the water and which was adopted as far away as the North Sea. The Oriental compass was a standard piece of equipment in all Christian ships prior to 1350 and it allowed, indeed obliged, the use of sea maps. Cartography was born around 1296 in Spain, more particularly in the Balearic Isles, and soon influenced peoples' ideas and methods of navigation. A Pisan map of 1300, the 'portulans' of 1325–1340, and especially the famous Catalan Atlas ordered by Charles V, which covers an area from Dakar to Japan and from Sweden to Mali, all demonstrate that a decisive step had been taken in Europe, without which the modern age would never have begun.

Whether in town or on the sea, these refined techniques affected the flow of business. Socially speaking, the result was ambiguous; as with every introduction of new machinery or skills, they were followed by the dismissal or disqualification of many workers, and those who had been left behind by progress had no intention of being forgotten. Clearly, it was absolutely in the employer's interest to reduce unnecessary expenses hampering his business. The accounts of the Datini family in Prato, to the north of Florence, show that the selling price of a woollen cloth broke down as follows; 38 per cent represented the price of the wool, 16 per cent the cost of processing it, (both percentages approximate the earliest ones we know of) but the cost of making the cloth and sundry expenses had shrunk to 35 per cent, allowing the employer to make a clear profit of 10 per cent on every sale. Freight charges shrank along similar lines; the cost of transporting wine by sea from La Rochelle to Bruges fell by 10 per cent, whereas the cost of carrying wine by land from Auxerre to Flanders added 40 to 60 per cent to its market price, according to the itinerary taken. It was hardly surprising that the sea route from Genoa to Bruges, for instance, should have been preferred to the Alpine passes, to the great loss of the Champagne Fairs, or that the techniques of maritime insurance contracts, as drawn up by the notaries, should have improved beyond all measure. The Genoese notary Bagnaria insured up to 200,000 florins worth of merchandise in 1427 alone.

Western businessmen were aware, sooner than the country people, of the need to adapt their training and projects to meet these possibilities. Pegolotti's *Practica della mercatura* (1340) and Uzzano's *Libro di mercantie* (1432) were accompanied by the opening of accountancy and management schools. According to Villani, there were six such in Florence by 1338 and we know of some in London, Bristol, Bruges, Bremen, Milan and Genoa by the beginning of the fifteenth century. The improved bookkeeping techniques seem to point to improved merchant procedure; double-entry bookkeeping was adopted, involving keeping a current cash-book, a book showing every customer's debits and credits and a book of current accounts, which not only allowed mistakes to be spotted and adjusted, but also allowed a balance sheet to be drawn up on a day-to-day basis, funds to be transferred from one account to another, and branch accounts to be cleared. Double-entry bookkeeping is possibly a Venetian invention, and was known in Florence around 1277–80 and in Genoa by 1339, remaining a purely Italian skill for a long time, not encountered in the Low Countries or Germany until the fifteenth century.

It is surprising, given this mastery of complex financial problems, that commercial enterprises were not better structured and organised. They multiplied, it is true, but often at very mediocre levels; in Toulouse, for instance, 67 per cent of the businesses had capital funds of less than 200 livres, and 56 per cent of them were only drawn up for a year, without a binding contract. Even in Italy, the homeland of mercantile associations and companies since the tenth century, such groupings were generally limited to the members of a family and were of short duration; they might involve a dozen relations pooling their funds, the *corpo*, and issuing shares for external financial support, the *sopra corpo*. The total invested capital was moderate, amounting in the biggest cases to less than 100,000 pounds. To make matters worse, Genoese and Florentine companies tended to keep only 25–30 per cent of their capital in liquid assets, which meant that in the event of a branch folding or of panic among the shareholders, their bank reserves failed, hence the term *banca rotta*, bankruptcy. The avalanche of bankruptcies around 1340–5 did not appear to have taught anyone a lesson. At the most, greater numbers of short-term public associations were formed; huge financial enterprises which lasted only a short time, such as the Florentine *monti* or the Genoese *maona*, which amassed vast capitals – 300,000 ducats in Genoa were invested in the alum business. Portugal and Catalonia had until then been little tempted by these forms of commerce, but now they attempted to form several such associations in order to fund cork, mercury and agricultural enterprises, but they lacked the financial backing provided by the wealthy Italian communes. Finally, these various enterprises were still at the mercy of fluctuations in the volume of gold and silver supply, called *larghezza* and *strettezza*, which mark the history of minting money. The stage of central clearing banks or even of credit mechanisms such as the bill of exchange or the cheque had not yet been reached, and the artisans and merchants of Europe still had a little way to go before they could take on the world.

The towns in agony

This is just one side of the picture; the towns were growing and the countryside was surrendering to them, business was flourishing and techniques were improving, but none of this was enough to cover the cries of the rioters and the crackling of incendiary fires. Although a paradise for businessmen, the fourteenth-century town was hell for the poor.

The structure of artisan work in the town had not been modified in the way work on the seignorial estates in the country had been. The guilds, the *arti*, remained the normal framework of employment and security. They showed a growing tendency towards rigidity, maybe because the improved techniques mentioned above meant that it became more necessary to supervise the quality of the merchandise and to eliminate competition, two requirements of urban manufacture. This was behind the Italian towns' decision to make it mandatory for their citizens to enroll in a guild, an organised trade, a regulation

The pharmacist adds up his accounts. A fresco from
the Castello of Issogne at the end of the fifteenth century.

In order to qualify as masters, apprentices had to produce a master-work. Here two candidates for
mastership in carpentry are working under the attentive eye of an elder. (Ms. Roy, The British Library.)

which was almost inevitable in other countries. In Germany, in Cologne, Magdeburg, Hamburg and Lübeck around 1379, 62 to 70 per cent of the inhabitants were inscribed in a trade – an *Amt* or a *Gewerke*; in England, perhaps rather fewer were inscribed in the guilds. In Languedoc, after 1360, towns tried to vet workers who wanted to enroll in their guilds, because they could now vote for the officers who represented the craftmasters in the consulate, and it was important to eliminate possible factious elements. This attitude can be called Malthusian, and in Ulm, for instance, it took the form of a five years' residence requirement and a high entry fine. The same state of mind presided over the growing number of requirements to be met before promotion within a trade was granted; the usual way of achieving the status of master was by producing a 'master-work', but this qualification became more difficult and expensive to achieve, and was finally reserved by preference for the masters' own sons. The masters closed ranks very early on in northern Germany and the trend then spread to north-western Europe and resulted in the position of master becoming hereditary. In Ghent at the beginning of the fifteenth century, 213 brewers out of 280 inherited their fathers' positions. In other places, the number of apprentices was restricted for the same reason; in Paris after 1351, only one was allowed per workshop.

In the long run, the towns ended up with an extremely delicate situation: on the one hand, the trades remained the controlling factor in the life of the town, because one had to enroll in them, – Villani counted no fewer than 200 textile workshops in Florence around 1340. But, on the other hand, working conditions and even the entry conditions they imposed created tensions in the towns, which emanated as much from the *sottoposti*, the unemployed, as from the unskilled workers. For them, although their wages were rising steadily and so put them above the country workers, this was offset by the rising price of manufactured goods. Whereas the peasant could buy his seed cheaply because of the agricultural depression, town prices were subject to great leaps and bounds (bread went up by 800 per cent in Paris in 1419–20), which put them out of the reach of the *popolo minuto*, the labourers and common people. On top of this, things which could, when necessary, be manufactured in the villages – wooden or iron objects, clothes, tools – were steadily getting more expensive, and though this was a slow process, it was still faster than the rise in wages (the price of worked iron rose from a base line of 100 at the onset of the fourteenth century, to 160 after the Plague, and to 350 at the beginning of the fifteenth century). Here too the ordinances of February, June and October 1351 for England, France and Castile respectively, further aggravated the situation in the towns, even if the governments of the last two kingdoms did accept an overall price rise of 30–50 per cent above the prices of 1347, something Edward III refused to do in his island. Little as production was stopped by the military troubles, they should not be disregarded, because any drop in the profits made by the big people, the *poorters*, the *popolo grasso* as they were known, could be important. Italian textiles are a case in point; profits there fell from 15 to 6 per cent in 1375 – in the ship-building industry in Rouen, they fell from 50 to 7 per cent in 1380. These circumstances created an atmosphere of class conflict; the master ironsmiths of Reims called on the municipal forces to disperse workers demanding employment, and indeed the

William Wenemaer, magistrate and Captain. A
fourteenth-century tomb plaque (Ghent, Musem of
the Biloque.)

public authority was called on to intervene in most of the movements we will be discussing.

To intervene, or in some cases to leave be, notably when one of those astonishing battles within the ranks of the workforce took place – between well-paid and underpaid workers, between workers and unemployed. Absurd vendettas, watched over with obvious satisfaction by the employers, as they have always done. The unhappy history of Ghent and that of Liège is riddled with fratricidal conflicts, as in 1349–50, when the fullers and weavers massacred one another. There are so many facets to these urban events that it would be silly to impose an order on them, an order which contemporaries did not perceive and which may not have existed.

Sorcerer-apprentices

Out of this jumble of events, we should pick out those in which the political and even the clan dimension is most obvious, two blanket terms which have often been applied without discrimination. Generally, in towns with a strong franchise, it was a matter of obtaining access to the magistrature, the *Rat*, the consulate, by securing representatives for the middle-ranking workers, the members of guilds which had until then been kept apart, because they were considered, on account either of their particular product or of the level of their clientèle, to have no role in the government of municipal affairs. Among these were the livestock guilds, or those representing the lower stages in the manufacture of woollen cloth. Riots, however, tended to be sparked off more often by local circumstances; an outside event such as the arrival of foreign armies, or an internal outburst, such as a battle between two political factions, could suffice. Often, a leader would emerge – a member of the more leisured classes, a draper, a minor noble or a clerk leaning on the support of the common people – to further the interests of his own class or caste. Such a leader would happily adopt a democratic manner of speaking, but his aim would at best be only to broaden the census-paying base of bourgeois power. There are very many examples of this, not all of them equally well-known; among the most famous was the case of 1293 in Florence, which brought about the expulsion of the Albertis, that is the 'Ghibelline' party, theoretically hostile to the Pope, and which, by means of the 'Ordinances of Justice', opened the Signoria to a few new guilds, but in so doing handed it over to a new merchant stratum: the Albizzi and Strozzi. In Bruges, at the beginning of the fourteenth century, the Leliaerts, partisans of the *Fleur de Lys*, a handful of *poorters* and some drapers, several of whom were killed, were led by Peter Deconink to rise up against the French and their collaborators (1302), before the royal army exacted its revenge. Similar events happened at Speier in 1304, Brussels in 1306 and especially Liège, where Henry of Dinant held out for a few years. These north-western regions remained very unstable until the coming of the Plague in 1350, which was accompanied by pogroms. Mainz, Strasbourg, Cologne and Basle had their upsets between 1332 and 1336 as did Genoa and Florence in Italy. When the draper Jacques van Artevelde rallied to Edward III, who made him captain of the town from 1338 to 1345, was this socially significant? Artevelde made promises to the textile workers and, because he did not keep them, he was assassinated in a riot, which took place before the internal struggles of 1349–50 at the time of the Plague.

Maybe the Plague was also responsible for one of the most original attempts of this kind; in 1347, a Roman notary called Cola di Rienzo assumed the title of censor in the manner of antiquity, and in the general despair brought on by the Plague and in the absence of the Pope, he claimed to restore the Roman Republic. This time, the language employed was 'popular'; the men of Trastevere were invited to sack the palaces of the fleeing Roman nobility and an attempt was made to set up a direct government with elections in the *rione* of the city. Cola's vision was however defeated by municipal reality; he had neither the stuff of emperors nor the means even to gain control of the fortress of Sant Angelo. When the Latin aristocracy cut him down in 1354, there was no outcry.

The Étienne Marcel episode was of the same kind and is familiar to Frenchmen, who are brought up to believe that this clumsy draper was a founder of popular, or at least Parisian, democracy. What happened was that, when the Estates were summoned by Philip the Good to grant him some money, they dealt him some hard words; the Bishop of Laon, Lecoq, and the Provost of the Paris merchants, Marcel, a member of the city's wealthiest family, led the criticism against royal taxation and the merchants' lack of representation at court. There was nothing in all this about the poor. The capture of the Valois king at Poitiers, the demagogy of Charles, King of Navarre, who wanted to seize the throne, the apparent weakness of the Dauphin Charles, all drove Étienne Marcel to speak up; in 1357 he imposed a check on public finances – but he was only thinking of Paris. Work on town walls was begun, which Charles V was to complete; Paris was split up into quarters and a militia was drawn up. None of the measures unseated the Dauphin, nor did they satisfy the populace. In February 1358, Marcel attempted a last effort against the young Charles, which resulted in the famous and misunderstood scene of the Louvre being invaded by a rabble, which slaughtered royal counsillors at the feet of the frightened prince – who was from that day on mortally insulted. Like Petion, who offered Louis XVI a bonnet on 20 June 1792, Marcel put his hood on the Dauphin's head, but this was surely to protect him rather than to humiliate him.

It is fairly clear that the Provost had not wanted events to take such an extreme turn, and afterwards, events moved very fast; the Dauphin fled, the Jacques were crushed, the people turned against Marcel, who was assassinated by a false friend in July, at the moment when the Provost had lost his mind and was about to open the city gates to the English.

The list of urban movements in which the common people were led on by men of another class, who only duped them with empty promises, is far from ended. In Germany, during the powerful revolutionary movement of 1378–82, nothing other seems to have happened in Brunswick, Mainz or more to the West in Metz. During the Ghent rising of 1382, Philip van Artevelde, Jacques's son, had the artisans with him, as in 1302 or 1328, but he was aiming at municipal power. He was left behind among the dead at Roosebeke in November, when they met the royal army, and during the difficult negotiations which followed until 1385, the only question discussed was the statute of the magistrature. As for the Parisian movements of 1413–14, the result of rivalry between the partisans of Bernard d'Armagnac and those of John of Burgundy, these certainly included some 'popular' members – butcher boys, messenger boys, fullers and cloggers formed part of the Duke's escort, shook his hand and followed the rich master-butcher, Simon Caboche. In spite of their numbers, the **105**

Étienne Marcel, the provost of the merchants, was assassinated in Paris on 31 July 1358 by a partisan of the Dauphin, the future Charles V. (Paris, Bibliothèque nationale.)

discussion turned on the state of the kingdom and on the Estates. Indeed, the Parisians went on slaughtering one another until 1418, without improving the lot in life of a single one of them. In Brussels, the Hoek, who opposed the Kabiljauws when Jacqueline of Bavaria was expelled in 1423, and in Seville, the partisans of the Ponce, who were in opposition to the Guzman, were all just as deceitful.

The volcano rumbles

In the long run however, those social classes which had every reason to complain of their lot could not go on being aroused without something changing. Although Cola, Marcel and Caboche were democratic only by the standards of their times, they did act as sorcerers' apprentices. As did those splendid well-intentioned individuals, who were aware of the poverty of the people at the beginning of the fifteenth century; Gerson, Jean Petit, Alain Chartier moved the princes to pity and made them weep. The Franciscans took up their theme, and harangued the crowds for hours at a time from a post or a platform, like Fra Richart in Paris in 1429. By dint of denouncing the parasitical court; the nobility led by Pride; the war, which robbed the have-nots; the vacillating Church and, finally, the earthly riches which lead to Hell, they made sure that peace would not return.

The framework for a new society already existed: the *ateliers*; the fraternities; the *vicina* of the town quarters and even the *colloquia* – those more or less illicit associations, which did not admit masters and which had been denounced since the thirteenth century. As always, their most convenient weapon was sabotage – inertia and strikes, or *ristoppio* as it was called in Italy, *takehan* in Flanders. In France, it was known as *grève*, a name possibly derived from the Place de la Grève in Paris, and these occurred in 1311–13 in London and Flanders, 1332 in Strasbourg, 1337–45 in Ghent, 1346 in Florence, and, during the guided movements of 1354 and 1358, identical demonstrations took place in Siena, Cologne and London. The sequence of events was the same everywhere; the workers would refuse to accept arbitrary wages, the masters would withdraw and then recruit either loyal apprentices or endebted peasants. Blood seldom flowed, repression is hard to detect and the result was insignificant.

This is why the events of 1378–83 are so important, although they were not on the scale of Wat Tyler's effort in London, of the *remensas* of Aragon or of the agreements between masters along the Rhine valley. As it was, the common people of the towns of Europe were spontaneously and simultaneously aroused, albeit for different reasons; in Florence it was the wages freeze decided on by the Albizzi and Strozzi; in Metz, it was the prohibition of the iron workers' coalitions and the expulsion of the marginal people from the Champ at Seille; in Rouen and Paris, it was the reintroduction of *fouages*, which the dying Charles V had cynically abolished. This time, the greater part of the rioting and its leaders came from the common people. In Florence, in July 1378, after a split between the dominant Guelfic clans, in which Salvestro di Medici played an ambiguous part, agitation against the Signoria spread to the stall-holders, who took up arms. Bands were formed with a wool carder, Michele di Lando, at their head. 1,500 crossbowmen were drawn from the people and the palace of the Podestà was attacked, that of the Signoria was invaded and its tax registers burnt, the prisons were thrown open. Although the people obtained the admission of three new guilds to the council, one of which was the guild of the *popolo minuto*, of the people, which meant everything and nothing, they were unable to organise their government or even their food supplies. Lando himself was suborned by the authorities and the *arti maggiore*, notably the money changers and drapers, who made a splendid return to the town. By the end of 1381, everything was back in order. The same pattern of events occurred in France, if rather more rapidly; Paris revolted in the autumn of 1381 – when the people grabbed the leaden mallets used by the sergeants. The *maillotins* demanded that the *fouage* be abolished, that an edict be issued fixing maximum prices and that wages be raised; they were treated with feigned consideration by the regents – the uncles of Charles V. What they in fact did was firstly to crush the *harelle*, who had risen up in Rouen, before hurrying to break the Flemish revolt at Roosebeke. Returning to Paris, the royal army forced an entry, marching over the broken city gates. The repression was relatively gentle, since they did not intend to make the Marais desperate. As it was, the people had plenty of opportunities to work off their grievances after failing to obtain the freedoms they had wanted – during the long civil war, which broke out in 1407.

Contemporaries were not always impressed by the disturbances; towns were volatile places inhabited by different and unpredictable elements and there was no reason to be

The Palazzo Vecchio in the Piazza della Signoria, Florence, was built between 1299 and 1314.

surprised when they rioted. If things got out of hand, the towns called on the king. On the other hand, the peasant risings, which were really less serious, were much more frightening, because protesting serfs were always dangerous. Peasants were still considered fundamental to the established social order, and while urban troubles were worrying, country troubles were shattering. There was only one way of dealing with them – by using the army. Was it strong enough?

Authority at bay

The State was in a sorry condition in this period. The Popes were originally honourable but contested men, but then their reputations were impaired and they were hated. The

Emperors were swollen with ambitious projects, the western monarchies were in full disarray – old men, minors and madmen ruled alongside a motley array of podestàs, princes and captains, who had nothing in common apart from the brevity of their power and the impracticability of their projects. Nonetheless, it was in this period that some of the foundations of the modern State were laid.

The return of the 'republic'

The old dualism of the twelfth century – one Pope and one Emperor – did not survive beyond 1250. This symbol of the Christian West, the theory of the two swords, which had nourished so many university theorists, no longer applied; both were broken. Only a few Italians, Dante, Marsilius of Padua, Petrarch, retained a nostalgic feeling for the Empire. The coronation of Henry VII in 1312, that of Charles IV in 1355, and the occasion when Sigismund was presented with the golden rose were acknowleged by kings, even ones like Charles V of France, who had the gall to make the visiting Emperor ride a black horse. In Italy, however, the Emperor meant nothing; his vicars did as they pleased, called themselves Dukes like the Visconti in Milan in 1395, or ignored his summonses, like Amadeus of Savoy in 1406. There was nothing the supreme sovereign could do about it. In Germany, he had sold everything to the towns and the 350 princes, who shared out his regalian rights between themselves. He wandered around with a few officials, without an army and without any money; his income has been estimated at 7,000 marks per annum – half that of the King of Sicily.

So the State was now represented by the King, who was authorised by Roman Law. The King disposed of *auctoritas* and *potestas* and the lawyers of the end of the thirteenth century had told him he was Emperor in his own kingdom. Raoul of Presles invoked the City of God and the Old Testament. John of Terrerouge and Philip of Mezières even spoke of a royal religion. In the time of the ageing Charles V and Edward III, as well as under Peter of Castile and Peter of Aragon, royal entourages invested the ruler with a different and fairly contrasting physiognomy. Certainly, first Nicholas Oresme and then John Gerson told the King that he was the guarantor of good order; on him rested the *respublica*, but that from then on, he was both its provisional prop and accountable to it; his office was temporary and he had to render account of it to God and men. His actions, unless he was going to be a 'perfect tyrant', could only be the result of general consent, even if this consent was given only by representatives, clerics and nobles. Simon of Montfort had asked for nothing else in 1260 – and if he was chopped into bits for his pains it was only because he was ahead of his times. So the real sovereign was the body politic, which delegated quasi-universal power over life and property to the king, but which could demand that he render an account of his rule and reform his behaviour.

Whether aged or a minor, the kings of the time nearly always accepted this idea of a royal 'guild', but they were not disposed to take it to its logical outcome – the election or adoption of an heir as in the time of the Roman Republic, which everyone talked about without knowing much about it. Kings added a few sentences to their coronation oaths and they

Charles *le Téméraire* presides over a chapter of the Golden Fleece, an order created to gather the nobility around the Duke of Burgundy. (Ms. fr. 139, Paris, Bibliothèque nationale.)

renewed the old practise of itinerant rule. This was really a sign of their weakness; since the ruler was the people personified, he had to go to the people. John *le Bon* was permanently on the move. In 1389, the young Charles VI was paraded all around France. Even the Emperors could not stay still; the hostility meted out to the Castilian King Peter the Cruel was largely due to his self-isolation at Seville, where he surrounded himself with Moors. All the same, under this appearance of delegation, not to say leading strings, the kings retained most of the trumps of the old kingship. First of all, their authority was that of a clan, a family, and to this extent there was only a difference of degree between them and the urban factions. Everything fundamentally touching the fate of the crown was settled within the family; if the ruler was a minor, his mother and uncles ruled in France as they did in England, and no one contested this. If the succession was contested, as happened in England, France and Castile, the affair was settled by the royal relations in favour of a brother, a cousin or a nephew. The crowns of Hungary, Poland and Naples and a whole range of principalities were thus passed from hand to hand via marriage, distant inheritance or dynastic ascendancy. This allowed families like the House of Anjou, or the Wittelsbach of Bavaria, to extend their tentacles into territories lying very far away from their family lands. The settlement of grievances, the assassinations of Peter the Cruel, Louis of Orléans, of Giangaleazzo Visconti, of Richard II and John *sans Peur*, looked very much like vendettas. Women too, and Queens, although excluded here and there from essential successions like that of France in 1328, were in fact much more important than before. Their influence over their husbands, their children, their brothers-in-law and their lovers opened up careers of intense political activity for them, among whom were Jeanne of Burgundy, Isabeau of Bavaria, Jeanne of Penthièvre, Valentina Visconti, Yolanda of Aragon, Joanna of Naples and many others.

For all that the king's family shared his ruling role, the support, which the king was in principle entitled to expect from the aristocracy and his councils, had become somewhat ambiguous. The old feudal service and oaths of vassalage certainly still applied, and a ruler had to be able to count on the nobility. But, in the cold light of day, this social class looked less and less like the loyal followers of the Capetians. The king's council was now made up (apart from a few of his relations) of clerks and bureaucrats, his own creatures. It is quite interesting to study the changes in the flow and provenance of this amorphous personnel; in France, England and Bavaria, not to mention the Italian towns, different groups from different provinces rose to favour one after the other. When members of the real aristocracy did take part, such as Châtillon, Brienne, Lorris, Dormans, Marigny, they often represented dynasties of personal counsellors, breeding grounds for confidential officials and ambassadors. The nobility was really brought to heel by means of purely cosmetic privileges, amongst others the extremely exclusive 'orders', whose rituals invested their recipients with social and spiritual kudos. They included the Orders of the Garter, the White Lady, the Golden Fleece, Saint Michael, and many others. But where among this handful of friends, beneficiaries and technocrats was the 'Republic' to be found?

It was well concealed in the profoundly religious dimension of the public authority. Gerson himself said that the kingship was sacerdotal, and indeed the ceremony of annointment during his coronation was a sacrament which distinguished the king from the prince. A king could decide on matters of faith, as King Louis had already allowed himself to do. The case of the Capetians and Valois kings was exceptional in this respect; the canonisation of Louis IX in 1298 endowed his family with a nimbus of hereditary sanctity. The French rulers could heal scrofula; they decided against Gregory XI's advice on points of dogma at the synods of Rouen and Lyon (in 1373 and 1374). In 1378, Charles V unleashed the Great Schism after having openly, and no doubt sincerely, chosen in favour of Clement VII against the Urban VI. Nor did the people's devotion ever desert the king, even such a clumsy and unjust one as John *le Bon*, even the useless and mad ones like Charles VI. Indeed, probably no ruler has ever been loved and lamented as much as that unhappy lunatic, whose madness nonetheless cost his subjects dearly. Joan of Arc too, by spurring on the pusillanimous Charles VII right up to his coronation at Reims in 1429, well understood that the self-styled Dauphin was from that moment on unassailable.

It is a fact that none of these rulers saw any of his subjects lift a hand against him – and this could not be said for the Spanish, English or Italian kings. The Emperor was the only ruler to share this aura; Sigismund considered it his duty to convoke and preside over the Council of Constance in 1415–18, but how can this parvenu emperor be compared to the sons of Saint Louis?

Indeed, although the French kings have been allotted first place in this survey because their situation was the most characteristic of the lot, the final picture is very confused; the theorists stated and the people no doubt believed that the king personified the *respublica*, the common good. His sincerity was beyond doubt, as were his merits; he was at worst ill-advised. But in practice, his entourage of familiar and familial persons, and the religious aspect of his mission prevented the institution from evolving naturally, and slowed the process down by hanging onto a past, which had not been abolished and which it preserved. At the same time the instruments of government, which the State was clumsily attempting to control, themselves dragged the power towards 'tyranny'.

As yet unmastered weapons

In the fifteenth century, nobody doubted but that the king's primary function was the exercise of justice. It was his principal *raison d'être*. Whether this justice was dealt out in the narrow circle of his residence, of his audience, or in the large circle of one of those courts and parlements whose development I have traced earlier, or whether justice was delegated to local officials, sheriffs, seneschals and bailiffs, it demanded the ruler's whole attention, or rather the attention of his clerks, to whom he had practically delegated justice. A process abetted by the proliferation of transcripts of customary law, of manuals and treatises on jurisdiction, of procedural styles for setting up inquiries, in addition to the flowering of an important stratum of men of justice, which robbed the king and his handful of loyal advisors of all real responsibility in the application of the rules of ordered society.

If there had been but one source of justice, and one disposing of a competent and devoted body of executives, the plaintiff would have had only the delays due to the ever-weightier procedures and the costs involved in dealing with doorkeepers, prosecutors and the council for the defence, lawyers and pen-pushers at all levels, to complain of. And so it was in principle; the Exchequer and the King's Bench of the English king, the Grand' Chambre and the Requêtes of the Hôtel de France, the Audience and the Amannies of the Low Countries should have been enough. The ruler would then have had a first class instrument of control to hand. However, this was far from being the case, firstly because public justice failed to penetrate to the level of the lowest order in society, the villagers. The sheriffs and bailiffs held assizes, *grand jours* and diets fairly regularly in the towns, but it was a question of being able to get to them. Furthermore, local seigneurial jurisdictions were still valid; we saw how in England 350 hundred courts out of 620 were held by landlords. As in France since Saint Louis' reign, justices in eyre had been sent out on circuit, who tried to get people to appeal to the royal tribunals – but these were lightning visits. The fourteenth century showed a progressive decentralisation of royal justice in direct contradiction to royal wishes. In most of the principalities, institutions were established in the mid fourteenth century, or afterwards, which were almost free of any control by a central authority. This was the case in the Gallic Marches, in Bavaria, in Brandenburg and on the Habsburg lands; in the Duchy of Burgundy the *grands jours ducaux* appeared in 1352, as did the Parlement in Brittany, followed by the 'États' in the Dauphiné in 1357, and in English Guyenne; that of the Black Prince in 1366; a Grand Council in Gascony which became a Supreme Court in 1370, and a Council of the Estates in Flanders in 1390. Within his own domain, the ruler could take advantage of distance or particular local customs to double the organs of central justice. Already by 1291–1303 it had been useful to organise a Parlement in Toulouse to determine the written law for the seneschalships of the Land of Oc, and it was renewed in 1319 and after 1355; sessions were held almost regularly, drawing in cases sometimes as far away as Berry. The royal power carried out a few supervisions in 1366, 1369 and especially in 1389, when dishonest judges were executed. Finally, when the Dauphin Charles sought refuge south of the Loire after the Treaty of Troyes in 1420, he took with him and installed in Poitiers about half of the clerks of the Paris Parlement, thus doubling their numbers, because the gaps in the Poitiers ranks were filled by him, and those in Paris by the regent Bedford.

Although public justice in its application and especially its exploitation did not procure all the means of action the central power might have dreamt of, he could at least count on getting them from his fiscal powers. I pointed out how, well before 1300, the accrued cost of all kinds of expenses had gradually made it impossible, even for the most richly endowed rulers like the King of France, to follow the ancient and healthy practice of living off his own land. It is thought that the king's personal expenditure around 1340 on dowries, gratuities, the upkeep of his Hôtel, his travels and his wardrobe, absorbed the whole of his income from his own domain. We know that in difficult circumstances, he would resort to harsh expedients such as melting down plate and alienating revenues, which were frequently employed between 1337 and 1355, but were obviously only temporarily effective. As for the occasional confiscation of the property of a criminal vassal or of bankers and Jews, the eventual disaffection this gave rise to proved a considerable deterrent. Taxation was the only other resource, and the slow and painful reintroduction to the public of the idea of paying taxes was a major feature of fourteenth-century history. As Oresme stressed, since the king was responsible for the common weal, his subjects were logically bound to contribute to his work. As the nobility could only be called on to contribute their blood, this meant that for all the others, contributing meant paying taxes. Contrary to what is too frequently asserted, the Church had been the first to do so, albeit not without jibbing. Since Philip the Fair and Edward I, kings had extorted *decima*, an action, which along with the distraints effected in Castile and Germany, was gradually accepted. The demands of the

Local justice: a condemned man is taken to the gallows, 1389. (Bidpai, *Fables*, Ms. 6807, Chantilly, Musée Condé.)

Avignon papacy were already so high that it was sometimes difficult to raise the expected contributions in some dioceses. But this is not the main point; the ones who had to pay were not the powerful but peasants and townsfolk, who also paid indirect taxes – on merchandise and salt – which were introduced between 1290 and 1340. At the same time, rigorous central accounting offices were set up in the shape of the Court of Accounts and the Treasury. Indirect taxation was known to be unreliable, so they had to dig deeper and tax hearths. The hearth-tax or *fouage*, later known as the royal *taille* was the foundation on which the sure and ample revenues of the modern state were built. The original principle was that it was an extraordinary imposition and, even though 85 per cent of the government and war funds in France around 1375 came from this regular source, it was still understood to be exceptional. The next step was introducing the principle of consent, when John *le Bon* asked for a heavy fouage in 1355, and it was agreed that elected men should be responsible for spreading the load over all parts of the kingdom. This principle was adhered to and around 1390 the country was divided up into *éléctions*, which were made up of a few bailiwicks grouped together for purposes of taxation, very similar to the English counties. The vocabulary used was peculiar, and was in fact used during the whole of the Ancien Régime, since the tax collectors in the *éléctions* were appointed by the State, whereas the Estates, that is the appanages and principalities, elected their own tax collectors. It was in France that the system acquired its greatest strength and effectiveness, due to a particular predicament – the crushing ransom imposed on King John could not be paid all at once. Previously, *fouages* had been levied for a variety of reasons in 1337, 1342, 1349, 1350, 1355, 1356 and 1357, but this time, after 1360, and because the annual installments had already been set, this debt of honour (which was also a public debt) could only be settled by imposing annual *fouages* from 1361 to 1404 – more than 40 successive years of taxation. This arrangement could not have been more legal because of the obligations of loyalty to the ruler. Five or six 'General Treasurers of the Aid' were appointed to supervise the whole thing, over and above the *éléctions*: the beginnings of the *généralités* of the Ancien Régime. The Court of Accounts was now flanked by a Court of Aids. When the ransom was finally acquitted, the renewal of the war justified further levies, and from then on taxation became customary.

Poitiers had saved the French fiscal powers, but in England the opposite happened, precisely because the French payments allowed the English kings to be less demanding and less regularly extortionate than their neighbours.

Before Henry V decided to introduce regular taxation in 1405, the English kings were reduced to levying occasional taxes, as in France prior to 1360, and we have seen the disastrous results of excessive impositions like the polltax of 1378. We can assess how unevenly this extraordinary taxation developed by looking at the annual incomes of the principal political powers in 1420, where they have been estimated; taking the income of the Papacy and the Emperor as our base line of 100, the Kings of Sicily and Aragon received 150, the King of Naples and the Duke of Burgundy 200, the King of Castile 300, that of England 500, but the Valois king received as much as all the rest together – 1,500!

Such a list would be misleading, since the French ruler was no more able to control his fiscal powers than he could fully exercise his judicial powers. Without dwelling on the sometimes disastrous social and economic consequences of royal taxation, it must be pointed out that the king was unable to implement a coherent fiscal policy as long as he was unable to get his money. We saw the origins and features of this situation above, which did not improve at all during the period from 1350 to 1420. On the contrary, it worsened, causing general disorder. The price of precious metals peaked and the gold/silver ratio swung disastrously from 1:11 to 1:5, accompanied by inevitable speculation. Under these conditions, different forms of currency manipulation followed rapidly on each others' heels – 85 such have been counted in the Valois kingdom between 1337 and 1360 and then 30 between 1417 and 1423. In France, the royal coinage was devalued step by step, falling in 1359 to less than 0.1 gm of silver per 4 gm coin, valued at 24 deniers instead of 12 deniers, and in 1422 to 0.02 gm valued at 30 deniers, with the gold coinage bearing up rather better. Our written sources of information provide us with a whole range of prices drawn up, not according to the currency used in payment, but according to a pound–shilling– pence scale whose practical value in every day market terms is not always known. Contemporaries were aware of these inconsistencies. This is doubtless the reason behind the practice of referring to, and sometimes even drawing up the sum in terms of the Florentine florin, one of the few currencies stable enough to provide an international monetary standard.

States and 'Estates'

If the ruler was incapable of controlling his mercenaries, his coinage or his judiciary, if he allowed himself to be influenced by coteries and lived a bad life generally, two ways were open to those who wanted to discipline the power. Such people included a number of clerks, burghers and nobles, and Chartier, Étienne Marcel and John *sans Peur* turn up here again in the search for new political bases.

First of all, they had to consult the 'people', that is to say, themselves, those privileged by wealth or the members of the dominant 'Orders', particularly about those matters which concerned them closely – taxation and the ruling body. Although convocations, 'Estates', Cortes, Assizes and Diets had been held sporadically in the thirteenth and the beginning of the fourteenth century, the kings had always avoided allowing them to become established bodies. Unfortunately, the expenses of war meant that they had to be increased and inevitably, the kings had to listen to harsh words about the State's extravagance, its ill-prepared military campaigns, and the incompetence of court officials. From 1340, Edward III had to reform his Parliament in order to beg for subsidies, but this was an old tradition in England and all he had to do was show a little compliance. The Valois were less amenable and when, for instance, they summoned the '*États*' from 1355 to 1357, they got money from them, but they also had to put up with remonstrances and long reforming ordinances, notably that of 1355 and the 'Cabochian' Ordinance of 1413 (a very silly name for it, because the butcher Caboche did not have a hand in it), which outlined a sort of parliamentary government, after having secured the dismissal of all the existing officials. These texts, like those which the London insurgents wrested from Richard II's counsellors in 1381, are extremely interesting stages in the evolution of political ideas. However, none of them was granted an order of execution due to lack of royal good will, no doubt, but also due to the shortage of manpower, money and time. Anyway, after 1360, with the exception of a brief interlude in France between 1407 and 1418, the rulers were careful not to go beyond the level of the provincial 'Estates' in order to limit their concessions, and at no slight risk of encouraging a local perspective of problems. What we know of convocations of this sort outside France and England suggests they belong to the same type; the Dukes of Burgundy, Tyrol and Austria, the Bishop of Liège, the Duke of Savoy and the Kings of Castile also summoned 'Estates' between 1362 and 1420, while carefully extirpating all dissolutionist tendencies.

Most of the detainers of important public power found themselves in a position, which could only be improved by holding these regional assemblies; principalities and mini-states were emerging once again in Europe. They were autonomous, even independent, and this last phenomenon finally destroyed the illusion of kingship by mutual consent.

In reality, most of these groupings had rather different origins to their distant precursors of the tenth century. Although they did not necessarily lack a regional base, it was more likely to be part of their heritage from olden times, as in Lorraine, Tuscany and the Pyrenean valleys and Brittany. In fact, human intervention was a more obvious factor, and could involve reassembling neighbouring lands and similar previously separate entities, like Gaston Phoebus' attempt between Foix and Béarn. Otherwise straightforward military conquest was the means employed, as in the case of the Marquisate of Brandenburg or the Duchy of Milan. Or else it could be an old fief spared by the kings because of its isolation or specific features, like English Guyenne or Brittany. Finally, it could be an appanage, either exploiting a straightforward governorship as Louis of Anjou did in Languedoc, or the careful and lengthy acquisition of unconnected lands united solely by their common rulers, presiding over a finely-spun web of marriages, alliances and exchanges, the most famous example of this being that of Philip of Burgundy, who ruled from the gates of Lyon to the Rhine estuary.

All these constructions had one thing in common, in that they involved the creation of a State equipped in every way like a kingdom, with royal palaces, a network of garrisons, its troops of mercenaries, its Hôtel and Chamber of Accounts, its *Jours* or Parlements, its bailiffs and its own receivers, even its own Chancery, secret seal and coinage. It is scarcely surprising that this emancipation was accompanied by a personal form of politics, with the Counts of Armagnac–Fezensac, the Sires of Albret, the Kings of Navarre and Gaston Phoebus (dead in 1391) playing off the Black Prince against Charles V, or the other way around. The Duke of Brittany refused to pay him homage, and the Duke of Burgundy extended his political influence into Lorraine. The disintegration of the kingdom occurred, rather surprisingly, at a time when its natural evolution was pushing it towards centralisation around one person. Should this process be seen as a final struggle before falling into the arms of an uncontested monarchy, or as one of the proving stones of modern kingship? In 1420, when everything seemed to have reached its lowest point, nobody would have dared predict the answer.

The 'popular' element was however less indifferent than the courtiers of the time believed, and it was aware of this uncertainty. In the same way as individuals were attempting to supplement the failing spiritual and moral institutions, they also dared to think about the nature of power and the 'Republic'. At first, they restricted themselves to grumbling about the governing class, an ancient tradition which goes back to the *Romance of the Rose* and, encouraged by rousing sermons, they vituperated rulers who 'rifflent et happent' (pare coins and grab money) and the 'puteries de la reine Vénus' (that was Isabeau of Bavaria), and counsellors who had neither sense nor soul. They damned pride and pomp, which led the world, and Charles of Navarre, Henry of Lancaster and John *sans Peur* needed to indulge in only a little demagogery to be acclaimed as reformers. None of this went very far; it was the clergy or the 'Estates' who spoke of the separation of powers and of purging. Neither the social order nor the monarchy were questioned. This led in return to the awakening of political awareness; in Italy, certainly since the mid thirteenth century, being Ghelph or Ghibelline, black or white, did not just mean belonging to the party of a great personage whose interests had led to such and such options. In Florence, at the time of the Villani and of Boccaccio, the people were for order or for liberty; whole quarters and guilds were overtaken by these rivalries without any homogeneous social message emerging clearly. Armagnacs and Burgundians in France were the same; behind the violet flag of Burgundy, they prided themselves on more than 'democracy'. These were the timid

The political emblems of the Dauphin's party and that of the Burgundians. (Paris, Musée de Cluny.)

beginnings of political parties, possessing no doctrines, no recognised objectives, no leaders and no passwords, but nevertheless they were the promising stirrings of popular consciousness, suggesting that the spirit of nationalism, previously unknown to the Middle Ages, should be associated with them. Nationalism was possibly the religion which recruited the Czechs to Huss, stirred the loyalty to the king which awoke Joan of Arc; behind these vain attempts this new message began to resound – that they belonged to an established entity, a national group. It is not the least of the age's paradoxes that when all spirits were in disarray, when humanist emancipation was in full spate, that one of the most durable ideas to be born at that time was the feeling of being part of a whole.

Different values and authorities 3

The idea of 'crisis' is not easily applied within the framework of mentalities, beliefs and values; being both convenient and suggestive it is liable to facile analogies. Ever since the romantic historians and since John Huizinga, it has been used to excess to describe the last centuries of the Middle Ages, painting them in autumnal colours and plunging them into the 'mingled scent of blood and roses', while suggesting that beneath the decadence and decay, the Renaissance was germinating. However, when trying to grasp as much as possible about collective mentalities and behaviour, this approach is partial, founded on a few arbitrarily selected and assembled cases, and, more particularly, derived from a rather superficial aesthetic or even anecdotal point of view. Now, less than in any previous age, the descriptive mode is inadequate and the many examples I have taken from literature or art or from mundane daily life, such as costume or funerary rites, are meaningful only when carefully related to the complex play of social patterns, class interaction, political structures and economic fluctuations.

Therefore it is not a matter of denying that the crisis of the end of the Middle Ages, the 'crisis of feudalism' analysed above, did profoundly affect men's minds, their religious convictions and their portrayals of life and death. On the contrary. But we should treat simplistic explanations with caution, since we find the origins of this collective mental evolution at many different levels. We should refrain from speaking of a transitional period referring to a sterile inventory of 'ancient elements' which 'survived' or 'collapsed' and of 'new forces' already rising to assume their full potential. Finally, we should take the trouble to view the last centuries of the Middle Ages as they actually appeared to contemporaries, that is to say, as being modern.

Ancient and modern ways

'War, pestilence and famine': this sinister trilogy was evoked, not by present-day historians, but by certain contemporaries to describe the fifteenth century. The great pandemics of 1348, 1360 and 1374 struck down a quarter to a third of all Europeans in a few months. Subsequently a series of more localised but desperately regular outbreaks reduced the population of many areas, so that by the beginning of the fifteenth century it was scarcely half that of a century earlier. In spite of the lucid accounts of storytellers like Boccaccio and chroniclers like Jean de Venette, we should not forget that many sources closer to daily life and the ordinary man, such as the preambles to wills or municipal deliberations, are extraordinarily reticent about the Plague. It is however hard to imagine that these brutal bursts of mortality, the sinister images which accomplished them and the shortened life expectation they entailed did not vividly impress contemporaries.

It comes as no surprise then, to find a priest of Cahors, under interrogation by an Inquisitor around 1390, saying that throughout his life, he had seen only war in the country and diocese of Cahors and that he had never known peace in those regions. It is clear that this man, like many others in the period, was painfully aware that his age was one of misery and extreme uncertainty, in contrast to a bygone age of peace and tranquility. From the beginning of the fourteenth century the *bon temps de Monseigneur Saint Louis* was regretted, but seventy-five years later, even the reign of Philip the Fair was looked back upon as a golden age.

It is clear that the demographic, economic and political conditions of the fourteenth century were awful enough to disturb people and induce bewildered and resigned behaviour. This should not lead us to draw any summary conclusions. Where mentalities and religious attitudes are concerned, especially in traditional societies, ideas and behavioural norms evolve slowly to a secular, even plurisecular rhythm. An event, however spectacular, was never more than peripheral and external, devoid of any direct and immediate impact on the world-view of the contemporaries. If the event reccurred with sufficient regularity, it might certainly accelerate, slow down or deflect an existing trend, but a long time would pass before it would become a really permanent feature of existence, one moulding people's images and their imaginary world. As far as we are concerned, this means that we should look back into the twelfth and thirteenth centuries for the origins and orientations of the great evolutions we shall speak of, and which were only partly affected by the events of the fourteenth century.

On the other hand, the fact that the premises on which collective mentalities were founded (particular 'models' of the Church or the family or of death) ended by collapsing, victims of centuries of erosion and of the blows of a few recent catastrophes, does not allow us to consider this just as a crisis, as a phenomenon with purely negative results, generating anguish and panic. Of course, the collapse of well-established social and political frameworks, the bankruptcy of traditionally recognised authorities, always has a disorientating effect. In the event, some people prefer to deny the evidence and try to maintain a semblance of life along meaningless lines, and others despair. The majority, however, react in a necessarily clumsy, sometimes excessive and often retrospective way. At the end of the Middle Ages it was obviously not the idea of progress, as we understand it, which was behind the contemporaries' successful reorganisation of their anxious energies. They looked more often backwards to a distant and mythological past, hoping to find there models and values with which to replace those disappearing under their eyes. The bankruptcy of university scholasticism restored life to Saint Bernard's mysticism, and those who were vanquished at Poitiers sought to revive the virtues and epic feats of

A refuge from the wars; the Saintes-Maries-de-la-Mer is a fortified church on the Camargue coast. The apse was built in 1140–80 and a lookout tower was put on top in the thirteenth century. It was extended in 1394 and the machicolation was added in the fifteenth century.

Charlemagne's age in their Orders of Chivalry, while waiting for the humanists to resuscitate the mirages of antique grandeur, as recorded by Livy and Valerius Maximus and in the *Deeds of the Romans*. Although we should not be seduced by these anachronisms, they did entail a certain liberation. Faced with the collapse of the old structures, some managed to clear new ways in doubt and tears and others in their dreams; and they broke, in spite of themselves, with the old certainties and status quo, which had proved to be illusions. The men of the fourteenth century were not the last witnesses of a twilight world they are sometimes represented as, but new men. *Via moderna* and *ars nova* were expressions used to describe the currents renewing theology and music; they could also be used to qualify all the mental and religious attitudes and images of the time.

The great shake up

Fourteenth-century man of course never existed. Although the search for global explanations is a legitimate exercise, it will never reconstruct the diversity of the real world, a diversity which also applied to time, so long as we are as attentive to the slow rhythm of generations and centuries as we are to the brief staccato pattern of catastrophes. There was a diversity of space: fourteenth-century Europe included the old lands, which had long been prosperous and densely peopled, and were rich in culture and in artistic traditions. These lands suffered most harshly from the crisis and were most painfully affected by the collapse

121

of established structures. Northern France, with her cleared lands, her rich harvests and cathedrals and cloth-producing Flanders are good examples of countries whose ancient vitality was impaired. But the new, formerly somewhat peripheral lands were in consequence relatively spared by the armies and the Plague and they benefited from the shifting trade routes, the changing fashions, the discovery of new mines and technical inventions, from the appearance of younger and stronger political organisms. It was these regions – Castile, Lombardy, Southern Germany, Bohemia and Poland – which gave birth to new centres of art and culture and which continued to create new universities and to build cathedrals. They gave new life to traditions which were dying out in other places and imbued them with their particular character.

There was diversity, finally, in society. As we know, the huge mortality rates and the economic crisis were factors which encouraged social mobility, whether on an individual or a collective level. Whole groups had seen their traditional bases of wealth, power and prestige gravely threatened; the monetary disorders, the fall in agricultural revenues, the devastation of the countryside, and the aggravation of the political struggles between clans and parties, struck in the first place at the feudal nobility, the traditional clergy (both regular and secular) and the old urban patrician families. It was these people whose recognised scale of values was most deeply disrupted by the problems of the age, as was shown by their tendency to indulge in all kinds of excesses, and in their irrational fondness for increasingly fantastic representations of moribund ideals. But this century was also a century of new men, *nouveaux-riches* and *nouveaux-pauvres* and to a greater extent of lay persons entering the hitherto inaccessible worlds of culture, art and prayer. It was these two movements, the social promotion of numerous *parvenus* of every kind, newly ennobled or enriched, and the vulgarisation of an until then largely clerical culture, which converged and gave birth to a whole new set of values, relationships and behaviour, aimed at fostering the success and self-awareness of these new groups. They could be mercenaries and captains enriched by the luck of war and by ransoms; merchant adventurers breaking new routes for transalpine commerce and Atlantic navigation; skilful manipulators of money, who made their profits from the fluctuating exchange rates and the beginnings of modern taxation; princes and ambitious holders of *appanages* surrounded by their courts and their liveries; successful preachers of the new piety; or finally and above all the lawyers and the officials. These scribes, notaries, graduates with a smattering of Latin and Law, were growing in number all over the place as a result of the proliferation of State bureaucracies, and the list of these newcomers who were projected to the forefront by the economic and political changes is very long.

None of this was new. These men were less concerned with inventing cultural forms, which would immediately have betrayed the originality of their role and their way of life, than with reviving the legacy of the traditional élites, and finding mythical references to themselves in the antiquated rituals of Chivalry and the mannered graces of *courtoisie*, which allowed them to forget how recent their success was, as well as the harshness, even the brutality, which might have accompanied it. We should however learn to distinguish, beneath the affected charm of elongated figures and borrowed myths, the robust dynamism of conquering social groups with their appetite for life and for possessing the world. Even their anxieties reveal the desire to escape from ancient constraints and former destinies.

The decapitated Church

Having attempted to mark out a field of research in these preliminary comments, I will pass on to examine concrete changes in the collective mentalities, culture and religious beliefs and practices, which were typical of the fourteenth century, and which continued into the first half of the fifteenth century. The most widely felt changes were those affecting the whole range of Christian life.

From the eleventh to the thirteenth century – to give the Gregorian reform and its very many extensions their largest dimension – the essential feature of the history of Western Christianity was the strengthening of ecclesiastical institutions, which provided the faithful with an improved framework of pastoral care. The Church began to feel that she had achieved a measure of stability, with the definitive victory of the Popes over the Emperors, who had long contested their pretensions to Universal Rule, in the time of Innocent III (1198–1216) and his successors. The Oecumenical Councils (Lateran IV, Lyons I and II) further provided the Church with exceptional opportunities to elaborate and broadcast her reform legislation. The dazzling success of the Mendicant Orders, the universities and the Inquisition, and finally, the publication of great compilations and commentaries of Canon Law, were the fruits of two centuries of trying to impose the moral and political values she defended onto the West, in order to turn it into Christendom. Her success, which the Gothic cathedrals still symbolise, did not however extinguish all tensions nor did it settle all contradictions. The following centuries would determine the fate of these institutions. Were they to survive the rigours of the 'crisis'? Were they capable of adapting to new economic, social and political conditions?

The last breath of the old Church

Let us begin by looking at the overall picture. That means seeing things from the viewpoint of the Papacy, because it was precisely its exaltation and the multiplication of its means of action, which had been one of the major features of the preceding era.

The dramatic pontificate of Boniface VIII (1294–1303) ended the era of the great reforming Popes. Celestine V's 'great refusal' had been a warning signal; he was a hermit who was elected Pope in July 1294 and abdicated five months later, crushed by his responsibilities and the weight of the intrigues entwining themselves around him. His decision revealed that the strains inherent to his office had reached an unbearable level. His successor Boniface VIII was not a weak character; he affirmed nothing other than traditional principles, even if he did so with a harshness which reflected not only his temperament, but the very spirit of the age. 'It is absolutely necessary for the salvation of every human creature to be subject to the Roman Pontiff' (*Unam Sanctam*, the Papal Bull of 18 November 1302). On the other hand, the Jubilee of 1300 showed that the Papacy was

123

A statue of Pope Boniface VIII by Manno di Bandina, 1301, Bologna, Museo Civico. Its archaic style and hierarchic stiffness suggest the ideal of theocratic power which the Pope believed he could impose, and which King Philip the Fair demonstrated to be empty.

still perfectly capable of understanding the most profound religious aspirations of the faithful and of using them to serve its own glory. Under these conditions, when the Pope was trounced by Philip the Fair, King of France, at Anagni (7 September 1303), contemporaries were struck less by the scandalous aggression of William of Nogaret and Sciarra Colonna's henchmen than by the humiliation of the Papacy. Henceforth the whole theocratic structure, which had been built up over the last two centuries, was undermined. A rich and daring ruler, jealous of his sovereignty and resolved at all costs to raise taxes and to control his bishops only needed the skill to orchestrate all the grievances, both old and new, which were directed against the Papacy, and to suggest appealing for a General Council as a possible alternative to the abuses of the Roman See, for the Papacy's spiritual sanctions, which had checkmated Emperors, to become ineffectual. Faced with the rise of the nation states and of monarchical administrations, the Church could no longer defend her freedom in the sense intended by the Reformers of the eleventh and twelfth centuries, that is to say, as the affirmation of the absolute primacy of the ecclesiastical institution and its right to control and correct all human activity.

For the time being, Boniface VIII's second successor Clement V (1305–15), an Augustinian, managed to solve, without glory if not without skill, the crisis between the Papacy and the King of France. Prepared to sacrifice the Templars in order to save

Boniface's memory from formal condemnation, he agreed to summon the Council of Vienna (1311–12) for this purpose, which was conducted under open pressure from Philip the Fair.

Clement V was restrained by diplomatic necessity and by his fear of the warring factions, which were then terrorising Rome, so he led an itinerant existence during all his pontificate, first in Aquitaine and then in Provence. The following Pope, John XXII, broke with this nomadic life style, which was anyway nothing really new, and established the Papal See in Avignon, where it remained firmly fixed for the next sixty years. These years represent a new phase in the history of the Church.

This is not the place to give a detailed account of the six pontificates which covered this period (John XXII, 1316–34; Benedict XII, 1334–42; Clement VI, 1342–52; Innocent VI, 1352–62; Urban V, 1362–70; Gregory XI, 1370–78). I shall only attempt to draw a general picture of what it meant in terms of the functioning of the ecclesiastical institution and of contemporaries' conception of it. The change did not necessarily affect terminology; traditional statements about the universal authority of the Supreme Pontiff, and his 'fullness of power' over the totality of the faithful, including rulers, which was his as Vicar of Christ, abound in the writings of these Popes and of some theologians of the time. The fairly anachronistic struggle which set the Avignon Popes against the Emperor Louis of Bavaria between 1322–46, showed how even the old debate about *sacerdotium* and *imperium* was still capable of arousing passions and of clouding concrete political interests. For all that, Christendom was no longer a reality. Reality belonged to the monarchic States: to France, England, the Iberian Kingdoms, the Italian *Signorie*, to the Free Towns of Germany, and the Papacy was forced to negotiate with these new entities, which were resolved not only not to submit to the tutorship of a supreme spiritual authority, but also to exercise efficient political control over the Church in their own territories and, eventually, to impose certain taxes on her.

Whether open or concealed, these tendencies towards forming national Churches were to be found all over Western Europe in the fourteenth century, and the Avignon Popes could not do anything to stop them. In England, Parliament passed two Statutes in 1351 and 1353, which gave the King the powers, potentially at least, to replace the Pope in almost all matters concerning investiture or ecclesiastical jurisdiction. In France, the *Dream of the Rood*, which was composed around 1376–78 in Charles V's entourage, shows clear 'Gallican' tendencies in its treatment of the nature of royal sovereignty and the exercise of ecclesiastical jurisdiction. A Gallicanism, which remained moderate and very respectful of Papal dignity; but it was true that the King of France prided himself on his privileged relationship with the Avignon Popes, a relationship as bitterly resented by the English, who were prompt to suspect the Popes of granting diplomatic and financial favours to France during the Hundred Years' War, as by the Italians, who denounced the new Babylonian captivity and the exile of the Papacy far from Rome and the See of Saint Peter. These accusations were to some extent justified by the fact that the Avignon Popes were all French, some of them even former loyal servants of the French King, and that among their entourage, 83 per cent of the Cardinals, 60 per cent of the administrative staff and 81 per

The antipope Nicholas V, who had originally been supported by Emperor Louis of Bavaria, begs Pope John XXII's pardon in Avignon with a rope around his neck. (Anonymous chronicle of the end of the fourteenth century. Besançon, Bibliothèque municipale.)

cent of the Palatine and domestic staff were also French. For all this, we should not forget that other nationalities, especially the Italians, also retained considerable access to the Papal Curia, and on the whole, the Avignon Popes should be recognised as having been very careful of their independence.

In practice if not in theory, all this meant that the Papacy of the fourteenth century had to relinquish a considerable part of its theocratic pretentions of the previous era. However, what it lost in political clout and ideological power, the centralisation of the Papacy made up for in teams of administrative efficiency. The institutional network established by the Church in the eleventh to thirteenth centuries was still made up of pretty broad and flexible links. Local particularism remained strong and Papal authority, although enjoying unrivalled prestige, was occasionally hard put to make itself felt on an everyday basis: whence the need to resort to relatively exceptional procedures (legations, oecumenical councils) or to create special centralised organisations, alongside the existing institutions, which were dependent solely on Rome (the Mendicant Orders, the Inquisition, the Universities).

The fourteenth-century Church, on the contrary, did not need to affirm principles other than those established in the previous era, and witnessed the development of very detailed administrative systems and procedures, which allowed the Papacy to exercise its centralising and monarchical authority in a much more permanent and efficient manner. From then on, she really did have the means to intervene at practically all levels of the local Churches' daily existence. This organisation owed much to Pope John XXII's real administrative genius, and, without going into detail, it developed along three lines which were inextricably entwined. Firstly the Popes managed to nominate a considerable number of posts and offices (canonries, priories, parishes, etc.) to the obvious detriment of ordinary beneficiaries, especially the Bishops, by extending Papal powers over more and more categories of benefices and by granting more and more generous reversions.

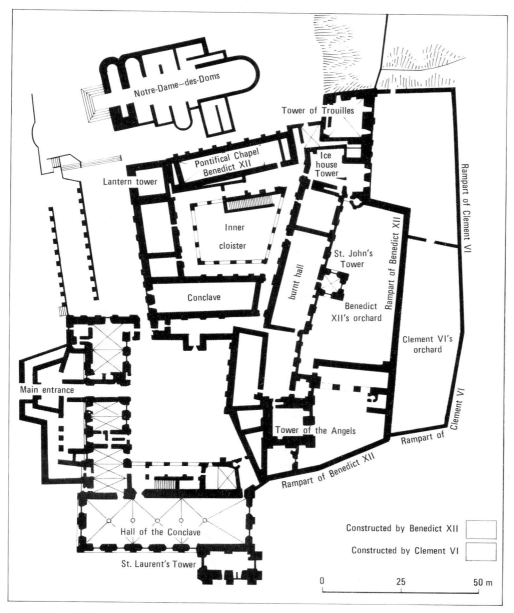

3 The Palace of the Popes at Avignon

The Palace of the Popes in Avignon, an enormous and majestic construction and 'the loveliest and strongest house in the world' according to Froissart. Built in 1334–52, it combines military austerity with an elegant and sumptuous interior.

Secondly, taxation was both cause and effect of this increase in the number of Papal dispositions. The Avignon Popes were able to set up a complex system of taxation, whose most profitable features (common services, 'annates', 'spolia') were precisely those levied on beneficiaries appointed by the Pope. Thirdly, jurisdiction: by juggling appeals and reserved cases, the Papal Tribunals (Rota and Penitentiary) extended their jurisdiction over a whole range of different cases.

The development of Papal centralisation was obviously accompanied by a considerable increase in the administrative staff, especially at Avignon. Without even considering the Cardinals and their followers, the Chancery, the Apostolic Chamber, and the Papal Tribunals employed nearly three hundred clerks in the fourteenth century.

The vices and virtues of Avignon

The achievement of the Avignon Popes is certainly not without merit. They could rely on a competent staff often trained in the Academies of Law, and they succeeded in setting up, on an immense scale throughout western Christendom, an administrative apparatus which was perhaps more efficient than that of the most modern monarchies of the period. They had the same limitations; local resistance often put paid to the rules laid down by Avignon, if only through inertia. In spite of its complexity and apparent weight, Papal taxation in fact returned only a mediocre income, and its unpopularity was due rather to the often niggling or arbitrary methods used by the collectors than to the harshness of its exactions.

Did the Papacy actually achieve any of the aims it pursued? The immediate aims certainly; the monarchic centralisation of the Church and the stream of men and wealth to Avignon allowed the Popes to turn the town into a real capital. They took advantage of its excellent position, which was much more central than that of Rome in relation to the rest of Christendom, and turned it into one of the crossroads of the West, a great commercial centre and also a university town and a centre for the arts and culture, to which Parisian men of letters, Italian painters and Flemish musicians thronged. The Palace of the Popes has survived almost intact, and was certainly one of the loveliest in Europe. The Avignon Popes were also able to use their financial resources, in the difficult task of gradually pacifying their Italian states with a view to eventually returning to Rome. But these successes did not in themselves justify the effort required. In fact, the Church's centralising drive was much older, going back to the Popes of the eleventh century. It had originally been conceived as the vehicle of Reform and as a weapon for defending the liberty of the Church against lay encroachment. But by the fourteenth century this Reform was no longer the great hope which had fired the clerics and laymen of the Gregorian age with enthusiasm, but had become a ritual reference, which gave rise only to regulations of a particular and ineffectual nature. Sadly, the centralising process had, perversely, become an end in itself. The particular genius of the Avignon Curia was to guide the movement to a new level of perfection at the very moment when the profound religious need for it had faded.

When one tries to come to a general conclusion about the Avignon interlude, its negative aspects tend to come to the surface, although individual Popes and their auxilliaries were sometimes exceptionally meritorious, lacking neither in education nor intelligence, nor even devotion. John XXII, Benedict XII and Urban V have even been accredited with a deep and sincere piety. Their fault was rather that of allowing the Papacy to become the head of a vast governmental machine. They were concerned above all with good administration and good justice, and they lost contact with the religious aspirations of the faithful, even as they forgot the dynamic nature of pastoral care. In the spiritual sense of the Reform, they allowed an administrative and eventually repressive conception of Christian life to predominate.

This evolution was all the harder to resist, because it had got rid of the controls and warnings which might have been able to stop it. The Avignon Popes stopped summoning oecumenical councils, at which the regional Churches could make themselves heard and could create a dialogue between themselves and the Roman Church. The Curia became a closed shop. By abusing the facilities they had obtained by developing apostolic 'reserves' and 'graces', the Popes and Cardinals resorted to remunerating their servants and intimates with the revenues of their very many benefices, without giving a thought to the resentment aroused locally by the ensuing invasion of absentee Avignon clerics. Accustomed to exercising absolute authority, they thought that they could throw themselves into the joys of nepotism and the struggles of clans and factions with impunity.

Pontifical luxury. This golden rose is supposed to have been offered by Clement V to the Prince-Bishop of Basle in the fourteenth century (Paris, Musée de Cluny).

These abuses did not give rise to more than limited forms of opposition for quite a long time because the system, which allowed many people to better themselves, functioned fairly efficiently. A group of 'spiritual' Franciscans, who had split with their Order and had regrouped for a time around Louis of Bavaria, denounced the Antichrist reigning at Avignon. Some intellectuals showed how perverse was this concentration of the *plenitudo potestatis* in the hands of the Supreme Pontiff and, reflecting on the nature of the Church's authority, they demanded that it should be returned to the Christian people, who were to be represented by the General Council, while their rulers were to be protected from abuse by the Pope's spiritual authority in their own lands. The most daring authors were Marsilius of Padua and John of Jandun in their *Defensor Pacis* (*Defender of the Peace*, 1324) and the Franciscan William of Ockham who wrote several treatises around 1330–40, in which he leant towards a purely spiritual conception of the Church: the exercise of authority would be limited to properly pastoral functions (preaching, sacraments) and all forms of coercive power, even for maintaining ecclesiastical discipline, would pass into the hands of the ruler, the defender of both civil and religious peace.

These critics were in a very small minority, belonging to restricted intellectual milieux or to isolated heretical circles. Most of the clergy and the faithful indulged as yet only in subversive attitudes, a latent discontent which gradually substituted defiance for veneration.

The Papacy in the mire

In 1376, when Pope Gregory XI decided against the wishes of most of the members of the Curia to return the Papal See to Rome, he showed that he did have a certain awareness of this situation and that he wished to restore part of the Holy See's lost prestige by satisfying the profound longing of a great number of Christians who, in the image of Catherine of Siena, remained faithful to a mystical conception of the Church, and could not accept that the Vicar of Christ, the mystical body's earthly head, could be permanently separated from the Holy City, the place of jubilee, and the tomb of the apostles and martyrs. However, the premature death of Gregory XI on 27 March 1378 prevented his initiative from bearing fruit, and precipitated instead the crisis of the Schism.

It was not the first time that the medieval Church had experienced two rival Popes at loggerheads, but the Great Schism of 1378 was different on account of its length – nearly 40 years – and of the profound unrest, which it engendered among many clerics and faithful. It was one of the most obvious elements of the crisis of the end of the Middle Ages and certainly one which had a decisive effect on the formation of modern Europe. It is worth our while to tarry here, and to leave the many side-issues for a moment.

Individual responsibilities were not especially important at this point: those of the Cardinals on the one hand, and those of the Christian rulers, especially the French King, on the other are the most obvious. Nor are the details of the episodes leading up to the double election of April–September 1378, which divided Christendom into two patently equal allegiances. On one side, there was Urban VI and his successors, who were more or less

131

masters of Rome and of the Papal States, from which they drew most of their revenues. They were acknowledged in Italy, Germany, Eastern Europe and England. On the other side, there were Clement VII (1378–95) then Benedict XIII (1394–1417) who quickly returned to Avignon, where they inherited its administrative machine and fiscal system, and whose supporters included France, Scotland, and the Iberian Kingdoms, as well as Naples. So the Schism of 1378 thus began as a crisis of the Papal institution, the almost predictable results of the inequities which the Popes of the fourteenth century had allowed to develop. The excessive power given to the organs of the Curia, especially the Holy College whose members, veritable princes of the Church, few in number but torn by irresolvable clan struggles, were ready to sacrifice everything to maintain their position. They had dug the gulf between the mass of Christians, who were instinctively faithful to the Roman See of Peter, and the Papal Curia, which had become incapable of detaching itself from its Avignon palaces, its administrative habits and its French associates.

From being a crisis of the Papacy, the Schism then expanded rapidly into a crisis involving the whole Church, a logical consequence of the systematic centralisation practised until then. To what extent did it really affect the body of the faithful? This was doubtless the case only in those regions were the two allegiances clashed, as in the Low Countries, where laymen could watch the spectacle of their rulers and bishops veering back and forth and where they saw rival clerics arguing over their duties and revenues. There, the scandal of the Schism and the peril in which it put their souls, must have been painfully felt by those anxious about their salvation. But, throughout Christendom, the clergy were aware of the drama. The bankruptcy of the Papacy was seen as the cause and sign of a profound corruption of the mystical body, the more so as it soon became obvious that the rival Pontiffs, locked in their intransigence and resting their cases on more or less equivalent authorities and political support, were not going to prevail one over the other. The intellectuals and the universities formulated the idea, that they had to go beyond the straightforward use of force, the only resort officially admitted by the Popes, and think up new solutions to impose on the two adversaries. Inspired by the critical ecclesiology of Marsilius of Padua and Ockham, they admitted among themselves that their solutions involved active intervention by the Christian rulers and the exercise by the community of the faithful, or their representatives, of a considerable part of that power, which had until then been monopolised by the one Supreme Pontiff. They also admitted that the Schism could only be solved in conjunction with resuming the Reform movement on a global scale, which had been abandoned for so long, and had resulted in the distress of the faithful and the perversion of so many institutions.

One solution: the Council

The first attempt at this came fairly late from the most powerful ruler in the Europe, the most Christian King of France, who was urged on by the University of Paris and a good many of his bishops to issue two successive 'Substractions of Obedience' in 1398 and 1408. By depriving the Popes of their hierarchical authority and their revenues they hoped to

Emperor Sigismund leads a procession at the Council of Constance. A fifteenth-century miniature. (Constance, Rosgartenmuseum.)

force them to abdicate or at least to negotiate. Benedict XIII's intransigence, the refusal of other States to join in this French 'Substraction', and the rapid weakening of Charles VI's government, undermined by the King's madness and the quarrels between the Princes of the Blood, all ensured that this attempt failed. The next attempt at a solution was that of the Council, advocated long ago by the universities, who had plenty of arguments for establishing its legitimacy and competence. The first Council, of Pisa (1409) was nonetheless a virtual failure. It was convoked by Cardinals who refused to acknowledge either authority, and its own authority was contestable. It neglected the urgency of the need for Reform and limited itself to condemning successive rival Popes without being able to eliminate them and to electing a further Pope, Alexander V (who was succeeded in 1410 by John XXIII). Under these conditions, the fact that the Pope of Pisa was soon able to get himself recognised more or less everywhere, leaving his adversaries only the rump of the allegiances (Spain for Benedict XIII, a few German and Italian principalities for Gregory XII), was not enough to permit a quick solution to the crisis. Neither the longing of the faithful for Reform nor that of the national Churches for the restoration of their liberties was satisfied by this hasty solution and John XXIII, discredited by his disputed personality and his clumsy methods, had to take stock of the situation quickly. He defended his own person by convoking a new General Council at Constance (1414–18), which however drew its legitimacy much less from the Papal Convocation, or from the protection which Sigismund, King of the Romans, had promised it, than from the sheer numbers of Conciliar Fathers (there were many representatives from the Universities and the Christian rulers as well as all the Abbots, Bishops and Cardinals) and from their conviction that they really represented the Universal Church in its diversity and unity, as was manifested by the way they divided themselves up by nations during the sessions. Having rapidly taken note of John XXIII's unwillingness to undertake the task of Reform, the Council deposed the Pontiff

133

and then decided, in an unprecedented move, that it would itself continue to preside with full authority: thus unequivocally affirming its superiority over the Pope and its ability to replace him in the exercise of the Church's sovereign power. In the following years, the Fathers of Constance conducted a dual campaign: that of ending the Schism (the deposition or abdication of the rival Popes and the election, according to an exceptional procedure which would stress the sovereignty of the Council, of the new Pope Martin V), and reforming the Church (which ended up, in practice, as a series of Concordats concluded between Martin V and the Conciliar 'nations'). The cornerstone of the system was the decretal *Frequens* (9 October 1417), which arranged for regular sessions of General Councils to enable them to control and direct the government of the Church. In fact, by allowing the Curia a free hand in the intervals between sessions and by not setting up a regular procedure for dealing with eventual disagreements between Pope and Council, *Frequens* was heavy with future confrontations.

The next Council at Siena (1423) was dissolved by the Papacy. In revenge, that of Basle, which opened in 1431, entered quickly into conflict with Pope Eugenius IV and finished by splitting in two (1438). The half faithful to the Pope held an assembly at Ferrara and then Florence, whose proceedings were controlled by him (1438–45). But another Council was held at Basle and then Lausanne until 1449 which, once it had deposed Eugenius IV and proclaimed the superiority of the Council over the Pope (Felix V, appointed Eugenius IV's successor was never more than a puppet), it produced important and interesting reforming legislation (on matters pertaining to benefices, taxation and ecclesiastical discipline); but it gradually lost all its authority and ended by dissolving in general indifference. The Fathers of Basle had been the victims of their own intransigence, of the confusion so often created by wordy and interminable debates, and of Eugenius VI's skill. From 1439 onwards, he was able to pride himself on his magnificent success, which included re-establishing the Union with the Greek Church at Florence. More encouraging still was the Christian rulers' lack of support for the Council (whereas in 1415 no one had risen to John XXIII's defence): though chiefly concerned with affirming their authority over the Churches in their States, they nevertheless ceased to associate this policy with the success of the Conciliar movement. On the contrary, rather than following the Council of Basle in taking its demands for Reform and its role as the representative of the Universal Church seriously, they now preferred to negotiate with a weakened Papacy for advantageous 'Concordats'. The 'Pragmatic Sanction', promulgated by the King of France Charles VII in 1438, is typical of their attitude. While it proclaimed its official attachment to the Council and to Reform, its actual content was directed towards reorganising the government of the Church in France by limiting Papal intervention as much as possible, and by re-establishing traditional procedures and 'liberties', which had the chief effect of clearing the way for efficient extortion by the King, his officials and law courts. To sum up, although the Conciliar movement allowed the institutional crisis to be solved, it failed in so far as it tried to be a Reform movement. After Constance and especially after Basle, the Church was ruled once again by a monarchic Papacy, which, in spite of being much diminished, was exposed to deviations analogous to those of the preceding centuries. In order to maintain their

High Church dignitaries: the Pope, a Cardinal, a Bishop and an Abbot conversing with monks. A detail from a fresco by Simone Martini (1283–1344), *The Church militant and triumphant*, in the Spanish Chapel in Santa Maria Novella, Florence.

command over Rome and their States, the Popes were forced to be directly and permanently involved in Italian politics. Since they were no longer able to exercise their tutelage over kingdoms like England and France, where strong sovereigns were working towards forming real national Churches, they were tempted to resume their taxation and administration in politically less coherent regions like Germany. For that reason it was there that resentment over the failure of Conciliarism and anti-Roman feelings were most virulent.

However, to avoid limiting ourselves to determinist and retrospective points of view, it should be stressed that the Councils of Basle and Constance represented a unique moment in the history of the Church. Those who took part in them were occasionally uplifted, and some, the university men – doctors of Law or Theology from Paris or elsewhere – even derived an inordinate pride from them. They were intellectuals intoxicated by the experience of direct action and by the possibility of acceding to sovereign power. In these extraordinary assemblies of men from all over western Europe (not to mention the Greeks present in Florence), distant Bishops and even simple priests and clerics were able to raise their voices, which had until then been stifled by the crushing machinery of the Avignon administration. For twenty years, Constance and Basle were truly the crossroads of Europe, bubbling with cosmopolitanism, diffusing ideas and manuscripts. The intellectual

135

experience of many humanists from Poggio to Aeneas Sylvius Piccolomini, not to mention the unclassifiable Nicholas of Cues, began there. Since they represented a universalist tradition which belonged both to medieval Christianity and to modern humanism, the Councils of Constance and Basle also embodied the sincere if rather incomplete longing of their age for Reform and the desire of the community of the faithful to participate in some way in the Church's work of salvation. Their failure was inevitable, but it was none the less a drama involving the whole Church, and the sign of a serious lapse in the process of reforming self-regulation, which had until then allowed the Church to surmount all crises.

Overflowing emotionalism

It is true that only a minority of clerics and administrators were really able to appreciate the profound repercussions of the Schism. The body of the faithful was not insensitive to the virulent criticisms levied against the Papacy and its agents, or to the hopes which arose from the very idea of a Council. For them, however, the essential framework of the Church, the one which encapsulated everyday Christian life, was provided by the diocese and the parish, which had been established and organised by the thirteenth century. Would this diocesan structure be able to resist the crisis of the end of the Middle Ages and to take on the most intimate religious aspirations of the faithful?

Church cadres hold out

Until fairly recently, historians have insisted above all on the 'desolation of the churches' as a reflection and consequence of the troubled times, which were supposed to have characterised the fourteenth and beginning of the fifteenth centuries, and to have seriously disrupted the religious life of the faithful. Nowadays, enlightened as we are by still insufficient research, we have come to alter this excessively pessimistic vision.,

Of course the epidemics and wars resulted in churches being destroyed, harmed or profaned. Parishes were depopulated, or remained without parish priests, and bishops were prevented by the disturbances from visiting their dioceses and ordaining new priests, and the impoverished ecclesiastical revenues made all efforts at reconstruction lengthy and hazardous. However, the extent of the damage varied considerably from region to region and there is no proof that they automatically resulted in loss of religious fervour.

But even without that, the quality of pastoral care remained well below the norms established by the Councils and Canon Law. There was never any real crisis in the recruitment of clergy, on the contrary, especially in towns with great churches, an extraordinary abundance of religious persons was to be found. In many towns one inhabitant in every ten or twenty was a cleric. However, this numerous clergy was badly distributed and often badly recruited, and badly trained at all levels.

Most of the bishops came from the nobility and the body of officials, and they were not necessarily models of knowledge and even less of pastoral devotion. In those times, when the national bishoprics were becoming increasingly domesticated by their States, many bishops lived at Court and did not reside in their episcopal towns, and even those who did were anxious to maintain their status as great lords, to provide jobs for their relations and protégés and, at best, to perform their office by safeguarding its revenues and prerogatives. In consequence, they often completely neglected their pastoral obligations (preaching, confirming children, holding diocesan synods, diocesan visits, organising the cathedral school, and controlling the education and recruitment of priests). Nor were the cathedral canons efficient seconders, since their principal occupation was generally quarrelling with their bishop. There were of course exceptions and prelates could be cited who showed some zeal, at least periodically, for re-establishing discipline among the clergy and improving Christian education and practice among the faithful. Many more could be cited who were to be recommended by their extremely honourable education – generally legal – their worthy manners and their practice of the traditional virtues of generosity and good works. But there were none who were really capable of animating the life of their dioceses; who could transcend the level of good administration and stimulate, by their example, an authentic movement of spiritual renewal, as certain Gregorian bishops had done and as certain bishops of the Counter Reformation would do.

Parish priests, especially the country ones, were by and large left to themselves. They have often been tried and condemned by the moralists of their age as well as by present day historians: first among the vices imputed to them were absenteeism (leaving the parish to be ministered to by a curate), ignorance and immorality. In the diocese of Geneva, for instance, it was established following a pastoral visit in 1411 that 31 per cent of the parish clergy was absentee; 35 per cent was poorly or very inadequately educated; and 40 per cent was attributed with behaviour unworthy of clerics (about half of which were cases of concubinage). These figures are important and their incidence rose still higher during the fifteenth century. In other places less worrying percentages were to be found, but the evil was real enough. We should remember that such pastoral inquests were conducted by inquisitors imbued with legalism and social prejudice, and give an accordingly pessimistic impression of the state of affairs. Many priests were merely inadequately trained (their education could involve mere apprenticeship to an older priest) and this was exacerbated by the inadequate diocesan structure and, more generally, by all the faults inherent to the system of benefices (lay patronage, pontifical collations, etc.). Finally it can be asked whether the faithful were really shocked by situations, which to us appear seriously decadent. In certain cases they definitely were, and this was one of the reasons for the violent and summary anticlericalism, which surfaced in some popular risings. 'Away with the priests' was a war cry of one of the leaders of the Flemish rising of 1323–8. More often however, it is likely that even a poor priest, present in person, close to his flock and accessible, was able to provide his flock with the services they expected from him; the distribution of sacraments, a form of village policing and supervision and the daily administration of the parish, which was as much the basic unit of society as it was the spiritual community.

This was a very ancient arrangement and many of its inadequacies, which were exposed by the increased use of the written word had existed for a long time. Obviously this did not

a) (above): a monk and his mistress have been caught *in flagrante delicto* and set in the stocks to be jeered at. (Ms. Roy. EIV 187, British Museum)
b) Monks' behaviour was criticised; fondness for wine (Ms. Sloane 1435, British Museum) and loose living.

exclude a certain deterioration towards the end of the Middle Ages, especially during the Great Schism, which profoundly disorganised the machinery of Papal administration. Since the earliest centuries, the Church had felt the need to reinforce the framework of pastoral care by leaning on structures other than those provided by diocese and parish.

A relay of mendicants

The ancient branches of the monastic and canonical orders: Cluny, Cîteaux, Prémontré, and others, no longer counted. Despite this, their great abbeys were still standing and their numerous rural priories, although obvious objects for every kind of pillage, were still a familiar part of the country landscape. The gloomy picture generally drawn of monasticism at the end of the Middle Ages (neglect of the Rule and of Communal Life; the ruin of their temporal possessions; the collapse of recruitment) should perhaps be altered. There were at least local reform movements. But it was clear that monasticism no longer fascinated contemporaries as it had the people of the High Middle Ages. The monasteries were no longer the chief places of sanctity and were no longer capable of animating great religious movements, as Cluny and Cîteaux had been able to do for pilgrimages and the Crusades. La Chartreuse was alone in maintaining its prestige intact, but precisely because the Carthusian Order was most removed from the world, most hostile to every kind of pastoral activity and its spiritual authors influenced only a tiny elite of the devout.

Let us for the moment leave the Inquisition to one side, (it was not very active in this period and had passed largely under the control of the bishops) and the University, (which had never played anything more than a marginal role in edifying the faithful and educating the bulk of the clergy), and move on to the really vital problem of the Mendicant Orders. Their founders and the Popes of the thirteenth century had conceived them as direct agents of Papal action, and so of the Reform. The purity of their manner of living, which was based on voluntary poverty, and the high level of their religious and intellectual education were supposed to enable the Mendicant friars, not only to lead the fight against heresy, but also to assume a major part of pastoral responsibilities. As preachers and confessors, consoling the sinners and the dying, they offered their privileged mediation at all the testing times of Christian life, when people must draw close to their Creator. In spite of the understandable lack of enthusiasm on the part of parish priests and bishops, their success grew from strength to strength throughout the thirteenth century, especially in the towns. But in the fourteenth century the Mendicant Orders experienced several trials. Some monasteries had been ravaged by the epidemics and their original rule had been somewhat relaxed, which had resulted, in the case of the Franciscans, in an irreparable rupture between the 'Spirituals', who remained faithful to the spirit of the founder and the letter of his Rule and to the superior merit of poverty, but were soon condemned and rejected as heretics, and the majority of 'Conventuals' who, in the name of obedience to the spiritual hierarchy, agreed to sacrifice part of their observance. In the time of the Great Schism, movements advocating Reform and strict observance appeared, but they never won more than part of the Orders to them. Further, the more or less overt hostility of the secular clergy to the Mendicant Orders was not relaxed, who in spite of all these problems continued to play their role. The extraordinary success of the great repentance sermons of Vincent Ferrer or Bernardino of Siena, which attracted immense crowds, are only extreme examples of the popularity which the Mendicant preachers enjoyed everywhere. The frequent appearance of funerary monuments in their churches is a sign that many people looked to them for comfort at the onset of death, that terrible journey, which so fascinated Christians at the end of the Middle Ages. In certain cases in the towns, the Mendicant monasteries, to which the faithful flocked, constituted a kind of anti-parish, confronting the traditional secular parishes.

These successes demonstrated the efficiency of the Mendicant friars' pastoral methods – but how far did their message reach? That it was often strictly conformist in social terms, calling on the wealthy to give alms and on the poor to have patience, is scarcely surprising. More surprising is the banality and traditional character of many of the moral and religious themes, even though they were skilfully presented. Not only were the Mendicants not present everywhere, especially in the countryside, but their instruction did not necessarily meet the anxious needs of the faithful. In short, the deficiencies of the framework for Christian living proposed by the Church in the fourteenth century were obvious. They were probably aggravated, especially after 1350, by the miseries of the age and the Schism. But just as damaging was the simple absence, even among the Mendicants, of real innovations on the pastoral level, as were the weight of routine, the tendency towards perpetuating antiquated structures, and the abusive resort to the facile weapons of regulation and sanction. The extravagant abuses of excommunication further served to caricature these

Saint Vincent Ferrer, a Spanish Dominican, travelled around Europe and aroused whole crowds to repentance and conversion by his preaching. (Domenico Morone's *Saint Vincent Ferrer preaching*, Oxford, Ashmolean Museum.)

tendencies. When seven or even nine out of ten inhabitants of some village in the Dauphiné were excommunicated at the beginning of the fifteenth century (one for blaspheming, the other for not paying his tithes, the third for failing to confess at Easter to his own parish priest, and so on), they may have been extreme examples, but, irrespective of the practical consequences of these excommunications, how could the situation have been considered other than abnormal, since the traditional demands of the law were seriously out of line with the Christian's experience of life?

Aspiring to new things

Concrete religious attitudes should be studied from this angle especially. We are less interested in the movements of despair and anger prompted by catastrophes and scandals than we are in the reactions or absence of reaction on an everyday level to the weight of routine, of the judiciary and of the mechanical play of institutions.

The problem was not new, but until then the most common reaction of those who were dissatisfied with the framework proposed by the Church – the only one to have been recorded in the documents, at any rate – was rejection, radical and sectarian revolt, and heresy. Almost all the heresies of the High Middle Ages and up to the thirteenth century aimed more or less at forming a Church of the pure, of *Parfaits*, of the poor of Christ as the only real Christians living in the Spirit and in charity, in direct opposition to the Church of the Antichrist, corrupted as she was by riches, violence and sex. The rupture would be total and the tension extreme, with overturned values and millenary hopes; such was the mental atmosphere of these heretical movements. By the fourteenth and fifteenth centuries it seemed that such movements were getting increasingly rare.

But some still existed, such as the 'Apostles' who were aroused in Lombardy by two popular preachers, Gerardus Segarelli followed by Fra Dulcino. Also belonging to this type of heresy were the groups of Spiritual Franciscans in Languedoc and Italy, who were imbued with the millenary visions of Joachim of Fiore and who revolted openly against the Papacy in the name of absolute poverty in the first quarter of the fourteenth century. They found the courage to stand up to hostility and eventual martyrdom in their belief in the coming of a Golden Age, which they announced in prophesies, heralding the advent of a completely spiritual Church, ruled by the teachings of Saint Francis almost as much as by the Gospels themselves. However, these movements never grew very large and the great heresies of the previous age faded out around the same time, their disappearance due as much to the exhaustion of their spiritual message and of their social bases, as to repression. Catharism was moribund and the last *Parfaits* were being tracked down by the Inquisition in the Pyrenees. The Waldensian communities were protected by the relatively discreet and peaceful nature of their practices, and so survived in certain Alpine valleys, but only as tumours in a decaying society. After the mid fourteenth century, the Inquisition found that there were only a few isolated spirituals and *Fraticelli* left for it to pursue, who expressed their resentment in apocalyptic prophecies against the Avignon Papacy, and a few individuals accused of practising magic or sorcery, who were henceforth to be its prey.

More typical of the fourteenth century were the spectacular but relatively unimportant Flagellants, who first appeared in the Rhine valley and in the Low Countries in 1349 along with the Black Death and who made the occasional come-back. They could still be called a great spontaneous mass movement. Preachers who had lost their licences would summon the Flagellants to repentance; while emphatically rejecting the authority and sacraments of the Church, they prided themselves on performing miracles and based the sanctity of their movement on a letter which was supposed to have fallen from Heaven, which suggested to crowds prey to panic and enthusiasm that they relive directly the sufferings and the very gestures of Christ's Passion. Assuming forms which ranged from the extravagant to the extreme, this bloody Christocentric movement was nevertheless well suited to the new devotional trends. This meant that the Church, while condemning these mystical and violent outbursts, which never lasted very long, agreed to introduce certain of their features into the normal penitential practices of properly drawn up confraternities.

None of this implied that heresy, as a collective and radical way of rejecting official

Saint Dominic presiding over a tribunal of the Inquisition, painted by P. Berruguete around 1465. The condemned men are being led to the stake, dressed in the *san benito*, a grotesque yellow chasuble, with the *croca*, a sort of paper mitre, on their heads. (Madrid, Prado Museum.)

Flagellants; a spontaneous and mystically inspired pentitential movement. (Fifteenth century, Chantilly, Musée Condé.)

teaching and ecclesiastical institutions, had disappeared. But as far as its most important manifestations were concerned, it did assume new forms, becoming much more political and learned. Political because heresy was from then on inseparable from the awakening of national consciousness, which was stirring everywhere in the West.

Heresy was now no longer a purely popular movement sworn to abolish the Church and humble the ruling classes; from being a violent movement of religious dispute it turned into a manifestation of national identities seeking to define themselves. By attacking the strongly centralised Church, heresy was necessarily anti-Roman (and anti-Avignon) and could easily crystallise latent xenophobic feelings (against German theologians in Bohemia or against Italian clerics in England). To a much greater extent than in previous centuries, heresy could now arouse sympathy among all levels of society, and especially among those whose rise was linked to the appearance of national States, and consequently, it could secure lasting political and military support.

By the end of the Middle Ages, heresy was a learned beast, no longer led by *Parfaits* risen out of the mob, or by a haphazard collection of leaders, whose charisma was based on some mysterious revelation, but by highly educated clerics, university men trained in faculties of the Arts and Theology, who were familiar with philosophical speculation and biblical exegesis as well as with ecclesiological problems. Their longing for political and pastoral action was grafted onto rational ideas of moral and institutional Reform, onto a precise

143

programme, based on the conviction that it was a fundamental Christian requirement for each believer to gain direct access to the authentic basis of his faith, that is to say, to the Bible, which was largely diffused, preached and translated in vernacular languages. Although more popular variants of such heresies could rise up along their fringes, their leaders generally suspected such developments, being aware of the risks of social radicalism and the resurgence of more or less aberrant messianic tendencies.

Wycliffe and Huss: premises

The two most notable heresies at the turn of the fourteenth century were the English one launched by Wycliffe and the Bohemian one which grew out of the ideas of Jan Huss. Both movements clearly found that the disruption caused by the Great Schism proved particularly favourable to their own development.

Wycliffe's heresy had the richer doctrinal content. It was when he was about fifty, having let his thoughts mature over a long time, that this famous Oxford theologian and counsellor to the King during various financial negotiations with the Papacy, threw himself into an exceptional intellectual adventure. Within scarcely six years, he had produced an extremely abundant, even redundant, written work, which was shaped by a few central themes. The most important was that of the absolute greatness of God as Lord and Master. Faced with this Divine Transcendence, men could claim neither an inherent right nor any delegation of divine power, nor indeed could they earn any form of salvation by their own merits. Wycliffe thought that the efficient mediation of the Church and of good works were subordinate to the immediate claims of predestination. This meant that every ecclesiastical structure collapsed, that the Liturgy and the Sacraments were devalued, especially by his rejection of Transubstantiation. Wycliffe concluded by making Holy Writ into the only source and measure of the Faith and by claiming that it was immediately intelligible to all the faithful. As a corollary of his veritable desacralisation of the institution of the Church, both civil society and the State were newly enhanced, since they represented an order made necessary by the very existence of sin. It was by respecting this framework that the spiritual life of each Christian could develop. The origin of Wycliffe's basic intuitions is of little relevance, but it is clear that they showed a powerful revival of the Augustinianism which characterised the end of the Middle Ages. It is not certain that Wycliffe himself perceived the whole destructive force and revolutionary strength of his teaching, which were fully apparent when the Protestant Reformation put it into action one and a half centuries later. Its immediate effect was limited by the dry and negative nature of Wycliffe's thought, his lack of concern for popular anguish about salvation, and the very aridity of his writings and their weak diffusion, all contributed to restricting the direct impact of Wycliffism. Wycliffe was no mob leader and it was abusive to hold him responsible for the explosion of the great Peasants' Revolt of 1381. These calumnies allowed some of his thesis to be condemned in 1382, but Wycliffe himself was protected by his political connections and he died in the communion of the Church on 31 December 1384 in his parish of Lutterworth where he retired to.

During these years however, certain popular preachers (poor priests, Lollards) who have been called disciples of Wycliffe appeared in the English countryside. This was only partly true, because although the Lollard movement borrowed some of its members from Wycliffism: former Oxford graduates; some of his methods: direct and permanent recourse to the Bible, of which the Lollards supplied complete English translations; and some of his catchwords: hostility to the Church's wealth, to the Mass, to the Sacraments; nonetheless, it was still a fairly traditional political and anticlerical movement which immediately ensured it a certain success with the peasantry and the gentry. Several decades passed before the Bishops and the King of England were able to wipe out Lollardism; in the long run, the struggle (a strictly internal affair) contributed to the awakening and structure of the English national Church.

The most authentic successor to Wycliffism was to be found instead in Bohemia. For rather fortuitous reasons, Wycliffe's principal writings got there in the 1390s and were grafted onto a more traditional evangelical stream of moral and ecclesiastical reform, which had been nurtured for some time by popular preachers (who were often learned men) like Matthias of Janow. The social base of this movement was formed by devout members, who gathered in Prague around the Chapel of Bethlehem and the University, and especially by the Czech Masters and students. It was in this milieu that Jan Huss, the son of a peasant, became Rector of the University and a Theology lecturer. As a starting point for his movement, he read Wycliffe carefully and cautiously, retaining especially his criticism of the institution of the Church and his aspiration to a more personal and less mediated form of piety. On the other hand, he was more open than his instructor to the general feeling of the faithful of his age and he hesitated to accept Predestination and remained attached to the reality of the Eucharist. Although his preaching gradually became more radical in the popular sense, Jan Huss was not short of support in Czech society. Consequently, the Czechs felt bitterly insulted by the Council of Constance, at which Huss had voluntarily presented himself, which judged, condemned and executed him with implacable severity (6 July 1415). Several years later, all Bohemia revolted in unison against the German Emperor and against Rome. Since 1409, the expulsion of Germans from Prague University had demonstrated that the rise of Czech nationalism was closely linked with the idea of religious reform, and the complex nature of the movement, which combined national and religious, learned and popular elements, is clearly illustrated by the programme which the Hussites drew up for themselves in 1420. Some of the new ideas formulated by Wycliffe could be found in it, such as the first steps towards a universal priesthood (rejection of the mediation of the Church, criticism of her powerful political stance, recognition of the national State as guarantor of Christian order) as well as themes derived from a much more traditional form of evangelism. Hussitism drew most of its social and military strength from its national character; under the spiritual direction of the University of Prague it rallied a good part of the nobility and the Czech bourgeoisie to its cause, thus forming a real State apparatus, which resisted the German 'crusades' victoriously for the next fifteen years.

The Hussites had their own radical offshoot, the Taborites (who made a mountain, rebaptised Mount Tabor, the high point of their meetings). They took the popular and sectarian aspects of the movement, combining Wycliffian anticlericalism with ancient millenarian hopes to give birth to a sort of Utopian society, which attracted to it heretics of all kinds: Waldensians, Beghards and Adamites, at least for a while. But this extremist stream ended by splitting with the 'Calixtines' of Prague, so called because they called for Communion under both kinds and made the chalice the symbol of their movement. Once they had crushed the Taborite army in 1434, they negotiated an agreement with the Council of Basle which conceded them most of the 'Four Articles' of 1420, except for the abolition of ecclesiastical property (1436). This was a modest and disappointing end to a movement, which came too soon and was still too marginal for the Europe of its time. Luther was to call himself the heir to Huss, and rightly so, since it was his ideas and preaching, which had given birth to the first movement of religious protest capable of rousing an entire nation, and which was, at the end of the day, partly triumphant.

A simple and demanding faith

In the main, however, heresy often survived only as a relic from the past or as a sign of movements to come, and it did not really appear to characterise the religious life of the West in the fourteenth and beginning of the fifteenth centuries. Certainly, the anxieties they betrayed were shared by many of the faithful and as we will see, many were drawn in the general direction in which it was moving, although less daringly and without leaving the bounds of orthodoxy. It seems particularly significant that the great majority, even when a prey to troubles, adopted a different attitude to that of collective radical dissent. The religious anguish of contemporaries is an established fact. They were more acutely aware than before of the vices of the ecclesiastical institutions, which had possibly worsened. The troubles of the age, wars and epidemics, the social crisis which upset the traditional order, and finally the drama of the Schism, made the problem of Salvation more obsessive. Faced with a more mobile, less coherent and gradually more threatening world, they realised that ancient guarantees could be reassessed and that everyone was responsible, to a certain extent, for bringing about his own Salvation. It was no longer possible to count on the old solidarities of lineage or on the prayers of monks to tame death and to lead the soul serenely towards the place of rest to await the coming of the Judgement. Obviously not every part of the social and ecclesiastical framework had disappeared, but each person was increasingly left to himself throughout his life, to prepare for the 'art of dying well'. His relationship with God, his religious life, and inevitably, his social life were increasingly matters of personal choice. It is often in the midst of doubting and tears, in a more diverse and uncertain world, that new spaces open up to liberty and reason. Of course, the traditional framework and means of salvation proposed by the Church were not, except exceptionally, totally abandoned. Eventually reinvested with their original meaning, sometimes at the instigation of clerics, they remained the basis of religious life and the attributes of social conformism.

Popular adherence to the Sacraments, for instance, which has been well analysed, is significant. It remained massive and unanimous in the case of Sacraments corresponding to a rite of passage in life – Baptism, Marriage, Extreme Unction – and although Confession,

Jan Huss' degradation: the palms of his hands were scrubbed in order to remove all traces of his ordination; he was then taken in a procession, wearing a shameful bonnet showing pictures of devils; at the stake, his headdress was inscribed with the word 'Heresiarch'. His ashes were thrown into the lake to stop them from becoming a cult object. (*The Chronicle of the Council of Constance* by von Richental, 1465, Constance, Rosgartenmuseum.)

and especially Communion, were only little practised, often scarcely conforming to the minimal norms established by the Fourth Lateran Council (once a year, at Easter), this was not necessarily a sign of religious indifference, but was a mark, possibly inopportune but sincere, of reverence before the Transcendence of God, a form of hesitation before direct contact with the Divine Mystery, which was both sought after and redoubted. This led to the success of other less impressive practices and devotions, which were sometimes substituted for the Sacraments. The zeal for alms giving 'which extinguishes sin as water extinguishes fire' did not relax, even if its aims and means were not quite the same as in the preceding period. The Liturgy did not get any richer at the end of the Middle Ages and Sunday observance was far from regular, truly impoverished as it was by the routine and mediocrity of the current sermons. Elsewhere, however, Christians did not cease to seek in certain forms of prayer and ecclesiastical ceremony the means of intercession which their anxiety did not allow them to forgo. They arranged for hundreds and thousands of Votive Masses to be said. They crowded to processions and pilgrimages and filled the churches on certain feast days of high spiritual and emotional content (Maundy Thursday, All Saints, Christmas, and so on). They participated with intact fervour in the manifold expressions of the cult of the Virgin and the Saints. In short, there was nothing to show that the religious practice of the faithful had been permanently weakened, and if there was some falling off, it was due rather to ignorant, unworthy or absentee clerics who incurred the displeasure of the laymen.

147

Popular devotion; these pilgrims are kneeling in front of a reliquary containing relics of Saint Claude. (Coloured woodcut sold to pilgrims who had come to venerate the Saint in his sanctuary in the Jura.)

However, good works and the Sacraments were no longer enough to fulfil the expectations of the lay community. Apart from the fact that these practices kept them in strict and passive dependence on a clergy, whose mediation was anyway disputed, they certainly did not answer all the questions which emerged from a more acute anguish over the questions of death and salvation.

One of the fundamental needs of Christians at the end of the Middle Ages, which was expressed in its extreme form by certain heresies, was the need for immediacy, for contact with the Divine without the help of intermediaries, and for a closer relationship, even identification, with Christ as sufferer and saviour. The first condition of this closer relationship, and one perceived and expressed with increasing clarity, was an improved knowledge of Revelation and the Faith. The fourteenth and fifteenth centuries both witnessed an immense thirst for religious education, collective and individual, at very different levels of society. The Church responded very unevenly to this demand, and the faithful often came up against ignorant or aggressive clerics, who were unable to ensure the diffusion of a minimum of Christian teaching. In such cases, the faithful were forced to keep to their routine religious practices and remain ignorant, or to turn to the traditional resources of popular wisdom, imbued with folklore and magic, which were relatively free from clerical control. In other cases, though, the Church was able to undertake a real effort to provide people with religious and moral instruction. While very inadequate, the network of little schools controlled by Church authorities was greatly improved from the fourteenth century onwards. Doctors and devoted prelates, of whom Gerson is the outstanding example, compiled manuals for parish priests on how to perform their office and on sermons, and more general short treatises in the vernacular on meditation, prayer and the practice of Christian virtues for all literate Christians. The most efficient pastoral work was

a) The cult of the Virgin (wooden panel, thirteenth century, Paris, Louvre.)
b) Saint Maurice, patron of travellers (painted wooden statue, fifteenth century, from Montereau, in Paris, Musée de Cluny.)

being done by the Mendicant Orders, which were still growing in certain regions, in spite of their internal crises. Christians, especially the town dwellers, were able (on a regular basis or occasionally) to hear first class sermons by the Friars on subjects close to their hearts. They could watch theatrical performances on the steps of their churches, the 'Mystery Plays', which adopted and explained the most dramatic features of the Liturgy, especially those relating to the Passion. They could contemplate pictures, either the frescoes in their churches and cemeteries or the humble woodcuts in their homes, showing didactic illustrations, often related to the Mendicant Friars' sermons, of the great devotional themes which the Church was trying to teach the faithful. Finally, there was the privileged and still small elite of persons who knew how to read and were able to get hold of books. They were able to accede directly to the holy texts of the Liturgy and to the Books of Hours, which allowed lay persons to appropriate the rhythms and traditional themes of monastic and canonical prayer, to the short treatises of Christian spirituality, which invited the reader to examine his conscience and engage in private prayer, and finally to the translations of the Bible, which allowed direct meditation on Revelation. The clergy was not at all in favour of this direct diffusion of the Scriptures and lay persons could often only get story Bibles; simplistic and shallow summaries of the Life of Christ.

The intimate circles of the new piety

All that has been mentioned above – the fondness of the lay community for certain features of traditional conformist practice and their disappointment at seeing them poorly

149

maintained in the classical framework of the parish – explains a fundamental feature of lay religious life at the end of the Middle Ages: the search for new social groups. In general terms, one could speak of atomisation. The basic Christian unit tended to become the individual or the family, the privileged place of initiation to elementary religion, to the essential sacraments and daily observance (prayers and fasting). Over and above this minimum level, the Christians of the time tried to form other communal groups to set against the parish framework, groups which they felt to be generally more restrained and better able to ensure them satisfactory conditions for social integration, for the religious life and for personal edification. Some people entered into the mainstream congregations by joining the third orders of Saints Francis and Dominic. More often, they joined a brotherhood (or any similar type of pious association) which could be urban, parochial, professional or purely devotional, and whose numbers increased all over the place during the fourteenth century. They had an obvious social and political function by providing membership and shelter, and they remained under the control of the Church and, in particular, of the local lay elites. For all that, their properly religious role, which was intimately linked to the others, was not any the less fundamental. By efficiently coordinating their members' charitable activities, they guaranteed them in poverty, sickness, death and Purgatory, the material and spiritual solidarity which they feared their own families would not be able to provide in those troubled times.

Although their charitable and funerary function was essential, many of these communities tried to stimulate the piety of their members and to encourage them to pray and to perform religious exercises by arranging their own sermons and liturgy. While these were still conducted collectively in brotherhoods with a common or bourgeois member-ship, they became individual or family practices among richer folk, patricians and nobles, who were able to secure the services of a chaplain and confessor, and who owned libraries and private chapels, which served both as family mausoleums and as places for prayer and meditation.

Besides these relatively institutionalised and official forms, the end of the Middle Ages saw many other types of religious community rise up, which were more innovatory and informal, sometimes frankly borderline, and were eventually considered suspect by certain civil and religious local authorities. They included embryonic congregations gathered around a few saintly individuals – like the *famiglia* around Catherine of Siena, who called herself their *mamma* – which disappeared quite early on to evolve towards a more conventional monastic form. There were fairly spontaneous groups of pious laymen to be found all over Germany, the Low Countries and northern France from the end of the thirteenth century, which were known collectively as *béguins* and *béguines*. The most stable groups were controlled to a certain extent by the Mendicant Orders; they were the female *béguinages*, which gathered women together to live, in little adjoining cells under the supervision of one of their members, lives of austerity, manual work and prayer, but without taking perpetual vows. Other *béguins* or *béghards* ended up badly and were condemned towards the end of the thirteenth century and again at the Council of Vienna (1312) along with other groups of the Brethren of the Free Spirit. Their principal enemies

The Bruges Béguinage: home for a new group of pious lay persons.

were the Rhineland Bishops, who accused them of the worst vices. They seem to have been particularly keen on meditation and direct union with God, and tended to detach themselves from the Sacraments and all institutionalised forms of meditation. Other *béguins* and *béguines* escaped this condemnation, for instance, those very informal communities called the Friends of God, who gathered for prayer and meditation on the Bible, and were to be found in the Rhineland in the mid fourteenth century. It is often difficult to understand what actually differentiated the orthodox groups from the heterodox, apart from purely local and personal factors. Both lots seem to have been inspired by the writings of some German Dominicans. Master Eckhart (*c.* 1260–*c.* 1328) was the greatest, but his boldness eventually earned him condemnation by the Pope. As a theologian of the Mystical Union and Transcendence of God, he was reproached with deifying man and leaning towards a form of pantheism. Tauler (*c.* 1300–61) and Suso (*c.* 1296–1366) were more prudent in their conception of the union with God, but they expressed the incomparable richness of the inner life with even greater sensitivity. They were very popular with the predominantly female groups which cultivated Rhinish mysticism. Ruysbroeck the Admirable (1293–1381) played a similar role in the Low Countries, where the *béguins* and the Brethren of the Free Spirit were equally numerous. He

151

John Gerson preaching on the *Imitation of Jesus Christ*. This devotional work was written in Latin for religious persons, but its many translations were given an astonishing welcome by the laity. (John Gerson, *Sermons on the Passion*, Valenciennes, Bibliothèque municipale).

was closer to simple lay persons if rather less sure of his theology and correspondingly in danger of 'glorifying' the human soul by claiming that it could find a meeting place with the Divine in its own depths. His influence can be found among the Brothers and Sisters of the Common Life and the Canons of Windesheim, who had been founded in Holland around 1379 and 1386 respectively by two friends, Gerardus Grotius and Florentius Radewijns. These two communities – the one an association of laymen leading lives of austerity and work rather similar to those of the *béguinages*, the other a canonical order of more classical form – may be remembered as the perfect realisation, in an orthodox sense, of those tendencies which went to make up the *devotio moderna* so typical of northern Europe. The Brethren of the Common Life and the Canons of Windesheim had a considerable success in the Low Countries in the fifteenth century. They created many communities, many endowed with schools in which children were educated according to the principles of the new devotion. Among the abundant literary production of these circles, the *Imitation of Jesus Christ* stands out. It was apparently composed between 1420 and 1427 by Thomas à Kempis, a canon of the Windesheim congregation, and it is a perfect expression of spirituality in its concern for perfect ecclesiastical and sacramental othodoxy (especially in Book IV, on the Eucharist); in its praise of asceticism and renunciation which allow the soul to draw near to God in prayer and solitude; in its Christocentralism; in its underlying pessimistic vision of the world; and finally, in its relative indifference to the social dimension of Christian values, especially to poverty. The Imitation is a wonderful work, and the first illustration of modern Christianity, which by means of austerity, retreat and meditation, found other ways of salvation than those of religious conformism and the accumulation of good works.

Latent anxiety and fear

Can this renewal of pious forms be summed up in terms of concrete religious attitudes and mentalities? Too often, only the relatively superficial elements have been recorded, which has impaired our interpretation, because by emphasising the excessive and even the baroque and extravagant features of certain manifestations, we run the risk of seeing only abberration and perversion in what was also a clumsy attempt at liberation and invention.

The desire for direct contact with God resulted in certain restrained groups of religious and lay persons, often predominantly female, engaging in a sort of popular mysticism, which was suceptible of turning into quietism and even pantheism. Our only evidence is provided by the enemies of these groups who were prompt to bring out the old weapons of patristic polemic against them.

More in evidence are the abuses which certain devotional practices gave rise to, especially those associated with death and salvation. Religion at that time was obsessed with death, giving rise to a profusion of macabre images (the wounds of the Dead Christ, the Apocalypse, the Triumph of Death, the *Danse Macabre*, skeletons and *transis*) which served to appease a dolorous form of piety. Christians would provide in their wills for pious funds and foundations for hundreds and thousands of masses to be said for their souls. If they had the means, they would arrange their own funerals and decorate their own tombs with a manic care and an attention to detail approaching the absurd. The success of the belief in Purgatory, the systematic search for the indulgences offered by the Church, the development of the cult of a growing number of very specialised intercessory saints, all these rather anarchic forms of piety which proliferated at the end of the Middle Ages, originated in this arithmetic of salvation, adding up points for the next life, which people firmly believed would give them the courage to face the mysteries of the Last Rites, at the price of losing some of their sense of transcendence and holiness. Practices of this kind did not necessarily reveal anguish, panic and morbid delectation, since they also expressed the greater part assumed by the lay community in the work of their own salvation, over and beyond the traditional reassurances of the Church. Christians no longer accepted to be totally dependent on others to prepare their souls for, and accompany them on, the journey into the next world. Their obsession with individual death and judgement, which is so evident in the prayers and art of the period, was not merely due to the terrible mortality, though of course accentuated by it, but to the profound collapse of social and ecclesiastical structures. Georges Duby has written that 'it was not the poverty of the times, the recurring scourges, wars and epidemics, which ensured the triumph of the new macabre but the development of the lasting movement which had over the last two centuries gradually

153

The effigy of the Black Prince in Canterbury Cathedral, which sports all the attributes of his temporal power. The Black Prince (so called on account of his black armour) was the great English war leader during the first period of the Hundred Years' War.

reconciled Christianity with popular religious aspirations.' Although these manifestations were often clumsy, and often ended by bringing despair rather than consolation, one can still discern behind the delirium an individual rationality seeking to express itself, a new freedom trying to emerge from the ruins of the old world.

Anyway, is it still permissible to speak of the Christians of those times, even of the lay community, in general terms? The above remarks apply equally to the urban milieu, animated as it was by the fraternities and Mendicant friars' sermons. The aristocracy was especially affected by the economic, social and political crisis and must have been very receptive to these new forms of religious anxiety. Its wealth allowed it to play a capital role in transforming the artistic taste and the funerary rites which expressed and permitted this particular privatisation, atomisation, and in a sense, declericalisation of Christianity which we have already discussed.

Two further levels may be identified, separate from but not unconnected with the first. On the one hand, a religious elite consisting of secular and regular clergy and also of pious laymen and devout persons often gathered in those discreet little communities mentioned above (*béguinages*, Friends of God, Brethren of the Common Life, etc.) Adept at reading the Scriptures, examining their consciences, at meditation and personal prayer, these Christians were distinguished by their need for the inner life and their more intimate contact with God. This led to the ideal of the austere, grave and well-regulated life, which made them very reluctant to perform the more external acts of piety (such as pilgrimages) and the ostentatious devotions of their contemporaries, retaining only those ecclesiastical meditations which seemed really useful to their spiritual nourishment. They were also, it

154

The emaciated face of the Crucified Christ of
Perpignan; fourteenth-century Rhenish art.
Religious emotion attained its greatest heights when
contemplating the death of Christ and from then on
the Crucifixion was to dominate popular
imagination. (Perpigan, Chapelle du Christ.)

must be said, somewhat indifferent to the social problems of charity and in any case,
strongly conformist politically. Attitudes like these, in which it is difficult not to see a
certain individualism and a desire to appropriate personally the whole range of Christian
piety, suggest an outline of the sociology of the *devotio moderna*. It is tempting to explain its
success by connecting it with certain social groups in full ascendancy, whose rise was
typical of the end of the Middle Ages. These were university men, tired of the abuses of
Scholasticism, the rulers' officials and lawyers and great merchants preoccupied with
defining a way of Christian life which did not immediately condemn their professional
activity, men in short who had in common their practice of reflection and respect for the
written word, along with a sense of their individual achievement. It seems however that
the social scope of the new devotion extended beyond these bourgeois circles and put its
mark equally on the simple and austere Christianity recorded in certain common circles,
among which the families of Gerson and Joan of Arc are well-known examples. These
centres of devout laymen (which seem to have been more numerous in northern Europe)
were active in forging the social bases for Erasmianism and the Reformation.

Alongside this elite and the faithful of the already much more numerous town churches,
there was an immense crowd of predominantly rural and very often illiterate Christians
who remained dedicated to a much more traditional and essentially collective religion. One
should be careful when attacking the legend of the Christian High Middle Ages, since the
innovatory tendencies we have just studied did end by penetrating these circles as well,
albeit tardily and imperfectly. They were in a way helped by the universal impact of the
economic and social crisis. On the other hand, we must avoid anachronisms like assessing

155

these Christians' piety by the standards of twentieth-century Christianity, and even by those formulated by the Councils and learned canonists of the age. The fact remains that, whether or not the consequence of irregular religious practice and inadequate preaching, popular religion often remained a religion of fear and of obscure forces, which ended by denuding the most fundamental Christian dogma of their meaning. Although the authenticity of these Christians' religious feeling is incontestable and the moralising indignation of some Catholic historians does not apply here, it is true that many aspects of the Christian message were completely hidden in this rural and static religion.

Whatever social level we consider, a final remark is appropriate. Apart from a few ultra-minority and finally suppressed groups, the ecclesiastical framework held out, in spite of its inadequacies and critics. The vitality of the ecclesiastical organisation in the Mediterranean countries could be set against its already advanced decay in the Germanic and Anglo-Saxon areas, precisely where most of the heresies (Lollardism and Hussitism) developed, as well as popular movements (Flagellants) and informal lay associations. These disparities could be examined and the respective responsibilities of the Avignon Papacy with its technocratic blindness, of the States and of the general social and economic evolution, which favoured precisely those nordic regions, be weighed up. In all events, the ecclesiastical structures resisted attack and even gave evidence of their capacity of adapting, no negligible feat. On the whole, the Mendicant Friars remained worthy of their pastoral and missionary vocations. More generally, by adopting the brotherhoods, by organising the distribution of indulgences, by democratising all the forms of votive and funerary piety, the Church was able to do justice to a good number of the new religious aspirations, although it is certain that she was forced at the same time to leave laymen, especially the richer and better educated ones, a hitherto unknown margin of initiative and freedom. She remained virtually in control of the diffusion of Revelation – until the printing press introduced its immense power of duplication – and of the Sacraments, and succeeded in keeping the West Christian. A Christianity criss-crossed with signs foretelling the Reformation, but it is important to note, while tracing these signs, that the Reformation did not happen then.

A freer way of thinking

The same agitation as that which shook the structures of religious life was felt in the spheres of thought, theory and science. This period has been defined as that in which the medieval world vision dissolved. An evolution, which involved the (incipient) reorganisation of all the spheres of intellectual activity, cannot be attributed to the crisis of scholasticism. Further, this phase in the history of ideas cannot be envisaged in isolation and must be placed within the larger context of the change in mentalities and practices studied above (which should not conceal the relatively autonomous and often innovatory nature of truly speculative thought).

The Christianity of the professors

The social and institutional framework for intellectual activity had itself changed somewhat. The great universities of the early thirteenth century – Bologna, Paris, Oxford – and more particularly their faculties of the Arts and Theology, remained the most intense centres of intellectual life, without their syllabuses or their pedagogical methods having much evolved. They all continued to recruit thousands of students from a very wide area. Their prestige was intact and various social and political bodies agreed in recognising in them a sort of superior magistrature, whose effective authority was immense and gave rise to the most immoderate pretensions among the university men themselves. The University of Paris, especially her theology faculty, claimed to be the 'mother of the sciences and the light of the faith' as well as the counsellor and immediate auxiliary of the Papacy. The Great Schism raised these Parisian doctors' and Bolognese canonists' elevated idea of their role in Christendom to its paroxysm; since all the other traditional sources of authority were crumbling, they thought it was up to them to define for the Universal Church the 'way' to exterminating the Schism and to direct the Council's deliberations over dogma. Formerly covered with Papal favours, they became the theoreticians of Conciliarism. Their pretensions were no more modest in the spheres of law and politics, in which the doctors' opinions were recognised as a source of law. In serious crises, the Kings of France turned to the University of Paris for advice and support, and she in her turn affirmed on several occasions her right to participate in the general Reform of the kingdom. The University of Prague was veering in the same direction, spiritually at least, as the Hussite movement.

There are many more such examples, but it is questionable to what extent these interventions were really effective. They certainly revealed the intellectuals' attention to the present and their sense of political responsibility, which were in themselves admirable. University men were not remotely revolutionary types. Their ideal was that of a Reform, which they would inspire and which would re-establish the harmony of a providential social and political order. In the meantime however, the universities did not profit from this extension of their sphere of action. Apart from other factors to do with the general crisis and the antiquated teaching methods, it continued to disrupt their normal pedagogical work, and involved them in sometimes unfortunate partisanships (remember the pro-English masters of Paris who condemned Joan of Arc) and it ended with the rulers curtailing their traditional privileges and submitting them to strict political control.

Even before they were reduced to this subordinate status, the masters had had plenty of time in which to give assurances of their sense of obligation towards the established power. Since the beginning of the fourteenth century or even earlier, the trend had been to limit the recruitment of students and professors, which was intensified as the economic difficulties worsened. As with the other guilds, that of the Universities was moving rapidly towards hereditary membership, or in their case, towards reducing the requirements for members of the masters' families. For their part, the instructors ended by winning their way in the essential matter of their remuneration: the students paid and paid heavily for instruction in theology and law. The effect of this was doubly pernicious. When Francesco Accurso in Bologna and Pierre d'Ailly in Paris owned lands and houses it was hard to believe that their words were impartial. They had chosen their camp, that of the establishment, and over and above their undoubted honesty and real emotion, they would always draw the line at all violence and disruption. Froissart was quite right at the end of the fourteenth century in calling them *chevaliers en lois* (Knights of the Law), because they did indeed belong to that class. As for the other effect, it was perhaps worse; not everyone who aspired to knowledge could afford to pay the masters and the effervescent universities of the thirteenth century began to see their poor students leaving. Those who did hang on were assisted financially and rootless, like Villon, or they were future clerks.

In spite of their prestige, the great universities no longer monopolised the learned tradition, as they had done in the time of Saint Thomas Aquinas. During the fourteenth and fifteenth centuries, more than forty new universities were created everywhere in Europe, nearly always on the initiative of the rulers. The number of these foundations is explained by the divisions resulting from the Schism and the rise of national states and territorial principalities. Most of these new universities were limited to training competent clerks and lawyers without claiming any sort of intellectual originality. There were some however, in the Empire (Erfurt, Vienna) and the Slav kingdoms (Prague, Kracow) which responded to their countries' growing national self-awareness and were capable of taking up and enlarging on certain philosophical and theological debates initially launched in Paris or Oxford.

Within the ancient universities there were some colleges fairly independent as to their recruitment and function, like the College of Navarre in Paris, where the first French humanist circle gathered in the time of Charles VI, which welcomed teachings, ideas and books generally excluded from the more traditional faculties. Other such circles were more removed from the properly scholarly world: the new religious communities on the one hand and certain royal or civic courts and chanceries on the other, which also became centres of intellectual life and literary creation. Avignon, where the Popes assembled the most beautiful library of the age, rich not only in religious but also in classical works; Paris, where Charles V had the Bible, St Augustine's *City of God*, Aristotle, Livy, Valerius Maximus and others, translated into French for his library in the Louvre; Munich in the time of Emperor Ludwig of Bavaria; Prague, in the time of Emperor Charles IV: Naples, Milan, and Florence whose communal chancery was, under Coluccio Salutati and Leonardo Bruni, the centre of Petrarchian humanism, and many other capitals were in their time centres of art and culture, not to mention the more ephemeral but equally brilliant part played by Constance and Basle during the Councils.

To sum up: by the end of the Middle Ages, the places where the learned tradition was elaborated had been increased and diversified. Of course, the same men often circulated from one to another, and the weight of university traditions was felt in all of them. Nonetheless, they did indeed enjoy new conditions, which were more favourable to certain forms of intellectual daring and to the cultural diversity of the nations. They were also more conducive to unscrupulous intervention by the political powers.

William of Wykeham (1324–1404) giving an open-air lecture in front of New College, Oxford, founded in 1379. (Ms. C 288 Oxford, Bodleian Library.)

Founding a new ethic

The great contribution of the thirteenth century, which may properly be called scholasticism, had been not only to provide an interpretation of the Faith within the patristic tradition, which made use of the forms of expression of Antiquity (grammar, rhetoric and logic), but to attempt, much more ambitiously, to reconcile Faith with Reason, Revelation with Philosophy, and to integrate them within one unified scheme of knowledge, whose architecture was largely borrowed from Aristotle, that of the Creation and the Creator, of nature and the supernatural. Not that this perspective, whose most elevated interpretation is still the *Summa* of Saint Thomas Aquinas was ever the dominant theory in the thirteenth century. It was opposed by the more traditional theologians, who remained faithful to Augustinian thought, and to its suspicion of the material world. Even with Thomas himself this thought induced moments of caution or remorse, which trapped him in certain dead ends, and it was precisely this which the 'Averroists' in the Arts faculty like Siger of Brabant (*c.* 1240–*c.* 1283) crudely exposed. An achievement which led to the condemnation of Averroism by the Bishop of Paris in 1277, which not only applied to teaching already under attack from inside, but also to Thomism; and contemporaries, whether they were pleased or sad about it were perfectly aware of this. It jeopardised a whole philosophical orientation, over and above the more or less skilful application of Aristotelian texts. An optimistic orientation, which was based on the positive and dynamic conception of a science which could explain the whole of Creation and the Creator, in the rational terms of a harmonious structure established on the necessary hierarchies and mediations. It was also a humanist orientation, as unwilling to exclude the foundations of anthropology and physics from rational analysis as it was the economics of grace.

The 1277 condemnation was essentially local (even though it was taken up rather later in Oxford) and it could not deal a death blow to Thomism, which continued to be taught in the Dominican Order, nor even to Averroism, whose main centres moved to the Arts faculties of Bologna and Padua. But it did turn them into minority or marginal doctrines, which were destined to remain that way for a long time, and from them on it was precisely those themes, given prominence in the condemnation of 1277, which became the mainstays of the most innovatory philosophical and theological debates.

Oxford rather than Paris was the scene of these debates in the fourteenth century, especially since the first great theologian of the new era, the Franciscan Duns Scotus (*c.* 1266–1308) taught successively in both universities. Even though he still accepted God as a necessary Being, accessible to metaphysical speculation, Duns Scotus refused to see the world as an emanation of the divine intellect, according to the tenets of Aristotelian causality. By demonstrating the emptiness of a philosophy which wanted to apply these shackles to what was after all a natural dimension, he restored to God, in the theological sense 'the full powers of a freedom without bounds'.

Duns Scotus' criticism of Thomism was subtle, but William of Ockham radicalised it (*c.* 1290–*c.* 1349). This English Franciscan has already been mentioned on account of his part in the struggles of the Spiritual movement, from 1328 onwards, counselling the Emperor Ludwig of Bavaria against the Avignon Popes. As the author of very many

The English Franciscan William of Ockham (1290–1349/50) disputed Thomas Aquinas' theological construction. A fourteenth-century drawing (Cambridge, Gonville and Caius College.)

pamphlets, he was one of the most virulent critics of Papal supremacy. Ockham derived the ecclesiology which emerges clearly from these texts, (although it was elaborated in the course of the struggle) from the philosophical and theological theses, which he had taught at Oxford until 1324 when, even before he got his Master in Theology, he was summoned to appear at Avignon whence he escaped four years later to join Ludwig of Bavaria.

Ockham's thought was based on a logical premise, which he borrowed from the nominalist tradition; all knowledge comes to us via the senses. Only immediate and intuitive knowledge can be real. Theoretical knowledge, which is founded on words and concepts, is completely bound up in the rules of language; on the ontological level, such knowledge is completely confused and uncertain. Ockham's epistemology ended up as empiricism. Under these conditions, it is clear that every philosophical attempt to ascend from the creation to God the Creator collapses. No reasoning and no concept allow us to speak of God, to prove His existence, to describe His attributes, to restore the workings of His grace. Ockham affirmed with exceptional conviction the absolute liberty of God, which left the question hanging as to the nature of man's freedom both on the level of knowledge and morality. What was the point of restricting man and the whole of the natural world in institutions, with rules and determinisms, when we can perceive only contingencies beyond the individual realities which alone are accessible to our understanding, and when these restrictions are only empty constructions of the mind and do not form part of an objective hierarchy?

The destructive force of such notions is clear, since they led not necessarily to scepticism, but definitely to individualism. They devalued the Church as the visible society of such institutional mediations, and led to the demand for immediacy through the only channel whose authenticity Ockham considered guaranteed, that is, through the revealed message of the Scriptures, which even he did not doubt.

Conceived in line with the daily demands of teaching and then of anti-Avignon polemic,   **161**

Ockhamism is not a coherent doctrine. Ockham was nowhere near to drawing all his premises to their natural conclusions, philosophical as much as moral and religious, or to replacing all that he destroyed. He did feel the need to restore a certain cohesion to Christianity, which he had so totally atomised, but the formulae he proposed lacked rigour; holding property in common, the consensus of all the faithful. He was less familiar with law and political theory than was Marsilius of Padua, and he did not manage to formulate the notions of popular sovereignty and representation (for example by the Council); the opinions he professed on the Papacy were thus hesitant, criticising it harshly without daring to deny it all primacy. Like many of the heterodox thinkers of his age, he turned on the whole to the ruler (in the circumstances, to the Emperor) to ensure the regularity of civil and religious life and the preservation of the common weal.

In spite of its practical limitations, Ockhamism had immense appeal, and it cannot be reduced to the old quarrel between nominalism and realism, nor even to criticism of Thomism. In fact, Ockham pushed all these problems aside by giving first place to the problem of free will. By braving the simultaneous pitfalls of scepticism and of authority, he rejected the lures of a rational theology and placed a terrible dilemma at the heart of his anthropology; he gave man the philosophical means of achieving freedom, while confronting him with the absolute authority of Revelation and the crushing menace of the absolute freedom and omnipotence of God. With Ockham the medieval vision of the world dissolved and the drama of the modern world took shape, that of a philosophy which both liberates and crushes man.

Though Ockham was himself condemned and died around 1349, carried off by the Great Plague without being reconciled with the Church, his work was nonetheless extremely influential. Without joining him in all his daring speculations, a majority of theologians ended by adopting the general lines; defiance of a too facile accord of theology and philosophy, a sense of the unlimited sovereignty of God, giving special attention to the problem of freedom and justification. These were the elements of a nominalist *koiné*, which was adopted by most European universities in the second half of the fourteenth century. Obviously the partisans of the *via antiqua* (themselves divided into different camps, Albertists, Thomists and Scotists) continued to oppose those who advocated this *via moderna* but, with a few exceptions (for example the University of Cologne, created in 1388, which remained the rallying point of Thomism) the *moderni* were everywhere preponderant. So it was they who, in the eyes of the humanists, were soon to incarnate medieval scholasticism in its driest aspect, attracting their complaints and sarcasms. The trial of Ockhamism is still going on, with Catholic historians adding for their part the reproach that directly or indirectly, it paved the way for the Lutheran Reformation.

Scholasticism or anti-intellectualism?

This debate has the advantage of stressing the central position of what is far too narrowly termed nominalism, but it certainly demands a more detailed treatment.

162   At the end of the Middle Ages, scholastisicm was imprisoned in the framework of

immutable teaching practices – lectures, tutorials, disputations – which often gave it a feeling of sterility. The indefinite reassessment of the same questions, the empty play of hypotheses, whose arbitrary nature was recognised *a priori*, often reduced the instruction of theology to a purely dialectical virtuosity which expanded into increasingly formal exercises. Nominalism may well have precipitated this evolution, by assuming the scholastic tradition after having previously emptied its philosophical and theological debates of all certainty and almost all real content, and thus becoming a caricature of what it had itself denounced. But other schools of thought did not escape this process either. In any case, it is true that many theologians of the end of the Middle Ages appear to have avoided scepticism only by resorting to a fairly platitudinous eclecticism. Although this did not lead to religious indifference, it must be admitted that the standard of theological thought was lowered in this period, involving a flight away from synthesis, which was only compensated for, even among the most learned, by the return to more simple emotional and trusting forms of piety.

Ockhamism might have brought theology back onto the rails of scriptural exegesis since Ockham had proclaimed the primacy of Revelation, without denying all the value of tradition and of the rule of faith elaborated by the Church throughout history. However, it must be noted that right up to the beginning of the fifteenth century, in spite of a few interesting attempts, for instance to improve knowledge of Greek and Oriental languages, this Biblical revival did not take place among the theologians, but only among a few marginal or heterodox movements such as Wycliffism. It was to be the great contribution of Humanism, beginning with Lorenzo Valla, to relaunch the edition and commentary of the Holy Writ in a truly theological perspective.

Nominalism, however, by which we mean not so much a precise doctrine as a general intellectual attitude, also had obvious positive effects. By extricating itself from the constraints imposed by the coherent and more or less Aristotelian system of the thirteenth century *Summa*, nominalist thought was able to free itself and open up new paths by the end of the Middle Ages. Although none of these developments got very far by itself, and although their 'precursive' character has been emphasised rather anachronistically, they should be mentioned as one of the facets of the profound renewal of the mental structures of the West in this period.

At this point we should be wary of giving too much emphasis to labels which are still honoured: Realists, Thomists, Nominalists, etc., and to the disputes between schools and orders: Franciscans against Dominicans, secular against regular clergy. In this jumble of varyingly successful attempts, in this multitude of works in which analysis takes obvious precedence over synthesis, each person was actually going his own way and taking his material where he could find it. But almost all of them, and this is the interesting thing from the historical point of view, expressed in their own way some of the fundamental tendencies of the age.

The first aspect to underline is the appearance, even among men of science and scholarship, of a certain anti-intellectualism, manifested by the eruption of mysticism, morality, and pastoral concerns into the sphere of learned theology. In other words, people were becoming more interested in active participation, in the affective part of the life of Faith, in the concern for personal salvation, in the powers of freedom and will, in the expectation of grace and in the certitudes of intuition and illumination, and they had less confidence in the few resources of discursive and speculative knowledge. Nothing in all this is to be found in Ockham himself, who does not appear to have been a mystic and whose criticism of rational theology remained very dialectical. But in fact, already in the previous generation, in a Dominican context (one still marked by the rationalist and optimist vision of Saint Thomas) the first demands for a mystical theology had been made by Master Eckhart. His mystical theology was a dialectic of time and eternity, of being and essence, which by taking bold short cuts, tried to restore the conditions for immanence and inwardness and for turning back, for the soul's loving union in God, for the birth of the Word in the soul, for the awareness of the Creator which lies in the deepest recesses of the creation. These extremely bold objectives were echoed in a few popular movements, (they were more intelligible in Master Eckharts's German sermons than in his Latin writings) and were condemned at Avignon, which meant that they were not to be found among the masters of theology in subsequent generations.

John Gerson (1363–1429) professor and then Chancellor of the University of Paris, was typical of this more moderate orientation. He was ready to warn against the illusions and dangers of mysticism and could only envisage making the spiritual life of Christians more profound within the context of the Sacraments and good works recommended by the Church. But, at the same time, Gerson, having inherited nominalism, took up its criticism against rational theology. He refused to accept that straightforward philosophical reasonings wanted to bring God back within the natural order, to impair His sovereign freedom and complete His Revelation. He considered that theological discourse ought to aim less at demonstration than at persuasion and emotion in order to guide the soul towards contemplating and loving a God, who made Himself felt in the heart, and was accessible through meditation, prayer, and the Eucharist. Gerson's doctrine thus ended up by making specific demands. In his Latin thesis as well as his many French sermons and manuals on pastoral care and prayer, he explains that his mission was not simply intellectual, but that he also aimed at clarifying the religious practice of the faithful, (including, on the political level, that of the rulers) in order to infuse their lives with the precepts of the Gospels. It followed that he should also supervise the education of simple priests and prepare them for the duties of their office. Gerson's personal involvement in the Council of Constance, at which he acted both as the exponent of a moderate conciliarism and as the vigilant guardian of dogmatic orthodoxy, is a good illustration of how this theologian saw himself, who wanted to be both pastor and moralist, man of action and spiritual director, while remaining fundamentally prudent and conformist.

With Gerson and contemporaries of similar inspiration, speculative theology developed a practical dimension, which, although it cannot be called mysticism, introduced a new concern with psychology and spirituality, an attention to individuals (including the simple, as well as women and children) and has allowed certain historians to refer to it as Socratic Christianity. So it is not surprising that they looked for inspiration less to the great

164

The art of navigation improves: The compass combined a needle with a mariner's card by fixing them one above the other on a pivot in a box. (Miniature from the end of the fourteenth century from Marco Polo's *Livre des Merveilles*.)

scholastics of the thirteenth century than to the Fathers of the Church and the spiritual authors of the twelfth century, like Saint Bernard or the Victorines.

Science rattles its chains

In the domain of natural philosophy and science, the liberating effects of nominalism were also felt. By cutting God off from creation, by refusing the rigid causalities and implacable determinisms which bound a universe entirely arranged according to its first cause, this doctrine had shattered the illusion of a necessarily ordered world, in which philosophy could have no other function than that of deciphering, behind the many appearances, enigmas and symbols of the temporal world, the pre-established dispositions of the Divine Plan. For nominalists, however, reality was only concrete and singular. Words, concepts, symbols and every ideal form had no existence. The philosopher thus had to fix his attention on the physical world, in its diversity and contingency. Scientific knowledge would be derived from the minutiose observation of real things and from experience, which alone are capable of extricating not causes or laws but regularities from simple empirical physical phenomena.

It is well known that, in spite of this favourable context, the natural sciences really had not progressed much by the end of the Middle Ages. Scientists, for instance, were able to improve their astronomical measurements considerably by rallying to the Ptolemaic theory of the movement of the planets, which was more complex than that of Aristotle, and explained appearances rather better. By trying to express certain theses of Aristotelian physics in mathematical terms, Thomas Bradwardine, a Master of Oxford (*c.* 1328) and

165

some of his students, the 'calculators' of Merton College, followed by John Buridan in Paris (before 1352) and Nicholas Oresme (1350–77), managed to expose the absurdity of several of the Philosopher's propositions and the experimentally untenable nature of certain of his deductions, for instance relating to dynamics. But these promising intuitions, which attempted to renew the very methodology of physics, did not lead very far. Although direct observation and experience were firmly established as necessary, 'one cannot attain a certain degree of certitude except by applying one's mind to the study of things and not of the Philosopher (Aristotle) or the Commentator (Averroes)', as Nicholas d'Autrecourt, the most systematic of the Parisian nominalists wrote around the mid fourteenth century. He was a decided precursor of modern empiricism, but in practice such precepts could not do anything to improve the existing techniques of experimentation. The advances in mathematics were equally limited because their attempts at quantifying were still strongly qualitative, 'taking into consideration degrees of intensity rather than the expanses of time and space'.

Under these conditions, it would be anachronistic to honour these doctors and especially the *École de Paris* of the time of John the Good and Charles V, by arbitrarily taking a few formulae out of context, and identifying them as the premises of some of the fundamental discoveries of modern science. The invention of the infinitesimal calculus cannot seriously be attributed to the author of the *Centiloquium theologicum* (who has been identified, on suspect grounds, as Ockham), nor that of the principle of inertia to Buridan, nor that of analytical geometry or of the diurnal rotation of the earth (a hypothesis he did in fact formulate, only to reject it explicitly) to Oresme.

In fact, these various authors, while they benefited from the collapse of Aristotelianism provoked by nominalism, were not able to break out of the framework whose powerful logic, on top of a thousand years of tradition, continued to impose its qualitative concepts. In view of the excessive mental and social gulf which divided 'mechanical' workers from the clerics, the latter, victims of the inadequacy of their experimental technology, were not able to break this 'union of a determinist metaphysics with common sense empiricism' which gave traditional science its strength. The scientific revolution of modern times did not take place in the fourteenth century any more than did the religious Reform.

Were there no spheres in which knowledge and technology, speculation and professional expertise might have converged? It is hard to tell from the present state of documentation. Although architecture, military genius and the art of navigation (one thinks of the Genoese and Catalan sea charts of the fourteenth century or the Portuguese expeditions of the fifteenth) seem to have acquired a little science, it is difficult to know just how it was done. It is improbable that they had significant and direct contact with the knowledge of the universities since, in spite of the nominalists' rehabilitation of observation and experiment, the clerics were prevented by social prejudice and problems of terminology from understanding the material potential of the world around them. Once the indefinite play of symbolic meanings had become unfashionable, the initial impulse towards encyclopaedic literature was dissipated in minutiose and repetitive works, though it could have given the schoolmen a chance to assimilate and theorise about the already immense technical information available to them.

Medical science remained empirical. Here some doctors are administering medicine to Louis VI the Fat (*le Gros*). (*Chroniques de France ou de Saint Denis.*)

Medicine was represented in the reputable universities – Montpellier, Bologna and Padua – but it could not shake off the crushing weight of the Greek and Arab authorities, which formed the basis of instruction. Such timid progress as was made in anatomy and surgery was due to a few physicians like Mondino dei Luzzi and Guy de Chauliac, who dared surmount the intellectual reticence of their colleagues and the Church, and the more professional reserve of surgeons and barbers, whose ability was essentially empirical and routine. But that did not take them very far.

The State breaks away from the Divine

The liberation of scientific and philosophic thought is part of a general trend which also included the development of the Law and of political literature as autonomous (albeit not laicised) disciplines at the end of the Middle Ages. The revival of Roman Law, which Canon Law had largely absorbed, started in the twelfth century and continued in the later Middle Ages, getting more precise as attempts were being made to apply it more specifically to the realities of the time. Political Aristotelianism had for its part been known at least since the thirteenth century. The work of improving these acquisitions was undertaken by the first humanists as well as by Latin historians and orators, and their efforts made it possible to reflect more completely on the nature and aims of the State (essentially the monarchic State) and of the organisation of civil society. However, the end of the Middle Ages produced no original political theory; the diversity of the sources and the conditions under which doctrine was elaborated effectively prevented originality, since it emerged not only from the Schools but also from chanceries and law courts. Although nominalist influences very often produced 'democratic' ideas about the rights of individuals, of whom the State is only the sum, and the common good which is the sum of individual interests, other influences

167

insisted more on the organic nature of the social hierarchy and on the absolute necessity of the Rule of Law as defined and imposed by the ruler. In any case, nobody was still thinking in terms of a pure theory of the natural State. Everything in the Augustinian tradition directed it towards more or less providential ends, compatible with the salvation of its members. Even Marsilius of Padua, although represented as one of the elegists of the sovereignty of the lay State and the primacy of Natural Law, was also heir to an ancient political tradition, whose ideal was a Christian Empire and an all-spiritual Church.

The origins of this liberation go far back in time and it is easy to uncover the premises of a similar notion of the 'common weal' in the mid thirteenth century. When the English barons waxed indignant about the neglect or the nepotism of Henry III, they invoked precisely that idea; when Beaumanoir drew his ideal portrait of a ruler, he used it as his framework. But these men of action and Law did not rid themselves of the idea of the ruler's sacred mission. The moment he pronounced his oath, the King assumed the *respublica*, becoming its defender and its incarnation. There was nothing 'Gothic' about all that. On the contrary, the lawyers who gradually invaded the Capetian and Plantagenet courts around 1300, men from Italy and the south of France were imbued with Roman Law and knew what *imperium* and *potestas* meant and did not worry in the least about God's little finger. It was the ruler, as judge, legislator and potentate, whom they wanted to succeed and whose schemes they served. Now that the German Emperors had been definitely thwarted and the warlike Papacy morally disqualified, what had they to fear? Only Kings could be attributed with sovereign right, and we may assume that Nogaret did not hesitate when he forced his way into the apartments of a Pope and laid hands on him. These zealous servitors, Pierre Flotte, Guillaume de Plaisians, could double as theorists; Pierre Dubois sketched the outline of a terribly materialistic rule for the King of France, which masqueraded as Christian Leadership. In Paris, where Philip the Fair or even Philip VI and Charles V were in control, this was easy, but less so in Italy, where there was a desperate need for a centralising power, and a shortage of candidates. The Pope was by definition excluded, and anyway he had gone away. The Angevin, who was tied to the south in his disputed lands and the Valois, who was watching in the north for his moment, were both 'Barbarians', and, so, like the Ghibellines of a former age, the exiled Dante had only the Emperor to appeal to, when, sick at heart, he wrote his *De Monarchia* around 1315 – he whose homeland was Guelph. But his cry of anguish over an embattled Italy did not include a programme of action. This was supplied by Marsilius of Padua almost two centuries before Macchiavelli, who traced the ideal portrait of the *Defensor pacis* in 1324, when a contested Emperor was attempting to revive the Hohenstaufen and the Ottonians. According to him, politics had to be freed from morality, and temporal things from spiritual: with the law of the heart and the soul pertaining to the Church, and the social body and the Law to the Ruler; because society was in itself legitimate and could vary according to time and place, independently of the will of the Church and maybe of God. This meant that the fulness of power devolved on the rulers of society and, Marsilius added, on the Emperor, evidently.

The lesson was not lost. Even though the Emperor was no longer effective, the States, although not quite nations, were girding themselves with their newly legitimised monarchies. The theorists could go even further, by espousing the democratic ideas which had blossomed in the towns at the beginning of the fourteenth century, or by urging the ruler towards an 'antique' form of tyranny. But the aristocracy was drawn up in the front line with its muscle-power still formidable, despite its financial set-backs and military disarray. It was because they did not understand this that men like Artevelde of Ghent, Marcel of Paris, and Rienzo of Rome were crushed when they tried to seize power in the middle of the fourteenth century. It was only in the nineteenth century, when the bourgeois perception of history created its particular illusion of the past, that their attempts appeared democratic. However, once this crisis had passed the teachers came to the fore again: Nicholas Oresme, Jean Gerson, Pierre d'Ailly came to reproach the people and to advise the rulers between 1370 and 1420. They were fine speakers and were heard with all the emotion then fashionable, and some, like Jean Petit went so far as to excuse crime carried out for reasons of State; or like Alain Chartier, condemned the apparent weakness and hypocrisy of the rulers who themselves remained unimpressed, regarding these intellectuals as their creatures. The advance towards the monarchy of the modern age had begun.

Even Italy was not yet ready to take the road to tyranny. Nevertheless, tyranny could be seen in Milan in the time of the Visconti and the 'free' Florentine Leonardo Bruni stigmatised it in 1402, fearing its contagion. More than one humanist was tempted by it, seduced by the glamour of absolute power. Although the amiable Salutati could discourse on the comparative charms of the *via contemplativa* and the *via activa*, it was a rhetorical exercise; the era of the Sforzas had not yet come.

Man as the centre of the world

We have already used the expression 'humanism' several times. Although more characteristic of the previous period, it also flourished in the intellectual atmosphere of the crisis-ridden fourteenth century. Indeed, a humanist tradition had been a permanent feature of the whole of the Middle Ages in the West: sometimes vigorous and creative, as in the ninth and twelfth centuries, and sometimes almost silenced. Humanism was to some extent aware of its legacy, as it would demonstrate by researching into Carolingian manuscripts, and in restoring numerous twelfth-century authors to honour (Saint Bernard, John of Salisbury). But by the fourteenth and beginning of the fifteenth centuries, humanism was endowed, not only with exceptional vigour, but also with its own particular character.

Geographically and socially, it was a very localised phenomenon, found first in Italy and more especially Florence. The first Tuscan humanists emerged on the fringes of the Universities and the Church, more or less linked to the world of commerce and chanceries in a relatively laicised milieu. Petrarch (1304–74), Boccaccio (1313–75), and Salutati (1331–1406) were simultaneously lovers of fine language and rhetoric, and sincere Christians, who like all their fellow men aspired to reform the Church. Humanism for them

169

started out as a form of protest against certain dominant cultural tendencies; in this it shared in the general atmosphere of the age. The humanists protested against the theological pretensions of Aristotelian and Averroist philosophy, the barbarous Latinity of Scholasticism, and the abuses within the Church. In contrast with a culture invaded by confusion, formalism and impostors, they extolled the purity of the writings of Antiquity. Like Poggio, they tracked them down with passionate intensity in monastic libraries, selecting and 'editing' the most authentic manuscripts to absorb and imitate their contents. They also offered the positive contrast of a rhetoric designed to move and convince and not, as with dialectic, to distract the mind by leading it along the detours of arbitrary demonstration and analysis. Their final contribution was to return to the Bible and the Church Fathers and to free them from their glosses. Clearly, by going back to the original texts, the humanists came up against the problem of reconciling the aesthetic and moral values of a resuscitated 'paganism' with Christian religion. But they found their answers in the works of Saints Jerome and Augustine; pagan ethics were fulfilled in Christianity, and so the study of Grammar and Rhetoric enabled a better understanding of the Scriptures.

Passing via Avignon, humanism reached Paris, where it had already been grafted onto native traditions. It was in Charles VI's reign, especially between 1380–1410, that the beginnings of French humanism can be most clearly distinguished. It was adopted by little coteries of friends gravitating around the Royal Court and the College of Navarre, whose main preoccupations stress its relationship to the Tuscan variety, which it imitated with varying degrees of skill. Characterised by an even stronger allegiance to Christianity, it also had a specific national tinge, expressed by its interest in the vulgar tongue, enriched by contact with Latin, and by its exaltation of national, patriotic and monarchic values in a heroic perspective loaded with references to the grandeur of Antiquity. Gerson and Jean de Montreuil are good examples of this, since they both put their rhetoric at the service of political action and in spite of the former's allegiance to a fairly traditional form of religious morality, they formed part of the same intellectual current.

Other more modest centres of humanism could be pointed out in Europe at that time. But even those in Italy and France were fragile; the last convulsions of the Hundred Years' War interrupted Parisian humanist tradition for thirty years. Vigorous resistance made itself felt everywhere, whether by the Averroist and Nominalist universities, or by monks and Mendicant friars, who maintained their traditional suspicion of the false lure of a 'pagan' culture. Understandable connivances were also established with the communities of the *devotio moderna*.

In Italy the movement was stronger, and it grew steadily during the first half of the fifteenth century. The works of Lorenzo Valla (1407–57, the son of a Roman notary, who became professor of Rhetoric at Pavia and counsellor to the King of Sicily and then to the Pope), and of Leon Battista Alberti (1404–72), heir to a Florentine patrician dynasty, are typical of this evolution. They show us a humanism which had reached its full philosophical maturity. A process aided by the rediscovery of Greek, which was taught in Italy from the end of the fourteenth century by Byzantine refugees whose model and protector was Cardinal Bessarion. This enabled Valla, after he had written his Ciceronian

This thirteenth-century miniature illustrates the *Liber divinorum operum*, written around 1160 by Abbess Hildegarde of Bingen. Man is already at the centre of the world and associated with it. God, who envelops the universe, communicates his creative power to man. (Lucca, Biblioteca Statale).

breviary (*Elegentiæ linguæ latinæ*) to attack the very text of the Bible by exposing the inadequacies of the Vulgate and more specifically the corrupt versions in current use. Humanism also began to develop a coherent doctrine and methodology, capable of formulating a project for the global reform of the Church and society. The humanists used their command of the texts and their rediscovery of the values of Antiquity to criticise ecclesiastical institutions and traditional pedagogical practices, suggesting in their stead a new educational approach which was soon given form in pioneering foundations (Alberti wrote his book *Della Famiglia* in 1433–40) and in universal peace projects, drawn up by Valla and Cardinal Nicholas of Cuso (1401–64). The latter also drafted a vast programme of syncretism, which would unite Christian wisdom, medieval knowledge and the universal values of Latinity in an immense scholarship, which would contain both the need to transcend its own limits and the intuition of Divine Transcendence.

However, certain features of emergent humanism were already hardening. Its elitist nature was expressed by extolling wealth, creative work and action, all of which fitted in harmoniously with (comfortable) retreats into solitude and with the cultivated recreations

171

of aristocratic minds. Such optimism was sometimes a bit short-lived, and its social conformism was accentuated to accommodate the rise of the great monarchies and the Italian *signorie* to 'absolute' power, even when the ruler had the good taste to show some consideration for literature and its harbingers.

Thus, as with the other intellectual streams of the age, humanism itself very soon traced the limits of the liberation which it had originally demanded and propelled with such force.

The birth of a lay mentality?

Now that we have tried to reconstruct the various learned and popular, religious and intellectual, emotional and rational components which went to form the images and manners of Western Europeans at the end of the Middle Ages, let us now look at them from a global point of view; and consider in particular the birth of the secular mind.

Naturally, there was no question of any slackening off of faith or increase in unbelief. Although this was not necessarily inconceivable at that time, and not just as the blustering of a few *condottiere* and 'blasphemers', the fact remains that just as in the preceding centuries, the texts reveal a Christendom, that is, a society in which the Church sought to permeate the individual and collective lives of all its members, and in which Christian moral and eschatological references continued to dominate practically the whole of culture. Even the timid attempts at dialogue which the Christian West had broached in the twelfth and thirteenth centuries with Judaism, Islam and 'paganism' (that of the Mongols) by means of controversy and missions, had come to an abrupt stop in the first half of the fourteenth century. The internal collapse due to the crisis, together with the irresistible pressure of the Turks in the Eastern Mediterranean, tended to revive within a newly shrunken West the ideals of the Crusade. They tended, it is true, to be ineffectual and ill-conceived, involving fanatical anti-Semitism, with its miserable list of pogroms and enforced conversions.

Far from being the precursors of a de-Christianising process, the aspirations of many people to a more extensive religious and moral education, to a more personal form of piety, to the Reform of ecclesiastical institutions, all witness on the contrary to the fact that the great majority of men in the Middle Ages continued to seek in their faith for the answer to their existential anxieties, which had been quickened by the troubled times and the failure of the old social and political structures. The various heresies themselves seem to have been more in the nature of extreme forms of authentic religious protest than resurgences of traditional popular and pre-Christian attitudes, rebelling against clerical discourse and demands.

Having said that, it is just as certain that this period saw a profound adjustment in people's forms of expression and in social and individual practices, and a new interpretation of the profane and the sacred, of everyday concerns and the expectation of the next life.

Putting the symbols to flight

In numerous spheres there seems to have been a greater awareness of the essential distinction between temporal and spiritual things, between affairs of the world and the realities of the Above. This was the case with the learned tradition, in which theology tended to be clearly differentiated from philosophy, physics and law. This was equally the case in politics, in which the sovereignty of the States and the independence of the rulers in regard to the Papacy were growing stronger everywhere in the West. One may also consider that the spectacular progress achieved in the sphere of mercantile and financial expertise, especially in the great Italian towns, was evidence that the Church was relaxing her long-standing suspicion of these forms of activity, which had invariably been associated with certain forms of sin. From then on, such activities were considered justified by their accounting efficiency and their obvious social utility alone, and were developed independently of religion. The evolution of artistic and literary taste is surely also proven by the appearance of a specifically profane type of inspiration. Many more examples of this trend could be supplied. In short, the evidence suggests that people were becoming more acutely aware of the concrete reality of creation, of the irreductible individuality of each of its components and of its sometimes weighty resistance, as well as of its charms. The other side to this awareness is obviously to be found in the tendency of individuals to lead more profound religious lives and to go beyond the limits of simple social conformism, in order to live according to the revealed message and to engage in precise exercises leading to personal sanctification.

This process Huizinga calls a 'decline in symbolic ways of thinking'; in the sense that the physical world did in fact cease to be perceived as a forest of symbols; from the heart of which the soul's vocation was to ascend by means of love and illumination. A mysterious motion, by which he who desired could in some way participate in the object of his desire. This form of Platonism, or if one prefers, of the 'realism' so typical of the High Middle Ages and especially of monastic spirituality, no longer corresponded to the common mentalities of the fourteenth and fifteenth centuries, which were much more concerned with empirical practice, with concrete and individual perception, and with direct knowledge.

Having said this, although they were more clearly aware that nature and the supernatural constitute two distinct orders of reality, each with its own consistence, nevertheless the men of that time did not envisage a radical separation of the two. On the contrary, they constantly interacted with and contaminated one another. So it is not the case that society really became laicised, but only that its ancient symbols were fading and becoming vulgarised in a baroque and anarchic proliferation of signs, a clumsy and belittling approach to the Mysterious, in short a confusion of values. Which brings us back to the idea of crisis, which can be aptly employed in the history of mentalities. Not just as a simple echo in the minds and manners of contemporaries of the sudden disasters in the population and the economy, but as the expression of an internal tension, itself the result of the rupture of a world vision, which had until then been relatively coherent. I will mention but two examples which seem to illustrate this phenomenon.

173

Federigo III, Duke of Urbino (1422–82), a portrait by Piero della Francesca, 1465. From being a *condottiere* leading Francisco Sforza's militia, he passed into the service of Ferdinand I of Naples, and then of Pope Pius II against Malatesta, and finally defeated Colleone's Venetians. He became one of the most brilliant Italian patrons of art of the fifteenth century.

The new men

The growth of individualism is often mentioned in connection with the end of the Middle Ages. And indeed, the area of personal responsibility was certainly widened and individual success was enhanced. As the object of the moralists' attentions, proven by the birth of casuistry in the devotional treatises and confessional manuals, the individual, perceived as morally and physically unique, acquired more initiative, as much regarding his mundane existence as in preparing his own salvation.

The social effects of this liberation of the individual are clearly, in the documents at least, most perceptible among the upper classes. Rulers ceased to be simple emblematic figures whose personality was concealed behind the charisma of their office and the permanence of their line, and became, in our eyes as in those of their contemporaries, beings of flesh and blood. Their power became more personal, they were portrayed both after their death and even during their lives no longer as ideal figures but under their authentic features, on tombs, paintings and medals. The impressive effigies of the English kings and princes at Westminster and Canterbury, and the equestrian statues of the Visconti and Scaligeri in Milan and Verona demonstrate this new way of glorifying the ruler.

Indeed, the multitude of individual successes is one of the features of social history at the end of the Middle Ages. Ancient constraints were relaxed, meaning the rules of lineage and of religious inevitability, and the intangible hierarchy of the 'orders' was replaced with the complex diversity of the 'estates of the world' in the common representations of society. A diversity of worldly elements were readily swept under the cloak of the Virgin of Mercy by the iconography of the age, unless they were abandoned to the whirlwind of the *Danse Macabre*. There were individual successes such as the university graduate, sometimes of

The People's Palace (Palazzo del popolo) in Orvieto, 1157.

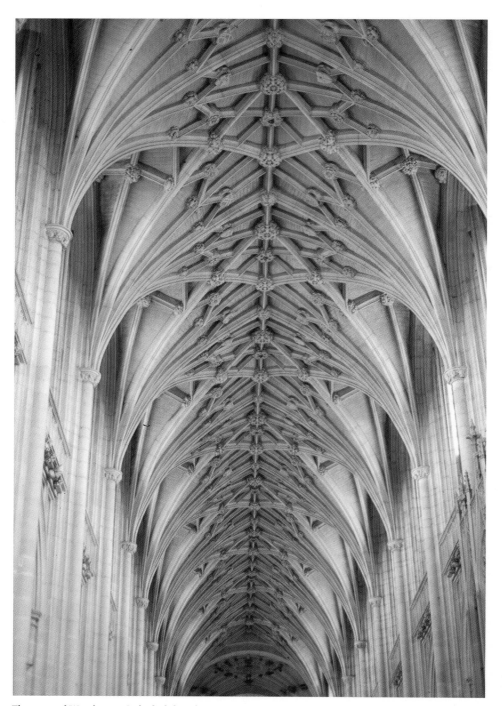
The nave of Winchester Cathedral, late fourteenth century.

The castle of Lassay, fifteenth century (Mayenne).

The front of the Ca'd'Oro, the house of a rich patrician. 1440, Venice.

The art of miniature painting: *Les Très Riches Heures du Duc de Berry* (April) by the Limbourg brothers, *c.* 1415. (Chantilly, Musée Condé.)

'The Romance of the Holy Grail', fifteenth century, showing a tournament with two knights fighting before the king. (Dijon, Bibliothèque municipale.)

Jean de Wavrin's *Chroniques d'Angleterre*, fifteenth century. An assault on a castle during the Hundred Years' War. (Paris, Bibliothèque nationale.)

'The Garden of Youth', a miniature from the *De Sphaera*, *c*. 1470. (Modena, Biblioteca Estense.)

Timurid art in Turkestan; 'The Hunt'. End of the fifteenth century (Istanbul, Topkapi Sarayi.)

Floral arabesques; detail of a tile mosaic of the Safavid period.

The new men: these voracious and unpredictable men of the law lengthened legal proceedings and increased chicanery. This painting by Marinus van Romerswael (1493–1567) depicts a lawyer's office.

lowly birth, whose knowledge and diplomas propelled him into the elite of officials and especially of the Church; or the Genoese merchant or Florentine banker, who could make a net profit of nearly 20 per cent in a good year by speculating in the spice trade or in the money market. Probably even more relevant were the three social types to whom Chaucer applied his caustic wit: people were especially aware of the man of law, because the rapid increase in this type of person was the visible sign of their alienation; notaries were employed throughout most of North-West Europe after 1425 or 1450 (though this was not such a remarkable feature, because their services in drawing up contracts were considered more useful than onerous). Not so the crowd of counsels, doorkeepers, procurers, sergeants and others, those voracious and unpredictable men of justice, who were behind the extravagant formulae employed in the texts and procedures stored in our archives. They lengthened legal proceedings and increased chicanery; the overloaded law-courts became an aspect of daily life in the towns. Both the plaintiff and the defendant were obliged to resort to a body of law which had become unintelligible to common people. It was by his obsessive presence that the man of war first came to the fore; with the bands of adventurers, who were paid by contract, a *condotta*, which tied them to their employer. Such bands included men of Navarre, Brabant and Genoa, who lived off the land and turned to brigandage with the 'Companies' when they had to; but also the mercenary captains, whose rich booties, fat ransoms and royal pensions soon lifted them up to the higher echelons of the aristocracy. The case of Du Guesclin is well known in France, but everywhere in Europe those interminable wars (struggles between Italian cities, the Prussian 'crusades' and the first Portuguese naval expeditions) provided adventurers and needy nobles with opportunities to make their fortune quickly. They were all uprooted men, cut off from their familiar environment by a fine, an escapade, a bankruptcy; petty landowners rejected by their lineage like Auberchicourt or Du Guesclin, or leaders of daring bands like Cervolles or Villandrando; the intimates of a great man like Chandos, Talbot or Campo Basso, or professional street fighters, like Colleone, Hawkwood, Knolles, and even high-ranking bastards, like Dunois and Malatesta. Francesco Sforza was the only one to achieve lasting power, proving when he became Duke of Milan that the adventurer was by the mid fifteenth century no longer an outlaw. Lastly, the men of letters emerged as a new class of intellectual particularly favoured by the rulers. Admittedly, these successes could sometimes be precarious. Spectacular crashes feature regularly in the financial history of Siena, Lucca and Florence. And many *condottieri* found only death and dishonour at the end of the road.

However, a few clearly more marginal characters managed to squeeze themselves into the space thus opened up to personal initiative, alongside a majority of individuals who enjoyed in spite of everything a minimum of initial advantages: burghers owning family patrimonies and ambitious petty nobles. The growth of anti-Semitism and xenophobia may not have left many opportunities for Jews and foreigners, but the weakening of certain moral constraints, the collapse of lineages, the imperious demands of war, pushed bastards into the limelight, especially those belonging to the high aristocracy, along with their mothers, courtesans and royal mistresses. They were treated almost on a par with legitimate children and were entrusted with great responsibilities – the bastards of Burgundy, Armagnac and Orléans were numerous in the episcopacy and the French high-level administration from the 1370s onwards. People went so far as to invest them by virtue of their irregular birth with mysterious attributes. However, the extent of this phenomenon must not be exaggerated. There is nothing to indicate that there were more bastards than before, nor should we disregard the disapproval of burghers and ecclesiastics, which bastardy continued to elicit. But it is interesting to observe, through the behaviour of a few great families, if not a 'veritable exaltation of the fruits of sin' at least an awareness and acceptance of a clear distinction between the traditional norms of the Church and the values proper to a social group.

New alliances

However, just as much as the affirmation of individualism, what one sees at the end of the Middle Ages is the search for new alliances, which is only another aspect of the same phenomenon. The liberation of the individual may well have been more often imposed than desired, involving not a Promethean exaltation of self but disorientation and solitude, the result of the collapse of ancient social and mental structures. We have already mentioned the shortcomings of the ecclesiastical structure. No less shattering was the collapse of rural interdependencies, peasant or feudal, which were based on the continuity of lineages and the relative stability of inheritance. The economic crisis, the war, the Plague, the exodus towards the towns, the terrible epidemics, the new forms of civil and military service and of

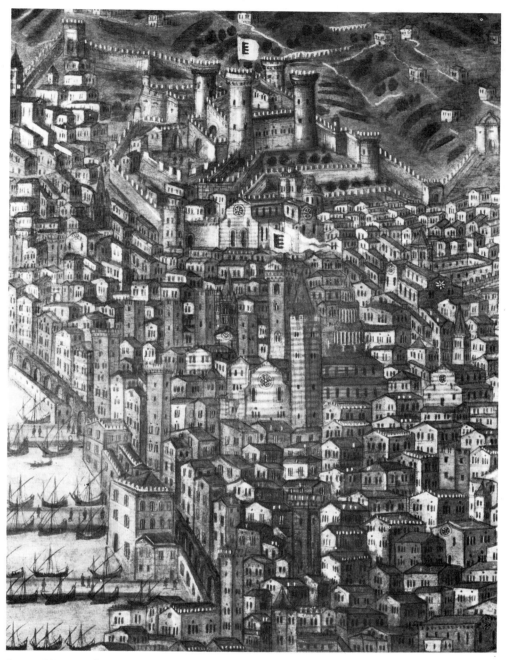

Squeezed between the mountains and the sea, Genoa was forced to grow upwards. This fifteenth-century painting shows how the densely packed houses cover the slope from the town walls to the port. (Detail: Genoa, Museo Navale di Pegli.)

the State, tore many individuals from their familiar context. Some of them slipped backwards into a marginal existence, others on the contrary resorted to the hitherto repressed forces of self-expression, which made them search even harder, under many different guises, for new forms of association guaranteeing mutual help and welcome.

We have observed this tendency in the sphere of religious life, through the proliferation of fraternities and all kinds of new communities. But in fact, the phenomenon was absolutely general. If, for instance, the old model of the family, solidly anchored on the couple and perpetuated by the unfailing sequence of generations, stood up badly to the economic reversals, to the deadly blows of the plagues and to the ascent of new men (as a certain degradation of the legal position and the image of women seemed to show), it tended to be replaced by other models. These emerge as much from actual practice as from the genealogical literature of the age, well represented by the Italian merchants' accounts books. In all cases, it was fairly clearly a matter of substituting efficient new alliances for the old and muddled traditions: regrouping a maximum of brothers and cousins under the aegis of an elder member, eventually ramifying to include bastards or completely unknown members of the lineage, attached to it by the artificial legal bonds of clientship and interest, as in those vast *alberghi* which dominated the town of Genoa in the fourteenth and fifteenth centuries, where they controlled whole districts. In the countryside from Aquitaine to Tuscany the attempts at restoring agricultural production (in the periods when the crisis slackened off) were often the work of large groups rather than isolated persons – fraternities or tacit communities assembling up to ten or twenty members, who were much more robust than the mutilated hearths could be, consisting as they did of widows and widowers, whose numbers were increasing as a result of the Plague and poverty.

The world of merchants, which is sometimes presented as one of triumphant individualism, did not escape this tendency. Here too individual achievement seldom rose above mediocrity, and would disappear at the first serious reversal. Big business was done by companies which were structured around the family. We should also remember that everywhere in the fourteenth and fifteenth centuries the guilds and *arti* were growing in number in the towns. They were rigorously organised and, at least in theory, ensured that their members were protected against competition from outside as well as regulating the reciprocal obligations of the craft masters, servants and apprentices. No milieu was more aware than the aristocracy of the proliferation of new forms of association. The Orders of Chivalry and the courts of love of the Kings of England and France, the liveries and retinues of the Cardinals and great lords, the factions and parties in the Italian cities or in the service of princes of the blood, were very different forms of association. Some emphasised the fairly mythical exaltation of a bygone chivalric past; others were solidly founded on written contracts and payment in kind and were incontestably efficient in political and military terms. Like the professional or fraternal organisations already cited, most of them had a mystifying role, aimed at winning greater acceptance of the hardening socio-professional hierarchies, or of the taming of the aristocracy by the rulers. But they all, as the richness of their rituals proves – ceremonies, banners, uniforms, colours – had the merit of guaranteeing their members a minimum form of mutual help, of representing an acceptable substitute for the old ties of man to man, of constituting efficient instruments of social regulation. By the end of the Middle Ages, the States relied as much on the complex play of oaths and contracts, which had come down to them through the old feudal structures, as they did on the organs of a still very incomplete bureaucracy, to ensure the cohesion of the many heterogeneous groups which they comprised.

In fact, may not the very emergence of these States be interpreted as the ultimate sign of this search for alliances and collective identity? Maybe the beginnings of national feeling and of a dynastic cult, like the growing success of ancestral myths (such as that of the Trojan origin of the Franks) also betrayed this desire to re-establish the continuity of broken lineages and lost ancestors.

Bursts of artistic activity

The most remarkable evidence we have of particular individual achievement is to be found in art. Right up to the thirteenth century the West had only had a religious art, one which contributed towards praising God; both from the point of view of the patrons, who were highly cultivated prelates and rigorous organisers of iconographic programmes, and from that of the artists, who were generally anonymous, and whose very work was perceived as an ascetic and holy activity. At the end of the Middle Ages, however, there was a rapid increase in lay patronage and in the diversification of inspiration. To start off with this increased clientèle often only had the effect of diffusing and vulgarising the themes and forms of the religious art of the preceding period, which sometimes led to standardisation and mediocrity. The best it achieved was a stylistic and precocious emphasis on prettiness and luxury expressed by a profusion of gold, jewels and ivory. Derived from the great French art of the thirteenth century, 'International Gothic' invaded Europe in the fourteenth, spreading from Prague to Naples via Paris and Avignon, in a profusion of works of art, frescoes, statues, hangings, metalwork, whose graceful forms, refined colouration, and technical perfection should not conceal the repetitive nature of their inspiration. Buildings certainly kept close in design and principle to those of the High Gothic period, but Rouen, the chapels of Amiens and Mans, the Breton churches and the lovely chapels of the English colleges did not claim to rival the colossal achievements of the thirteenth century. It was in the overloaded decoration, which sometimes stretches technical ingenuity to its limits, that art achieved yet higher summits. By a curious transference of interest, it was the homes of individuals (meaning rulers of course) which appeared to absorb the artist's whole imagination. Whether ruined or restored – though intact in the Books of Hours of the Duke of Berry and other Maecenes – Pierrefonds, Mehun, the new Louvre as well as the Palace of Poitiers, the Hôtel Cœur in Bourges, the Hôtel de Cluny in Paris and so many other buildings were all erected in that exceptional half century from 1400 to 1450.

It would be to misunderstand this 'flamboyant' art to see it merely in terms of the stone tracery around Gothic doorways. Once again, Italy went her own way, and not without reason, given that Florence has been the cynosure of curiosity and admiration right up to our day; her particular aestheticism blossomed after 1350–5, mingling copied Roman

The flamboyant style in religious architecture. The Jacobins' Church (fourteenth century) in Toulouse is vaulted with arches which spread out with almost disconcerting verve.

skills with Romanesque decorations. Although the Duomo of Milan was rising up a Gothic building, the foundations of Florence's Duomo showed a different intention. When Brunelleschi finished Santa Maria del Fiore *c.* 1421 and San Lorenzo in 1432 to the designs of eastern or paleao-Christian basilicas, he had opened the way for the Renaissance's royal progress. It was then the humanists began to belittle the original art of the West, that of Vézelay and Rheims, the *opus francigenum*, disparaging it as 'Gothic' or 'Barbaric'. Rather too precipitately, when one thinks of the Loire valley, but also of Florence herself, where the Palazzo Pitti was completed in 1440. As well as its elegant floors modelled on the style of Antiquity, the palace boasts a powerful façade of rusticated blocks in the dreary 'feudal' style.

This dual evolution affected decoration generally; statuary was escaping from its monumental format and becoming individual, even trying to achieve verisimilitude. Jean

The dome of the Cathedral of Florence was built in 1417–46 by Brunelleschi and is the perfect expression of what Italian architects were striving after in the Middle Ages.

de Marville (died 1389) then Claus Sluter (died 1404) at the court of the Valois Dukes of Burgundy at Dijon combined (as did other artists in Poitiers, Avignon or Amiens) the sumptuous gravity of Flanders with the naturalist detail of Burgundy: refining wrinkles, smiles and gravity, overloading dukes and prophets with heavy robes and cut jewels. The artists in Florence had different aims. Already in the Baptistery and then in their individual works of art for Or San Michele and the Bargello, Donatello (died 1466) and Ghiberti (died 1455) aimed at nudity and grace, captured in the vivid gestures of their sculpture which divested itself of all symbolism in order to bring the stone to life. There were perhaps two visions, two ways of thought, but whether made for dukes or *signorie*, art was no longer anonymous or even free, involving instead a fee, a commission and a patron.

In fact, art was becoming increasingly identified with its benefactor or patron, who was delighted to see his name and his face inscribed on the works which were to adorn his   **181** home, his library or his chapel. He was happy to be installed with an almost embarrassing familiarity beside the Divine actors in the Nativity or the Passion. He might even be turned into the central figure of the work, perhaps with the trappings of the gallant knights and heroes of Antiquity, like Emperor Charles IV in the frescoes of Karlstein or the Dukes of Burgundy on the portal at Champmol. The age of the portrait had arrived, the ultimate achievement of that glorification of self through funerary pomp – probably the great art of the age. Everything in the arrangement of the funerals of nobles and princes was conceived to exalt the dead man's personality and to guarantee his survival as an individual. He would have determined the details of the ceremony, arranging it to recall his success and his fortune. The effigies exposed on the funeral chariot; the armorial bearings and statues carved on his tomb, sometimes a monumental structure, erected where possible in a private chapel, even, in certain Italian towns, in the open air, admitted him among the numbers of those who live on in this world, serenely asleep on their state beds or even, eyes wide open, vested with all the attributes of power and office. However, art was not just responding to the new demands of society. People's apprehension of earthly realities had quite simply changed.

In destroying the link between Creator and creation, nominalist thought had exposed the accidental and particular nature of the physical world, but in so doing, had restored a place for freedom, or at least, freedom from determinism. It had assigned to every individual thing its proper quality, from being the material sign of an immaterial reality, participating mysteriously in a providential order of the universe, to existing as a physical entity, knowable only as such. The analytical realism of so many works of art at the end of the Middle Ages, which painstakingly delineate the physical world, the flowers, foliage and fauna of the countryside, the furniture and utensils of interiors and the sometimes unprepossessing faces of its subjects, can be attributed not so much to a new 'bourgeois' attitude, as to an Ockhamist philosophy of objective observation.

It may be suggested that the fourteenth century experienced (closely linked to the laicisation of art and culture which we examined above) not the discovery of nature, which was already present in the poetry of the twelfth century and in the cathedrals of the thirteenth, but a new appreciation of nature, which was less symbolic and more attentive to the immediate charms and diversity of the physical world, its medley of colours and indefinite renewal of forms. Although a number of fairly flat and dainty works were produced in this period, in which one's attention wanders through a profusion of bland detail, what actually saves them from a certain artistic vulgarisation, is that the best artists and writers retained a sense of that holy mystery and awe, which alone makes for true art. The Gothic inheritance, with its long tradition of idealising figures and its virtuosity in the play of colour and line, its feeling for lightness and light, was strong enough to ensure the spiritual continuity of inspiration, as the tapestry of the *Apocalypse of Angers*, designed by Nicholas Bataille *c.* 1380 and the *Très Riches Heures du Duc de Berry* illustrated by the Limbourg brothers (*c.* 1415) perfectly demonstrate. These works reveal a universe distinct from that of everyday life; a world of elegance and fantasy in which religious emotion and the mystery of things are suggested with infinite subtlety. Italian art shared this distinction,

The sculptor Claus Sluter was of Flemish origin. He worked for the Duke of Burgundy and gave new life to Gothic forms. He finished decorating the Chartreuse de Champnol at Dijon in 1393, which was intended by Philip *le Hardi* to serve as a dynastic necropolis, as Saint-Denis did for the Kings of France. These two statues represent the prophets Jeremiah and Zachary at the well of Moses (1395–1405) and were intended to decorate the cloister well.

although it experienced a slight regression in the second half of the fourteenth century with the coming of a new less cultivated clientèle. The revival of iconographic programmes by the Mendicant Orders, the lessons of Giotto (*c.* 1266–1337), with his monumental feeling for composition and for the plasticity of the body, were not forgotten and emerged again in Masaccio's (1401–29) frescoes in the Brancacci chapel in Florence, whose powerful, grave and tragic figures are presented in extreme relief. In Van Eyck's paintings around 1430–4, such as the 'Adoration of the Lamb' or the 'Arnolfini Marriage', a complex allegory of Christian matrimony, there is a devout piety fairly typical of northern Europe, expressive of his restrained mysticism.

However, the simple pleasures of contemplation and narration plainly dominated people's artistic taste at the time, calling on art to show them the infinite wealth of the physical world. Where the architects of the thirteenth century had exposed the powerful architectonic structures of the Cathedrals, models of the very structure of the universe, those of the fourteenth and early fifteenth centuries buried them, as in the vaults of Ely or Gloucester Cathedrals, beneath the arabesques of stone ribbing and the exuberance of stone foliage. Where the Parisian sculptors of Saint Louis' time had placed simple and majestic figures against plain geometric backgrounds, those of the following period inserted them, even drowned them, in sumptuous surroundings – the towns and fields of Tuscany or Flanders, the greenery of the closed gardens of *courtoisie*, the mysterious forests of hunters and knights errant.

The new spirit of old literary forms

The new forms of artistic expression were paralleled to a surprising degree in literature. This may not have been 'flamboyant' in the fourteenth and fifteenth centuries, because it has not come down to us on account of its brilliance and virtuosity; but it was animated by the same feeling for description and individualism and there was nothing particularly Antique about it; old literary genres were being repeated, but a new spirit was blowing through them. The poets and romancers did not find it easy to laicise their work; Dante's ghost stood in their way, and his cry of anguish could still be heard. Exiled from Florence because he thought as an Italian and not as a partisan; because he aspired to a Christian unity whose only hope lay in an inadequate German, he remained faithful to the old imperial order while all the values which could have upheld it foundered around him. Dante Alighieri sums up in himself both the universalist thought of the thirteenth century and the changes of the wrecked fourteenth century. His *Divine Comedy*, as the hundred songs of his journey beyond the tomb were later called, was written between 1304 and 1320. It is a work built around a scholastic structure, with its harmonious and firm architecture, in which symbols predominate and moral order triumphs, but also a completely personal vision of man's struggle against nature and against destiny. There seems to have been a silent period after this 'testament' appeared. Those who took up their pens after 1350 or 1360 knew neither Dante nor Saint Thomas. They were as if delivered from their metaphysical burdens, and they gave a new look to the old literary genres. In a troubled age people are impelled to seek more forcible tones, to provide lavish spectacles and to take part in them. The patronage of Charles V, Jean de Berry, Philip *le Bon* and René d'Anjou was partly theatrical, emotive and in the last analysis fairly artificial, especially when the princes were personally involved. The rondeau, ballad, the dancing songs of France, the sonnet or the innovatory *Stil nuovo* in Italy, though they might deal with prowess and *courtoisie*, were only court entertainments and complaisant vehicles for self-advertisement. Guillaume de Machaut (*c.* 1375) Charles d'Orléans (*c.* 1425) and François Villon (*c.* 1450) himself, the court flatterer, the prince of the blood and the delinquent scholar, spoke of nothing more than their feelings and anguish. The Italians may have been more stylish, and the English more restrained, but they all shared the same egocentric dimension. Petrarch was shedding his sonnets like leaves between Florence and the Fountain of Vaucluse, pursued by the flattering murmurs of princes and their comfortable prebends; Boccaccio, with the security of his paternal allowance behind him, was free to mix scabrous adventures with political epigrams – he watched Florence expiring from the Plague from the heights of Fiesole. And Chaucer's 120 Canterbury Tales (of *c.* 1385) are very personal works, as well as blistering portrayals of society.

These were artificial genres, you may say. But the theatrical performances which were staged by civic pretensions spoke to the people. Although the religious Mystery plays, like Arnoul Gréban's triumphant *Mystère de la Passion* seemed to cling to the past, his 80,000 verses – enough to entertain the crowd for three consecutive days – are actually full of profane scenes, human characteristics and real introspection. History escaped this bias even less; it began by concentrating on the immediate, but soon emerged as the mirror of the ruling class, showing events as they appeared to the men of letters. Not that the standards of history writing fell; both Villani in Florence and Froissart in France before the end of the fifteenth century were among the very best observers of society. But their accounts served to describe the people, as a means of governing them and of serving the master.

Literature, like art, thus showed the same inclination to observe the world, as the success both of the anecdotal story and of technical works like the famous *Treatise on Hunting* by Gaston Phœbus demonstrate. Here too the rediscovery of nature was aimed less at supplementing banal didacticism than with furnishing a public, which was essentially aristocratic (by birth or, at any rate, by taste because aristocratic fashions generally set the tone in bourgeois circles) with material for its nostalgic fantasies and the background for its dreams.

So the lay culture which emerged at the end of the Middle Ages demonstrated people's new attitudes towards the world, life, and finally, death. Attitudes which acknowledged external realities and were hungry for life and possessions. Certain chroniclers noted, sometimes to their surprise, that the great epidemics did not induce a general prostration but gave rise to bursts of vital energy, to social dynamism and to the demand for immediate pleasures and joys. In the prologue to Boccaccio's *Decameron*, Pampinea makes a splendidly bucolic suggestion to her companions, who had left plague-ravaged Florence with her:

We could go and stay together on one of our various country estates, shunning at all costs the lewd practices of our fellow citizens and feasting and merrymaking as best we may without in any way overstopping the bounds of what is reasonable. There we shall hear the birds singing, we shall see fresh green hills and plains, fields of corn undulating like the sea, and trees of at least a thousand different species, and we shall have a clearer view of the heavens which, troubled as they are, do not however deny us their eternal beauties, so much more fair to look upon than the desolate walls of our city. (Transl. G. H. McWilliam; Penguin Classics 1972.)

Joy and death

The new forms of wealth and luxury, often the attributes of parvenus, also reflected these attitudes. They were flashy and ostentatious. Men and women covered themselves with sumptuous clothes in brilliant colours, with jewels, and they filled their rooms with costly ornaments. Everything became collectable and was owned and enjoyed on a personal level: the libraries and with them the very knowledge contained in the books; the bronze sculptures, the paintings, the tapestries, the works of art, even objects of religious and liturgical significance (portable reliquaries, ivory diptychs, Books of Hours).

Court life was clearly the milieu in which the taste for luxury and show developed most rapidly. The almost permanent parties that went on there gave rise to excessive dissipation, in which the traditional practice of extravagant display and the new joys of possession were

The city's showpiece: Siena's communal palace was built between 1297 and 1310, and its splendid tower, 102 metres high, around 1340. It is the most elegant civic building in the Gothic style in Tuscany.

combined; feasts and nocturnal or rustic balls, in which men and women rivalled one another in elegance and extravagance, hunts and banquets, princely *entrées* and all sorts of performances, tournaments and ritual passage of arms, the ceremonies of the chivalric orders, not to mention the extreme pomp of coronations and royal funerals, were all occasions for displaying a profusion of gold, furs, weapons, banners, wine and spices. These celebrations, which were generally arranged according to scenarios overloaded with allegories and historical reminiscences, were clearly dedicated to furthering the glory of the ruler and his dynastic ideology. They had a further role, which was quite simply that of demonstrating, without any sort of restraint, the extent of his power and his wealth. Court life first assumed this brilliance at Paris, when Charles VI was a young man. The fashion then spread everywhere, beginning with the princes of the *fleur de lys*, especially the Dukes of Burgundy who, right up to Charles *le Téméraire* (1467–77) did not cease to astonish their contemporaries with their sumptuous court and very active patronage, although their tastes were rather traditional.

The ruler's glory and his wordly power were also expressed through his buildings. While not many great churches were built at the end of the medieval period, it was the age of princely and communal palaces, which although real fortresses were remarkable by virtue of their courts, their state-rooms and their chapels, such as may still be seen today at Mantua, Siena and Avignon. This last example is particularly rich because it also symbolised the invasion, one could even say the laicisation, of ecclesiastical circles by the life style of the aristocracy, and all that this implied about the Papacy's will to dominate and its attachment to the earthly insignia of power. Juxtaposed to Benedict XII's austere Cistercian palace was Clement VI's princely dwelling; the hunting scenes in the *Chambre du Cerf* (Room of the Stag) had their place there as much as did the religious frescoes in the *Chapelle Saint-Martial*, in the same way as classical authors sat on the same shelf as the Church Fathers in the library and as profane receptions alternated with religious ceremonies. Maybe the chapel, in spite of John XXII's initial formal condemnation of 1322, resounded with the compositions of the *Ars nova*, that new music, whose composers sought to escape from the constraints of traditional polyphony and did not hesitate to upset the rhythms and to mingle musical expressions borrowed from the most varied sources, profane as well as sacred, in an inextricable confusion.

The same tendencies were rather less obviously at work in bourgeois and popular circles. In the Italian cities the houses of the patricians were adorned with proud towers, competing with church towers and communal belfries. Feasts, like the famous *Palio* race in Siena, were privileged occasions when civic particularism could express itself. Almost everywhere the growing success of sports and worldly games could be observed, whose increasingly precise rules determined their symbolic and social function.

So the civilisation of the end of the Middle Ages was now characterised by men's increased desire to impose the ephemeral or lasting mark of their presence on nature; to inscribe her concretely in space and even in time. Previous generations had thought time should be controlled by God alone, but now the mechanical clocks stuck on the façades of communal buildings made time move to the rhythm of human labour.

187

The concert, a tapestry of around 1500. (Paris, Musée de Cluny.)

A game of chess; the reverse of a mirror. Beginning of the fourteenth century. (Paris, Louvre.)

An Italian oliphant in ivory, from the end of the
thirteenth century. (Paris, Musée de Cluny.)

The cult of beauty, wealth and power made the idea of individual physical death intolerable. This effigy plumbs the depths of this revulsion; toads are nibbling at François de La Sarraz's face, while worms wriggle through his limbs. (Detail of the tomb in the Chapel of La Sarraz, Vaud, Switzerland, *c.* 1400.)

It would, however, be paradoxical to claim to find in these resolutely humanist attitudes the last word of the fourteenth and fifteenth centuries. The great fresco of the Campo Santo in Pisa (*c.* 1350) shows happy scenes of courtly life (the garden concert and the forest ride) together with terrifying scenes of the triumph of death, a great winged reaper, and the discovery of three decomposing cadavers in their open coffins. In his 'Legend of Saint George and the Princess' (fresco at Saint Anastasia of Verona *c.* 1435) Pisanello placed aristocratic figures richly dressed and full of grace and distinction in the foreground, but the background is sinister and heavy with menace; dark bushes, dream or nightmare architecture, condemned men hanging from the gibbet, an evil sea and stormy sky. These famous works serve to remind us that awareness of death and fear of obscure forces and of Hell still dominated the mental horizon.

This obsession had begun as concern for individual salvation, which as we have seen was being increasingly mishandled by traditional ecclesiastical and social structures, obliging each person to consider his personal responsibility and the imminence of his appearance before the Heavenly tribunal more directly. The old reserve towards this agonising prospect, which Pope John XXII echoed in 1332 when he maintained that individual judgement and the Last Judgement were separated by a long repose of the soul and not by the direct vision of Divine Reality, was dismissed by the theologians. An evolution illustrated by the neglect of the iconographical theme of the Last Judgement in favour of that of the dead man, naked and alone, appearing before his Judge, as in the famous miniature of the *Heurs de Rohan*.

The agonising over salvation, the social crisis and the terrible mortality rate were the first causes of these obsessions. But the acuter awareness of individuality and the growing attachment to terrestrial realities, to wealth, power, beauty (consider Villon's *Testament*) also contributed towards making the idea of the death of the self and the annihilation of the body almost unbearable. The sinister defiance of the *Memento mori* might be answered either by the grating derision of the *Danse macabre* or, at least for the more powerful, by a proud statement of terrestrial immortality, the temptation to hero worship. For most people, however, merchants and warriors, for instance, whose social success was more glaring, it is clear that their final recourse was still 'conversion' *in articulo mortis*, the erection of a tomb near to the relics of the saints, and the prayers of monks or friars. In short, they turned to the Church, to its sacraments, to its funerary liturgies and its discourse which, in spite of everything, could still assure them of their final rest. We know how the Church, for the soundest reasons, attempted to invest macabre iconographical images – the 'Tale of the three dead and the three living' or the 'Triumph of Death' – with brutal detail in order to emphasise the ineradicable horror of putrefaction in contrast with the consolations of scorning the world, pious almsgiving and indulgences. Such discourses were doubtless effective but they still had to settle with the profound change of mentalities and the shifting emphasis in Christian outlook this implied. Elements of the spiritual and the human meanings of death seem to have been juxtaposed rather than fused. Consider the tombs which show the dead man simultaneously in the form of a macabre *transi*, an image of decomposition, and in that of his living and immortal body. But what sort of immortality was this? During the crisis of the end of the Middle Ages, Western man was divided between the unease and the joy of living, between the *Imitation of Jesus Christ* and the possession of the world.

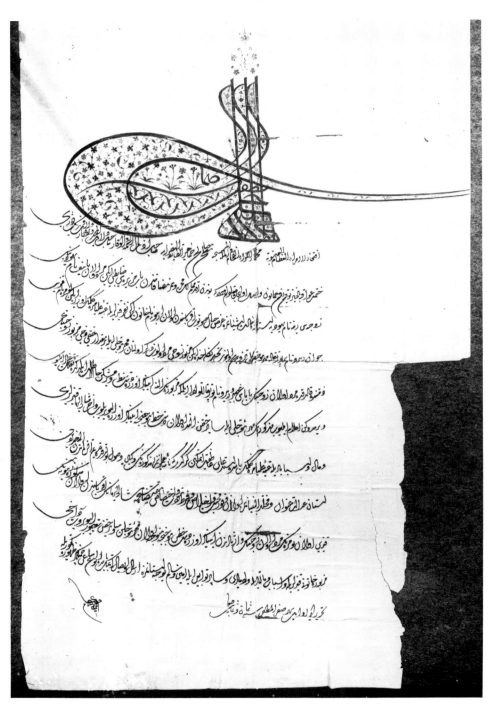

The *tughra* of an Ottoman sultan (Murad III, 988 AH?). From now on, the rest of the world would have to reckon with a new imperialism, installed on the ruins of Byzantium.

PART 2

A new deal in the East and South 1250–1520

A reprieve for Byzantium? 4

The last two centuries of Byzantium's existence (1261–1453) can be divided roughly into two periods which were shaped by events whose influence decided the final fate of the Empire. From 1261, the date of the reconquest of Constantinople by the Byzantines, to 1354, the date of the Ottoman Turks' permanent installation on the European lands of the Empire, and during the following period until 1453, the reigning Palaeologus dynasty was interrupted only by the Cantacuzenus episode. This occured when John VI was proclaimed Emperor at Didymotichum in Thrace in 1341 and managed to ascend the throne of Constantinople in 1347. He held it until January 1355, while his son, Matthew, who was proclaimed co-Emperor in 1353 and was crowned in 1354, kept his title until 1357. Within this first period, Michael VIII Palaeologus' reign (1259–82) was distinguished by his vigorous resumption of control over the muddled situation left over from the Latin occupation, unlike the reigns of his successors, which were dominated by the loss of Asia Minor, by the civil wars and by Serbian hegemony in the Balkans. From 1354, the history of Byzantium is that of a slow progression towards death, punctuated by successive and unhoped-for reprieves, which only served to anticipate the Ottoman Empire. This picture is all the more striking when contrasted with the reassuring panorama of the Western world, where in spite of the crisis of the fourteenth century, splendid progress was clearly being made, a progress especially well illustrated by the expansion of the Italian cities. Indeed, it was both Venice and Genoa's command of the sea and their stranglehold over Byzantium's economic mechanism which lay at the root of her decay.

Surviving in spite of everything

With the recovery of Constantinople, the Empire resumed her international dimensions and her crucial importance on the chessboard of Mediterranean politics. The Empire of Nicea, that peripatetic State founded in Asia Minor after the Latin conquest of Constantinople, had never ceased to work towards this end and finally achieved it. For all that, the re-established Empire lacked territorial cohesion; while it retained Bithynia along with its adjacent islands and Rhodes in Asia Minor, its European territories included (apart from Constantinople and its region) Thrace and Adrianople, Macedonia and Thessalonica as well as the fortress towns of Mistra, Monemvasia, Maina and Geraki, which then formed the core of its future reconquest of the Peloponnesus. After 1262–3 the important ports on the western side of the Black Sea, Anchialos and Mesembria, were taken from the Bulgarians. All the rest of Greece proper and the Greek islands remained under Latin control, with the exception of the independent entities; the Despotates of Epirus and Thessaly (which separated from Epirus in 1268). The northern part of the Balkan peninsula was divided between the two Slav kingdoms of the Serbs and the Bulgars. As for Byzantium's command of the seas, it had been lost to the Italian maritime cities, whose colonies and entrepots were scattered over the whole eastern basin of the Mediterranean. Worse still, Byzantium was soon embroiled in the bitter war waged between Venice and Genoa in her territorial waters, powerless to react and subjected to their recurring hostilities. Her control over trade and the maritime routes, which linked Italy with the Latin possessions in the Mediterranean and linked Constantinople via the Bosphorus and beyond with the Black Sea, was at stake.

'Restoration' and 'union'

Once in Constantinople, Michael VIII had to deal with the most urgent concerns; rebuilding and repeopling the capital, which had been bled dry and devastated by the Latin occupation and had been abandoned by a great many of its inhabitants. He installed a colony of Tzakonians (inhabitants of the eastern flank of the Peloponnesus) in a district of the town in order to supplement the population. They supplied him with the vessels and sailors he needed to create a new fleet, capable of confronting the Venetians without always having to resort to using the allied Genoese fleet. Ships for the fleet and rowers were also supplied by the Gasmuli of the capital, who were of mixed Frankish and Greek origin. It is significant, that alongside measures taken to stockpile great quantities of supplies against an eventual siege, Michael VIII also decided to increase the cultivated area within the city, a reminder of how rural Byzantine cities, including the capital, appeared in those days.

After the reconquest, the Emperor decided on two principal objectives; one was to confront the great enemy coalition preparing in the West with Charles of Anjou 'King of Sicily and Naples' at its head (a title he had claimed since 1265 and won when he defeated Manfred of Hohenstaufen at the battle of Benevento in 1266); the other was to re-establish the Empire in its territories prior to the Latin conquest, by eliminating the Despotate of Epirus and the Latin islands of Greece and by securing the renewed submission of Bulgaria and Serbia. The first objective was principally a matter for diplomacy, while the second presupposed above all military action, without neglecting the arms of diplomacy. It was in this field that Michael VIII excelled, deploying his exceptional skills as a negotiator. Charles of Anjou turned out to be a redoubtable adversary. In him, immoderate ambition went hand in hand with the expansionist policy of the Norman kings and the Germanic Emperors who had preceded him. These two men conducted a strange duel lasting over twenty years which tied and loosed alliances and was capable of upsetting the various balances of power in Europe at any moment.

The dromond, long, light and fast with its high decks and oars, was clearly evolved from the Roman trireme and was the precursor of the Venetian galley. It remained the most effective warship until the end of the eleventh century and never stopped being used by Byzantium. (a model in the Hellenic naval museum, Athens.)

During this period, Byzantium was in particularly acute danger on two occasions, when total catastrophe threatened. These occurred in 1273 and 1281, when the interests of the western powers and those of the Balkan lands converged against the Empire. Charles of Anjou had conquered Corfu at the beginning of 1267 and had trampled all over Manfred's possessions in Epirus. In the same year, the two treaties of Viterbo ensured on the one hand, his sovereignty over William II of Villehardouin's lands and on the other, his participation in a future partition of the Byzantine Empire with the Latin ex-Emperor Baldwin II under the aegis of Pope Clement IV and with Venice's much sought-after assistance. At the same time, having made every effort to create a Balkan coalition of Serbs, Bulgars, Hungarians and Albanians, Charles managed to get himself proclaimed 'King of Albania' in 1272 and in 1273 he induced the Bulgarian Tsar and the King of Serbia to recognise his title.

For his part, Michael VIII threw himself into a race against time aimed at breaking the western coalition. He brandished appropriate weapons before each of his many adversaries: with Popes Urban IV, Clement IV and Gregory X in the first phase and with John XXI, Nicholas III and Martin IV in the second, Michael used the major argument of the Union of the Churches, which, along with that of the liberation of the Holy Land, had become the principal objective of the Papacy's eastern policy as a whole after the fall of the

Latin Kingdom of Constantinople. With Hungary and the Tartars of the Golden Horde (1272) he implemented his policy of matrimonial alliances, thus neutralising Serbia and Bulgaria respectively. Meanwhile, successive Byzantine embassies attended the court of Louis IX, King of France, who was preparing a Crusade against Tunis (1270). Negotiations were started later with Alfonso X, King of Castile and with the Pisans. On the debit side, he pursued the by now almost obligatory policy of granting treaties to the Italian maritime towns and thus drove Byzantium still deeper into a vicious circle of economic dependence. The treaty of Nymphaeum (1261), by which Genoa took over dominance of the eastern trade from Venice, was reaffirmed by Michael VIII after an attempt at squashing it, with the additional concession of Galata, a district on the Golden Horn which remained a Genoese entrepot right up to the Turkish conquest. In the same way, Michael renewed relations with Venice by negotiating a treaty in 1265, which was ratified in 1268 with a five year time-limit and a revoking clause, in line with the Republic's new tactics. This intricate policy enabled the Emperor to undo the western alliances and to thwart Charles of Anjou's projects, thus effectively neutralising him. But, inevitably, events led to the Council of Lyon in 1274, when the Union of the Churches was finally proclaimed in what constituted a spiritual triumph for Gregory X as well as a diplomatic success for Michael VIII. On the Byzantine side, the great Logothetes George Acropolites represented the Emperor, while among the westerners the Franciscan theologian Bonaventure distinguished himself.

From the Council of Lyon to the resurgence of the Angevin menace, Michael VIII moved to counter-attack, both on the diplomatic level (the renewal in 1275 of the treaty with Venice) and especially on the military level. Apart from the reverses he incurred against the Sebastocrator John Angelus of Thessaly, who ended by leading the opposition to the Emperor, Michael reaped only successes in Egypt. The Byzantine fleet, commanded by the Veronese admiral Licario (after defeating the Frankish fleet at Demetrias in 1275), imposed Byzantine hegemony over the Aegean by grabbing Euboea and several other islands.

Once again, the fragile balance of power, which had been so painstakingly secured, was upset by disaster. This time the Roman Curia gave Charles of Anjou the go-ahead; the new Pope Martin IV differed from his predecessors in that he followed a policy totally subordinated to Charles' projects. Once again alliances were forged at Orvieto in 1281 between Charles and the titular Latin Emperor Phillip, the son of Baldwin II, and Venice (pressurised by the Pope, who for his part denounced Michael VIII as a heretic) was unwilling to renew her expiring treaty with Byzantium. As in the first phase, John of Thessaly, the Serbs and the Bulgars were at the rendez-vous. The Empire was saved at the last minute thanks to a 'coincidence' which had really been set up long before: the revolt of the Sicilians against the French during the 'Sicilian Vespers' (March 1282) and the intervention of Peter, King of Aragon. These simultaneous events were to a great extent due to Michael VIII's diplomatic manoeuvring and his support, especially his financial assistance.

Although the Emperor was fully successful in his first objective, he was not in the second, because the separatist Greek states, Epirus and especially Thessaly, a land of great magnates, continued to resist reunification with enthusiasm. After the Council of Lyon, the

Charles of Anjou portrayed with the airs of a
Roman Emperor. He played a major role during the
second half of the thirteenth century in the central
and eastern Mediterranean. (Rome, Museo del
Palazzo dei Conservatori.)

Sebastocrator John set himself up as the guardian of Orthodoxy and he even convoked a
synod which declared the Emperor a heretic. As for the Slavs in the Balkan peninsula who
were, according to the original plan, supposed to be part of the restored Empire, they proved
totally uncooperative and made particular use of the menacing rise of the Serbian nation.
Latin presence persisted in Attica, in Boeotia, in the adjacent islands and to a great extent in
the Peloponnesus, while the command of the sea was resumed after a brief respite by the
maritime republics of Italy.

The East adrift, the West shaken

Michael VIII's eastern policy was determined by his western policy. He gave most of his
attention to the latter, upsetting the balance of the Byzantine sphere of influence in favour
of the European provinces. As a result Asia Minor was progressively neglected, with
dreadful consequences. Nonetheless, the Emperor had been in touch with eastern powers
from very early on; with the Seljuks, the Mongols of the Golden Horde in the Crimea as well
as the Mamelukes in Egypt, concluding treaties and even matrimonial alliances which
transgressed the bounds of religious considerations. In so doing, the Emperor pursued a
dual aim: that of neutralising attacks against his territories in Asia Minor while fanning the
flames of hostility in Hulagu's Mongols against the neighbouring Sultanate of Iconium,
and, still within the framework of his western policy, that of annihilating the Bulgarian
menace by rousing the Crimean Tartars against her, a policy which was not always
successful. Nor was it always free from economic considerations, as a treaty drawn up with
the Mamelukes of Egypt in 1281 demonstrates, which was vitally important to them: by

promising them passage through the Bosphorus and the Propontida to the Black Sea, it opened the only possible route to Central Russia to them, their principal source of slaves for supplementing their population and maintaining its present level.

In spite of these positive aspects, Michael VIII's eastern policy sinned through lack of coherence and continuity. This, however, is to play down the gravity of the imminent danger coming from the West, which prevented the Emperor from assessing correctly the long-term threat building up on his eastern frontier, with the Mongol invasions and a new instability in their relations with the Turks. Only towards the end of his life was Michael VIII aware of the breadth of the catastrophe which had struck the populations and the towns of Asia Minor and which he attempted, too late, to stem.

As it was, his choice was dictated also by ecclesiastical and dynastic problems concerning his illegal accession to the throne. It was precisely in the eastern provinces and principally in Bithynia that the Arsenite revolt broke out, so-named after the Patriarch Arsenius, a partisan of John IV Lascaris, the legitimate heir. This revolt, with its openly popular character, was directed against the central authority and the higher Church hierarchy. It was severely repressed and the *akrites*, the guardians of the eastern frontiers, were particularly hard struck, as were the great landowners of Bithynia, who were subjected to semi-confiscation of their lands, by means of heavy taxation and military levies exacted from them. As a result, the country's old system of defence was destroyed and it was taken not long afterwards by successive waves of Ottomans.

The Council of Lyon and the proclamation of the Union only served to crystallise all latent hostility to Michael VIII and to exasperate the people and the greater part of the Church, whose forcefully expressed conservatism fell on favourable ears. Zealots, the extremist members of the clergy, priests, monks and other exalted persons, roused town crowds by circulating derogatory pamphlets, while the Arsenites united with the Josephites, partisans of the former Orthodox Patriarch Joseph. Few people, especially among the upper classes, accepted the principles of the Union, with the exception of some high officials like Chartophylax John Beccos, who was raised to the Patriarchal throne for these reasons, or Constantine Meliteniotus and George Metochites. However, most of them had been opposed to it beforehand, as indeed the Patriarch himself had been. According to them, as indeed to Michael VIII, the submission to Rome was only an act of *oikonomia*, a minor concession, which could be made in political or ecclesiastical affairs as a last resort. It was thus a perfect instrument of official State or Church strategy. But no general consensus had been obtained: as far as the people of Byzantium were concerned, infringing the rules of Orthodoxy meant sacrificing all that they held most sacrosanct for all time. It meant drawing divine anger onto their heads; a danger, according to them, far more terrible than the armies of Charles of Anjou. Their Emperor had betrayed the True Faith, he was a *latinophron*, someone who thought the Latin way. Their hatred for the Franks, nourished by their humiliation at the fall of Constantinople in 1204, by the crusaders' destructive behaviour and by their anger against the new plans for conquest which rose up one after the other in the Christian West, had not yet been consumed. In December 1282, the man who had succeeded in restoring the Empire and in renewing its prestige, in eyes of the West at least, by means of a policy which was certainly costly but very far-reaching and who had also saved it from a second fall, died in a Thracian village and was buried under a sod of earth; not having officially disavowed the dogma of the Union, he was not honoured with a Funeral Mass by the Orthodox Church, and he was still excommunicated by the Latin Church.

The collapse of the State's bases

Once Michael VIII had gone, his successful European policy collapsed before Byzantium's lamentable situation. The State had been exhausted both militarily and economically by the exaggerated weight of the effort undertaken and slipped a bit further downwards. However, at the same time as the great political activity of Michael VIII's reign was fading away, cultural life in Byzantium, despite the relative inactivity and the obvious disorientation of his successors, was on the contrary fired by an urge to survive and continued to shine as never before – and even to assume the attributes of a new renaissance.

The long reign of Andronicus II (1282–1328) which featured great catastrophes and definitive territorial losses, had in fact begun ten years earlier when Michael VIII issued a decree proclaiming him co-Emperor (1272). By this act, which was of high constitutional significance, the rank of associate Emperor was invested with particular importance, with effective powers as well as legal status. The participation of the co-Emperor in the affairs of State was increased at the same time as he was granted the right to bear the title of Autocrator. These were the beginnings of what was to become (in the teeth of the strictly centralised power of those times) the new statute of the ruling dynasty, whose members were in future to share the government of local administrations. The influence exercised by western feudal institutions over this change has been stressed because Andronicus II's second wife Irène of Montferrat had demanded the division of the theoretically united territory of the Empire so that it could be distributed among her sons, an 'unheard of thing' as the contemporary historian Gregoras wrote, referring to the sacrosanct Roman idea of the indivisibility of the State. But, given the increasingly slack links between the central power and the provinces it could not remain indivisible. The lack of territorial cohesion imposed decentralisation, which was effected at first by members of the Imperial family or by the Emperor's closest relations, but this process also ended by benefiting the great local landowners, who in consequence became almost, or totally, autonomous.

The victory won by the great Byzantine aristocracy was sealed by the ascent of the Paleaologi to the throne and the broadening of the *pronoia* system to include even hereditary *pronoia*. This was detrimental to the finances and the military organisation of the State. The period also saw the fortunes of the peasant classes and those of the minor nobility decline still further. Their lands, which had until then been the basis for effective recruitment, were remorselessly absorbed by great magnates who were able to avoid the military obligations which normally devolved on the *pronoia*. Matters ended inevitably with the army being swamped with foreign mercenaries, thus creating a vicious circle.

201

Constantinople, the tower of Galata in the Genoese quarter. Built under Anastasius I in the fifth century, the old tower was destroyed in 1261, according to the conditions of the Treaty of Nymphaeum, which Michael VIII imposed on the Genoese. They were allowed to rebuild it in 1349.

Andronicus II's foreign policy, as opposed to that of Michael VIII, inclined as much through necessity as through conviction towards Asia Minor and the Balkans and emphasised the Balkan element of the Empire rather than its relations with the West. The Turkish advance on the one hand and the Serbian drive on the other constituted the Emperor's main concerns. Parallel to this, the rivalry between Genoa and Venice constituted another worrying factor, since Byzantium was forced to get involved. Andronicus was caught between two fires and opted unconditionally for Genoa, so that the Veneto-Genoese war, which broke out in 1294, soon developed into a war between Venice and Byzantium. The Empire suffered loss of lives and property (1302) from this war and was forced to renew its treaties with the two belligerents. Venice extended her control over other islands of the Aegean, while Genoa consolidated her position in Constantinople by building a strong wall around her colony in Galata. A little later (1304) Genoa added the island of Chios to her possessions, close to her colony in Phocea on the coast of Asia Minor. Andronicus II's foreign policy had been a total failure.

His eastern policy fared no better, in spite of Andronicus' obvious concern with saving Asia Minor, notably in the period from 1293 to 1295, when he sent in Alexis Philantropenos, a very capable military leader. After a series of brilliant victories against the Turks, he was urged on by his soldiers and the local population to rise up against Constantinople, additional proof, if such were needed, of the anti-dynastic attitudes prevailing in these regions. Since Michael VIII's repression of the Arsenites, there had been a stream of defections to the Turks from them. This also occurred among the ships of the fleet once it had been dispersed. In short, when the disintegration of the defence system reached the point of no return with the destruction of John Vatatzes' military improvements, all Andronicus' efforts were crushed on the points of the advancing Turkish lances. The cost of maintaining these divisions bore unbearably on the State's inadequate finances and Andronicus II was inspired to reduce the army and, in addition, to disperse the fleet. The result was on the one hand, that Byzantium became incapable of lining up more than a thousand men on the battle-field, which made a mockery of the Byzantine army, and on the other hand, that their sea defences were abandoned to their Genoese allies. Military dependence was thus added to their economic dependence and augmented Byzantium's vulnerability to the sea power of Genoa and Venice at one stroke. In the place of the powerful armies, which the Empire had previously been able to raise by the sea on land, it could by this time envisage maintaining a permanent force of only 3,000 knights and a fleet of twenty ships on the proceeds of a series of fiscal measures introduced by Andronicus to increase the revenues of the State. The greater part of the expenses of the public treasury were destined to pay off foreign powers and to neutralise their aggressive plans which the State could no longer counter by military strength – a very significant fact, which tells us much about Byzantium's position on the international scene.

The weakness of the State under Andronicus II contrasted with the strength of the Church, which, once the evil effects of the Arsenite schism had been surmounted, entered a period of full bloom thanks to the extremely Orthodox policy of the Emperor who, from the moment of his accession, hastened to disavow the Union of Lyon, which had already expired. The Church was granted new concessions – not least of which was the direct submission of the monastic community of Mount Athos to the Patriarch of Constantinople, formerly subject only to the Emperor – and its spiritual influence spread out and was consolidated throughout the Orthodox world, from Asia Minor to Russia and to Lithuania via the Balkans. The Church's own authority gradually supplemented the henceforth too compromised prestige of the Empire. By 1300, the Byzantines held only a few isolated towns in a countryside dominated completely by Turkish tribes belonging to different emirates, with the Ottomans in Bithynia. The Battle of Bapheos (1302) near Nicomedia, showed that the loss of Asia Minor 'a fruit ripe for the picking' was final.

Following his policy of forming 'alliances beyond the frontiers', as Gregoras called them, against the Turks, Andronicus II employed mercenary troops in a final attempt at defending and reconstituting the territory, but this proved only an ineffectual half-measure. After the Turks had defeated his bands of Alan mercenaries, he resorted to the services of the notorious Catalan Company and its adventurer leaders, who acted like a boomerang against Byzantium. Apart from a few ephemeral victories over the Turks, these Catalan allies delivered not only Asia Minor but also the European territories and notably Thrace over to pillage and devastation, their aim being none other than that of finding somewhere to establish themselves. The abolition of the Duchy of Athens and Thebes by the Company at the Battle of Halmyros of Phthiotis (1311), following their destructive advance across Macedonia and Central Greece, and the creation of a Catalan duchy in its place, had nothing to do with the Emperor's intentions. The only positive thing to emerge from this rampage was that the western plans for reconquering Constantinople which Charles of Valois (who had concluded a brief alliance with the Catalans) had fostered, were abandoned, as were those of Philip of Tarento, both of them feeble caricatures of Charles of Anjou's grand projects.

After the threat of the Catalans and of a western Crusade had receded, Andronicus II recognised that he was powerless to stop the course of events in Asia Minor and instead he took greater interest in the European provinces as well as in his relations with the West. Where the independent Greek states were concerned, their decline followed closely on that of the central State. After the Angeli had disappeared from Epirus and Thessaly, Janina and some other towns in Epirus and in northern Thessaly submitted to the Emperor while the South was annexed to the Catalan Duchy of Athens at the same time as the Venetians seized the port of Pteleos. For all this, the most important development to occur in Thessaly at that time was the Albanian immigration, which began under a purely military guise, but subsequently evolved into a permanent installation, providing an inexhaustible supply of warriors to serve the great lords of the land.

Civil war

From 1321 to 1354 the doom-laden Empire underwent two civil wars, the second one being by far the most disastrous. Although it was about dynastic quarrels on the political level, it had an undercurrent of social and spiritual conflict, which at the most critical moments turned it into a real class war. The first civil war lasted, with a few interruptions, from 1321 to 1328; the second began in 1341 and appeared to end in 1347 but in fact did so only in 1354. They subjected the Empire to unprecedented economic, social and political disintegration while providing the Turks and Serbs with a favourable terrain for carrying out their plans of conquest and expansion.

The first civil war is called the 'War of the two Andronici' because it broke out between Andronicus II and his grandson, the future Andronicus III. It did not feature any great battle, but it involved a permanent state of emergency and the incessant movement of troops, which interrupted the normal flow of trade and disrupted agriculture at the expense of the countryside, notably in Thrace. Andronicus III's strategy against his grandfather was remarkable in that he did not aim solely at rallying the privileged classes of Byzantine society to his cause (to whom he distributed further privileges and *pronoia* lands, which secured him the allegiance of several powerful men, especially of younger ones, the most prominent among them being John Cantacuzenus) but he also tried to secure the support of the lower classes by exploiting their deep discontent with the heavy taxation imposed by Andronicus II. In Thrace Andronicus III promised – a promise he did not subsequently keep – the town and country inhabitants that he would exempt them from taxation, and so won the population over to his side. That was why the whole of Thrace was allotted to the young Andronicus 'as an Imperial title' when the two adversaries signed their first treaty in 1321, thus creating the first official partition of the territory – a proceeding which Andronicus II had until then fiercely resisted.

The most striking thing about the last phase of this war, which began in 1327 and took place principally in Macedonia, was the active intervention of the Balkan Slavs, whose own rivalries led them to chose different Byzantine sides. The Serb king, Stefan Dečanski, followed up the Serbian court's old alliances with Andronicus II and joined his side, while the Bulgarian Tsar Michael Šišman, joined Andronicus III to fight both the old Emperor and the Serbs. By May 1328 the Macedonian towns and Thessalonica had already joined Andronicus III's camp for the same reasons as the Thracian towns had so done and the first civil war ended with the young Emperor's entry into Constantinople. His advance guard was made up of soldiers drawn from the middle classes in order to attract the loyalty of the capital's inhabitants.

Andronicus III's reign (1328–41) was, insofar as was possible, a time of recovery. The young Emperor's foreign policy (inspired apparently by Cantacuzenus) was not essentially opposed to that of his grandfather, although he relegated relations with the West to second rank and was orientated towards the Balkan Slavs and the Turks of Asia Minor. At the same time, Andronicus tried to give Byzantium some sort of territorial homogeneity by basing it on Greece proper, where he solved the problem of the independent Greek states of Epirus and Thessaly by annexing them to the central power. Despite being considered one of Byzantium's last achievements, it did not have lasting results. This was due to the advance of the Serbs, who, once they had neutralised Bulgaria at the crucial battle of Velbǎžd (1330), soon extended their control over Epirus and Thessaly, the very regions which the Emperors of Constantinople had so long had their eye on. At the time, Andronicus was at least able to profit from his ally the Tsar's debacle by occupying several fortresses on the Byzantine–Bulgarian frontier as well as Mesembria and Anchialos, the Black Sea ports.

Elsewhere Andronicus, obviously influenced by Cantacuzenus, took a decisive step in the southern Aegean and in Asia Minor with regard both to the Ottomans and to the activities of the Genoese and the new western League formed at Avignon (1334). He entered into close collaboration with the small Turkish emirates, who were often as hostile to the Ottomans as they were to the Latins. This policy, which established the Turks' and notably the Ottomans' hold on the internal life of Byzantium, contributed towards building a new fleet and allowed Andronicus III to recapture Chios from the Genoese (1329) and to rally the Genoese of Phocea to him. He also succeeded in repulsing the attack against Lesbos by the Christian League (France, Venice, Rhodes, Cyprus, and the Pope) and they, instead

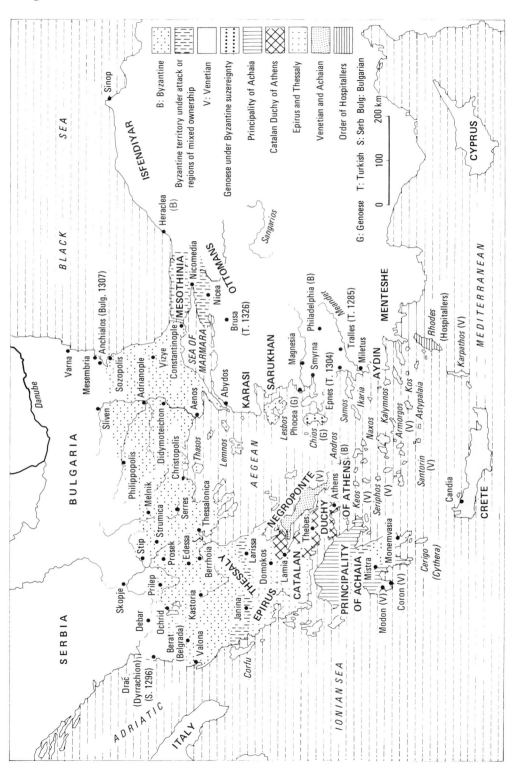

4 The Byzantine Empire in 1328

of fighting the pirates based in the Turkish emirates, turned against an island, whose overlord, the Emperor, was supposed to be a member of the League. Although one of the objectives of his eastern policy had succeeded and had even resulted in an alliance with the Emir Umur of Aydin, drawn up at the Cape of Erythraia (Kara Burun) in 1335, this was not the case with another of his objectives, that of preventing the Ottomans from moving into Bithynia. The first direct confrontation between a Byzantine Emperor and an Ottoman Emir was at Pelekanon when Orkhan defeated the Byzantine army, led by the Emperor in person and by John Cantacuzenus in 1329. Their personal encounter resulted in a treaty by which Byzantium was obliged to pay an annual tribute for what land she still held in Bithynia and which sealed her definitive loss of that part of Asia Minor. This led to the Byzantines' gradual awareness of the futility of their military efforts. In effect, the loss of Bithynian towns such as Nicea, Brusa and Nicomedia (1331–7) put a full stop to Byzantine rule on the coast of Asia Minor and also unleashed Ottoman attacks on the European coast of the Empire and the islands of the northern Aegean. Philadelphia and Heraclea of Pontus withstood winds and tides for some time yet and were the last towns to survive in the midst of the Turkish masses.

In spite of all these set-backs, Andronicus III's legal reform was built into the framework of his State reorganisation and constituted the cornerstone of the Emperor's internal policy. He followed up Andronicus II's attempts at stemming the proverbial corruption of the Byzantine legal system, by creating the institution of the 'Judge Generals of the Romans' in 1329. This was a college with four members, two churchmen and two laymen, who were directly responsible to the Emperor. Their powers were very extensive and their sentences irrevocable. This body was quick to accuse itself of corruption, but it endured until the end of the Empire, undergoing certain alterations. The most important of these was the appearance of local Judge Generals (in Thessalonica, Lemnos and the Morea), following the process of decentralisation. The presence of churchmen at its centre was only one indication of the growing influence of the Church in the law courts, another being the extension of the jurisdiction of the Patriarchal law court, which exercised powers parallel to those of the secular law courts.

Portrait of a dying State

Despite the general climate of decline and possibly even because of it, Byzantine towns grew considerably in importance during the last two centuries of the Empire. One of the effects of the destabilisation of the State was the so-called emancipation of the towns, which happened gradually as decentralisation increased and State control over the communes slackened. The towns certainly continued to function as administrative centres, but it was now a function limited to the town itself and its surroundings, an administrative unit known as a *katepanikion* (which sometimes designated a larger area) whose governor, generally called *kephalon*, was responsible for many duties, for instance that of registering tax payers (*apographe*). The *kephalon* was often not a State representative but a local agent tolerated by the Emperor; in the last period of the Palaeologi, he was even transformed into an autonomous detainer of his administrative territory, in which more and more of his private property was to be found.

One remaining attraction of the towns

As well as Constantinople and Thessalonica, the great towns of the Empire, there were still cities of fairly considerable size on the European side, whose populations grew following the strong influx of refugees from the countryside in the troubled period of the fourteenth century. The towns (some of which were not continuously part of Byzantium) were Philippopolis, Adrianople, Ainos, Heraclea, Selymbria and Mesembria in Thrace; Christopolis, Serres, Kastoria and Berrhoia in Macedonia, Janina and Arta in Epirus, Larissa, Trikkala, Demetrias, Lykostomion and Halmytos in Thessaly; Corinthia, Patras, Monemvasia and Mistra (this last a creation of the thirteenth century which was completely destroyed around the mid fourteenth century) in the Peloponnesus. Most of them were real fortified towns, maintaining strong garrisons in their acropoli as evidence of their military function. The predominant type of town in this period was a fortified entity consisting of an acropolis built on a raised ground (*anopolis*) and a lower town (*katopolis*). Servia in Macedonia is often cited as an example of the type, but her distinctive appearance is in fact due to her particular position and is representative of towns in mountainous hinterlands. There is a whole range of variants on the main type, among which the *kastra*-towns (*palaeokastra*) of the Aegean islands are memorable.

For lack of quantifiable figures, the population of these towns cannot be calculated, but they do seem to have shared in the general decline. This was particularly pronounced in the fourteenth century due to repeated attacks of the plague and in spite of the artificial increase due to the influx of rural populations in war time. We are best informed about Constantinople and Thessalonica; the former counted between 50,000 and 70,000 inhabitants on the eve of the Turkish entry, whereas the population of the latter was reduced, according to one source, to 40,000 and, according to another, to 25,000; and it fell to 7,000 a few years later when she was definitely lost in 1430.

Social differentiation attained precise forms in the cities at this period, as was eloquently demonstrated by the distribution of the social classes among different town quarters. Some districts were also given over to foreign trading colonies, mainly Italian, as well as to ethnic or religious minorities, for instance the Jewish quarters. The existence of quarters for foreign merchants where they conducted their business soon soured relations with the local population, as the great number of protests from nationals of the maritime republics, especially from the Venetians, about acts of violence against them, testify.

The distribution of trades in the towns (in Constantinople and Thessalonica at least) was concentrated in certain distinct districts, for instance the sailors of Thessalonica occupied a district giving onto the port. Most of the trades at Constantinople were gathered in certain parts of the market or even in certain streets of the capital. This phenomenon has recently been analysed; it has been convincingly shown, contrary to what has hitherto been believed, that during the thirteenth and fourteenth centuries Byzantine trades or at least

Aerial view of Mistra and the Eurotas valley. As the capital of the Greek Despotate of Morea (1348–1460), Mistra was a place of refuge for many representatives of Hellenic genuis before their exile in the West. The ruins of the palace and of beautiful Byzantine churches are spread out over the hillside.

some of them were formed into bodies of guilds along Western lines, although they were structured differently from the corporations of the ninth and tenth centuries registered in the Book of Eparchus. On the other hand, the guilds of the later period resembled those of the mid Byzantine period in their very great differentiation. Apart from the ever present notaries (*tabullarioi*) there were the guilds of perfumers (*myrepsoi*), butchers (*makellarioi*), construction workers (*oikodomoi*), saltmakers (*alykarioi*), belt makers, cobblers, tanners, blacksmiths, nail makers, furriers (*gounareis*), and so on. Apart from the lay *tabullarioi* whose principal was nominated by the Emperor, the leaders of the other guild bodies were more like employers directing their employees while exercising the trade themselves at a level higher than that of their subordinates.

One of the characteristic features of Byzantine towns of the thirteenth and fifteenth centuries should be stressed; the presence of great landowners in the towns as city officials. Although their lands might lie close to the towns they preferred to live inside them, where they owned urban properties and participated intensely in the towns' economy. Their political role varied according to their ascendancy within the municipal senate, but their control did not slacken during the fourteenth century in spite of having to come to grips with the relative growth of the urban population's economic role and the greater importance of the *deme* assembly, in which an increasingly large proportion of the population was beginning to participate, including artisans, tradesmen and the lower classes. This trend was reflected in the way the Emperor granted franchises and statutes giving the towns autonomy. The best known are those granted to Thessalonica, Janina and Monemvasia. When this last was reintegrated within the Empire (1259) it is noteworthy that the first Palaeologi did not hesitate, contrary to Villehardouin's previous practice of granting concessions exclusively to the local aristocracy, to enlarge its fiscal privileges to include the middle classes and even the town's shopkeepers and artisans.

The town franchises of this period do appear to have been drawn up in response to actual needs rather than as legal statutes responding to new social forces. Any comparison with the charters granted to the 'free' towns of the West would show the profound differences between them. In different historical circumstances the tardy revival of the Byzantine towns might perhaps have evolved into a real renaissance. But the fatal point at which this revival was halted by the Ottoman conquest revealed merely the result of the decomposition of the central authority and not the fruit of a new social and economic order.

The aristocracy devouring the land

The major characteristic of Byzantine society in the age of the Palaeologi was the decentralisation of the State on the administrative level which ended by abolishing the function of the ancient themes and by replacing them with smaller units, the *katepanikia* mentioned above, known also under vaguer terms such as *topos*, *meros* (named places) *chora* (countryside) *periohe* (region), etc. What was more, after the 1320s, this decentralisation brought about the creation of autonomous or semi autonomous principalities (*appanages*) which were ceded to members of the ruling dynasty or even to

Theodore Comnenus Ducas Synadenos and Irene his wife. He was one of the great landed proprietors of his age, and he and his peers were in many ways counterparts to the great feudatories of the West. (From a manuscript containing the regulations of the monastery of the Virgin of Sure Recourse in Constantinople; Oxford, Bodleian Library.)

other nobles. Thus in 1321, the region of Christopolis–Selymbria passed to Andronicus III while the sons of Andronicus II, Constantine and Demetrius, governed Thessalonica, which fell into John V's hands after 1350. The same town devolved later onto the heir to the throne, Manuel, who added Serres and eastern Macedonia to it after 1371. He governed there in such an independent manner that he even conducted a foreign policy contrary to the Emperor's, as will be seen later. In 1381, the northern coast of the Propontida, along with Selymbria, was ceded to Andronicus IV and his son John VII who bore the title 'Heirs to the Throne'. John VII in particular became master of Thessalonica in 1403 with the title of 'Emperor of all Thessaly' and he lived there until his death in 1408. A little later, Manuel II's three sons, Andronicus, Constantine and Theodore, received Thessalonica, the Black Sea towns Mesembria and Anchialos, and the Despotate of the Morea respectively. This last

211

was by far the most important of these appanages. Before it was made into a Despotate it was governed by the so-called *cephale* of the Morea from 1262 to 1348 when it was given to the Despot Manuel Cantacuzenus to govern. Examples of appanages devolving onto members of the nobility (generally related in some way to the Imperial Family) include the towns of Chrysopolis and Anaktoropolis and the island of Thassos, which was ceded to the brothers Alexios and John Palaeologus, respectively Grand Stratopedarchus and Grand Primate, in full ownership, by Emperor John V (1357).

Incidentally, the term *appanage* is used in a conventional sense to designate Byzantine reality, for the western institution known under this term differed in several ways from what is meant by the same word when used for the Eastern Empire. Apart from the hereditary principle, which did not exist in Byzantium, the very function of the Byzantine *appanages* as expressions of the decentralisation of the State distinguishes them from their equivalents in the West, which contributed towards the concentration of power in the person of the king.

The existence of great domains in Byzantium under the Palaeologi was the dominant feature of this period and formed the basis of the economic, social and political power of the aristocracy, as represented by a few very powerful families who dominated the State mechanism in all its forms, from the civil service to military and sometimes ecclesiastical posts. These families' great landed estates were accumulated from one generation to the next by means of inheritance, marriage, purchase or especially Imperial gifts, and they were distributed over most of the Empire's provinces, beginning with Asia Minor and after the reconquest of Constantinople and the loss of the lands in Asia Minor, in the European part. Their owners were the great magnates of Thessaly, the Melissenoi, the Strategopouloi, the Raoul, the Gabrielopouloi, in Macedonia and in Thrace, the Angeloi, the Tzamblakones, the Synadenoi, the Tornikioi, especially the Cantacuzeni. Some of these families were very old, such as the Tornikioi, who went back to the tenth century, the Asanes, to the eleventh, or the Cantacuzeni, to the twelfth century. Their power was exercised through the State functions which they practically monopolised, as well as through the administration of the provinces, even of provinces where they held landed property. Apart from the Palaeologi, who were particularly strong in Thessalonica, the Cantacuzeni possessed vast domains not only in the Serres region but also in the region of Didymoteichon, which was to become John VI's temporary capital, and the Synadenoi controlled Bizye where they owned great properties. Unlike its counterpart in the West, the Byzantine aristocracy did not have a special legal status, not did it constitute a class with hereditary rights. Membership of the Senate no longer meant what it had in the old times; it did not presuppose heredity and was derived simply from the functions performed by the senators, which were not transferable. It was not impossible, albeit difficult, to gain access to the ranks of the aristocracy, and this could be managed by climbing through the ranks of the army or the civil service, where we do indeed know of several newcomers (Chumnus, Metochites, Sphrantzes).

The monasteries as a whole were the other great proprietor in Byzantium. They had acquired vast concentrations of lands, often comprising whole villages, together with their inhabitants and ground rents, especially the monasteries of Mount Athos, which held huge domains in Macedonia and Lemnos, and also derived revenues from Lake Poru in Thrace. One of the ways the monasteries acquired their estates was through individuals bequeathing them their property, for a variety of reasons and generally on joining one themselves. This could include any number of different things, from a clothes factory to bread ovens, blankets, winding-sheets, cloths, tools and vessels, not to mention pairs of oxen, vineyards and houses. Other sources included all sorts of sales by third persons to the monasteries as well as litigation, generally at the price of a long court case, about lands adjacent to their own. Imperial donations made up by far the most important source, heaping riches on the monasteries and often involving immunity from taxation. Andronicus II's pro-monastic policy has already been mentioned. This policy was not altered during the first years of the *philolatin* Emperor Michael VIII's reign, from which a long series of *chrysobulls* survive, confirming ancient possessions or granting new ones to several monasteries on Mount Athos as well as to the monasteries of Saint John of Patmos, of Makrinitissa and Nea Petra in Thessaly, of Nea Mone on Chios and of Saint Demetrius in Constantinople, and so on.

Between the two extremes of the social scale, the very wealthy aristocrats and the so-called urban proletariat (who were to a greater or lesser extent given over to delinquency), there was the great mass of the population made up of small craftsmen, the workers and the poor peasants. They formed the *deme*, the protagonist of social conflict in the fourteenth century. The *deme* was preceded by another class, which the texts describe as the middle state (*mesotes*) or the middle part (*mese moira*) or again the third group (*trite moira*) whose members were called middle people (*mesoi*). These people and their attitude during the revolts of the fourteenth century will be discussed further on. The urban populations of Constantinople, Thessalonica, Adrianople or Didymoteichon were generally made up of layers of variously wealthy people, principally involved in trade and manufacture and often combining these functions with administrative duties and running landed estates. These people can be considered a middle class or an urban bourgeoisie, which had emerged as a result of contact with westerners.

On the other hand, from the middle of the fourteenth century onwards our sources cease to use the term 'middle', due to the irruption of members of the aristocracy into these trades. These were former landowners who, once the greater part of the cultivated lands of the Byzantine territory (including their own landed estates) had been lost, turned to trade as the only sector in which they could invest their capital profitably. By identifying to some extent with the *mesoi*, the Byzantine aristocrats rendered this term inapplicable. For good reason, because their own family names, illustrious as they were, were amply sufficient. We know a good many of them, names like Notaras, Palaeologus, Angeloi, Argyroi, Cantacuzenus, Lascaris, Synadenoi, Ducai, Radenoi, Asanes, Melissenoi, etc. They formed a class of wealthy and aristocratic burghers who collaborated closely with Italian businessmen. Several of them went so far as to disregard the feelings of the Byzantine and Orthodox majority of the population in demanding and obtaining Genoese or Venetian nationality, or both at once, and in allowing themselves to live in the western manner; but

213

A plough drawn by a pair of oxen, or *zevgarion*: this term was also applied to the area under cultivation and to the most heavily taxed – and wealthiest – peasants (*zevragatoi*). (Ms. grec 2736, *Oppianos*, fifteenth century, Paris, Bibliothèque nationale.)

in the long run they were obliged to resign themselves to playing a very minor role in trade compared to the Italians.

Feudalisation

Although predominantly rural, the Byzantine economy was based on the use of money, even in the countryside itself, if only due to the pressure of taxation. As it was, the fraction of taxes and dues which had to be rendered in coin could only be obtained from the producer's contact with the market. This monetarisation did not appear to affect the essential character of the mainly subsistent rural economy. The economy was based on the family unit and did not change when these units were absorbed into great landed properties, whose expansion was one of the features of this period. The nuclear family was both the unit of production and the unit of taxation and was based on the indivisibility of property between brothers. These units of production were classed according to their productivity. Given the existence of many factors determining the reality of peasant incomes in the fourteenth century, the system of taxation employed, which assessed productivity mainly according to the number of plough oxen per unit, seems to show that the land as a unit of production no longer belonged to the primary producer. Nonetheless, the peasantry was beginning to grow complementary crops on their own plots, notably vines, which became one of their main sources of monetary income. This did not mean that the peasants did not dispose of plots of land for growing cereals, but these generally lay within the great landed estates belonging to private individuals, pious endowments or the Crown.

Their surplus was appropriated in two ways, by raising taxes and by collecting ground rents. The second method of appropriation of the surplus already presupposes the existence of a landowner other than the peasant farmer; it consisted of a proportional rent in kind or of a fixed sum of money. The two methods of appropriation overlapped, since taxes were levied from cultivators who also paid ground rents for working someone else's land. The ground rent generally corresponded to a tenth of their cereal crop and a third of their wine production, although some contracts between landowners and peasants specifically applied this proportion to cereal production as well. The second method of appropriation seems to have been extended notoriously during the era of the Palaeologi. It was enforced more strictly not only in private properties, where it was the norm, but also in *pronoia* lands. In the Latin possessions it also formed part of the revenues from the fiefs and was eventually applied throughout the baronial system, notably in Corfu.

The formation of great landed estates was to a great extent attributable to the changes introduced to the system by which *pronoia* lands were alloted. *Pronoia* lands were tax-paying estates which the State granted to beneficiaries in return for military service. Once the estate had been granted, it could also be made to pay ground rent, like the Crown properties, which was levied by the proprietor under the form of *morte*, a proportion of the peasants' produce. These grants were considerably extended under the Palaeologi, who also made them hereditary. The Latin conquest had the same effect by creating fiefs, which from the economic point of view, succeeded in perpetuating the methods of appropriation of surplus produce which were applied in Byzantium. In the Latin possessions in the Morea, particular attention seems to have been paid to improving the seigneurial reserve, which meant intensifying labour services (distinguished sometimes as services rendered by individuals or by their plough oxen) which were not a significant part of the Byzantine system.

The pious foundations were just as successful in forming great landed estates, due to the deliberate policy of the State, which handed over a considerable number of properties and rents to them by means of repeated grants. Individuals participated actively in this process and monasteries were sometimes founded by members of the provincial nobility. People of middle standing and the poor also contributed, making donations to the monasteries and also selling them their property. Within the great landed estates, whether monastic or lay, the contribution of the peasant cultivator lay not only in farming such land as was already viable, but also in enlarging the property by emphyteusis. This also resulted in the creation of small and middle-sized peasant properties, as the example of Corfu clearly demonstrates. According to fifteenth-century Corfiote accounts, vineyards and olive groves were planted within the framework of the feudal estates by peasant cultivators, who by these means also became co-proprietors. On the other hand, the growing disproportion between farmland and manpower led, at least in the Latin estates, to significant changes. In Latin Morea, the population was so reduced by desertions and the Plague that the feudal lords were obliged to grant uninhabited feudal lands against purely nominal rents, a situation which was perpetuated over a long period in Corfu, where feudal lands and other estates owing merely minimal rents were to be found.

The exhausted peasantry

The mass of the Byzantine peasantry continued to be classified by distinguishing between those who owned a pair of plough oxen or a team of several oxen and those with only one, or none (*zeugaratoi, boidatoi, aktemones*). This type of classification was also applied in the Latin possessions where, however, certain taxes, which had previously been assessed according to the different peasant classes, were now applied uniformly and labour services were generally commuted into cash.

Farming did not just concern the rural communities; towns too were well supplied with farms belonging to the citizens, both within the urban area and around villages. Occasional records of practices aimed at safeguarding this rural patrimony and the socio-economic balance have come down to us: the inhabitants of Janina, for instance, owned lands in many villages and in 1319 they reaffirmed the practice by which these lands could not be sold to local *archons* and soldiers (*pronoiars*), land transfers being allowed only between citizens. However, the presence of landed proprietors living in the towns does not imply that they were more than just rentiers. Although this was not a new phenomenon, it does seem to have been linked to the disintegration of the rural community. In effect, the penetration of powerful men within the community disrupted the stabilising function of communal solidarity as regulated by the 'preferential' law (*protimesis*) which the new elements could now use to their own advantage. On the other hand, the practice of granting whole villages to particular *pronoiars* and monasteries had the same effect and weakened links between the State and the rural community. Nonetheless, the concentration of pockets of habitation around the land of a single tenant (*metochion, zeugelateion*), who was dependent on a pious foundation or a particular person, is an indication of the extent to which the community had disintegrated and of the changes in the methods by which the area of cultivation was enlarged. These pockets of habitation were no longer offshoots of a dynamic community (a dynamism which was well illustrated by the Fiscal Treatise of the tenth century) but were now brought about by external forces.

These many changes did not involve the attrition of the rural community as an institution, which continued to survive in the midst of the new realities and perpetuated its ill-defined function within the new feudal entities implanted by the Latin conquest as well as in the heart of *pronoia* lands. The Ottomans were to find solid foundations there on which to build their administration.

During this period, when the rural populations were subjected to a feudalising process, they relied on a strong family structure as the basis of production. As it was, from the end of the thirteenth to the middle of the fourteenth century, peasant populations fell sharply as a result of a combination of factors. Invasions, wars, and the Plague all harmed rural populations and led to a shortage of manpower in the country. It is also clear that the population crisis had internal causes, as illustrated by the reduction in the average size of families and in the declining birth rate. We have some quantitative figures for a number of villages in Macedonia which reveal that between 1300 and 1314, the size of the average family fell from 4.7 to 3.7 members. From the economic point of view, this decline was to a certain extent due to population mobility, as indicated by the difference between the average sizes of well-off families and poor families. Families owning draught oxen shrank in size from 5.86 to 4.33 members between 1310 and 1341, while those owning none shrank from 3.80 to 2.65 members.

Religious art was also able to depict certain aspects of real life, such as these tax assessors. A detail from a fourteenth-century mosaic inspired by the life of the Virgin. (Constantinople, Kharije-Jami.)

Among the factors affecting population growth, monasticism should be mentioned; the practice of celibacy seems to have had a considerable impact on Byzantine society in the period. However, monasteries certainly had a positive effect where organising agricultural production and improving the land were concerned, by attracting the rural work-force to settle on their vast landed estates.

Empty coffers

The monetary and economic crisis was the result of a disproportion between the State's fiscal resources and its need for cash. This cash shortage was connected to the political crisis as well as to changes introduced to the economic and social structure of the Empire. It was clear, both within the rural sector and the commercial sector, that the State's fiscal resources had been exhausted and that this was aggravated by the loss of income from its mines and the annihilation of its metal reserves – another corollary of the Latin conquest.

The political crisis forced the State to release great sums of money for the military needs of the Empire as well as for paying tributes to the Ottomans. These expenses led the State into external debt and forced it to grant much of its revenue from taxation, notably from its customs, to its creditors. The ensuing shortage of ready money was met by depreciating the

217

Two gold hyperpyrs: one of Michael VIII (1259–82) of 15 carats and the other (right) of the reign of the two Andronici (1325–8) of 11 or 12 carats. (Paris, Bibliothèque nationale, Cabinet des médailles.)

national currency and, starting with the reign of Manuel II Paleologus, by striking an exclusively silver coinage, which also rose in value in relation to the national gold currency. The *hyperpyra*'s gold title had fallen from 20.75 to 20.25 carats between 1081 and 1143, and was reduced to 11.25 under John VI (1347–54). This depreciation was accompanied by the emission of depreciated coins of different alloys, which led to a clear differentiation between current money and the preferred (old or Venetian) coins. In the long run, this resulted in the subordination of the national currency to stronger foreign currencies, the former being used to pay wages. Worse still, the State came to demand its taxes in foreign coin.

We not not have quantitative figures allowing the whole extent of the external debt to be established. Such information as has been handed down does allow us to realise that it was not the size of the debt that hamstrung the Empire, but the drying up of its income from taxation. We know for instance that in 1343 and 1352 the debt was in the order of respectively 35,000 and 5,000 gold ducats and that the annual tribute paid the Turks came to 10,000 *hyperpyra*. If these sums are compared with the gross income of a cereal growing unit in Byzantium, based on the price of wheat in the market at Constantinople, an approximate but significant result is achieved.

The average production of a Byzantine cereal unit would be about 300 *modioi*. At 5 *hyperpyra* the *modios*, a sum of 40,000 gold ducats would correspond to the gross produce of some 53 farms, or to the ground rent paid by 530 family units, which would represent a population of about 2,200 persons. A tribute of 10,000 *hyperpyra* thus corresponded to the gross produce (calculated on the Constantinople market of the middle of the fourteenth century) of almost seven family farm units. Around the same time a ship's cargo would be worth around 40,000 *hyperpyra*. Even taking into account the strong differential between local prices and those of the market in Constantinople, the sums mentioned above cannot be considered catastrophic. What made them so was the disintegration of the rural economy. These sums should be appreciated in terms of income from taxation. For instance, the 10,000 *hyperpyra* tribute was equivalent to the income the Byzantine customs secured in Constantinople (12,000 *hyperpyra* in 1328 and 10,000 in 1355) as against the 200,000 *hyperpyra* which the Genoese got from their customs at Pera, according to Gregoras, and which contrasted with the highest prices obtained in Genoa when the farm of their customs was put up for sale. The Byzantine historian may have exaggerated the difference, but it does reveal the great gulf between the nominal price and the real income of the Pera customs controlled by the Genoese. However, even in the case of the Genoese tax returns at Pera, which anyway began to fall off in the 1360s, they never brought in enough to meet the entrepot's need for cash.

The economic crisis was of course an off-shoot of the political crisis; as the cultivated area shrank, tax returns necessarily dwindled. The loss of territories in Thrace increased the capital's dependence on grain imports, which gave the Italian cities a still greater edge over the Byzantine economy. The population crisis also seems to have contributed to the decline. The harm done by these disadvantages was not repaired by the various expedients which were resorted to in an attempt to deal with the financial crisis. Emperor John VI Cantacuzenus took some measures, which were aimed on the one hand at encouraging commerce, and on the other at increasing his income from taxation, which he was just as keen on boosting in the agricultural sector. That these measures were also meant to encourage commerce appears to be the most likely interpretation of the Emperor's decision to replace the 10 per cent purchase tax with one of 2 per cent. This measure was accompanied by another which struck at foreigners importing grains; they were charged half a gold coin on every *modios* of wheat, which represented a duty of between 10 and 17.5 per cent of the value of the commodity, depending on whether it was calculated according to normal market prices in the capital or those in the local markets of Romania.

John VI also taxed the production and sale of wine by levying a *hyperpyra* on every fifty measures of wine. By comparing the normal price of wine in local markets with the market price at Constantinople it appears that this tax represented only 4 per cent of the latter price. Those who bought wine directly from the producers had to pay twice this tax, since buyers were qualified as 'richer than farmers' by the Emperor and as people who realised great profits. They exploited 'effortlessly the labour of others' that is, of the peasant-farmers. These people were middlemen, merchants who purchased directly from the producers and were liable to pay purchase tax on the spot. This fiscal measure, together with other measures in favour of the Navy led, according to the Emperor, to the revival of Byzantine maritime trade and increased the traffic in the port of Constantinople. The State tried to profit from the commercialisation of agricultural produce, notably of wine, a major ingredient of urban consumption, and from the difference between local prices and the prices demanded in the market of the capital. A differential which allowed the Emperor to apply purchase tax inequitably, since the purchaser could, in his turn, benefit from the reduced customs dues.

Foreigners as masters

There is no doubt that the manufacturing crafts were still being practised although they were dying out in centres like Thebes and Patras. The same applied to trade and transport. They were, however, all orientated only towards the internal market; the movement of commerce was concentrated along the eastern fringe of the Mediterranean and part of the Black Sea. Long-distance trade had come under the control of the Italian towns, Venice, Genoa, Pisa; with a few ports of the French Midi, Catalonia and Dalmatia in second place. What was more, Venice and Genoa dictated the capital's commercial strategy. The impact of the West on what was left of the Byzantine Empire's economy was also felt in the internal market, on one hand through the import of manufactures and on the other by the capital's dependence on imported foods following the loss of the cereal growing region of Thrace, which had fallen under Ottoman control by the end of the fourteenth century. The economic crisis, which had put an end to minting gold coins and led to the depreciation of the national currency, led them into monetary and even economic dependence. This dependence was just as much the result of their military impotence as of the political crisis, and may be attributed to an inability to adapt the economy to the new territorial realities: a situation which applied as much to the declining Byzantine Empire as to the Latin settlements in the East.

The capital was not the only consumer of wheat imported by Western merchants; the West also imported this commodity to meet its own requirements, which were of course mostly covered by its own wheat; in Genoa's case mainly from Spain. Nonetheless, there was a western demand for wheat from their colonies as well as from regions outside Italian control. This trade could have disastrous consequences for the city's provisions, either because it would cause terrible food shortages, or because it affected prices and consequently the general stability of urban society. This meant that a threshold had to be established below which grain could not be exported and so would not have a harmful effect on the internal market's supplies. The Veneto-Byzantine treaties of 1265 and 1285 stipulated that wheat was to be exported only when its price did not exceed 50 to 100 *nomismata* respectively per 100 *modioi*. The first sum may refer to bumper harvest prices and the second to high or normal prices (because the difference between them is not accounted for by monetary depreciation between the two dates), but the important thing about these agreements was that the civil authority was trying to ensure that the internal market was provided with grain at a price the consumer could afford. In effect, the 1285 price was practically the same as the 1343 price; taking the silver to gold ratio (1:7.45) into account, the 1285 price would correspond to 616 mg of gold as against 639 mg for the 1343 price, while the 1265 price would be the equivalent of 323.6 mg of gold. According to the few prices known to us for the fourteenth century, we can conclude that they doubled during the second half of the century in Crete. There were several abrupt price rises reported in Constantinople during the second decade; sudden price rises also appeared in provisioning markets such as Caffa, a Genoese colony. All this was reflected on the markets of Constantinople and Pera (the price of wheat in 1401 was four times that of 1390 in Pera, and fell in the following year at Constantinople to 37.5 per cent of the 1401 price, which was only 50 per cent more than the 1343 price: equivalent in gold terms to only the maximum price of 1285). Nonetheless, the Byzantine State, since it no longer controlled its sources of provisioning after the 1370s, was not able to exercise the self-sufficient policy it had tried to implement by means of treaties. Further, the abrupt price rises for essential commodities had a far harsher impact on consumers than is apparent from converting prices into gold. This led to complaints about speculators and lamentations about the continuous fall in the purchasing power of the national currency.

Within the framework of the Byzantine economy, merchant and financial capital was becoming just as dependent; merchants were orientated not only towards the internal market, but they also became middlemen supplying western merchants who controlled the long-distance trade. This restriction of the range of trade and its national agents resulted in the creation of a few pockets of commercial activity, linked either to the maritime traffic serving the internal market or working the international routes. The typology of the thirteenth- and fourteenth century towns corresponded in part to these imperatives, while the political realities accentuated their regional particularities as well as their specific economic functions, by means of a preferential policy which was expressed by conceding privileges.

In this sense, a town like Monemvasia could obtain franchises which encouraged her to exercise her specific function (which was sea-faring trade within the Empire) and to establish contact, under a privileged statute, with distant markets. Under the same title, Janina could secure immunity from paying customs duties even in Constantinople, which allowed her merchants to trade over a vast area. The town's privileged status included not only a number of exemptions concerning the rural economy and commercial traffic, but also a special clause protecting the town from all alterations to its currency. This was partly an attempt by the commune at protecting itself against the disorders following the repeated issues of depreciated monies, and partly the result of economic regionalism leading to a kind of autonomy guaranteed by the central civil authority. This economic regionalism (or simply the existence of centres ensuring contact between the hinterland and the main flow of trade) could also be attributed to the strategy dictated by the buying power of the European merchants there, who, as we have seen, exported a proportion of local produce using local agents. In a larger context, however, these merchants also established their own bases; the Venetian and Genoese colonies.

Latin colonisation in the East was a legacy of the crusades and, once it had lost its vital links, it did not prove cost-effective. This was due as much to its expense as to the destruction that had been inflicted on the conquered land. Venetian colonisation escaped this pattern to a great extent, being a source of prosperity for the *Dominante*, and so generating a certain degree of prosperity in the regions where it had taken root. Still, rigorously attached to the principles of the *Dominante* as she was, Venice simply annexed the economies of her eastern colonies to her own interests, while attempting to establish them as self-sufficient, particularly on the agricultural level, so that they could produce surpluses. Venice's encouragement of agriculture was simply an attempt at rationalisation; whole plains were dedicated to agriculture and controlled by a system of fortresses; the distribution of water was supervised, and woods and vineyards were planted; rural populations were also increased by importing slave workforces (e.g. Crete). The lack of cereal-crops in some territories was compensated for by the direct links they provided with regions beyond the orbit of the colonies; Canea and Modon and Coron, Candia with Salonica and Negropontus, Negropontus and Crete with the islands of the Duchy of the Archipelago and, for their extra-colonial links, Crete with the coast of Asia Minor and Alexandria. There were also links, over and above their common and complementary interests (the Contarini family), between Crete and Cyprus, between Corfu and Epirus. As for the *Dominante*, her need for grain forced her to follow up her links with the regions of Thrace and Central Russia; Syria and Alexandria were the sources of spices, sugar and silk.

This traffic was made possible by the Venetian ships; the produce of their colonies and that of other regions travelled straight to Venice or it might be stored in one of her colonies, to remain there or to start out again towards other markets. The only wares to escape this pattern were those whose movement was determined by inter-colonial requirements. For instance, the colonies contributed little wheat and the bulk of the *Dominante*'s provisions came from the cereal-growing regions of Thrace and Central Russia. Cyprus was a tributary of Crete, and its traffic with Venice was based on imports from Asia (which were carried there by Armenian and Syrian merchants) and on the produce of its saltworks. Genoa's seizure of Cyprus (1373–4) benefited traffic between Crete, Syria and Egypt. The Negropontus and Salonica absorbed part of their agricultural and manufacturing produce from their respective hinterlands and from neighbouring regions (central Greece and the Peloponnesus for the Negropontus, which produced increasing quantities of seasoned timber). These products were exported to Venice in exchange for cloth, which was stored in the Negropontus. The Peloponnesus also received considerable quantities of cloth and metal in exchange for its cereals, oil, honey, silk and raisins.

As opposed to Venetian colonisation, which was based on huge territories and required permanent supervision to organise the economy and the population of these rural expanses, Genoese colonisation was dispersed and depended on an uncontrolled hinterland. They relied either on securing a steady supply of produce from its sources of origin or on exploiting one product (for instance mastic or alum), but this did not mean that Genoa's economic hold over the Levant was less strong than Venice's.

One permanent feature of the Levant was the slow circulation of money within it, which also affected Genoese commercial operations: this was remedied by the practice of drawing up contracts in which funds which had not been repaid were re-invested. Prices were not always competitive and sometimes the purchase of wheat at Caffa was profitable only during the slack season, while other commodities were guaranteed only middling profits. On the other hand, the same products (for instance alum) commanded advantageous prices elsewhere: wax, for instance, secured considerable profits and furs too were very good investments; in other cases the trade was set up on a permanent and lucrative basis, as for instance with mastic. Genoese traders were experts in handling heavy merchandise and they were equally specialised in the slave trade, exchanging agricultural produce for exports of wax, furs and skins, alum and non-ferrous metals, slaves, cloths and canvas, metallic objects, silver (both in bars and worked) as well as foodstuffs: the wines of Italy and Provence went to Pera and Caffa as did the wines of Romania; Italian and Andalusian oil went to Chios and Pera. The profits oscillated between 10 and 30 per cent; furs, mastic and wine could command more than twice their purchase price. The gold to silver ratio favoured the westerners, and the predominance of their currencies as well as their freightage and service charges tipped the balance of payments in favour of Genoese commerce.

The Byzantine economy could not escape the impasse it had been relegated to and, in spite of the measures taken by the public authorities, it was unable to resist the maritime and even the economic supremacy of the Italian cities. Attempts were made to revive the old system of small military estates in the Empire of Nicea; to create a self-sufficient

Venetian merchant ships, the Republic's driving force. A detail from Vittore Carpaccio's *Legend of Saint Ursula*, executed in 1490–6 for the Scuola di Sant'Orsola in Venice. (Venice, Accademia Art Gallery.)

economy and to encourage urban economies by conceding privileges; other attempts were directed towards reducing Latin activity in the heart of the capital, including John Cantacuzenus's efforts at improving the fleet; none of these had lasting results.

It is extremely significant that the philosophical thought of the period, that of Plethon or Bessarion, proposed radical solutions. Inspired partly by the Platonic model, they were also aware of Byzantine reality and of the mechanics of the agricultural economy, and they adopted a utopia which laid emphasis on restructuring the agricultural economy, but only managed to perpetuate the traditional repartition of the surplus by means of taxation (paid to the public sector) and ground rents (paid to the private sector). The first utopias were discredited as much by their underlying assumptions as by their retrospective character. The same retrospection applied to other forms of social criticism, for instance in the polemic against usury. Nonetheless, this radicalised thought did have its counterpart in the West and it did speak of technological transformations and modernisation, while focussing on the fundamental problem of the agricultural economy.

The humiliation of Byzantium

The first half of the fourteenth century ended with the accession of Andronicus II. The age of renewal which had been achieved under Michael VIII, when Byzantium had once more become a power with an important role to play in the history of Europe, was now definitely over. The period succeeding it had been latent in the previous one and saw the Byzantine State transformed into a second-rate State, singularly limited territorially and deprived of any international influence, in spite of the occasional diplomatic approaches, which had already been initiated, towards the Turks and in spite of their renewed dealings with the West, directed towards the Union of the Churches and an alliance against the Ottomans.

Internally, social antagonisms were growing stronger, the more so given the State's inability to safeguard its territories and their inhabitants' possessions. The feudalising process finally burst the last bounds of a centralised State, thus concentrating economic power and, in the long run, political power in the hands of the great military and landed nobility and certain ecclesiastical institutions such as the great monasteries.

Who profited from the second civil war?

The second civil war broke out in 1341, after the death of Andronicus II, between the Palace Chamberlain John Cantacuzenus and the party of the Emperor's mother, Anna of Savoy, and proved to be the high point of the crisis of fourteenth-century Byzantium. It was a significant war in many complex ways since the social problems and the ecclesiastical schisms were grafted onto dynastic struggles, thus dividing the people and splitting the State. The war was long and had a disastrous effect on the economy because it reduced State revenues to their lowest level yet and destroyed the country's productivity. On the political and military level, it allowed the Serbs and Turks to intervene and once these people had arrived in Macedonia and Thrace, they never left. Serbian and Ottoman settlement in these regions (the former was at least ephemeral, the latter permanent) was consolidated, as it was in Epirus and Thessaly, and is considered one of the most important results of this war. For all this, the social aspects of this conflict dominated all the others; this was most forcibly expressed by the truly dramatic episode of the Zealot revolution in Thessalonica, where the class struggle, which also shook the other towns of Macedonia and Thrace, was revealed in all its breadth.

The first and most important phase of the war, starting with Cantacuzenus's entry into Constantinople in February 1347, may be divided into three periods (1341–2, 1342–5 and 1345–7) so that its many complicated factors may be relatively clarified and understood.

John Cantacuzenus was by far the most dominant Byzantine personality of this war, if not of the whole fourteenth century. He belonged to a great family of the Byzantine nobility whose members had held military and political office since the twelfth century. He himself was the greatest and richest aristocrat of his age; he owned an immense fortune calculated in thousands of heads of cattle and made up of great domains concentrated especially in the regions of Serres and Didymoteichon as well as in Thessaly and Constantinople. A first-class statesman and diplomat, he was also a man of letters whose historical writings, in spite of their bias, rank, alongside his theological works, among the essential sources of fourteenth-century history and literature. His opponents included Patriarch John Kalekas and Alexis Apokaukos, who were defending not so much the interests of Anna of Savoy and her son, John V Palaeologus, as their own. Apokaukos, unlike Cantacuzenus, was sprung from a poor and obscure family; in some ways he represented the middle classes, newly enriched in the service of the State. Cantacuzenus, who was Regent in all but name at Andronicus II's death, clashed with the Patriarch's and Apokaukos' personal ambitions. These two took advantage of the Palace Chamberlain's absence in Thrace to proclaim an official regency with John Kalekas at its head and to pronounce Cantacuzenus an enemy of the nation. Apokaukos, promoted Grand Duke (Admiral of the Fleet), went so far as to destroy Cantacuzenus's personal property in Constantinople, inciting the *deme*, over whom he seems to have exercised a certain influence, to rise against the Grand Domestic. Cantacuzenus then got himself proclaimed Emperor at Didymoteichon by a party of nobles, who had fled Constantinople, and by the representatives of the great landowners of Thrace, whom he leant on in order to build up another army with which to confront the capital. The protagonists of this drama did not appreciate the forces they had unwittingly unleashed by this series of hostile actions, until they were no longer able to control them.

From the beginning of the crisis, the opposing forces were dragged into a religious and spiritual crisis brought about by the Hesychast dispute. It could not in fact have been otherwise because politics in Byzantium were closely linked to theology and it is well known that the Byzantines were above all religious animals. The mystical tendencies partly inherent in Byzantine society were accentuated and developed in the fourteenth century, particularly among the monks of Mount Athos. The Hesychasts (or Quietists) strove for the vision of Divine Light, which the disciples had contemplated on Mount Tabor, and to achieve this they employed strange methods of prayer, which somehow required the participation of the human body. Both the methods and the basis of this doctrine were

225

The triumph of Hesychasm and its definitive insertion into Orthodox belief. John VI Cantacuzenus presides over the Synod of Blachernae (1351) surrounded by the new Patriarch Isidore of Monemvasia and members of the Synod and his guard. (*The Theological Works of John Cantacuzenus* 1371–5; Paris, Bibliothèque nationale.)

strongly opposed by Barlaam, a lucid and rational Greek monk from Calabria, who found a redoubtable adversary in the person of the great theologian and fervent Hesychast, Gregory Palamas. Under his influence, Barlaam was condemned by the synod of 1341, but the controversy did not stop there. It was chiefly concerned with the question of the eternal visibility or otherwise of the light on Mount Tabor: impossible, according to Barlaam, who insisted on separating the eternal from the temporal world, whereas Palamas advocated the distinction between Divine Essence and Divine Energies such as Love and the Light of Tabor, which act as intermediaries between God and man. The Hesychast system thus became the means of expressing that very old nostalgia of Greek religiosity, for a bridge connecting the Beyond with the here and now.

Cantacuzenus's social origins as much as his personal leanings made him as great a friend of monks and Hesychasts as the Empress's western origins made her hostile to them, as was

Alexis Apokaukos, Cantacuzenus's adversary during the second civil war, belonged to the new rising class of top civil servants. The Grand Duke is shown here holding a manuscript specially executed for him. (*The works of Hippocrates, c.* 1345; Paris, Bibliothèque nationale.)

Patriarch Kalekas for other reasons. It would be too simple to identify the partisans of Cantacuzenus with the partisans of Hesychasm, but they were indeed sympathetic to one another. The proof is that Cantacuzenus's victory over his adversaries in 1347 led to the consecration of the Hesychast dogma, the deposition of Kalekas and his replacement by a Hesychast monk Isidore, while Palamas was promoted Archbishop of Thessalonica. Nonetheless the opposition to the Hesychasts was not disarmed and the quarrel raged on with the historian and theologian Nicephorus Gregoras at the head of the anti-Palamist party. It was only in 1351 at the Synod of Blachernae convoked by Cantacuzenus, that the adversaries of Hesychasm were definitely condemned, at the same time as the Palamist theories were recognised as conforming completely to the Orthodoxy and the Tradition of the Church Fathers. Gregory Palamas was canonised shortly after his death (1357/8): the opposition gradually faded out and around the end of the century, Hesychasm had been incorporated fully into the teaching of the Orthodox Church.

A new social dimension

Although the religious dissentions served to aggravate political divisions, the acute social struggles which gave rise to the civil war were revealed from the start by the way the aristocrats rallied to Cantacuzenus. Apokaukos's response in confiscating their property in Constantinople showed that the Grand Duke was capable of exploiting the hostile feelings of the *deme* against his opponent and his party. The *deme* was made up of the elements of a sort of middle class, of shopkeepers and sailors, the first of which seems to have played a more important part when Adrianople's *deme* rose up against the *dynatoi* ('powerful') of the city, although only one of the three leaders of the revolt, Phrangopoulos, is known to have belonged to the trading world. This may explain why the revolt and the resistance against Cantacuzenus were better organised, Adrianople being one of the last towns in Thrace to surrender. A further explanation may be sought in the attitude of the city garrison, part of which at least went over to the insurgents, as also seems to have been the case in Bizye and Thessalonica, cites which resisted just as long if not longer. Whatever the case, the revolt in Adrianople spread like wild fire and was taken up rapidly in almost every town in Thrace, except Didymoteichon, Cantacuzenus's capital, and thence to Macedonia, ensuring for a while that the legal dynasty of the Palaeologi was in the ascendancy, as the insurgents demanded. During this phase of the war, the towns' importance increased as refugees flocked to them, fleeing before the enemy troops and from the pillaged countryside and thus adding excessive crowding to the economic and social problems already present in them. From then on, both camps concentrated their efforts on the towns and on gaining possession of them.

1342 was a critical year for Cantacuzenus, whose power, which was that of the aristocracy, was everywhere, from Constantinople to Thessalonica, in decline. It was in Thessalonica, the most flourishing city of the Empire after the capital, but also the one in which social inequities were at their most provoking, that a popular rising known as the Zealot Revolution grew most strongly. Unlike the other towns, where anti-aristocratic risings occurred fairly spontaneously, Thessalonica had in the Zealots a well organised political party, which prepared the revolt carefully. The proof of this is that, after they had evicted their governor Theodore Synadenos, who had joined Cantacuzenus's party, they succeeded in taking over power and in imposing their own rule and, what was more, in keeping it until 1350. Although they recognised the legitimate Palaeologus dynasty, whose representative shared the government of the town with the leader of the Zealots, during all that time the Thessalonians were completely independent and autonomous. In the same year (1342) Apokaukos came to the city's aid with a fleet he had assembled with the proceeds of Cantacuzenus's confiscated wealth. The opposing forces varied in this respect; Apokaukos depended on his fleet and on the sailor and merchant elements in the coastal towns, later adding new property confiscations and new taxes to this foundation. When Cantacuzenus wrote his History, he attributed him with the intention of creating a 'tyranny' based on islands and coastal towns. As for Cantacuzenus himself, he had from the beginning built up his army from the military bases established in the hinterland of Thrace and Macedonia.

Thessalonica, part of the defences of the acropolis dominating the town. These ramparts had been constantly reinforced since the fourth century, especially under the Palaeologi, and they reveal much about the Byzantine town's relations with the outside world and about the internal organisation of the city.

The gravity of the situation forced Cantacuzenus to undertake the journey to Serbia to appeal to Dušan for help. From that moment in particular, the Serbs began to get involved in the civil war and, far from bringing the support Cantacuzenus had counted on, they smoothed the way for Dušan and the Serbian aristocracy's plans for conquest. However, Cantacuzenus's particular interests were served towards the end of 1342, when the strongly feudalised land of Thessaly rallied to his camp. The new governor nominated by Cantacuzenus soon succeeded in controlling Epirus, Acarnania and Aetolia. This sequence of events gave the war the appearance of a conflict between the ancient provinces of western and central Greece, which were at the heart of Cantacuzenus's plans for reconstructing a centralised state stretching unbroken from Byzantium to the Peloponnesus.

229

Although the situation had turned in Cantacuzenus's favour, it suffered a setback when Dušan grew suspicious of the over-powerful Cantacuzenus and changed sides, joining the Regent in Constantinople. This was the moment for the second foreign power, Cantacuzenus's old ally, Umur, to appear in Thrace and Macedonia and supply some sort of military solution to the conflict. From then on the war was conducted principally between the respective allies of the two Byzantine parties, the Serbs and the Turks, who were both chiefly interested in winning towns. There was however an essential difference between Dušan (and later Ivan Alexander, who was also allied to the Regency) and Umur; whereas the former aimed at winning territorial prizes on their own account, Umur (as opposed to the Ottoman Orkhan whose intentions may well have differed), in spite of all the loot collected by his troops and the revenues he drew from taxing certain towns, did not appear to have planned a permanent settlement on European soil.

The decisive phase of the war, which presaged its end, began in 1355 at Constantinople with the assassination of Apokaukos by his political opponents. A few months later a major event occurred; the capture of Serres by Dušan, which paved the way for his conquest of the rest of Macedonia, with the exception of Thessalonica still held by the Zealots. In Thrace after Umur's unexpected departure, Cantacuzenus concluded an alliance with the Ottoman Sultan Orkhan by giving him his daughter Theodora in marriage, enabling him to subdue the country by directing his new allies against it. They devastated the countryside and pillaged the farms, which were subsequently totally abandoned because of the shortage of labour, thus forcing the towns to surrender in order to avoid being starved out. The Empire had already lost the northern part of Thrace around Philippopolis, which passed into the hands of the Bulgarian Tsar Ivan Alexander in exchange for helping the Regency – assistance which, as it turned out, he did not supply. In Constantinople, the Regency's other Bulgarian ally was the Voivode Momčil, who had announced his autonomous rule over the region of Rhodopes and had already been crushed under the walls of Peritheorion by Umur. This time the balance was tipped in Cantacuzenus's favour and he was able to enter Constantinople in February 1347, where he was proclaimed Emperor, while respecting John V's rights to the throne. Cantacuzenus treated him as a 'special son' and married him to his daughter Helen. The civil war might have been considered over, but this was not the case.

The Zealot revolution

Thessalonica, with her revolution and her Zealots, was still there. Given that the term 'Zealot' has assumed more than one meaning during the course of Byzantine history, a few explanations are in order. The word in its literal Greek sense means one who holds faithfully to orthodox dogma and belief; whence it means the conservative spirit in society as opposed to the one known as 'political' and was considered to combine moderation with a progressive and open attitude, further inspired by the love of literature. The Zealots themselves, however, ended by splitting into two parties, the religious Zealots, fervent partisans of Hesychasm and consequently of John Cantacuzenus, and the political Zealots who were opposed to the Hesychasts and were classified by the Church as the disciples of

Barlaam. It was this group which set itself up as the leaders of Thessalonica, whose population was truly multi-racial, although the great majority were Greeks.

The city enjoyed a particular form of urban autonomy which went back to the Roman period and was known as 'political law' (*politikos nomos*), translated in Serbian documents by the term *gradski zakon*. The town's status as a commune allowed her to elect her own magistrates who were authorised to promulgate laws concerning the city and local property, agriculture, commerce and the manufacturing trades as well as local customs. This presupposed the existence of a senate (*gerousia, synkletos* or *boule*), which, it is true, was dominated by noble and wealthy citizens, and an assembly of the people called *ekklesia tou demou* (a term derived from Antiquity), which was convoked by civil or even Church authorities or by party leaders or demagogues. The town was governed by two archons, one representing the Emperor and the other the commune. These were the real privileges of a free town, which flourished particularly in the fourteenth century with the relaxation of centralist rule, and which were confirmed by each of city's supreme rulers when they changed over. This was the case when the city was captured by the Latins, as it was after the Fourth Crusade when it was conquered by John Vatatzes in 1246, or when it passed into Venetian hands in 1423. But these privileges did not count for much in the eyes of the Zealots when the Revolution took place.

The assassination of Alexis Apokaukos in Constantinople in 1345 precipitated the bloody phase of events at Thessalonica. The co-governor John Apokaukos, Alexis's son, whose power, compared with that of the second archon and leader of the Zealots, Michael Palaeologus, was only illusory, had him assassinated and decided to hand the city over to Cantacuzenus. This was when the Zealots, in collaboration with the sailors' guild, counter-attacked with Andrew Palaeologus at their head and with all the townspeople behind them and forced John Apokaukos, along with 100 of his wealthy followers to lock themselves up in the acropolis. When the Zealots and the people stormed it, the co-governor and his partisans were thrown over the walls and lynched by the Zealots gathered below them. From then on the power passed entirely into the hands of representatives of the lower classes and the city was governed entirely independently of Constantinople, obeying no orders from the capital. They even refused entry to Gregory Palamas, who had been nominated Archbishop of Thessalonica by the Patriarch. It was only at the end of 1349 that one of the two governors, Alexis Metochites managed to overthrow his colleague and rival Andrew Palaeologus and expelled him from the city. Supported by a few Thessalonians, he appealed to Cantacuzenus while the Zealots appealed to Dušan. This proved a double-edged weapon, because it cost them the sympathy of the majority of the population. Cantacuzenus was the winner in this sequence of events and was finally able to enter the town accompanied by John V, and Gregory Palamas was at the same time able to take possession of his episcopal throne. The leaders of the Zealots were arrested or expelled and, after addressing the population and accusing the Zealots of treason, Cantacuzenus returned to Constantinople leaving John V in charge (1350). This was the end of the Zealots' rule in Thessalonica, the most interesting revolutionary movement in the history of Byzantium.

Though the lack of written sources and the biased accounts of their opponents makes it difficult to be sure of the insurgents' social origins, it is most likely that they came principally from the lower classes (the *popolo minuto* of the Italian towns), the *demos*, which revolted against the powerful classes. Their main strength lay in the Zealot party which, unlike the rest of the population, was well organised and was closely linked to the sailors' and the dock workers' guild, which included the fishermen, and which, like the Zealots, were armed and rebellious. Both groups seem to have been involved in trade and piracy. Rather surprisingly in the circumstances, the Zealots were led by Michael Palaeologus during the first phase of the Revolution. He was related by marriage to the Imperial family and his successor, Andrew Palaeologus, was also a member of the nobility. At the time, however, these two leaders served more as spokesmen than as real revolutionaries, which the Zealots and sailors definitely were. In Thessalonica and certain towns of Thrace, notably Adrianople, part of the manufacturing and trading middle classes seem to have been on the side of the *deme* and so were distinguished from the towns of eastern Macedonia, which were deprived of important commercial activities and where for the most part the struggle was limited to two factions within the local nobility – with the *deme* adhering to Cantacuzenus's faction. Constantinople herself belonged to the first category since the Regency was supported by the Gasmuli (sailors and particularly oarsmen) whereas Apokaukos tried to secure the support of the city's tradesmen by introducing favourable legislation. This meant that the money-changers (*argyramoiboi*), who were considered real bankers by the Italians, were from the beginning opposed to Cantacuzenus and in 1347 they rejected his appeal for funds.

We must however be careful not to simplify the attitude of certain classes of the population, who in spite of sharing fairly similar social origins behaved differently. In Adrianople the money lenders were accused of 'Cantacuzenism' by the *deme*, which serves to distinguish them radically from the money-changers of Constantinople. This was the case too with the middle classes who were called 'the middle people among the citizens' (*oi mesoi ton politon*) or the 'middle part' of the social body (*e mese moira*) and whose behaviour was, to say the least, ambiguous. The *deme* turned against them, either because they were not on their side or because of the hatred their social and economic superiority aroused. At Thessalonica they even had a victim in the person of a certain Gabalas, executed by the Zealots during the events of 1343. They were subsequently forced to make a pact with the people against the powerful classes.

As for the Revolution and especially the Zealots' programme for government and their ideology, the only thing to emerge at all clearly from the sources remains the merciless persecution they conducted against the ruling classes and the confiscation both of their property and that of religious establishments whose revenues they used to provision their army and to supply the fleet. The movement's strength lay in the particularly strong hatred aroused in the working classes (workers, artisans, peasants) by the huge social injustice and the concentration of wealth in the hands of a small group of landed proprietors. This resentment was expressed by the new administrations in the disaffected towns, especially in Thessalonica, which removed all power from the rich and made the urban institutions more liberal, with the people taking part in the organisation and defence of their towns.

For all the differences between this fourteenth-century Byzantine revolutionary movement and the popular risings which shook the towns of Flanders and Italy in the same century, there were certain analogies between them in the general context of urban social conflict. It is interesting to note how Cantacuzenus's take-over mirrored Simone Boccanegra's seizure of power in Genoa in 1339. According to Cantacuzenus, that had been a case of the *deme* getting the better of the ruling classes (*dynatoi*) and the 'better' elements (*aristoi*), whom it either expelled or deprived of office, thus expressing its desire for self-government (*demokrateisthai*) and for electing one of their own members, *Boukanegra*, as their leader. Cantacuzenus thus used the same terms to describe the events in the Italian town which he applied to situations in Byzantium he considered analogous. As for any real connections that might have existed between the Zealots' and Boccanegra's revolt, for instance the little Genoese or even the Venetian colony's influence on the course of events at Thessalonica, they are most unlikely. In view of the particular conditions within the Byzantine Empire which did provoke the revolutionary movement there is no need to look for external factors to explain it. The conclusion is that any connection between what happened in Byzantium and the urban risings in Italy would be tenuous because there was no flourishing class of tradesmen and artisans in Byzantium and the landed nobility controlled the towns, thus preventing new social elements from developing and succeeding politically.

Byzantium open to the Turks

The coming of John VI Cantacuzenus to the throne of Constantinople ensured the triumph of Hesychasm and so renewed links with the conservative politics of Andronicus II, who had been loyal to Orthodoxy, and put an end to the leanings towards Western culture which had emerged during the reigns of Michael VIII and Andronicus III and, before them, of Manuel I Comnenus.

John VI was fully aware of the deplorable situation the Empire was in. The country, especially Thrace, had been devastated by the civil wars and pillaged by Turkish troops, making farming and consequently taxation impossible. The State coffers were almost completely empty and he depended increasingly on the liberality of rich citizens or on the charity of foreign rulers and states in the form of gifts or loans. Even the crown jewels had been sent to Venice by Anna of Savoy in pawn for a loan of 30,000 ducats, which the Serenissima was constantly demanding be repaid. In 1347 the Black Death spread through the capital. Cantacuzenus has given us a terrifying description of its effects, modelled on Thucidides' account, telling how it took innumerable victims especially in Constantinople, where the mortality was so high that a Western source went so far as to estimate it at 8 or 9 per cent of the city's population. Cantacuzenus's previously conceived plans for forming a continuous State from the Peloponnesus to Constantinople, now appeared completely unrealisable. The Byzantine Empire was limited from then on to Thrace, to the northern islands of the Aegean, from Thessalonica to the Byzantine Morea at the other end of the Hellades. The principal winner of the Byzantine civil war was Dušan, who had extended his control over all the rest of the Greek provinces up to the frontiers of the Catalan Duchy.

Cantacuzenus did achieve a system of government which replaced the sole rule of the Emperor with the collective rule of members of the Imperial family. This was determined by the new requirements created by the Empire's territorial situation, rather than by the Emperor's personal wishes, opposed as he was to Irène of Montferrat's demands for partition along the Latin model. Nonetheless, John VI's action was not devoid of political considerations, seeking to weaken the Palaeologus dynasty and favour his own. His oldest son Matthew was thus made ruler of western Thrace while his younger brother Manuel was put in charge of the Byzantine possessions in the Morea, which were arranged into a sort of principality enjoying administrative autonomy while recognising the Emperor's sovereignty. This was how the Despotate of the Morea was created in 1348.

Cantacuzenus's foreign policy can be summarised firstly as pursuing his agreement with the Turks and secondly as attempting to match the superior strength of the Genoese. The latter aim depended more on the internal situation, given that the Genoese had gone so far as to create a sort of state within the State. Cantacuzenus, by making great financial efforts, managed to build a fleet which he then used to defy the Genoese, on whom the greater part of the revenues from the Bosphorus devolved, as well as lowering the customs duties of Constantinople in competition with theirs. This led to a war which Byzantium lost, her fleet defeated and dispersed by the Genoese in 1439. Cantacuzenus's attempt at restoring her economic and military autonomy had failed. The Emperor's subsequent involvement in the new war which broke out immediately afterwards between Genoa and Venice proved yet again, if proof were needed, that the Byzantines were irrevocably caught up in the web of circumstances. Cantacuzenus sided first with Venice and Peter IV of Aragon but was forced, after the Battle of the Bosphorus in 1352 on his allies' withdrawal, to capitulate to the Genoese. The Venetians took the opportunity to ally with John V, who promised them Tenedos, the island dominating the entry to the Hellespont and the Propontida, in exchange for 20,000 ducats destined to finance hostilities against his father. Civil war was about to be resumed.

In trying to combine the principle of dynastic legitimacy with his desire to establish himself against the Palaeologi, John VI sought to arrange matters at the last moment by redistributing Thrace between his son and John V, who had gathered all the opposition around him. In spite of this, the situation deteriorated rapidly and the two sides declared war, which was resolved by the armies they summoned. On his side, John V appealed to the Serbs and the Bulgars, while Orkhan sent his son Suleyman to Constantinople at the head of a considerable army. The Turks emerged as victors in the battle which took place near Didymoteichon, a few months after the sea battle of the Bosphorus. Strengthened by this outcome Cantacuzenus ignored the claims of legitimacy and excluded John V from the succession, crowning Matthew as co-Basileus at the beginning of November 1354. His own reign was nearing its close. John V meanwhile secured the help of a Genoese pirate, Francesco Gattilusi, by promising him his sister in marriage and the cession of the island of Lesbos as dowry, and managed to enter Constantinople in the same month, where he was triumphantly welcomed. The Emperors negotiated a few initial settlements, which then

An earthquake. The Greek peninsula is frequently shaken by such tremors, which explains the realism of this sixteenth-century fresco depicting the earthquake announcing the Last Judgement. (Mount Athos, Dionysiou Monastery.)

collapsed, after which Cantacuzenus decided to abdicate under pressure of public discontent. He assumed the habit of a monk and retired from the political scene, without however ceasing to serve as counsellor to John Palaeologus until his death thirty years later at Mistra. As for Matthew, he held on to Rhodopes for some time before he was beaten by the Serbs and was forced to abdicate by John V in 1357.

Cantacuzenus's downfall is closely linked to the limitations of his policy of alliance with the Ottomans, that is to say, with his inability to dictate to them just how far they were to go. The age of straightforward incursions and raids conducted by Turks on Thracian territory was definitely over, and those coming now from different points in Asia Minor, with the Ottomans in the forefront, came to stay. This was the beginning of the European phase of their history. They were already installed around 1352 in the fortress of Tzympe in the Chersonese in Thrace, the principal point of passage to the hinterland, which Turkish bands of varying origins had invaded earlier on – some of whom had come long ago with Umur, others independent raiders with Ghazi leaders who had wandered over. They were only waiting for an opportunity to install themselves permanently and this came with the great earthquake of March 1354, which destroyed the fortifications of several towns in Thrace. Some of them, like Gallipoli, were abandoned by their inhabitants and passed into the hands of the Ottomans and other Turks without a blow being struck. In vain did Cantacuzenus offer Suleyman great sums of money for the return of Gallipoli, which was on the contrary subsequently transformed into a strong base for the Sultan's future expeditions against the interior of the Balkan peninsula. Cantacuzenus had indeed opened the door to the Turks by summoning them to his assistance, but the Regency had also pursued this policy, which failed simply through lack of means and of competent men of Cantacuzenus's calibre. The irruption of the Turkish enemy was only precipitated by the decay of the whole Byzantine system since the Turks would have discovered Europe even had they not been invited there.

The Byzantine Empire had only around a hundred years of life left; it was to deploy these years in 'descending the stairs of evil down to the last step' to paraphrase the neo-Greek poet Kostas Palamas, while their cultural Renaissance soared to yet greater heights.

Begging for a last reprieve?

Of all the Byzantine Emperors, John V Palaeologus reigned the longest, if one calculates from his coronation in 1341. During this period, he was twice evicted from the throne by his son Andronicus IV (1376–9) and his grandson John VII (1390). He was a weak Emperor, unable to face up to conditions which were beyond remedy. The decisive factor in this period was of course the Ottoman advance, which also affected the Latin possessions in the East and the interests of the Italian maritime towns, who responded by relegating their mutual antagonisms to second place.

The Byzantine Emperors' foreign policy was henceforth orientated towards the West in a continual quest for help against the Turks, in exchange once again for the Union of the Churches. This subject never ceased to preoccupy the Emperors, even after the failure of the

Council of Lyon. There had been attempts at negotiation during the civil wars by Andronicus II, and by Andronicus III around the end of his reign, as well as those by Anna of Savoy and Cantacuzenus himself. In 1348 he submitted plans for a Christian expedition against the Turks to the Pope, in which he promised to participate, and which, he claimed, would create within the hearts of the Byzantine people feelings favourable to the future resumption of the question of the Union. John V drove matters still further by reversing the previous thesis which gave priority to military aid over the Union and by dropping John VI's demand for the convocation of an oecumenical council.

The Emperor offered an initial phase involving his personal conversion to Catholicism and that of his family, even the heir to the throne, Manuel. He suggested proceeding in stages because of the hostility of the majority of the clergy and his people to the union, starting with the conversion of his ecclesiastical partisans and of those nobles who would submit to his decision. These propositions went even further than those of his forefather Manuel VII, who had negotiated the demands of the Papacy in a much more restrained manner. As it was, the problem had changed fundamentally since Michael VII's day, given that the danger now came from Infidels, against whom the Papacy could not deploy the same balancing act it had applied in Charles of Anjou's case. In this sense, the propositions formulated by John V in a letter he sent to Pope Innocent VI at Avignon (1355), thus constituting a first step towards his conversion, did not have the military results he had hoped for. The Christian League which was formed at Smyrna in 1359 to fight the Turks and free the Holy Land was really only concerned with defending the commercial interests of Venice, Cyprus and the Rhodes Hospitaliers in the eastern Mediterranean.

In the meantime the situation in the Balkans had reached its most critical stage. After Dušan's death in 1355 his empire collapsed and was shared out between his successors, who formed little independent or semi-independent enclaves, while Bulgaria, divided as she was, was neutralised by her serious internal problems. The Ottomans turned up beneath the walls of Constantinople in 1359, after which the most important towns of Thrace, such as Didymoteichon, Adrianople (1368–9), Philippopolis, fell one after the other into their hands. It is very difficult to establish the exact dates of the capture or recapture of these towns since several of them passed back into Byzantine control before submitting definitely to the conqueror. Matters were precipitated under the new Sultan Murad I (1362–89), who moved towards the Slav territories in the peninsula and began a vast programme transferring the peoples of Thrace to Asia Minor and vice versa. Starting with Murad I, the course of events in Byzantium and the Balkans began to be measured according to the length of the Ottoman sultans' reigns rather than those of the Byzantine Emperors, and even less those of the Serb or Bulgar rulers.

When his advances to the Pope failed, John V turned to the Italian sea-faring republics and then to the Slav states in an initiative conducted by the Patriarch of Constantinople, who favoured a Balkan entente as opposed to collaboration with the West. The Patriarch Callixtus's journey to Serres to talk with Dušan's widow was interrupted by the prelate's unexpected demise, while negotiations with the Bulgarian Tsar, one of whose daughters had married Andronicus IV, came to nothing. Added to this, hostilities broke out between the Bulgarians and the Byzantines, who took the port of Anchialos from them. On the other side, a real crusade had begun under the leadership of Peter I, King of Cyprus, and had set sail for Egypt, thus disappointing the Emperor, who had expected it to serve his interests. Finally despairing of his cause, John V undertook the long and painful journey along the Danube to Hungary at the beginning of 1366 to solicit King Louis the Great for help.

This proved the first of a long series of journeys across Europe undertaken by the Emperors of Byzantium in their desperate attempt to save their country from the cataclysm. The Emperors responded to the needs of the times by making urgent appeals for help rather than by deploying their forces beyond their frontiers. Another and no less telling sign of the times was John V's detention by the Bulgarians at the Hungarian border on his return from Buda, where he had anyway been unable to obtain anything. This new humiliation imposed on the Emperor of Byzantium by the Tsar of Bulgaria, who was no less exposed to the Turkish danger, already answers the question as to why the Turks entered eastern Europe so easily.

John V was able to return to his capital thanks only to the intervention by his cousin Amadeus VI of Savoy. The 'Green Count' as Amadeus was known, had previously carried out, with the help of Francesco Gattilusi and a small Byzantine force, the important exploit of regaining Gallipoli from the Ottomans in 1366. What was more, by taking the ports Mesembria and Sozopolis from the Bulgarians, he contributed to the strength of the Byzantines, who already controlled Anchialos on the western shore of the Black Sea. Amadeus's activities however, fervent partisan that he was of the Crusade against the Turks, were not exempt from ulterior considerations about the outcome of the Union, since he brought with him a Papal emissary in the form of Paul the Latin ex-Archbishop of Smyrna, recently promoted Latin Patriarch of Constantinople. The position of the Byzantine Church was expounded to Paul, in the absence of the Orthodox Patriarch Philotheus, by the ex-Emperor John VI, now the monk Ioasaph, who insisted on discussing plans for convoking the oecumenical council he longed for, at which the Pope and the Patriarch of Constantinople would assist along with all the eastern Patriarchs and the leaders of the Serbian, Bulgarian and Georgian Churches.

Finally, in spite of the lively protests of the Byzantine clergy, and Amadeus's threats to return Gallipoli to the Turks and to attack Constantinople, John V undertook a second journey to the West, to Rome, in the company of several high dignitaries, among whom the neoplatonic philosopher Demetrius Cydones. There was no churchman in the Imperial entourage. The Emperor's official conversion to the Latin dogma took place in Rome in October 1369 in front of Pope Urban V, but it was a personal undertaking which did not implicate the Church in any way and did not contribute to the Union. Worse still, it produced no military assistance for the Empire. John V had to submit to a further humiliation in Venice, where he was retained as a debtor of the Republic. It was only following a further intervention by his son Manuel, that he was able to return to Constantinople in October 1371. The purpose of his journey had not been achieved; the West was too involved in its own affairs to concern itself with the very serious military problems of Byzantium, whose solution, it was thought, depended on theological considerations.

Murad I reclines under a poplar after reducing a stronghold. (Ms. Øttoman Hünername, 1584; Istanbul, Topkapi Sarayi.)

Too late

At the same time the 'Balkan entente' was collapsing. Its great protagonist had been the Patriarch Philotheus and it was directed at what Louis Bréhier called 'The Orthodox Crusade'. The Patriarch did succeed in bringing the Serb and Bulgarian Churches back within his jurisdiction, but the Balkan states were too weak and divided, internally and among themselves, to come to an effective and realisable agreement. This is what the battle of Tzernomianon (Čirmen) on the Hebron in September 1371 demonstrated, at which the exclusively Serbian armed forces of King Vukašin and his brother, the Despot Uglješa, were crushed by the Ottomans. This defeat did not only seal the fate of Macedonia, whose various autonomous princes became tributaries of the Sultan and submitted to the ban levy. It also meant that the defence of the whole Balkan peninsula had crumbled. A little later, both Byzantium and Bulgaria became tributaries of the Sultan and were obliged to supply him with troops. The slight advantage Byzantium drew when Manuel Palaeologus retook Serres after the death of Uglješa could not compensate for the humiliation of being reduced to a minor state, paying tribute to the Ottomans, which she was from then on.

John V was soon to accompany Murad on his expedition against the Seljuk emirates of Asia Minor. His son Andronicus chose this occasion for his first revolt against him, allying himself unhesitatingly with Savji, the Sultan's son, who also rebelled against his father.

John V was forced into a horrible and degrading position when Murad, after crushing the revolt and blinding his son, ordered him to inflict the same punishment on his own son and his grandson John. The Emperor executed this order rather more mercifully, since his two victims did not lose their sight completely, whereas Savji died of his wounds. As for the government, Andronicus lost his claim to the succession and was replaced by Manuel who was crowned Emperor in 1373.

These events inaugurated a new period of conflict within the Palaeologus dynasty, in which Andronicus made a series of attempts at deposing his father, closely linked with the problem of Tenedos, which determined relations between Byzantium, Venice and Genoa during the second half of the fifteenth century. The island of Tenedos had become a vital strategic point for controlling the Hellespont since the Turks had dominated the Straits and was the cause of a bitter conflict between the two Italian cities, which was fought out within the area. The antagonism of the two opposing Palaeologi parties only served to further the opposite interests of the two cities, with the Sultan as arbiter. The Italian cities were anxious to preserve their economic and financial acquisitions and had made the entente the pivot of their policy towards the Ottomans ever since they had begun to extend their hegemony into Europe.

The Genoese had helped Andronicus IV to win his throne in 1376 but they were unable to retake the island, which had been conquered by the Venetians, John V's allies. This was when Gallipoli, liberated ten years previously by Amadeus of Savoy was returned by Andronicus IV to the Ottomans in exchange for their support. Murad I responded to John V's and Manuel's promise to resume their obligations as tributaries and re-established them on the throne in 1379. By bestowing his favour on Andronicus as well, he forced John V to recognise him and his son John VII as heirs instead of Manuel and to abandon the principal towns of the northern shores of the Propontida. This served to tear the Empire still further apart and to reduce the Emperors of Byzantium to despicable pawns on the Sultan's chessboard, moved about at his whim. As for Tenedos, it was proclaimed a neutral territory and handed over to the Count of Savoy, according to the peace treaty concluded between Venice and Genoa in Turin in 1381. Its fortifications were to be destroyed and its population transferred to Crete and Euboea. This treaty was put into effect only in 1383–4, although Venice had not stopped using the island. Byzantium was the only interest not to be represented.

The only gleam of light in this gloomy period was the policy of the Despot of Thessalonica, Manuel Palaeologus, which was the reverse of his father's, especially during the second phase of his government (c. 1382–7). Manuel defied the Turks' tributary law and tried to transform Thessalonica into the centre of defence in Macedonia and Thessaly, which he had brought back within the Empire. He did not hesitate to confiscate half of the Church lands belonging to Mount Athos and Thessalonica and to turn them into *pronoiai* in order to give himself the means with which to supply his military needs. In this sense, Manuel took up John V's attempt at secularising certain Church domains in order to strengthen his army against the Turkish menace, an attempt opposed by the Church, which cited holy canons. Murad I reacted quickly to Manuel's political independence; he took Serres – for the second time – and besieged Thessalonica, which surrendered in 1387. The city was allowed to exist under a relatively autonomous regime, which Bayezid I abolished in 1394, as well as imposing *devshirme* (taking children away) in 1395.

In fact, the period from the beginning of the reign of Andronicus IV and the war of Tenedos to the end of the latter (1376–81) is considered one in which the Ottomans consolidated their conquests in the Balkans. Murad I established the foundations of the Ottoman State mechanism and reorganised his army. He also implemented a vast policy of immigration and colonisation in the occupied regions, while arranging for the distribution of lands among his soldiers and the creation of fiefs. After retaking Gallipoli, Murad officially transferred his seat to Andrianople (*c.* 1377), which became the Ottomans' first European capital. Further conquests were soon undertaken and other important towns such as Niš (1386) and Sofia (1387) fell into his hands before he invaded eastern Bulgaria. There he occupied Tărnovo for a while before reaching the Danube, where he took several fortresses and forced the Tsar to hand over Silistra.

Next came the turn of Serbia. After checking a rebellion in Bulgaria, Murad turned towards Kossovo, the seat of Vuk Branković, a member of the anti-Turk coalition, which had been formed on the initiative of Prince Lazar of Serbia. The Battle of Kossovo in 1389 went the same way as that of the Hebron and put an end to the Slav nations' last attempts at stopping the Ottomans from crushing them in the peninsula. Murad's death (he was probably stabbed by Lazar's son Miloš Kobilić) did not affect the outcome of the battle, which was won by the superior strength of the Ottomans under the leadership of Murad's son Bayezid. Prince Lazar and his nobles were put to death and his successors had to submit to paying tribute and to raising auxiliary troops. Bayezid also imposed a poll tax (*kharaj*) on all the non-Muslim population in the country. The monasteries of Mount Athos, which submitted in 1386, were not exempted from this tax, which they also had to pay on all their landed estates, including those outside the boundaries of their community.

A matter of a few years

Under Bayezid I (1389–1402), known as the 'Thunderbolt' (*Yildirim*), affairs both in Europe and in Asia Minor reached a crisis, when, after triumphing over the Turkish Emirs, the Sultan accorded himself, with good reason, the title of 'Emir of Rum'. On the western side, Byzantium's total isolation increased with the annihilation of Serbia and the Serbian defence, when their capital Tărnovo succumbed to a ferocious siege in 1393. Bayezid was now able to play at cat and mouse with Byzantium and to exploit the disagreements within the bosom of the Imperial family, as the Byzantines had previously done when they had raised up foreign pretenders against their established sovereigns. Thus in 1390 John VII was able with the Sultan's help to dislodge his grandfather from Constantinople for several months, at the end of which Manuel implemented his return by bringing back John V, with the Sultan's agreement of course, and at the price of still greater concessions. John V was forced to destroy the fortifications near the Golden Gate which he had built up to defend the capital. Manuel and John VII were obliged to accompany the Sultan on his campaigns in

241

Asia Minor and, in spite of his revulsion and bitterness, Manuel had to take part in the conquest of Philadelphia in 1300, the last Byzantine city to remain free. It was in the Ottoman camp at Brusa that Manuel learnt of his father's death (1391) and he managed to escape and reach Constantinople in order to make sure of his throne and to take over his diminished Empire.

Between the accession of Manuel II Palaeologus in 1391, and the Battle of Ancyra (1402) and Murad II's accession (1421) and Manuel's death (1425), the Empire was on the verge of collapsing. But the intermediary period was a relative lull before the storm, marked by Manuel's noble efforts to remedy the situation. The Emperor certainly showed himself worthy of his time and, unlike his father, he was determined to resist the enemy. He even managed to improve the situation, but much of this was due to the Ottoman civil war, which broke out after the battle of Ancyra, and after that, to Mehmed I's peaceful policy towards Byzantium.

Bayezid convoked all his Christian vassals to a meeting at a Serres (1393–4) by individual summons so that each one was unaware of the others' presence up to the last moment, thus sowing terror among them and making them understand what was to follow. In the spring of the same year, Bayezid laid siege to Constantinople by setting up a land blockade lasting eight years (with brief interruptions), which reduced the stores of food inside the capital to rock bottom. All that the West offered the famished population of Constantinople were the empty counsels addressed to them by the Venetian Senate; later they sent a cargo of wheat for the people and an offer of asylum for Manuel.

About the same time, along with abolishing Thessalonica's clement regime, the Ottomans completed the conquest of Thessaly, which Evrenos Bey had begun in 1393, and they invaded southern Greece and the Peloponnesus, where they defeated the Despot of Mistra, Theodorus I Palaeologus, in front of Corinth. The Turkish advance was considerably eased by the complete absence of solidarity among the Christian rulers (Navarrese of Thebes and Achaia, Acciajuoli of Athens, the Byzantine Despots of Mistra). They moved almost simultaneously into the Balkans, where they overthrew the Voivode Mircia of Wallachia, who, in spite of winning the violent Battle of Rovina in 1395, became a tributary of the Sultan. As a result, the Ottomans became masters of Dobrudža and controlled the nerve points along the Danube.

The West now grew really worried. King Sigismund, whose country was in immediate danger, was the first to react by appealing to Christian solidarity. The first to respond were the French knights who came in a considerable contingent led by Count John of Nevers, in which John le Meingre, known as Marshal Boucicaut, took part. The Wallachians came with Mircia, and various companies of knights from Bohemia, Poland, Spain and England came to swell the land army, while Venice, the Genoese of Lesbos and Chios and the Rhodes Hospitalers lent war galleys to safeguard the Black Sea and the mouths of the Danube. In spite of their very considerable numbers (around 100,000 men) the lack of agreement between the French and the Hungarians on the one hand, and the Ottomans' mettle on the other, made short work of this army at Nicopolis in 1396, when the last crusade of international dimensions ended in a bloody failure. Most of the prisoners were massacred, though Sigismund managed to get away in a Venetian ship; on passing through the Hellespont he was treated to the sight of what was left of the Christian prisoners stuck up along both shores by the Turks.

The truth was that the organisers of this crusade had not been in the least concerned with the critical situation of Byzantium, but had aimed only at defending Catholic Hungary and, at the very most, at throwing the Sultan out of central Europe. The problem of freeing the Holy Land had occurred to only a few of them and, as for delivering Constantinople, no one had given it a thought.

Bayezid resumed his blockade of Constantinople after a brief hiatus. This was when he built the famous fortress known as Anadolu Hisar on the eastern shore of the Bosphorus, which, together with its twin, which was built later on the European side, was to be for ever associated with the capture of the city. At the same time Evrenos Bey's troops were invading Greece again; they occupied Athens for a while and travelled as far as the Venetian colonies on the southern Peloponnesus, ravaging the countryside as they went. Manuel's despairing appeals to the Doge, the Pope and the Kings of France, England and Aragon, had no effect – apart from the derisory force of 1,200 soldiers led by Boucicaut, which Charles VI had consented to send. There were other reasons why Basil I, Grand Duke of Moscow, did not involve himself. Although the Russian Churches remained solidly anchored to the Orthodox faith and recognised the supremacy of the Patriarch of Constantinople, they did not want to have anything to do with an Emperor who had become the 'vassal' of the Turks. Since the Byzantine Church had maintained and even intensified its network over the Orthodox countries, it was up to the Patriarch Antonios IV to refute this argument in the name of the ancient and undying doctrine of Imperial oecumenicalism.

In these circumstances, Manuel had no choice but to resume where his father had left off, at Boucicaut's insistence. With the fundamental difference that he did not go to Rome to offer any conversion or to discuss the Union; he quite simply addressed the two western powers France and England, asking them to provide adequate military assistance and at the best, to organise a Crusade to drive the Turks out of Constantinople and Europe.

He was very well received in the courts of Europe, since the West had begun to appreciate the extent of the Turkish danger, and also because the humanists credited the Byzantines with being the natural retainers of Greek culture. For all that, the only material support Manuel secured was the sum of 3,000 marks (2,000 pounds) given him by Henry VI of England, which represented the sum total of monies raised in the country's churches by the sale of Papal indulgences. There was no question of mobilising an international Crusade. The only positive aspect of this peregrination, and this only in the long term, was that greater contact began to develop between Byzantium and the West, where, in spite of the Hundred Years' War, the Renaissance was flourishing. Constantinople was abandoned by all and, gradually whittled down to her own suburbs, was irretrievably condemned. It was a matter of a few years at the very most.

The Slavs, both oppressors and oppressed

Serbs, Bulgarians and even Russians intervened many times in Byzantium's last agony. Their role was ambiguous; they were suffused with Imperial culture and felt that they were the natural heirs of a moribund Empire, to which they aspired. But, like their ancestors of the tenth or eleventh centuries, they thought they could achieve this by force, easily summoned up from their ethnic, linguistic and psychological traditions. To achieve their end they had to raise their heavily armed hands, like disrespectful sons, against the one who enabled them to achieve self-awareness. In so doing they were playing their Islamic neighbour's game by contributing to the fall of Byzantium, which would bring them down with her.

The ascent of the Serbs

The main stages in the development and expansion of the Serbian States were also stages in its relationship with the Byzantine Empire, and each one represented a struggle: for independence under the Nemanja, for the heart of the Macedonian Balkans since the time of Milutin, and for hegemony over the Balkan peninsula in Dušan's time. During each of these periods, Serbia's progress was conditioned by the contrasting and gradual decline of Byzantium.

The end of the internal troubles, which had erupted when Stefan the 'first-crowned' died, and the beginning of a relative stabilisation with the accession of Uroš I (1242–76), coincided with the start of the intensive exploitation of the mineral wealth of Serbia, the driving force of the country's progress. German miners from Hungary, probably from the territory of the self-styled Saxons of Zip (who were generally known as *Sasi* in Serbia, Bosnia and Bulgaria) had stimulated the productivity of the mines, and by the end of the thirteenth century, they had developed them very considerably. The mines were behind both the commercial expansion and the stable currency which enabled the Serbian kings to implement their policies.

Byzantium soon became aware of the effects of Serbia's economic development when Stefan Uroš II Milutin (1282–1321) began to realise his plans for expansion, with the active assistance of the Serb nobles, who were behind his annexation policy. The Serbs seized northern Macedonia with the towns Skopje (Skopia in Greek), Štip (Stypeion), Veles (Belesos) Debar-Debra (Dibre), and it was only after painful negotiations that the Emperor's representative Theodorus Metochites managed to satisfy the demands of the Serbian nobles who had benefited most from the confiscation of Byzantine lands. Milutin was to marry Andronicus II's daughter Simonis, aged 5, who would bring him the regions he had already conquered as her dowry (1299). Serbia herself, as was only fair, began to feel the strong impact of Byzantine culture, which was adopted in court circles and grew more intense as more Byzantine territories were incorporated into the Serbian State. Even the Byzantine *pronoia* system was adopted by the Nemanjides, probably even before Milutin's reign, whence the first references to it in Serbian documents. The Serbs had only legalised

244

Queen Simonis. She was five years old when her marriage was consummated and the unhappy woman was never able to have children. (Detail of fresco, Gracanica, *c*. 1320.)

the system already existing in their conquered lands, by which the properties of local *pronoiars* were administered, and which subsequently spread into Serbian lands as well and to Zeta, where it was still to be found under Venetian rule.

Serbia took an active part in the Byzantine civil wars from their first phase, trying to extract maximum profit from them while consolidating their alliance against the Bulgarians. The victory they achieved over Tsar Michael Šišman at Velbăžd (nowadays Kjustendil in Bulgaria) in 1330 put an end to the Bulgarian–Byzantine alliance and contributed to strengthening Serbian hegemony in the Balkans. The victor of Velbăžd himself, Stefan Uroš III Dečanski (1321–31), shortly afterwards fell victim to the avidity of the Serb nobles who, seeking to extend their territorial gains, had the king assassinated and replaced by his son Stefan Dušan (1331–55) who owed his political existence to them. The

245

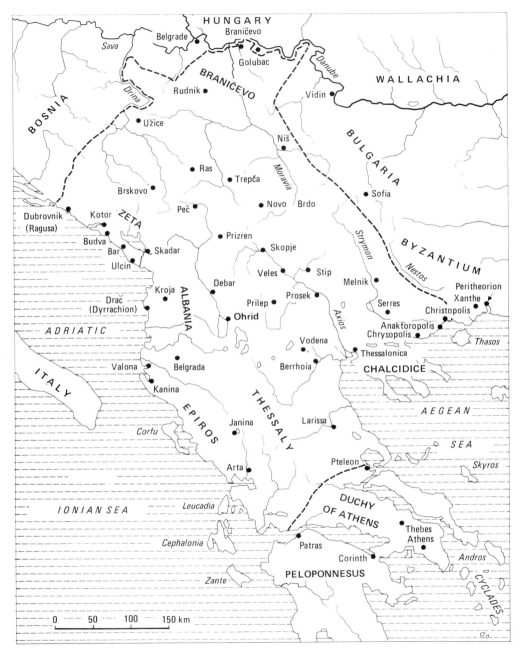

5 Serbia in the reign of Dušan (1331–1355)

nobles effectively imposed their grand schemes for Serbian expansion on the new king, whose advance into eastern Macedonia, seizing Prilep (Prilapos), Strumitsa (Strimvitza, Stromnitza), Vodena (Edessa), Ohrid (Achrida) and Kastoria, was temporarily halted when Dušan and Andronicus III signed a peace treaty in front of Thessalonica in 1334. Hostilities were quickly resumed with the outbreak of the second Byzantine civil war, which was really won, as we know, by the Serbian king. Dušan was able to complete his conquests in Albania and Macedonia at the expense of a disunited Byzantium without really having to fight a battle, as well as taking several towns such as Kroja, Berat (Belegrada), Avlona, Berrhoia, Serres, Drama, Philippoi, Chrysopolis and even Mount Athos. Thessalonica thus became a Byzantine island isolated in a vast countryside occupied by Dušan, soon to become Lord of Epirus and Thessaly as well as Aetolia and Akarnania (1347–8).

The moment had come when his ambition to suppress the Byzantine Empire and to replace it with a new one in which Serbs would hold political power, but which would retain the same form, could be realised. It was a replay of the same struggle over the Imperial title that Charlemagne and the Carolingians, the German Emperors and the Bulgarian rulers had conducted earlier. Dušan referred to himself in his charters as 'Basileus and Autokrator of Serbia and Romania' (Greek charters) and as 'Tsar of the Serbs and Greeks' (Serb charters), which expressed his particular ideology very adequately. As a natural consequence of these changes, the Archbishop of Serbia Ioannikios was nominated 'Patriarch of the Serbs and Greeks' thus endowing the Serb Empire with its own Patriarchate and responding to its new needs. It assumed its greatest symbolic significance with the solemn coronation of Dušan at Skopje in April 1346 in the presence of the Patriarch of Tărnovo, the self-appointed Archbishop of Ohrid, and even representatives of Mount Athos, whose monasteries were soon rewarded for their voluntary submission. The third move necessary to consolidate his new authority was to establish a legal foundation by promulgating the Code of 'the Blessed Emperor Stefan', which also guaranteed Serbian and Greek landed property. The State was officially divided into Serbian territory (*Srpska zemlja*) made up of the ancient lands where old Slav titles such as *župan*, *knez* and *voivode* were *de rigueur*, and into 'Romania', the conquered Byzantine territory where the institutions and titles of the Byzantine administration were retained (for instance the term *cephale* to designate the governor), to the extent of setting up Judges General similar to those in the Greek provinces. Although the first territory had been officially handed over to Dušan's son, King Uroš, he was still so young that the arrangement was purely nominal and the real master of the whole Empire was still the Tsar.

The legal system, like the administration, was generally copied from Byzantine models, with the basic difference that the main detainers of power were now Serbs, with Greeks being retained only exceptionally in the civil or military service, or indeed in ecclesiastical office. The principal effect of this was to transfer most of the lands of the Byzantine nobility into the possession of the Serb feudal lords, as allods (*baština*) or as *pronoia* estates, as in the case of the land granted, probably from the time of Dečanski, to the Protosebastus Hrelja, in the Štip region, part of which at least had belonged to Byzantine *pronoiars*.

Dušan's foreign policy was directed towards securing an alliance with Venice in view of their common enterprise against Byzantium. This did not interest the Serenissima in the least, since she was concerned above all with fomenting Dušan's hostile intentions towards Hungary, against whom he was obliged to maintain a defensive stance, having given up Belgrade and Golubac. As for his relations with the Papacy, for all his intransigence towards the Roman Catholic 'semi-faithful' whom his Code prohibited from marrying Orthodox Christians, Dušan did make a few approaches to various Popes with the obvious object of harming Constantinople. These came to nothing and anyway the Tsar's premature death put an end to all his grand plans for hegemony over the Balkans.

Turkish interference

As the ephemeral Serbian State fell apart, the power of certain feudatories increased. Such were Hrelja, who had maintained his independent rule over the Štip region and Strumitsa during Dušan's lifetime, or Hlapen, the lord of Berrhoia and Vodena. Tsar Stefan Uroš (1355–71), Dušan's son, ruled in name only and could not prevent the division of his vast territory into several independent feudal units. Dušan's half-brother, Symeon, known as Uroš Palaeologus (1355–70) got himself proclaimed 'Emperor of the Serbs, the Greeks and all Albania' but was able to impose his authority only in Epirus and Thessaly. After his death and a brief reign by his son Jovan Uroš, the country was governed by the Philanthropenoi, a great Byzantine family, who recognised the overlordship of the Emperors of Constantinople. In Macedonia, Vukašin, also styled 'King of the Serbs and the Greeks', was lord of the regions of Prilep, Skopje, Ohrid, and Prizren, while to the East lay the lands of his brothers Constantine Dragaš and Constantine Dejanović with the towns of Kratovo, Kumanovo, Štip, Strumitsa and Velbǎžd. Serres, finally, with her surrounding region stretching beyond the Nestos up to Peritheorion, was part of the share of Despot Jovan Uglješa, Vukašin's brother.

The same state of affairs prevailed in the original Serb lands: the most powerful lord there was the Despot Lazar, who tried to consolidate his positions in the Morava Valley, in the teeth of Župan Nikola Altomanović, lord of the northern region between Rudnik and Ragusa, while at Zeta the three Balšić brothers had seized power. This fragmentation of authority was aggravated by the death of Tsar Stefan Uroš in December 1371, and was the main reason for the lack of coordination in the attempts to fight the Ottomans. One attempt had already been made when the brothers Vukašin and Uglješa led a fairly strong attack on Adrianople before being crushed in the Battle of Čirmen when both brothers were killed, in September 1371. Vukašin's son, the *kralj* Marko, who lives on as a popular hero in Serb epics and whose deeds have been perpetuated in Bulgarian, Croatian and even Albanian songs and stories, was in fact reduced to being a tributary of the Sultan as were the brothers Dejanović. It was while fighting under the command of Bayezid I that King Marko and Constantine Dejanović perished in the Battle of Rovina (1395) after which their respective lands were annexed by the Ottoman state.

During this period, the rapprochement of the Serb Church of Peć and the Patriarchate of Constantinople was an important event, and was agreed to in exchange for recognition of

Emperor Stefan Dušan was carried to power by the Serb nobility and for a while was able to fulfil the dream of the southern Slavs by removing Constantinople's hegemony over the Balkans. (Detail of fresco, Lesnovo, 1349.)

Peć as a Patriarchate in 1375. This solved the controversy, which had begun when Stefan Dušan created the Patriarchate of Peć unilaterally, as part of the general move towards a Balkan coalition which the then Patriarch Philotheus Coccinos had fervently advocated. As it was, the Serbs again took the initiative in organising the resistance, particularly the Despot Lazar (1371–89) who had extended his lands at the expense of the Župan Altomanović. Lazar created a network of alliances by establishing matrimonial ties with Vuk Branković of Kossovo and George Stracimirović Balšić of Zeta, and by his close collaboration with King Trvtko of Bosnia, and he managed to create a vast anti-Turkish bastion, which however suffered its well-known fate at Kossovo in June 1389. Miloš Kobilić, who killed Murad, and Prince Lazar, who was assassinated after the battle, have been assimilated into Serb legend, while Vuk Branković is remembered as a traitor.

The subjection of the Serbs had not only political and religious repercussions; in fact the Ottomans won control over one of the peninsula's fundamental economic resources, which had maintained the ephemeral success of the independent Serb principalities. The creation of several mining industries in the fourteenth century had made the Serb State rich and flourishing. The industries had generally merged with merchant colonies and were grown into little burghs or agglomerations around fortresses (*podgradje*) or into small towns of some importance with populations of often diverse ethnic origins – Saxons, Ragusans, Cattariotes, Spalatians, Venetians, Florentines, Albanians, Serbs, Wallachians, Greeks, and so on – each group with its own particular rights. The Saxons even possessed a 'Mining Code of the Saxons', which corresponded to the German 'mining code' of Chemnitz and the 'Law of the Mines' of Kremnitz. They were, however, few and were soon assimilated into the local population by the preponderance of mixed marriages, to the extent that by 1600, German was no longer spoken in the mining towns.

Most of the burghs and villages were found around the mountain Kopaonik (from *kopati*, to dig) where great quantities of lead, copper and iron ore were extracted. Apart from the burghs Brveniek, Trepča, Plana, Janjevo, and Koprici, the most important locality in this region in the fourteenth and fifteenth centuries was Novo Brdo (Novus Mons, Novomonte, the Nyeuberghe of the Saxons) whose mines produced silver ore known as *glama* which also contained grains of gold. Mints had been set up in the mining centres, especially at Novo Brdo, Rudnik and Brskovo (Brescoa), all flourishing little towns frequented by Ragusans and Cattariotes. Another centre of mining activity was at Kratovo in north-eastern Macedonia, where traces of Saxon settlers have been discovered.

Among other variously important towns, Prizren was a meeting place for Greek, Dalmatian and native merchants, especially during its annual fairs. These were also held at Peć, in front of the monastery, seat of the Archbishop and later Patriarch, Priština, on contrary, was described by Cantacuzenus as a simple unfortified burgh (*kome*) with a royal residence.

An echo of the importance of the Serbian mines and especially those of Novo Brdo may be found among Byzantine authors such as Ducas, Chalcocondyles and Critobulus, according to whom, gold and silver nuggets superior in quality to those of the Indies could be extracted in great quantities by digging anywhere in the country. Elsewhere, Constantine the Philosopher, a Bulgarian scholar from Kostenec who had fled to the Serbian court after the fall of Bulgaria, said of Novo Brdo that it was 'truly a town of gold and silver'. The French monk Brocard had established the number of mines owned by the Serb king in 1332 (somewhat exaggeratedly) at five gold mines, five silver mines and one mine producing both metals, while Bertrandon de la Broquière estimated the revenues of the mines at 200,000 ducats per annum in 1433. As for the mines of Bosnia, which were as important as the Serbian mines, the Bosnian documents of the fourteenth and fifteenth centuries speak of exporting gold and silver and refer particularly to the gold of Vrbas.

Some old towns of Greek, Roman or Illyrian origin fell into another category of Serbian towns, which had managed to retain considerable autonomy and held their own communal assemblies and had their particular municipal laws. Their rise occurred between 1250 and 1350, after which growing social unrest led to their rapid decline. Among them, Dulcigno (Ulocin in Old Serb) was a centre for ship building, and its inhabitants also often resorted to piracy. In the thirteenth century, it even held a little court, a temporary place of sojourn for members of the royal family. The most important of these towns was Bar (Antivari in Greek, Tivari in Albanian), which in the fourteenth century had a 'Grand Council' with members of the great Bazan, Žaretić, Boris, Samoili and Rugi families taking part in it. Scutari's population was mostly Albanian, whereas the inhabitants of Budva, a castle of ancient Illyrian origin, bore Slav and Albanian names and grew vineyards and olive groves and fished, occasionally going in for piracy, like the Dulcignotes.

In occupied Byzantine territory, with the exception of Serres which played such an important role in Dušan's new state, the most important town was Skopje in northern Macedonia, where a certain number of Greek families are known to us (Lipsiotes, Skopiotes, Apokaukos, Skropolites, etc.) Along the Danube the predominant towns were Braničevo and especially Belgrade, whose prosperous period dated back to the rule of the Despot Stefan Lazarević, who contributed to transforming this town into a cultural and religious centre, influencing all Serbia. *The Life of the Despot Stefan Lazarević* by Constantine the Philosopher contains a description of medieval Belgrade which compares the town to Jerusalem and the Danube to a river of Paradise.

Bulgarian interventions

Certain aspects of Bulgarian history in this period resemble Byzantine history, the more so since she never ceased to define herself by reference to Byzantium. Her steady political decline was punctuated by acute social conflict; the weakening of central authority only served to strengthen the boyard class and contributed to the subsequent collapse of the State. These numerous negative phenomena were contradicted by the country's flourishing spiritual and cultural life.

Ever since the accession of Michael VIII Palaeologus, Tsar Constantine Asen Tih (1257–77) had opposed him, driven on as he was by his wife, Irene Lascaris, the sister of the little dethroned and blinded John IV. Those ports (especially Mesembria, Anchialos and

Sozopolis) which enabled their intermittent rulers to control the shipping on the Black Sea and notably those ships bringing wheat to Constantinople, were a permanent source of discord between the two States during these years. Tih subscribed to Charles of Anjou's plans for conquest, as subsequently did George I Terter (1280–92). In the meantime, attacks by Hungarians and Byzantines, recurring Tartar raids destroying crops and rustling cattle, and the rapacious behaviour of the Bulgarian boyards towards the peasantry, all contributed to a popular rising which broke out in the north-east, led by an enlightened swineherd called Ivajlo. After holding the throne for a while (1278–9), he had to give way to a pretender imposed by the Byzantines, Ivan Asen III (1279–80), who in his turn was forced to give up the crown to Terter, a boyard of Cuman origin.

The Tsar's power was limited towards the West by an autonomous entity centred on Vidin which, in a larger sense, comprised western Bulgaria. This area had passed at odd times under the control of Hungary, but recovered its independence under the Despot Jacob Svetoslav (1272) and again under the Despot Šišman, shortly before submitting to the Serb king. Towards the end of the thirteenth century, Bulgaria was divided among several principalities and seems to have been wholly dominated by the Tartars. It was only at the very beginning of the fourteenth century that she was freed from the foreign yoke by the new Tsar Theodor Svetoslav (1300–22). He took advantage of Bulgaria's critical condition and succeeded, with the help of Eltimir Lord of Krăn (Krounos in Greek), to extend the frontiers of his state south of the Balkan mountain range and to recuperate the Black Sea ports. He was then able to prevent wheat from being exported to Constantinople, where people were starving because the crops in Thrace had been destroyed. This measure forced Byzantium to agree to peace, which was prolonged until the outbreak of the second Byzantine civil war, and allowed Bulgaria to enjoy a certain degree of economic development; which basically meant trading between the Black Sea ports and the Italian maritime towns.

The advent of the Šišman dynasty, the Despots of Vidin, to the throne in 1323 reunited Bulgaria for a while. They threw out the Boyard Vojsil, who had been installed in the sub-Balkan regions of Sredna Gora, from Stilvnon to Kopsis, by the Byzantines as 'Despot of Moesia'. Michael Šišman (1323–30) took an active part in the internal affairs of Serbia as well as in the Byzantine civil war and he was negotiating with Andronicus III about making a joint attack on the the former, when he was defeated at Velbăžd. His death put a sudden end to his projects. The new Tsar Ivan Alexander (1331–71) managed, in spite of his weakened state, to secure his western frontier by allying with Dušan, who was married to his sister. He resumed hostilities with Byzantium by winning back the Black Sea ports, which had previously been conquered by Andronicus III. At the beginning of the second Byzantine civil war, Alexander was actively involved on the side of the Regent of Constantinople, which secured him the considerable advantage of being able to extend his lands southwards to the upper valley of the Hebrus, that is to say, to the northern region of the Rhodopes which had until then formed the front line of defence of the Empire's European provinces.

252   In contrast to these achievements, the internal situation in Bulgaria did not stop

A view of river Asenitsa in the mountain range of the Rhodopes, a territorial stake between Byzantium and Bulgaria.

deteriorating. Like Byzantium, the Bulgarian State underwent a decentralising process and was broken up by her feudal lords into small autonomous units. The first to go were the north-eastern regions between the lower Danube valley and the Black Sea, which detached themselves from the Tărnovo government. The Boyard Balik, of Cuman origin, set himself up there as an independent ruler. He was succeeded by his brother Dobrotica, whose name was later given to part of his lands, called 'Dobrudža'. Around 1357 Dobrotica enlarged his territory towards the south-easterly foothills of the Balkan range (Stara Planina) by seizing the fortress of Emon and later that of Varna. These bases allowed him, with the help of his own fleet, to extend his activities into the Black Sea, where he thwarted the Genoese and even got involved with the Empire of Trebizond. His successor, the *magnificus et potens dominus Ivanko*, the *Juanco* of Genoese sources, concluded a treaty with Genoa through the mediation of a Genoese embassy from Pera, conceding a whole set of privileges to the Genoese merchants, including freedom of movement within his territory and the right to build churches and their own houses. He had been preceded in this by Tsar Ivan Alexander who had drawn up the same sort of treaty, but with the Venetians, in 1352.

After the north-eastern region had broken away from the central State, Vidin's turn came again. This time, however, it was Tsar Ivan Alexander himself who divided the greater part of his land between his two sons, following the example of the last Palaeologi. The region of Vidin (between the rivers Timok and Iskăr) was granted to his oldest son, Ivan Sracimir, (1365–96) while the capital Tărnovo with the Drăstăr region (Distra), Nikopol (Nicopolis) on the Danube, Sredec (Serdica, Sofia) and Diambol (Yampolis) fell to Ivan Šišman (1371–93), born of a second marriage. One noteworthy aspect of this arrangement was the advantage the Church of Constantinople derived from it, since, after his proclamation as Tsar, Sracimir brought his Church back under the jurisdiction of the Patriarch of Constantinople, as did Ivanko, lord of Dobrudža. In spite of Sracimir's difficult relations with the King of Hungary, which for a while reduced Vidin's kingdom to the status of *banat* (*banatus bulgariae*), where Franciscan monks began to operate, this did not deter him, after he had recovered his throne and after his brother's death, from his ambition to control the region around Sophia (1371).

As in Serbia, many towns in Bulgaria, besides the great number of originally Greek and Roman towns, had developed from the burghs which had grown up around the *boyards'* fortified dwellings. Their inhabitants were invested with privileges and enjoyed a degree of autonomy. The most important of them was Tărnovo, the capital of the second Bulgarian State, which was built on a high escarpment of the Balkans, solidly fortified and surrounded on three sides by the River Jantra. Bulgarian texts refer to it as 'Čarigrad Tărnovo', the Queen of towns, glorious Imperial city, truly second after Constantinople'. North of the Balkans other important towns rose up: the Danubian towns of Vidin (Bononia in Latin, Baudins according to Boucicaut), Nikopol (the ancient Nicopolis), Orjahov (now Rjahovo) and Drăstăr (Durostorum in Latin, now Silistra) on the one hand, and on the other, Preslav, the ancient Bulgarian capital, Provad (now Provadija) to the east and Lovăč (now Loveč) to the west. In the north-west of the southern Balkan basin, Sredu (the ancient Serdica, Triaditza to the Byzantines) was a fortified town but had no acropolis. On the Rila massif, Kostenec (Constantia in Greek, not to be confused with the Constantia of the eastern Rhodopes), Constantine the Philosopher's place of origin, and Kosteneki; in present-day Macedonia, the fortress of Stob (Stoumpion in Greek) on the lower course of the river Rila.

On the eastern shore of the Black Sea, the high-point of ancient Greek colonies, the towns preserved traces of their Byzantine past and character for a long time (especially the coastal towns south of Varna), due certainly to their frequent reintegration within the Empire: towns such as Karbona (now Balčik), Kavarna, Kaliakra, Konstanca, Kellia-Kilia and Likostomaion; these last on the Danube delta and mouth; Varna (the former Odessa), Anchialos, Mesembria (Nesebăr now and in Old Bulgarian), Sozopolis (now Sozopol), Pyrgos (now Burgas) Agathopolis (now Ahtopol). South of the Balkans, on the constantly fought-over border between Byzantium and Bulgaria, the important towns were Sliven (Stilvnon in Greek), Boruj (Beroe in Greek, now Stara Zagora) and Diambol (Yampolis in Greek).

As for the Bulgarian mining burghs, such as there were (not as many as in Serbia) had also been founded by Saxons from Wallachia, where they used to live in the fourteenth century. They settled mainly around the mountain town of Kiprovec (now Čiprovci) in the eastern Balkans, near the sources of the river Ogosta. They processed the minerals (iron,

The fortified town of Tărnovo. As capital of the second Bulgarian State and seat of its autonomous patriarchate, the town flourished under the first Asenides, with whom its name is still associated. The town was burnt in 1393 after being conquered by the Ottomans.

silver and gold) as they dug them up and their work lives on in the names of neighbouring villages like Željazna (from *željazo*, iron) and Srebărnica (from *srebro*, silver).

Bogomilism featured very strongly in the inner life of medieval Bulgaria, and the movement grew stronger still during the reign of Ivan Alexander and spread through the towns. At the same time, new religious sects like the Adamites or the partisans of Barlaam, the anti-Palamist champion, caught on and brought down on them the Emperor's fierce anger. He summoned two councils, one in 1350 and the other in 1360, to Tărnovo to move against the heretics. A period of persecutions and harsh repression followed, which ended with the adoption of Hesychasm as the official doctrine of the Orthodox Church, in line with what was happening in Constantinople at the same time. But peace did not return to the hearts of the clergy or the Bulgarian people, as the Anchoritic movement which spread all over the country demonstrated.

255

The end of the Bulgarians

Bulgaria's independence was soon to end; she was the first Balkan country after Byzantium to be invaded by the Ottomans on their way into Europe. As it was, she had already suffered from incursions and pillage by Turkish troops allied to Cantacuzenus during the second Byzantine civil war. In the region of Rhodopes, the Bulgarian chief Momčil, who had driven the boundaries of his autonomous principality towards the Aegean as far as the towns Xanthe and Peritheorion, rose to the occasion and fought Umur's Turks in front of this last town, dying at the head of his warriors in June 1345. *Momčil-voevoda* has entered Bulgarian legend and the songs of Rhodopes as a hero who had tackled obscure and treacherous enemies to fall at the end, a victim of a base betrayal. The Ottoman conquest of the region of the Rhodopes proper appears to have been effected after the Battle of Čirmen (Tzernomianon) in 1371, at the same time as the Bulgarian Tsar, like the Byzantine Emperor, became a tributary of the Sultan.

Matters came to a head a few years later. In 1388, Sultan Murad I invaded eastern Bulgaria and the Danube region in order to quash Tsar Ivan Šišman, who, emboldened by the success of the Serb Despot Lazar, had refused to pay his annual tribute. The final fall of the Bulgarian State of Tărnovo took place in 1393, after the Imperial town was subjected to a fierce siege by Bayezid who gave it over to the fury of his troops. In 1395, the Sultan annexed the Danube region, including Nicopolis, and decapitated Tsar Šišman who had taken refuge there. As for the State-like entities of Vidin and Dobrudža, they succumbed in their turn, the former in 1396 after the defeat of the Christian crusade, in which Ivan Sracimir took part, at Nicopolis, and the latter definitively around 1417, after a period of Wallachian occupation.

For those who could remember Krum or Symeon, Nicephoras Phocas or Basil II, the pitiful and mutual deterioration of the two great Balkan adversaries must have been poignant. Of the greatness that had been the eastern Roman Empire, all that remained were a few posts manned by Italians ready to compromise their honour in return for permission to stay on, a handful of castles whose garrisons were partly made up of westerners, and the besieged city herself, disregarded by all, drifting in a Turkish ocean towards her inevitable end.

A Turkish or Mongolian Islam 5

The Mongol wave released a material and spiritual catastrophe onto Islam and interrupted the course of Muslim history. The Ayyubid State was annihilated by its mercenaries who installed a military government in Egypt, which soon spread to include Palestine and Syria. Further north and east, the Mongol expansion brought about the disintegration of the Seljuk Sultanate in Asia Minor and the occupation of Iraq by the Mongols, who destroyed Baghdad and forced its new Abbasid Caliph to seek refuge in Cairo (1258). It also led to the creation of the Mongol States of the Kipchaks and the Ilkhans and to the appearance of the Turcoman kingdoms, with their various destinies, from Asia Minor to Afghanistan. In all this, the Mameluke Sultanate was alone in conserving a certain link with the past, in spite of internal politico-military incidents, and proved to be the most solid, best organised and administered of them all. The Sultan also benefited from his control over the ports of the eastern Mediterranean and the Red Sea, which gave him a considerable supremacy in international trade. The great prosperity of this Sultanate was particularly well reflected in its splendid buildings in Cairo. The situation in the Near East gradually evolved during the fourteenth century, especially in the second half, when the Ottomans rose to power. This rise was momentarily compromised when Tamerlane's Turco-Mongolian troops invaded and when the Egyptian regime was replaced by a new series of military leaders; by the turn of the fifteenth century, the Muslim world was plunged into new vicissitudes.

During this period, the Europeans abandoned all their territorial possessions, with the exception of Cyprus where the Kingdom of Jerusalem had taken refuge, and they no longer took part in politics. To compensate for this, they, especially the Venetians and the Genoese, stepped up their economic activity. In the Eastern Empire, in spite of winning back their capital in 1262, the Byzantines were reduced to watching their supremacy in eastern Asia Minor dwindle and disappear and in the Balkans be whittled down by Bulgarians, Serbs and finally Turks, to whom John VI Cantacuzenus unwisely appealed for help. By the end of the fourteenth century, there was only a temporary reprieval for the Byzantine Empire.

The death of the Crusade

Four crusades were carried out with varying success in the first half of the thirteenth century, with the purpose of re-establishing the Kingdom of Jerusalem in the Holy Land.

Although the Fourth Crusade stopped half-way and ended by creating the Latin Empire of Constantinople, the Fifth (1217–19) came to a sticky end in Egypt as did the Seventh, that of Louis IX (1248–50). On the other hand, the Sixth Crusade, led by Emperor Frederick II, restored Jerusalem to the Franks by reaching an agreement with the Ayyubid Sultan al-Kamil in 1229. Fifteen years later, however, the Muslims retook the town and thus restricted the Frankish 'States' to a few towns on the Syrian and Palestianian coastline and their immediate surroundings. Louis IX's expedition to Egypt did nothing to improve the situation, which deteriorated when the Mameluke Sultan Baibars, who had defeated the Mongols at Ayn Jalut (1260), undertook the systematic reconquest of Frankish positions; the Franks' most telling loss was that of Saint-John of Acre in May 1291, which had been a vital commercial base for the Genoese.

The end of the Palestinian dream

The loss of the Latin possessions put a definitive end to the dream of Palestine and to all hopes of reconstituting a Kingdom of the Holy Land. The causes were many; following the policy of reconquest and Muslim unity initiated by Nur-al-Din and Saladin, the Ayyubid Sultans manoeuvred pacifically and skilfully, preferring to conclude treaties with the Europeans when this served their purpose in the short term and attacking them when circumstances permitted. Later the Mameluke Sultans, with a view to controlling Egypt and Syria, halted the Mongols and prevented all contact with them by the Latins. A more far-seeing policy might possibly have enabled the Franks, by seeking an alliance with the Mongols sooner than they did (Louis IX attempted one unsuccessfully), to keep all or some of their positions in Syria and Palestine. As it was, the Ayyubid enterprises and especially those of the Mamelukes, were further served by the rivalries between Frankish families and between Italian merchant cities.

The Latins retreated to Cyprus, where the Kingdom of Jerusalem was perpetuated, thus introducing two new notions; that of turning the island into a base for the eventual re-conquest of the Holy Land, and that of maintaining the island as a Latin enclave in the eastern Mediterranean, where merchant ships in this area could call. As it was, until the Turks took it in 1571, Cyprus did constitute an eastern bastion, which, especially when the Venetians occupied the island, concentrated on trade rather than on conducting a military offensive against Islam. Cyprus was also a centre of Latin culture, the effect of which may be traced in the literature and especially in the religious and military architecture of the island.

A bit further West, the Knights of Saint John of Jerusalem had found an asylum in the Island of Rhodes, which they took in 1310. They turned the island into a naval and military base against the Muslims of Asia Minor and Syria, occasionally occupying other islands (Cos, for instance) and various strongholds on the coast of Asia Minor, such as Halicarnassus (nowadays Bodrum). The Ottoman Turks captured the island in 1522, forcing the Knights to leave first for Tripoli, and then Malta.

When the Byzantines reconquered Constantinople in 1261 and Michael VIII established the Palaeologus dynasty in the capital, the Latins were affected in ways which transcended

The island of Rhodes, the acropolis. This powerful stronghold was held by a few Knights of Saint John of Jerusalem at the head of a Greek garrison.

the loss of their Empire. The Venetians were momentarily evicted in favour of the Genoese, who were to turn Galata into the great centre of their trade in the eastern Mediterranean and the Black Sea; the Byzantine Empire was gradually pieced together again and, more particularly, Charles of Anjou, brother to King Louis IX and himself King of Naples, tried in vain to win back the throne of Byzantium. His definitive failure, which occurred when all his hopes were destroyed by the Sicilian revolt of 1282, put an end to the Latin presence in the East, except in the Morea where the Principality of Achaia kept going for a long time and, like Cyprus, became an enclave of Latin culture in a Greek world.

It is symptomatic of the fourteenth century that their expeditions, which were still incorrectly described as Crusades, no longer envisaged the reconquest of the Holy Places. They gradually took on new aspects; until the 1360s they were badly organised coalitions, which aimed at defending Christian interests in the eastern Mediterranean, either against Turkish emirates and pirates, as in 1345, or against the Egyptian Mamelukes, who controlled the trading posts along the Syrian, Palestinian and Egyptian coastline. The capture of Alexandria in 1365 by Peter I of Cyprus, who wanted to safeguard this port's commercial significance, turned into a failure which rebounded against the Christians of

259

Egypt and the European merchants living there. The Venetians and Genoese subsequently discouraged this sort of expedition. A second aspect emerged when the Ottoman Turks established control over Balkan Europe; expeditions carried out against them were designated anti-Turkish crusades. Their purpose was to protect Christians living in the Balkans against the Muslim onslaught. The expeditions of Nicopolis (1396) and of Varna (1445), which will be discussed later, were cruel failures for the Europeans, who resumed their offensive against the Turks only in the sixteenth century in the form of clashes between the Spanish and Austrian forces and the Ottomans.

Although the religious aspect was not completely missing from these Latin expeditions into the eastern Mediterranean, it was subordinated to their commercial motives. This attitude was especially well exemplified by the behaviour of the great mercantile cities of the age; Venice and Genoa. Anyway, what other justification could the westerners find for their actions in the East? The Latin States in the Holy Land and Byzantine territory had mostly disappeared and with them all kinds of properly political problems. As for human problems, these were practically non-existent in Syria and Palestine, where contact between Latins and the local people had been reduced to a minimum and gave rise to no continuity. There were some exceptions, such as Cyprus, the Principality of Morea and a few Aegean islands held by the Venetians, but centuries had to pass before even fairly close relationships were established between westerners and easterners. Although certain twelfth-century chroniclers did feel that the Latins had indeed been grafted onto the local populations, noting what their Latin masters had assimilated from local customs and languages, this process did not survive the Muslim reconquest. Although the religious orders and some lords struggled for most of the thirteenth century to defend the territories which had been left under their control, in the end they had to give up. All that remains of their sojourn in Syria and Palestine are the castles they built along the Christian–Muslim boundaries, the occasional reference to Arab writers in the chronicles and, finally, the presence of certain merchant communities, mostly Italian, in various Syrian, Palestinian and Egyptian ports. In the West, the benefits were equally limited; although the spirit of the Crusade still prevailed with some popes (Boniface VIII, John XXII), some rulers (Philip VI of Valois, Peter I of Cyprus), and especially some religious orders (notably the Dominicans, with Ramon Llull, Burchard, William Adam and Ricoldo of Monte Croce), it is significant that knowledge of Islam and Muslims made no progress at all; false notions and incomprehension remained the rule.

The Italian interests

Although political and religious endeavours in Muslim territory, and partly in Byzantine territory, failed, commercial enterprise did not. During the twelfth century, the conquest of the Syrio-Palestinian ports allowed colonies of Italian merchants to be established in them, but the activity of these merchants was limited to local trade, which they supplemented by trading with Egypt.

Trading conditions changed between the first half of the thirteenth century, when the Venetians dominated the Mediterranean market, and the second half, when the Mameluke

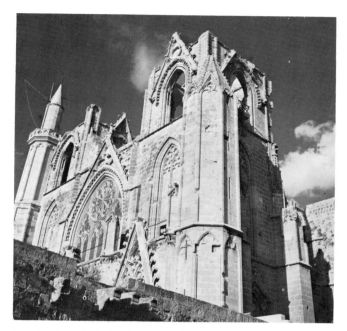

The Gothic Cathedral of Famagosta. The Lusignan kings were crowned here, who originally came from Poitou and who reigned over Cyprus for nearly three centuries.

regime took over Egypt and Syria and got control of the transit trade between the Indian Ocean and the Mediterranean as well as the export trade in local and East African produce. The Genoese were able to profit from the reconquest of Constantinople by the Greeks in securing certain temporary advantages over the Venetians, not least the permission to settle in Galata in 1265, where they gradually built a Genoese town. They also secured the right to trade on the Black Sea and so established trading posts in the Crimea, at Caffa and Tana. They established themselves with equal strength in Cyprus (at Famagosta) and, in spite of the fall of Acre, they maintained their positions in several ports on the Syrian coast. The Venetians reappeared, after their temporary exclusion, in Constantinople in 1268, and were found a little later on the Black Sea. They also succeeded in turning Alexandria into one of their main ports of call in the East. Since they still occupied Euboea and Crete and various points in the Adriatic, they were able to set up a communications network, by implementing their policy of establishing their presence and influence in a number of places, which amounted to an economic and political empire, known as 'Venetian Romania'.

The wars conducted by Michael VIII Palaeologus against Charles of Anjou and those which his successors engaged in against the Bulgarians, the Serbs and the Turks, weakened the Byzantine Empire still further, fraught as it was with considerable social problems. The Venetians and Genoese profited extensively from these by gaining control over almost all of Byzantium's foreign trade and thus depriving the Empire of important revenues. By the beginning of the fourteenth century, the volume of trade passing through

261

Galata was almost ten times that passing through Constantinople. The trade in the most remunerative export goods (wheat, wood, leather, alum, precious cloths, and especially slaves from the Caucasus, who were intended for Mameluke Egypt) was controlled by the Italians, some of whom, like the Genoese Benedetto Zaccaria, had considerable economic power.

The Venetians and Genoese were not consistently successful and on more than one occasion they suffered the hostility of local administrations in Constantinople as well as in the Crimea, where after initially welcoming them, the Mongol Khans of the Kipchak turned very anti-European. Their attitude was communicated by the hostility of the locals, who accused the Latin merchants of ruining them and, more particularly, of looking down on them. Furthermore, the Empire's financial difficulties induced the Basileus to devalue the hyperpyr (the gold solidus) several times, from 24 to 9 and then to 5 carats. Byzantine money in consequence lost its role as the international coinage to the new Italian coins, the *Genovino*, the *Florin* and finally to the Venetian *Ducat*, which was called a *sequin* and enjoyed total supremacy for centuries. This ascendancy was perfected by the creation of a network of bankers who avoided cash transfers and introduced maritime insurance, which secured merchants, traders and ship owners definite advantages.

When the political situation in the Near and Middle East disrupted the trade routes to China and Turkestan, the Venetians and Genoese, without totally abandoning their outposts on the Black Sea and in Anatolia, concentrated more on their Mediterranean trading posts and on the ports of call of international trade. The internal stability and security of countries under Mameluke rule induced them to strengthen their merchant colonies in Syria, Palestine and Egypt, with the port of Alexandria playing an essential role. Cyprus and Crete were also involved in this process; the former even commanded a strategic position in the eastern Mediterranean. When its ruler, King Peter I, led his expedition against Alexandria, his motives were not simply religious but included commercial considerations. His attempt failed and this rebounded momentarily against Frankish merchants living in the city. There were in consequence no further attacks on Alexandria and a commercial *modus vivendi* was established between Eygptian officials and merchants and Italian merchants and ship owners, which was to endure until the Ottomans conquered Syria and Egypt at the beginning of the sixteenth century.

In the long run, the dream of the knights of the First Crusade, that they would establish a Latin State in the East, was a complete failure. Instead the Latin presence made itself felt in a form which gave a particular turn to relations between westerners and easterners. There could be no question of territorial control, but, under the cover of trade, the question of controlling economic activities which concerned both Europe and Asia arose. A form of mercantile capitalism thus appeared in the Mediterranean, which developed steadily throughout the centuries and would make the fortune of the Near Eastern States, or ruin them, according to their strengths or weaknesses.

Egypt, a sanctuary

In the second half of the thirteenth century, profound changes appeared within the Muslim world of the Near East; in Syria and Egypt, the Ayyubids, Arabised Kurds, had already

A delegation of Venetians is received at Damascus (and not at Cairo as this picture by a follower of Bellini was long considered to represent). In effect, the whole of the Mameluke world was affected by the implantation of Italian merchant colonies. (End of the fifteenth century, Paris, Louvre.)

altered the situation locally, while further north and east, the Seljuks, Islamised Turks influenced by Arab and Iranian culture, had supported the Caliph of Baghdad and had extended Muslim hegemony up to Byzantine Asia. Shortly before the mid thirteenth century, the Mongol menace arose; Genghis Khan's successors had penetrated Muslim territory and threatened the ruling dynasties in Iran, Iraq, Azarbayjan, and Anatolia, as well as northern Syria.

A military 'coup d'état'

The Egyptian ruler, al-Malik al-Salih, recruited his horsemen among the Khwarasmian Turks, who originated from between the Caspian and the Sea of Aral, and had been driven forwards by the Mongol advance. He directed them into Palestine and Syria with the idea of rebuilding Ayyubid unity, as in Saladin's time, and of organising them as a bulwark against the Mongols. The Khwarasmians however distinguished themselves by massacring the local populations, notably in Jerusalem, where they decimated the Christian

263

inhabitants (1244). In order to get rid of them, al-Malik al-Salih resorted to buying slaves from the Black Sea ports, who came from the Turkish peoples around the Lower Volta. These tribes were now controlled by the Mongols, who did not scruple to sell them to Greek and Italian merchants. After receiving a military training, these slaves, or Mamelukes, formed the core of al-Malik al-Salih's army, they were also called al-Salihs, after their master. They performed their function perfectly by eliminating the Khwarasmians and then by defeating Louis IX's crusaders, who had landed at Damietta in 1249. The sudden death of al-Malik al-Salih allowed them to assume control; dissatisfied with their new leader Turanshah's intentions towards them, the Mameluke chiefs suppressed him and recognised the Sultana Shajar al-Durr, al-Salih's widow, as their new sovereign and set up one of their men, the Emir Aybeg as her advisor. Aybeg took over the supreme power and assumed the title of 'Sultan' in 1250, thus inaugurating a new dynasty of Egyptian rulers: the *Bahri* Mamelukes (from the Arab word *bahr* (sea) which was applied to the Nile; one of the Mamelukes' main garrisons was on an island in the Nile), which lasted until 1382. From then until 1517, other Mamelukes, mainly of Caucasian origin, ruled Egypt and were called *Burjis* (from the word *burj* (tower) because they were quartered in the towers of the Cairo citadel).

The seizure of power by the military and the consolidation of the new regime were due to different factors; the first was the new Frankish threat, Louis IX's crusade, which was eliminated in the Nile delta, and the second was the Mongol menace from Iraq, led by the Mongol Khan Hulagu, who took Baghdad in 1258, destroyed the town and invaded Syria. The Mameluke Sultan Baibars (reigned 1260–77) managed to defeat the Mongols at Ayn Jalut in 1260, a victory which won him the immeasurable esteem of the Muslims, who considered him as the saviour of Islam and of the Caliphate – one of the Abbasid Caliphs having escaped to Cairo. Finally, the Mamelukes' success in reuniting Egypt and Syria into one political entity allowed them to set themselves up as the successors of Saladin. Thus a regime, which owed its existence to the play of circumstance and the ambition of military leaders, managed to establish its legitimacy fairly rapidly. Their power was the surer in that they constituted Egypt's and Syria's sole defence against the threat of Mongol invasion, given the extinction of the Ayyubid dynasty.

Since their rise to power had been alien to Muslim tradition, these soldiers imposed a political system based on their own organisation; membership of a specific Mameluke cadre, which formed the basis of the State. The Sultan was the leading representative of this military caste, but he relied for any real power on the emirs, with whom he had been recruited and trained – his companions, to whom he was only *primus inter pares*. These emirs were entrusted with *iqtas*, the revenues from lands, whose size varied according to their holder's status and to his military or administrative importance. The emirs were supposed to use these revenues to maintain their own Mamelukes in battalions of ten to forty or a hundred men, ready to be called up at any moment by the Sultan. For his part, the Sultan drew almost half the State revenues; this was justified by the importance and the size of the Sultan's functions. He represented central government, along with the services provided by the court. Although these revenues secured the Sultan considerable prestige and made him the real head of State, they were not great enough to give him absolute power or even to allow him to ensure his son's succession. Like those of his emirs, his revenues were in fact personal, temporary and not transferable. The hereditary principle did not exist, and consequently, it was very rare for the son of a Sultan to succeed his father, although this did happen in the fourteenth century, when Sultan Qalawun (1279–90) was succeeded by his son Muhammad al-Malik al-Nasir, who, however, only reigned from 1310 to 1314. The same condition applied to the emirs' *iqtas*. This system had its inbuilt faults; the Sultan and his emirs were members of a caste, which, once it had confiscated the power, was not prepared to relinquish it to other social classes. This meant that they were obliged to maintain and, where necessary, to increase the membership of their caste, in other words, the Mamelukes. It followed that, since the Sultan and the Emirs represented only a minority within this caste and that their descendants were prohibited from the succession (the sons of Mamelukes, who had been born in Egypt or Syria, were, by definition, not Mamelukes), they could be replaced only voluntarily or by force. This explains the number of *coups d'état* which occurred during the Mameluke regime and the absence of a real dynasty.

The reflection of ancient Islam

In spite of these constraints, this regime enjoyed a strong authority and administration, which it had inherited from the Abbasid and Fatimid Caliphates. The Sultan was the temporal leader and the presence of the Abbasid Caliph, the spiritual leader of Islam, in Cairo guaranteed the legitimacy of his rule. Of course, the Mameluke Sultans were careful to confine the Caliph's mandate within extremely narrow limits; he was unable to exercise real power (except on rare and brief occasions) beyond that of being the guardian of the legitimacy and continuity of Islam, as far as the population was concerned.

The Sultan resided in Cairo; his buildings and palaces were in the Citadel, from which Saladin had previously ruled. The Sultan and the emirs were mostly of Turkish origin and spoke Arabic badly, but nonetheless, the holders of the aulic posts, which formed the Sultan's council, were appointed from among these emirs, who were then summoned to discuss and decide on State policy. Among these posts, there was the Master of the Sultan's household (*ustadar*), the head of Chancery (*dawadar*), the emir of the army (*amir silah*), the commander of the guard (*ras nawba*), the emir of the stables (*amir akhur*), and the emir responsible for the Sultan's safety (*amir djandar*). In practice, when the Sultan led his army on expeditions outside Cairo, he delegated his powers to a lieutenant (*na'ib*) who took over the administration. As under the Fatimids and Ayyubids, this administration was split up into departments (*diwan*), each one controlled by a *nasir*, dealing with the Empire's revenues, its expenditure, the army and the internal administration. As under the previous regimes, the *diwans* were often staffed by Christians and Jews. Orders and decrees were issued by the chancery, which was controlled by the 'secret secretary' or *katib al-sirr*. Details of its organisation appear in the chancery records, the most famous of them being the *Subh al-a'cha* compiled by Qalqashandi (1355–1418) and finished in 1412. From the

265

fourteenth century onwards, the chancery also had a rider messenger service (*barid*) which had started life as a military service, but was later handed over to the administration and became remarkably efficient, especially for keeping in touch with the provinces.

These provinces were not constituted uniformly; two great spheres of power existed in Egypt, one in the Egyptian Delta and the other in Upper Egypt or Sa'id. These were split up into two provinces, each administered by a governor, or *wali*. Syria had six regencies (*mamlaka*) or lieutenancies (*niyaba*), each one commanded by a *na'ib*, the Sultan's representative, with his own emirs, administrators and governors. This arrangement did not prevent inspectors (*kashif*) from being appointed in Egypt in the second half of the fourteenth century; this function was performed by emirs, whose duties included ensuring that the irrigation system functioned properly, that the tax collectors were protected and that the harvests were supervised. The *kashifs* eventually became extremely important in provincial administration and politics.

The State was particularly concerned with the administration of the countryside, because most of its income came from it, either in the form of agricultural produce (cereals, legumes, sugar cane and fruit) or in harvest taxes. So it was normal for the State to supervise agriculture, especially in Egypt, where everything depended on the flux of the Nile, and where this could be used to advantage only if the irrigation system was properly maintained. In Syria and Upper Egypt, the peasants had to be protected from frequent pillage by Beduin tribes. The Mameluke State encouraged these tribes to concentrate their expansionist energies in Nubia, which had until then been partly Christian, but was progressively Islamised as a result of Baibars' conquest and the incursion of Arab tribes. The islamisation of Nubia was of capital importance to Egypt and the Mameluke regime, because this country was the gateway to Central and East Africa with all its riches, first among them being the trade in black slaves.

The wealth of the Mameluke Empire went in part to the Sultan, in part to the emirs. Their income was derived from their *iqtas*, whose revenues were supposed to provide them with a generous subsistence as well as funds for purchasing, feeding, training and equipping their own Mamelukes. These emirs generally lived in the capital, Cairo, or in the great towns of Syria, Damascus and Aleppo, and they entrusted the administration and supervision of their *iqtas* to intendants, who were often hard on the peasants. Like the Sultan, the emirs surrounded themselves with a court, which varied in importance according to their rank. They were encouraged to use the rest of their income to build themselves palaces and tombs of great size; to dedicate funds towards religious buildings (possibly a mosque or a *madrasa*) or military works, and, finally, in order to ensure their own and their families' material future, to build or buy housing blocks, baths, shops, khans (*wakala*) and lands. They protected these acquisitions from future distraint or confiscation by turning them into *waqf*; pious foundations, whose revenues were dedicated to maintaining the religious edifices which the emir had erected, but which also enabled his descendants to draw an income from them. The *waqf* system was clearly applied very extensively under the Mameluke regime, as much in Egypt as in Syria, and the registration (*waqfiyya*) of these donations, where it has been preserved, constitutes a precious record of the economic and social history of the Mameluke towns.

Aerial view of Bab al-Hadid, or the Iron Gate (fifteenth century), one of the five still extant gates in the walls of the Aleppo citadel, which were rebuilt on Byzantine foundations in the Mameluke period.

Towns and town life were important features of this State, because the rich and powerful lived in them and spent their essentially agricultural revenues in them. Economic life improved remarkably under the Mamelukes and contributed to the development of the towns – especially the great ones; Cairo, Damascus, Aleppo – in spite of the Black Death of 1349, which hit Egypt hard. The population grew and buildings, shops and workshops rose up to provide lodgings and employment for the increasing numbers who had been attracted by the pickings to be made from the emirs' lavish expenditure. New quarters also had to be built, with their characteristic features; their indispensible religious monuments, mosques, *madrasas* and such like, and their commercial districts, whose importance depended on their location. In certain cases, entrepots; *khans*, *wakala*, *qaisariya* and *funduks*, multiplied in the town centres (seldom on their edges) in response to the great commercial activity in Cairo, Damascus and Aleppo. The towns did not all develop in the same way; nor did their internal organisations keep up with the growth of their population and their many

267

different activities. The guilds themselves do not appear to have been very well established; in any case they were very restricted. The *futuwwa*, which developed under the Abbasids, survived only as a formality in Mameluke Egypt and Syria, deprived of political or social influence, and which eventually disappeared. It was replaced by the *ulamas* (plural of *alim*; learned man versed in Theology), whose influence over urban society grew as a result of their role as intermediaries between the ruling power and the people, and they functioned both in legal and religious matters. Trained in the *madrasa*, they meant more to the people than did the Mameluke Sultan and emirs, who were still considered foreigners. They stood for Arabic–Moslem tradition, religious orthodoxy and they were seen, perhaps even more so in lower-class districts and the countryside, as their true spiritual mentors, in liaison with the religious societies (*tariqat*). Some *ulamas* and pious persons were revered as saints – and their sanctity was sometimes recognised even by the emirs, who were careful to establish links with their people and not to appear different from them.

The Islamisation of Egypt appears to have made advances in this period; although Christians and Jews were not persecuted or harassed, it is clear that Islam was endorsed as the fundamental bond which united the people and the rulers of the Mameluke Empire – rulers who were themselves often fairly recent converts to Islam. The first Mameluke Sultans used the theory of the Hanbalite theologian Ibn Taymiyya (1263–1328) – often contested by other Muslim theologians – which justified the indissoluble union of religion and a strong State, capable of ensuring observance of the religious law, of promoting social improvement and of developing harmonious relations between the various communities in the population. The religious character of the regime was demonstrated by the profusion of pious monuments built by the Mameluke Sultans and emirs in Cairo, Damascus and Aleppo and other towns: mosques, *madrasas*, hospitals, tombs, schools, fountains (*sabil*) and so on, whose original architectural style is a feature of the Mameluke period.

The great route to the Indies

The Mameluke State was successfully established both within the political administration of Egypt and Syria and without, where it took advantage of favourable circumstances. The failure of Louis IX's Crusade and, soon afterwards, the defeat of the Mongols at Ayn Jalut won the Mamelukes security in Syria. A security which was strengthened at the end of the thirteenth century by the eviction of the last Latin Christians from the Middle East following the capture of Saint-John of Acre in 1291, and which was made concrete when the Mongols agreed to a peace treaty in 1323, after suffering further defeats. In the same way, the defence of the Syrian frontier was ensured by the elimination of the Armenian Kingdom of Cilicia. Finally, the decline of the Mongol States in Iran, Iraq and Asia Minor during the greater part of the fourteenth century forced merchants to abandon the trade routes which passed through these countries. In Syria and Egypt, on the contrary, peace and stability reigned, which made the routes leading from these regions to the Indian Ocean all the more attractive. Consequently, greater interest was paid to Central and East Africa; Nubia was already directly controlled by the Mamelukes through their Arab tribesmen. Egypt thus

A masterpiece of Mameluke architecture, Sultan Hasan's *madrasa* in Cairo (fourteenth century), in which the central court is enclosed by four *iwans* of noble dimensions, with an octagonal fountain in the centre, capped by a bulbous dome. (Watercolour by David Roberts, 1839.)

became the pivot for trade between the countries of the Mediterranean and those of the Indian Ocean; an important transit trade crossed the country from Aydhab in the South, along a road leading to the Nile Valley at Qus and then down the river to Cairo and finally Alexandria, where western merchants took up the relay. This trade in spices, pepper, precious cloths and luxury items like porcelain, brought the Mameluke State considerable revenue from its customs, import and export duties and tariffs on ships and transactions. This revenue paid for the import of materials such as wood and metals and sometimes cereals, and also for buying young slaves, who were vitally important to the Mameluke army.

From the Ayyubids until the mid fifteenth century, all important trade was controlled by the *karimi* merchants, whose grandest period was during the fourteenth century. These merchants were organised into family associations in which free men and slaves participated as agents, market prospectors and as representatives in local trading posts on the East coast of Africa, in Arabia, in India and even further afield. By the fourteenth century, *karimi* merchants or their agents were probably in contact with the inhabitants of Java and Sumatra – where Islamisation had already begun, especially in North Sumatra at Atjeh – and with the Chinese. They shipped the products of the Far East to Egypt and made

269

the fortune of the Mameluke State as well as their own (*karimi* worth several hundred thousand dinars have been recorded), and they contributed to the remarkable economic progress of Cairo's commercial quarters and souks, in which a number of emirs were also involved.

The *karimi*'s monopoly of the Red Sea and the Aydhab-Qus road was slowly attacked, partly by the Beduin tribes of Upper Egypt, who were avid to draw some profit from this wealth passing under their noses and began to make trouble. This was exacerbated by the Black Death and by the activity of pirates lurking in the southern end of the Red Sea and along the African coastline. Before the end of the century, the *karimi* had consequently abandoned Aydhab and transferred their port to Suez.

On the Mediterranean side, Alexandria was the great crossroads of international trade. The elimination of the Latins from their positions in Syria and Palestine made it easier for them to establish intensive commercial relations with the Arab world. These relations were momentarily compromised when Peter I of Lusignan attacked Alexandria in 1365, and was violently denounced by the Italians for so doing, but once that threat had disappeared, the former situation reasserted itself. Alexandria, like the other ports along the Syrian and Palestinian coastline where other European merchant colonies were to be found, was the furthest place where these merchants could trade, since the Mamelukes forbad them all commercial activity in their territory and, with more reason, beyond it in the Red Sea. It was only along the Turkish–Mongolian border that Europeans were able to establish some contact with Asia. Given that Venice and Genoa were far from able to compete with the power and wealth of the Mameluke State, and on the other hand, that the Italian, Provençal and Catalan merchant cities monopolised transport across the Mediterranean, they were able to draw substantial advantages from this at the least expense, by projecting an image of themselves no longer as conquering warriors, but as merchants seeking friendly contacts. Apart from the Lusignan episode, the foreign colonies lived peacefully in the Mamelukes' ports, where they were able to add the final links to the network of trade they had set up all around the Mediterranean.

Apart from the merchants, other Europeans crossed Mameluke territory as pilgrims. Although some people were inspired by their pilgrimage to recall the crusades with a degree of bitterness, others looked at the East with new eyes. Gower rejected the idea of killing Saracens as contrary to Christ's teaching in his *Confessio Amantis*; Langland wrote that the religion of the Muslims was not totally opposed to that of the Christians. Honoré Bonet admitted in his *The Tree of Battles c.* 1387, that the Pope was justified in preaching the Crusade, but he considered that war against unbelievers was unjust on two accounts; firstly, God had given them their religion, so why remove it by force rather than letting them live freely? Secondly, God's will was not to be countered. John Wycliffe castigated all Crusades as undertakings of brigandage and pillage.

The Mameluke State was thus the dominant power in the eastern Mediterranean before the end of the fourteenth century, although incidents tended to show that it was not proof against all problems. As for instance when the supply of Mamelukes dried up after 1360, which forced them to look for new recruits in the Caucasus, or when Aydhab was

The tombs of the Caliphs. This astonishing necropolis of the second Mameluke dynasty (the Circassians), stretches out, deserted and hauntingly strange, in north Cairo. The mausoleum of Sultan Barquq is one of the best preserved buildings in it. According to Mameluke tradition, it served also as a *madrasa* and a mosque.

abandoned, or when the Black Death ravaged the country in 1349, followed by a series of epidemics. There were also the troubles in Upper Egypt and, at the end of the century, a preliminary clash with the Ottomans along the Cilician border. None of these events was, however, serious enough to disrupt the Empire and it was to carry on, almost always as splendidly, for the whole of the fifteenth century.

The end of an original Egypt

The second period in the history of the Mameluke Sultanate belonged to the *Burji* or Circassian Sultans, because contenders for power now had to be Caucasians. Although they did not constitute a real dynasty, almost all the Sultans between 1382 and 1461 came originally from Barquq, the Zahiri Mamelukes, so that the reigns of Barquq (1382–99), Shaykh (1412–21), Barsbay (1422–37), Jaqmaq (1438–53) and Inal (1453–61) constitute a lineage in that these Sultans all belonged to the same ethnic group. A little later, a Mameluke from Malik al-Ashraf Barsbay's group, Qa'it Bay (1468–96), and then

271

one of his Mamelukes, Qansawh al-Ghawri (1501–17), formed another line of Sultans. Compared with the first phase of the Mameluke Sultanate, the second was very different, not only because the successive Sultans all belonged to the same tribe, but because their reigns were much longer than the previous ones, evidence both of the stability achieved by the Mameluke government and of the authority the Sultans had won over their military and civil administrations. At the very least, this showed that they had turned their emirs into reliable collaborators, to whom they assigned notable revenues and privileges. They made sure that the emirs enjoyed particularly enviable circumstances and were not drawn into palace revolutions. On the contrary, they defended the regime which brought them wealth and responsibilities. In this context, the Sultans appeared not only as powerful rulers but, what was more, as rulers who showed concern for their subjects' interests, especially those subjects who came highest in the hierarchy and whom it was sensible to favour. The Sultans also seem to have grown closer to the Egyptian people, not only because they ruled for longer and so were better known, but because they were more arabised than the Sultans of the first phase had been. Under these conditions, from the beginning of the fifteenth century, the Abbasid Caliphate was no longer anything more than a religious symbol devoid of political influence.

Important changes also occurred in the administration. The serious economic problems at the end of the fourteenth century and the increased authority of the Sultan over his entourage led to one of the emirs close to the ruler becoming especially important. He was the *ustadar*, master of the Sultan's household, who ran the administration from the centre, supervising it as a sort of Grand Vizir. He remained dependent on the Sultan, who was henceforth more of a political than a military leader and who was responsible for the good functioning of the State. Besides the *ustadar*, another emir held a high position in the hierarchy; the emir of the armies (*atabek al-'asakir*), for whom an old Seljuk title was revived instead of Fatimid or Ayyubid titles. This was significant and should be seen in context with the contemporaneous rise in power of the Ottomans, who also claimed to be the heirs of the Seljuks and who, like the Mameluke Sultans, were also Turks. The two great dynasties were neighbours within the confines of Anatolia and Syria–Cilicia, and they recruited the petty lords in these regions as clients or allies. Thus the rivalry between Mamelukes and Ottomans erupted in more than one domain.

When new problems emerged at the end of the fifteenth century in the political and economic life of the Mameluke State, another emir rose in his turn to great importance; he was the *dawadar* (literally, portable desk) who took in hand the administration of the Sultanate, supplanting the *ustadar*. Here too, comparison can be made with the Ottoman State, where the *defterdar* (literally, keeper of the registers) controlled the administration of the finances under the authority of the Sultan and the Grand Vizir and was one of the highest Ottoman officials. The marked personality of these Circassian Sultans, who were deeply conscious of their power and role, and the presence of a very small number of high-ranking emirs on whom the basic offices of the administration and the protection of the State devolved, meant that this period was one when power was centralised and when the authority of a small number of rulers over the emirs and functionaries was enlarged. This process accentuated a phenomenon, which had appeared in the first half of the fourteenth century; the confusion between the Sultan's household (where the emirs came from) and the State, which was unquestionably to the advantage of the latter. The centralisation and increase of power was also marked by the fact that the Sultan, during the main part of the fifteenth century and until the beginning of the sixteenth, remained in Cairo and was no longer obliged to go on expeditions to defend the State's territories. Residing in his palace in the Cairo citadel, where dwellings, garrisons and administrative offices huddled together, he was henceforth a real 'head of State' (as Sultans Barsbay and especially Qa'it Bay demonstrated perfectly). Apart from making frequent grandiose appearances in the Capital, the Sultan demonstrated his power in the provinces through his inspectors (*kashif*), who had begun as mere controllers of agricultural revenues and land maintenance, but were then supplied with military assistance by the capital and were promoted to keep order in the provinces; they ended up supplanting the governors. The *kashif* were nominated directly by the Sultan and so represented the central authority, which they helped to strengthen.

The germs of disintegration

The Black Death which raged through Egypt in 1349 dealt a serious blow to the country's population and economy, the more so since the epidemic reappeared in 1374–75 and from then on fairly periodically. Although the scourge struck at town dwellers – and among them many Mameluke recruits who had not developed immunity to it – it did not spare the country people and this had important consequences for the Mameluke State. Since the State drew the bulk of its financial and material resources from the countryside and since it could replace the lost recruits only by buying them in at inflated prices, (all the higher since humans in the Caucasus and other countries were getting rarer), it felt obliged to maintain and even increase the pressure of taxation and surveillance of agricultural production. This provided the *kashifs* with the scope to extend their powers in the countryside; they were now required to control the maintenance of the irrigation canals and dykes, vital to a high level of production, and to protect the tax collectors, to prevent exaction by the emirs and to forbid incursions by the Beduin into settled territory. The problems of the rural population had increased as their numbers decreased, due to the additional burden of taxation and to depradations by the Beduin of Syria and Upper Egypt. These nomadic peoples were probably less affected by the Black Death because they were remote from the areas where the epidemic was fiercest, and they did indeed profit from the fall in the sedentary population, which they constantly raided. It was under these conditions that the *kashifs* were called on to extend their brief in the provinces, with the idea of protecting the fundamental resources of the State. This led to vigorous repressive action against the Beduin and they, who until then had provided an element of protection for trade between Africa and Egypt crossing Upper Egypt, which they had drawn financial advantage from, were no longer able to do so. Further, in order to avoid this dangerous region, the merchants abandoned the sea route to Aydhab and adopted a new port at Tor, near Suez, which was already active before the end of the fifteenth century. Further serious events occurred at the beginning of the fifteenth century; the invasion of Syria by Tamerlane's Turco-Mongolian troops; famine in Egypt; the resurgence of the Plague in 1405 and the war of the emirs against Sultan Faraj, which went on until 1412. These events contributed towards the break up of the Sultanate and the withdrawal of its political and economic authority from several regions. The situation was improved only in the reigns of Sultans Shaykh (1412–21) and especially Barsbay (1422–38), who introduced new measures, those of strengthening the powers of the *kashif* to the detriment of the emirs, and increasing the State's control over foreign trade. This last measure was beneficial; from 1425, Barsbay turned the spice trade into a State monopoly, controlling both the unloading point at Tor and the loading point at Alexandria. He thus increased his income at the expense of the emirs, who could no longer profit from the transit of these goods through Upper Egypt and along the Nile Valley. This situation was further improved by the fact that eastern Asia Minor, Upper Iraq, Northern Iran and Afghanistan were in this period areas of conflict, where merchants chose not to go. Consequently, Syria, which was enjoying a period of peace after Tamerlane's invasion, benefited from the troubles of its neighbours and also welcomed some of the trade destined for the West. The wealth of the Mameluke Sultanate definitely increased, a wealth which lasted until the end of Qa'it Bay's reign (1468–96) and gave new life to Egypt and Syria as well as widening commercial relations with Western Europe, because the Mamelukes' wealth allowed them to buy more numerous and more varied European products. These included luxury and consumer goods as well as materials indispensable to the Mameluke armies. The increased strength of the Mamelukes' economy and finances is illustrated by the penetration of European products; a penetration which sowed the seeds of competition by encroaching into a domain which had until then been fairly well protected. As long as the Mamelukes were able to protect the sea route to the Indies and the Far East, along which merchandise came to Egypt, they had nothing to fear. Even when the Portuguese established themselves along various points in the Indian Ocean, at the beginning of the sixteenth century, they were not yet strong enough to blockade or turn away trade en route for Egypt, since they did not have enough bases and contacts.

These economic factors have been considered the root cause of the Mamelukes' weakness *vis-à-vis* the Ottomans, but they are not the main reason for their collapse. The reasons for it are found in the regime's internal difficulties at the beginning of the sixteenth century, in Egypt as much as in Syria, and in the rise in power of the Ottomans, who then possessed the most impressive and efficient armies in the whole Near East and eastern Mediterranean.

The trend towards urban development, which we remarked on for the first period of the Mameluke regime, continued during the second and was even intensified. Although the Plague of 1349 depopulated the towns as well as the countryside, the towns seem to have recovered better and faster from its effects. The presence of a strong centralised power in the

The Tayruzi bath (1444) in Damascus, one of the oldest baths still in use. The heating system supplies three connecting and increasingly hot chambers; the last and hottest is flanked by little side chambers for bathing, while the central area is reserved for sweating.

fifteenth century allowed a large court to grow up in Cairo, while emirs of various ranks continued to live in the capital or the great provincial centres and to draw their revenues from the countryside, through the *iqta* entrusted to their keeping. Like their predecessors, they spent this money on their own Mamelukes, on building themselves residences, even palaces (some of which have been wholly or partly preserved and which reveal many aspects of urban life then), or participating in commercial enterprises. Some was spent on public buildings; religious (mosques, *madrasas*, tombs), or utilitarian (baths, fountains), or commercial (*khans*, *souks* and shops). The Sultans were not slow to dedicate their wealth to urban activities and many monuments were built in Cairo and Damascus which testify to the splendour of their regime. Numerous peasants were attracted by the chances of employment provided by the Sultans' and emirs' wealth, keen as they were to escape the depradation of tax collectors and the rigours of working on land which successive epidemics had sometimes left profoundly depopulated. These uprooted peasants came and

275

settled in peripheral shanty towns and in the courtyards of central buildings, in fairly miserable dependence on the palaces. The citizens, workmen, traders, craftsmen, employees of the Sultan's administration, and Mamelukes in the emirs' service enjoyed higher incomes and lived either in collective housing with several floors (*rab'*) or in houses rented from the emirs.

Building activity was intense in the fourteenth and fifteenth centuries and was engaged in not only by Sultans and emirs but also by shopkeepers and important businessmen, the successors of the *karimi*, who built entrepots, places for selling merchandise in bulk (*khans*, *wakala*, *funduks*) as well as their own homes. Another way of using the income from the *iqta* and from trading, administrative or economic activities, was to build or buy shops, blocks of flats and baths and to draw income from them. As before, these properties were safeguarded from eventual confiscation by being included in pious foundation schemes or *waqf*, and were made inalienable, thus protecting the interests of their founders' descendants.

Towns were also lived in by the *ulamas*, men of religion and learning. Trained in *madrasas*, they performed religious, legal and even pedagogic functions as well as serving as intermediaries between the authorities and the people. The increase in arabisation and the growth of Islam made them increasingly important, the more so since the Cairo Sultans were keen on proving themselves good Muslims in the eyes of the people and provided the *ulamas* with their own specific buildings.

On the whole, towns led a quiet existence during most of the fifteenth century, free of revolts and unrest, thanks to the administration and the authority of their Sultans and to the benefits of trade both within and without the State, which reflected on all town dwellers.

The Turkish menace

The period of the Circassian Mamelukes started off with a few difficult moments, however: while Tamerlane and his troops had invaded Syria in the fifteenth century, occupying and devastating Damascus and Aleppo and threatening Egypt herself, he turned his attention subsequently to Anatolia and the danger withdrew. It remained none the less present in the minds of the Mamelukes, who feared the return of the Mongol troops; a return which never took place. During the whole of the fifteenth century, the decline of the Byzantine Empire and of the Khanate of Kipchak meant that the Mamelukes were deprived of allies, or at least partners, who had been very useful to them. Ottoman power grew gradually out of the ruins of the Byzantine Empire, but was dealt a severe blow by Tamerlane in 1402. This encouraged the Cairo Sultans to underestimate the real danger to them from the Ottomans, the more so since they seemed to be aiming no further east than Anatolia and to be directed more towards Balkan Europe, even after they had recovered from their defeat. In the eastern Mediterranean, Peter I of Lusignan's ill-advised attack against Alexandria in 1365 had left a bad memory; so, once Sultan Barsbay had established his authority, he did not hesitate to launch an attack on Cyprus, devastating Limassol in 1425. In the following year he invaded the island and took King Janus prisoner, whose son John II (1432–58) became his vassal. Once the security of the Mameluke State had been ensured on their sea front, it had to be secured on the northern and north-eastern frontiers, on the Syrian borders. The adjacent territories were now largely ruled by the Turcoman horde of the Black Sheep (*Kara Koyunlu*) in the second half of the fourteenth century. After being defeated by Tamerlane, they recovered their importance only in the mid fifteenth century and did not present a threat to the Mamelukes. The Black Sheep State was annexed in 1467 by the White Sheep State (*Ak Koyunlu*), which had also appeared in the second half of the fourteenth century and reached its apogee under Uzun Hasan (1466–78). Once established in eastern Asia Minor, and then in the Diyar Bakr, they rivalled Mameluke influence over these regions, some trying to attract the allegiance of rulers established in the buffer zones Cilicia and Central and Eastern Anatolia against the Ottomans. The White Sheep were later to turn their faces further to the East, where they finally established their rule, leaving Anatolia to the Ottomans. From then on they became the Mamelukes' principal rivals in this whole area of the Near East.

At the death of the Ottoman Sultan Mehmed II, the Conqueror of Constantinople, one of his sons, Jem, revolted against his brother Bayezid II and tried to persuade the Mameluke Sultan Qa'it Bay to help him, who avoided getting involved. However, sporadic fighting did erupt around the principalities of Cilicia (Dulgadir and Ramazan) between 1485 and 1488. The century came to its close without much change in the situation. The sixteenth century brought the accession of Sultan Selim I to the Ottoman throne, who was to change the political aspect of the whole of the Near East. After crushing the Safavid ruler of Iran and occupying all eastern Anatolia and western Iran in 1514, he turned after a brief respite against the Mameluke State. His army's superiority and especially his artillery won him victory over the forces of the Mameluke Sultan Qansawh al-Ghawri at Marj Dabiq in North Syria in 1516, which delivered all Syria and Palestine over to him. He invaded Egypt without a blow being struck and triumphed over the young Sultan Tuman Bay. The conquest was accomplished in 1518, giving the Ottomans absolute control over the eastern Mediterranean and the countries around it.

The collapse of the Mameluke regime cannot be explained simply in terms of its economy, although Egypt and Syria certainly suffered greatly from the Black Death in 1349 and its periodic resurgences during the fifteenth century, which served to inhibit population growth. Further, the supply of Mamelukes from the Kipchaks had dried up and was not replaced by deliveries from the Caucasus, which meant that the Mameluke army was not as strong in the fifteenth century as it had been in the fourteenth. Although the Mamelukes feared the eventual return of the Mongols, the death of Tamerlane and the dismemberment of his Empire and the struggles between Black Sheep and White lulled the Mamelukes into thinking that the danger from the East was receding. As for the danger from the Ottomans, it was clearly perceived only with the accession of Selim I in 1512. His attack on Syria in 1516 was not anticipated because Selim had led them to believe he would attack Upper Iraq.

On the other hand, although the Sultans of the fifteenth century were generally good

277

rulers and good Muslims, they were still foreigners in the eyes of the Arab peoples of Egypt and Syria, before whom they appeared only in ostentatious guise. They do not appear to have done much to defend the Mameluke Sultanate when the Turks attacked and indeed certain Mameluke governors in Syria had already had dealings with the Ottomans.

Finally, Qa'it Bay's brilliant reign, which brought peace and ease of life, also led to the relaxation of military discipline and of concern about defence. Further, the desire to indulge in material pleasures was particularly developed in this final period and the will to resist was correspondingly reduced. Their awakening in 1516–17 must have been all the more brutal and their defeat the more complete.

Not everything in Egypt that had distinguished the Mameluke Sultanate disappeared. The Ottomans were to resume a great proportion of the country's administration on their own account and to leave social institutions as they were. Even the term Mameluke went on being used until the beginning of the nineteenth century, but without evoking the importance and the glory that had been theirs for two and a half centuries.

Young Turks

At Genghis Khan's death in 1227, the Empire he had carved out was divided into four principalities or Khanates; China–Mongolia, Turkestan–Central Asia, Afghanistan–Iran and eastern Turkestan with southern Russia, each one granted to one of his immediate descendants. It was during the expeditions which resulted from this division, starting with Afghanistan, that the Mongols came into direct contact with the Middle States and then the Near East. Thus the Khwarasmian ruler, Jalal al Din Mengubirdi, was defeated in 1230, before being eliminated by the *noyon* (ruler) Tchermogan in 1232; which left open to him the way to western Iran, and then to Azarbayjan (1233), Georgia (1236) and Greater Armenia (1239). The Mongols were then at the frontier of the Seljuk Sultanate of Asia Minor, which was invaded shortly after, and whose Sultan Kay-Kusraw II was defeated at Kose Dagh in 1243, a defeat which allowed Bayju Noyon to install a Mongol protectorate over eastern Mongolia.

Further north, the Mongol advance was pursued across Russia as far as Poland and Hungary (1236–41), but the death of the Great Khan Ogodai and the ensuing disputes over the succession halted their offensive in Europe. It was not resumed and the Mongol territory of the Kipchak Khanate did not extend beyond the Ukraine. These conquests gave the Mongols control over the northern and eastern shores of the Black Sea, and so over the trade routes to Iran, Central Asia and China, all countries which were anyway subject to them. A little later, Hulagu, the brother of the Great Khan Mongke, invaded Iraq and pillaged and destroyed Baghdad (1258). His lieutenant Kitbuga pursued the advance into Syria, where he was killed at the battle of Ayn Jalut by the Mameluke Sultan Baibars. Syria, Palestine and Egypt consequently stayed outside the Mongol sphere of influence and when the heir to the Abbasid Caliph, who was slaughtered in Baghdad, took refuge in Cairo, this city became the new centre of Islam.

The end of the Seljuks

The Mongol advance in the East, which started in Upper and Central Asia, immediately displaced the Turcoman tribes there, who were unwilling to submit to Mongol rule and managed to reach Asia Minor by successive stages, where other Turks were already installed and were able to offer them brotherly hospitality. During the 1230s and the beginning of the 1240s, these Turcoman tribes penetrated Seljuk territory, where they were not particularly welcome either as settlers or as nomads, especially since these tribes did not prove very peaceful and did not submit without friction to control by the Seljuk administration, as well as adhering to their own cultural and religious traditions. Although they were converts to Islam, they had not abandoned their former shamanic practices and their form of Islam seemed rather heterodox. All these factors meant that the newcomers did not feel as welcome as they might have wished and some of them reacted against the Seljuks' reserve and even their restrictions by revolting under the aegis of their *babas*, or religious mentors. One of these, Baba Ishaq, unleashed a real social and religious uprising, which took advantage of the problems of the Seljuk leadership at that time. It was however rigorously suppressed and its leader captured and strung up (1241). Kay-Kusraw II (1241–6) was unwilling to see such movements reappear and undertook to send these tribes gradually to the frontiers of his State bordering the Byzantine State, granting them lands and tax concessions on condition they directed their energy firstly towards installing themselves locally and then, should the opportunity arise, against Byzantium. These tribes were able to establish *uj*, little marcher territories, but were temporarily prevented from raiding or attacking Byzantine lands by the Empire of Nicea, which was firmly established in western Asia Minor.

The arrival of these tribes added noticeably to the population of Asia Minor, at the very least on its central plateau, at the expense of the Greek population, which had hitherto been in the majority. These population changes were accompanied by economic changes, which were however less significant, because the Turcoman tribes, in spite of practising nomadism (to a certain extent obligatorily), adapted fairly readily to a form of semi-nomadism and even became sedentary to a certain extent. Their adaptation was slow and occurred during the whole thirteenth century, taking advantage of the problems the Byzantine State was suffering under Andronicus II (1282–1328) and of those the Seljuk State was undergoing.

As it was, the Mongol irruption into eastern and central Asia Minor resulted in their victory over the Seljuk Sultan at Kose Dagh (26 June 1243), which led, after an attempt at ruling co-jointly, to the division of the Sultanate into two States; one in the West with its capital at Konya and the other in the East with Sivas as its centre. Sivas was controlled fairly weakly by the Mongols, a situation which Vizir Mu'in al-Din Pervane tried to turn to his advantage. He was an ambitious Turkish notable, who aimed at restoring the unity of the Seljuk State, and he succeeded in so doing when the Sultan of the West was forced to flee and to seek refuge in Constantinople. This unity lasted until 1277, not without a few

279

A nomad camp. The rough life of the steppes is evoked here in quite a different manner to that of visionary Persian art. Several details illustrate the Mongols' life style; their eating habits, clothes, tools, weapons, luggage, mounts and even the social distinctions within a group. (A leaf from the *Siyah Qalem*, Turkestan, fifteenth century; Istanbul, Topkapi Sarayi.)

problems with the Mongol Khans of Iran; it was their relative retreat which incited the Turkish emirs and Mu'in al-Din Pervane to revolt openly against them and to appeal to Baibars, the Mameluke Sultan. The Sultan was worried by the Mongol presence on the frontiers of Syria and he was not keen to see attacks on Aleppo and Damascus start up again, so he supported the revolt. His army triumphed over the Mongol army at Albistan, and he then advanced on Kayseri (Cesarea of Cappadocia). He stopped there, content with putting Cilicia under his direct control and turning it into another buffer zone for the Mameluke State. In Asia Minor, the Mongols retaliated against Mu'in al-Din Pervane and executed him in August 1277, thus consolidating their authority over the eastern part of the country, which became a protectorate in all but name. Seljuk Asia Minor was subjected until the first years of the fourteenth century to constant fighting between pretenders and rulers striving to secure the Mongols' favour; fighting which resulted in the disintegration of the central power. In 1303 Masud II died, who is considered to have been the last Seljuk Sultan. In the East, the Mongols maintained their rule by setting up a governor, but in the

West, the Turcoman tribes felt themselves free from all control and began to act on their own account. By the beginning of the fourteenth century, the unity of Turkish Asia Minor was a thing of the past.

One consequence of the Mongol invasion was the way it transformed the economy of Asia Minor. The changes wrought by the arrival of the Turcoman tribes very probably affected agriculture and stock-raising, and perhaps also the local markets, since the first tribes to arrive probably did not have the same needs and did not offer the same produce as the earlier inhabitants. This may have led to problems between the older populations and the newcomers, disturbing their social and economic structures and giving rise in certain places to confrontation and conflict, leading to the expulsion of Greek communities into Byzantine territory.

Their impact on the 'international' market and the transit trade through Asia Minor was more serious. The wars and the disappearance of Seljuk authority and the security it had ensured forced the merchants to abandon this route for the Syrian and the Egyptian routes, to the Mamelukes' delight, or, better still, for the Constantinople–Black Sea–Crimea route, which was controlled by the Greeks, the Genoese (from 1375 onwards) and the Kipchak Mongols, and which opened the way to China to merchants and missionaries. The Seljuk Sultans were thus deprived of their income from this traffic around 1240–5, and they had also lost a great part of their revenues along with so much of their territory. In spite of holding on to their title, they were no longer able to impose their authority over the Sultanate, and still less to withstand of the Turcoman tribes' first moves towards independence. The Seljuk Sultanate of Asia Minor was soon no more than a memory.

The flowering of the new Turkish Emirates

As we have seen, the Turcoman tribes installed by the Seljuks along their frontiers formed *uj*, military marcher lands, under the authority of their chiefs and dependent on the Seljuk Sultan. These *uj* were generally situated alongside Byzantine territory. Before the Sultanate of Konya collapsed and during most of the second half of the thirteenth century, the tribes tended generally to take up waiting positions; beginning to settle without abandoning their nomadic activities and their offensive against Byzantine territory. The main *uj* were along the northern and western sides of the Anatolian plateau, reaching as far as the Black Sea. This was the case with the Isfandiyar (the Jandar) at Kastamonu and the Pervane at Sinop. To the west, they did not overflow onto the Aegean plains before the end of the thirteenth century, a process which involved tribes from north and south, those of Ertughrul, of Karasi, of Sarukhan, of Aydin as well as those of Menteshe.

The disintegration of the Seljuk power gave these tribes complete freedom of action and, under the command of their beys or chiefs, they formed independent principalities or *beyliks*. These *beyliks* emerged both on the edges of the former Sultanate and within it, where their beys appropriated fairly enormous territories, such as the *beyliks* of Sahib Ata,

281

Germiyan, Hamid, Karaman, and further to the east, in the Cilician Taurus, of Dulgadir and Ramazan.

These *beyliks* were not formed uneventfully and although this did not amount to anarchy, the Turcoman beys strove to control greater stretches of territory, at the expense of either the Byzantines or of their own brothers and neighbours. The Byzantines suffered even more from these attacks because Emperor Andronicus II had abolished the tax concessions which had previously benefited the peasant soldiery of the frontier marches (the *akrites*), and they either failed to offer resistance to Turcoman attacks, or they abandoned their lands and sought refuge in the towns. Pressurised by the beys, the Greeks were increasingly incapable of defending the Aegean plain and they tended to crowd into the ports and the towns in the interior: Heraclea of Pontus, Nicomedia, Nicea, Brusa, Sardis, Phocea, Magnesia, Nymphea, Smyrna and Philadelphia. A Greek army led by Andronicus' son, Michael IX, suffered total defeat (1301) and the Emperor attempted another campaign of reconquest a little later. He appealed to the Catalan Companies led by Roger de Flor, who arrived in western Asia Minor in 1304 and harrassed Turks travelling to the Cilician ports – but he achieved nothing more decisive. When the Turks set out again for Constantinople, they had no difficulty occupying the abandoned terrain and pushed much further beyond their old limits. Over the next two decades, the Ottoman beys moved westwards as far as the Aegean coast, where they fell under the lure of the sea. The *beylik* of Karasi, for instance, controlled the eastern shores of the Dardanelles and its bey threw himself into piracy: the Bey Sarukhan took Magnesia of the Sipyle (Manisa) for his capital and took part in sea raids with his southern neighbour. The *beylik* of Aydin got hold of Pyrgion (Birgi) in Ephesus, of Koloe (Keles) and the acropolis of Smyrna before 1326 and expanded its sphere of activity the moment Umur Bey took over as leader and occupied Smyrna (1327). This port became the base for launching attacks on the Byzantines in the Aegean as far as the Peloponnesus. Later, John Cantacuzenus was driven by his struggle against John V Paleaologus for the throne of Byzantium to appeal to Umur for his help, asking him to send Turkish troops into Thrace (1341). Already in September 1332, however, Andronicus II and the Lords of the Archipelago had concluded a Union with Venice and the Hospitallers of Rhodes against the Turkish corsairs in the Aegean, a Union which was joined by Philip VI, King of France, and the Pope in March 1334. It had almost no effect at all.

The Anatolian plateau was controlled by various *beyliks*, among which those of Germiyan and Karaman were the most important; the first because it occupied a relatively prosperous zone of passage to the outer world and the second because it dominated the whole southern zone of the plateau, notably the town Konya, on the strength of which it claimed to succeed the Seljuk Sultans. A series of victories over Turcoman neighbours and certain Mongol governors allowed it to increase its territory – and to become the principal State in Central Anatolia by the first quarter of the fourteenth century. This success was illuminated at Konya and especially at Karaman by a surge in artistic and intellectual vitality, which effectively picked up from where the Seljuks had left off. Further north, Ankara and its region were governed, not by a Turcoman bey, but by a group of men representing corporations associated with the *akhi* fraternities. They were a completely new element and very probably represented an evolution of the *futuwwa*, which already existed in the preceding century, when the leaders of the religious confraternities and the corporations established their control over more volatile elements. In eastern Anatolia, finally, the Mongol protectorate was represented by a governor whose name, after 1327, was Ertena, who turned his governorship into an independent state with its capital first at Sivas, then at Kayseri. The *beyliks* in the north led a quieter existence for most of the fourteenth century, although they occasionally indulged in fratricidal struggles or in attacks on the Greek state of Trebizond.

A considerable fragmentation of power was taking place over the whole of Asia Minor; the growing number of *beyliks*, each one enjoying an independence which made up for what they had lost in Central Asia; the rivalries between *beyliks*; their religious and political dynamism, which drove them to attack the country of *Dar al-Harb*, the increasingly weak Byzantine Empire; the invasion of lands inhabited by Greeks – all these factors contributed to the disruption of Asia Minor during the first forty years of the fourteenth century, in complete contrast to the situation a century earlier. The Mameluke Sultanate was much more peaceful, ruled as it was by a single authority and administration, and the flow of trade between the Mediterranean and the Middle and Far East abandoned Asia Minor for Syria and Egypt, and further away for Constantinople and the Crimea. This meant that the economy of Turkish Asia Minor declined, a decline which certain *beyliks* exploited to their own advantage, among which the Ottomans.

The emergence of the Ottomans

The *beylik* which was to emerge as the Ottoman State also started off as a Turcoman tribe, whose beginnings in Asia Minor are not well known and have been embellished by later historiographers and chroniclers. This tribe was probably also driven west by the Mongols, shortly before the middle of the thirteenth century. One of its chiefs, Gunduz Alp, had a son called Ertughrul, who was given the region of Seuyut as an *uj* by the Seljuk Sultan around 1270, on the middle course of the river Sakarya (Sangarios), north of Kautahya on the eastern frontier of Bithynia, a Byzantine province, against which he probably led expeditions. He died *c.* 1290 and was succeeded by his son Osman (Othman, hence the name of their dynasty; *Osmanli, Othmanli* in Turkish, Ottoman in European languages). Osman was probably a member of a *ghazi* confraternity and the chronicles record that his father-in-law, Edebali, was a *shaykh* with considerable influence over him; as with the other *beyliks*, Islam's part as a catalyst in Ottoman expansion cannot be denied. Although we have little information about the period when Osman was leading his tribe, we may assume that his command was of the same nature as the Seljuks' and other *beyliks*', where power belonged to a particular family, one of whose heads had the right to rule the rest of them, as well as assigning duties, tasks or important benefits to the principal family members.

Osman may have launched his first expeditions against Bithynia in 1291. The   **283** chronology of these campaigns and conquests is very little established, but his army seems to have occupied the whole of eastern Bithynia around 1320, threatening the important towns of Brusa (Bursa) and Nicea (Iznik). The exact date of his death is not known either, which took place between 1317 and 1326; he seems to have handed the command of his army to his son Orkhan in 1317. Orkhan captured Brusa in 1326 and Nicea in 1330, establishing his capital in the first of these towns, where he built two mosques in 1337–8 and 1339–40 and where Osman was buried – acts which illustrated Orkhan's involvement with Brusa. This interest was given another dimension when Orkhan built or renovated a commercial district in 1340, with a *bedestan* (a special place for trading in valuable goods). Ibn Battuta noticed this when he saw Bithynia and Brusa in 1333 during his travels all over western Asia Minor around 1330–5. Brusa was also the most important town in this wealthy province and a lively commercial centre.

Orkhan pursued his expansionist policy by seizing Nicomedia (Izmit) in 1337, and thus reaching the Sea of Marmara, controlling more of its shores as far as the Dardanelles when he occupied the *beylik* of Karasi a little later (1340–5). His brother Ala al-Din seems to have seconded him by dealing with civil affairs and sometimes leading military expeditions; he died in 1333. Some time after this, Orkhan enjoyed good relations with John Cantacuzenus, to the extent of marrying his daughter Theodora in 1346. Cantacuzenus needed allies in his struggle against John Paleaologus and, after Umur's death at Aydin, he appealed to Orkhan, who responded by sending troops under the command of his son Suleyman (Soliman). They entered Thrace in 1348 where they then fought – notably against the Serbs. A few years later, the Ottomans made a new incursion and occupied Tzympe (1352) and Gallipoli in 1354, which gave them a bridgehead onto the European shore of the Dardanelles. Over the next few years, they took advantage of the growing weakness of the Byzantine Empire to control all eastern Thrace; the date of their capture of Adrianople is disputed, with 1362–3, 1369 and 1372 put forward. The same uncertainty applies to the Turks' first appearance in Thrace; some historians consider that when Amadeus of Savoy temporarily retook Gallipoli in 1366 the Ottomans were forced to abandon Thrace, leaving only a few independent bands to raid Byzantine, Bulgarian and even Serb towns. These bands are supposed to have captured Adrianople. This is unlikely, because Andrianople was an important place and could have been reduced only by the Ottoman army.

Orkhan's offensive succeeded thanks to his army, which was made up partly from the personal and regular troops or the *beys* and members of his tribe, called *yaya* or Fantassins, and partly from irregular troops or *azab*, who were only called up occasionally, and finally from troops recruited among former prisoners of war, called the 'new troop' (*yeni tcheri*, the Janissaries). The cavalry was composed of regular horsemen (*sipahis*) and irregular horsemen or raiders (*akinjis*). On top of this, Orkhan's successes secured him the support of the religious confraternities and of scattered Turcomans, eager for a share in the loot. Orkhan himself was a *ghazi* and bore the title of 'Sultan of the conquerors, soldier of the Faith' as well as that of Bey.

The assassination of Murad I. To the right of the Sultan, the Serb Miloš Kobilić can be seen plunging a dagger into his victim's heart. (Ms. Ottoman Hünername, 1584; Istanbul, Topkapi Sarayi.)

By his death (*c.* 1262/3) the Ottomans were already spreading over what was left of the Byzantine Empire in the southern Balkans. The young Ottoman State was able to act like this in Europe only because it had no particular standing in Asia Minor and because the principal Anatolian *beyliks* of Germiyan and especially Karaman were preoccupied with building up their power locally and with fighting one another.

Murad I (1362–89) continued his father's work in Balkan Europe by occupying most of Bulgaria and Serbia. In spite of being defeated by a Bulgaro-Serbian coalition in 1387, he took his revenge at Kossovo in 1389 and was killed during the battle by a Serb. Bulgaria was nonetheless annexed to the Ottoman State, while Serbia was subjected to the Ottomans but allowed to keep its own ruler. In Asia Minor the Ottomans implemented a policy of marriage or subjection which allowed them to annex the emirate of Germiyan and part of the emirate of Hamid bordering on the *beylik* of Karaman. All these regions were turned into provinces and were divided into a number of estates or *timars*, which were assigned on an individual and revocable basis to military persons and civil and religious

285

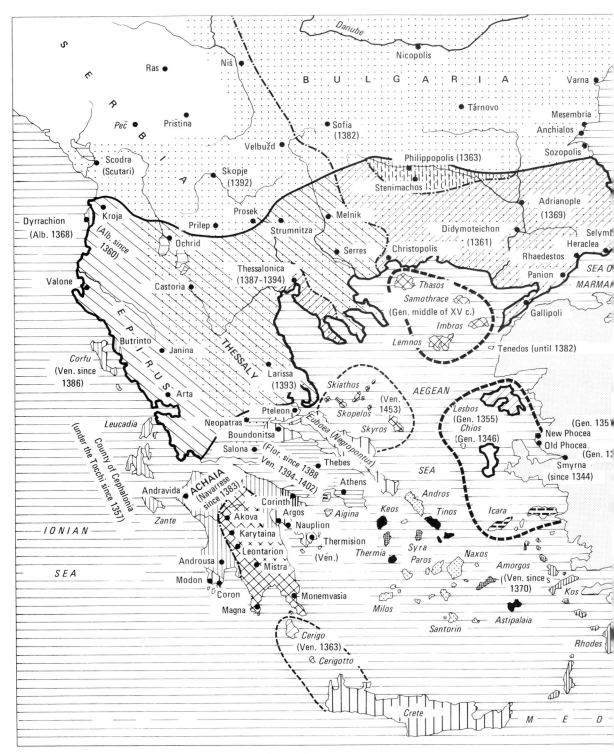

6 The extent of the Turkish advance in the XIVth century

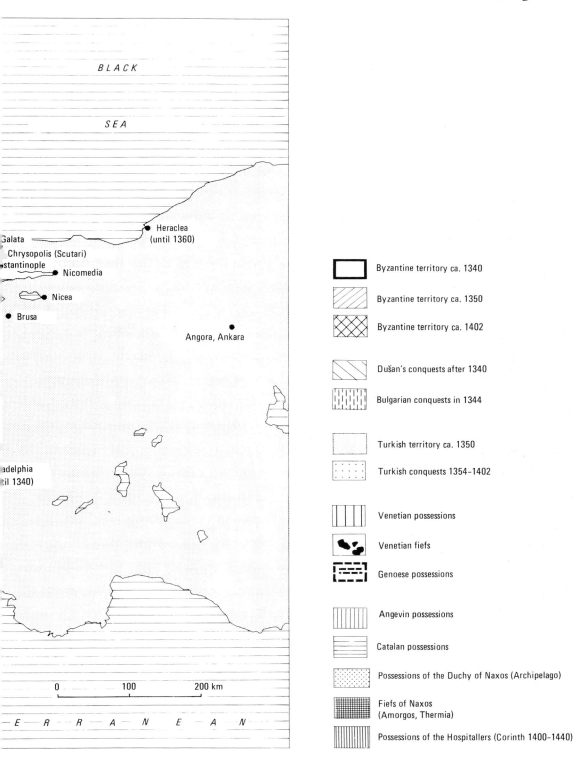

BLACK

SEA

Galata

Heraclea
(until 1360)

Chrysopolis (Scutari)

stantinople

Constantinople

Nicomedia

Nicea

Brusa

Angora, Ankara

adelphia
til 1340)

0   100   200 km

E   R   R   A   N   E   A   N

☐	Byzantine territory ca. 1340
▨	Byzantine territory ca. 1350
▨	Byzantine territory ca. 1402
▨	Dušan's conquests after 1340
▨	Bulgarian conquests in 1344
☐	Turkish territory ca. 1350
⬚	Turkish conquests 1354-1402
▥	Venetian possessions
◣	Venetian fiefs
▦	Genoese possessions
▥	Angevin possessions
▤	Catalan possessions
⬚	Possessions of the Duchy of Naxos (Archipelago)
▦	Fiefs of Naxos (Amorgos, Thermia)
▥	Possessions of the Hospitallers (Corinth 1400-1440)

functionaries. They were responsible for improving their estates and for raising taxes, most of which went to the State. The *timar* system was not unlike that of the Seljuk *iqta* and it developed considerably from the fifteenth century onwards.

The Ottomans' first expansionist stage was largely abetted by the religious activities of the Muslim fraternities. They made it easier for Turkish 'colonies' to establish themselves around urban centres conquered by the Muslims, particularly in Balkan Europe, by setting up mosques, *madrasas* and places of prayer (*zaviye*) and pious foundations (*vaqif*). This religious movement was considerably extended during the last thirty years of the fourteenth century.

The Ottoman expansion was pursued by Bayezid I (Bajazet), who was called *Yildirim* (the Thunderbolt). To start off with, the new Sultan had his brother Ya'qub killed in order to ensure unity and above all to avoid conflict within the family. He thus inaugurated a practice which has been called 'the law of fratricide'. This allowed him to throw himself into expeditions in the Balkans and Asia Minor. From April 1390, he intervened in Byzantine affairs by facilitating the ascent to power of John VII Palaeologus, subsequently dropping him in favour of the future Manuel II. He constantly stepped up his pressure on Constantinople and even occupied a great stretch of the eastern coastline of the Bosphorus, where he built a fortress, the castle of Anatolia (*Anadolu Hisar*), to watch over shipping passing through the straits (1395).

In the Balkans, Theodorus, Despot of Morea, declared himself a vassal of Bayezid's between 1391 and 1395, as did the Hospodar of Bosnia. The Prince of Achaia ceded various towns in exchange for Ottoman help; Wallachia became Ottoman territory; Bulgaria was defined as a province and Stefan Lazarević was able to accede to the throne of Serbia only because Bazeyid intervened. By the end of 1395, the Turks occupied almost all of Balkan Europe and were massed at the frontiers of Hungary, whose King Sigismund begged the Europeans to organise a Crusade to drive the Turks out of Europe. This crusade clashed with the Turks near Nicopolis on 25 September 1396. The crusaders were confronted with a particularly homogenous and well-commanded Turkish army, which inflicted a crushing defeat on them, giving rise to the Turks' reputation for being strong and invincible.

Bayezid next undertook a brief siege of Constantinople (1397) but did not push his advantage to the limit, whereas Larissa, Patras and Athens in Greece were all captured.

In Asia Minor, after 1390, he occupied the *beyliks* of the Aegean coast (Sarukhan, Aydin and Menteshe), part of the *beylik* of Isfandiyar beside the Black Sea and, a little later, central and eastern Anatolia, where the Karamanid Ala al-Din had to cede him the main towns of his *beylik*, after which the old Mongol territory of Sivas and Kayseri fell into his hands. By 1400, Bayezid had reached the Bosphorus. He already ruled over a vast domain which, with the exception of Constantinople, stretched from Bosnia to the frontiers of the Mameluke State and the principalities of eastern Anatolia. The fate of the Eastern Empire was apparently sealed.

The fortress of Anadolu Hisar. The first Turkish fortification to be built opposite Constantinople on the Asiatic side of the Bosphorus, under Bayezid I.

A supple and overwhelming domination

The Turco-Ottoman expansion did not initially bring about many changes in the Aegean regions of Asia Minor, where the *beyliks* had already set themselves up in the early fourteenth century, apart from introducing the concept of one single government, which must have been a fairly hazy one in the period between 1390 and 1400. Changes to the population were also limited, because they had been effected during most of the fourteenth century, when Turks were superimposed on the Greek populations in the *beyliks*, dominating them on account of their strength if not their numbers and setting up the

289

rudiments of institutions, which were intended to favour the establishment of a Turkish population. Landed estates were removed from their former Greek detainers and were probably assigned to members of the beys' families or to their followers. It is also possible that certain Greek proprietors held onto their estates in return for their allegiance to the new rulers. Finally, other lands were assigned to pious foundations (*vakif*, plural *evkaf*), in order to ease the transition to Islam. All these lands were then considered as personal property, or *mulk*, which was transferable and unalienable.

When the *beyliks* passed under Ottoman control, the *mulk* properties were repartitioned between members of the Ottoman family, vizirs and high civil and military functionaries, members of old bey families as well as religious and legal-religious personalities. Many of these detainers also enjoyed *timars*, which were assigned to them on account of their particular functions. This practice gave rise to a dominant class in Asia Minor at the end of the fourteenth century, which belonged to the ruling circles of the Ottoman State and controlled most of the landed wealth of this region; this involved, to a great extent, a revival of the Byzantine heritage. The *mulk* estates were subject to regular Muslim taxation (*zakat* or tithe) while the *timars*, whose detainers changed about and belonged to different social categories, contributed precisely fixed revenues (in all forms of payment).

The Ottoman conquest of Balkan Europe was implemented directly, without the mediation of the *beyliks*. This meant that the Ottomans immediately took over great stretches of land, part of which remained in the hands of its old Bulgarian, Serb and Greek proprietors. Another part was assigned as timars to military persons of all ranks and to civil functionaries, constituting the essential part of their remuneration and thus obliging them to make sure that their *timar* was productive. Their State taxes were defined in coin or in kind on registration of their *timars* and they were also obliged to supply the Ottoman army on request with soldiers, their number being determined by the size and the revenues of the particular *timar*. A further part of the land fell to members of the Sultan's large family, to the principal rulers of the State and to religious confraternities, as their own property as *mulk* possessions. These estates were defined 'territorially' but not 'financially' as the *timars* were; consequently their owners had complete freedom of action over these lands, especially where their workforce and their farming methods were concerned.

By dividing up the conquered land in this way, the Ottoman government meant to ensure optimum conditions for their political domination and their revenues. The first two forms of tenure were strictly controlled by the (newly established) provincial and central administrations, and if their detainers failed to carry out their duties or performed them unsatisfactorily, they could quite simply be deprived of their possessions or their *timar* estates along with the advantages tied to them. As it was, these estates represented the government agents' remuneration and often their personal profit as well, which explains their concern that the lands assigned to them, whatever their size, should be as productive as possible. Christian owners also had an interest in doing the same, since this ensured them both material revenues and their continued authority over their peasants as well as fairly privileged relations with the Ottomon rulers, who in their turn were able to use them as intermediaries for carrying out their orders. Later in the fifteenth century, when the Ottomans stepped up the demands of their administration and its presence, some of these Christian owners were converted to Islam and became Ottomanised.

Owners of *mulk* lands also tried to make the most of them. During the recent past, these lands had suffered from the wars between Byzantines, Serbs and Bulgarians as well as the Ottoman campaigns, and they were sometimes depopulated and impoverished. The Ottoman government encouraged the movement of populations from one region to another to the advantage of some *mulk* proprietors, or else prisoners and slaves were installed on their lands and were occasionally freed. This governmental action was often performed directly by the *mulk* proprietors who could only benefit from it. Later, Turkish populations in Asia Minor were moved to the Balkans to replace Greek and Bulgarian populations who had been sent to Asia Minor. This system progressively increased the Turkish population in part of the Balkans. As for their Islamisation, this was achieved by the religious confraternities, who were assigned properties where they installed *zaviyes*, places of worship and assembly for Muslims, many of whom had moved voluntarily from Asia Minor to participate in the expansion of Islam, hoping either for war or for some of the manna which had fallen on the Ottomans.

By the end of the fourteenth century, some of the *mulk* properties seem to have been turned into *vakif* (*waqf* in Arabic), that is to say religious possessions, which were in principle inalienable. This took two forms; one called *hayri*, in which the revenues of the *vakif* were dedicated solely to pious works; the other called *ehli*, in which the revenues could also be used to support one or more persons designated by the donor. This procedure was not as yet very widespread by the end of the fourteenth century.

By these different means, the young Ottoman State controlled its conquered territories both directly and indirectly. This control was exercised by the army and the administration, both of which had been strengthened and developed by the extension of the Turkish dominions. Ottoman administration only really grew to proper size and shape in the reign of Murad I, who was not content with being a bey and assumed the title of Sultan, without any reference to the Caliph. Under him was the Vizir, the first one being Ali Pasha, the son of Kara Khalil Jandarli, who had established the foundations of the Ottoman State under Orkhan. The Sultan appointed the Grand Vizir (*sadr-i azam*) who was answerable to him and was the next most important State official, responsible for all civil and military affairs, although the Sultan still kept the initiative and his priority in these matters. By the end of Murad I's reign, the increase in the territory and consequently in the Vizir's duties led to other vizirs being appointed to second him. Both he and his aides were chosen among members of the Ottoman family or among great families close to them, and later among high-ranking dignitaries. They took part in the daily sessions of the *diwan*, which the Sultan presided over, assisted by the *qadi 'asker* (or *kasasker*; the judge of the army with authority over the religious and legal staff, taken from the *ulama* class trained in the *madrasas*), the *nishandji* (head of the civil functionaries, and originally entrusted with applying the Sultan's Seal – *nishan or tughra* – onto documents emanating from the Sultan or the *diwan*), and the *mustevfi* (later called *defterdar*, keeper of the registers of the State revenues: taxes, levies, various revenues, legal impositions, *kharaj* or land rents, *zakat* or legal alms, *ushur* or tithes, extraordinary taxation – still rare in the fourteenth century – *pendjik resmi* or the right to a fifth share in prisoners, customs dues, commercial taxes, and so on).

So long as the Ottoman *beylik* only covered the territories of Asia Minor, the bey had appointed only one military leader to take charge of the conquered lands and to extend them, as well as more general military matters. His title was *sanjak beyi*, the *sanjak* corresponding to an administrative unit under the authority of a military leader, generally the son of an Ottoman ruler. There must have been several *sanjaks* in Asia Minor before the expansion into Europe, which in turn created more *sanjaks* on European land and in Rumeli. This increase in their number led Murad I to introduce a higher echelon in the administration of the provinces, the *beylerbeylik* (governorship) under the command of the *beylerbey* (governor), who was invested with military and civil powers.

The first governorship to be created was in the province (*eyalet*) of Rumeli around 1362–5; the second was created in the province of Asia Minor, or Anatolia, in 1393. Each province was divided between the *qadi* (judge) the *alay beyi* (responsible for military matters) and the *subashi* (responsible for administration and finance). Their various functionaries were granted their own *timars*, but they also organised the repartition of other *timars* in liaison with the central administration, assigning them particularly to the soldiers and horsemen of the Ottoman army.

The army was also transformed during the reign of Murad I, when its numbers were increased to allow for further expansion and for defending the conquered territories. A new form of recruitment for the armies of the Sultan and the beys was devised around 1380 to supplement the old system of using prisoners. This was the *devshirme* (collection), an operation by which Christian children were rounded up in a certain number of villages and towns in the Balkans and removed. The number levied was fixed each time and probably did not exceed a few hundred children; nor did *devshirmes* take place every year. The children were sent into Anatolia where they were assimilated to their Turkish surroundings and were Islamised. After which they were sent on to Gallipoli and formed the corps of the *ajemioglan* (foreign children); there they received a special education according to their intellectual and physical abilities. Some of them became *ichoglan* (children of the household, or pages) and passed into the service of the Sultan's household, where they could rise through the hierarchy and attain high administrative positions. Others were incorporated into the Janissaries (Fantassins, armourers, artillerymen); along with the cavalry (*suvari*) they formed the 'Slaves of the Gate' (*kapi kullari*) or, more precisely, the Sultan's personal and devoted servants. One feature of the Janissaries was that, from this period of their development (1380–90), their organisation was closely linked to the Bektashi confraternity, which was created about sixty years earlier by Hajji Bektash Veli and was gradually considered to be on the borderlines of Muslim heterodoxy. Its ritual did in fact incorporate proper Muslim practices, traditions coming from Eastern or Central Asia and, after the second half of the fourteenth century, with elements drawn from Christianity. The manner of these Janissaries' original recruitment may have driven them

The Janissaries. These elite troops formed the iron hand of the Ottoman infantry. They had originally been created in the fourteenth century to make up the Sultan's personal guard, and were recruited from among the children of subject Christian peoples, torn from their families and subjected to harsh training. (Sixteenth-century Ottoman Ms., Istanbul, Topkapi Sarayi.)

to follow the way of Bektashism rather than that of regular Islam; as it was, Bektashism flourished in Rumeli.

Another part of the cavalry, the *sipahis*, was also improved and became one of the major elements of Ottoman domination, since each *sipahi* received a *timar* estate appropriate to his rank for his own upkeep and that of the soldiers he had to supply; whence the name 'timariote' frequently applied to them. These soldiers were subordinate to the *subashi*, who was dependent on the *alay beyi*, who answered to the *sanjak beyi*. The Sultan also had his own cavalry, under his direct command, which was formed partly from *ajemioglan* and partly from former converted prisoners and non-Ottoman Muslims.

293

On the level of the economy, the young Ottoman State was careful to avoid disrupting the established structures, whenever this was possible. Peasants on lands whose former owners had fled and had been replaced by new proprietors (*mulk sahibi*) or by timariots, found that only their masters had changed and that the Ottoman government demanded no more in taxes than the Byzantine government had before them. The same process was applied in Rumeli after its conquest. Indeed later documents, given that only a few survive from the end of the fourteenth century, give the impression that the decision had been made to maintain the economic life of the conquered regions and to avoid all profound disruption, which may explain why some local lords were kept on. This process subsequently evolved and gave rise to *qanum-name*, which were regulations proper to each province, defining the rights and duties of its inhabitants and constituting a form of customary law juxtaposed to Koranic Law. Trade with foreign powers, especially with Italian merchant cities, does not appear to have been very important to the Ottomans until the end of the fourteenth century, apart from maintaining relations with the Genoese in Chios and with the Venetians along certain points of the European Balkans, basically for trading in wheat. In Asia Minor, however, the Ottomans controlled the principal ports and towns of eastern Anatolia until the end of the fourteenth century; Brusa, Smyrna, Ankara, Konya, Alanya, Antalya. Also, part of central Asian and Iranian trade destined for Europe did not pass through Syria or Egypt but took the route through Anatolia and so benefited the Ottoman bases, especially Brusa, which was already an important centre for the silk trade.

Although the Ottoman State had not yet achieved greatness, it was important because of its geographical position, its well-organised administrative and military structures, its political and religious dynamism and its conception of a strong and centralised authority. But it was also capable of a fair amount of tolerance towards the people in its power. In short, all that was to be the grandeur and the prestige of the Ottoman Empire was already present, even though its momentum was momentarily halted by a new obstacle.

The 'Mongol peace'

Before his death in 1227, Ghengis Khan had already divided his Empire between his four sons, each one receiving part of the territory (*ulus*). During the next two decades, new Mongol offensives were conducted, one against southern Russia, the other against the Near East. After a series of incursions into Poland, Moravia and Hungary under the leadership of Khan Batu, the first offensive concentrated on lands which had until then been occupied by Kipchak Turkish tribes, called *ulus* or the Khanate of the Golden Horde in Russian chronicles. This khanate stretched from the mouths of the Danube to lake Balkhash, including most of the Ukraine, the Crimea, the northern regions of the Caucasus and the steppes between the Caspian and lake Balkhash. It was not initially in contact with the Muslim world, but later on played a political role which influenced it.

The second Muslim thrust, led by Tchermogan, then by Bayju, and lastly by Hulagu, took the Mongols from central Asia to eastern Asia Minor and reduced Afghanistan, Iran and Iraq, essentially Muslim countries. This khanate, known under the name of Khanate of the Ilkhans, evolved differently in many respects to the Khanate of Kipchak.

The Golden Horde

The creation of the Khanate of Kipchak (from the name of the Turkish people who had succeeded the Comans and the Polovtzians and were defeated by Batu's Mongols) or of the Golden Horde (*Altin Ordu*) was the result of Khan Batu's expeditions. Between 1227 and 1255 he established himself not just as the instigator of Mongol expansion and settlement in eastern Europe and the creator of a Mongol State stretching from the Danube to lake Balkhash, but also as the most important personality of the Mongol world in the mid thirteenth century. His power extended much further than the bounds of his own khanate and the rulers of a number of Russian principalities (Ryazan, Tver, Suzdal, Kiev, Galicia) acknowledged him as overlord. This was the case with the Grand Prince of Vladimir, Alexander Nevsky (1252–63). Although Batu established his reputation as a redoubtable master, especially where taxes were concerned, his reign was nonetheless distinguished both by the way he favoured economic and commercial activity and by his tolerance, himself a shamanist, towards the different religions practised in his khanate; Nestorian Christianity, Orthodox Christianity, Islam, Judaism. His own son Sartaq, was a Nestorian and enjoyed very good relations with Alexander Nevsky. It was possibly Sartaq's brutal death in 1256, which prevented the Khanate of Kipchak from going over to the Christian camp.

After the brief reign of Ulaghchi (1256–7), the power passed to Batu's brother Berke (1257–66), who conducted a pro-Islamic policy. He himself converted to Islam, without abandoning his predecessors' tolerance towards other religions. When Khan Hulagu's process in Azarbayjan threatened the Kipchaks, Berke sought to make the Mameluke Sultan Baibars his ally. They exchanged embassies (1261) and concluded an alliance against Hulagu in 1263. Baibars was further allowed to recruit mercenaries in the Khanate of Kipchak for the Mameluke army. Hulagu's expedition into the Caucasus proved a failure and he took his revenge by massacring Kipchak merchants in Persia, to which Berke responded by killing Persian merchants in Kipchak. Berke's nephew Nogay then led an expedition which also failed; the two khans were in fact making a bid for control of all Azarbayjan, at that time divided in two. Neither of them was able to win it. Berke also founded a town, Saray, on the lower Volga, which he made his capital; it remained the capital of the khanate until 1395 when it was destroyed by Tamerlane.

Berke was succeeded by Mengu (Mongke) Timur, Batu's grandson (1266–80), who intervened on several occasions in the quarrels of the Mongol Khans of central Asia as well as maintaining good relations with the Mameluke Sultans of Egypt and the Basileus of Constantinople, Michael VIII Palaeologus. Himself a shamanist, he had great tolerance for all religions and he granted immunities to the priests of the Orthodox Church in the

A charge by Mongol riders. This miniature shows the influence of the Ilkhans, who encouraged the art of illumination in Persia and enriched it by their connections with the Far East. (*Universal History* of Rachid al-Din, 1314; Istanbul, Topkapi Sarayi).

khanate as well as allowing the Genoese at Caffa, in the Crimea, to set up a consulate and a entrepot on the land he had granted them. He was succeeded by his brother, Tode Mengu (1280–7) who, with his successor Tole Buqa (1287–90), were rulers in name only because Nogay held the real power until his assassination in 1300. Nogay was fairly favourable to Christianity, including Latin Christianity, since Franciscan monks were able to establish themselves in Saray. As an ally of the Byzantines, he intervened in Bulgaria, where he installed a new ruler, George Terter, who was a real vassal of the Mongols. Nogay's authoritarianism was however unpopular and he was finally attacked by Khan Tokhtu (1290–1312); soon after being defeated, Nogay was killed.

At the beginning of the fourteenth century, the Khanate of Kipchak (the Golden Horde) was in a very firm position. It profited from the intestinal struggles wrecking the Byzantine Empire; the Russian and Bulgarian rulers were its subjects and it enjoyed good relations with the Mamelukes of Egypt and Syria and even with the Ilkhan Khans of Persia. The presence of Genoese and Venetian merchants gave rise to an important trade, starting from its Crimean bases – although the Italian merchants in Caffa and Sughdak were occasionally subjected to the Khan's hostility, particularly in 1307.

With the accession of Ozbek to power (1312–40), the Kipchaks adopted new guidelines; the new Khan converted to Islam and from then on all their rulers were Muslims, which, however, did not mean that other religions, especially Christianity, were repressed. Relations with the Mamelukes suffered a few setbacks, but to make up for this, the Genoese and Venetians were well treated. This was not the case at the beginning of Janibeg's reign (1340–57), a reign distinguished by a certain emphasis on Islamisation and by two important events; one was the appearance of the Great Plague around 1346, which decimated the population and appreciably impoverished the khanate; the other was the struggle against the Ilkhans of Iran. Azarbayjan, momentarily reconquered by Janibeg in 1355, was lost to them three years later. In the last years of his reign, Janibeg was exposed to the hostility of his Mongol lords, which even gave rise to conflict, while on their side, his Russian vassals tended to relax their links with the Mongols.

This reign seems to have been a turning point in the history of the Khanate of Kipchak; the memory of Ghengis Khan's great empire was no longer enough to rally the Mongol lords to their Khan. Once they were established in ethnic and religious circles where they formed only a minority group, the Mongols came under the influence of these circles – to a certain extent. Finally, their vassals began to shake off their subjection. However, the Kipchak Mongols continued to dominate the northern shores of the Black Sea, which were crucial to their existence.

After Janibeg, power was no longer held by the Khan but by Mamay, the 'mayor of the palace' (1361–80), who tried to reestablish the unity of the khanate, which had been disrupted by several emirs, especially in the eastern part. From 1370, the Russian rulers withheld their allegiance from the Khan and a little later, they refused to pay him tribute. The Mongols were defeated at the battle of Kulikovo Polje (8 September 1380) and, in the Crimea, they were obliged to let the Genoese take possession of part of their territory.

At this time Tokhtamish, the Khan of the White Horde (the eastern part of Kipchak), who had imposed his rule over this region with the help of Timur Lenk (Tamerlane), ruler of Transoxania, triumphed over Mamay and became Khan of the Golden Horde, thus reuniting the whole of the Kipchak. He then invaded the Russian principalities and destroyed various towns (Vladimir, Suzdal and Moscow in August 1382) and reestablished Mongol suzerainty. Strengthened by his victories, Tokhtamish then envisaged reconstituting the empire of Ghengis Khan, but he found Tamerlane in his way, who in the meantime had become lord of Transoxania, Afghanistan and Persia. The ensuing war lasted from 1387 to 1395 and ended with the defeat of Tokhtamish and the destruction of the Khanate of Kipchak, notably the destruction of its principal towns. However, Khan Timur Qutlugh (1398–1400) joined Tamerlane's side in 1399 and was placed by him at the head of what was left of the khanate to the east, where he established Mongol domination over the Russian principalities, a domination which lasted a century, whereas Kipchak itself split up into three smaller khanates around the middle of the century; those of Crimea, Kazan and Astrakhan.

A shaken Persian world

In 1255, the Great Khan Mongke confided the task of unifying all the territories from Afghanistan to Syria under the Mongol authority to his brother. Hulagu eliminated his adversaries systematically: the Ishmaelites of Persia in 1256; the Caliph of Baghdad in 1258, when the town was destroyed. The Mongol advance into Syria was finally halted by the Mamelukes at Ayn Jalut in September 1260; this battle established the boundaries between Mongol and Mameluke territory, with the Mamelukes stretching as far as northern Syria and the west bank of the middle Euphrates. The Mongols' failure is partly explained by the alliance which Berke, Khan of Kipchak, drew up with the Mameluke Sultan Baibars in 1261, and which threatened Azarbayjan. To the east, the Khanate of Jaghatai presented a threat to the Mongols of Persia, who responded by making sure of their authority over the regions from eastern Asia Minor to west Afghanistan. Hulagu was a Buddhist and was married to a Christian (a Nestorian). His successors Abaka and Argun were Buddhists as well; until Argun's rather more tolerant reign, Muslims were less well regarded and the rulers manifested hostility towards the Sunni Muslim States.

Hulagu set up his capital at Maraga in Azarbayjan; Abaka (1265–1282) fixed his at Tabriz. During his reign, the Nestorian Church grew in importance and in March 1281, the elected Nestorian Patriarch, Mar Yahballaha III, was of Uigur if not Mongol origin, which made relations between Church and government easier still.

Abaka succeeded in eliminating the Kipchak menace hanging over Azarbayjan in 1266, and that of Jaghatai in 1270 and 1273. He was less fortunate in his moves against the Mameluke Sultan Baibars, victor over the Mongols at Elbistan (1277), against whom he solicited the support of the Pope, the King of England and the King of France – in vain (1274–7). A further Mongol army commanded by Abaka's brother, Mengu Timur, was defeated in October 1282 near Homs by the Mameluke Qalawun.

Abaka's death on 1 April 1282 caused a great crisis among the Ilkhans; his successor Tekuder converted to Islam, taking the name of Ahmed, and began his campaign to Islamise the Mongols by driving the Nestorian Church leaders away and drawing closer to the Mamelukes. However the opposition party, which embraced Mongol traditionalists, the Nestorians and the Buddhists as well as Armenian and Frankish vassals, ended by winning and allowed Argun, another of Abaka's sons to take over power in August 1284.

The new Khan was a Buddhist, who showed very great tolerance for all religions, including Islam, allowing Muslims to be judged according to Koranic Law. His minister of finance, Sa'ad ad-dawla, was a Jew, who restored order to the finances and administration of the Ilkhanid government by raging against the abuses and pillage of the Mongol lords and military leaders. Argun was however hostile to the Mamelukes and wrote Pope Honorius IV a letter in which he proposed organising a Crusade against the Sultan of Egypt. He followed this up by sending a Nestorian monk of Turkish origin, Rabban Çauma, on a mission to Europe. He went to Rome, France and England where he was given, apart from an excellent welcome, only fair words. Argun sent two further ambassadors to the West, who were not more successful, and the project was abandoned.

Argun's death in 1291 gave the Mongol lords an opportunity to revolt against his administration, which ended with the accession of his brother Gaykhatu to power, a man of no attainments, who attempted to stem the serious financial crisis by introducing paper money (*tchao*) on the Chinese model to Persia in 1294. This paper money system had the effect of immediately stopping all commercial activity and was rapidly abandoned. Gaykhatu was overthrown in April 1295, but his successor Baydu (April to November

The citadel of Tabriz. The town was a Mongol capital from the end of the thirteenth century and was very soon endowed with walls by the Khans (fourteenth century), of which this door remains, pierced in a redoubtable wall 40 metres high.

1295) proved just as incapable of reestablishing order and the authority of the Khan. Ghazan (1295–1304) brought about a profound alteration to the Ilkhan state; a convert to Sunni Islam, he was carried to power by the Muslim party and the emir Nawruz, and opened his reign by reacting violently against all religions other than Islam; violence which was instigated and executed by Nawruz, whose excesses and those of his followers drove Ghazan to retaliate; he had them arrested and executed in 1297. From then on, Ghazan proceeded to reorganise the administration and the country's economy, in which he was supported notably by his Vizir, Rashid al-Din Fadl Allah, who was also the great historian of the Mongols. He was able not only to reestablish the Khan's authority in the face of the Mongol emirs' opposition, but also to encourage farmers at the expense of nomads and to restore life to trade. He was also the first Ilkhan to undertake a programme of religious building, especially at his capital Tabriz. Finally, he demonstrated a degree of good will towards the Shiite Muslims. His foreign policy was a continuation of that of the great Khans of the thirteenth century; he attacked the Mameluke Sultan in Egypt twice, without positive results, and he opposed the expansion of the Khans of Jaghatai towards the West.

His brother and heir Oljeitu (1304–16) had been a Christian initially, but once converted to Islam (1310), he subscribed at first to the Shiite doctrine. Christians, Mazdeans and even Sunni Muslims suffered annoyance, discrimination and sometimes even persecution, which created a climate of civil war in the khanate. Outside it, Oljeitu appealed in vain to the Europeans to fight against the Mamelukes, and led a few expeditions against them. He also intervened in central Asia Minor, where the Bey of Karaman acknowledged him as his overlord. To the east, he took eastern Afghanistan from the Khan of Jaghatai (1313), which involved several years of fighting on the confines of the two khanates. Oljeitu installed his capital at Sultaniyya (1305) where he undertook building programmes without however neglecting Tabriz, where Rashid al-Din was doing the same thing.

Abu Sa'id (1316–34) became Khan when he was twelve; his power was confiscated by the emir Tchuban who got rid of Rashid al-Din by having him executed in 1318. He had to wage ceaseless war against factions, some of which were led by his own sons, such as Timurtash in Asia Minor. His death in 1327 served only to aggravate the internal rivalries, which were amplified by Abu Sa'id's death in 1334; the emirs quarrelled over the power or over parts of the Ilkhan territory, which was no longer headed by a Khan. The Persian State of the Ilkhans disappeared with a whimper, cut up and dismembered and would regain only a shadow of its former glory when it was annexed by Tamerlane at the end of the century. Among the local dynasties which rose up around the middle of the fourteenth century, the more predominant ones were the Jalayrids in Iraq and southern Azarbayjan, the Kara Koyunlu in eastern Asia Minor and northern Iraq, the Sarbadarids in the Mazandaran, the Muzaffarids in Fars and Kirman and the Kert in Afghanistan. Turks, Turcomans, Persians, Arabs and Mongols divided the ruins of a State, which had been on the verge of uniting the whole region from Asia Minor to central Asia, among themselves.

A deeply divided world

The coming of the Mongols to western Asia and southern Russia has been seen as a historical phenomenon which deeply disrupted these regions. In fact, what happened at first was that new people with new masters were imposed on them, and that shamanism, Buddhism and various forms of Christianity (Nestorian, Orthodox, Latin) subsequently took root there and were occasionally stronger than Islam, although Islam had been the dominant religion there since the seventh to eighth centuries. However, these roots did not go deep enough and most of the populations remained faithful to the Muslim religion, which the Khans eventually adopted, out of either conviction or political opportunism. For a while, though, the spirit of tolerance did prevail and non-Muslim communities were able to live in security until the first decades of the fourteenth century.

This picture can be improved on; at the beginning of the Mongol expansion, the conquerors were borne on a wave of enthusiasm which was derived from their belief that they had been called to these conquests by a divine will. They felt that they had been chosen as its instruments and that their victories were evidence of this. In reality, the Mongol religion was not a very profound one, and it was certainly less profound than the religions of certain people who had proved totally resistant to their own religious convictions. Instead, the opposite happened and the Mongols adopted the dominant religion, dictated by external or family circumstances (the Khans' wives played a part in this matter). The first Khans of Persia were Buddhists, while those of Kipchak were shamanists, but their wives tended to be Nestorians. Nestorian Christianity was widely diffused over central Asia and as far as eastern Asia and was adopted by several Mongol and Turkish tribes. Both the Ilkhan Oljeitu and the Khan of Kipchak Sartaq were Nestorians (the former finally adopted Islam). Buddhism also prevailed at the beginning of the Ilkhan dynasty, since Hulagu, Abaka and Argun were adherents of this religion, which seems to have lost its importance and influence by the end of the thirteenth century. Orthodox and Latin Christianity also had their moments of glory; among the Khans of Kipchak a great part of their populations in Russia were Orthodox, and under Mengu Timur the Russian Church was granted privileges which almost made her into a real power alongside that of her rulers. The Christians of the West, for their part, sent missions (generally Franciscans) not only to the Crimea but into the regions of the lower Volta, notably the capital Saray. When the Kipchak became Islamised under Ozbek, the spirit of tolerance continued to reign.

The Nestorians were equally well received by the Ilkhans, as the existence of their Patriarch Mar Yahballaha III proved almost until his death. The Latins themselves were generally more involved with politics than religion and their presence in Persia was represented by a bishopric in Sultaniyya.

Before Islam carried the day in the two khanates, it experienced a few vicissitudes, especially with the Ilkhans in the time of Hulagu. In his eyes, this religion did indeed symbolise the essential adversary, the Caliph, and when he invaded Iraq and Syria, a number of Muslim towns were not only pillaged but also destroyed, and their populations

301

often massacred. There too, however, tolerance prevailed, possibly through neccessity, because the Mongols were obliged to resort to Muslim governors and administrators in regions populated by Muslims. Islam gradually recovered the lost terrain and even more, since the Kipchak as well as the Persian Khans were converted to Islam, generally without losing their tolerant attitude to the other religions. The subsequent disintegration of the Khanate of Kipchak led to the total disappearance of religions other than Islam from the whole of its territory; a few kernels of Christians of different rites did survive, but only to play a much reduced part in society.

Religious problems were only one aspect of the relations established between Mongol governors, local rulers and emirs and the different elements making up the population, since the khanates were made up of heterogenous collections of ethnic groups and societies. For some time after their invasion, the Mongols continued to behave like nomads, until owning lands, controlling towns and founding capitals turned them into semi-nomads, sometimes even settled people. Although at the beginning of their expansionist drive they tended to turn agricultural regions into steppes better suited to their way of life, the Khans subsequently perceived the error of this way of thinking and began on the contrary to encourage agriculture, especially in southern Russia. This new policy benefited those Russian princes who were vassals of the Khans as well as the notables and members of the rulers' families, who were detainers of these lands. These persons were all-powerful in their lands and over their inhabitants as well as being among the most important army leaders. In fact, the pre-eminence accorded to these feudal begs and the rivalries between begs, were among the principal causes of the dimunition of the Khans' power and the weakening or collapse of the Mongol khanates.

An open world from the Crimea to China?

Almost all economic development was effectively prevented by the conflicts with the Mamelukes of Egypt and the Khanate of Kipchak, by the progressive disappearance of the Latin states of Palestine and Syria, and by the pre-eminence of nomadic or semi-nomadic elements among the peasantry and settled peoples until first part of the fourteenth century. As for relations with Europeans, the only ones to be maintained were with the Khanate of Jaghatai, in so far as there was no fighting going on there. Although the Christians had been well received until the beginning of the fourteenth century and Genoese merchants had been able to establish themselves in northern Persia, and although Ghazan had encouraged the renewal of agriculture, nevertheless, after his death and still more after Oljeitu, the disintegration of the Ilkhan State put a stop to economic relations with the Italians and closed the route to central Asia through Asia Minor, northern Iraq and Persia. As the Seljuk Sultanate spread over Asia Minor and independent and often rival *beyliks* fought over this region, routes which had crossed it in the thirteenth century were abandoned for those passing through the Mameluke Sultanate, which was much more stable and safe, or the route via Constantinople, the Crimea and the Khanate of Kipchak.

302

This last seems to have enjoyed favourable conditions very soon; firstly, it did not have to fight the Muslim populations residing on its territory as violently as the Ilkhans had done. The Russian elements were not sufficiently organised or strong enough to oppose the political and economic decisions taken by the Khans and the same applied to the Turks or Bulgars along the Volga. The traditional social structures of the Mongol tribes found a favourable terrain in the steppes of southern Russia or of Decht-i Kipchak. However, agriculture was finally encouraged (if only by using slaves taken from a wide area, a practice reminiscent of feudal societies, but which bears no comparison with European arrangements), because its produce was not only indispensible to the subsistence of the inhabitants, but was also an important export sought after by the Italian merchants in the Crimea. A further inducement lay in the fact that the bulk of taxation was raised from the peasantry, who were far more easily controlled than other social categories. Another aspect of the Kipchak economy is the slight interest which the Khans took in their towns. Not until the fourteenth century did they acquire permanent residences, but the only towns they recognised were those of China and Mongolia and they did not hesitate to send the Russian artisans who had made the glory of Kiev and other Russians towns to them. This practice resulted in the degradation of urban institutions and to the preponderance of the Mongols' customary laws in the Russian principalities.

The Khanate of Kipchak succeeded best in its commercial relations with the Empire of Constantinople and the merchant cities of Italy. Constantinople was a port of call for Greek and Italian ships sailing to the Crimea or to Trebizond, where the route leading to Tabriz via Erzurum, the ex-Theodosiopolis, began. Until the end of the thirteenth century, the Genoese and to a lesser degree the Venetians used this port and this route, taking advantage of Michael VIII Palaeologus's opening the Black Sea to the Genoese. This traffic does not seem to have harmed Genoese trade with Persia and Armenia, which started from Lajazzo in the Gulf of Alexandretta and crossed eastern Asia Minor. By the beginning of the fourteenth century, however, the disintegration of the Seljuk Sultanate and the ensuing political and military disorder made this route considerably more difficult. The first route too was considerably disrupted by the evolution of the Khanate of the Ilkhans.

From then on, the Greeks and Italians concentrated their efforts on the Crimea. Since the earliest times, the Byzantines had practically monopolised Black Sea trade, especially the trade in wheat, which was immensely important to Constantinople's food supply. Their monopoly was broken by the coming of the Genoese and the Italians; already in the time of the Latin occupation of Constantinople, Italian merchants had sought to trade with southern Russia, which was by then controlled by the Mongols. In 1247 a missionary called John of Piano de Carpine met Italian merchants in Kiev; these merchants were perhaps more interested in trading in products from the Baltic countries. In 1253 another missionary, William of Rubruck, mentioned that Soldaia (or Sughdak) in the Crimea was the *rendez-vous* for merchants from Russia and Turkey. In 1260, Nicolo and Matteo Polo, uncles of the traveller Marco Polo who later became so famous, found a number of Latin merchants at Sughdak who had made this port the centre of their trade. Sughdak was administered by a Greek Sebastocrator but was subject to the Mongol Khan; it had retained a measure of autonomy and its political, commercial and religious relations with the capital of the Greek Empire and with the ports of the Asia Minor littoral had made it into the most important market in the Crimea. Rubruck mentioned that at Sughdak, silks and cotton cloth and spices from Turkey and elsewhere were exchanged for Russian furs.

The Genoese colony at Caffa was founded back in 1266, when the Genoese were granted a bit of land on which to set up their consulate and an entrepot. Their installation was made easier for them by the Treaty of Nymphaeum with Michael VIII, which opened up the Black Sea to them, and by the treaty of 1263 between Michael Palaologus and the Mameluke Sultan Baibars and the Mongol Khan of Kipchak, which essentially concerned Egypt's trade in slaves from Russia, Georgia and the Caucasus. The Genoese played an important part in this trade, often acting as intermediaries. Although Caffa was twice destroyed (in 1296 and 1308) the town was rebuilt in 1316 and flourished greatly. Alongside the Genoese, who were the most numerous, merchants of all origins could be found there: Europeans, Greeks, Arabs, Turks, Persians and Mongols. A *codex comanicus* survives from this period, a dictionary translating Coman words (the name of a Turkish tribe) into Persian and Latin, which was probably meant for the merchants and missionaries there.

The principal rivals to the Genoese were the Venetians, who were present at Sughdak around 1285. They were also involved in the slave trade, as well as in all the trade coming to Saray from the Crimea and travelling from there as far as central Asia and China. At the beginning of the fourteenth century, John of Montecorvino was sent from Rome to Peking to be its Archbishop; he considered the Caffa route via Saray and Elmalig to Khanbalik (Peking) the most practicable 'when not too troubled by wars'. Pegolotti has provided us with a detailed itinerary from the Crimea to China, with practical notes about customs, means of transport, currencies, and so on. In 1333, Khan Ozbek allowed the Venetians to establish themselves at Tana on the Don estuary. From then on they equalled the Genoese in the Black Sea and indeed ended by bettering them during the fourteenth century. Italian trade was anyway ruined by Khan Tokhtamish, who ravaged Saray and Astrakhan, seized Tana and massacred the Italian population there. The silk trade with China, which the Italians had engaged in across the Crimea, was interrupted by the disappearance of their points of contact. Caffa did continue to play a role, however, especially in exporting the produce of the Russian hinterland; wheat, wood, salt, furs and of course slaves, who were still in demand in Egypt.

As long as the 'Mongol peace' reigned over Kipchak, the khanate was to a certain extent prosperous, and allowed human, religious and commercial exchanges. The Mongols managed to maintain their domination for over a century by demonstrating their strength and by their tolerance in dealing with very different peoples. Their adhesion to Islam, which might have improved their relations with their neighbours and might have brought them religious unity, did not in fact solve all the problems they were confronted with during the fourteenth century. They were too different from the peoples they had subjected and were finally assimilated to them rather than the other way around, and the elements of the civilisation they had introduced into the Near East gradually disappeared. When the Ottomans established themselves over the whole of Asia Minor, western Persia, Iraq and the shores of the Black Sea at the end of the fifteenth century, what was left of the Mongol State was by then completely separate from the western world. Already by the close of the fourteenth century, Tamerlane's offensive had put an end to what had been the Mongol Empire.

6

A confrontation in the East: Turks and Europeans

Although Western Europe gloried in its undoubted progress and in its remarkable expansion, especially from the last part of the fifteenth century, this expansion generally did no more than touch on lands lying outside the bounds of the Old World: everywhere else it came up against the Ottoman Empire – in the Maghrib and in the Near East. This Empire represented an insurmountable obstacle and to make matters worse, the Turkish offensive prevailed until *c.* 1575–80. Although in the long run this obstacle was overcome on the economic front, this was not really effective until the seventeenth century. In spite of all that has been claimed for it, the discovery of the sea route round the Cape of Good Hope did not effectively impair the economy of the Ottoman world before the second half of the sixteenth century. It should be stressed at this point that the success of the Turkish Sultans contributed greatly towards reuniting the Muslim world and that the other Islamic countries (apart from Morocco, which was subjected to European influence), including Iraq and the Persian Gulf, were dependent on Constantinople, soon to become 'Istanbul'.

The Ottomans put an end to the Byzantine State during the fifteenth century, a task in which they were well supported by the Venetians and the Genoese. They also extended and strengthened their authority over Balkan Europe, and then over the shores of the Black Sea. The Mameluke State was still at the height of its brilliance and still played a leading role in the world of commerce, but its internal affairs were slowly deteriorating and by the beginning of the sixteenth century, it could no longer withstand Ottoman aggression. The same degenerative process applied to the Turcoman States of Asia Minor and western Iran; heirs in part to the Ilkhans. In short, from the frontiers of Hungary and the Danube to the Persian Gulf and the Caucasus and from Algeria to the Red Sea, an enormous political, military, economic and even religious block (in so far as Islam was the dominant religion in it) impeded the Europeans' progress – sometimes so successfully that they had to abandon those bases which they had been able to create, for instance in the Maghrib. Once they had been thrown out of this zone, with its Black African and Asian connections, the Europeans had no alternative but to circumvent it and to establish direct relations with these regions.

The demise of Byzantium

The annihilation of the Greeks shocked and pained Christendom and was certainly the most notable event of the fifteenth century in the East. Although this august ruin had been whittled down over the fourteenth century until it was no more than a fairly obsolete symbol and represented only a minor threat to the Turks, people both East and West were aware that the Turks needed to occupy Byzantium in order to obtain the capital and the legitimacy which would round off their achievement. During Bayezid's triumphant campaign, this was thought to be only months away. However, a brutal and unexpected event gave the Greeks a half century's reprieve.

A thunderbolt called Tamerlane

Tamerlane liked to compare himself with Ghengis Khan and indeed, the Turcoman conqueror did rival the Mongol in the number of decapitated heads his soldiers collected as trophies and in the wave of irrational terror which swept before him. But unlike them, he was not accompanied by a tribe or an ethnic group, or any form of organisation for exploiting the subjected lands; consequently, he achieved nothing that endured – only a dozen years of savage turmoil and abominable massacres. His religious pretexts did not stand up to examination and there is no evidence he had formed any sort of preliminary plan of conquest and settlement.

Timur Lenk, the Lame, was the chief of a Turcoman tribe of Samarkand, which he led between 1380 and 1393 on a campaign of conquest and pillage across the Iranian plateau, where the last Mongol dynasties were dying off. Herat, Shiraz, Ispahan and Tabriz were taken and their destruction was accompanied by the systematic execution of their male populations. Horrifying numbers of decapitated corpses, which served to heighten the panic, have been recorded; as many as 70,000 in one place. Tamerlane then pushed on into the Caucasus and to Mesopotamia, where he occupied Baghdad. The emirs and beys of Dyar Bakr and eastern Anatolia prudently submitted to him, but this did not inhibit the conqueror from sacking Sivas, for instance, and having 4,000 Christians buried alive on his way through in 1400 before descending on Damascus, which he almost entirely destroyed.

In the meantime, he had been tempted by India; he crossed the Indus in 1398 and reached Delhi, which he left a ruin. Since his campaigns were not followed up by an organised occupation, he had scarcely turned his back when revolts broke out against his atrocities. This also happened in Asia Minor during his occupation of Damascus, especially since the Ottoman Bayezid had no intention of being ousted. Their inevitable confrontation took place at Ankara on 20 July 1402. The Ottomans were crushed and Bayezid was captured with his eldest son; he was tortured and thrown into a ditch where he died a few months later. This tragedy was accompanied by the usual scenes of carnage. As might be expected, the whole of Anatolia including Smyrna where the Knights of Rhodes had fled came under Tamerlane's control, allowing him to confront Byzantium.

The West was enthusiastic. The scheme of things of the time of Saint Louis rose up from its ashes; here was the saviour come to destroy the Turks, contain the Mamelukes and succour Constantinople. Marshal Boucicaut was given the job of contacting Tamerlane; the Castilians and French hurried some Franciscans off to find him at the end of 1403. They had some difficulty joining the conqueror, because he had since changed his objective and

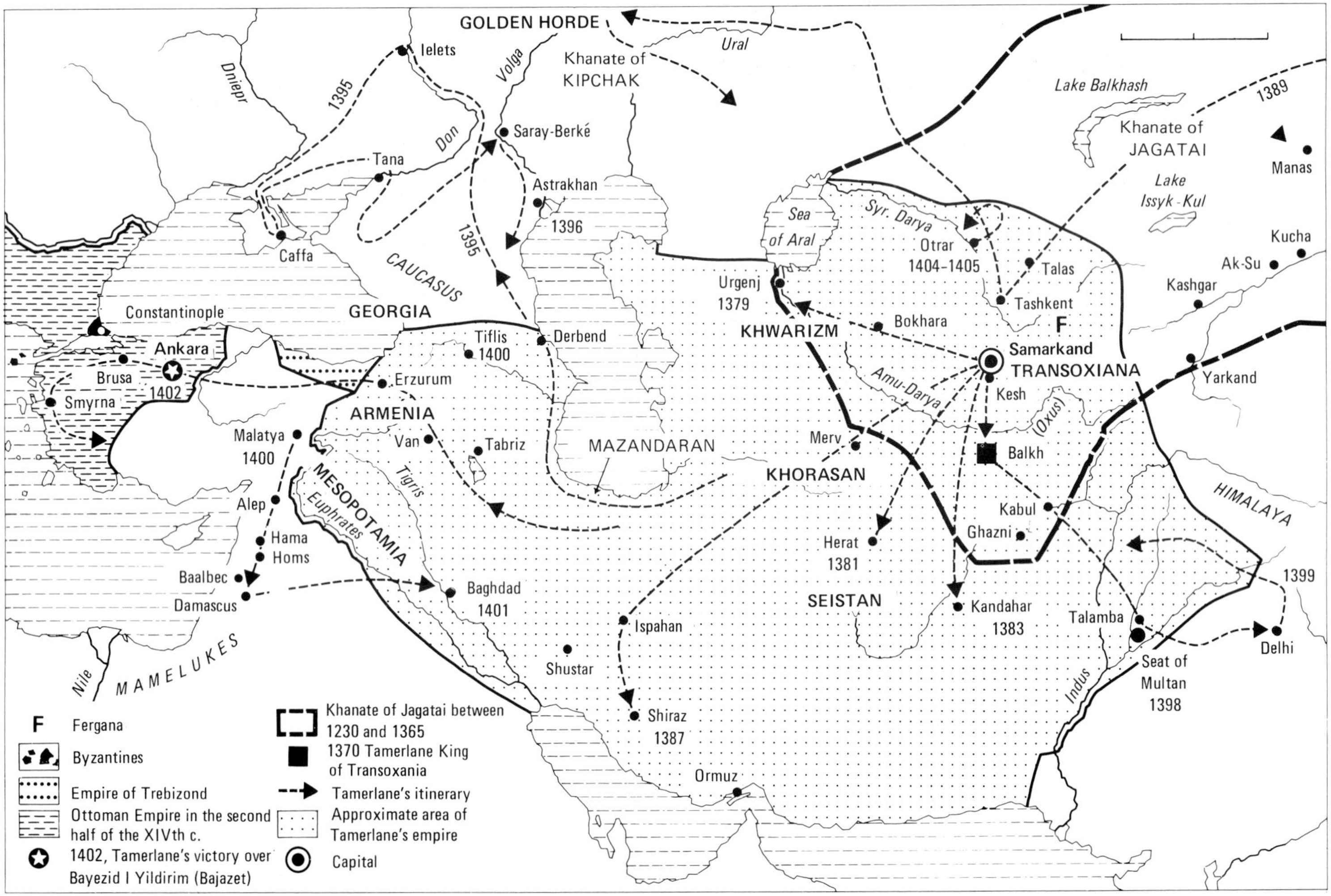

7 Tamerlane's empire

Map labels:

1389
Manas
Kucha
Ak-Su
Kashgar
Yarkand
Khanate of JAGATAI
Lake Issyk-Kul
Lake Balkhash
HIMALAYA
1399
Delhi
Seat of Multan 1398
TRANSOXIANA
Talamba
Indus
Talas
Tashkent
F
Samarkand TRANSOXIANA
Kesh
Balkh
(Oxus)
Kabul
Ghazni
Kandahar 1383
Otrar 1404-1405
Bokhara
Syr-Darya
Amu-Darya
Merv
SEISTAN
Herat 1381
KHORASAN
Sea of Aral
KHWARIZM
Urgenj 1379
MAZANDARAN
Ispahan
Shiraz 1387
Ormuz
GOLDEN HORDE
Khanate of KIPCHAK
Ural
Volga
Astrakhan 1396
Saray-Berké
1395
Derbend
Shustar
CAUCASUS
Tiflis 1400
Erzurum
Van
Tabriz
Tigris
Baghdad 1401
Don
Tana
Ielets
1395
Dniepr
Caffa
GEORGIA
ARMENIA
MESOPOTAMIA
Euphrates
Malatya 1400
Alep
Hama
Homs
Baalbec
Damascus
MAMELUKES
Nile
Constantinople
Ankara 1402
Brusa
Smyrna
Fergana

Legend:

Khanate of Jagatai between 1230 and 1365
1370 Tamerlane King of Transoxania
Tamerlane's itinerary
Approximate area of Tamerlane's empire
Capital

F Fergana
Byzantines
Empire of Trebizond
Ottoman Empire in the second half of the XIVth c.
1402, Tamerlane's victory over Bayezid I Yildirim (Bajazet)

308

The legend of Tamerlane. The ravages effected by
this cruel man's lighting invasion were long
remembered in Europe, inspiring either caricature
or idealisation, as in these Italian, German and
French engravings of later centuries.

was no longer interested in the West. He had set off for Iran, where the envoys were brutally brought, understanding nothing, because they found there a Muslim and a Turk, not an animist Mongol. He was getting ready to attack the Chinese when, luckily for the Ming, death overtook him in January 1405. Since he had achieved nothing apart from destroying all he came across, except for his capital Samarkand, his conquered Empire fell apart after three or four years. Nothing remained of this passing scourge, except for one town which had been enriched by the booty of fifteen years of pillage.

Tamerlane's invasion of Asia Minor and his victory over Sultan Bayezid I were none the less real catastrophes for the young Ottoman State, for not only had it lost the greater part of its Asian territories, where previously conquered or annexed *beyliks* were reestablishing their independence, but especially because Bayezid's sons launched a series of fratricidal wars over the succession to the Sultanate, which lasted over eleven years. Before this was resolved, Tamerlane's desire to break up Asia Minor had been realised. It is however remarkable that no significant movement of rebellion started up in the European part of the Ottoman State, and that these newly subjected Christian countries did not seek to shake off the Turkish yoke. Did this mean that the Ottomans, in spite of their defeat at Ankara, were strong enough to impose respect for their authority, or that the conquered countries were too weakened to resist the Turks, or again, that their yoke was not after all so intolerable? In any case, no rulers in the Balkan provinces intervened in the Ottoman civil war and the Byzantine Emperor Manuel II was able to draw only limited advantages from the situation. This war finally ended in 1413, with the victory of Mehmed I (Muhammad), who then had to restore the Ottoman hegemony, reconstitute their territorial unity against the countries of Anatolia and prevent the Karaman prince of Konya from taking advantage of their temporary weakness in Anatolia. Mehmed I succeeded in doing all this three years after his brothers' triumphs, and by 1416 he was not only the sole ruler of a reunited State, but he had also defeated his Karaman rival and had reaffirmed the Ottoman presence in the Balkans. His only danger lay in the emergence of a pretender to the throne called Mustafa, who was supported by a rebellious emir.

Two major factors emerge from this troubled period; the definitive superiority of the Ottomans over every other power in eastern Europe and Asia Minor, and the solidity of their State's internal structures, which managed to keep going during the difficult and disruptive years and were able to function again in the interest of the State when it was fully reconstituted.

A reprieve but no new trumps

During his second visit to Paris, Emperor Manuel II learnt of Bayezid's disaster at the Battle of Ankara (1402), which altered the balance of power in the East and procured the Empire a reprieve lasting fifty years. During the dynastic crisis which confronted the Ottoman State after Bayezid's death in exile and during the reign of Mehmed I (1413–21), Byzantium experienced relative peace for the last time and was able to undertake a final attempt at righting herself. New contacts were established between the Empire and the dismembered

Ottoman State, allowing the former to recuperate Thessalonica and the coastal regions of the northern Aegean, west of the Black Sea and the Propontida, as well as rescinding on the annual payment of tribute to the Ottomans.

Manuel concentrated his efforts on consolidating the Despotate of Morea, which had passed from the Cantacuzenus family to the Palaeologi in 1383–4. The problems of the Despotate were summed up by the bitter antagonisms of the numerous potentates in the Chersonese, who included of course Byzantines, Navarrese, Venetians, the Order of the Hospitallers of Rhodes, and the local lords, who were perhaps the most recalcitrant of them all. During these last years of the Empire's decline, however, and in spite of it, the despotate experienced a revival of Hellenism and a new cultural ferment; this was expressed in the writings of the period and it prefigured a renaissance which was not allowed to reach maturity, being brutally curtailed by the Ottoman conquest.

Manuel went twice to the Despotate of Morea, and it was during his second visit (1415–16) that, emulating the practices of Antiquity which Justinian I had revived, he erected the Great Wall of Hexamilion between the Gulf of Salonica and the Gulf of Corinth, which was meant to act as a strong barrier against Turkish attacks by land. Raising the funds and the workforce required for this major construction, in which a large number of the population took part, incited certain local lords to resist and they even tried unsuccessfully to demolish the wall. Among the other inconveniences which ensued was the emigration of many Greek and Albanian peasants (and consequently of an important workforce) to the Venetian colonies, in order to avoid liability to taxes financing the construction. After the Emperor's departure, his eldest son John, the future co-Emperor and his other son, Theodore II, Despot of Morea, were able to extend the territory of the Despotate at the expense of the Latin Principality of Achaia, which was saved at the last moment by Venetian intervention.

Manuel was fully aware of how precarious his peace with the Ottomans was, which was why he had not given up seeking for western help, in circumstances unfavourable to Byzantium. Venice and Hungary were at war and the Papacy was too preoccupied with the internal problems of the Latin Church, which the Council of Constance (at which the Emperor's personal envoy, Manuel Chrysoloras, himself a convert to Catholicism, was present) attempted to resolve, to pay any attention to Manuel's embassy. In fact, his embassy only managed to persuade Pope Martin V to draw up special Indulgences for financing the construction of the Hexamilion, and to consent to the marriage of Catholic princesses with members of the Imperial Family. Such measures drew the two worlds closer together only superficially, and brought Byzantium no comfort in her present serious danger.

The Italians could no longer be relied on for support either. Although the merchant republics' interests in what was left of the Empire were not negligible, the whole hinterland was now Turkish, which gave them the opportunity to negotiate with the Sultans, as indeed the Sultans were doing with the European merchants. Since the Fourth Crusade, the Venetians had systematically installed bases along the maritime route linking Venice with Constantinople – at Zara, Corfu, Cephalonia, Zante, Modon, Corona, Crete, the

Aegean Islands and Euboea, as well as Salonica and Patras at certain times. They also controlled Constantinople and the Bosphorus, the gate to the Black Sea, having driven the Genoese towards Asia Minor, and were able to set up a real empire, known as 'Venetian Romania'. When the Greeks retook Constantinople in 1261, the momentary revenge exacted by the Genoese scarcely affected the Venetians at all since Michael VIII Palaeologus granted them a district in the capital and permission to trade. Besides the Venetian *Bailo* representing the Serenissima at Constantinople, other Venetian representatives were established in the Levant (at Trebizond, Cyprus, Syria and Alexandria). A whole commercial network was extended over the hinterland and Venice drew enormous advantage from the particularly efficient organisation which had been established by her Senate and her economic bases. The Venetians' privileged situation was largely due to their commercial dynamism, but also to the progressive withdrawal of the Byzantines and, at certain moments, of the Genoese. As long as their interests were not directly threatened by the Turks, thus allowing them to keep their expenditure on defence to a minimum, Venetian commerce could only expand. Looking at these bases, it is noticeable how trade with their hinterlands and more distant countries was almost obliged to pass through them. This situation was modified somewhat when the Turks took up a more threatening and demanding stance, occupying Bosnia, Albania and Salonica and reducing the Peloponnesus to tributary status and controlling practically all of the western and southern coastline of the Black Sea. The Venetians then tried, if not to restore life to the Byzantine State, at least to prevent it from collapsing. Their efforts were however never more than tentative because they had no intention of coming into direct conflict with the Turks; Salonica had been an exception. Reading the Venetian documents allows us to realise that the help they afforded the last Byzantine Emperors was limited, even during the siege of Constantinople; Venetian Romania was far too precious an investment for Venice to allow it to be sacrificed to a lost cause. This did not prevent the Venetians from keeping up their offensive against the Turks, but by then the Byzantines were past caring. The Genoese, who had profited from the events in 1261 and immediately afterwards in Constantinople and the Greek Empire, initiated the commercial expansion of the West into the Crimea and the Khanate of the Golden Horde; as masters of Phocea and the islands of Lesbos and Chios, their contacts with Byzantium were reduced in line with the loss of her territory to the Turks. Although a Genoese contingent came to the help of the Greeks at the siege of Constantinople, and fought there valiantly, the Genoese were also the first to recognise Ottoman supremacy and thus persuade the Sultan to confirm their old privileges in Galata, Chios and Lesbos.

So Byzantium could count only on herself in the first half of the fifteenth century; the Lusignan Kingdom of Cyprus had too many problems of its own with the Mamelukes and the Genoese to concern itself with the Byzantines, the more so since old grievances between the Empire and that Kingdom still rankled. Although the Greeks were able to reestablish their rule over the Latin part of the Peloponnesus at the beginning of the fifteenth century (the Principality of Morea), this situation lasted only thirty years and they did not succeed in taking the Duchy of Athens from the Acciajuoli, magnificent Florentines who invested Athens with a new splendour; but it was an Italian, not a Greek, splendour.

Finally the Hospitallers – or Knights – of Saint John of Jerusalem, who had been definitively driven out of the Holy Land in 1291, first settling in Cyprus and then taking over Rhodes from the Byzantines in 1306–8. They turned the island into the seat of their Order and the base for their intensive maritime activities in the eastern Mediterranean. They took part in the Crusade of 1344, which ended with the conquest of Smyrna, which the Knights then occupied until the town was taken by Tamerlane in 1402. They then got hold of ancient Halicarnassus (nowadays Bodrun) where they built the Castle of Saint Peter from which they launched a few sea raids. The immediate proximity of the Ottomans prevented them from being very intensely active, and indeed they made a conspicuous target; there was no question of their bringing the least help to Byzantium.

When Murad II (1421–51) came to the throne of the Sultans, the Emperor's apprehensions were justified. In June 1422, Murad laid siege to the capital in spite of the efforts of John VIII, the new co-Emperor, to stop him by setting up a pretender against him. This siege was a short but particularly violent one (three months), giving the population, which had resisted bravely, a bitter foretaste of what would happen thirty years later. Murad was forced to raise his blockade by the appearance of yet another pretender set up by Manuel; shortly afterwards he moved towards central Greece and the Peloponnesus, where he destroyed the fortifications which Manuel had so painstakingly erected at Hexamilion, before advancing as far as Mistra in a flurry of destruction. He finally concluded a treaty with the Byzantines, which forced them to resume paying their annual tribute and to abandon the Black Sea ports, except for Mesembria and Derkon, and which allowed them to retain the Peloponnesus only on condition they did not rebuild the Hexamilion. Thessalonica, which had been under seige since 1422 and was wracked by famine, was ceded by the despot Andronicus Palaeologus, Manuel's third son, to the Venetians, who promised to safeguard the town's privileges and to take charge of it. However, Venice was able to stay on in Thessalonica for only seven years; after Murad had rejected all their offers of very high annual tribute, he took the town on 29 March 1430 and let his men loose on it for three days. Affairs thus returned to the situation prior to the Battle of Ankara.

Manuel II died in July 1425, clothed in the habit of a monk, having handed the power to his son and co-Emperor John VIII in 1421. The people were grateful to him because he had been able, while preserving them from captivity, to avoid compromising his faith with the West. He had maintained contact with the Papacy, but had insisted on his point of view, which was basically the same as that of Cantacuzenus and that of the overwhelming majority of Byzantines and their Church: the priority of an oecumenical council, which would discuss in all equality the question of Union before deciding about it; and the need for immediate assistance, without which the council would never take place at all, for lack of a free Constantinople.

Hope in the Morea and the West?

John VIII (1425–48) reigned *de facto* over the city state which Constantinople and her adjacent region had become, while his brothers divided the wreckage of the Empire among themselves, which they governed as autonomous despots: Constantine in Mesembria and

313

Anchialos, with the consent of the Sultan; the Despot Demetrius at Lemnos; while Theodore II ruled the Despotate of Morea on his own until 1427, when he shared the power with Constantine and Thomas Palaeologus. Following the example of his father, John VIII paid particular attention to the only vital force in the declining Empire; the Peloponnesus, where Byzantine power had been reestablished over the whole peninsula, with the exception of the Venetian possessions (Modon, Corona, Nauplion and Argos) and Patras, which belonged to the Latin Archbishop. In 1430 Patras too gave itself up to Constantine Palaeologus, which meant the beginning of the end for the Principality of Achaia. In the north, on the contrary, the Empire was in process of losing its remaining free bastions, Thessalonica, as we have already seen, and Janina. The latter was handed over to Sinan Pasha by its own inhabitants who did not want to undergo the fate of Thessalonica and so succeeded in preserving certain privileges concerning their freedom, the landed property of the Church and their own protection.

Faced with the gravity of the situation, John VIII resigned himself to playing the 'Union' card once more, in order to bring about a Crusade for the salvation of the whole of the Christian Orient. It was undoubtedly a game of dupes; the Emperors offered the Papacy, in exchange for the help they requested, the Union of the Churches, which basically meant the submission of the Church of Constantinople to Rome, an undertaking which their people would not even consider. On their side, the Popes stressed the priority of submission over aid, which anyway ran a strong risk of remaining theoretical. It is true that there had been some new thinking on the subject of the Union among the aristocratic circles of Constantinople and especially in intellectual milieux, where the movement of the partisans of the Union (*philenotikoi*) took shape, as opposed to that of its adversaries (*anthenotikoi*). They had been impressed by the different consequences of the capture of Thessalonica and the reduction of Janina and began to get used to the idea of the latter solution, because in their eyes it represented the lesser of two evils. In the meantime, living conditions in the capital were growing increasingly precarious; western travellers of this period drew a picture of a town abandoned to despair and neglect. Several churches and palaces were falling into ruin, the town appeared to be overrun by the poor and destitute and a new onslaught of the Plague in 1435 contributed further towards the decimation of the population. It was in this atmosphere that John VIII (who had already travelled to the West as co-Emperor) was won over to the cause of the Union and in November 1437, he undertook the journey to Italy, the last Byzantine Emperor ever to tread its soil.

The Byzantine delegation was headed by John VIII and the Patriarch Joseph II, and included the Emperor's brother, the Despot Demetrius, and several civil and ecclesiastical personages, among whom Bessarion, the Metropolitan of Nicea and future Cardinal of the Latin Church; the philosopher George Plethon; Gennadios Scholarios, who would become the first Patriarch of Constantinople after its fall; even the Russian Church was represented by Isidore, the Greek Metropolitan of Kiev. They arrived in Venice in February 1438, and went first to Ferrara and next to Florence; it was only in July 1439 that the Union was proclaimed in the presence of Pope Eugenius IV in Latin by Cardinal Cesarini and in Greek by Bessarion after long and minutiose debates, during which the two sides of the oecumenical council had occasionally been at loggerheads. The Byzantine recognition of the primacy of the Pope was formulated in a certain spirit of moderation, but taken as a whole it did indeed mean the submission of the Orthodox Church to Rome. With the exception of the Metropolitan of Ephesus, Mark Eugenikos, who was resolutely opposed to the Union, the *Tomos of Florence* was signed by all the Greek prelates and the Emperor – an occasion which the triumphant Roman Church wanted to invest with great significance. All the Florentines took part in the ensuing celebrations, ensuring that the treaty was perpetuated in certain works of the Renaissance, among which are Vittorio Pisano's medal with its double portrait of Emperor John VIII, and Antonio Filarete's rendering of the Council on the central doors of Saint Peter's in Rome. The greatest masterpiece is undoubtedly Benozzo Gozzoli's fresco on the walls of the Medici–Riccardi chapel in Florence (painted between 1459 and 1464), which depicts the procession of the Magi. Among the illustrious members of the Medici family shown taking part in the procession and alongside the Patriarch Joseph, John VIII can be seen on horseback wearing sumptuous clothes and surrounded by fabulous scenery. The painting dates from some time after the event, and a certain poignancy may be read in the expression on the face of the last Byzantine Emperor to venture into the West in search of the solution to a cause that had already been lost.

As it was, the Union of Florence did not produce any concrete results and, compared with the Council of Lyons, which had, at least provisionally, averted the danger to the West, it proved to be completely insignificant. Instead it had the negative effect of splitting the people of Byzantium into two profoundly opposed and irreconcilable parties, which confused religious disputes with political questions and especially with quarrels between members of the Paleaologus dynasty. In the Orthodox world of the Balkans and especially in Russia the reaction against Constantinople's apostasy was equally lively; Isidore was deposed by Basil II, Grand Duke of Moscow, and from then on the Russian Church decided to elect her prelates herself. In the East too, the Orthodox Patriarchs of Antioch, Jerusalem and Alexandria repudiated their representatives at the Council and abjured the Union. Gradually, in the face of popular anger, certain of the Union's protagonists ended by retracting, while Bessarion and Isidore, the leaders of the Unionist party, definitely adopted Catholicism and became Cardinals of the Latin Church.

The Crusade which the Union of Florence had failed to give birth to began to be realised a few years afterwards, as the Ottomans drew closer to the borders of Hungary. The Jagellonian King of Poland, Ladislas III, who had been crowned King of Hungary in 1440, accompanied by his vassal the Voivode of Transylvania, John Corvin Hunyadi, and the Serbian Despot Giorgi Branković, put himself at the head of a great army which had come to join Prince Vlad of Wallachia and for which Venice, the Pope and the Duke of Burgundy had promised to procure ships. As with the Crusade of Nicopolis, the principal object of the enterprise was to repulse the Turkish menace looming over Hungary and to liberate the neighbouring regions of Serbia. No less vivid was the notion of reaching Constantinople, which the Pope and Cardinal Cesarini fostered. The timing of these projects was propitious, since Murad was then at war in Anatolia with the emir of Karamania, an ally of the

315

John VIII Paleaologus arriving in Florence, by Benozzo Gozzoli. Eastern luxury was demonstrated by the clothes worn by merchants visiting Florence in the period, and so impressed the painter that he reproduced them in his magnificent fresco of *The Procession of the Magi* (1459–64) in the Medici–Riccardi Palace.

Crusaders. At the same time, George Castriota Skanderbeg organised the resistance in Albania, while the Despot Constantine rebuilt the Hexamilion in the Peloponnesus and he forced the Duke of Athens, Nerio II Acciajuoli to become his tributary while he was crossing the Isthmus.

Since the Crusaders were following the plan of the Crusade of Nicopolis, the allied army of 25,000 to 30,000 men crossed Serbia and Bulgaria, where they carried off a few victories. In order to gain a little time Murad hurriedly agreed to a ten year armistice at Adrianople, which Ladislas III ratified at Szegedin in July 1444. This imposed certain limits to Ottoman expansion in the Balkans and allowed Giorgi Branković to recuperate his territories. Satisfied with these arrangements, he did not budge when the other leaders of the crusade decided to renew hostilities, urged on apparently by the Venetians and by Cesarini, who is supposed to have released King Ladislas from his oath. They reckoned without the speed with which Murad reacted; he rushed from Anatolia with an army of between 80,000 and

100,000 men and crushed the allies at the battle of Varna in November 1444. Ladislas and Cesarini were killed; Hunyadi fled to Hungary where he went on planning anti-Turkish alliances, before being beaten in the plain of Kossovo in 1448. The battle of Varna broke up the last attempt at an united European enterprise and John VIII was obliged to congratulate Murad on his success against the Christians.

An island lost in Turkish Islam

From then on, Western Europe got used to considering the fall of the Empire a *fait accompli* and to accepting a status quo which established the boundaries of Ottoman conquest along the frontiers of Hungary and the Albanian massif. Constantinople was reduced to no more than an island in the Turkish desert, and would sooner or later be swallowed up in its sands. The Union of Florence only served to accentuate Byzantium's isolation from the rest of Western Christianity; while certainly pitying the fate of the errant sheep, the Latins bolstered their consciences by telling themselves they had at least succeeded in winning them back into the spiritual fold just in time before their elimination.

Contacts between Constantinople and the West grew increasingly rare after the catastrophe at Varna, and it was only shortly before his death that John VIII ratified the sempiternal treaty with Venice. In the meantime, Murad II had invaded the Morea, once again destroying the Hexamilion with his artillery and once more forcing the Despots Thomas and Constantine Palaeologus to pay him an annual tribute – the elder Despot was soon to leave the Peloponnesus to take over the throne. His accession illustrated the shift in political emphasis from Constantinople to the Morea, where he had been brought up, and where the last Paleaologi found their principal support. It was in the Morea that Constantine had risen to political significance and, having secured the necessary forces there, it was as a Morean prince that he came to Constantinople. After all, the capital was still an international city soon to be invaded by the Ottomans, whereas the Morea was much more of a Greek homeland, a more real *Rhomais*, where Greek political life survived several years after Mehmed II's conquest of the Bosphorus.

Constantine XI arrived in Constantinople on 12 March 1449, having been crowned at Mistra in January. The man who was to be last Emperor of Byzantium showed himself worthy of his destiny and was able to invest the last hours of this Empire of a thousand years with the spiritual exaltation it had so lacked towards the end of its existence. Constantine at once undertook desperate approaches to the Western powers, begging them to save Constantinople, stressing the danger which its fall would bring down on the rest of Christendom. Rome, Venice, Genoa, Ragusa, Hungary, France, the German Emperor, the King of Aragon and Naples – all were solicited in vain. The last of these, Alfonso V, went so far as to appropriate the few sums provided by the Pope for the defence of the city, using them instead to further his plans for establishing a new Latin Empire of Constantinople on his own account. The fact was that historical circumstances did not allow the hypothesis of a new Latin occupation in the East or of safeguarding Constantinople to be realised, and indeed, given that the forces of Christendom could not be mobilised in favourable

317

circumstances, there was no chance of anything being achieved under the prevailing conditions. The Italian maritime cities were already adjusting to the future; the Venetians were beginning to trade in the markets of Adrianople, thanks to their friendly relations with the Sultan. Elsewhere the Genoese in Galata and Chios took steps to ensure that the fall of the Empire would not harm their commercial activities in the Aegean and the Black Sea.

Nonetheless, Constantine spent himself in ceaseless demands for help, turning especially to the Pope, whose Apostolic Nuncio, Cardinal Isidore, the ex-Metropolitan of Kiev, arrived in the capital to assist at the proclamation of the Union in the Hagia Sophia during a celebration in which the clergy of Constantinople had refused to participate (December 1452). As for the last Patriarch of free Constantinople, Gregory III, he had already taken refuge in Rome, sickened by the opposition to him in ecclesiastical circles. Most conspicuous by their absence were the people of Constantinople, who were ready to lose all save for their Orthodox Faith. Strengthened and even exacerbated by their imminent fate, their Faith was their sole solace. Seen in this perspective, the words attributed to Grand Duke Lucas Notaras (himself a naturalised Genoese who was involved in Genoese trade), according to which he preferred to see the Turkish turban in the capital than the Latin mitre, expressed the feelings of the majority. His words are invested with a fully tragic significance in the light of the fate inflicted on this same Notaras by the Turks, who forced him to witness the execution of his sons before following them to the grave.

The new Sultan Mehmed (Muhammad) II the Conqueror (1451–81) was determined to finish with Constantinople, since he needed its unique strategic position to join the two parts of his State and he wanted to make it his new capital dominating both sides of the Bosphorus. He built an enormous fortress on the European side of the Bosphorus, which he called *Boghaz-Kezen* (a pun, meaning both narrow passage or straits, and 'cutter of the throat' – the Rumili Hisar of today) thus making plain his intentions towards the terrorised inhabitants of the town. Constantine protested several times about it before resigning himself to it and, according to the contemporary historian Ducas, he expressed himself in a message thus: 'Since you have chosen war and I can dissuade you neither by oaths nor by flattery – do as you wish; as for me, I take refuge in God and if it is His Will to give you this city as well, who can go against it? . . . from now on I have closed the doors of the city and I will protect its inhabitants as far as possible; may you exercise your power by oppressing everything until the Good Judge will give each of us, to me and to you, our just judgement.'

The end of the New Rome

Abandoned by everyone, Constantine was at least able to supplement the town's food supplies and to proceed to the necessary repairs of the walls before the blockade began, as it did on completion of the Rumili Hisar fortress. The forces present were hopelessly unequal. The tens of thousands of men in the Turkish army (the sources differ, giving from 165,000 to 400,000 men – the first figure being the most probable), surrounded by dervishes and followed by a host of irregulars and noncombatants confronted only a few thousand Greeks

The Rumili Hisar, or the new fortress. Built by thousands of masons and craftsmen to match the Anadolu Hisar on the Asian side of the Bosphorus, this castle allowed Mehmed II to control the Straits and cut Constantinople off from the corn growing regions of the Black Sea. The last blockade of the city was thus inaugurated.

(4,773 according to the contemporary historian Sphrantzes; 6,000 to 7,000 according to Italian sources) and some foreign contingents; 200 archers who had come with Archbishop Isidore and Leonardo, the Genoese Bishop of Chios, and 700 men recruited in Genoa, Chios and Rhodes under the orders of Giovanni Guistiniani Longo, the famous Genoese from Chios. Sphrantzes mentions 2,000 foreigners (over and above a total population of not more than 50,000 in the city). Whatever the facts, the ratio of defenders to attackers seems to have been around 1:15. The inadequately armed defenders were distributed among crucial points along the walls, while outside them twenty-six war ships were anchored at the Golden Horn, as opposed to the great Turkish fleet (around 400 ships) drawn up in the Bosphorus around Diplokionion (nowadays Beshik-Tash). Given their inadequate equipment, the Byzantines disposed of only two advantages – apart from

319

their city's strategic position. One was the chain which closed the Golden Horn and prevented the foreign fleet from sailing into the port and thus rendered their sea wall unassailable, and the other was the great land wall of Constantinople, four miles long, which traced the town limit from the Propontida to the northern point of the Golden Horn and which had never been crossed by force since its construction in the fifth century by Theodosius II. However, the main advantage lay with the adversary; the Turkish army was equipped with weapons developed by the new military technology, which was applied for the first time against so great an obstacle. Accounts of the efficacy of the 'Royal Cannon' are probably exaggerated; it was built along with other cannons by a Saxon from Transylvania, possibly called Urban, who abandoned Constantinople for the greater remuneration offered him by Mehmed, and whom Ducas described as a 'terrible and extraordinary monster'. In any case, the firing power of the whole of the Turkish artillery was too much for a fifth-century construction, with a few later repairs, to withstand. The defenders themselves had only arrows, lances and catapults, while the few small cannon they possessed were short of projectiles. Times had changed and the Byzantines were a century behindhand.

The moment came when the city was totally cut off by land and by sea. Hunyadi's diversionary manoeuvres on the Danube, which were supposed to enable him to relieve Constantinople – at least provisionally – were not carried out; on the contrary, some of his men appear to have acted as technical advisors to the Turkish army on how to make better use of their cannon. The warships and soldiers promised by Venice and Genoa were reduced to two Venetian ships with 800 soldiers on board, which arrived only in April 1453, and to one Genoese ship, while Giorgi Branković sent Mehmed the contingent of soldiers he owed him as a vassal. On his side, Mehmed prevented Constantine's brothers from coming to his help by sending troops from Thessaly under Turakhan to invade the Peloponnesus, which they devastated as far as Messania.

Within the capital, a spirit of resistance and exaltation inspired by the long-suppressed knowledge of their imminent end, took hold of the defenders and the people, with Emperor Constantine and the highest dignitaries of the Empire, including some of the Cantacuzenus family, at their head. The *Bailo* of the Venetian colony of Constantinople and his men, along with two Venetian captains, offered to take part in the fighting, as Nicolò Barbaro recorded in his diary of the siege. The Catalan consul did likewise, and some of the Genoese in Galata came forward to swell Guistiniani's forces. Besides him, there was also an engineer and sapper called John Grant, whom the Greeks considered a German, but who could well have been a Scotsman.

The siege grew more intense after 7 April 1453, when the bulk of the Turkish troops had been moved from Andrianople and were posted in front of the land walls of the capital. A first attack accompanied by bursts of cannon fire was repulsed, while the Genoese ships, full of men and provisions, succeeded in pushing through the blockade and in entering the Golden Horn. This was enough to make Mehmed decide to follow a famous precedent and construct a land route, apparently with the help of Italian engineers and using his immense resources in manpower and machines. About twelve kilometres long, this route linked the

Bosphorus, where his fleet was moored with the Golden Horn. About seventy of his ships were then dragged along it, to turn up in the Golden Horn on 21–22 April. The sight of these ships sliding down the slopes of Pera 'as if they were sailing on the sea, with their anchors, their masts and the rest of their fittings' aroused stupour and despair among the inhabitants of the city, as described by the contemporary historian Critobulus. The walls of the city were already badly damaged and some people had been killed by the Turkish bombardment, the inhabitants of Constantinople being the first Europeans to feel its effect. On 18 May, a mobile wooden tower (*helepolis*) was erected outside the walls, but the defenders managed to set it on fire. On 23 May, Mehmed sent an embassy to demand the surrender of the city but it left with this answer from the Emperor, its high moral content telling much about the spirit of resistance manifested by them all in the hour of supreme sacrifice: 'The act of giving this city to you is not for me or for anyone else among its inhabitants to perform, for we are all going to die in a common decision, of our own volition, and we will not save our lives.'

The final dispositions in the Turkish camp were taken on 27 and 28 May at the same time as the whole population of the city, Greeks and Latins, gathered in the Hagia Sophia to attend the last Mass. On the morning of 29 May, the general attack was unleashed in three waves. The elite corps of Janissaries was thrown into the third wave, when the fighting was at the height of its violence. This was when Giustiniani received the wound which forced him to abandon the battle, thus spreading confusion among the ranks of the combatants. Constantine tried desperately to retain them, but already around fifty Turks had entered the city through the little door of *Kerkoporta* and had forced a passage for the others. A fight to the death followed, with was most violent by the doors of Saint Romanos, where Constantine was seen for the last time. He had removed his Imperial Insignia and he died fighting as a plain soldier in front of one of the gates of the town of which he was Emperor. The resistance collapsed and the Fall of Constantinople was proclaimed when the Ottomans hoisted their standard above her walls. The Sultan made his solemn entry into the city, which he delivered over to his soldiers' fury, having expressed his wish that the walls and the houses be left intact. They ransacked the city for three days; the historian Critobulus of Imbros, who entered the Sultan's service and became the apologist of his exploits, acknowledged that the Turkish army 'evacuated and devastated the whole city, to such an extent that no one could have believed that it had ever contained inhabitants, or riches, or urban prosperity, or anything else in the way of furnishings or magnificence'. Only a small number of inhabitants were able to get away in the Venetian ships. The colony at Galata handed its keys over to the Sultan, who granted it privileges as a reward for its surrender.

Liquidation

Once he had removed the principal obstacle to establishing the unity of his new Empire, Mehmed proceeded with lightning speed to the conquest of the Greek, Latin and Slav wreckage of the Balkan peninsula and the East. The fate of the Despotate of Morea was

The Turks made massive use of specially constructed cannon, which put paid easily to Constantinople's ancient walls and inadequate means of defence. (Ms. Ottoman Hünername, 1584; Istanbul, Topkapi Sarayi.)

decided in 1460. Despot Demetrius Palaeologus, a fervent opponent of the Union of the Churches, surrendered with his family to Mehmed and was given certain islands in the northern Aegean and the town of Ainos off the Thracian coast as appanages. Thomas Palaeologus on the contrary reached Italy, where the Pope granted him a pension and Venice responded to his offer of subsidies by allying with him against the Turks. His daughter, Princess Zoe, married Tsar Ivan III of Russia as her second husband (1472) while her daughter, Helen, was married to King Alexander Jagellon of Poland in 1513, but had no children by him. Thomas' oldest son, Andrew, the protégé of Bessarion, was considered in the West as the legitimate heir to the Byzantine throne and the Despotate of Morea. The Pope granted him the title of Despot, which figures in the titulature of his Bull *Andreas Palaeologus Dei gratia despotes Romeorum*. In a Chrysobull of 1483, issued by Andrew, he even styled himself: *Andre(a)s Pateologus Dei gratia fidelis imperator Constantinopolitanus*. As for Manuel, Thomas' younger son, he eventually left Rome to rejoin the Sultan, who offered him an appanage and a pension. The younger of his two sons converted to Islam.

The Comneni State of Trebizond had already had to withstand the Turks during John IV Kalojoannes' reign (1429–58): after taking in Greeks fleeing from Constantinople, Trebizond in her turn was captured by the Turks and John IV had to acknowledge the Sultan as his overlord and pay him tribute (1454). He formed an alliance with Uzun Hasan, ruler of the Turcoman State of the *Ak Koyunlu* (the White Sheep, established in eastern Asia Minor and Azarbayjan) in an attempt to recover his independence, but this came to nothing. However, his successor and brother David renewed the alliance and even appealed to the West for help. Vainly, as it was, because Mehmed II took the offensive and defeated Uzun Hasan before laying siege to Trebizond, which surrendered on 15 August

1461. Its Emperor was executed along with several members of his family at Adrianople, accused of having plotted against the Sultan (1463). The end of the State of Trebizond marked the complete disappearance of all that was once Byzantine territory. In the place of the Greek Christian Empire, and over practically the same territories, there now stood a Turkish Muslim Empire which was poised to grow even larger. In the Balkans, what was left of Serbia had been conquered in 1459, as was Bosnia in 1463, and towards the end of the century Ottoman domination extended as far as the Adriatic. In Greece proper and the Aegean, Lesbos fell in 1462, Samos in 1475, Phocea on the Asiatic coast in 1455, Euboea in 1470 and the Duchy of Athens in 1456. The Parthenon, which was then a church dedicated to the Virgin Mary, was turned into a Turkish mosque. The Venetian colonies of western Greece and the Peloponnesus succumbed in their turn towards the end of the century. Rhodes was taken from the Knights of Saint John in 1522, Chios and Naxos in 1566, while Cyprus surrendered in 1571. Crete and the Ionian islands, except for Leucadia and some of the Cyclades, were all that was left of the Latin Empire in the East. They succumbed later, except for Corfu which alone remained within Venetian territory.

And silence

The news of the capture of Constantinople stunned the western world. Its easy conscience had been soothed by the capacity of the capital's walls for withstanding attack, which had been so often tested and proven, and by the recent supply of provisions which had reduced the famine. The westerners hoped that a new pretender to the Sultanate would emerge, who would give rise to civil war – they even hoped for the advent of some new Timur-Lenk in Asia, who would force Mehmed II to raise the siege of the city, all of which helped them to lessen their concern over its imminent destruction; an attitude reinforced by the confessional gulf between them and the Byzantines who clung obstinately to their Orthodoxy.

So their surprise at the breadth of the catastrophe and at the death of the Emperor was all the greater wherever the dreadful news arrived. It was brought to Venice on 29 June 1453, when the letters from the Castellan of Modon and the *Bailo* of Chalcis announcing the capture of the city were read aloud during a session of the Grand Council of the Republic. From Venice, the news was brought to Rome in a letter on 8 July, where shortly afterwards a report on the events dated 15 July arrived from Crete, addressed to the Pope by Cardinal Isidore, who had taken refuge on the island after his happy release from captivity. Another report from the same time was drawn up for the Pope by the humanist Lauro Querini, who had interrogated several inhabitants of Constantinople, eye-witnesses to their city's capture, who had subsequently been sold and redeemed. The Pope also received a letter from an eye-witness, the Latin Bishop Leonardo of Chios, while Aeneas Silvius Piccolomini, the future Pope Pius II, then secretary to the German Emperor, sent him a description of the fall of Constantinople and of the 'second death of Homer and Plato'. The contemporary Polish historian, John Dlugosz, ended his description of the siege and fall of the city:

The destruction of Constantinople, as unhappy as it was predictable, was a great victory for the Turks, but also the end of Greece and the shame of the Latins. By it, the Catholic faith was struck, religion was confounded and the name of Christ insulted and denigrated. Of the two eyes of Christendom, one was blinded; of its two hands, one was cut off. Libraries were burnt, books destroyed, the doctrine and the knowledge of the Greeks, without which no one can call himself learned, went up in the smoke.

As for the Greek people, one has but to refer to the great cycle of *threnes* and popular songs which served, as they became part of the traditional repertoire, to transmit the ideals which the humiliated nation had aspired to, and which helped it to survive the long centuries of occupation.

The uncertainties of the Western world were succeeded by consternation and anguish; when Cardinal Bessarion learnt the news at Bologna on 23 July, he hastened to write to Doge Francesco Foscari in Venice, lamenting the Byzantines' fate and exhorting the Doge to put an end to the disputes in Italy and to unite the Christian princes in a new crusade. The Papacy, whose interests in the East – apart from the problem of the Union of the Churches – were linked with those of Venice and Genoa, was also concerned, and on 30 September 1453, Pope Nicholas V issued a Bull proclaiming a European Crusade. But his appeal did not have the results he had counted on; Venice had already begun treating with the Sultan, the better to safeguard her acquisitions. It was only the efforts of Aeneas Silius Piccolomini, who became Pope in 1458, which induced the Christian rulers, more particularly their representatives, at long last to assemble at Mantua – but they spread their arrivals out over a whole year from the beginning of 1459 to January 1460. His pontifical Bull, which was promulgated after much equivocation, proclaimed three years of war against the Infidel – and was to remain a dead letter. It had become impossible for European rulers to collaborate in a Crusade, due as much to the ravages and changes wrought by the Hundred Years' War (especially in France, whose king, to make matters worse, was then at war with the King of Naples), as to the war between the German Emperor and Bohemia and to the opportunistic policy of the Doge, who had changed sides more than once.

Soon afterwards, following Mehmed II's new military successes, the disappearance of Hunyadi and Skanderbeg and the deaths of Pius II and Bessarion, Europe, near the end of her own crisis, found that she now had to tolerate the presence of a non-Christian empire on her soil. She was forced to modify her traditional policy of confrontation and instead, to negotiate with the enemy, resuming the confrontation under different forms and in the service of her new States' expansionist ambitions. It has been pointed out that, although the world of the First Crusade and of 1204 was governed by the idea and the spirit of the Crusade, the world which had to face up to the Turkish problem was a world of compromise. In this sense, the capture of Constantinople in 1453, a decisive event for the future of the East, is a date of oecumenical importance, since a new political Europe was born of it.

While the capture of Constantinople by the Crusaders had not resulted in the creation of a viable Latin State, her capture by the Ottomans on the contrary, gave birth to a new empire, which was solidly established over almost the same area which the Christian

Empire had covered in its most flourishing period. However, the very fact of possessing this supremely global city, which was subsequently repeopled by transferring Greek populations from all the subjected regions, to a certain extent determined the way relations between the Sultan and his Greek subjects were organised. In submitting to Byzantine ceremonial when he invested Gennadios Scholarios with the title of Oecumenical Patriarch, Mehmed II, who prided himself on his title *amiras Turkorromaion* (Emir of the Turko-Romans), meant to stress the fact that he had replaced the Byzantine Emperor at the head of a multi-ethnic Empire, rather than to demonstrate that he intended to rule over a Turko-Greek empire. Even if he had intended this, it would have been impossible to realise, since society was divided into dominant and dominated parts, the latter being all the subject peoples. The political, fiscal and legal privileges which he granted to the Church of Constantinople were due to the fact that she had been entirely subjugated. Further, by putting a sworn enemy of the Union on the Patriarchal throne, such as Scholarios was, the Sultan intended to raise a barrier against the penetration of Western influences among the Orthodox peoples, and thus against eventual European attempts at restoring their freedom to them – or at least at striking against Ottoman domination in the Balkans.

Seen from the point of view of internal government, the privileges he granted the Patriarchate of Constantinople were destined to facilitate the exercise of his power over populations already well ensconced within the framework of the Church organisation. However, the Church was also the sole institution to survive the fall of the Empire. She emerged from it united and strengthened, the transmitter and preserver of the Greeks' cultural legacy and of Byzantine tradition. She provided not only the Greek people, but also the subject peoples of the Balkans and the Slav lands, whose independent Churches had been suppressed, with the means of surviving in a dynamic way by preserving their cultural inheritance. A heritage, which later served as the foundations on which their national identities were built.

The Turkish Balkans

By the time of the fall of Constantinople in 1453, the Greek Empire had already lost much of its territorial significance. Its past grandeur and its political role did however invest Mehmed II's victory with symbolic content and anyway, Constantinople was the Turks' crossing point between Europe and Asia and an important economic centre. Above all, it symbolised the final unification of the Ottoman State. From then on, it was really possible to speak of an Ottoman 'Empire', although the Turks themselves had as yet not used the term. It is worth pointing out that from then on, the Turks emerged as the greatest power in Europe, by virtue of their army and artillery, and the internal organisation of the State.

Mehmed II pursued his usually victorious expeditions until his death in 1481. From then on, there were no more semi-dependent territories within the Ottoman State; instead, there was one properly unified State, with the Ottoman Sultan as its sole ruler, supported by a centralised administration headed by the Grand Vizir and the Governors of Rumelia and Anatolia.

325

Mehmed II's capture of Constantinople inaugurated a change, which however was more symbolic for the West than it was significant for Turkey. The Ottoman Empire reached its highest point with the reign of Suleyman the Magnificent, above (sixteenth-century Ottoman Ms.; Istanbul, Topkapi Sarayi.)

Towards a new Eastern Empire?

Although there was a slight pause in the expansionist drive during the reign of Bayezid II (1481–1512), the reigns of Selim I (1515–20) and Suleyman the Magnificent (1520–66) saw the Ottoman Empire attain its greatest extension and reputation.

After Mehmed II the Conqueror's death, the rivalry between his sons Bayezid and Jem caused a few minor problems, since Bayezid enjoyed the support of the Janissaries, whereas Jem first tried to interest the Mamelukes in his cause and subsequently applied to the Knights of Rhodes. They sent him to France and then Italy, where he died in 1495. The Ottomans had grounds at one moment for fearing that the Europeans might use him as a pretext for intervening. At the Hungarian end of the Empire, peace reigned almost uninterruptedly, although the Ottomans made an unsuccessful attempt to take Belgrade. On the other hand, there were endless disputes with the Venetians who lost their bases in the Peloponnesus, and with the Mamelukes who controlled Cilicia and feared the Ottomans now that they were their immediate neighbours. Some indeterminate struggles also took place over the sovereignty of the two little principalities of Ramazan and Dulgadir, situated on the furthest borders of the Empire and subject to the Mamelukes. Above all, Bayezid's reign was one of consolidation and organisation within the State.

Under Selim I and Suleyman the Magnificent, however, Ottoman expansion began again for a variety of reasons. After Selim came to power (as a usurper) religious and political unrest broke out in eastern Anatolia. The Turcoman tribes (who were *Alawi* Muslims, similar to Shiite Muslims, and so were heterodox) had resisted being conquered or assimilated by the Ottomans and had gathered under the leadership of one of their tribal chieftains. Shah Isma'il had declared himself independent following the fall of the *Ak Koyunlu* and had set up a state in what is now eastern Anatolia and western Iran. He exploited the Turcomans' anti-Sunni and anti-Ottoman feelings and got them to acknowledge him as a reincarnation of Ali, son-in-law and cousin to the Prophet. He took advantage of the quarrels between Bayezid's sons over the succession and even intervened in support of Prince Ahmed, Selim's elder brother, who was also backed by the heterodox tribes of Asia Minor. These revolts ended with the death of Ahmed, and Selim then unleashed a violent military and orthodox religious offensive against Shah Isma'il, who was defeated in the battle of Chaldiran near Lake Van in August 1524. This success was partly due to the superiority of the Ottoman musketry and enabled Selim to occupy Azarbayjan and its capital Tabriz. He made no attempt to push his advance any further forward, being well aware of the problems which Anatolia still held for him and of the danger that the Mameluke Sultans might still come to Shah Isma'il's help. In 1515, he took the further decision to occupy the principality of Dulgadir (Dhu'l Qadr), although its overlords, the Egyptians, had been careful not to take sides in the dispute between the Ottomans and Safavids. The Mameluke Sultan, Qansawh al-Ghawri, was sufficiently worried by this to send an army to northern Syria, but, since he also refused to let the Ottoman army cross his territory in southern Anatolia, Selim took advantage of this to accuse him of collusion with the Shiite Moslems. He attacked him at Marj Dabiq near Aleppo on 24 August 1516, and inflicted a crushing defeat on the Mamelukes, in the course of which the Sultan was killed and his army decimated. Syria and Palestine fell quickly and in December 1516 a further victory at Gaza opened the way to Egypt; the new Mameluke Sultan was defeated near Cairo in January 1517. Within a short time, practically the whole of Egypt was controlled by the Ottomans, what was more, the *sharif* of Mecca rallied to their side and the Abbasid Caliph was taken prisoner and sent to Istanbul. Selim in fact never assumed the title of Caliph, merely that of 'protector and servant of the Holy Places'.

Once he had organised the governments of Egypt and Syria in their new role as Ottoman provinces, he returned to Istanbul, intending to undertake new expeditions against Shah Isma'il and against the Knights of Rhodes. Instead he died unexpectedly in September 1520.

Although his reign was brief, it was important not only because he strengthened the

State's eastern frontiers but even more because he established Ottoman rule over some of the wealthiest provinces of the Arab world. Moreover, his conquests gave the Ottomans total control over all commerce from the Mediterranean to the Indian Ocean. His son Suleyman succeeded him without any dynastic disputes and continued his policy of expansion in a different way. For example, he immediately lifted the blockade on the Safavid frontier, thus re-opening trade with Iran and the countries further east. Shortly afterwards, in 1521, he took Belgrade from the Hungarians and conquered Rhodes, thereby ensuring the safety of shipping in the eastern Mediterranean from 1522. He led thirteen expeditions during his reign, ten in Europe and three in Asia, which stretched the Ottoman State to its furthest limits. Hungary was in particular the target of his attacks and one of them brought him up against the walls of Vienna, which he besieged for two weeks (September to October 1529).

Or towards a new Abbasid Empire?

The Mamelukes and the Ottomans were not, however, alone in influencing the course of history in the Near and Middle East in the later Middle Ages and the early Modern period. The Turcoman dynasties who emerged in their neighbourhood, both before and after Tamerlane's invasion, also played a fairly important role in the region, and, in the same way as had the Khanate of Kipchak or the Golden Horde, the Mongol State established on the northern shores of the Black Sea, they saw themselves change from being the dominant power in the area to mere vassals of the Ottomans. During the course of the sixteenth century, the latter finally emerged as the uncontested masters of the whole Near East and of certain neighbouring lands.

The Turcoman Black Sheep (*Kara Koyunlu*) appeared in eastern Anatolia at the beginning of the fourteenth century, but it was only towards the middle of the century that they made themselves felt between Mosul and Erzurum under the command of the Emir Bayram Koja around 1350–80, when they seem to have had a lot of adventures with the Uyrat, the Artukids and the Jalayrids of eastern Anatolia and Upper Iraq. His successor Kara Mehmed (1380–9) freed himself from Jalayrid suzerainty, clashed with the Artukids and the White Sheep (or *Ak Koyunlu*), defended his territory against Tamerlane and even conquered Tabriz, but he was finally killed fighting against his own rebellious emirs. After a few unsettled years, Kara Yussuf (1391–1420) became head of his dynasty, with its glorious destiny. He had first of all to suffer the consequences of Tamerlane's invasion and took refuge with the Ottoman Sultan and then in Iraq and finally in Damascus where he was temporarily imprisoned by the Mameluke Sultan, but escaped the death sentence imposed on him thanks to the intervention of Shaykh, the governor of Damascus. As soon as he was freed, he regained his lands in Anatolia (1404) and continued to expand them systematically by occupying Azarbayjan, eastern Iran and Iraq. These successes worried the Mameluke Sultan Shaykh, who did little about it, whereas the Sultan of Jaghatai, Shah Rukh, encouraged the other Turcoman tribes, among them the White Sheep, to attack Kara Yussuf. He followed this up with an unsuccessful attack of his own. Kara Yussuf then died, leaving to his son Iskandar an immense domain which he defended successfully against the White Sheep and Shah Rukh. He also had to face serious fights with his brothers, one of whom, Shah Jihan, sought the help of Shah Rukh and ended by defeating Iskandar, who was assassinated in 1438, having hoped in vain for support from the Egyptian army. Jihan Shah (1438–67) raised the prestige of the Black Sheep to its highest point, extending his empire in Iran at the expense of the Jaghatai and concluding a treaty of friendship with the Timurid Abu Sa'id. He was moreover an enlightened ruler who attracted literati and scholars to his court at Tabriz as well as being a keen builder. But an expedition which he led against Uzun Hasan Beg, King of the White Sheep, ended tragically for him and for the Black Sheep dynasty, whose lands passed over to the White Sheep in 1469, all of Jihan Shah's sons having been killed too.

The Turcoman dynasty of the White Sheep appeared in the region of Dyar Bakr during the fourteenth century and lasted until 1502. The first great individual to emerge from this line was Kara Yuluk Uthman, who, after several battles with the Black Sheep under Kara Mehmed and Burhan al-Din of Sivas, sided with Tamerlane and was confirmed in his possession of Dyar Bakr. They were subsequently restricted to this territory by the power of the Black Sheep and it was only under Uzun Hasan Beg (1466–78) that the White Sheep, who were confined to the West by the Ottoman advance, turned eastwards. They triumphed over Jihan Shah and the Timurid Abu Sa'id and extended their domination over the whole of Iraq, Iran and western Afghanistan. His son Yaqub (1478–90) had an easy reign, but after his death internal dissention and above all the rising power of the Safavids in eastern Anatolia and western Iran, which had the additional effect of rallying the Turcoman tribes in the region to Shiite Islam, led to war in 1502 and to the total defeat of the White Sheep in Armenia. Murad, one of Yaqub's sons, later took refuge with the Ottomans and participated in Sultan Selim's expedition against the Safavid Shah Isma'il in 1514, dying shortly afterwards.

During the great period of Uzun Hasan's and Yaqub's reigns, the White Sheep appeared to certain Western powers, notably the Papacy and the Venetians, as possible allies against the Ottomans, but nothing came of this. Uzun Hasan was nonetheless considered as one of the great rulers of his age, as much on account of his power and his ability as a legislator and administrator, as on account of his commercial enterprises, centred on Persia, and his taste for the arts and for literature. Under him, as under the Black Sheep, Tabriz became a brilliant capital where Turkish, Arab and Persian cultures mingled happily.

These two Turcoman dynasties, which managed to survive Tamerlane's expeditions, were also close to potentially dangerous powers, the Mamelukes and the Ottomans, but they managed in the long run to avoid confronting them. Instead they directed their aggressive energies towards the East, where they contributed, the White Sheep in particular, to put an end to what was left of Mongol power between Turkestan and the Near East. The struggle between themselves, followed by that between the White Sheep and the Safavids, made sure of the Ottomans' eventual victory.

This brief survey of the main stages of Ottoman expansion, to which will be added a few necessary remarks about the progressive organisation of their conquest, does not absolve us from taking a closer look at these 'new Balkans', which the Turks controlled during the following three centuries.

The fall of the Albanian fortress

The Albanians have to be treated as an ethnic group simply because, more than any other Balkan race, they have never had a national organisation with which to identify. Precisely because the history of medieval Albania does not coincide with the development of any one state, it is the history of a nation formed by a very old ethnic element in the Balkans, based on a common language and spiritual *habitus*, expressed in its civilisation and based on a common territory. Thus their history is that of a nation, which has long been clearly distinct from the other nations which developed in the Balkan peninsula at the same time.

The geographical formation of the country, with its coastline lying open to Italy, has indeed favoured the interplay of different factors, from the claims of the Holy See on the Church of Illyria to the territorial pretensions of the Normans in Italy and the Angevins in Naples. In 1272 Charles of Anjou was able to use these to found the ephemeral 'Kingdom of Albania'. Throughout the period, Venetians, Greeks and Jews as well as merchants from Amalfi and Ragusa took part in the economic and commercial life of Albania. For this reason, the coastal towns of Dyrrachion (Durazzo, ancient Epidamnos and nowaday Durres), Avlon (Valona) and also Kanina, held to have been Avlon's acropolis, were important naval bases and active cosmopolitan ports, frequented and indeed inhabited by an entire cross-section of races. Nevertheless the long-lasting influence of the Despotate of Epirus and the importance of these places for the western defence of Constantinople once the Palaeologi had been restored, meant that Byzantine influence was preponderant in thirteenth- and fourteenth-century Albania, and possibly as early as the eleventh century. Apollonia (an ancient colony of Corfu, replaced by the medieval burg of Polina) and Belegrada (the ancient Pulcheriopolis and modern Berat, described as a fortress of 'Romania', meaning Byzantium) retained active memories of Hellenism until recently. The impact of Greek culture was felt as far afield as Albanon (or Arbanon) with its centre at Croya; the original home of the Albanian race, in the high mountainous region between the Mati and Isamo rivers, which had reached the line delineated by Antivari, Podgorica and Prizren in the North by the fifteenth century.

Of all the Balkan peoples, the Albanians were the last to enter recorded history. In fact, Byzantine sources only start to mention this famous and ancient people in relation to other events in the eleventh century and it is principally from the same sources that we learn of the great adventure of the fourteenth century, namely the expansion of the Albanian people towards southern Greece, which seems to have been the most crucial phenomenon in their whole history. According to Cantacuzenus, under the reign of Andronicus III the Albanians already occupied the mountainous part of Thessaly and lived far from the towns in remote villages, where they suffered from the rigours of winter and from Byzantine attacks. They were not organised as a State but they called themselves by the names of their

The gateway to the citadel of Berat (Belegrada), rebuilt in the thirteenth century by Michael Angelus Comnenus. The Albanian town was a frontier post of Hellenism and Byzantine governors resided there until the fifteenth century.

tribal chiefs (*phylarhoi*, according to Cantacuzenus), namely Malakasioi, Mbuioi and Mesaritai. There is no doubt that their many contacts with the Despotate of Epirus and the Europeans, who landed on their coasts with the idea of advancing into the interior, must have given them the idea of moving South. They were even encouraged in this and invited by Greek and Latin landowners, who were short of farm labour and recruits in wartime. Not surprisingly, their rebellious natures soon reasserted themselves, as for example in the case of the Albanian tribes around Belegrada and Kanina and in Thessaly, whom Andronicus III could only control by bringing in Umur's Turkish troops in 1337.

The collapse of Dušan's Serbian State was followed by the defeat of the Despot of Epirus by the Albanians in the battle of Acheloos in 1358, in which Despot Nicephorus was killed. This allowed small Albanian principalities to rise up alongside others led by non-Albanian princes, but ruling over territories mostly populated by Albanians. In the first category came the principalities founded at Epirus and Aetolia–Arcanania, one under Peter Ljosha at Arta and Rogoi and the other under Ghin Bua Spata at Acheloos and Angelocastron. They were abolished in 1418 by Carlo I Tocco, Duke of Leucadia and Count Palatine of Cephalonia, as was the principality of Karolo Thopia, the *princeps Albanie*, with its centre at Durres. In the second category one might include the small principality of Comnenus at Vlore, and the essentially Serb principality of Zeta, belonging to the Balšić brothers, in that these had succeeded in dominating a large part of Albania as far as Himara and Belegrada

331

to the South, before losing their capital Skadar (Shkoder in Albanian, Scutari) which finally fell to the Venetians on the death of the last Balšić brother in 1421.

Albanian colonisation in the Peloponnesus was implemented in two waves, the first under the reign of Despot Manuel Cantacuzenus (1348–80) and later under Theodore I Palaeologus (1383–1407), who allowed 10,000 Albanians to settle with their families and their cattle. With regard to them, Manuel II Palaeologus wrote that 'the newcomers installed themselves in uninhabited cantons; they cut down the forests and the countryside was rendered hospitable and cultivated. Many of these wild areas served no purpose beyond that of harbouring brigands, but once in the hands of capable farmers, they were sown and planted with various crops.'

The Albanians of the Morea fought alongside the Greek inhabitants on various occasions against the continual waves of Turkish invaders, at Tavia, at Hexamilion and elsewhere. However, the fall of Constantinople in 1453 was the signal for a general revolt by the Albanians in order to impose their hegemony over the Peloponnesian peninsula, which was led by Manuel Cantacuzenus, Governor of Magna and Emperor Matthew's eldest son, whom they had invited to be their general. This revolt was only squashed with great difficulty by Turakhan Bey, who lent Thomas and Demetrius Palaeologus his support. It is an indication of the Albanians' curious position in the Morea, that, in spite of their privileges, they remained peripheral to the life of the native population and formed totally separate groupings. On the other hand, the fact that they chose a genuine Greek prince and not an Albanian chief as their ruler, sheds light on the depth of the antagonism between Paleologi and Cantacuzeni, which clearly did not incite the Albanians to rise, but equally clearly served their purpose.

In Albania itself at this time, the population continued to hold off the Ottomans under the leadership of George Castriota Skanderbeg (1405–68), the Capitanus Generalis of the 'League of Albanian lords', which had been formed at Lesh with the objective of coordinating its members' armed forces. Like the Byzantine emperors, Skanderbeg tried at first to ally himself with the Hungarians, with the Kingdom of Naples or with Venice, but he was obliged instead to continue, alone at the head of his people, a hopeless and soon legendary struggle. As the 'athlete of Christ' he could make marvellous use of the rugged nature of his highlands and his people, and for some time, he made light of the Ottomans' efforts. A surprise attack allowed him to destroy a Turkish army at Alessio in 1457, which prompted the West to get excited and to proceed on a quest. But the help promised by Mathias Corvin of Hungary did not materialise, any more than did the King of France's and Alfonso of Aragon's vague promises – in 1461, 1464 and 1465. Skanderbeg was forced back step by step before the enemy in a series of truces and ambushes. In 1466, he was blockaded at Korja without hope or provisions and gave up the fight. He died two years later. In Rome, they put up a statue to him. Ten years later a few small risings gave witness to Albania's continuing existence – and then silence fell.

The elimination of the Serbs

After the defeat at Kossovo, Serbia finally became a tributary of the Ottomans. Lazar's son and successor, Stefan Lazarević (1389–1427) took part in all the Sultan's great expeditions, in Wallachia in 1395, at Nicopolis in 1396 and at the Battle of Ankara in 1402. The Serbs did nevertheless make the occasional brief attempt at freeing themselves from these humiliating obligations, especially after Ankara, and in connection with the relations developing between them and the Hungarians, to whom Lazarević preferred to submit. During this period he regained Belgrade, made it his capital and helped King Sigismund against Bosnia. As a reward for his help, the king gave him the Hungarian mining town of Srebnica, which became a bone of contention between the Serbs and Hungarians until they were both finally occupied by the Ottomans.

On the other hand, the Ottoman civil war which followed the Battle of Ankara allowed Serbia to extend her influence over Zeta, thus breaking a passage to the sea. In spite of this achievement, Serbia never managed to compete effectively with the Venetians, whose interests had always led them towards the East coast of the Adriatic and who managed to take the towns of Skadar and Dulcigno, and later Bar and Budva from the Serbians.

Giorgi Branković (1427–56), who succeeded Stefan Lazarević, ceded Belgrade to the Hungarians according to the terms of a treaty drawn up by his predecessor, and was obliged to accept the overlordship of the Ottomans, who advanced unremittingly into Serbia, taking the towns of Niš, Kruševac and Gobulac. So Smederevo (Semendria) became the last capital of the Serbian nation, on the banks of the Danube near the Hungarian frontiers, where Murad II gave them permission to build a fortress. Smederevo was not to remain the last bastion of Serbian independence for long; it yielded to Murad after a siege lasting three months (1439) and was once more ceded to Branković as a reward for his stance during the Christian Crusade of 1444. The town was definitely conquered by Mehmed II in 1459 after the fall of Constantinople. In the meantime the whole of Serbia – Novo Brdo, Trepča, Priština, Prizren, Peć, Golubac, Resava, and others – fell into the Ottomans' hands under her last ruler, Lazar Branković (1456–8). The mountainous provinces of Zeta were alone in prolonging their independence for a certain time under the leadership of the Černojević family, who even founded a capital called Cetinje, where the first Serbian printing press was put into operation. The Černojević finally succumbed to the Sultan in 1499.

As for Belgrade, known in the West as the 'bastion of Christianity', having heroically resisted two sieges in 1440 and 1456, she survived for nearly a century under Hungarian overlordship as the 'Banat of Belgrade', of which the fortresses Zemum and Slankamen were also part. The town fell to Suleyman II on 29 August 1521 only after violent fighting and artillery bombardment.

The only State in the Balkans which managed to escape Ottoman domination was the aristocratic republic of Ragusa in Dalmatia, which submitted first to the Venetians (1205–1358) and later to the Hungarians (1358–1526). They went on paying the Ottomans a small annual tax which allowed them to continue their existence and their well-known enormous enterprise in the fields of finance and trade, right up until the beginning of the nineteenth century.

Bosnia did not offer much more resistance; its last king, Stefan Tomašević (1461–3) refused to become a tributary of the Sultan and, at the instigation of the Byzantine Emperors, he tried to get help from the West by submitting to the Pope. This did him no good, since his vassals abandoned him and gave themselves up to Mehmed (which did not save them from the death penalty). The king himself was taken and assassinated by the Conqueror, while his kingdom and his capital Jajce were absorbed into the Ottoman State.

The Turks beyond the Danube

When the Ottomans eliminated the Bulgarian State at the end of the fourteenth century and were established along its Danube frontier, they came into contact with two young, in fact practically new-born Romanian States. Wallachia had only just freed itself from the Hungarian grasp under the leadership of its Voivode Bassarab in 1330, who managed after a long and successful struggle, to beat Charles Robert, King of Hungary, in the Carpathians and thus consolidate the foundations of his State, which had been laid by his predecessor, Radu Negru. Even more recently, the infant State of Moldavia, encouraged by Bassarab, took advantage of the threat of Mongol invasion to resist the Hungarian yoke and to declare its independence under the Voivode Bogdan (1365).

Wallachia and Moldavia both adopted Orthodoxy in reaction against the Catholic Hungarians; in 1359 and in 1401 respectively, they were attached to the Patriarchate of Constantinople, which stressed the identity of these nascent Romanian States by granting them both the status of Metropolitan Bishopric. The Metropolitan Sees of Suceava, capital of Moldavia and Curtea of Arges in Wallachia were destined to play an important role, not only in the spiritual life, but also in the political development of their two principalities. Moreover the introduction of Slavonic as the official language in the administration of both the Church and the State made relations between Romania and the Slav countries, especially Bulgaria, much easier. By the same token, it facilitated the penetration of Byzantine influence.

As for the province of Transylvania with its large Romanian population, its few attempts at political organisation came to nothing as a result of its being annexed to the Hungarian Crown of Saint Stephen.

The geographical position of Wallachia and Moldavia and a number of economic factors, among which the development of agricultural and manufacturing production and of trade were not the least important, contributed to the rise of these States during the first two centuries of their existence. The creation of trade routes across Romanian territories intensified their commercial relations, and the central town of Brasov became an important knot in the network of contacts linking Wallachia with Moldavia and Transylvania. The Romanian countries anyway played a part in international trade by providing a land route from Western Europe to the Balkans and the Black Sea, and to the eastern colonies of Italian maritime towns like Genoa.

Murad II indulges in a scornful gesture by splitting the helmet of John Hunyadi, the Romanian and Hungarian hero, one of the last to resist him. Hunyadi's courage earned him the attribution of a second Alexander the Great in a popular Greek song. (Ms. Ottoman Hünername, 1584; Istanbul, Topkapi Sarayi.)

As the two new States began to establish themselves in spite of continuous Hungarian pressure and, in the case of Moldavia, Polish pressure, they came up against the more serious problems presented by Ottoman expansion in south-east Europe. From then on their foremost concern was to check this expansion north of the Danube. Into this struggle Mircea the Old (1386–1418) threw himself heart and soul, winning the battle of Rovina in 1395, and for a time he even managed to extend his power south of the Danube into the lands of Dobrudža, which had previously belonged to the Bulgarian prince Ivanko. Although Mircea the Old and King Sigismund of Hungary, who was his tactical ally on this occasion, were defeated by the Turks at the Battle of Nicopolis in 1396, Mircea did not stop fighting the Ottomans or involving himself in their internal quarrels, trying to draw maximum advantage from them. Nevertheless, after the re-alignment of the Ottoman Empire under Mehmed I, the Voivode of Wallachia was obliged to become a tributary of the Sultan in 1417, shortly before his death.

An intermediate period followed, during which John Hunyadi (Iancu of Hunedoara), the Voivode of Transylvania who later became Regent of Hungary, took over the leadership of the Romanian anti-Ottoman forces from Mircea, and Vlad Dracul, the Impaler, won his series of impressive victories over Mehmed II in 1461–2. The weighty task of leading the resistance fell on Stephen the Great, ruler of Moldavia (Stefan cel Mare, 1457–1504). First of all, he made his position clear by swearing allegiance to King Casimir of Poland and by repudiating the efforts of Mathias Corvin, King of Hungary, to bring Wallachia under his sovereignty. He then began a long war of attrition against the Sultan in order to throw the Ottomans out of Wallachia and to make the frontier along the Danube inviolate. However, in spite of some military success, including the victory of Rahova in 1475, which won the praise of the Pope and the admiration of the Western world, Stefan could not reverse the situation, which became particularly oppressive after Bayezid II had consolidated his position on the Ottoman throne.

In the summer of 1484, the trading towns of Kilia on the Danube Delta and of Cetatea Alba, on the Dniestr Delta (namely Akkerman, Monokastro or Asprokastro), which the Moldavian ruler had defended as important outposts, fell to the Ottomans. After which Suceava, the capital, was burnt for the second time (the first was under Mehmed II in 1476). Stefan cel Mare was told to pay tribute, but as he never agreed to this, it was only after his death that Moldavia finally became a tributary of the Sultan.

In this way the last outposts of Christianity, both Slav and non-Slav, which had formed a protective buffer for central Europe, collapsed one by one. Ottoman power was not the only cause, as the resistance in Hungary and the Germanic nations was soon to demonstrate; it was in fact the inadequate social structures of these emergent states which led to their downfall after ineffectual resistance.

It is true of the Slavs in particular that during the whole period of their existence as independent States, they were in continual conflict with the Byzantine Empire. They did not cease to suspect the Byzantine cultural influences which infiltrated their society, while being simultaneously attracted by them. But this attitude was modified as soon as they lost their political independence and the Slavs recognised that Byzantine culture had become fundamental to their own identity. The feeling of hostility which existed between the Byzantines and the Balkan Slavs had largely disappeared by the first quarter of the fourteenth century, even before the Turks began their conquests, and there came into being in various places in the Balkan peninsula a sort of Slavo-Byzantine culture. Thus the Patriarchate of Constantinople regained all the influence over the religious and cultural life of the Christian people of the Balkans which the Empire had lost. As far as the Bulgars and the Serbs were concerned, Byzantium still existed after 1453 in the institution of the Orthodox Patriarchate. But, as satellites of a State which itself was hemmed in on the edges of a fully expanding Western Europe, the southern Slavs ceased to exist for over four hundred years.

Ottoman success

It was a fact that from the middle of the sixteenth century the Ottoman Empire was a considerable power, enforcing its authority from the Moroccan frontier to the Persian Gulf, from the Danube to the edge of the Sahara, and from the Black Sea to Arabia. A vast empire, whose power was admired and respected, a seemingly unshakeable Colossus against which Europe had achieved only defensive successes, but had more often to circumvent.

By uniting practically the whole Arab–Muslim world, the Sultan became not only its temporal ruler but also 'Emir of the Faithful' and its spiritual ruler (although he still did not call himself Caliph).

In relation to the Christian world, he represented the power of Islam, which did not mean that he wanted to crush Christians, and certainly not those within his Empire. Europe however, was bent on conquering the world by the end of the fifteenth and beginning of the sixteenth centuries, and came up against an insurmountable obstacle in the shape of an adversary present in all parts of the Ancient World; the Mediterranean, Eastern Europe and the Near East. Spaniards, Austrians and Hungarians, not to mention the Venetians, all realised that their defeat merely increased Ottoman prestige, which reached its highest point at the end of Suleyman the Magnificent's reign.

The Sublime Gate

The Ottoman Sultan was the incarnation of the Ottoman regime. He wielded absolute power, was temporal ruler, leader of all Muslims and protector of Jews and Christians. The Sultan appointed the Grand Vizir, the important functionaries of the *diwan*, the provincial governors and the court dignitaries. He was Chief of the army, he nominated the great religious personalities (the *shaykh al-islam* and the chief muftis of the main towns). Although he himself could not break Koranic Law (the *shari'at*) he could add customary laws to it for the various provinces (*kanun*), on condition they were not contrary to Koranic Law and had been approved by the *shaykh al-islam*. The Sultan delegated his administrative powers, and where appropriate his command of the army, to the Grand Vizir. The Vizir's power was a measure of his standing with the Sultan who appointed him, but could also depose him if it so pleased him. The Vizir presided over the *diwan*, where the vizirs 'of the cupola' met, who were chosen from among the Vizir's assistants and the high functionaries of the Empire. They were the Head of the Ottoman chancery (the *nichanji*), the two military judges (*kadi-asker*) who represented the religious hierarchy (apart from the *shaykh al-islam*), the *defterdar* who was responsible for finance, the Grand Admiral or *kapudan pasha*, and the governor of Rumelia (the *beylerbey*). The *diwan* was the central organ of the government but in certain circumstances it could also constitute a court of justice.

The administration was in the hands of civil servants, either graduates of the *madrasas*, colleges of religious law, or selected from the corps of pages collected from the Christian villages in the Balkans (*devshirme*), who were promoted through a hierarchy. Even those of

337

Christian origin were Muslims, and after Mehmed II almost all the Grand Vizirs for instance, came from the ranks of palace officials, which did not, of course, make them any less loyal to the Sultan. The provinces were governed by *beylerbeys*, whose rank and statute varied according to the importance of their provinces. They were fully responsible for the civil and military administration of their provinces and consequently played a great role in Ottoman politics. The *sanjak beys*, or *subashis*, were under their orders, each administering a smaller subdivision of a province. The provinces of Algiers, Tunis and Tripoli had a special statute which was more military than civil.

Most of the administrative staff (*kalemiye*) were paid a salary when they held a modest rank within the administration. Functionaries of a certain rank benefited from a further income, the revenues from a *timar* or *arpalik* (literally, money from barley) which varied in importance according to their position in the hierarchy.

As in the preceding centuries, the army played a leading role in the power of the Empire. It carried out conquests, and ensured defence where required. It could also be an instrument of power in the hands of a candidate to the throne; this was the case with Bayezid II and Selim I, who were supported by the Janissaries. The military class, or *askeriye*, comprised firstly the *kapi kullari*, or slaves of the gate, who were recruited by means of the *devshirme*. The bulk of the army was still made up by the corps of Janissaries, who formed the infantry, henceforth supplied with fire arms as well as their traditional white weapons. Added to them were specialised corps of cannoners (*topçu*), or escort soldiers (*top arabaci*); of armourers (*cebeci*), of sappers (*lağimci*) and of bombardiers (*humbaraci*); along with the cavalry, they made up the permanent army and were all paid wages.

Another part of the army consisted of the provincial *sipahis*, free cavalry officers endowed with *timars* of varying importance, who had to support a number of soldiers proportional to their income from them. There were about 15,000 Janissaries in Suleyman's time and about 25,000 to 30,000 *sipahis*. There were finally groups of soldiers who were either fairly regular or attached to specific duties. As for the navy, it played an important part from Bayezid II' reign, thanks to the corsairs, but Suleyman and after him Selim II turned it into a real fleet with more than 200 vessels – of varying dimensions, it is true. The Kapudan Pasha drew his revenues from the maritime provinces of the Aegean; the *shiurme* was recruited among their prisoners of war, condemned men or mercenaries; soldiers called *levend* could also be embarked on these ships.

Finally, the Ottoman army was equipped with an excellent administration which included services for the upkeep of roads, bridges, fortresses and relays. Arsenals (for the navy and the artillery) were built at Istanbul and there were others in different ports in the Aegean and the Black Sea.

The Ottoman government also used its administration to manage the Empire, which meant imposing upon its subjects (*reaya*); peasants, craftsmen and merchants. They were supposed to supply either the State or their timariot with contributions in kind or money. It is certain that the *timar*-holders or the agents of the administration abused their power to profit from their exactions. In theory, however, the revenues of the *timars* were precisely laid down, and the taxes and contributions imposed on the *reayas* were noted in registers or

The Suleymaniye mosque in Istanbul (1550–7) was built on the model of the Hagia Sofia by the architect Sinan, a Christian imbued with Greek culture. It is one of the first Islamic mosques to be directly inspired by the Byzantine basilica.

mentioned expressly in the regulations (*qanun-name*). These regulations may have existed from the end of the fourteenth century, and they multiplied under Mehmed II, under Bayezid II and especially under Suleyman. They constituted the legislation proper to each province and were written texts to which the administration and the subjects could refer. They had been instituted after the conquests in order to maintain economic and social continuity in the conquered countries and to avoid disruption. The tax collectors were either the timariots themselves (or their agents) or the financial agents of the provinces; the *qadis* or their adjoints (*na'ib*) could eventually be called on to intervene against recalcitrants or against extortionate functionaries. The revenues were then collected in the provincial capitals and a part was sent on to Istanbul to the Sultan's treasury. At each stage of the proceedings, checks were implemented, in accordance with the registers' instructions and in conformity with the *qanun-name*.

The Sultan's subjects were classed into two principal categories; Muslims, who enjoyed all the rights specified by Koranic Law and were not liable to certain taxes, and the non-Muslims, essentially Christians and Jews, who were subordinate to their own religious leaders (Patriarchs, Metropolitans, Grand Rabbis) and formed the class of 'protected persons' or *zimmi*. Each great religious group, whether Christian (Greek Orthodox,

Armenians of various rites) or Jewish constituted a *millet*, or 'nation'. In exchange for the freedom of religion and protection granted them by the Sultan, they paid him a specific tax, the *jiziye*, often confused with the *kharaj*. This protection was no empty word; even though exactions did occur, they were infrequent and restrained, and there do not seem to have been religious persecutions. The different Churches certainly had to pay taxes to the Treasury as well, but this was a lesser evil. The Ottomans' tolerance was indeed well known in the Mediterranean world, and when waves of Jews were expelled from Spain in the sixteenth century, they found a safe refuge in Constantinople and Salonica. In the Arab countries, their inhabitants remained under the authority of their traditional leaders and retained their traditional structures, on which a higher Ottoman administration was superimposed and enforced by a few detachments of Janissaries.

From privileges to Capitulations

Before the conquest of Constantinople, the Ottomans had little contact with Western powers, with the exception of the Venetians in the Peloponnesus; nor had these contacts always been peaceful.

Their capture of Constantinople established much closer relations, on the economic level, between the Ottomans and the Italian merchant cities; Genoa, Venice, Florence and Ragusa. However, as they expanded during the sixteenth century, the nature of these relations was altered; they had come into conflict with several military powers, and had also been approached by others with the view of concluding political alliances and of facilitating trade. Wealth poured into the Ottoman State both in the form of booty and of revenue from its new provinces. But this wealth also created new needs among the ruling class; the Sultans were constantly striving to turn their capital into a city unparalleled in its monuments and splendour, which resulted in the considerable growth in the population of the capital. All this created a demand for products and goods which the East did not produce or which were of a better quality in the West. To a certain extent it became necessary to open the Ottoman market to foreign goods, which of course proved no less useful to the Western nations, who profited from this opening and brought their particular produce to this market. Development was slow, but Venice was the first to secure a strong position for herself in spite of some difficult moments. Her precedence, her familiarity with the East, her trading posts and her relations with local merchant or manufacturing centres all helped. Genoa was the first to profit from special trading conditions and a settlement, and, without disposing of a network as important as Venice's, she cut a good figure in the East.

Suleyman the Magnificent was approached at the beginning of his reign by Francis I, who solicited an alliance with him and preferential conditions for French merchants. The Sultan saw no reason to object; what did France mean to Ottoman trade? Very little and consequently the French had no problem securing the conditions of residence and trade which are known as *Capitulations* (1535). These must be seen as a generous gesture of good will on the part of the Sultan, who asked for nothing in return. On the military level, the

The bazaar at Istanbul. The presence of notables and foreigners among the crowd illustrates the international role of this urban market. (Ottoman miniature of the fifteenth century; Istanbul, Topkapi Sarayi.)

only tangible but limited manifestation of this pseudo-alliance, was the siege and capture of Nice by Ottoman and French fleets in 1543. The French on the other hand, found it much more useful than did the Ottomans, who could expect nothing from it, since it relieved the pressure on them from the Habsburg States. The most striking consequence of the alliance was however the introduction of diplomatic missions and the installation of French consuls in a few of the Empire's ports of call. It is significant that from then until the middle of the seventeenth century, these consuls and sometimes even the ambassadors were nominated by the French traders – which illustrates the general character of the institution. At the same time, however, these French representatives intervened in defence of their nationals against the Turkish administration, and their relations henceforth took a new turn, at least on the local level, and included relations between the ambassadors and the principal dignitaries of the Empire, as high up as the Grand Vizir. This new aspect would be enlarged with time, and what could be called the voluntary diplomatic isolation of the Ottomans and the disdain of the Turks (but not their Greek, Armenian and Jewish subjects) for international commerce would be transformed; the former into the search for alliances, the latter into individual collaboration with the foreigners, but with the very precise purpose of implementing their resources and making their personal fortunes. This would be the case from about the second half of the seventeenth century. In the meantime, these French, Dutch and English merchants installed themselves in the ports and a few towns of the interior, where they of course did business but also established links, especially with the minorities, to whom they felt closer and whom they needed to act as intermediaries with the indigenous producers and traders. In the longer term, this would lead to intervention in the affairs of the Ottoman Empire.

A new equilibrium

The economy of the Ottoman Empire rested on the importance and the variety of its production, and on the existence of a consumer market in the great cities and especially in the palace and the army. The most important production was of course agricultural, with Christian and Muslim peasants paying dues in kind to their local authority (which could be a timariote, an agent of the administration, a manager of pious endowments, or an intendant of the Sultan's estates). These dues varied between one eighth and one third of their produce. The peasants' methods were traditional and their production poor, consisting (according to the region) of cereals or of various forms of stockraising, sheep being the most common. However, they could also grow fruit, olives, spices, rice, sugar cane, honey, and they bred horses, buffalo, camels, goats and pigs. They grew linen, flax, cotton, produced silk for textiles and used metals such as iron, lead, silver and copper. However, their manufactures and trade could not compare with those of the towns, where the bazaar was the most important place and where these activities were regulated by guilds or corporations. Controlled by the *qadi* and the *muhtesib* (chief of the market police) they formed a fairly restrictive cadre, from which competition and initiative were excluded. Manufactured goods were generally intended for local markets, but some products were sought after by foreigners; fleeces, skins, leather, carpets, silk and ornaments as well as other goods from further east which passed through the Ottoman State, such as perfumes, spices, calicos and furs. This important trade was effected by means of caravans and ships, and controlled by businessmen (*tujjar*), who manipulated capital from various sources, and some of whom were high government dignitaries.

The wealth of the Sultans, who controlled the Treasury, contributed to the economic life of the Empire, not least by maintaining a palace, where hundreds if not thousands of people lived, and by keeping up an army. They also had a natural propensity to embellish their capital by building huge and splendid mosques. From this point of view the end of the

The Mopti mosque in Mali testifies to the penetration of Islam into black Africa.

Granada; the famous palace of the Alhambra (fourteenth century) and the surrounding area.

Nicolas Bataille; a detail from *The Apocalypse*, *c.* 1380. (Angers, Musée des Beaux Arts.)

Donatello (1386–1466); bronze statue of *David*. (Florence, Bargello Museum.)

Fra Angelico; a detail of the *Descent from the Cross* showing a view of Florence. (Florence, San Marco Museum.)

Opposite, above. Enguerrand Quarton; *Pietà*, fifteenth century. (Paris, Louvre.)

Opposite, below. Pisanello; *Saint George and the Princess, c.* 1435. (Verona, Sant'Anastasia.)

The Master of Flémalle (Robert Campin?); the right panel of the Triptych of the *Annunciation* showing Saint Joseph, *c.* 1420. (New York, Metropolitan Museum of Art, the Cloisters Collection.)

Jan Van Eyck; *Arnolfini and his Wife* c. 1434. (London, National Gallery.)

Hieronymus Bosch; *The Hay Wain*, the central panel of a triptych (1500–2). (Madrid, Prado.)

fifteenth and the whole of the sixteenth centuries saw an extraordinary building boom in a remarkable architectural style, especially in the great towns of the Empire, not only at Istanbul but in all the provinces. Until the 1560s at the earliest, their wealth did not suffer from the Europeans' progressive exploitation of the sea-route round the Cape of Good Hope, because centuries-old currents of trade cannot be turned in a few years or even a few decades, especially when too many people have a vested interest in their continuation. In the same way, the part played by international trade in the Ottoman economy should not be exaggerated, since it consumed products and commodities of all kinds. It was only towards the end of the century that the first characteristic signs of a financial crisis appeared, due to the influx of American silver, which led to the devaluation of the *asper*, the basic Ottoman coin. This was followed by the beginnings of an economic crisis and especially of a social crisis, exemplified by the first revolts of the Anatolian people, who were most affected by the heavy taxation and the demands of the State. But this is another period in the history of the Ottoman Empire. The Sultans and other great persons were not concerned solely with war and the territorial expansion of their empire. Of course, its grandeur and prestige were to a great extent the results of its military strength, its huge size and its wealth; however the Ottomans did not exclude all intellectual and artistic activity.

Mehmed II the Conqueror was a very cultivated man who spoke several languages and wrote poetry. He invited Italian artists, such as Gentile Bellini who painted his portrait, and Greek and Italian writers like Amirutzes of Trebizond, Critobulus of Imbros and Ciriaco of Ancona to Istanbul. Suleyman the Magnificent was also an educated man; in his time, some of the greatest Turkish writers were alive, such as Fuzuli (1480–1556), the first truly historical and even critical Ottoman chronicles were compiled and travel accounts and maps were drawn up by navigators like Piri Re'is and Saydi Ali Re'is. The study of the sciences and medicine was not at all neglected and of course, religious science, the greatest of them all, was widely practised in the *madrasas* of the capital and the great towns of the Empire.

This period is most famous for its architecture; the great mosques of the time of Bayezid II, Suleyman the Magnificent and Selim II in Istanbul and Edirne (Adrianople) are some of the greatest examples of the art. Many of them were designed by Mimar Sinan (1489–1578), a brilliant architect, who used the Hagia Sophia as the model for a specific type of Ottoman mosque, which was then copied throughout the Empire. This art was complemented by the decorative arts, which made striking use of glazed tiles, generally made in Nicea, with flower and leaf patterns executed in pure lines and subtle colours and characterised by a 'tomato red', which is a feature of this period only.

Suleyman the Magnificent's reign was justly known as the golden age of the Ottoman Empire and he was an object of wonder for the European travellers who crossed it.

As a result of all this, the Christian nations were still incapable of imagining any sort of withdrawal by the Ottomans on the diplomatic or political level, in spite of the propaganda which was emerging in the sixteenth century. Even on the economic level, their relations were never exceptional and certainly did not amount to 'penetration'. The demand came from the West rather than the East, as the *Capitulations* demonstrate.

Thus, in the period between the battle of Ankara in 1402 and capture of Tunis in 1574, a   **343**

State gradually took shape, invested with increasingly considerable powers, which won the respect of the Western nations. This is perhaps one of the reasons why they looked elsewhere in the world for room to implement their need for political and economic expansion and sailed round that once impenetrable rock that was the Ottoman Empire.

The taming of central Europe

North of the Danube and east of the Elba another essentially Slav world was waiting for its fate to be determined: Germany. Was it to become a satellite of a dominant Western Europe, in the hope of its future independence, or was it to be the heir to Greek culture, the successor to Byantium? We have scarcely mentioned the Germanic world until now because it lay on the margins of the Christian world until the beginning of the fourteenth century. We are only just beginning to realise how splendid this civilisation was from the many stupefying archaeological discoveries now being made. Perhaps it was not so much marginal as neighbouring; Poland, Bohemia and the Baltic lands had been penetrated by missionaries from Germany, by soldier–monks known as Teutonic Knights or Sword-bearers and of course by merchants. Since the tenth century the Polish plains had been crossed from the coast to Krakow, and then to Byzantium via the Moravian back door. Since the eleventh century, Englishmen, Flemings and Teutons had reached Novgorod, south of Lagoda; Gdansk and Riga were lively trading points, as were Prague, Krakow and Buda in the interior. Old and solid cultures, both Slav and Hungarian, developed in these places, but on the whole, these western outposts were cut off from Europe; they were suddenly integrated to the West when the Greek bulwark lying further to the south collapsed.

A new 'Drang nach Osten'

By throwing its peasantry and merchants into the assault on Silesia, Brandenburg and Greater Poland in the twelfth and thirteenth centuries, Germany had already largely implemented that 'drive to the East', which had always been the Germanic response to its needs for population or economic expansion. After 1300, this penetration beyond the Oder and into the Prussian and Masurian marches seemed to have ground to a halt – not so much because of local resistance, but because the original population pressure had reached its natural limits. So another, more subtle, dangerous and effective form of penetration was operated through the infiltration of German culture, laws and power. In this respect, the case of Bohemia was the most obvious. The Czech rulers of Prague had long ago been rather condescendingly admitted among the nations of the Empire. They had even been allowed the title of 'King', which they alone in the Holy Empire might bear, apart from the King of *Germania*. This particular status became increasingly blurred in the course of the thirteenth century; the German language was increasingly used, and when the University of Prague was founded, most of the students spoke it. The language of the rulers' laws vacillated between German and Latin, but the common languages did at least find a refuge in popular literature. This is an important sign because it is proof of the permanence of the feeling for

Emperor Charles IV, King of Bohemia. He was crowned Emperor with the help of the Papacy but dedicated himself to Bohemia, which he turned, by founding the University of Prague, into an important cultural centre. (Imola, Cathedral Treasury.)

Czech and Moravian identity. Nonetheless, men who were related neither by blood nor by feeling to the Slavs had no problem climbing on to the throne of Bohemia. The House of Luxemburg is the most famous of these, even supplying Germany with an Emperor in the person of Charles IV, since it developed very strong links, notably on the religious level, between Prague and Germany. But these rulers were not very interested in local affairs. Although Charles IV did indeed give Bohemia an official entry into the German world by including the King of Bohemia in the list of electors to the Imperial title established by Golden Bull of Eger, this was in order to stifle the 'national' feeling which was beginning to emerge in Bohemia. As it was, the blind King John of Bohemia was so concerned with the affairs of his country that he was killed at Crécy in the army of the King of France, a relation and ally, as part of his involvement in a war which did not obviously further Bohemian interests. A little earlier, this rallying movement went through a surprising phase when the Angevins, who were then installed in Hungary, introduced part of the essentially artistic and literary influence of the Italian courts to the Czech land. Of course, the constant

345

pressure exercised by the West and especially by German infiltration elicited suspicious and hostile reactions, but it began as a matter for intellectuals. The Hussite episode has already been related; Jan Huss's revolt was religious but also Czech, and the extremist movement of the Taborites, who persisted right up to the end of the German reconquest, had an obvious regional dimension. When Rome acknowledged part of the insurgents' claims, this was, much as the revolt itself was, a victory for the Czechs. The people of Bohemia went on challenging Rome under King George Podiebrad, a local man this time, who seized the throne in 1458. They even broke completely with Pope Paul II – but this did not compare with the revolt of the White Mountain in the seventeenth century. In reality, Bohemia at the end of the fifteenth century was only a stake between the Empire (which was temporarily out of the fight but which, once in the Habsburgs' hands, surrounded Bohemia) and Poland, their voracious and ambitious neighbour, who did in fact manage to install herself there for a while.

The situation in Hungary was much more complex; firstly because it concerned recently installed non-Slav populations, with 'exotic' cultures. Also because the Germans of the Ostmark and of Austria still had vivid memories of the 'ogres', even after the Magyar raids of the tenth century had definitely stopped and their chiefs were mostly converted, and they kept a healthy distance from Hungary. This allowed her to remain a docile neighbour, free from German penetration for a long time. Further, the Hungarians showed no inclination to align themselves with Western practice; in the middle of the twelfth century Conrad III's army, while marching to the Holy Land, was dealt some nasty shocks by that part of the population which did not pay more than lip service to kings. The magnates, masters of enormous stretches of the *puszta*, were extremely dangerous horsemen and pillagers. In the long run, however, contacts were established; the Danube was after all a busy trading route, if less so than in the tenth century and earlier. Buda too was a trading centre of considerable repute, where German merchants from Bavaria and even the Rhineland were installed. A King of Hungary even took part in a crusading expedition to Egypt; another one, Andrew II, travelled through Europe in his search for support when he was threatened, and worse still, crushed by the Mongol invasion in the middle of the thirteenth century. He was received like an inopportune scrounger, but not like a savage. The decisive step was taken after 1290, when the fate of the Latin principalities in the East and in the Byzantine lands had been determined. Hungary's potential role as a link in the chain of solidarity between Europe and the Latin East evaporated; at the end of a series of battles, the details of which do not concern us, the Angevins of southern Italy became Kings of Hungary. This illustrates the curious irony of dynastic concerns; during fifty years, precisely those years in which the Ottoman danger materialised, Hungary under her Franco-Italian rulers deliberately turned her back on the Balkans. The Angevins' preoccupations with Bohemia, Poland, Serbia and the Adriatic were purely family ones; they embroiled themselves in a complicated network of dynastic alliances in which Hungary had no place. This phase ended in 1387 and was in no way a parenthesis; on the contrary, it provoked a dual and major evolution. On the one hand, as with the Luxemburgs in Bohemia, Louis the Great's reign was accompanied by Western influence;

the court at Buda copied those of the Valois and Naples. Italians and Frenchmen thronged to it instead of Germans; the architecture of the palaces and churches evolved from 'Gothic' to the Italian style and the mingling of cultures began. Inversely, on the political level, Louis the Great had tried, as a good Frenchman, to reduce his magnates to obedience by promulgating statutes which were supposed to reduce the ramifications of the aristocratic hierarchy to one level, the 'equestrian' or 'chivalrous' order. He then imposed a sort of poll tax on the nobility which provoked hostile reaction against his power, but did not bring about his immediate downfall; since the Angevin kings took no interest in Hungarian matters, they could be disobeyed without risk of punitive measures. This is what the Boyards did, which in the long run only made them more autonomous.

A new step was taken when Louis of Anjou's son-in-law Sigismund inherited the Hungarian crown. Although he took a greater interest in Hungarian and Balkan affairs than his predecessors had done, Sigismund, a German this time, spent most of his reign in the Empire until his death in 1437. His part in the pontifical schism, in the Hussite business, in the expeditions of 1385–6 against the Ottoman Sultan Murad, which ended in the disaster of Nicopolis, have already been discussed and need not be recalled. His personal involvement as Hungarian King in the West gradually turned the Pannonian Waste into a sort of march, which became increasingly vulnerable as the Ottomans came closer. It may have been the feeling of being at the front line of Christendom which aroused a defensive and autonomous reaction among even those aristocrats who drew positive advantages from royal absenteeism. This new awareness also affected the Poles who were moving with increasing vigour into the Danube region; the Hungarians participated rather unwillingly in the crusade launched by Ladislas Jagellon in 1443–4 against the Ottomans, which ended in the disastrous Battle of Varna on the Danube. The Hungarian aristocracy was able to recover soon enough to proclaim one of its leaders 'regent' in the place of one of Sigismund's descendants, a minor called John of Hunedoara, or John Hunyadi as he is known in the West. He blocked the Turkish advance in front of Belgrade in 1456 and beyond the Iron Gates. After the sudden death of Hunyadi, Mathias surnamed the Crow, *Corvin*, was designated second regent and drew up a strong barrier of continuous principalities and little forts from Bosnia to Moravia between 1458 and 1463, which momentarily prevented the passage of the Sultans' troops. Unfortunately Corvin – and this attitude shows how profoundly Westernised the Hungarians had become – fixed the centre of his power at Vienna and threw himself against the Poles in an attempt at establishing a dominion stretching from the Adriatic to the Moravian pass, even making a bid for the Empire. His death in 1490 marked the end of Hungary's hopes for autonomy; the magnates preferred to leave the crown to the Pole Ladislas, already King of Bohemia. Already those unifying elements were emerging, which, by bringing Hungary and Bohemia within the Habsburg patrimony, definitely tied them to the Germanic world. The Boyards had no other option but to give evidence of their military heroism against the Infidel in the sixteenth century, and of their responsibility as soldiers of Christ along the borders of those Christian lands which were subjected to Turkish attacks. A strange reversal in the fate of an originally Turco-Mongolian people, whose first actions were as Asian invaders of Germany

347

and whose last were as the defenders of the Germans against Asiatics of the same race as themselves.

The birth of Poland

This is a provocative heading and one liable to shock a people proud of its ancient culture and of the indisputable evidence of its ancient history. What is more, this heading exaggerates not only in terms of the realignment and political origins of Polish history, but also in terms of her economy; have not the oldest ploughshares been found in Poland and even in Moravia, and the most technically perfect ovens of the medieval centuries? Have not wooden structures of remarkable quality and size, urban and otherwise, been uncovered at Biskupin, Gniezno, Krakow, Opole and other places? Finally, had these vast plains not been traversed and exploited by merchants of all origins since the ninth century, if not earlier (as Muslim travellers testify)? Notwithstanding all these facts, my heading stands because, as with the Romanians, the Hungarians and even the Czechs, this collection of people lived on the fringes of the Christian world of the West. The general line of this book is to show the progressive integration within the sphere of control of Western Europe of zones which remained beyond its reach until a given moment in time. Poland fits this bill; for a brief moment, between around 990 and 1050, one has the impression that the Slav peoples living in the plains of Lesser and Greater Poland and even in Pomerania, which had just been federalised by the Miesko and the Boleslas families, were going to turn immediately and definitively towards the West. In the year 1000, Emperor Otto III placed a royal crown on Boleslas' head at Gneizno; Christianity came from the West in spite of a few Byzantine attempts, and the cereal growing plains of Poland seemed to carry on naturally from those in Germany, the Low Countries and France. Unfortunately this trend was interrupted after 1100 and Poland fell back on herself, distancing herself from the European scene. There is little doubt about the motives for this phase of contraction in her history; on the one hand the brutal Germanisation of her most westerly regions, accompanied by expulsions and seizure of lands, which mark the whole period from 1130 to 1230, certainly provoked a defensive reaction giving rise at the same time to that mutual suspicion between Germans and Poles, with consequences which are still with us today. The Christianisation which accompanied this drive was sometimes no less brutal and only served to aggravate the situation, with the Teutonic Knights grabbing Prussia and the Sword-bearers the regions of Estonia and Lettonia. Moreover, the ceaseless and unsuccessful wars conducted by the soldier-monks against the Russian rulers of Novgorod and elsewhere, who had been converted to Christianity by the Byzantines, or against the tenaciously pagan Lithuanians, combined to bring an insupportable burden to bear upon the Polish peasantry. Finally, the development of the Hanseatic ports and the strict control exercised by the German merchants of Lübeck and elsewhere drained the Polish interior of its riches and gradually reduced Poland to the status of a colony.

The effects of all this on the social and economic structure of Poland were very clear: to the extent that most of the products bought and resold by the Germans – wheat, shipping timber, linen, pitch and furs – were derived from the forested and cereal-growing regions in the north, Poland's centre of gravity moved away from the southern area of Krakow to that of Posnania or of the lower course of the Vistula; Warsaw was created in the middle of the thirteenth century. But because the rulers went on patronising the southern regions, the aristocratic elements in the centre and the north acquired a spirit of independence, or at any rate of indiscipline, which paralysed all new attempts at strengthening public authority. Associations of nobles, called *szlachta*, probably a variation on the German *Geschlecht*, were able to keep their peasant labourers and artisans in a state of acute dependence, when what we know of the peasantry in the eleventh century indicates that it was as well poised for independence as was its counterpart in the West. This meant that the social development of an initially particularly well-endowed country was now retarded. Serfdom became harsher; the *kmetes* were almost slaves; seigneurial taxation grew unbearably heavy and the kings were incapable of ensuring observance of their laws.

This disastrous situation, which was so unworthy of Poland's brilliant beginnings, began to unfold at the start of the fourteenth century, when the pressure from Germany was relaxed. King Casimir I (1333–70) managed to restore a certain lustre to the royal office by bringing a huge programme of ennoblement to bear on the townsmen and the less redoubtable elements of the aristocracy. This 'new nobility' naturally supported the king; Casimir granted this aristocracy of both money and function statutes in 1372, 1374 and 1379, thus securing loyal subjects for himself, on whom he could base his administration. Alongside this, the foundation of the University of Krakow in 1364, and subsequently the orthodox zeal demonstrated by the Poles over the schism, gradually showed Poland to be a fully fledged partner in the European consortium. However two elements were still lacking to this 'birth': the immense territory of Lithuania covering the zone from the Baltic to the confines of the Black Sea, almost the whole of White Russia and part of the Ukraine, without being entirely pagan, were still on the fringes of the Polish and Russian worlds. Mongol authority over the area had gradually evaporated. From 1337, the Jagellonian family, who held the ducal title, drew closer to the Polish kings; their union was realised when Ladislas Jagellon acceded to the throne of Krakow, a union which frequently had to be renewed due to the ill will of powerful nobles. In 1410 this fusion was consecrated by the Perpetual Union of Radom, which immediately turned Poland into the second-largest power in Europe, after the Empire. The other obstacle was resolved simultaneously; control of the Baltic coastline which the Teutonic Knights barred all access to; in vain did Ladislas urge the monks to move to Podolia and contain Mongol domination there. He took advantage both of their refusal and of the general dissatisfaction with their repressive attitude to break with the Germans. The Knights were crushed and dispossessed at Tannenberg in 1410. Unfortunately for Ladislas this success encouraged his family to launch themselves into enterprises beyond their control. As promoter of and participant in the crusade against the Ottomans, Ladislas III was in his turn defeated and killed at Varna.

The reign of Casimir IV Jagellon marked the apogee of this second Polish renaissance. The Varna expedition had induced the Polish ruler to draw closer to his neighbours in central Europe in a first step towards the vast enterprise of uniting the Slav and Hungarian

349

The wheat trade. Wheat was grown in Poland and distributed by the Germans, transported down the Vistula. (Detail from the ceiling of the Town Hall in Gdansk by L. Van de Luck, 1608.)

territories of this part of Chistendom under Polish control. In the first place, Casimir settled the problem of German influence; he returned part of the Teutonic Order's lands to them in fief, while retaining the vital approaches to the Baltic, notably in Pommerania (1466). Then he attempted to establish some sort of order in the relations between the Polish aristocracy and the royalty: firstly by increasing his power by a massive programme of secularising Church possessions, and then by organising a system of minor 'diets' – regular but glittering assemblies of the local aristocracy. These assemblies were summoned one after the other in various localities with the intention of getting royal decisions ratified. On the occasion of the general diet of Nieszawa in 1454, Casimir had already affirmed royal support for the minor aristocracy, as the Angevins had done in their time in Hungary. Finally, as a result of agreements with the Germans of the Hanse, he tried to take back in hand part of the internal trade of Poland; cereal production and forestry exploitation passed to some extent under his control and the impulse this gave to the economy was certainly behind the notable rise in the standard of living. Western travellers passing via Krakow or elsewhere were now astonished by the exceptional luxury with which the Polish nobles surrounded themselves. Above all, after the failure of his Hungarian experience, Casimir felt that the moment had come to set himself up as the defender of Christianity in the East. He pursued a domineering and tortuous policy from 1479 to 1492, which led him to put his son Ladislas on the throne of Bohemia and, when Matthias Corvin died, on that of Hungary. In principle Ladislas should then have stood in line for the Polish throne. If this concentration of territories had been achieved, an enormous power stretching from the Baltic to the Adriatic and from the Oder to Kiev would have been realised in central Europe. In his care to endue these grandiose projects with the cultural dimension they so obviously lacked, Casimir zealously developed the University of Krakow. Students flocked to it from all over the place and Casimir also encouraged Polish students to study in Paris and Italy; the education of a man like Copernicus cannot be understood outside the context of Casimir's achievement.

Such ambition may have outstripped the means at the Polish royalty's disposal; in any case, it did not interest the landed aristocracy who were primarily concerned about securing their profits from the trade with Germany. This meant that when Casimir died, Poland, instead of assuming control over a third of Europe, began to decline; a process which, interspersed with a few remarkable recoveries, would reduce her power and allow her neighbours to prey on her. First to founder were Casimir's political projects; it was obvious that his 'imperial' construction could not hold together, even without the revolt of Lithuania, which rejected the control of Krakow for a while at least. On the level of royal authority, the *szlachtas* could not be kept to heel: the new King John Albert was advised to adopt a policy worthy of Italy – a sort of princely tyranny – by the many Italians in Poland (who had flocked there when the new Slav power emerged, notably the Florentine Buonacorsi), but in vain. The nobility had grabbed most of the ecclesiastical offices and provincial governorships and opposed the King's despotic proceedings. In 1505, he was forced to issue an act of effacement which would mark the whole of Poland's subsequent history; no royal decision could be taken without convoking the Diet and securing its approval. This was undoubtedly akin to the 'parliamentary' regime to which several other royal families had been able to accommodate themselves, but the Polish royalty still required an effective administration which, in spite of Casimir's efforts, it did not possess. Last but not least, economically speaking, the Germans and English managed to secure concessions and privileges – at Gdansk from 1490 and a little later in other places – which reduced the impact of the customs legislation instituted by Casimir. They resumed the export of wood, wheat and pitch on a larger scale than before, which certainly enriched the aristocracy on the lands where these products were harvested, but ruined the royal treasury and reduced Poland to a land colonised by international trade and dependent on the good will of merchants from Lübeck and London. As with Hungary a little earlier, Poland, which had been poised on the threshold of European power, fell back to being a satellite of the West. Although her distance from Byzantium had never allowed Poland to pretend to be its heirs, in the situation after 1500 this could not even be imagined; in the seventeenth century, when a Sobieski saved Christendom, it was merely as a marginal potentate working for the Bourbons and the Habsburgs. However, in the midst of this disintegration which carried on over several centuries, for instance when Lithuania revolted, in the midst of this repetitive and wearying process, a new power rose up out of the gloom – that of Moscow.

The shadow of Russia

Beyond Riga, after Brest-Litovsk or Lvov, the landscape changes: the rivers become wider, the horizon recedes, the space becomes immense and there are no landmarks. These are the plains of Russia and the Ukraine, a different world and culture, with its different languages. The history of the Russian plains does not enter our discussion until the fifteenth century. The Scandinavians in the tenth and eleventh centuries had dragged them from their tribal oblivion, and several dynasties of Kiev and Vladimir had demonstrated their aggression towards their Greek neighbours in the south; Byzantine monks had brought Christianity to them and so in theory had attached these savage Christians to the Hellenic world. But were the Russian principalities which emerged here and there during the thirteenth century and before, parts of the European world? The trade in furs and slaves, and employment as mercenaries in the pay of the *Basileus* or perhaps some Muslim ruler, were activities without shape or purpose. The culture and even some original features of Russian society are doubtless worthy of interest, but, as with the other populations mentioned above, these worlds were extraneous to the development of European power. Further, the Mongol invasion and occupation of the mid thirteenth century served to isolate the rival principalities still further. Alexander Nevksy's victory over the Teutonic Knights may well be celebrated as a semi-popular exploit; it did absolutely nothing to change the shape of European history.

Here too, the perspective was altered in the fifteenth century and this can only be understood in terms of what went before; the failure of Polish ambitions, or perhaps originally the danger they had entailed for the Russian rulers, acted like a spark in arousing the awareness of these rulers, albeit not of their peoples. In any case, Muslim domination of the southern zones was weakening and the Russians' obsession with being besieged – a permanent state of mind – was slightly relaxed. This awakening was presided over by Ivan III, ruler of Moscow (1462–1505); he was the first to be aware of the Polish menace. He put paid to Casimir Jagellon's pretensions in Lithuania and he even caused a revolt in these border zones on his death. He too started the move to the south, initially towards Istanbul, which marks the whole of Russian history. We must pause at this point.

Following its defeat and almost total destruction by Tamerlane in 1395, the Khanate of Kipchak, or the Golden Horde, did not disappear completely, because Tamerlane entrusted what was left of it to Khan Timur Qutlugh (1398–1400), whose minister and general Yedigey managed to put paid to an offensive led by Grand Duke Witold of Lithuania (1399) and to make the Muscovite rulers accept the overlordship of the Khan. After Yedigey's death in 1419, Witold resumed his attacks and got as far as the Black Sea, where he integrated the region between the Dniepr and the Dniestr into his state, at least until his

The Kremlin in Moscow: the Cathedral of the Annunciation (1484–9).

disappearance in 1430. He tried to intervene in the affairs of the Khanate of the Golden Horde (the name adopted by the Russians) but the different clans which it comprised managed to preserve their independence and unity until 1438. At this date, an unlucky candidate to the Khanate, Ulugh Mehmed, withdrew to Kazan on the Volga, which he made into the capital of a new State, the Khanate of Kazan, while in the south the Khanate of the Great Horde spread itself out under the leadership of Kuchuk Mehmed. Finally in

353

1441 a third Khanate appeared in the Crimea under the authority of Khan Hajji Giray, the founder of a dynasty which lasted until the eighteenth century, while further east the Khanate of Astrakhan was formed, on the mouth of the Volga.

Thus was the great Khanate of Kipchak dismembered. Its remnants experienced varying fortunes, the more so since it no longer threatened Europe. This situation favoured the development of the Muscovite and the Polish–Lithuanian States: the Great Horde was subjected fairly rapidly to the Grand Princes of Moscow, as were the Khans of Kazan a little later. The Muscovites also tried to subjugate the Khanate of the Crimea, but there Hajji Giray, allied to the King of Poland, resisted their pressure until his death in 1466. His son and successor Mengli Giray turned the situation completely upside down by allying with Ivan III, Prince of Moscow, while Casimir IV, King of Poland, allied with the Khan of the Golden Horde. As it was, each of these sovereigns was acting in his own interest; Ivan III was trying to consolidate his position in Russia and to increase his territories, which he achieved by conquering Novgorod in 1478, by triumphing over the Khan of the Great Horde in 1480 and by forcing various Russian rulers to pay tribute to him instead of the Tartar Khans.

For his part, Mengli Giray aimed at eliminating the Genoese presence in the Crimea, where they were solidly installed along the coast, notably at Caffa. Their economic activity in this sector had diminished since the Polish–Lithuanians occupied part of the Black Sea coastline and controlled the routes from Moldavia and Podolia, and also since the Ottomans had conquered Constantinople, in spite of the favourable commercial agreement the Genoese had secured from them shortly after the conquest. Closer relations between the Genoese and the Poles made Mengli Giray decide to attack them; after taking all the Genoese bases one by one, he finally reached Caffa in 1475 and reduced it, thus putting an end to Latin presence in the Crimea, which the Venetians quitted long ago. Mengli Giray had taken Caffa with the help of Ottoman troops, in exchange for which he recognised the suzerainty of Sultan Mehmed II. This had the immediate effect of strengthening his authority and prestige over the whole region. In the longer term, the Khans of the Crimea remained vassals of the Ottomans until the eighteenth century (1783) and so contributed towards ensuring the domination of the Sultans of Constantinople over the Black Sea, where they had taken territories occupied by the Poles in 1484. A Polish venture into Moldavia failed in 1497 and Sayyid Ahmed, Khan of the Great Horde, who had supported the Poles, was subsequently completely defeated by Mengli Giray in 1502 and his Khanate ceased to exist. As for the Khanate of Kazan, it became increasingly subject to Russian domination before being taken by Ivan IV the Terrible in 1552.

Within the properly speaking Russian world, Ivan III put an end to the autonomy of the Tver principality (1485), occupied part of Lettonia and Pskov and moved its inhabitants to Moscow (1490). These were works of war and intimidation; better was to come. Hostile to the pretensions of the German merchants of the Hanse, who were used to dealing with Novgorod and Riga as they pleased, he taxed them or threw them out – as part of a policy of suspicion and xenophobia which has also become traditional. At least it had the effect of leaving the Russians to themselves, a situation which struck both Pope Sixtus

IV and Emperor Sigismund; their embassies proved that Russia was in theory now part of the European scene; but their representatives were dismissed without receiving any explanation. In fact, the ruler of Moscow felt much closer to the Eastern world, especially the now defunct Byzantine world. In 1472 he married Zoe Palaeologus, one of the last members of that branch of the Greek family which had settled in the Morea. He adopted the Imperial title, which had fallen into abeyance since the disappearance of Bulgaria, and called himself Caesar or Tsar, a title which Mehmed II, more concerned with Islam than with continuity, had disdained. His Patriarchate considered itself the authentic continuator of the Christian Church in the East, in the place of the Church in Constantinople which had become dependent on the Sultan. What had the heir to Constantinople to do with such an alien Europe? Better still, Moscow was to be the 'Third Rome'; between 1485 and 1508, Ivan abandoned his palaces of mud and wattles and employed Italian architects (because they were familiar with the art of princes) to build him a fortified palace, a Kremlin, girdled with Guelfic battlements, espousing the shape of the Sforza stronghold in Milan. In the centre of this fortress, the palaces and churches were spread among pavilions and scattered dwellings in the manner of the Sacred Palace, and the main church there, the Cathedral of the Dormition of the Virgin, was built by the Bolognese Fieravente to a Byzantine design.

The birth of the Kremlin, just when the Slav principalities in Central Europe, including Poland, were fading out and when Byzantium was giving way to the Turks, was a major event in the history of Europe. From then on, Europe stopped at the Duna and the Dniepr; beyond them a new world gradually grew up, a world which claimed to succeed Constantinople, looking towards the Black Sea and the Straits, from which many years of effort still separated it. Without making facile prognostications, it can be said that Western Europe ceased to make any progress here for a long time, having reaped but the memory or reflection of the Greek heritage and having abandoned the land and its inhabitants to Islam. But a Christian, Eastern and powerful heir was emerging on the horizon – not yet the Russia of Peter the Great or of the treaty of San Stefano, but one in which Ivan encouraged Russian trappers to cross the Urals and to venture into inviolate Siberia, where there was plenty to keep both soldiers and pioneers busy. Next, the approaches to the seas had to be won back, Poles and Germans had to be repulsed, the Turks defeated, and the Mediterranean reached – but all that is another story.

7 Africa opens up to the old worlds

The middle of the thirteenth century brought considerable political upheavals to the Muslim world of the West, some of which resulted in the disintegration of States which had previously known grandeur and power. Before the middle of the thirteenth century, the westerly side of the Almohad State experienced many internal and external problems which led to its final dismemberment. The defeats inflicted on the Muslims in Spain since 1212 had left them only the region of Granada, which became a kingdom ruled by the Nasrid dynasty. In the Maghrib, three States were created; Abu Zakariyya made himself independent in Ifriqiya in 1228 and founded the Hafsid Kingdom; in Morocco the Banu Merin gradually established themselves between 1242 and 1269 and founded the Merinid Dynasty, fixing its centre at Fez; lastly, western Algeria was transformed into the kingdom of the Abd al-Wadids with Tlemcen as its capital (1235–6).

A new Maghrib

The Maghrib began to establish its political frontiers, which it was to maintain until the twentieth century, with minor changes. These divisions invested the various kingdoms with their own identity, which was felt both in their internal governments and their external relations. The concept of an united Maghrib no longer existed and would reappear momentarily only when the Ottomans ruled over Algeria, Tunisia, and Tripolitania in the middle of the sixteenth century. As it was, Morocco tended to isolate herself from the rest of the Maghrib and maintained economic links with Spain, whereas the other kingdoms turned more towards Catalonia, southern France (notably Marseille) and the Italian ports, Genoa being the most important. The really essential event, however, which was to become so extraordinarily important in the future, was when Islam turned around towards Black Africa.

Three dynasties, enduring for centuries

In Ifriqiya (Tripolitania, Tunisia and eastern Algeria), the Hafsid governor, Abu Zakariyya (1229–49), assumed the title of Emir once he had become independent and took pains to establish his power by exploiting the rivalries between Arabs and Berbers, and by trying to settle nomadic Arab tribes, such as the Banu Sulaym, to whom he granted the right to establish themselves along the whole of Algeria's eastern frontier.

His son Abu Abdallah al-Mustansir (1249–77), after repressing a few rebellions by the nomads, had to repulse Saint Louis' expedition of 1270, but, when it came to its abrupt end, he was able to devote himself to governing his kingdom and to maintaining good relations with neighbouring Muslim States (Morocco and Sudan) and various Christian States. Andalusian Muslims driven out of Spain by the Reconquistà found a welcome in Ifriqiya and Tunis became an important intellectual and artistic centre, over and above her economic role. Al-Mustansir assumed the title of Caliph around 1259, probably following the sack of Baghdad by the Mongols and the death of the Abbasid Caliph. He was not recognised as such by Muslims in the East, in spite of his considerable renown.

After his death, the Hafsid State entered a period of political turmoil brought about by rivalry between the heirs and claimants to the throne, by conflict between the various tribes, and by Christian attacks such as the one led by Roger de Lauria, a military leader in the service of Peter of Aragon, King of Sicily, who seized Jerba (1284). Hafsid unity collapsed and Tunis and Bougie became the centres of two rival kingdoms. Unity was restored by Abu Yahya ibn Abu Bakr II (1318–46) but did not survive his death, allowing the Merinids to advance as far as Tunisia (1347–8 and then 1353–8). After their departure, three new States were formed around Tunis, Bougie and Constantine. Unity was restored in 1370 by the Hafsid Abu l-Abbas (1370–94) who made use of both force and diplomacy to consolidate his power.

In central Maghrib, the Sultan of Tlemcen, Yaghmurasan, managed to govern for nearly fifty years (1239–83) without any internal difficulties, which allowed him to resist attacks led against him from outside. His son Abu Sa'id Uthman (1283–1304) had to repulse the Merinid Abu Ya'qub Yussuf, who besieged Tlemcen for eight years and built the new town of al-Mansura opposite it. The siege came to an end when Abu Ya'qub was assassinated in 1307. Once he had restored the kingdom's armed forces, Sultan Abu Tashfin (1318–37) launched a series of expeditions against the Hafsids in the East, but before he had achieved more than a few successes he had to deal with a new siege of Tlemcen by the Merinids, in the course of which he was killed. The Merinids turned the Abd al-Wadid kingdom into a protectorate for more than twenty years, and, although the Abd al-Wadids shook off their control in 1359, they were subsequently unable to govern their domain properly and were generally at the mercy of the Arab tribes. However, they did manage to keep going until the middle of the sixteenth century, in spite of attacks from the Hafsids and the Spaniards, and later on from the Turks.

The Banu Merin, who had led the struggle against the Almohads since the beginning of the thirteenth century, ended by winning and occupied first Meknes and Fez, the towns of the interior, then Rabat and Salé, the coastal towns (1248), and finally Marrakesh, the Almohad capital (1269). This struggle must be seen in terms of a semi-permanent war between the Zanata Berber tribes and the Arab tribes, which the Almohads had favoured in order to secure their power, installing them along many points of their territory, up to the

Interior of the Bou Medina Mosque in Tlemcen. Built in 1339, it is a remarkable example of Merinid architecture.

Moroccan south. The founder of the Moroccan dynasty, Abu Yussuf (1258–86), established his capital in the new town of Fez (Fez al-Jadid) at the gates of old Fez (Fez al-Bali). As the successor of the Almohads he tried to reconquer the lost territories in Spain and his interventions served at least to protect the Nasrid kingdom of Granada (1275 and 1284–5).

The sovereigns who came after him had to deal with internal revolts by their Arab tribes as well as with attacks by the Nasrids, who occupied Ceuta (1302–9), forcing the Merinid Abu Thabit to found Tetuan nearby.

The Merinid dynasty reached its apogee with Abu l-Hasan (1331–51). His conquests extended his kingdom from Algesiras to the Gulf of Gabès, but in Spain he was defeated by the Castilians and ended by losing Algesiras to them (1344). After suffering a serious defeat at Kairouan in 1348 he lost control over the whole of the Maghrib. Revolts sprang up in Morocco, one of them led by his son Abu Inan. Abu l-Hasan died in 1351 after having abdicated, but was posthumously considered to have been especially revered. Abu Inan (1348–58) retook Tlemcen and raided Ifriqiya, but his reign marked the end of Merinid expansionism and of the internal stability of the realm, which was now prey to rivalries between Sultans and great rulers in the East, to such an extent that two Sultans were created, one at Fez and the other at Marrakesh. Abu l-Abbas (1387–93) restored unity to the Merinid kingdom and even launched expeditions against the Abd al-Wadid territory, but his death was followed by new troubles which made Christian intervention in Morocco feasible. In 1399 Henry III of Castile seized and devastated Tetuan, while in 1415 the Portuguese occupied Ceuta. From then on Spanish–Moroccan relations entered into a new phase.

On another level, the Almohad State had bequeathed certain institutions to the kingdoms which succeeded it, notably the Hafsids. Here, beside the sovereign were found the ten *Shaykhs al-muvahhidih*, as well as the *mizwar*, originally guardian of morals and then chamberlain. In practice, the power lay with the vizirs (of the army, the finances and internal affairs), and then especially the *hajib*, who had been promoted from majordomo to acting as intermediary between the sultan and his functionaries, and who eventually became the real head of government. One of the functionaries played an important role in the towns; he was the *mutasib*, guardian of morals, who was also responsible for controlling the markets and so a part of economic life.

The Hafsid sovereign was in theory an absolute ruler, and the fact of his having appropriated the title of Caliph reveals the extent of his political and religious pretensions. He also bore the title of *amir al-mu'minin*, commander of the faithful; the *khutba* was proclaimed in his name; he surrounded himself with ceremonial pomp and strict etiquette; he resided apart from the population, either in the *qasba* or in his new residence in the Bardo.

Among the Abd al-Wadids, the institutions and tribal power of the Beduins seem to have been in decline, but at the same time, starting with Abu Hammu I, a new trend emerged with the presence of a vizir and chamberlain of Spanish origin and the growing influence of an Andalusian-style administration. As for the Merinids, whose sovereign bore the title of *amir al-mu'minin*, he surrounded himself with a pomp identical to that of the Hafsid sovereign and resided at Fez al-Jadid. There were some differences in that there was no *hajib* and that the government offices were concentrated in the hands of the *mizwar*, especially after Abu Inan's reign. One vizir specifically was in charge of the army (where Zanata and Arab contingents were found alongside mercenaries of various origins and the ruler's personal guard) and military operations. The higher functionaries were generally recruited from the same families – sometimes coming from educated Andalusian circles but also from other parts of the Maghrib; thus, Ibn Khaldun had served the Hafsids before moving over to the Merinids.

Berbers or Arabs?
Towns or countrysides?

One of the problems confronting the States of the Maghrib was that of getting the Zanata Berber tribes to live in peace with the Arab tribes and of maintaining internal peace. The sovereigns and their viziers tried to solve it by allotting lands under the form of *iqtas* to these tribes, especially to the Arab tribes on whom some of their sovereigns had already leant for support (for instance in Morocco). Their collaboration had favoured their settlement in various parts of the Maghrib where until then they had not set foot.

The period which came after the Almohads has been considered one in which the Berbers, no longer the Sanhajas but the Zanatas, emerged as the real holders of power in the Maghrib. But such an interpretation is inadequate; in Tunisia the Berber tribes were driven off the plains, and in the mountainous regions they fled to they were unable to unite, thus leaving the field open to the Arab tribes. In central Maghrib, the Banu Badin, ancestors of the Abd al-Wadids, came to Yaghmurasan's aid. In Morocco, the Banu Merin were originally nomads from the region of Figuig and Sijilmasa; as enemies of the Almohads they appeared initially to be more interested in acquiring lands than in creating a kingdom: circumstances forced other ambitions on them.

As far as the Arabs are concerned, their expansion into the Maghrib had stabilised; most of the plains and the middle mountain ranges were occupied by nomadic tribes, who established relations with urban Arabs and Arab newcomers from the countryside. In Tunisia too, the Arab tribes dominated the neighbourhood of Tunis, the northern plains and large parts of the interior. In central Maghrib, they found themselves in the locality of Constantine, the Mitija, the region of Jabal Amur and various other regions, as well as in the Algerian-Moroccan border country. In Morocco where the Arab tribes, in spite of being less numerous, played an important role, like the Khlot, who formed the backbone of the Merinids' militia, these tribes generally preserved a marked spirit of independence, recognising only their own chief and incapable of uniting. They could on occasion also foment anarchy and their sovereigns had to manage them somehow. In order to keep the peace, they granted them privileges or else tried to incite them against one another. Although the Arabs were in control of the situation all over the Maghrib, their efforts were uncoordinated and in the long run tended to serve the interests of the Berber dynasties.

Among the other communities, the Jews endured conditions which varied from place to place. In Morocco already in the time of the Almohads, the Jews of Fez were established in a special quarter, the *mellah*, and this example was followed in other towns. This did not stop them from working in the Muslim quarters during the day in the same groups of trades as the Muslims, and especially in commerce, manufacturing and, of course, banking. In Tunisia, Jewish communities existed in all the big towns, except for Kairouan. Their number was growing because so many of their correligionists were coming from Castile and Aragon, an exodus which started in the last years of the fourteenth century. They brought with them new trades and skills, and effected a remarkable commercial revival in Tunisia, especially in Tunis. The Spanish Jews enjoyed more extensive rights than the native Jews (they could own and sell goods, and keep non-Muslim slaves). They did not have their own quarter, but they probably lived close to the synagogue. The Jewish community of Tlemcen was also strengthened by Jews from Spain, and Algiers possessed a Talmudic school of considerable repute.

There was no longer a native Christian community in the Maghrib. The Christians there had come from Europe, mostly from Italian merchant cities, and lived in their *funduks*. Some of them had consuls who intervened with the government authorities. As well as these, the Merinids and the Abd al-Wadids employed Christian militias made up of volunteers. There were also Christian prisoners captured either in the course of battle, especially in Spain, or by pirates, who were made into slaves. Missions for redeeming them began to be formed, which enabled missionaries to come into contact with North Africans. The most characteristic example of this trend is Ramon Llull, who became an excellent arabist and conversed with *ulamas* before his death at a very great age, assassinated in Ifriqiya.

Although the Maghrib experienced political and human upheavals, its economic life did not suffer any dramatic consequences as a result. On the contrary the presence of the nomads apparently influenced many regions, but not in an exaggeratedly negative sense, because the nomads definitely contributed to the development of stockraising, although in various places this entailed a decline in agricultural production. In the Hafsid State, for instance, agricultural produce from the Mejerda and the Algerian Sahel had to be imported to feed Tunis. Generally, however, agricultural production was kept up and made trade possible. Fruits, olives, leather and skins were exported, which endowed the coastal towns with an enhanced importance as ports.

The most important feature of this period was in fact the development of the towns and of their economic, intellectual, religious and artistic activities. In the Hafsid Sultanate, Tunis became the most important town, to the detriment of Kairouan. She was not only the political capital, a fact emphasised by the construction of palaces (the *Qasba*, the *Bardo*), but also the great economic centre of the country, dealing with the Italian mercantile cities, who owned *funduks* there, as well as with the other ports of the Maghrib. *Souks*, buildings intended for commercial purposes, were erected around the Great Mosque and grew very large. In comparison, Kairouan showed signs of stagnating although the Hafsids went on considering her as a great religious centre. Trade had however turned away towards the coastal towns, especially Tunis, leaving Kairouan behind as no more than a crossroad, a stopping place for merchants. She owed her continuing prestige to her religious role.

Tlemcen, the town of the Abd al-Wadids, also underwent a great development, due to the temporary presence of the Merinids. She had a prosperous working class, one of whose specialities was processing wool, and another was monumental construction. Most of the buildings which we can still see date from this period. Tlemcen was also a centre of Mediterranean commerce and Venetians and Genoese came there to trade. Bougie also took part in this economic development. However, the most remarkable town of the Maghrib in those days was uncontestably Fez, having dethroned Marrakesh as the capital of the western Maghrib. She reached the height of her glory in the fourteenth

361

century with magnificently built and decorated palaces, mosques and *madrasas* in the town of Fez al-Jadid, where everything that could contribute to and participate in the city's intense economic life was encouraged. Fez was not the Merinids' only active town: Meknes and Taza, in contact with the Atlas mountains and the plains, and Salé on the Atlantic, were just as prosperous, trading either with the hinterland or with foreigners.

The Maghrib of Ibn Khaldun

Two phenomena more peculiar to the Maghrib than elsewhere emerged during the fourteenth century. One was the progressive Arabisation of all its regions and the other – a consequence of its economic development and the resulting wealth – was the appearance of rich patrons, who encouraged not only literature but all cultural disciplines. The most famous example of this cultural activity is of course Ibn Khaldun (1332–1406). He was born in Tunis to a family of Andalusian origin and died in Cairo. He lived in various North African countries, in Nasrid Spain, and in Egypt. He filled political offices among the Merinids and the Abd al-Wadids, where he was awarded marks of his contemporaries' appreciation, to a greater or lesser degree. He was also involved in various plots from which he always managed to extricate himself without too much damage. In 1402 he arrived in Egypt, where he became a great *maliki qadi*, gave lectures and was perhaps entrusted with a political role by the Mameluke Sultan. In any case, he found himself in Aleppo when Tamerlane occupied the town and so met this famous person. He died shortly afterwards in Cairo. Ibn Khaldun was judged harshly by his contemporaries, who considered him an ambitious opportunist, driven by his lust for power.

Whatever the case, his duties and his travels and the difficulties he encountered allowed him to acquire, better than any other Maghribian scholar before him, a considerable and profound knowledge of Muslim society. He displayed this knowledge in different works, the most famous among them being the *Muqaddima* (the Prolegomenes) and the *Kitab-al-Ibar* (the Book of Happenings, or Universal History) which followed it, but which lacks the breadth and the depth of the first. Ibn Khaldun described himself as a historian, and his Prolegomenes constitute his considered opinion as to the information and methods indispensable to whomever undertakes to write history. His analysis led him to tackle complementary scientific disciplines, some of which, like philosophy, were derived from Antiquity, and others of which, like economy and sociology, appear on the contrary as necessary innovations, which allow contemporaries to understand society and the links uniting the causes and effects of events, and their consequences. Thus was born a new science, the *umran*, which enables human civilisation and the whole of society to be studied. From this it emerged that the behaviour of a group depends from the start on their *asabiyya* (family solidarity and identity of interests). This is followed by an evolution which aims at imposing the rule (*mulk*) of the group by making use of religion under the form of *da'wa* (ideological propaganda). The list of contents for the six chapters of the *Muqaddima* furnish details of this new science: Introduction; History and its purpose; Methodology; chapter 1. Study of human society, influence of the environment (geography, ethnology, anthropology); 2. Rural societies (*umran badawi*); 3. Governments, States (*mulk*), theory of institutions; 4. Urban societies (*umran hadhari*), the city, urban civilisation; 5. Industries, economic facts, social categories; 6. The sciences, literature, pedagogy, culture.

The *Kitab al-Ibar*, which was supposed to be the practical application of the theories outlined in the *Muqaddima*, is not as original and profound. It is none the less compelling because of its author's knowledge and analysis of the history of the Muslim world in North Africa and Andalusia. Ibn Khaldun's work was rediscovered by Europeans in the nineteenth century and has frequently given rise to passionate debate. Although he did indeed open the way for new disciplines, some people have gone too far in calling him the inventor of sciences, which could only have developed in different historical and economic contexts, and in comparing him with much later political writers and sociologists (including Hegel and Marx). He was a splendid thinker, but he was on his own and, to a great extent, in advance of his time and his immediate influence in Muslim lands was almost nil. He remains nonetheless one of the bright stars of Muslim thought and, in a larger context, of all humanity.

Although he outshines all his contemporaries, Ibn Khaldun was not the only writer. Among the other historians were Ibn Idari, author of a history of Ifriqiya from the Arab conquest until the Almohad government; Ibn Marzuq, who had also been a traditionalist, a lawyer and a poet; Ibn Abu Zar and many others. Geographers and travellers were no less important, such as Ibn Sa'id, Ibn Rushayd, al-Tijjani (who described Tunisia) and above all Ibn Battuta (1304–77), that extraordinary traveller who journeyed across the world from the Atlantic to Central Asia, India, Indonesia and China. Though the traveller may not have seen all that he describes, and his accounts sometimes betray an excessive imagination, and his descriptions occasionally err on the side of enthusiasm (some of these faults can certainly be ascribed to Ibn Juzayy, who actually wrote the text), the *rihla* (travel journal) is nonetheless a document extremely important to the study of the history and geography of the Muslim world in the first half of the fourteenth century. Finally, the name of the Moroccan mathematician Ibn al-Banna must be mentioned (1256–1321), who also took an interest in medicine, grammar, religion, astronomy and magic. Religious sciences and Sufism were also much studied in all the countries of the Maghrib.

The arts also flourished in these countries, and varied from region to region. In Tunisia, for instance, Andalusian architects and artisans brought their skills and techniques to the country, which can be seen in various buildings (the mosque of the Qasba in Tunis, the mosque of Testour, the mosque of Monastir) to which polychrome decorations were frequently applied; but the palace and gardens created for al-Mustansir have gone. The disappearance of a number of monuments of the Abd al-Wadids must also be deplored, such as the *meshuar* (palace–citadel) in Tlemcen; however, local art is exemplified in the mosque of Sidi ben Hassan with its stucco panels, its arabesques and its polychrome decoration. It was among the Merinids that artistic activity was most intense, especially at Fez where many essentially religious buildings arose: *madrasas* (al-Saffarin, al-Attarin, abu'Inaniya, etc.) which reveal the general desire for orthodox religious education. In the same context, the tomb of Sidi Abu Midyan in Al-Ubbad, a person venerated particularly in

363

The Merinids deployed their artistic and architectural skills to best effect at Fez, as the luxurious decoration of the inner court of the al-Attarin *madrasa* (1323–5) demonstrates.

central Maghrib, should be noted. Military architecture (walls and fortifications) can also be seen in Fez and Mansura. On the whole, the art of the Merinids is characterised by its architectural symmetry, but the pure lines of the buildings are obscured by excessive use of decorative motifs and by a superabundance of detail. All the same, this art form, the outward sign of the dynasty's power exercised a certain influence over western and central Maghrib and appears to have been influenced by local artisans to a far greater extent than was Hafsid art.

In short, the period at the end of the thirteenth and throughout the fourteenth century was one of political fragmentation, as far as the lands of the Maghrib were concerned. This may even have been necessary because the Almohad Empire had been spread over too vast an area. Each new kingdom corresponded to a human and geographical entity, which became more clearly defined as time went on. The Merinids did indeed try to reconstitute the Almohad State in the Maghrib, but in spite of their partial success in western Algeria, their final failure showed that the partition of North Africa had not been accidental. Not that the political evolution affected the economic activities of the area in any way, thanks to the progress made by Italian, Provençal, Catalan and other mercantile cities, which ensured that North Africa (especially Tunis) remained a relay between Africa and Europe. The Maghrib drew profits and advantages from this arrangement, which could be seen in the rise of a remarkable urban civilisation – and one all the more remarkable in that North Africa had been regressing since the eleventh century. Finally, the political upheavals and the arrival of the Arabs had not been irreparably disastrous for the Maghrib: on the contrary, they spurred the area on to experience a period of splendour in which the name of Ibn Khaldun shines with especial brilliance.

The jewel of Granada

The Nasrid kingdom of Granada had emerged from the disintegration and fragmentation of the Almohad State. However, as far as its external relations were concerned, it experienced conditions quite different to those in the Maghrib States. To start off with, the conquests of the Kingdoms of Aragon and Castile had very soon cut Granada off from the rest of Islam. This meant that it became the last Muslim bastion in European territory, but also that it became a place where contact and trade between the countries of the western Mediterranean and the countries of northern Africa was possible. Further, it was a wealthy State, whose inhabitants were profoundly conscious of their identity, perhaps because they were the objects of aggression from the other inhabitants of Spain, who were endowed with a different mentality and relied on a different dominant religion. While the other Muslim states of Spain had disappeared under the Aragonese and Castilian *Reconquistà*, and their Muslim populations had either been exiled to the Maghrib or had converted, Granada had remained stable and strengthened its presence and its faith, notably by building religious and civil edifices which bear witness to intense creative activity.

On the political level, the Kingdom of Granada appeared officially when the Treaty of Jaen was signed in 1246, but since 1232 Muhammad Ibn Yusuf Ibn Nasr (whence the name 'Nasrid') had fought a series of battles interspersed with treaties and had concluded frequently broken alliances with Castile, Aragon and the Merinids in his attempts at playing them off against each other. In spite of this, he lost territories in the west, north and east to the Christian kingdoms, and it was during his reign that what was to remain the Nasrid frontier until the end of the fifteenth century was gradually established. The outbreak of an internal rebellion forced him to appeal for help first to the Merinids and then the Castilians. It was Muhammad II (1273–1302), however, who put an end to this rebellion and consolidated the kingdom. The kingdom underwent its first internal crisis under Muhammad III (1302–9); a series of disturbances and plots were sparked off by it, which rebounded on the country's politics and also its internal stability. For the next twenty-five years, until the reign of Yusuf I (1333–54), the Kingdom of Granada was in difficulty and was attacked by the Castilians (who exacted tribute) and by the Merinids (who took Ceuta and Ronda). With the advent of Yusuf I and Muhammad V (1354–9 and 1362–91) internal stability was restored thus improving the Nasrids' ability to resist attacks from outside. They took advantage of the Merinids' difficulties to retake Ronda, Gibraltar and, temporarily, even Ceuta.

The population of the Nasrid Kingdom of Granada was mostly Muslim of Arab origin. The Berbers were few and were to be found in mercenary troops, recruited among the Zanata. This population felt very strongly about its specifically Grenadian identity; they were members of the Muslim community who governed and administered the country and

The splendour of the Alhambra in Granada: the Lion Court. Seldom has such a profusion of decoration been so successfully allied to subtlety and proportion as in these stucco carvings, whose surface reflects the light filtering from the patio.

towns and who thus provided political unity, except in cases of local rivalry or of serious internal crisis. The Christians were not numerous and were to be found in commercial circles both in the ports and in the inland towns. The Jews formed a very active community, engaged in trade as well as in certain aspects of agrarian life, in manufacturing and in various professions such as medicine.

On the whole, these different communities lived together peacefully without being harassed or persecuted. The Kingdom of Granada was famous for its tolerance, and for its liberal and easy way of life, with its many feasts and celebrations. From this point of view it provides an excellent example of an Islamic country coping with the Spanish *Reconquistà*, which drove so many Muslims and Jews to seek refuge, notably in the Maghrib.

It enjoyed a considerable and active intellectual life, with many *madrasas*, the most famous being the madrasa Yusufiya where many future scholars and men of letters studied: Ibn Marzuq, Ibn Juzayy, Ibn al-Khatib (the most famous of his time) and even Ibn Khaldun. Books were written on all the great disciplines and, although the Nasrids and Merinids were at war, the intellectuals of both kingdoms were able to engage in constant and often fruitful discussion with one another and with other countries of the Maghrib and even Egypt.

Finally, the originality and identity of the Nasrids of Granada were given form in their religious and civil architecture and the decoration of their buildings. The most famous example is the Alhambra of Granada, along with the Generalife. These palaces represent the quintessence of Nasrid art, and the final swan song of Hispano-Moorish art as a whole. It also stands for all that Granada meant in religious, spiritual, artistic and cultural terms and should be seen as the last achievement of that Islamo-Andalusian culture peculiar to Spain, which the *Reconquistà* could not destroy.

Farewell to Spain

The last century of the existence of the Nasrid Kingdom of Granada, the ultimate symbol of the old Muslim rule in Spain, was marked by events which led, ineluctably, to its annihilation. War, the progressive disintegration of the State, the intrigues within the ruling family and among the court dignitaries, a number of outside influences, the dislocation of society – they were all too much for a little kingdom which needed all its strength and the cooperation of all its inhabitants to resist the Castilians. However, at the beginning of the fifteenth century, it seemed as though the family of the Banu Sarraj (the 'Abencerages'), which played a pre-eminent part in politics, would be able to take charge of the resistance with some success. But in 1431 the Castilians defeated the Nasrid army, thus annihilating their attempts at defence. This led to internal conflict which developed into a real civil war between leaders of bands and various groups seeking to draw some advantage from the extremely unsettled situation. A ruler did emerge from this muddle, in the person of Abu l-Hasan Ali, called 'Moulay Hasan', to whom the Kingdom of Granada owed its last period of brilliance. After his reign, the Nasrid family fought among itself again; in 1482 Muhammad, the son of Moulay Hasan, known in the West as Boabdil, revolted against his father and his uncle Zagal and went so far as to solicit the help of the Christian kings. This

The Castilians' victory. In Higueruela, the remains of the Na͡srid army tries to reassemble in the castle courtyard. (Anonymous fresco, fifteenth century; Madrid, Escorial.)

was what is called the 'War of Granada', which served the *Reconquistà* because the opponents paid more attention to their own quarrels than to the Christians' advance. The towns passed one after the other into their hands; Loja (1486), Malaga (1487), Guadix and Almeria (1489) and finally, after a long siege, Granada, defended by Boabdil, fell on 2 January 1492: a fall which signified the end of the Nasrid Kingdom.

It is understandable that very little was achieved under such difficult conditions. The number of new buildings was very small, and such as there were had no innovatory features, displaying instead decadent ornamental decoration. Such alterations as were made to the Palace of the Alhambra consisted of platforms for cannon.

In spite of events, the local population continued to engage in a fairly active economic life, and when the Spaniards invaded they did not find a country in ruins. However the Christian conquest was not accepted by all the inhabitants; although the great majority of them stayed put, others emigrated to North Africa, especially to Morocco and Tunisia, where they formed distinct groups of 'Andalusians', who were eventually joined by other exiles.

368   The conquest of the Kingdom of Granada by the Spanish Christian kings was one of the

Baptising the Moors. The victors forced the Muslims to chose between expulsion and conversion and the majority submitted unwillingly to the latter expedient. (A bas-relief on Philip Vigarny's altar, 1520; Granada, Royal Chapel.)

rare occasions when Mediterranean Europe enlarged its territory. Their success encouraged Spaniards and Portuguese to cross the Straits of Gibraltar and to try to establish themselves in Algeria and Tunisia. There they came up against the Ottomans, who ended up dominating the whole area. Their only real achievement was that of uniting Spain – after two centuries of effort.

A new Morocco?

The Christian kings of Castile and Portugal were encouraged by their successes in Spain to extend their action into African territory and to occupy bases in western Maghrib, partly in order to prevent an eventual new invasion, and partly in order to fight North African piracy, which was then very active.

These aims, together with the anarchy reigning in the Maghrib, led Henry III, King of Castile, to seize Tetuan (1399), but he was driven out by a violent local rising. Somewhat later, the Portuguese took Ceuta (1415). In 1420 a civil war broke out on the death of the Merinid Sultan Abu Sa'id Uthman which resulted in a Merinid group taking over the power. These were the *Banu Wattas* (or Wattasids) who were established in eastern Morocco and in the Rif, whose chief Abu Zakariya became the real head of the Merinid government in the name of a helpless young Sultan. Until 1458, The Wattasids ruled Morocco in this way, successfully resisting attacks by the Portuguese (on Tangiers, even

369

retaking Ceuta in 1437), as well as a revival of Muslim fanaticism. The Christian offensive had elicited a strong Muslim religious movement aimed at buying back prisoners, but which was slowly transformed, in part into a spirit of Holy War and in part into a mainly mystical fervor called sufism, involving the veneration of local saints or *marabouts* and the creation of little centres of mysticism, the *zawiya*. The Merinids initially tried to limit this movement by favouring traditional Islam as taught by the *ulamas* and by building more *madrasas*, places for orthodox Koranic instruction. As their rule grew weaker, their policy was disrupted, and more and more people came to the *zawiya*, among which two centres or confraternities emerged, one based on the eastern mysticism of Abd al-Kadir al-Jilani (eleventh century), the other on a western mystic, Muhammad al-Jazuli (fifteenth century).

The Wattasids made use of this religious trend against the Portuguese and were comforted by the discovery in 1437 of the tomb of Moulay Idris, the founder of Fez. However this discovery encouraged the *shurfa* (plural of *sharif*) to emerge, who were more or less genuine descendants of Idris, and so of the Prophet Muhammad. Starting in 1458, a new period of anarchy and even of civil war broke out in Morocco, from which the Portuguese profited to take Ksar al-Saghir, near to Ceuta (1458) and to try to capture Tangiers, but in vain.

The last Wattasid ruler, Abd al-Haqq, was assassinated in 1465, after having arranged for Al-Jazuli to be killed – a *sharif* and mystic *imam* who was particularly popular in the region of the northern Atlas. Another Wattasid, Muhammad al-Shaykh, proclaimed himself the Sultan's successor, but he was unable to impose his authority outside the region of Fez. This situation enabled the Portuguese to take Arzila and Tangiers (1471) and the Castilians secured the monopoly of trade with the African coast. In 1520 they held the whole Atlantic coast of central Morocco by means of strongholds (*frontieras*) which, however, did not enable them to extend their control very far inland, apart from a few raids. The Spaniards seized Melilla in 1497, a place from which they could observe the Moroccan situation.

This situation was to develop considerably during the first half of the sixteenth century; in the south a tribe appeared consisting of a confraternity, the Banu Sa'ad (Saadians) who proclaimed themselves descendants of the Prophet, and so *shurfa*. They established themselves in the Sus, at Tarunda (1509) and then occupied Marrakesh (1525). From there they began their offensive against the Wattasids of Fez and against the Portuguese.

Although Europe had penetrated the western Maghrib by means of Portuguese and Spanish expeditions, and although the Christians did get hold of a few places, their offensive cannot be called worth-while. It allowed the Spanish to launch further attacks, but in the long run, it awoke a religious not to say national reaction in the North African populations, which was exploited by the Saadians and after them the Alawids. The presence of the Turks on their eastern frontiers further served to stress the Moroccans' isolation and so endowed the Moroccan State as geographically delimited with ever-greater reality; a State whose national identity was to grow stronger with time. The Morocco we know today is the result of this period from the fifteenth to the sixteenth centuries.

The soft underbelly of the Maghrib

After the reign of Abu Hammu II (1359–89), the Abd al-Wadid sovereigns had to cope with ever greater problems, as much on the internal level as on the external level. In the course of the fifteenth century, the Sultans of Tlemcen were obliged to abandon their capital on several occasions, due to palace intrigues, plots hatched by high functionaries and by the occasional deep-seated disturbance, to seek refuge with nomadic tribes. The Merinids took advantage of the situation to try to impose one of their candidates on Tlemcen and to turn this region into a vassal State. Their attempt failed since they had serious problems of their own to deal with; the Abd al-Wadid State had a tendency to split up into numerous territories, especially in the south and in mountainous regions, while their ports turned themselves into independent 'republics' who relied on piracy, both to ensure the life of their port and as a means of expressing their religious hostility to the Christian enterprises. The disappearance of the Nasrid Kingdom of Granada meant that many Andalusians came and settled there and encouraged this hostility by giving a new lease of life to piracy. The revolt of the Muslims in the mountainous region of Granada in 1501 was considered by the Spaniards to have been instigated by the North Africans and it incited them to intervene more energetically on African soil in order to reduce this danger.

This was how the Spaniards seized Mars al-Kabir in 1505, and then the Peñon of Velez (1508), Oran (1509), Bougie (1510) and the Peñon of Algiers, where they set up garrisons (*presidios*) whose authority did not extend beyond their walls. Nonetheless, the Spaniards controlled the greater part of the coast of the central Maghrib. At this point, the Algerians appealed to the Turkish corsairs to free them from the Spanish stranglehold. These corsairs, Aruj and Khayreddin Barbarossa, intervened, and from then on the coastal towns became stakes fought over by Spaniards and Turks. Inland, the region of Tlemcen was conquered by Turks (1515–17) who subsequently also interfered in the affairs of eastern Morocco. The following decades were marked essentially by the rivalry between Spaniards and Turks, who occupied the whole of central Maghrib, except for Oran and Mars al-Kabir.

After the invasion of Ifriqiya by Merinid Abu Inan (1352–8), which had no lasting effect, unity was restored only under Abu l-Abbas (1370–94). His son Abu Faris (1394–1434) carried on his work in the interior. He was however more interested in his neighbours to the East and intervened among the Abd al-Wadids of Tlemcen, in Morocco and even in Andalusia. He was a very strict ruler and also a very devout and pious Muslim, which endeared him to his people, whom he freed from all non-Koranic taxes, and to religious circles to whom he granted many favours. Furthermore, he encouraged piracy with enthusiasm, considering it a just and meritorious enterprise against the Christian powers.

His grandson Uthman (1435–8) tried to follow in his footsteps; he succeeded in religious matters but was unable to prevent struggles between members of the Hafsid family and revolts in the Arab tribes of the south from breaking out on various occasions. He nominated governors (*qaid*) from among his freed slaves to rule the country, as his grandfather Abu Faris had done. But when some of them showed a tendency towards independence, he gradually replaced them with members of his family, some of whom took   371 the opportunity to rebel. Uthman also imposed his sovereignty over the Sultans of Tlemcen and even, for a moment, over the Wattasids of Fez. These successes gave Ifriqiya the appearance of being the most secure and well-governed State in the Maghrib.

But his successors proved themselves incapable of pursuing the same policy: Abu Abdallah Muhammad (1494–1526) could not stop the Arab revolts nor prevent the Spaniards from seizing Bougie and Tripoli in 1520. The situation under Abu l-Hasan became even more dramatic (1526–43), since he was no more than a pawn in a game played between Khayreddin Barbarossa and Charles V.

Turks or Spaniards?

Since the middle of the fifteenth century, following the failure of the Varna Crusade and the capture of Constantinople, the Christian world of the West had been confronted by the Ottoman Turks in Central Europe and the Balkans. It seemed then as if they had reached the furthest limits of their expansion into these regions, the more so since they seemed to be concentrating on the shores of the Black Sea and on eastern Asia Minor.

Over and above their military operations on land, however, the Ottoman corsairs did not refrain from making incursions into the western Mediterranean. This was how one of them, Kemal Re'is, uncle to the famous Piri Re'is, raided the eastern shores of Spain and those of the Maghrib before 1495. Piri Re'is refers to this several times in his *Kitab-i Bahriya* (Book of Nautical Instructions). Equally certain is the fact that, in the very first years of the sixteenth century, the Barbarossa brothers also made a few successful sallies along these lines. Although they acted for the Ottomans, these were nonetheless individual initiatives. We may consider to what extent they were responsible for arousing in the Portuguese and especially the Spaniards – borne along by the euphoria of conquering the whole of Muslim Andalusia – the desire to drive this danger as far away as possible; for instance, by occupying the principal ports of the Maghrib, from Morocco to Tripolitania, which were also bases for North African corsairs. Spanish designs on Algiers incited the Algerians to appeal to Aruj Barbarossa, a notorious pirate with the added attraction of being a Muslim. He took advantage of this appeal to get total control over first Algiers and then the greater part of north-west Algeria.

The situation was modified a little later, when the Ottomans had conquered Syria and Egypt (1516–17) and when, in 1518–19, Khayreddin Barbarossa, Algiers' new master, put himself under the direct command of Sultan Selim I. He thus created the military province of Algeria, termed *ojak*, of which he was made governor (*beylerbey*) by the Sultan, who sent him reinforcements in men and equipment. This allowed him, after a few failures, to strengthen his authority over western Algeria. But eastern Algeria and Ifriqiya still escaped him; the weakness of the Hafsids meant that the latter was a potential base for rival Spanish and Ottoman operations. They fought out their rivalry during the following decades along two fronts; western Algeria, where the Spanish ended up keeping only Oran and Mars al-Kabir (1563) and the Jerba-Tripoli region, where the Turkish corsair Tugut (the Dragut of Western sources) operated with especial brilliance.

By the sixteenth century it was clear that the opposition to Christian encroachment in Morocco, and that the extension of Ottoman control over the Nile and the central Maghrib, were no longer merely political phenomena devoid of a religious dimension. Europeans were driven to employ means other than those provided by normal terrestrial warfare in order to penetrate the African continent – and even to seek out routes around Mameluke or Turkish Egypt. By so doing, they were suddenly confronted with immense new worlds.

The black world and its promises

Black Africa, in the Sudan and elsewhere, has been inhabited for millennia, and is generally agreed to have been the cradle of mankind. Glimpses of its continuous history have however been visible only since the tenth century, in the West at least, in the sources and records which began to be drawn up then. Among these are descriptions of Africa by Muslim geographers, or accounts by Arab travellers who, along with many others, had crossed the Sahara and had visited the edges of the Sahel and the Sudan. Liturgical or holy accounts have also been transmitted, sometimes through many centuries, by traditional story-tellers in certain ethnic groups (the Malinke and Soninke); there are the medieval ruins of famous agglomerations (Awdoghast and Kumbi-Salih in Mauritania and Niani in Guinea) or of villages (in the Senegal valley) which have recently been dug up. The civilisation of the Sahel steppes and of the savannas, from the Senegal to Chad, is slowly beginning to emerge from these accounts, in spite of much conjecture and hypothesis. If we look at this civilisation at the end of the Middle Ages, when the Europeans were about to appear on the scene, we see it at the height of its secular development, the result of the progressive taming of the soil, the more effective organisation of society and power, and the still marginal but fruitful confrontation of the old civilisation of black Africa with the material and cultural contributions of the Mediterranean worlds, starting with Islam.

The adolescence of central Africa

The first thing we know for certain from archaeological discoveries is that trans-Saharan Africa's command over the basic skills of material existence (agriculture, manufacture and commerce) had served to support a very elaborate form of social, political and religious life – a civilisation in the deepest sense of the word.

Although the climate of Africa had been deteriorating for several millennia, it still allowed settlement along the edge of the Sahel, thanks to a brief climatic improvement in the eleventh to fourteenth centuries, when these regions appear to have been blessed with rainfall and with a landscape similar to landscapes now found between 200 and 400 kilometres further south (for instance, between 400 to 500 mm of rain per annum fell in southern Mauritania in the eleventh to thirteenth centuries, as compared with 200 or 250 mm nowadays). Over the centuries, human settlements gradually covered this country-side, which was then considerably more hospitable than it is today, so that by the fourteenth to fifteenth centuries, the distribution of the population was less disjointed and

373

denser than before. This was the result of migrations mostly towards the south in order to escape from their ancient northern territories, where the desert was encroaching more and more. All these groups, most of which had held for generations the ethnic characteristics – languages, customs, social structures and mythology, even the names – which they still possess (Soninke, Malinke, Serer, Peul, Songhay, Mossi and many others), spread out over the vast areas of the Savanna and the Sahel, a process accompanied by recurring confrontations which are far from resolved in our generation. The Wolof (in the north) and the Serer (in the middle) have divided present day Senegal between them since the twelfth to thirteenth centuries, the south being occupied by a patchwork collection of ethnic groups which follows the coastline as far as Liberia. The Soninke dominated what were then the greenest steppes of southern Mauritania around Kumbi-Salih, but war (notably Almoravid aggression) and catastrophic periods of drought or the spirit of adventure scattered several of their clans eastwards towards the loop of the Niger and south-westwards towards the central valley of the Senegal. The Malinke came from the north (from Wagadu, according to oral tradition) and before the thirteenth century, they had colonised the upper valley of the Niger, upstream from what today is Bamako, and the hills south of· this town, which dominated the western bank of the river. The political disturbances of the thirteenth century drove many of them southwards either as fugitives or as conquerors (to present-day Upper Guinea) or westwards (to the upper course of the Gambia). Some may even have settled in the Kong region and as far as the cliffs of Bandiagra from that date – in any case from before 1500 – where some groups, which started out from the Mande, are supposed to have elaborated the extraordinary Dogon civilisation. On the eastern flank of the primitive Malinke homelands, the Bambara had begun their peaceful colonisation of lands along the Bagoé and Baulé rivers since the twelfth to thirteenth centuries, coming either from the south-east, or from Wagadu in the north-east. Further east, the Bozo, the Sorko and the Songhay had settled in successive stages along the Niger, while the Mossi had encroached into the immense area within the curve of the river between the thirteenth and the fifteenth centuries. The Peul, on their side, after having been progressively driven back by drought towards southern Mauritania, had begun their migrations in the thirteenth century. They settled in groups in the eleventh to fourteenth centuries in full Malinke territory, and by the fifteenth century they were installed in Macina (south-west of Timbuktu) and in the mountains of Futa-Jallon. In the sixteenth century they imposed themselves by force on Futa Toro, the middle valley of the Senegal. This was not the end of nomadism; many Peul clans followed their flocks around and were content with less fertile land. As well as this, all the Sudan kingdoms had to contain pressure from the nomadic Berbers of the Sahara along their Sahel borders. From then on, however, black African societies were massively village-based.

During the twelfth to fourteenth centuries, the no man's lands dividing the ethnic groups from one another were gradually whittled down and although the great valleys of the Senegal, the Niger and the Gambia, the old agrarian centres (the inner delta of the Niger) and the principal trading centres (Ghana) remained more attractive and more populated, in those days the cultivated areas also extended over mountains of southern

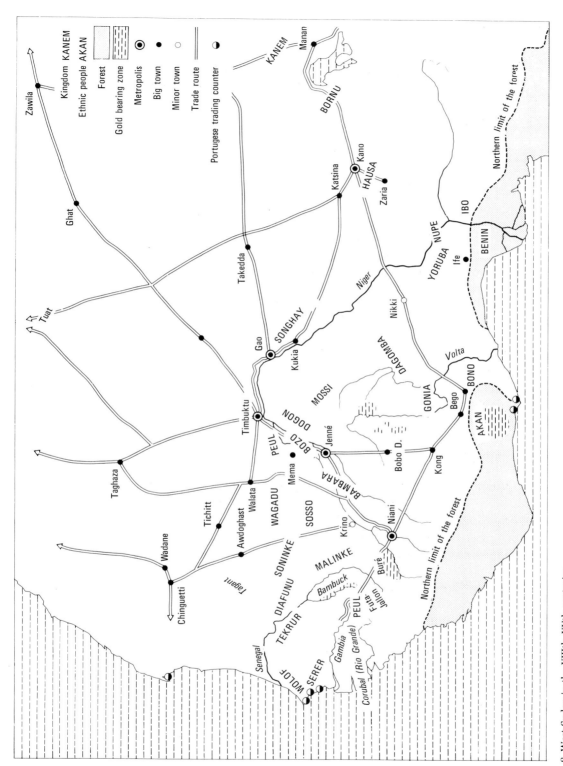

8 West Sudan in the XIIIth–XVth centuries

Legend:
- Kingdom KANEM
- Ethnic people AKAN
- Forest
- Gold bearing zone
- ◉ Metropolis
- ● Big town
- ○ Minor town
- — Trade route
- ◑ Portugese trading counter

Zawila
Ghat
Tuat
Takedda
KANEM
Manan
BORNU
Kano
HAUSA
Katsina
Zaria
NUPE
IBO
YORUBA
Ife
BENIN
Northern limit of the forest
Niger
Nikki
SONGHAY
Gao
Kukia
DAGOMBA
Volta
BONO
MOSSI
GONJA
Bego
AKAN
DOGON
Timbuktu
BOZO
PEUL
Jenné
Bobo D.
Kong
Taghaza
BAMBARA
Mema
WAGADU
SOSSO
Niani
Walata
Tichitt
Awdoghast
Krino
Wadane
Tagant
SONINKE
MALINKE
Buré
Chinguetti
DIAFUNU
Bambuck
TEKRUR
PEUL
Futa
Jalon
SERER
Senegal
Gambia (Rio Grande)
WOLOF
Corubal (Rio Grande)
Northern limit of the forest

Mauritania, which are now abandoned to nomads and the desert (Tagant, Affolle), over the now infertile steppes of the Maritania–Mali borderland, as well as over many hills and savannas wrested from the wild. Between the Atlantic and the Niger, the areas of untouched bushland seemed much smaller than before. Systematic surveys of ancient habitats allow the density of the populations of Yatenga (Upper Volta) in the twelfth to fifteenth centuries to be reckoned at about fifteen inhabitants to the square kilometre. In the Mema plain, south-west of Timbuktu, which is nowadays deserted, 280 ancient sites have been spotted and 404 around Jenne.

So from the tenth to fourteenth centuries, African life styles changed. Certain ethnic groups still concentrated exclusively, or nearly so, on fishing, such as the Bozo or the Sorko of the Niger. Hunting was still practised and conferred great prestige on the best huntsmen, who were the Simbo masters of the Malinke lands. The general practice of stockraising, which was so widespread in the Sahara of prehistory, had been steadily continued by the Peul, who lived from it, and countless sedentary groups kept cattle, goats, pigs and chickens. But since the tenth century, in the North Cameroons, around Jenne and elsewhere, agriculture was almost everywhere the main source of food. Bambara, Malinke, Serer, Wolof, Songhay and all the great ethnic groups were formed by peasants. As today, priority was everywhere given to one cereal, millet, or to its variant sorghum, which were both sown broad-cast, and these cereals apparently already supplied the basic daily dish. Attempts at crop rotation, the use of iron in tools such as hoes, the use of flood areas and strips of silt along river banks (a proceeding improved on by the Songhay in the fifteenth century), more systematic irrigation around certain points of the rivers, allowed production to be varied and eventually intensified. Rice was grown in flooded fields in the inner delta of the Niger and in the plains and swamps from the Corubal to the Volta. Products such as kidney beans and a variety of green vegetables (onions, garlic, aubergines, cucumbers, watermelons) were common in some areas (e.g. Senegal). In spite of the persistence of archaic agrarian techniques which knew nothing either of harness or of fertiliser, agriculture managed to feed the peasant world, except in periods of exceptional drought, and it even provided sufficient surpluses to allow crafts to flourish. We know about these artisans from travellers' accounts and from archaeology. In a larger sense, they formed only one element in a complex society of non-productive persons supported by agriculture, which we will examine shortly.

Peasant demand stimulated these crafts, which were sometimes derived from very ancient traditions, to become more diversified. Clay, leather and wood were the traditional materials from which the objects of daily use were made (vessels, clothes, quivers, house posts, dishes, and religious objects) but with Islam came the fashion, or the obligation, to wear woven clothes. Cotton is known to have been planted since the eleventh century (Senegal valley) and the weaving profession was no longer a rarity by the fourteenth century. The use of metals expanded rapidly: copper, the traditional metal for jewelry and ritual dowry ornaments, had long been made by a complex metallurgic process, and used in pure form or as a bronze alloy (Awdoghast in the tenth to eleventh centuries) and seen in admirable art forms – for instance the Ife brass heads in the thirteenth century. Iron had

Ropes of shells or cowries (left) were used as money for a long time in African societies, especially in West Africa. In the Ivory Coast, looms (right) are still used for weaving long strips of material which are then sewn together.

been known in Africa several centuries before our era, and it became more common from about the tenth century. Remains of furnaces can be found close to the ruins of even small villages (e.g. in the middle valley of the Senegal from the tenth to thirteenth centuries) and weapons such as spears, arrows and harpoons were generally made in iron and worked with remarkable skill. Some jewelry was also made in iron – arm and ankle rings – and by the tenth century, iron began to be used in agricultural tools. This was when the production of African gold, the gold which bewitched Europe, was stepped up (in the gold mines of Bambuk, of Buré, close to the Volta – Poura –, to Bito, and still further south in the fifteenth century) and was worked on the spot by goldsmiths attached to the forges. It was probably the most talented among them, close to royal courts, who turned out those elaborate jewels in their thousands which embellished the ruler, his wives and concubines, his *griots*, his heralds, his knights and palaces and which so forcibly impressed the visitors to and subjects of the famous court of Mali in the fourteenth century.

African craftsmen and peasants did not work only for local markets. Along the Senegal and in the Jenne region, bush markets, which are recorded for the fifteenth century, allowed peasants to exchange their produce for salt fish, cloth and other objects manufactured locally. But dug-out canoes on the rivers and stable pathways across the bush opened up the whole of the black world to the produce of these villages. The activity of professional pedlars, who were either Malinke – the Wangara (recorded in the thirteenth century) – or Hausa (fifteenth century), and the introduction of money (such as cowries in

377

This village furnace is to be found in the Ivory Coast near Korogho, where ancient metal-working skills are still preserved, as in many regions of black Africa.

Mali in the fourteenth century) and of many initiatives and mechanisms, stimulated and regulated such exchanges, directing and amplifying them on an inter-regional scale. Rice was transported from the Gambia to the interior, millet brought from the interior to the Niger fed Timbuktu and even Walata, and cola-nuts from the forests reached as far up as Jenne.

Animism and its associations

Like its economy, traditional black society at that time seems to have been greatly diversified, and even complex, because its hierarchy was founded on family, religious and military origins as much as on economic ones.

The first level in the hierarchy normally corresponded to the artisans whose work we discussed above, because in those days, and probably since long ago, they had given rise to professions. Within the various ethnic groups, although most of their people adopted the occupation proper to each group – stock raising for the Peul, fishing for the Bozo, agriculture for the others – some individuals and their families, the *nyamakala* (a Malinke term) among them, adopted complementary and indispensable occupations in a permanent, hereditary and professional manner. According to the traditionists, these professions were clearly circumscribed from then on. The smiths were masters of iron, gold and copper while their wives made pots. Other craftsmen worked leather, others wood.

Fishing was a trade. One particular function proper to certain ethnic groups in the black world (e.g. the Soninke and the Malinke) was performed by the *griots* (*dyali* in Malinke). These 'masters of words' were simultaneously poets, genealogists, chroniclers and messengers who were attached to great families on a hereditary basis to serve them as heralds and as living archives. Another, somewhat different professional group consisted of the Malinke traders mentioned above (the Wangara): their activity was professional in the full sense of the word, but involved no constraint or social subjection at all.

While these might have remained straightforward professional groups, they were in fact inserted into a larger social hierarchy, which defined each person's position and rank – a complicated, constricting and permanent hierarchy, which was accepted by all. The bottom of the social ladder was occupied by captives or domestic slaves whose existence, recorded in the seventh century, probably goes back far in time. They had been numerous in Ghana since before the eleventh century (one oral tradition provides the possibly symbolic number of 404 clans of slaves). They were also numerous in Malinke country and among the Wolof in the thirteenth to fifteenth centuries, and were settled in whole villages in the Songhay Empire in the fifteenth century. Their condition was hereditary, except for enfranchisement, and their master, to whom they were closely tied, employed them commonly in domestic or agricultural work (the Songhay and Wolof), less often in crafts or in the mines (such as in the copper mines at Takkeda). The origin of their subjection was frequently tragic – wars and raids – and their condition was precarious; sales, legacies and gifts of slaves were common daily occurrences. In Mali, for instance, their fate was made more tolerable in the peaceful atmosphere of the villages. The fate of the kings' captives was profoundly transformed by their situation in the courts, where they participated brilliantly in the feasts and were enrolled in the army, where some of them acceded to the highest ranks and on two occasions even to the supreme power. No such thing happened in Songhay, but there too, the subjection of the rural slaves was attenuated. It could happen that families and even villages reduced to servitude were transplanted without being broken up and that their obligations were defined, and so limited, by custom.

Without suffering the same lack of status, the craftsmen and *griots* were also badly integrated socially. Their groups were made up of castes, which were sometimes feared – smiths and *griots* were in league with spirits and their knowledge was redoubtable – and were always despised and separated by taboos. They could not marry out of caste. People refused to serve under their orders; tradition tells that this was the unanimous attitude of the Malinke chiefs in the thirteenth century, to whom the king–smith of Sosso, Sumaoro, proposed an alliance against their neighbouring slavers. There could be no question of such a thing. However, consideration and familiarity generally tempered the disdain with which these powerful, prestigious and close people, masters of forges and words, were treated. The *griots* of powerful men and kings were overwhelmed with presents and wives, they lived in opulence and their notoriety eclipsed even that of their rulers (e.g. in Mali in the fourteenth century). In the same way, the technical and economic thrust of iron and gold was strong enough among the Soninke in the thirteenth century to make one of their smiths king.

Free persons were also allotted their place in the community by the hierarchical   **379** structure of society. Just as today, the family provided the child's first social environment and education – around the mother especially, because polygamy seems to have been the norm, in powerful families at least. At the beginning of the thirteenth century in Malinke country, the young Sundiata lived and grew up with his mother, under the sufferance of his father's first wife (according to oral tradition). The conjugal family was only a ramification of lineage. By insisting, in Sundiata's case, on the instruction he received from his mother, Sogolon, and on her totems, the custodians of the past emphasised the strength of his maternal ancestors as well as his paternal blood. In their renderings of the story, however, they did give first place to the clans, the collections of lineages through the male descendants of a common ancestor (although there were certainly matrilineages too, for instance among the Serer). From the tenth to the fifteenth centuries, the clans, each with its own name, did indeed form the basic structure of ethnic groups such as the Soninke with its 44 clans, the Malinke (33 clans) and the Peul (12 clans and then 4, from the thirteenth century onwards, according to oral tradition). Each clan had its own form of worship, its territory and its chief. The social importance of each member was defined according to his position within his lineage and, more strongly, within his clan. The young, the unmarried, and the clumsy were inferior to Simbo master huntsmen, the initiated, the elderly and the wise. These held the power: each lineage had its chief, each clan its *mansa* and its council; they owned the gold and enjoyed many wives (according to oral tradition in Mali in the thirteenth century). However, a pecking order was already being established among the clans, according to their history or their totem and the chiefs of the most illustrious clans – among the Malinke, for instance, the Keita with their triple totem: lion, buffalo and panther – enjoyed still greater authority within the ethnic group.

This black society was of course imbued with religion. It was totally animist until the eleventh century and was still mainly so in the fourteenth to fifteenth centuries, which meant that the beliefs and the practices of the animist world still profoundly impregnated those centres where Islam had taken hold between the eleventh and fifteenth centuries. Certain traits of these beliefs and these medieval practices can be glimpsed among the Soninke and the Malinke. *Genii loci* (such as wells, sources and trees) or wandering spirits (gusts of warm air, will-o'-the-wisps) animated the world. Some of them were associated with animals (vultures or hyenas) or assumed animal forms (snakes). They could be conciliated by certain objects such as drums and altars, talismans and practices; certain skilful magicians, male or female, who were capable of taming animals and objects and even of assuming their forms, acquired considerable power. Ancestor worship was also general, and their spirits sometimes survived in objects which gave rise to feasts and libations. It seems that some famous secret societies, like the *Komo* among the Malinke, have their roots in this distant period. Religion, so deeply rooted in the land and so tied to ancestors, was the strongest bond between the many forms of association in which each had his place. Houses had their fetishes as did villages. The supernatural powers of their chief magicians guaranteed the survival of a lineage or a clan in the midst of perils, the worst of which came from the spirits. Within the ethnic group, each member was able to take part in the seances of the initiation societies or to attend public liturgies dedicated to

This moving funerary sculpture of a chief is far removed from the abstract geometrical current of African art, but its naturalism should not conceal its religious significance. (Stone, from Sierra Leone, thirteenth to fifteenth centuries.)

ancestors or tribal spirits. Everybody was exalted when the story of their common origins was recited either straightforwardly (*kokoro* in Malinke) or veiled in mythology (*maana*). Finally, the sacred and magic powers which were conferred on the monarchs of the first animist states (Kanem, Ghana, Sosso and Mali) were the basis of their authority and their ascendancy. The people of Kanem saw their king as a divine being from whom life, death, health and illness emanated. The king did not feed himself, it was said. Those who came across the caravans which brought his supplies were killed on the spot (eleventh century). The same divine aura emanated from the Emperor of Ghana and guaranteed him the same protection. A sacred serpent, emerging from a pit, was closely linked with the destiny of the ruler, who chose that this should be so (prior to the eleventh century). Sumaoro Kante, King of Sosso was reputedly invulnerable. His upbringing, it is said, was undertaken alternately by his mother and by a fairy; he could see things from far away (thirteenth century). Sundiata, the founder of Mali in the thirteenth century, was the incarnation of a supernatural power; he was protected by powerful *genii*; he disposed of sacred objects – the platform for great ceremonies (*bambe*), a staff, clothes and secret thaumaturgical objects – which maintained this power (according to oral tradition).

Islam undertakes the conquest of black Africa

Despite the hostile immensity of the Saharan frontier, reports and echoes of the brilliant Mediterranean civilisations soon made their way across the desert to the shores of the Niger and the Senegal. Men, merchandise and ideas crossed the Sahara early on and mingled with the black world, sometimes profoundly altering its civilisations and destiny. All these influences, or most of them, were derived from Muslim lands, or were transmitted by them,   381 as is well proven by the interest so many Muslim geographers and travellers since the seventh century took in the Sudan.

Crossing the desert

This was initially on account of trade. Soon after they were formed, the young countries of the Maghrib paid attention to this mysterious trans-Saharan world. Merchants ventured into it: they arranged itineraries dotted with wells and stages, which were stable enough to be described in writing by al Bakri (in the eleventh century). By the thirteenth to fifteenth centuries, camel caravans navigated the sands at established times with monotonous regularity. These crossings were indispensable to both sides, since they served to link them closely with one another, as their complementary merchandise was transported to and fro. Islam amassed leather, musk, feathers, ivory and spices for herself and her neighbours, notably the Christian world. Slaves and gold, however, had absolute priority. Black slaves were found everywhere in the Middle East, where they filled the armies, the shops, the dwellings and harems of Islam, and the first cargoes of black captives began to be unloaded in Sicily in the thirteenth century and then in Spain and Portugal in the fifteenth. As for gold, the growing monetary needs of the Muslim and the western States sharpened the importers' acquisitive urge. For its part, the black world demanded various luxurious objects and ornaments which it did not produce – clothes, delicate foods, art work – for its elite of kings, princes and merchants. Horses were needed for the kings' cavalries, the new strategic weapon of the thirteenth century. Copper and some plain cloths were lacking, and salt even more so – that essential condiment, which was found only along the coast and in great Saharan salt mines controlled by the powers and merchants of the Maghrib.

Thus over the centuries a solid network of routes developed across the Sahara. They were not all active at the same time, but their potential was enormous and they made it possible to penetrate all parts of the Sahara by the end of the Middle Ages. In the north, great caravans were assembled in Sijilmasa (western Morocco), in Wargla and Ghadames where men and merchandise from Fez, Tlemcen, Tunis, Kairouan, Tripoli and the whole of the Maghrib converged. Further east, other convoys set out from Cairo, the crossroads to the Sudan for the whole Muslim East. On the way, other Saharan centres developed as indispensable watering points: Zawila (Fezzan) to the east, an international transit point for the slave trade; the Oasis of Tuat in the middle, animated by active Jewish colonies; Taghaza to the west, a rich salt mine where camels were loaded with blocks of salt which they carried as far as Timbuktu; Takedda to the south, the centre for extracting and smelting copper. Once the desert had been crossed and the fringes of the Sahel had appeared with the first scrub trees, a cordon of 'ports' emerged at the end of the Sahara routes in the country of the black men. Merchandise was stored and exchanged in these places; men and animals could rest there; the return freight waiting in the warehouses was wrapped up there. They were also places where black slaves were parked in temporary enclosures before being sorted out and sent off again. The two most active 'ports' in the fourteenth and fifteenth centuries were Gao, a venerable city dating from before the ninth century, and

Timbuktu, a recently established town in full growth, first mentioned by Arab writers in the fourteenth century. As well as these, there was a whole range of towns from east to west from one end of the Sahel to the other: Tichitt and Walata in South Mauritania, Kukia down-stream from Gao, Kano and the Hausa towns, and the royal cities of Kanem and Bornu, near Lake Chad, Timbuktu and Gao owed their supremacy to the activity of the routes they controlled: the western routes through Awdoghast and Ghana, which had flourished in the tenth to thirteenth centuries, were now in decline (before their revival at the end of the fifteenth century with the Portuguese trade). This had benefited the central trans-Saharan connections and the most recently established route which led directly from the loop of the Niger to Cairo (fourteenth century).

This network of routes did not stop at the Sahel centres where they emerged after crossing the desert. In the fourteenth and fifteenth centuries they plunged deeply into the land of the black men by following old regional pathways. This was how the southern centres of Kong and Bobo were linked through Timbuktu, Jenne and Niani (the capital of Mali), and how Gambia and the Futa-Jallon were linked through Niani to the worlds of the Maghrib and the Mediterranean. Far away as they were, the savanna lands (the Ivory Coast and northern Ghana) and the forest lands (the Akan and Ashanti people and the Futa-Jallon) were penetrated by a long-distance trade from remote horizons. A profitable opening, which offered these lands a market for their cola-nuts, their ivory and their gold – but also a dangerous one, because it was among these 'Lam-Lam' pagans so despised by the Islamised peoples of the Sahel and the Savanna that the eastern slave trade was established and supplied.

From the Maghrib to the towns of the Sahel, the trans-Saharan trade was conducted by Muslim traders – Arabs, Berbers, even Egyptians – and only by them. There were no Europeans and very few black Africans. Everything passed through the hands of these intermediaries: salt, gold, slaves. Their field of action stopped in principle at the boundaries of the black African countries, and once they had reached the Sahel entrepots, their merchandise was transferred to Wangara or Hausa merchants, who sorted it out and traded it in the interior of the Sudan. In spite of this, the foreign merchants had an extremely stimulating effect in many ways on the black world.

Firstly on their trade. Arab merchants were very well acquainted with commercial skills, which they employed in the Sahara as they did elsewhere, and these they taught to the black merchants. They then formed societies or confraternities whose members spread out from their centre (Sijilmasa among others) to the principal caravan stops. They made extensive use of credit arrangements – a credit note for 42,000 dinars was signed at Awdoghast in the tenth century. They introduced specialisation on a large scale – in the fourteenth century there were businesses which traded solely in slaves. The whole of the economy of the Sudan – agriculture, trade and the extraction of gold – was stimulated from the tenth century onwards by these merchants' activity and techniques and by their ceaseless forward advance.

In more general terms, their profession led them to know the world of the Sudan thoroughly. From very early on (eleventh century), some of them, on their own or with

383

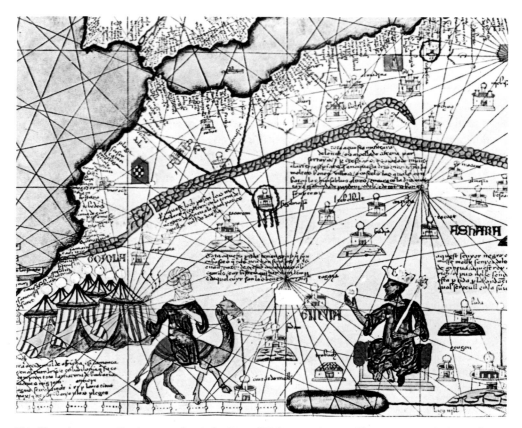

This fifteenth-century Catalan map shows the King of Mali presenting a gold nugget to an Arab merchant. Although some of the details are imaginary (the river is supposed to be a branch of the Nile) these maps were more accurate in other ways, showing for instance how dense urban settlement in the area was then. They were drawn up according to Arab travellers' accounts.

caravans, ventured as far as the gold sources. Many more were induced by their business to settle there permanently. In the fourteenth to fifteenth centuries their communities, which were often very prosperous, enlivened all the great black townships of the Sahel, where they lived in special quarters (at Walata, Timbuktu and Gao). They were also to be found in the smallest settlements and, trailing off to the south, as far away as Niani, the capital of Mali. They developed ties with the black population and intermarried. Subsequent generations of black populations were more susceptible to the properly Muslim tastes and ideas they brought with them. Arab eating manners and fashions in clothes were widespread – as well as everyday and artistic objects and architectural forms. The most decisive effects of Muslim penetration was however felt on the much more fundamental level of belief and religious practice.

Religion opens the way

Islam, the religion of the white merchants, was early on introduced by them to the black African countries. Once their fervent communities had taken root somewhere, the merchants immediately built mosques, in which the usual officiating team of meuzzins, preachers and the like installed themselves. Recent excavations have uncovered a ninth-century, possibly older, mosque at Kumbi-Salih (Southern Mauritania). Conversions did not start immediately in all cases; white Islam could dwell within the animist world without impinging on it for a long time. This seems to have been the case in the capital of Ghana where, still in the eleventh century, the proximity (within circa 10 kilometres) of a Muslim agglomeration with ten mosques and the presence of Muslim merchants and ministers at the court did not induce the Emperor or his followers to adopt the new religion. However the example and the apostolate of the Muslims did bear fruit. Black Muslims, beginning with the kings, are recorded at Gao in the tenth century, at Tekrur (the middle valley of the Senegal) in the eleventh century, in Mali around the same time, and the first conversions of Soninke in Ghana certainly took place before then (oral tradition speaks of the eighth century).

In the thirteenth to fifteenth centuries Islam had spread over large areas of the Sahel and had infiltrated into the Sudan, not without arousing strong local resistance from the animist centres; Sosso, Upper Gambia and Corubal, the heart of the Songhay country. The Kings of the Sahel States (Mali, Songhay, the Hausa cities and Bornu) along with their followers, their aristocracy, their merchant class and the whole of the urban populations as well as an indeterminate number of village communities, were converted to Islam (Manfara, the first Islamic village of Mali, was converted according to oral tradition in the thirteenth century). This Islam was fervent and structured: a stream of pilgrims was soon directed towards the Holy Places (Mecca), a practice which the Kings of Kanem, and then of Mali, sparked off in the thirteenth century. These repeated contacts with the prestigious heart of the Muslim world enabled ideas, books and literary men from the Maghrib and Egypt to be imported, a trend intensified by the establishment of structures common to Muslim communities within black African countries. Mosques were built in many black African agglomerations, especially since a building campaign had been started in the Empire of Mali by the zealous Mansa Musa on his return from pilgrimage (1324). These mosques were served by Muslim clergy and dignitaries (*ulmas, imans, katib, qadis*) who were frequently black men. These dignitaries were very learned; they knew the Koran and many of them were also deeply engaged in other branches of learning – exegesis (*tafsir*), jurisprudence (*fiqh*), and its interpretation (*hadith*) – either by frequenting *madrasas* in Morocco or even in Timbuktu, an extremely lively intellectual and religious centre in the fourteenth and fifteenth centuries. In certain ethnic groups (the Soninke and Malinke), holy individuals or marabouts (*murabit*), learned men who were missionaries, spiritual masters and qualified professionals, preached early on. Their words and example were effective in spreading the 'True Faith' more widely among the people. These masters met a   **385** real need and five marabout clans of Soninke origin acquired real influence over the Malinke in the thirteenth to fourteenth centuries (oral tradition). This impregnation bore fruit and when Ibn Battuta summed up his impressions from his African journey in 1352–3 he rejoiced in the urban populations' unanimous devotion to the Friday Prayer.

But he also immediately tempered his praises with regretful criticisms. The brilliant achievement of Islam in the fourteenth to fifteenth centuries was indeed in many respects incomplete. In the Wolof kingdoms around Lake Tchad, the countryside adhered massively to animism, a religion strongly tied to their territory, their families and to the local power. Even the courts and the kings neither wished nor were able to eliminate the animist basis of royal liturgies. In Mali, ceremonies included sprinkling dust in front of the king, mask dances, praises by *griots*, in fact all the practices prior to Islam. Naked slaves, young girls and servants, walked the streets of the capital – a shameful sight, before which Ibn Battuta veiled his face. In Songhay, the religion professed by King Sonni Ali in the fifteenth century was very suspect in the eyes of the faithful, who overloaded the King's memory with Islamic precepts. However, these animists survivals did not mean the same thing in all cases. Although, as far as the countryside, which largely underlay urban Islam, was concerned, they were dominant and often unanimous and ineradicable, with the Kings they were a matter of personal conviction and political choice. They were after all supposed to be the depositories and guarantors of the power they held over peoples, who were so deeply steeped in paganism that the accompanying rites and ancestral and magic practices were vitally important to them. Any king who gave them up would be depriving his people and himself of the magic and semi-divine force they conferred – and would be risking serious trouble, as happened in Kanem in the thirteenth century. By the fourteenth century, however, the King who integrated the manifestations of these beliefs into his liturgies no longer made them the pivot of his faith.

To sum up, two well-defined circles became more widely accessible to Islam: the towns and the courts. It was precisely these circles which were drawn, during the twelfth to fifteenth centuries, into the most decisive changes brought about by the dual and strong ascendancy both of the black world and of foreign Islam, to which they proved so receptive.

The towns of Africa and the advance of Islam

Towns formed part of the black world from early on, and they developed precociously in certain cultures. Towards the mouth of the Niger, tenth- and eleventh-century urban sites have been spotted at Yoruba (Ife) and some ninth-century remains in the Ibo Kingdom. The pagan Kanem of the eleventh century had their capital, Manan. Oral traditions testify to agglomerations prior to Islam in ancient Mali (Niani in the eleventh century, Kri and Krina, older still and the beginnings of Jenne which perhaps went back to the fourth century). The Arab geographers recorded the existence of flourishing towns along the Senegal before the local populations were converted (Silla, Tekrur, Barisa in the eleventh century). Contact with Muslims however, followed by the first conversions, the diffusion of Islam in the thirteenth century, and the intensification of trade, gave a new tone to urban civilisation in the Sahel-Sudan area.

Firstly, urbanisation appears to have been accelerated. This did not affect all regions, and the geography of the urban zones remained mobile and capricious. The cordon of towns which had been created in the ninth to eleventh centuries along the western trans-Saharan trade routes in Ghana (Kumbi-Salih), along the Senegal river and at their Sahel crossroads (Awdoghast), declined and was dismantled in the twelfth century. Elsewhere, many apparently more durable agglomerations changed their site several times between the eleventh and the fifteenth centuries (Krina in Mali and Gao). However, taking these geographical readjustments into consideration, which took place each time a commercial life-line shifted, the density of urban settlement did indeed increase between the twelfth and fifteenth centuries. Towns appeared to be more densely scattered along and near to the Niger valley, which from then on served as grain reserve, route and crossroads. The four towns, Niani, Jenne, Timbuktu and Gao were established as the uncontested metropolises of their regions, each with perhaps 20,000 inhabitants (Niani in the fourteenth century) or more (Timbuktu). Their prosperity stimulated and supported the emergence of a constellation of minor agglomerations of uncertain age, which have often been ignored until now. Some of these rose up along the last southern stages of the Saharan routes, like the venerable city of Walata; others were scattered around ill-defined sites in various provinces, where they sheltered the kings' representatives. Others grew up around mines (e.g. Takedda); still more were born near to the Niger. They followed its course (e.g. Krina) and rose up at the valley crossroads and along the great north–south routes (Zaghari, Karsahu, Mema and on the Niani–Walata route). They formed conurbations around certain metropolises (Kabara and Koriume around Timbuktu). Further east, urban constellations grew up in conjunction with the commercial development of the Hausa plateau. To the south, where the great Saharan trade routes carried on into the savanna and the forest, permanent settlements arose, notably those of Kong, Bego and Bono on the Jenne axis – in Akan and Ashanti country (nowadays lower Ghana). All these towns, especially those of the central Sudan, engaged in regular trade and served as so many stages along the same routes. They lived to the same economic rhythm and, in short, constituted the back-bone of a real urban network; this was most notably the case with Timbuktu, with Jenne and with their satellite towns, some quite far away (as far as Bego in the south).

The towns multiplied and prospered because, among other factors, their role grew under the determining effect of Islam and its prestige. Their economic function improved, especially that of the biggest towns. Niani, which had to feed and equip an illustrious ruler and his thousands of attendants, became an enormous entrepot and a manufacturing centre of exceptional vitality. Timbuktu took over from Walata around 1370 as the main caravan terminus and turned into an enormous permanent caravanserai, regorging wares from all parts, where troops of slaves were parked before setting off again. Merchants flocked from all directions to its three markets, where transactions were begun, and were then pursued in the town. The city was in permanent contact with the southern Sudan via its river port and its flotillas. Innumerable craftsmen transformed imported raw materials before sending them out again; iron, gold and coppersmiths worked alongside weavers of cotton, leatherworkers and many others. Jenne and Gao experienced an

387

analogous development and an even closer contact with the Niger due to their fleet of piraguas and canoes, which gave them command over the traffic coming up and down stream, generated principally by Timbuktu.

Towns were also places in which the main buildings and framework of Islam were concentrated. The mosque was an essentially urban monument, especially the great Friday Mosque with which Mansa Musa, stimulated by his pilgrimage, endowed so many cities in Mali and Songhay. These great monuments to prayer gave birth in their turn to Koranic schools, the most important of which were real centres of higher education, turning into towns which became established homes of the Muslim intelligentsia. Among the most famous of these was the capital of Bornu (fifteenth century) which influenced places as far away as the less well-equipped Hausa towns. Others were Gao, the seat of two great mosques (fifteenth century); Kabora on the Niger and especially Timbuktu, the uncontested intellectual and spiritual centre of black Africa in the fourteenth and fifteenth centuries, celebrated throughout the Muslim world. The city boasted three great mosques (Jingereber, fourteenth century; Sankore, fourteenth to fifteenth century and Sidi Yahya, fifteenth century) and active Koranic schools developed there in the fourteenth century. Initially run by *ulamas* from the Maghrib and spiritually dependent on Fez, these schools quickly emancipated themselves under the influence of their black clergy and scholars. They taught the Koran and Koranic law (*fiqh*) with such competence that they drew disciples from far away. The intellectual prestige of the city reached its apogee in the fifteenth and sixteenth centuries. Scholars crowded there – especially white Muslims – spurred on by emulation. In the mid sixteenth century there were 500 Koranic schools, distributed among the mosques, the squares and in houses, which offered instruction in all branches of law and theology.

The development of the towns also owed much to the formation of political and administrative structures within the great States. Certain cities had the good fortune to contain royal courts (Niani, Gao and a few others). Other, more numerous towns, which were not necessarily trading towns, owed their increased stability, prosperity and lustre to the provincial officials who were permanently installed in them, with their entourage and the entrepots in which they stored the taxes and tribute they levied.

By the fourteenth and fifteenth centuries urban society and environment were definitely distinct from the Africa of the bush, the fields and villages. The towns did not necessarily assume the form of homogeneous and dense agglomerations, enclosed within their walls. Many of them retained the fairly loose constellation formation, which seems to have characterised pre-Islamic cities among the Malinke and elsewhere. Gao and Kumbi-Salih were both formed in the tenth to eleventh centuries out of at least two agglomerations (royal town and trading town), a few kilometres apart. In the fourteenth century, the town of Niani stretched out in a haphazard manner over 20 kilometres, according to Arab writers, and preliminary oral and archaeological investigations have indeed come up with this configuration. As in the villages, many urban quarters consisted of mud huts, which doubtless sheltered peasants. But the towns also consisted of juxtaposed houses built of baked earth, and even partially (Niani) or wholly (Kumbi-Salih) of stone, collected within a limited area (Jenne, Timbuktu and Walata) and even fortified (the walls of Jenne). Towns meant squares, mosques, palaces, wharfs, and a whole kaleidoscope of stalls, hawkers, flotillas and bales. Towns meant crowds of people dressed in striped cotton cloth, among whom the naked were conspicuous; they meant a mingling of tongues; a confusion of physical and ethnic types; they were melting pots and provided openings for functions and careers, which often disregarded the old rural hierarchies. Thus Timbuktu, the most illustrious city, employed several professional categories which were unknown in the countryside; at the bottom of the social ladder came troops of slaves awaiting exportation, along with captive household slaves and servants; in the middle was a stable and varied bourgeoisie where black merchants, craftsmen (especially weavers) and *ulamas* lived cheek by jowl with foreigners, the communities of Maghribian and Egyptian scholars and traders; and the whole lot came under the aegis of the Sanhaja aristocracy around the governor (*tumbuktu-koi*). Timbuktu was a model town but she was not alone. Elsewhere, in more rural areas, courtiers and royal officials (minor folk at Timbuktu) were more numerous and, along with more restrained groups of Wangara and *ulamas*, these people would have set the pace in the local agglomerations.

A political Islam

In many ways, the opening of the Sudan to the initially Muslim Mediterranean world brought considerable impetus and support to the sacred kingships, which had been established in black Africa before Islam. This state of affairs was a major feature of thirteenth- to fifteenth-century black African politics.

Firstly, the kings were well placed to profit from the economic boom produced by the great trans-Saharan trade. They did so by combining various procedures. They reserved the monopoly of essential goods such as metals or horses (Mali); they confiscated nuggets found in the gold panning process (Mali, Ghana); they taxed principal imports such as cattle and salt (Mali; a tithe called the *canson*); they made the gold producers pay them tribute (Mali); they controlled and supplied the slave trade (Ghana, Mali, Songhay). As these kings grew more powerful, they extended the range of these levies to cover local surpluses obtained as a result of the economic growth; tributes, payable mostly in agricultural produce, were imposed on conquered provinces and kingdoms (Mali, fourteenth century, Songhay, fifteenth century); taxes were raised from servile populations dependent on the sovereign (Songhay, fifteenth century). In short, these monarchs laid the foundations of a new system of taxation, which was to determine all their subsequent political initiatives.

When these kings adhered to the model of kingship and the methods of government dictated by Islam, they secured another form of support. Muslim influence had been felt long ago, prior even to conversion, in military matters. Even pagan kings (the Sosso and the Mossi) had introduced cavalry units into their armies since the thirteenth century, which were certainly copied from the Arab world where the horses came from. Islam and its ideals followed. It would have been difficult and dangerous for the kings to abandon all references

389

The remarkable earth walls of the mosque of Jingereber, founded in 1325 by Mansa Musa in Timbuktu, Mali, after his pilgrimage to Mecca. Following the example of Jenne and Gao, the town soon developed into an unsurpassed commercial crossroads as well as a great religious centre.

to animist beliefs. For all that, the first royal conversions to Islam, whether due to conviction (the first Mali Mansa to be converted, in the eleventh century, is supposed to have been convinced by a miracle worked by a *murabit*, whose prayers ended a drought) or due to calculation, happened early on; in 1075 for Humai, King of Kanem; in the eleventh century for Mali. Their conversion did not necessarily entail that of their whole dynasty, due to reluctance on the part of the people and to the king's own responsibilities and convictions. Oral tradition makes Sundiata, still in the thirteenth century, into a totally animist king while Arab chroniclers introduce Dibbalemi (in the thirteenth century) as the first Muslim king of Kanem. In the fourteenth to fifteenth centuries, however, all the great monarchies of the Sudan, apart from the Mossi, had either adopted Islam or were very close to so doing (e.g. Dioloff, Mali, Songhay, Kanem-Bornu and the urban kingdoms of Hausa). Several of these kings then undertook the pilgrimage to Mecca as their ultimate act of piety. This was the case with Mansa Musa of Mali, who twice went on pilgrimage (according to oral tradition) and is famous for the ostentation of his second journey in 1324. Since the thirteenth century, Mansa Ule (son of Sundiata) and the usurper Sakura also went, as did various *mai* (kings) of Kanem in the thirteenth and fourteenth centuries; in Songhay the Askya Muhammad went in the fifteenth century. Kings found that their prestige was considerably enhanced by their adoption of Islam, in whatever form. Kings who had seen Mecca were infused with a sacred prestige and glory, which benefited everybody and which everybody, Muslim or otherwise, respected (hence the vogue for this undertaking among usurpers). However, a king who simply professed Islam and adhered to its principles without acquiring the charisma of the journey won the general sympathy of the Muslims and ensured the loyal support of the Islamic world in the administration of his State. This was not insignificant. Islam, together with the Koran, dictated a code of conduct and government for its kings; it put the prayers and preaching of the *ulamas*, the wisdom of its scholars and the legal skill of its *qadis*, whatever their origins, at their disposal. Mansa Musa brought back Egyptian scholars and experts (architects, for instance) from his second pilgrimage; other scholars streamed to his court from Libya, Morocco and different parts of the Maghrib, and they proved to be as loyal to the State as their black pupils and successors later were.

These skills, alliances and borrowings allowed these already rich monarchs to strengthen the instruments of their power, both in the centre and in the provinces. The centre included the court with its princes, officials, functionaries, its ceremonies and impressive luxury, all of which reflected and dispensed the king's sacred prestige. In Mali, the influence of the Sudanese entourage (brothers, wife, notables representing the great Malinke clans) on everyday life was very great. By the mid fourteenth century, court liturgies still included many pre-Islamic rites, which had grown up around the first sorcerer kings and were still to be found in the pagan courts of Ghana and Mossi. But these courts now contained many Muslim officials and when Ibn Battuta described one of these liturgies in 1352, it is clear that Muslims played a determining role in them. The *Iman* spoke the prayer; a preacher intoned a eulogy of the king; Muslim dignitaries processed in the midst of the emir-chiefs of the cavalry and the royal guard, where the pale faces of the Turkish soldiers were conspicuous. The court and official functions of Songhay also presented this mixture of local traditions and rites – developed out of their ethnic inheritance, which the royal family shared with the aristocracy – with supplementary borrowings from Islam. The monarchies of the Maghrib and Egypt seem to have inspired the creation of most of the administrative posts known in the fifteenth century. These consisted of twenty-six departments of very different natures, as much economic (finances, payments, crops, forests, fishing, floods, trade – ten in all) as military, legal or domestic (ten altogether), which reveal the force of the State mechanism at the end of the Middle Ages and the various ways in which it was supplied.

From the centre, the administrative framework moved outwards to cover the provinces very efficiently, in Mali (fourteenth century) as in Songhay (fifteenth century). In the Mali Empire, not all the provinces enjoyed the same statute. Such old kingdoms as had been peacefully absorbed (Mema) retained their chief or their monarch, who then became a vassal of the Mansa; others, which had been subjugated by force, were subjected to the authority of a governor nominated by the Emperor, as was also the case with a few strategically important towns (Walata) and with properly Malinke provinces. In order to unify the whole, the vassal rulers were supervised by a representative of the central power, and every year the Mansa summoned a council of the provincial chiefs to the capital. This council laid down the common Malinke law (*laada*) which would then be applied everywhere conjointly with Islamic law (*sharia*). The governors, who seem to have all been Muslims and some even former pilgrims (*hajj*), knew Islamic Law well and applied it locally, notably via the *qadis*, and this contributed powerfully towards structuring the Empire. The Songhay provinces were just as carefully administered in the fifteenth to sixteenth centuries. This was effected, on the regional level, by royal princes in the east and by a hereditary aristocracy in the west and, on the local level, by a multitude of specialised agents, better known than the Mali ones, who ran the royal domains, the river ports, the flotillas, the bearers, the markets, the servile class, and so on respectively. The army maintained order. It was dispersed among the principal strategic points and under the orders of the royal princes (*kurmina fari*, as the chief of the western front was called) or members of the provincial aristocracy (*dendi fari*, chief of the western front and many other regional commanders). The king secured the loyalty of all these persons, administrators, military men and *ulamas* by means of gifts, gratifications and donations of land or slaves.

Altogether, all the conditions necessary for the consolidation and development of organised and centralised States in black Africa were present in the thirteenth to fifteenth centuries. The preceding examples have shown that this was the case. From then on, kingships were the political structures habitually referred to by historical sources, which describe them as entities covering a specific area and consisting of several clans, the whole thing relatively stable and ruled by a monarch who generally acknowledged Islam, in spite of the animist and magical attributes of his power. A more complex and hierarchical society can often be glimpsed in the background, which was dominated by an aristocracy of royal officials, generals and *ulamas* enriched by princely gifts of gold, objects, people and lands. A landed aristocracy began to be consolidated (Mali, fourteenth century, Songhay, fifteenth century). In every case, executive agents, armies, commercial activity and towns emerged from the peasant masses and contributed to the established power. The first kingdoms we know of emerged from obscurity around the eighth to ninth centuries, before any sign of Islam. They developed in two distinct and different regions. Most of the towns were strung out in a long disjointed line from west to east along the sub-Saharan Sahel where the caravan routes ended, whose traffic contributed to their existence. Such were, for instance, the kingdoms of Tekrur, Diafanu, Diara, Wagadu, Mema, Gao, Kanem. The other towns

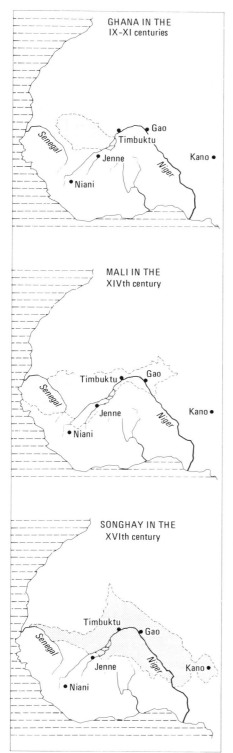

GHANA IN THE
IX-XI centuries

MALI IN THE
XIVth century

SONGHAY IN THE
XVIth century

Africa opens up to the old worlds

9 The medieval empires of the western Sudan

393

were grouped much further south, around the mouth of the Niger, in a little known political and economic configuration, which must already have been very lively. These were the Kingdoms of Ife, Benin, Nupe and Ibo. Then, in the twelfth to fifteenth centuries, in liaison with the advance of Islam and the great trans-Saharan trade and a few migrations, the line of states in the Sahel grew denser towards the South, where the more marginal or more southerly ethnic groups developed in their turn into the Wolof and Serer kingdoms (twelfth century) – which became the Wolof empire in the fourteenth century; into the Soninke states of the Sosso (twelfth century); into the Mossi kingdoms of the Yatenya (possibly thirteenth century); into the city-states of the Hausa country (thirteenth to fifteenth centuries) and, further east, following the political and population shift of the Kanem, into the Bornu. Around the fifteenth century, the most southerly populations, those of the savannas of Guinea and of the forests were affected in their turn. The Wangara traders, by thrusting south towards the gold mines of the Akan and Ashanti lands, contributed to hasten processes which were perhaps developing locally. They accelerated the establishment of the first real regional States, the kingdoms of Bono-Mansu, Dagomba and finally of Gonja, along their trade routes, the more isolated old Nigerian States in the south being less fruitful examples of the same trend.

Political unity was thus seen in terms of the kingdom, but these were not all equally wealthy, powerful or successful. Luck, a better organised power or society, a better commercial situation, a monarch's military or political skill and many other factors allowed certain States to dominate their neighbours and to form what are traditionally known as empires. The oldest of these were formed already before the eleventh century, east and west of this privileged zone of the Sahel, around the first great commercial crossroads. In the west was Ghana, enriched by the gold mines of Bambuk, and fairly firmly in control of the kingdoms of Mema, Diafanu, Sosso, Kaarta, etc., and of the caravan towns scattered around the south-western Sahara. In the east, Kanem controlled the Gezzan oases for a while. These empires then declined, and came unstuck (eleventh to twelfth centuries, Ghana; thirteenth to fourteenth centuries, Kanem). New political entities were formed from the new trumps we have seen above (trade, gold, Islam and administration), which were even more ambitious and endured for several generations with unprecedented brilliance. Of such was the Empire of Mali, founded by Sundiata Keita (died c. 1250), rich in gold from the mines of Bambuk and Bure, which reached its greatest size under Mansa Musa (1310–35), stretching from the Atlantic to the middle Niger and enfolding innumerable clans, kingdoms and ethnic groups within its firm but flexible grasp. After Mali came the Songhay Empire, which was formed after 1450 on an even vaster scale than the preceding one, because all the Sahel kingdoms from Bornu and Aïr in the east to Futa Toro and the Wolof lands in the west were momentarily induced to form a federation under its command. Ancient Mali itself, reduced to its Malinke and Gambian court, was also brought within its orbit.

By the first decades of the fifteenth century Africa was no longer an isolated world to be pillaged for slaves and gold. To the west, at least, the awakening of Africa had raised the Sudanese regions to the level of the Abyssinian kingdoms. Driven out of Spain and Sicily,

Islam opened a new route into Africa which has remained, five centuries afterwards, one of the great arteries of human life. This is a vital fact; it showed that, in spite of being mutilated and repulsed in the north, Islam still conquered and reigned in the south. It is difficult to assess how much Christendom knew about this, but she did not ignore it: already before the fifteenth century, her avid grasp was reaching out towards Africa.

Seeschiff vom Ende des 15. Jahrh., halb vor dem Winde segelnd.
Aus Bernh. v. Breydenbach, Peregrinationes. Mainz 1486.

A German ship with square sail and stern rudder. An engraving from the *Peregrinations of Brendenbach*, Mainz 1486. By this time, ships were considered as capital and shares in them could be bought and sold, and they were owned by several proprietors simultaneously.

PART 3

Towards the Modern Age in the West 1430–1520

Europe's second wind   8

The decade 1420–30 is one of the gloomiest in European history. All the elements of decay analysed in the foregoing pages seemed to have reached a pitch of virulence capable of destroying civilisation. This was how contemporaries felt, and long afterwards historians of later ages were similarly affected; Michelet discerned the potential implicit in the fourteenth century but he was only one among the many living or defunct denigrators of the 'crises' and the 'decline' of the Middle Ages. Why not lay down one's pen at this point, with Joan of Arc's pyre signalling the end of medieval times? It was only much later that the scene changed, after the age of Charles V, Francis I and Henry VIII, when Rabelais and Calvin were around, bringing us up to 1530 or 1540: there is a whole century, between Joan and Luther, to account for. This period used to be dealt with by winding up old concerns; the end of the Hundred Years' War, the fall of Byzantium, the Plague, without acknowledging that for some time already, caravels had been sailing down the coast of West Africa, that the Renaissance had begun, and that the modern State had been established. The past was divided up quite arbitrarily. Over the last fifteen years, however, the development of French regional economic studies and of research into art and thought in Italy, into German spirituality and English society, have exploded this concept. This slice of history definitely belongs to the Middle Ages. Between 1450 and 1540–50, Christian Europe was animated by an obvious reaction against her former regression; in spite of what some modern historians claim, there is no evidence, economically and socially at least, that she had recovered the levels of 1300 or 1320. This did not happen until the industrial revolution at the end of the eighteenth century. But it was in this period of revulsion and reaction that the foundations of Modern Europe were laid.

Recovery

When a business has gone through a depressed period and reopens its order books, it is said to have 'recovered'; in the fifteenth century, this was called 'reconstruction' but the two terms imply making good with old materials where the future is uncertain, both in general terms and concerning the success of the undertaking. It has sometimes not been possible to detect new forces at work, and the impression of revival was due to the natural elimination of impediments or disasters, with no structural changes. The century we are about to examine presented many of these features.

The 'copiousness of the people'

This rather excessive remark, with its faint overtones of dismayed surprise, was made by a moralist in 1520 and it points to a fundamental phenomenon without which all the others are meaningless: the attrition of human life had finally come to an end. There is so much information to be found in the archives after 1420 and especially 1470, that the first fairly certain population studies can be made. There were certainly more people, but the reasons for this are complicated and obscure.

The epidemics, whose brutal irruption had accelerated the population decline, were in retreat. The last great recurrences of the Plague were in 1437 and 1440, with a final haphazard appearance as late as 1465. Typhus was recorded in a series of epidemics between 1470 and 1560 in the Nantes area, for instance, where there were fifty-one years of recorded sickness out of ninety. Leprosy on the other hand, was only a bad memory and the disease had never swept through the population. Its disappearance has been attributed to the onset of tuberculosis – an unequal exchange, since the latter was far more harmful to the unprivileged classes of society – not to mention syphilis, a disease which the French and Neapolitans had the dubious privilege of spreading throughout their armies, and beyond, during the 'Italian campaigns' between 1498 and 1525. Compared with these, the Black Death lost its impact. The virulence of its bacillus was not attenuated by medical care, which was not to improve until after 1600, nor by any progressive immunisation of the natives, but by their improved physical condition. As with its success, the defeat of the Plague was a secondary phenomenon; it died because the individual no longer succumbed to it.

What role did wars play in this period? As with the Plague, the answer seems obvious. At various times and places, the disruption caused by cavalcades or by mercenaries' attacks was less constant; the retaking of Bordeaux (1453), the peace of Lodi (1454) in Italy, the end of the Hussite wars in Bohemia and the pacts drawn up between towns, which Emperor Frederick III encouraged around 1470, were all positive measures, as was the extermination of many mercenaries roaming around Alsace or their enrolment in royal armies between 1440 and 1450. But this was no reason for premature rejoicing. Although the war was in principle over in the French kingdom, between the Battle of Montlhéry, when Louis XI defeated the princes' troops (1465), and the beginning of the wars of religion a hundred years later, there was fighting in Artois and Burgundy until 1480, and right up to 1488, bands of *écorcheurs* (skinners) roamed around the countryside, in the Île-de-France, for instance. In England the Civil War broke out; in Germany the Knights, the *Ritter*, imposed the *Faustrecht*, the rule of the fist, over the whole of the Rhineland and central Germany, and Italy after 1490 was bathed once more in blood. Although war as we saw earlier, was the result of the nobility's deteriorating status, after the nobles had been eliminated, the politics of aggression were immediately resumed in the name of the king.

The sickhouse of Béthune approached by a leper with his clapper, and a cripple. (Detail from a fifteenth-century miniature; Paris, Bibliothèque nationale.)

Although the improvements in agricultural production meant that food shortages occurred less often, hunger still ravaged the Bourbon lands around 1465, northern France and the Low Countries in 1481 and 1492, and Alsace and western Germany between 1522 and 1525. These shortages were harmful because they reduced immunity to disease; there were few deaths as a direct result of starvation. All in all, these external factors can be said to have delayed the eventual recovery by failing to contribute to the atmosphere of relative security necessary to effect a rise in the birth rate.

Although our information is inadequate in this one fundamental point, it does suggest that two mainstays of population growth were gradually reinforced. Agriculture revived as a direct result of the collapse, both of the demand for land, and of an important part of the demand for peasant produce. Instead, the peasants were able to improve their production and the volume of foodstuffs produced by being better equipped and by working better-organised lands, which allowed them, as in the eleventh and twelfth centuries, to raise their overall standard of living and to reduce their mortality rate, especially that of children. Although the Florentine *catasto* of 1427 gives instances of families in which fifteen out of twenty children, or six out of eleven, died at a very early age (the returns were not falsified because the *catasto* took account of the 'family quotient'), the average number of surviving children in fertile households was beginning to rise again. In the Lyonnais, the average number of children per woman was 3.9 before the Plague; it fell to 1.8 in 1430, below the level at which the population remains stable, and climbed back to 4.5 or 5.1 in 1480. There is no doubt that the improved food supply played an important part in this recovery. But the return to the previous 'matrimonial model' was also important, in which girls were married off at an early age, favouring a high proportion of births. Bernardino of Siena stated in 1425 that there were 20,000 unmarried girls over the age of twenty in Milan, as

401

compared with the *catasto* of 1427, according to which 74 per cent of country girls were married by this age (only 58 per cent in the towns however). After 1480, the *Monte delle Doti*, a fund started in Florence for providing nubile girls with dowries, was almost obliged to close its doors for lack of customers. As we know, the man was always older in this sort of marriage but by the fifteenth century ages from between twenty-three and twenty-seven were considered suitable for bridegrooms, as compared with the over-thirties so frequently encountered before 1320 or 1340.

A final factor could be added, and one as yet not capable of being proven scientifically; the numerical preponderance of the female sex. Was this an accident of circumstance, due for instance to improved obstetric care and to fewer deaths in childbirth, or to a long-term biological trend which we cannot analyse? That this was a fact is confirmed by such censuses as were carried out. Although there were still rather more men than women in Tuscany in 1427, by 1455–70 the opposite applied in Basle, Nuremberg, Artois, and the Low Countries, where an average rate of 110–115 women to 85 or 90 men was the norm. Without pausing to consider the moral or economic implications of this state of affairs, it is worth recalling that since the marriage market was saturated with women, the age at which girls were married fell even lower and they started families earlier.

These being the probable material causes of this reversal of the population trend, can we measure or date it? There was after all no clear-cut break comparable to that of 1347–50: the general movement was slow, but also extremely diversified: in certain regions such as upper Provence, Catalonia and the Île-de-France population levels went on falling until the end of the fifteenth century; in others, like the Auvergne, Burgundy, the Lyonnais, Essex, Hainaut and certain parts of Languedoc the population increased dramatically from 1440. So there was no uniform quantifiable progress; if one took the averages for England, Normandy and Hainaut, one could state that the rhythm of population growth changed from being negative before 1410–20, to being positive again around 1420–40 in the best cases, with an annual growth factor of 0.15–0.30 per cent, and that real growth began after 1450–60, when factors of 0.50–0.65 per cent have been established. After 1475, the annual rate of growth stabilised at between 0.80 and 1.2 although figures of 1.28 have been given for Caux and 1.94 in Languedoc, which represent a doubling of the population in three or four generations. Unfortunately the figures supplied for the beginning of the fifteenth century show a tendency to level off and the number of inhabitants in most of the country was certainly only three-quarters or four-fifths that of 1310 or 1320. This is why it seems abusive to attribute 'copiousness' to the regenerative process, the more so since it began to fall off again around 1550. But this is outside our time-span and is mentioned simply in order to stress the indeterminate nature of the phenomenon.

A final and not negligible aspect should be mentioned. The situation in the towns seems to have been special; of course, this had always been the case and the crises of the fourteenth century had inflicted brutal bouts of inflation and depression on them. The great waves of urban immigration had left a residue behind them each time, and I have indicated that this growth preluded the towns' tyrannical exploitation of the peasantry. Once the most pressing danger was past, the attractions of the city did not dwindle because, behind

Birth and first bath of the baby in a wealthy household. (Quintus Curtius *The Deeds of Alexander the Great*. A French translation of the end of the fifteenth century; Chantilly, Musée Condé.)

their walls, both the unemployed and the refugee found welcome and perhaps work more easily than in the countryside. This was why even after 1450 immigration was almost everywhere so heavy as to present town councils with serious problems of assimilation. The flow of people changed direction at the whim of circumstance; in Paris around 1480 or 1500, immigrants from upper Normandy and Brittany (31 per cent) competed with those from the two formerly prolific areas of the lower Seine et Oise (29 per cent), with the people from the South of the Loire, who had until then kept away, making up 18 per cent of Paris immigrants. It is difficult to assess the volume of this influx; it has been estimated that between 1435 and 1455 it made up 25 per cent of the population of Rheims and 35 per cent of that of Strasbourg. Certain towns of differing importance were largely repopulated by the newcomers: Vannes, Rennes, Sélestat or Colmar; or else their social fabric was profoundly altered, as in Arles or Périgueux. On the whole, however, the population figures are not really evidence that fundamental changes took place, even if most of the towns in 1500 had as many and sometimes more men in them as in 1300, as in the cases of Lille, Dijon and Ghent. These increases came late, later even than in the countryside, and seldom before 1470. Under these new pressures, social attitudes hardened and rejected the undesirable part of this new population, assigning it to either suburbs or particular quarters. In order to obtain the *droit de cité* – the town franchise in Provence, in the Massif Central and along the Rhine – one had to acquire some land and obtain an *acte d'habitation*, 403

A peasant couple going to market to sell their farm produce. (An engraving by Dürer; Paris, coll. Dutuit, Petit Palais.)

even at Bordeaux, which had been much depleted by two successive sieges. These who did not secure these advantages were thrown out, as happened around 1460 or 1470 in the Burgundian States. Nor do I refer here to the few excessive and brief measures taken by certain rulers who thought that, by emptying a rebel town of her inhabitants and by forcibly replacing them with new ones, they could secure support, as happened at Arras and Liège during the Franco-Burgundian wars.

The countryside grows green again

The agricultural revival took shape in conditions parallel to those of the population revival, to which it was linked, although its general progress is hard to define because the disparities and contradictions are so great. Firstly, what is meant by the countryside growing green again is illustrated by the following example: around 1460, the average yield per hectare in the Cambrésis was around six hectolitres (16½ bushels), in stark contrast with Quercy, which in 1473 was still *tout en herm*, or neglected. Auvergne and Provence had to wait until the beginning of the sixteenth century before their deserted plots of land were worked again. Elsewhere, in the Estates of 1484 in France, or in 1489 when John Rouss and others presented King Henry VII with their complaint; in 1498 in Tuscancy, if Savonarola is to be believed, and in 1500 in Denmark, protests were still being voiced about the inadequacy of the revival. Nevertheless, its technical conditions can be discerned; it has been shown, in the case of Quercy for instance, that taxes were often assessed collectively (as much as 80 per cent of them for this region between 1450 and 1490), and so represented the combined efforts of various persons in a given sector. On the other hand, the price of corn levelled off after 1470, which made it profitable for the peasantry to grow more cereals on their patched-up lands. The more so since the wage rise slowed down as a new and more numerous generation of workers appeared on the scene. In England, wages even fell by 10 per cent and 15 per cent between 1430 and 1450, and again from 1470 to 1490 – maybe also as a result of competition from the towns.

Both the results and the phases of the revival as a whole may be presented thus; between 1440 and 1475, people concentrated on growing profitable crops, especially in Germany and Italy; linen, vineyards, orchards, olive groves. From 1475 to 1520 people began to clear empty plots on marginal land, but it was not before 1520 in Germany and in the Mediterranean regions that people began reclaiming the *Wüstungen*, which had been abandoned in the fourteenth century. Even in the best cases, however, only 20 per cent of this farmland was won back to the plough.

In spite of the slight rise in grain prices after 1460 or 1470, ploughland did not rise in value. The price of an acre of arable in England or in Neufbourg stayed at its 1420–5 level. The reason for this stagnation is clear: in their search for profit, farmers were experimenting with other crops and from the mid fourteenth century, a tendency towards soil specialisation was emerging. If a vineyard cost 20 livres to maintain and brought in 45 livres, as in Burgundy around 1450, why risk growing wheat? The practice of turning mediocre ploughland into profitable vineyards could involve stopping all production; around 1500 even the Junkers were trying to acclimatise the vine to Saxony. The *coltura promiscua*, mixed cultivation of vines and olives, vines and nut trees, which still characterises many southern European landscapes, was indeed much more widespread in those days.

Stock-raising was another aspect of farming which absorbed more and more of the peasants' interest. This investment was justified not only by the increased consumption of meat and milk products but also by the considerable growth in the manufacture of different sorts of wool-based textiles, which made sheep farming contracts exceptionally interesting, as much for the townsman, who would buy a flock and then lease it out, as for the farmer, who would sell its young and its produce every year and could thus safeguard himself against penury. The element of speculation, or on the contrary of alienation, in a great many of these contracts of *gasaille* or *nourkiage*, as they were called in different places in southern or northern France, or of *soccida* in Italy, should not be ignored. After 1460 in the southern Alps or the Pyrenees, many peasants were very often unable to meet their agricultural expenses and they would sell the ownership of their animals in return for cash, which meant that, while they still had to do the work, they could draw only a small proportion of the produce at the end of the year. It was probably as a result of these contracts becoming more common, that animals began to be kept apart, which seems natural to us but was very strange in the Middle Ages; no more promiscuous transhumance, no more animals rootling haphazardly in the woods, but instead, stables, piggeries, and specialised shepherds.

Among the factors which could have given stock-raising a hitherto unknown dimension was the ruinous competition from 'exotic' herds. Hungary exported so much beef and milk produce to the West circa 1480 that restrictive and even systematic protectionist measures had to be taken, as in Cologne in 1492. As for sheep, the introduction of long-haired breeds into southern Europe induced other places to take up regional sheep farming again. Although we do not know where the 'merino' sheep come from, they had been in Sicily since 1278 and in Spain from 1344. Their name may be derived from the Merinids of Morocco, or from a Berber tribe. The Genoese may have played a role in introducing them

Maintaining orchards; pruning and hoeing in the Spring. (*Les Heures de Rohan*, March; Paris, Bibliothèque nationale.)

alongside the Tyrrhenian Sea. Whatever the origins of their introduction, it did not mean that they were immediately and everywhere intensively farmed. In the Dauphiné, Cantal, and upper Provence, the destruction to the undergrowth and the erosion caused by the prevalence and voracity of these animals continued apace, or was resumed; the number of head of sheep in Provence largely exceeded that of humans. The Iberian Peninsula, where the traditions of transhumance were strong enough to survive centuries of neglect, was initially the only country able to organise a rational system for gathering, sorting, transporting and taxing flocks of sheep. The *Mesta* (the etymology of the word is still under

a) Sheep shearing by a trained shepherd. (London, British Museum.)
b) On the right, pigs are slaughtered on All Saints' Day. (A woodcut of 1491.)

dispute) began life around 1275 as a simple fraternity and grew into an economic and political power because its principal suppliers, the 'grandees' of Spain and the military Orders, were able to dictate suitable taxation and land appropriation policies to their kings. By 1360, the number of head of sheep was estimated at one million, and by 1450 the total number of sheep in all the flocks, which were gathered gradually within this vast association, reached three million head, and four million seven hundred thousand head in 1490, when Ferdinand of Aragon took over the Orders of soldier monks and so became the premier sheepraiser in Spain. This power not only secured him exorbitant privileges and

407

scandalous exemptions, but it also defended him against the peasants' claims for compensation for the damage inflicted on cultivated lands by the passage of flocks of several thousand head, because behind the sheep were drawn up the entire nobility and the king.

Disrupting the countryside

The situation was a little different in England, and analysing it will allow me to introduce a major fact in the history of European agriculture; the spread of coppices. In the British Isles, cattle and sheep had to be farmed without the advantages of transhumance. To make up for this, their wool was of such high quality that, before the introduction of merinos into Spain, it formed a major export commodity. From the reign of Edward III onwards, the situation changed, firstly because of labour problems in Flanders as a result of the wars (even after the English king had arranged a staple in Calais in 1362 where bales could be unloaded in complete safety), and secondly because many artisans from the Low Countries, Artois and the Rhineland came to England and enabled a properly English manufacturing industry to develop. We should pause a moment here: even if one disregards the totally ineffectual 'Navigation Act' of 1381, we see here the foundation stone of English economic preponderance in the eighteenth century. From then on, sheep farming became a much more profitable if speculative activity in the British Isles than before, since the duty payable on exports suddenly fell. The merchants one encounters at Saint Ives, Southampton, Stamford, Bristol and Winchester were no longer men of Picardy or Flemings, they were Englishmen. The Cistercians appear to have played a determining role in the development of sheep farming, because this had been one of their most traditional activities since the twelfth century. From now on, they concentrated their efforts on wool, even to the extent of organising convoys to Hull, freighting ships and providing work for neighbouring villages. Their example was followed by many members of the gentry. In the towns, a new category of woolmen emerged, who started off as more or less salaried brokers. They ran around the English countryside looking for proprietors in financial difficulties to whom they offered advance payment for their unshorn fleeces, which they then bought up cheaply (in view of the risks, the woolmen said) and then when sheep shearing time came up, sold them considerably dearer. Other sheep farmers managed to avoid these pitfalls and made sheep into a good investment in a country where, as the saying went, sheeps' hooves turned sand into gold.

This sheep farming, even without the massive movement involved in transhumance on the continent, needed lots of land. Voracious and untamed as sheep are, they do considerable damage to crops and woods, and the fields they are put in have to be enclosed. This led to the phenomenon known as enclosure, which could in practice be harmless and limited to individual decisions, but in the open-field landscape, which was that of England and of other lands now grassed over, enclosing meant disrupting the age-old communal agricultural practices and preventing other beasts from pasturing on common land by fencing it off. Enclosure ruined crop rotation and gradually destroyed the community; it is no exaggeration to say that English enclosures were in the long run as harmful to the peasantry of the British Isles as the abuses of the *Mesta* were to the peasantry in Spain. The kings soon understood the problem and already in 1235 King Henry III forbad the seizure and enclosure of common land, but this and other measures were swept aside after 1380–90 in the rising wave of stock-raising. This grew stronger still around 1430–50 when increasing agricultural profits allowed many families to implement vast enclosures. This phenomenon is often associated with that of the deserted villages, which in many cases had been ruined by the disappearance of the arable, or had been rendered incapable of pursuing a regular farming life, forcing communities to disperse and leave their sites. The mass of ruined peasants flowed to the towns to form a vulnerable workforce, ready for any work, providing a foundation for later English industrialisation. Between 1450 and 1489 around 2,000 areas were affected; in the Midlands and around Leicester or Lincoln as well as north of Newcastle, two-thirds of the villages were enclosed, but only half in Norfolk and the counties south-east of London. The York and Birmingham countrysides were less affected. Protests rose up and reached the ears of the ruler, notably the Grand Petition of 1489; inquests were ordered, as in 1517 by Cardinal Wolsey. But in fact, the King had an interest in developing the English wool industry. He turned a blind eye to the abuses and limited himself to issuing a few remonstrances. From then on the movement could expand at leisure. It reached its peak at the end of the sixteenth century in the reign of Elizabeth, outside our period.

The existence of similar phenomena on the continent poses a problem because they were not as widespread. In all the places where pasture increased noticeably, in Hainaut, Angoumois, Franche-Comté, Tyrol and Bavaria, both the age of their first hedges and the extent of the phenomenon remain uncertain. The only indisputable fact is that stock-raising in these regions had progressed, as well as in chillier parts like Brittany, Poitou or the Massif Central, where open *gastes* had surrounded the enclosed *coutures*, *trests* and *gaignettes* for centuries, and so had increased the number of hedges and walls. In England, enclosure was accompanied by an undeniable increase in the number of closed allotments.

Enclosing the woods

We are left with the problem of the woods which, as we saw, had spread over much formerly cultivated land. There is no evidence that clearance was part of the sixteenth-century agricultural revival. For this, we would have to move on to the eighteenth century, when wholesale felling of trees was resumed. In any case, the profits to be made from timber and culling increased to the extent of interesting efficient landowners. Around 1500, the seigneur of Neufbourg could get 907 livres income from his woods or *bosc* as compared with 400 livres from his *plain*. Even in Germany speculative enterprises sprang up with disastrous results. Around Nuremberg, for instance, burghers or timber merchants like the Hülpüchel felled the oak forests and replaced them with fast growing conifers whose wood could be used for all purposes. The progressive invasion of our deciduous woodlands by pines, fir trees and larches dates surely from this time. We have come to consider them as the native trees, but they are the fruits of urban speculation in the fifteenth and sixteenth

Hunting hares: dogs and greyhounds, possibly of Eastern origin, pursue their prey.

centuries; poisoned fruit too, because the thick and infertile carpet of needles lying on the forest floor rendered it sterile, and livestock could no longer feed from it. For different but no less catastrophic reasons, the German and Lorraine peasantry was reduced to mere labouring work, if not to wholesale flight.

The woods had maybe never stopped spreading: in Sologne in the fifteenth century, 72 per cent of farms, called *chézeaux*, contained woods. Where woods were not very extensive, they made up for this by becoming increasingly busy: charcoal burners, *boisilleurs*, woodlanders, *godins* (from the German *Wald*?) made their home in it, like the hermits and fugitives of the eleventh century, forming a whole population of 'wild' artisans, who, like their eleventh-century predecessors, probably played a fundamental part in reviving the 'secondary sector'. However, the owners of all these useful spaces suspected these woodlanders of real or supposed abuses and were probably behind two sets of measures, whose disadvantages seriously outweighed their advantages. In first place, the freedom of the chase, the ancestral privilege of all free men, which was fiercely defended by the peasantry (as is still the case today) was restricted. It had already been limited in so far as hunting wolves, bears, boar and stags required expensive weapons, packs of hunting dogs, nets and beaters, and so tended to become the prerogative of the aristocracy. However, the art of venery was increasingly cultivated in the fifteenth century and became more refined in line with the nobility's improved knowledge of zoology. They no longer thought of hunting as a necessary training for war or as a way of eating something other than lard; it had become a game of skill in which ladies could participate, thus obliging them to extend

410

a) Hunting boar, (left) from Gaston Phœbus' *Treatise on Hunting*. (Fifteenth century; Chantilly, Musée Condé.)

b) Falconry (right). Falcons, the pride and joy of the lords, were trained and kept by expert falconers. (Ms. Pal. Lat. 1071, Rome, Biblioteca apostolica vaticana.)

the exercise of the chase and the kill to less redoubtable beasts. Foxes, doe, roedeer, even hares and various birds, which until then had been gladly left to the peasants' bows, nets or traps, became the prey of the nobility, the more so since the adoption of falconry in western societies (after Frederick II's contact with Islam had taught him the rudiments of the art) required trained staff. Soon different breeds of dogs were developed for different sorts of hunting and setting. The nobility now demonstrated largesse by organising hunts lasting several days, as Louis of Orléans and René of Anjou did in the fifteenth century. Certain rulers even showed considerable talent for describing the techniques of the chase, and in the fourteenth century, a man like Gaston Phoebus could compose real treatises on hunting. Kings too, had always felt this form of activity to be particularly royal and were not behindhand: from Charles VII to Louis XVI not one French king failed to see it as his duty. This development ran counter to the obvious interests of the rustics; starting in 1450, legal proceedings, which had formerly been directed against poaching in the seigneurial preserve, started to prohibit customary practices. First to be attacked were the hunting methods used by the villagers, stating – not always wrongly – that they involved grievous depletion of animal life (the same procedure was applied to fishing). Then certain kinds of animals were reserved for the lord's hunting. Some rulers were well aware of the material advantages they could draw from these conflicts; in 1470 Louis XI sold some lords the right to monopolise the hunting in certain forests. This proved the starting point for the progressive exclusion of the peasantry from all forms of hunting in the woods. Claims that animal life did benefit from this were not without value, as the occasional need to organise

411

wolf or boar drives showed. But both the King's concern for his income and the nobility's concern for their art had a deleterious effect on the legal and economic rights of peasantry, reducing them to poaching and eating thrushes, tame rabbits or the vermin they trapped in their chicken runs.

Enclosing the woodlands by turning them into parks and breeding ranges was part of the new trend towards regenerating the natural environment. This concerned the general level of botanical knowledge; we have seen how from the end of the thirteenth century, even earlier for the Cistercians, people had begun to clear the undergrowth to encourage the growth of tall trees, and were allowing tracts of forest to be sectioned off from the peasants' pasturage and use, in order to promote growth. The extent to which the methods employed from 1340 or 1370 – and later along the Atlantic front and in Germany – to achieve this were effective, is arguable. Francis I issued an ordinance in 1516 which was widely imitated; it prescribed twelve-yearly intervals between fellings and yearly clearance of the undergrowth, referred to as *souille*. The sections surveyed were enclosed and after they had been felled, they were replanted at a rate of twenty saplings per acre for the more vigorous varieties like oak or beech, and were then left to grow. For the first three years after planting, the wood was a proscribed area. As with hunting, the beneficial aspects of these measures could not be denied, but they involved penalties and evictions, not to mention the effect of speculative fir plantations, all of which harmed peasant communities.

Thus the wooded part of the landscape, the second pillar of the medieval economy, tended to pass into the hands of masters who reserved it for themselves, albeit from excellent motives. The problem was complicated and peasant resistance was paralysed at the beginning of the sixteenth century by the inextricable muddle of seigneurial rights over any fairly important woodland. It was not only that prohibitions regarding felling, hunting, and reafforestation jostled one another, but surveillance agents in the form of wardens, verderers and provosts also represented well dug in and rival interests. Eighty-eight lords and ecclesiastics, for instance, not including the King, held rights to parts of the forest of Orléans. The example of the forest is fairly representative of the general revival at the end of the fifteenth century; although it certainly included elements of growth, its end was close and its benefits arguable.

A more secure artisan class

While the problems the rural sector was undergoing are interpreted in very different ways, especially if the extent of the troubles of the fourteenth century is taken into account, the urban sector presented an encouraging aspect, which goes some way towards explaining the ascendancy of the towns in the Middle Ages. The causes of this prosperity were many: there was no shortage of labour, albeit very unevenly skilled labour, neither in the towns where the country refugees flocked, nor in the villages where the most deprived elements now depended on getting piece-work to survive. Nor was there any shortage of work: one of the peculiarities of the history of labour in the West is the progressive subdivision of the stages in the preparation of manufactured goods. Refined techniques and a specialised workforce enabled a greater range of manufactured goods to be offered on the market to customers, who had also become more diverse and were certainly more demanding than before. Since the costs of producing particular sophisticated objects, such as precious textiles or metalwork, were mounting, an ever-widening distinction began to be made on the stalls between goods reserved for a moneyed elite and those destined for everybody else. In this respect, the manufacturing class played a very active role in promoting social discrimination and consequently class conflict. I will mention only one example, but it is striking; until the thirteenth century clothes were not a factor in distinguishing individuals from one another, and indeed, this could only be achieved by adding a band of fur, gold piping or stripes dyed an expensive colour, like red, to the common dress. From then on, however, peasants' clothing was not the same as merchants', who dressed like knights. The development of fashion in clothes (all the more extravagant because it became a sign of social promotion) served to divide individuals from one another. After all, this is a trait which has been familiar to the industrialised nations until fifty years ago and still survives here and there. I will of course not discuss crockery, furniture and tapestries here, whose evolution was of the same order.

On top of this, the vitality of the artisan class was sustained by the uninterrupted advance of technical know-how. I have mentioned mining, but in the textile sector, which has played a leading role for centuries, the innovations of the fourteenth century had become standard. Spinning wheels, looms and silk mills spread from Ypres to Florence before 1420. These tools not only enabled work to be done on a more regular basis, but they also facilitated the diversification of production which I mentioned earlier. For instance, cheap light serges (if rather rough and friable) had begun to be produced in the fifteenth century in England, near Bristol, Winchester and Salisbury, and more especially in the towns between the Meuse valley and maritime Flanders. Old centres like Arras, Tournai, Aire, and Huy were given a new lease of life; other burghs like Hondschoote, Menin, Saint-Trond and Armentières owed their existence to it. At the same moment the introduction of cotton from the East to Italy, Venice and Milan, and then to southern Germany, to Constance, Augsburg and Regensburg, encouraged the production of fustian, which was either a mixture of silk and cotton or more often of wool and cotton. This provided families like the Függer with a solid base from which to take off.

The manufacturing class already had two major sources of strength, which contributed to its growth. Firstly, the links between town and countryside were henceforth to be very firm. For a long time now, guild masters in Italy and then the Rhineland had been entrusting the execution of all or part of the manufacturing process to peasants. In Genoa at the beginning of the fourteenth century, 70–80 per cent of the textile workers employed by the town's entrepreneurs lived in the Appenines. This practice often reflected the masters' hostility towards their local apprentices, who were obliged to be more accommodating because village people were paid less than they were. From time to time, as in Flanders, the apprentices would rush into the hamlets to destroy the equipment of villages competing with them for work. By the beginning of the fifteenth century however, these savage practices were no longer current; on the one hand, the increased

413

specialisation of the apprentices had protected them against competition from peasants who were quite incapable of doing better than them, on the other hand the idea of a division of skills into two levels of different techniques became customary. The textile industry provides us with the best information about this: gathering, washing in running water, drying and spinning linen could only be done in the open air; everywhere this branch of the textile industry developed in the fifteenth century, in Ireland and in Wales, in Burgundy and the Bugey, in Swabia and Bavaria, skeins of linen were carried to the towns from the countryside, where they had been prepared. Woollen cloth, serges and *sayette*-weaving belonged to the countryside, while the town dealt with the finishing processes and dying, and kept the whole sector of *gros drap*, which had a low turn-over but was very highly priced, firmly to itself. Under these conditions constellations of villages were linked to the towns by the work they brought them, and grew up around the finishing centres; villages all along the shores of Lake Constance concentrated around Ravensburg, and the inhabitants of the Severn valley congregated around Bristol; at Prato around 1400 the Datini firm employed 317 workers in town and 453 outside it within a radius of 40 kilometres. Around Canterbury, 15 per cent of the rural population in almost 300 villages devoted some time to clothmaking. The progressive subjugation of the countryside was looming on the horizon.

A second aspect of the structure of the artisan class takes us forwards into the future; the progressive concentration of businesses. When Chrétien de Troyes described a hundred maids working cloth at the end of the twelfth century, he meant to stun his listeners thirsting for marvels. Two centuries later, this really did happen and even frequently. I have evoked the Bardi and just now Prato; at the beginning of the fifteenth century 2,000 workers were employed at the Zecca, Venice's arsenal and mint. A little later, 500 miners worked the alum mines at Tolfa. It is however the concentration of workshops under the same owner, rather than the massive reorganisation of men in a single place, which strikes the historian. Taken separately, each workshop employed only ten or twelve apprentices, even in the Florentine or Frankfurt textile industry, but these workshops formed part of a group; their equipment was often shared, purchases of products were made in concert and the link between these various parts was provided by a common family or a proprietor: the Buonacorsi in Florence, for instance, ruled over 300 workshops. These entrepreneurs were above all merchants; we will meet these leaders of men and financiers again.

The mining boom

The fifteenth century was the century of the mines. After 1460 in Central Europe and particularly in Germany, mining was organised along lines which determined its progress and viability until the eighteenth century and even later. It was because the Empire took the initiative in this process, which coincided with a moderate degree of internal peace, that the regions of the Rhine and the Danube achieved economic superiority even over Italy. It is not very clear just when this development began and there are plenty of historians who claim that it was only the result of a long period of growth dating from the thirteenth

414

Tailors were dressing noble and bourgeois clients, and fashion made its first appearance. From then on, the sort of cloth and trimmings worn – or allowed to be worn – indicated the wearer's position in society. (Three studies of women by Pisanello; Bayonne, Musée Bonnat.)

a) Spinning and weaving at the beginning of the fifteenth century. (A miniature in Boccacio's *Book of noble and famous women*, in a French translation. Ms. Roy 16 GV; London, British Museum.)
b) Raw cloth was bleached or dyed in large vats. (Ms. Roy 15 E III; London, British Museum.)

century. In reality, the problem of its origin is relatively minor; the essential fact is that on the eve of the age of colonial expansion, Europe was capable not only of fully exploiting her subterranean resources, but also of mastering techniques which would allow her to do this in other places.

This was not the result of an intermittent demand; it was not only iron ore extraction and alum mining that were progressing, but so was the search for all the products of the earth. Mineral salt was being mined in Saxony, Upper Poland and around Salins in Comté and such was the surge in the market demand for it, that the volume of salt produced was henceforth linked to the income accruing to the royal or princely treasuries from the *gabelle* or salt tax. This demand also served to increase the importance of the fairs and market places at Chalon-sur-Saône, Metz, Ravensburg and Basle – all situated on the Rhine–Rhone axis. From then on, the seaside salines, particularly those in Languedoc, were jeopardised. Venice was the only southern State which managed to face up to the

'Lotharingian' competition, which the Avignon Popes soon championed vigorously.

The Popes in Rome were themselves in charge of alum extraction, a chemical essential to the cloth-making process, which had fortuitously been discovered around 1461 at Tolfa, on the lands of Saint Peter. The semi-miraculous nature of its discovery (which meant that it was no longer necessary to go to Ottoman Asia Minor to fetch alum mined in Phocea, or to Egypt to buy it from the Mamelukes), together with the fairly scandalous nature of its exploitation (the Medicis of Florence took care of the extraction and marketing, and the Pope had the job of excommunicating anyone who refused to take it) have attracted a lot of attention. On top of this, Genoa and Venice, the traditional purveyors of Oriental alum, were overtaken by Florence; this was not the least of the Medicis' trumps in their rise to power. It is however fair to add that in northern Europe, wood-ash and crushed pumice stone had long been used instead of alum, making this a less profitable commodity than salt.

The extraction of copper also benefited from the discovery of deposits in Styria, where the silver-bearing lead mined there was found in an ore with a very high copper content (2 per cent), superior to Mosan or Iberian deposits. The importance of this metal in the development of both artillery and naval equipment, or more simply of cooking utensils, increased throughout the fifteenth century and especially after 1451, when a Saxon engineer called Funcken perfected a process for separating copper from silver, and copper from antimony. It was after all only two years later that Gutenberg tested the properties of this metal and chose it for casting the first movable characters for the printing press. The profits from the copper mines explain the interest the Függer took in them. They secured the concession of what amounted to the near monopoly of its extraction from Emperor Frederick III, which they kept until the discovery of the copper mines of Peru in the second phase of the age of discoveries.

Iron continued to hold first place among the more essential metals; as far as we can tell, iron production quadrupled between 1460 and 1530, but we can only guess at this from those urban or princely accounts, which do provide us with universal figures. Unlike many other minerals, it seems that iron ore extraction did not move away from its earlier sites. Nowhere do we hear of a boom comparable to the fever which took hold of Massa Maritima in the thirteenth century, where a sizeable town mushroomed between 1225 and 1250. Certain areas of production may even have dwindled, as on Elba, around Milan, in the Pyrenees, while Champagne, the Nivernais, Normandy, Lorraine, Harz and Thuringia stepped up their output. In Germany there were as many as 100,000 miners around 1525, half of whom worked in iron mines. The relative stability of the metallurgical map of Europe is perhaps derived from the fact that iron works were still strictly limited by the availability of fuel and the location of the mines. Other metals were also subjected to these restrictions, but since their volume was less, it eventually became possible to transport them. The processes were gradually perfected: ovens four or five metres high were loaded through an opening and ventilated by means of bellows, but in certain regions, especially in forested areas, work was obstructed by the need for clay for the ovens, wood for fuel, and water-courses for washing. This could lead to a bottleneck in production, as certain businessmen

A gold digger. (A miniature in the *Great Herbal*, fifteenth century; Modena, Biblioteca Estense.) The silver mine of Kutna Hora (right). The miners wear white clothes, use ladders and send the ore up by winch bucket. (Miniature of the end of the fifteenth century; Vienna, Österreichische National Bibliothek.)

like Jacques Cœur in France were aware. Since 25 cubic metres of wood were needed to obtain 50 kilos of cast iron, the risk either of a catastrophic destruction of the forests or of a production stoppage threatened. Coal, although it had been known since the twelfth century, was not yet systematically mined; it was widely used in the Liège countryside, but when the area was repressed by Charles of Burgundy in 1468, his followers were so unaware of its value that they had the coal-mining galleries destroyed and flooded.

Precious metals, on the other hand, were so scarce in Europe – the frequently referred to 'famine' – that energetic searches were undertaken to supplement the increasingly failing silver mines of Saxony or Poitou. The discovery of important mines in Bohemia, at Kutna Hora, at Plsen, allowed the demand to be met for a while. It has been suggested that European production amounted to a total of 85 tonnes at the beginning of the sixteenth century, considerably below requirement. Everyone knows that it was the need to find supplies outside Europe that drove the naval expeditions on their way; a need for silver and even more for gold, since after 1400 Christendom experienced considerable difficulty in reaching her usual gold supplies in the Maghrib, Byzantium and Alexandria. The discovery of meagre seams in Silesia and Moravia around 1475 gave rise to hopes, which were soon perceived to be excessive.

Glass making in Flanders or Germany at the beginning of the fourteenth century: showing sand extraction, ovens, glass blowers, and (left) checking the finished product. (A miniature of the *Journeys of Sir John Mandeville*, Ms. add. 24189, London, British Museum.)

Side-effects

Logically, we should now look at some of their essential products. But in fact, in every case, the actual volume of metal produced is less significant than the formidable amelioration of working conditions in mines, the *Bergwerk* or mountain work as the Germans call it. Since Antiquity it had been so difficult to dig a gallery and so dangerous because of the risks of collapse, asphyxiation or flooding, that only slaves, prisoners or the most deprived persons could be employed for this work. How could improved productivity be hoped for under these conditions? Mining had to be limited to open seams or to seams only a few metres deep. On top of this, Roman law accorded ownership of the substratum to the State and this last could be induced to act only out of good will or interest. In the twelfth century rulers like Barbarossa had included this right among their regalia, and had eventually delegated it, but it was little used. So the first mining codes of the Middle Ages to have survived, for instance that of Iglau in 1249, did indeed allow for the automatic intervention of the ruler.

The arrangement fell apart from the legal point of view in the fourteenth century when the territorial rulers began to appreciate the fiscal advantage that would accrue to them if they delegated their rights over certain mines in return for a sum proportional to their value. Emperor Charles IV did just that in 1366, with the proviso that at least 150 miners were to be taken on, as did Edward III in 1377, reserving the right of preemption at the

419

Money triumphs everywhere. (*Counting Money*, circa 1530–40 by Marinus van Romerswael; Nancy, Musée des Beaux-Arts.)

lowest market price on lead, which was an English monopoly. In France, the king granted mining licences piecemeal either to entrepreneurs like Jacques Cœur, or to local lords, who came to be known in Normandy and Perche as *barons fossiers*; pit barons. By the end of the fifteenth century, nearly all these concessions seem to have been turned into profit-making concerns. The mining master, the *Bergmeister*, generally kept a tenth of the production for himself; he set up a mining company made up (as with the Italian merchant ships) of capital investment and shares in the profits from part of the seam (this could involve as many as 130 burghers, clerics or small landowners investing their savings in the mines). Miners were recruited on a full-time basis and were consequently paid a proper wage. This was an important move in the history of labour, since it introduced a whole new element to the world of work. This sort of organisation could probably not have been as profitable, if it had not introduced a minimum of improvements which made the work possible if not easy. Around 1460 in Poland, pumping systems were perfected for clearing water seepage out of the galleries. About the same time pit props appeared in the more dangerous galleries and, together with the introduction of ventilation shafts equipped with bellows for circulating the air, miners were able to remain underground for several hours at a time. Mine shafts do not appear to have been dropped much below 20 metres because of the inadequate methods of excavation and soil removal. As it was, the list of accidents of all kinds was very long. When the German peasants revolted in 1525, many miners joined them, which is a rather telling indictment of their standard of living; low wages were among the many abuses they complained about. Like the peasants, which most of them were anyway, they

420   were forced to carry the increasingly heavy burden of a richer society.

The importance of money

Those historians who want to put the end of the Middle Ages before 1350 or 1400, would doubtless base their main argument on trade. The Europe of 1500 or 1600 bore no relation to that of 1250 or 1350, even if one refrains from looking beyond the seas; neither the consumer centres, nor the trade routes, nor the products, nor even the techniques were the same. But we are obliged to moved on into the sixteenth century precisely because this huge upheaval, this change in Europe's infrastructure, was effected over a long period and because it was a legacy of the 'crises' of the Middle Ages and prefaced the global explosion of Christianity.

Technical advances did not play a part in this upheaval: we suspected that this was the case in the eleventh and twelfth centuries, and now this was a certainty. Circulation on land did not progress much beyond the great advances of the thirteenth century: horse shoes, whippletrees and movable axles were already familiar things in Philip the Fair's time, but customs tariffs, in Sologne for instance, still went on listing unshod horses well into the fifteenth century. Carts could probably carry bigger loads; around 1350 we hear of 4 tonnes of stone and 2 tonnes of sand being transported in a carriage, the equivalent of a good lorryload – but how many carriages were up to this? Fewer complaints were being made about carts falling apart or potholes on the roads; Philip the Fair even had some stretches of the Lille highway paved. But couriers did not travel any faster than before, not even the fleetest courier service belonging to the Pope, or the *poste publique* created by Louis XI in 1471. One interesting and possibly English innovation dating from the 1320s was the travellers' coach. This was little enough with which to transform a continent.

On water, river navigation showed much the same picture; in many towns including Paris, Rouen and Lyon, the importance of water transport ensured that a few piers were maintained: in Flanders, the *vaarten* and the *overdrag*, canals and dykes, were dredged and enlarged. They could take big barques of 50 to 90 tonnes, with an infinite variety of names which enchanted erudite locals; barges, *tasches*, *aleaumes*, *plates* etc. As for the sea, which inspires many researchers, its booty was the most meagre of all. The Nordic ships, the *kogge*, with their triangular sails and rounded hulls could hold 300 or 400 tonnes; they could do five sea miles to the hour and better with good winds behind them. The galleys of the Mediterranean, with their seventy-five rowers, could not travel any faster and were forced to give way to the *nef*, with its freight carrying capacity of 150 to 200 tonnes, which had adopted the Indian compass and the Scandinavian stern-rudder since the thirteenth century. There must have been some cross-fertilisation between the two types of ship between 1420 and 1425 since war 'galleys' equipped with sails were found in the north, and in the south *caraques* were developed at Genoa to carry up to 900 or 1000 tonnes. Crossing the *nef* with the *kogge* produced a mongrel, the *caravel*, which appeared with her two or three masts and square sails around 1450–60. They had long been used to challenge the Atlantic. None of these innovations had changed the general situation, as the following figures show: in his will of 1423, Doge Mocenigo listed the ships in the Venetian fleet as 45 galleys of 300 tonnes, 300 *nefs* of 150 tonnes and 3,000 more modest barques – a derisory total: the leading merchant power in the Mediterranean could transport 60,000 tonnes at the very most; Genoa perhaps 20,000 at the same time; the whole of the Hanse perhaps 60,000; the Atlantic ports of Spain and France 15,000 and the English scarcely more.

To make up for this, the shifting of the centres of demand was all the more important, in that it was accompanied and often provoked by the establishment of a public authority. We have said that the fifteenth century was the century of capital cities; in many cases it was in fact the forseeable or fortuitous influx of a whole administrative, military and legal personnel which deflected established itineraries towards markets and centres they had not bothered with earlier. Where the old cities were concerned, this trend only confirmed their importance, as with Paris, Lyon, Barcelona, Milan or Rome, or their ascent, as with Florence, Rouen or Lille. But royal towns like Dijon, Bordeaux, Nantes, Southampton, Anvers, Basle, Frankfurt, Augsburg and Lisbon, which have continued to develop and towns like Poitiers, Avignon and Moulins which subsequently declined, expanded into urban agglomerations which had to be fed, where banks could set up business and where all roads converged. The most striking innovation of all was that this population growth was an urban, not a rural phenomenon.

The centres of production were not neglected either; many regions, which had formerly supplied agricultural produce, began to use it themselves, thus putting paid to a source of trade or changing the structure of trade, as with English wool, which stopped being shipped to Flanders. Other new regions stepped in to fill the gaps with their own surplus or rare products; Polish wheat and pitch, Spanish wool and saffron for instance, and took over from the traditional centres of trade, which died for lack of business and were wiped off the map.

New and old routes south and west

Since the overall picture of trade is very confused, I will pick out some of the fundamental innovations within the framework of the Mediterranean, mother of all commerce: indeed, the entire Muslim sea front from the Peloponnesus to Ceuta set the scene for this transformation. Between the Ottomans, with their great advance into the Balkans, and the Sultans, who were extending their power almost into Algeria, the Italian, Provençal, Languedoc and Catalan cities were chiefly concerned with maintaining regular contact with the places which served as outlets for the caravans from Asia or Africa. A tacit understanding grew up between them and smoothed the many exhausting and useless accounting regulations, which were implemented between Genoa and Venice, Palermo and Naples, Valencia and Marseille. Their new relationships were dominated by their common concern not to aggravate a now very perilous situation in the East – and were occasionally perturbed only by the ambitions of rulers like the Angevins, Aragonese and the House of Orléans, who were often strangers to the merchant cities. The Mongol drive into the Crimea, the total isolation of Constantinople and the excessive pretensions of the Mamelukes effectively forced the Italians to make very serious concessions in order to secure access to essential ports like Caffa, Trebizond, Byzantium, Cyprus, Lattakia for

The port of Genoa in the fifteenth century. Galleys, the long narrow war ships propelled by oars, which were mostly used in the Mediterranean can be seen in the upper right. In the centre, the caraques, with their high decks and poops fore and aft and three or four masts. These big ships made sea trade between Portugal and the Indies possible. (Detail from the painting by Cristoforo Grassi, 1485; Genoa, Civico museo navale.)

Genoa; Byzantium, Euboea, Crete and Alexandria for Venice, and the Maghrib for the Catalans. These were the traditional routes and they did not change at all during the fifteenth century. Dishonourable as the trade in black or Caucasian slaves was, it enriched the Neapolitans, Marseillais and especially the Catalans. 10,000 African slaves were counted in Catalonia around 1430 and we know precisely how much slaves of both sexes were sold for in the Christian ports of the Tyrrhenian Sea. This abuse, which gave rise after 1465–7 to a whole range of prohibitive legislation, was rather archaic both in its flow and in its extent, because almost at that very moment the Portuguese were introducing African slaves direct from the Senegal or the Ivory Coast. Other traditional items of Mediterranean trade were gradually leaving the holds of Italian ships; the alum of Tolfa supplanted alum from the East; pepper from Asia was soon competing with pepper brought directly from the Indies to Lisbon. Although they were still carrying pilgrims to the East, as well as wood, a few furs or some lead, it was little enough with which to procure some of that sorely needed gold. Venice persisted, trusting in her spices, cotton and silk, but in Genoa the Lomellini and the Centurione were looking further ahead, setting up bases at Alicante, then Seville, then

423

Venice, the arm of the Grand Canal with the wooden bridge of the Rialto. (A fragment of Jacopo de' Barbari's map, 1500.)

Cadiz and finally Lisbon. The future lay beyond the Straits of Gibraltar, not least because of the increasingly prohibitive nature of the duties payable on Eastern products (33 per cent for alum, 20 per cent for other merchandise) which made them impossibly expensive in Europe. On top of this, the Italians seem to have left the whole commercial exploitation of the Levantine hinterland, of Catalonia and Languedoc, to local shipping or even to the inland markets. They were not to be seen at the cattle fairs of Medina, Siguenza or Pizenas.

New forces were animating the Atlantic seafront. I do not refer to the fishermen and pirates hugging the coast from La Corogne to Plymouth – Basque, Gallician, Breton and Gallic sailors who had been doing this for ages. For many years too, boats had been taking 'claret' from Bordeaux and La Rochelle to Britain and bringing back soldiers. However two important changes took place over this whole area, which had until then been remote from the great trade routes, the first between 1350 and 1450 and the second after 1470. In the first phase Brittany and perhaps Navarre experienced a vitality and a dynamism, which were all the more surprising since the opposite was happening elsewhere. Whether one thinks of the Calvaries and the great monuments of Brittany, which almost all date from this time, or of the Pyrenean mercenaries, whose services were also secured then, it is not clear whether these were the effects of a particular demographic structure or the dawn of a new economy. The rise of Bayonne and the awakening of Nantes, Vannes and Saint-Malo all date from this time. After 1470, while this first phase was drawing to its close (Brittany and the Landes remained the concern of the Valois) a second began to emerge: having been the English throne's most cherished overseas city for three centuries, Bordeaux slipped out of its grasp and was apparently condemned to die; wine no longer left her shores and the whole countryside around her was hostile. In actual fact, the town recovered quickly, revived first by the pastel of Toulouse, then by the wines of Gaillac, and then by renewing their exports of Médoc wines. After 1475 she was reconciled with her ruler, who treated her with consideration. Matters were further improved when the whole maritime area from Bayonne to Saint-Malo came under the same authority after Normandy was assimilated – appeased after the last upheavals of Louis XI's reign. The population of Rouen tripled and at Dieppe it doubled. In spite of his general insouciance, Francis I did allow himself to be well advised in founding a sea port for Rouen, Le Havre de Grace, in 1517. The French kingdom seemed to be prepared for the onset of the Atlantic adventure ahead of England, as far as the island's Channel ports were concerned. It was from Dieppe that Béthencourt sailed at the end of the fifteenth century, from Saint-Malo that Jacques Cartier sailed in 1530. The Seine, the Loire and the Garonne had formerly been obstacles across the north–south routes but were now commercial arteries leading deep within the kingdom.

The revolution in the North

Further North the situation was similarly transformed; the 'Flanders route' and the Champagne Fairs were no longer viable. War, then the frontier along the Somme, loomed over the North and disrupted one of the primordial axes of European trade. This axis shifted further east and followed first the Rhine and eventually the Saône and Rhône, at least in the time of the Valois Dukes of Burgundy and the Avignon Popes. This new route had vital consequences. In the first place, Flanders and Liège faded away: these brilliant centres of European life, which had shone for almost three centuries, subsided into mere memories of greatness: Ghent and Liège did achieve a last flicker of life after 1500 but the end had come, brought on by a swarm of literati and ecclesiastics, who settled on the two proud cities and stifled them. The fate of Bruges was the result of irrevocable natural circumstances: the sea retreated, altering the shape of the coastline and silting up the Zwin. They tried everything in their efforts to save the pearl of Flanders – tidal basins, drainage, a new harbour channel in 1516, sophisticated port equipment – but the town fell asleep, no doubt for ever. Antwerp on the contrary perked up once the Escaut estuary had been dredged. The town, a small sea port, became an English staple. After 1480 Spanish wool started arriving and then English cloths and around 1515 a fair was created there. This was an important move, the more so in the light of another innovation, created when these southern islands and estuaries united with the northern ones to form Holland. Dordrecht grew up on the Waal, which had long been just a stockade; on the Lek Rotterdam was pushing up as the heir to Duurstede of former times. Further inland, at Delft, at Berg op Zoom, at Leyden and Maastricht, fairs and workshops were reaping the inheritance of Flanders and Liège. Although Amsterdam was still only a herring burgh, the birth of Holland was a big event in the history of commerce and of thought. Further upstream the *Pfaffenstrasse* of the twelfth century developed into a string of markets and fairs, ancient centres like Cologne and Frankfurt and new ones like Basle, Geneva and Chalon. As for Lyon, so long overshadowed by Avignon, the town flourished after the Popes had definitively returned to Rome. In 1464 the Italian banks set up counters there, and after 1470 Louis XI supported the installation of her international fair.

The current of European commerce now flowed from Antwerp to Lyon and Marseille: France was thrown back towards the west, a move which opened her up to the Atlantic. Italy tried to avoid being stifled by seeking bases in Spain and Portugal. There remained one place in the north of Europe looking onto the Atlantic – England. This brings us to yet another link with 'modern' history. It is part of traditional European and especially French thinking to associate England with the sea. Her situation, the origins of her Saxon and Norman inhabitants and her traditional, almost aggressive reserve towards the Continent all appear to justify the truism 'England is an island'. Too hastily spoken, because the English sailors had not yet achieved more than a certain aptitude for coastal fishing and a few of them had dared as 'Adventurers' to sail as far as Novgorod or even Pavia. The vessels frequenting the 'Cinque Ports' on the southern coast or London, in which wine, salt, pastel, ashes and skins were imported and wool or lead exported, were Norman, Breton, Spanish, Flemish and especially German – those 'Hanseatics' or *Österlingen* we have already met. When battles took place, including the Battle of the Sluys of 1340, the sailors were Bretons and their officers Genoese. There were no English sailors, apart from a handful of pirates, which is why the 'Navigation Act' of 1381, which reserved the right of trading with the archipelago to 'nationals' was a farce. A farce, but also portentous; it was immediately linked with the emergence of a woollen industry on the island and with the concentration

a) Antwerp (left) replaces Bruges; showing a port crane at the beginning of the sixteenth century.
b) A view of London at the end of the fifteenth century (right). In the foreground, the Tower; the Kings sometimes resided and held their councils there. In the background, London Bridge, rebuilt in stone in the twelfth century and entirely covered with houses, with Saint Paul's, the Gothic Cathedral, behind.

in the towns of a workforce, susceptible of being turned into artisans, miners or sailors, with the help of the land enclosures. This major reversal of policy, which could not have been considered under the Edwards, started slowly; after 1400, 38,000 pieces of cloth were exported to Calais, in 1480 it was 65,000 and in 1510, 90,000. These products left London but also Bristol, Southampton, Boston, Hull and Ipswich and landed at Lisbon in the south, at Bergen in the north and at the mouths of the Rhine in between. When Edward IV created the association of Merchant Venturers, a sort of official guild of English exporters, he conferred considerable privileges on them: 50 per cent control over trade within the island, 70 per cent outside it. This time they were Englishmen using English boats: by 1475 Normandy and Brittany could no longer be counted on and Charles Duke of Burgundy was hostile.

He was not alone. An enormous obstacle rose up in the way of English merchants and English expansion: the Germans of the Hanse. This great Baltic association reached its apogee in the first half of the fifteenth century, its sailors won all the trade from Novgorod and Bergen to London and Bruges. They could be seen as far away as Bourgneuf, on the shores of the Vendée; inside the Empire itself they rallied the whole hinterland up to the *Hellweg*, the great transversal route from Cologne to Magdeburg, as well as the big cities of the north-western area as far as Cologne. They were to be found along the rivers of Swabia and along the upper Rhine as far as the Alps; the number of German, Hanseatic or Bavarian merchants who regularly crossed the Brenner or the Saint-Gothard passes was so great   427 that they obtained a special quarter and hall in Venice – the *fondaco dei Tedeschi*. The Hanseatic empire comprised seventy-seven towns around 1375, but by 1450 it had grown to include over 200, from those parts of the Sund it had grabbed from the Danes, to all along the Baltic and Frisian coastlines and as far inland as Nuremberg and Strassburg. The English managed to penetrate this network only in two ways; their commercial techniques, mostly borrowed from the Italians, were more flexible than the Germans' credit mechanisms and accounting methods, which remained fairly archaic, and they quickly won the upper hand by selling their island's cloths in the market places of the interior. The English avoided direct confrontation with the Hanseatic fleets in the Danish waters or in the Baltic and instead they infiltrated the Rhine, the Main, and the Weser and opened warehouses in Frankfurt, Leipzig, Nuremberg, Basle and Constance. They were not seen in Gdansk before the sixteenth century, by which time they had won their freedom of action. Although the Tudors, especially Henry VIII, are credited with having created the English fleet, this was more in intent than in reality; for instance the Cabot brothers, whose ship left Plymouth for the Atlantic in 1497, were still Italians, and Elizabeth I deserves the final credit. However her vital achievement dates from the fifteenth century and does not concern us.

The recovery of coinage

Long before the hypothetical effects of prospecting in Africa or Asia could be felt in 1535 or 1540, Europe had to live through a hundred years of currency shortage, alleviated in the 1460s when a little more silver in Central Europe and a little more gold in Hungary allowed a whole range of coins of quality to be circulated. These new *testons, gulden, groschen* etc., provided a vital stimulus to trade, both in Europe and with the rich countries of the Levant. Venice, as a net importer of goods, was the major route for the loss of precious metals, but she lost her trading posts in the Peloponnesus between 1498 and 1503, and her merchants were forced, following the loss of Cyprus since 1473 and of the Black Sea since 1479 and 1490, to knock on the doors of Islam, which was notoriously unfriendly in the East and very unsafe in the West. In spite of these restrictions, costs rose in line with the appearance of royal fleets and armies, expensive buildings, a devouring administration and far-flung expeditions. Both the State and the individual amassed debts and borrowed, but the lenders themselves did not have bottomless coffers.

One solution was obvious; taking money out of its hiding places. There was no lack of Church treasure, workers' savings, merchants' deposits. The monetary dispositions implemented at the end of the fifteenth century, without which the *caravels* would not have been equipped, were called public taxation. The towns began it: Genoa and Florence from 1415 or 1420 put their public funds in the charge of a sort of State bank, which cashed the seizures, the indirect revenues, the taxed benefices and the income from levies imposed on revenues, known as *estime* in Languedoc. In Tuscany the imposition of a great tax on wealth led to the drafting of that enormous census of 1427 known as the *catasto*, but which was not repeated for twenty years. In Liguria on the contrary the Casa di San Georgio did function as public treasurer for a while, before the intrigues of the Consuls or the principal *alberghi*, who treated it like a sort of communal coffer, forced it to stop all payments in 1445.

At the same time a series of bankruptcies, like those of the Balbi and the Fioravanti, brought the companies' credit crashing down. The monarchies alone were able to avoid these disasters by forcing taxes upon their people, but since local conditions varied from one land to another, coordination was impossible before the end of the century. In France Charles VII and especially Louis XI managed to increase the *fouage* (hearth tax), turning it into a royal *taille* (*tallage*) worth four times its value in 1440. In 1471 a new regulation for indirect taxation allowed a new monetary recovery to be hoped for. But the Valois proved incapable of issuing a good coinage, unlike England, where the coinage was never debased, although her destructive civil war had just been ended and although the English money had suffered from the operation of Gresham's Law, when the Dauphin Charles flooded Normandy with poor French coins as part of his struggle against the regent Bedford in the dark days from 1420 to 1430. The Burgundian Duke Charles, conversely, who was well placed on the edges of the major commercial axis of the new Europe and was, above all, at grips with the glaring fiscal disparities from Mâcon to Frisia, aimed at new heights. The Empire could no longer be counted on, since, in spite of its proud motto which became the House of Austria's (*Austriæ est imperare orbi universo*, AEIOU: 'to Austria pertains the right to rule over the entire world') the Habsburg Frederick III was quite incapable of commanding anyone and his son Maximilian did not earn his nickname Max *ohne Geld* (penniless Max) for nothing. This left the Spaniards, but their involvement in buying out the military Orders, conquering Granada and soon after that, undertaking the Atlantic voyages, made them turn their backs on the rest of Europe.

So it was Charles the Bold who took the surprising initiative of summoning conferences at Bruges in 1469, where his finance ministers and those of Louis XI and Edward IV of York tried to establish firstly a common ratio of 1:11.3 or 11.4 between the two precious metals in order to limit speculation, and then to restore coins of better alloy to circulation on the security of their tax returns. In Germany, where a new 'florin' had been issued throughout the Rhineland since 1386, Charles obtained Frederick III's agreement, although it was never put into effect. Venice and Florence however did rally to this cartel; both the florin and the ducat remained the standard gold coins, further north as well.

Europe was ripe for this medieval version of Bretton-Woods. In Germany and Scandinavia and even Holland, the extreme scarcity of gold, together with the fiscal anarchy, made the gold–silver ratio climb to 1:12 and even 1:13 around 1505 or 1510. The gold coinages remained in principle tied to the Rhine or the Dutch florin, but even in Cologne or Antwerp its title remained low, 20 carats at best. As for the silver *groschen*, although its rate of exchange recovered briefly to a value of 40 *deniers* (It had been worth 20 in 1380, but 300 in 1433) it started falling again after 1488–9. Around 1500 the monetary situation was degraded to such an extent (with the *groschen* at 95 *deniers*, with an insignificant title) that this country became prey above all else to speculation. Without wishing to diminish the value of religious feeling, it is difficult to comment on the brutal conversion of all this area to Lutheranism a quarter of a century later, without denouncing what the near-bankrupt princes immediately resorted to – the seizure of the Church's property, a rich booty which filled their coffers anew.

Inversely, could one not say that in France, the relative fidelity of the Valois to the old ways was due to the fact that their financial position was greatly improved since Louis XI? Firstly by abolishing the last mint rights not under royal control (in 1481 for Anjou-Provence) and then by applying severe fiscal pressure, which nonetheless allowed the economy to pick up and so won the approval of the wealthiest men, especially in the towns. In 1475 the king had a new variant of the gold *écu à la couronne* struck, called the *écu au soleil*. As for the silver content of the *gros*, which had been adjusted in 1455 to 92/100 fine silver and was current at 30 deniers, it was fixed after 1472 at a rate of just over 3 grams of silver per coin, but was supplemented by poorer coins of different accounting values, *liards*, *blancs à la couronne* etc., until the creation in 1514 of a *teston* of almost 10 grams, of fine title, worth ten *sous*. The situation should be appreciated in the context of France's relative economic isolation from the beginning of the sixteenth century, taking account too of the crushing weight of taxation which bore on the taxpayer. To a certain extent the sequels of the great '*remuement*' of the fourteenth century can still be seen in our day.

England did not present a clear picture either. From the end of the War of the Roses until the taxes imposed by Cardinal Wolsey around 1517–19, her evolution was fairly similar to that of France. A new gold noble was struck and a shilling was put into circulation, which began to falter during Henry VIII's wars, and worried Cranmer and other royal counsellors. Although the Tudor king's rupture with Rome was due predominantly to personal motives, and the idea of seizing the monasteries' property does not seem to have occurred to him, Anglicanism nevertheless made a major contribution to the Exchequer.

Finally, it was on the southern flank of Europe that the complexity of the monetary problem was most evident. Not in Spain – where the conquest of Granada was much more instrumental than the pinch of gold brought back by Columbus in allowing quality coins like the gold *excellente* of 1497 to be minted, and where the effects of an influx of exotic products were first felt – but in Italy. Firstly because the continuous trickle of gold very quickly disrupted the Bruges arrangements. The ratio between silver, which was in very short supply, and gold, which was relatively abundant, was reduced by 1480 to 1:10.75 and even to 1:10. These conditions tended to drive gold north beyond the Alps or to ensure that it was immediately invested. It was this alternative, the impoverishment or headlong flight of gold, which explains the part the Italians played in launching the great expeditions which started after 1460–70, apart, of course, from their experience as sailors and travellers. The various currencies in circulation suffered from these ill-fated fluctuations: in 1472 Venice issued a *lira* which was supposed to represent 10 *grossi*, like Louis XII's *teston* in France later on. But these coins stood up badly against Spanish competition, which operated via Naples and Sicily from 1440, or against German competition. As for the florin, its legendary stability, which won it the name of 'dollar of the Middle Ages' from pre-1960s historians, caused its value to rise dramatically in terms of the Florentine silver currency; the debasements of the *quattrino* began at the end of Lorenzo the Magnificent's rule and were especially bad in the time of Savonarola (1490–8). Its old Venetian rival, the ducat, had already supplanted it as the standard currency by the beginning of the sixteenth century, due, among other reasons, to Venice's modest but regular supply of gold. This was another 'modern' feature. But the monetary situation in Europe was still precarious on the

Minting coins; the workman strikes the matrix with his hammer, which impresses the design on the coin. (*Treatise on the first invention of money*, by Nicholas Oresme, fifteenth century; Paris, Bibliothèque nationale.)

threshold of the sixteenth century. Indeed, we all know how Europe was spurred on by her recovered dynamism and by the weakness of her neighbouring continents, to leave her confines in order to seek a solution to these problems. Equally familiar is the explanation that it was those citizens, who controlled or rather were ruled by gold, who encouraged, supported and perpetuated the 'great discoveries'. Both in economic and politic terms, the 'merchants' were now the State's leading men.

The 'Wall of Money'

Because they controlled both ends of the chain of production, raw materials and distribution; because they controlled the various stages of the intermediary work by their power to lend or not lend money for wages and equipment; because they even controlled production at the family level by providing their only means of distribution, and finally because the State was their leading customer and servant (even if they did not necessarily appear at its head), the merchants, whom the Middle Ages had proscribed, were the new masters of society. One can argue over the nature of the 'mode of production' they gradually introduced into the economy, and whether it was or was not 'capitalism'. This is a theoretical problem of no particular interest to us, and we shall restrict ourselves to recalling that this word does not apply solely to the concept of profit and wages, but that it also implies the control of the public sector by private interest, social tension and class conflict in all sectors of the population, as well as the attempts to employ colonial, imperial or whatever sort of violence in order to maintain and increase profits. The handful of men I am about to discuss had assimilated many of these aspects, but the rest had not.

One of the most blatant features of the group, which turned it into the embryo of a

431

particular social class, was the legislation which protected them, and them only. Since merchants were excluded from the old social orders, since the eleventh century, or at any rate the twelfth, they had demanded and obtained protections, a *jus mercatorum*, a *Kaufmannsgericht*. Then, when the persistent troubles of the fourteenth century appeared alongside galloping taxation, they were granted here and there, for instance in the time of Philip the Fair in France, *cartae mercatoriae*, safe conducts which guaranteed steady trade. Better still, in an old city like Venice, the sea-faring expeditions, the *muda*, were given an armed naval escort because commerce was identified with the city herself. But it was in the fifteenth century that 'merchandise' managed to escape the common destiny: the merchants had their own law courts like the Florentine *Mercanzia*, their special quarters and their notaries; they were exempted from certain *tallages*; they were granted possession of royal lands by the ruler; they were delegated official work and parts of public revenues. Some commercial legislation even authorised groups of merchants, notably in Germany, to requisition armed convoys (*Schilddrake*) as their escorts.

It was the merchants who ensured that money circulated as widely as possible, but this money was perhaps not the same as the money they handed over or received when buying or selling. One has the feeling that they relied on the trade in money, the 'bank' as it was called from then on, for their most important profits and that this was their most important business, probably responsible for introducing distinctions into the merchant class, which had formerly been less in evidence. The merchant stayed put; he sent young men – trainees – out along the roads and over the seas who served him as letter carriers, employees and factors in his branches, while he limited himself to counting money and to frequenting municipal or royal palaces. This development – which was not without its perils on the eve of the global expansion of trade – had an immediate effect on the merchant's social position. He was in the town, close to his debtors and to the *Casa* where his money consolidated the public debt, to the Monte di Pietà where he would take up the unredeemed bonds, to the palace where his clients' funds were deposited. He was a man in the swim of things, who knew about everyone's affairs, and the step from there to the communal palace was easily taken. He used the money entrusted to him by the thrifty, by his colleagues and by rulers, to launch new businesses. After 1402 in Germany (in the forefront for once), in 1450 in Italy, the banker could even consent to loans on these monies. This was current practice in many places, which functioned as centres of credit and as bourses; Genoa, Florence, Rome, Venice of course, but also Frankfurt, Strasbourg, Nuremberg and Hamburg in the Empire, and Montpellier, Paris or Lyon in France, as well as Bruges and Antwerp, London and Barcelona.

Added to this, accounting techniques, which made such progress in the fourteenth century, continued to improve. It was as much a matter of simply perfecting old practices, as of ensuring that the best ones passed into common use. For instance, maritime insurance caught on everywhere north of the Alps after 1440, with premiums (settled in front of a notary) of between 3 to 5 per cent of the value of the merchandise. Contracts of the *colleganza* type, which enabled one individual's capital to enter into association with another's labour, also spread through Germany, where they were called *Wedderleging* or

432

Fürlegung, according to the locality. The itinerant merchant generally took a third of the profits, though this proportion could also vary, and in the larger sense, these contracts involved an agreement by which a whole sector of small proprietors could participate in, and who thus became involved in big business. As for the funds (*sors, loca*), which all sorts of people invested in these companies, they ended by becoming 'shares' which could be sold, bequeathed or placed.

It is surprising that, once this level had been reached, cheques were not introduced as part of the whole range of credit instruments available to accountants. But in fact, the fifteenth century had to put up with the bill of exchange; a practice which began in the thirteenth century, no doubt following the notarised contracts of exchange which were drawn up at the Champagne fairs or in the Italian piazzas, with the principal object of avoiding transporting coins, always a risky enterprise. The debtor would acquit his debt somewhere else, in the local coin, and the sum would then be debited from his bank account, at the local rate of exchange for that day. A customary delay, of two months between Genoa and Paris or Bruges, but three for Seville, four for London, allowed time not only for the letter of payment to be carried there, but also for the payer to arrange to supplement his account, if this was necessary. It is obvious that the practice could be extended; it was enough to gamble on the different rates of exchange between one place and another, or to send the bill of exchange on a round journey, returning to its place of origin to realise a notable increase in value between the sum previously advanced and the one which was cashed (bills of exchange and re-exchange). The bill then became an instrument of interest-bearing loans. However, here again, the ensuing stage, which involved endorsing and negotiating these effects, is not clear to us. Like Louis XI in 1463, certain rulers were in any case fairly hostile to what they considered speculative manoeuvres, and indeed they were based on the great variations in exchange rates at certain moments of the year when either the shortage of cash or, on the contrary, its abundance, allowed profitable calculations to be made. For instance, when the ships left Genoa in September or April, or when the Pope in Rome decided to appoint people to benefices, or to move to a summer residence, or in Valencia in July just before the wheat or rice harvest, money became unobtainable – and reimbursements could be arranged . . .

As for purely accounting practices, notably double entry bookkeeping, they spread very slowly beyond Italy, and were found in Toulouse or Cologne only in the sixteenth century. Arabic numerals on the other hand, were widely used in Italy or Spain before 1432 and in all Europe by about 1490.

Business

The age of companies like the Bardi has gone as surely as have the pedlars of ancient times. I pointed out just now that manipulating money was henceforth a systematic part of the wealth and activities of the rich, but this did not imply that there was a uniform type of mercantile association. There were always individual enterprises, scarcely even family ones, in that they did not appeal, as they had previously done, to their relations for financial

a) All transactions involved bargaining (above). Aristotle's *Political and economic ethics*, a translation by Nicholas Oresme, fifteenth century. (Rouen, Bibliothèque municipale.)

b) A banker and money lender. (J. Le Grant, *Le Livre de bonnes moeurs*, fifteenth century.)

and other forms of support. Although these were often embryos of bigger businesses, they could also include the personal achievements, either of an ambitious adventurer or of a dynasty jealously closed in on itself, concentrating the bulk of the business and profits in the hands of a single member. One famous and tenacious example comes to mind immediately, that of the Függer of Nuremberg, who next settled in Augsburg. The family had been known since the fourteenth century, but it was the brothers Georg, Ulrich and Jakob who launched it when fustian was introduced to southern Germany. The most active one,

434

Jakob II, managed to acquire shares in the gold mines of Hungary and the copper mines of Styria and Bohemia, thus controlling a notable part of the trade in these metals from Venice to Leipzig. In their case, they opened no branches and employed no agents, just a few diligent 'visitors'. Jakob II's energy enabled him to launch himself into banking thanks to his enormous concentration of capital which allowed him to do without intermediaries and 'business expenses'. He was esteemed by Maximilian I, to whom he had advanced loans at very high interest, at a time when nobody else considered the Emperor solvent. This earned him the position of personal banker to the Habsburgs. We know how he threw all his credit in every sense of the word into the imperial election of 1519, and so determined the success of Charles V. Following this, he continued to support the ruler's policies by paying both the Swiss troops which defeated Francis I at Pavia and the Germans who put Rome to the sack. This allowed him to influence imperial politics and it can be said that the fate of Luther and the Papacy lay in his hands. He died advanced in years in 1525.

This example is not the only one of its kind. But taken as a whole, the variety of business dealings led merchants to form groups, either on a regional basis or specialising in a particular commodity. This was frequently the case in the Empire. The Ravensburg Company, which was created by the Humpys around 1380, belonged to the first sort, with counters dispersed throughout Europe. By 1500 they had four in southern Germany as well as the mother establishment, five between Basle and Montpellier, three in Spain and as many in Italy and England. Each of these counters dealt on the spot with all the business which came their way. This could be wool, lead, saffron, wood, wine and of course loans. Hanseatic merchants like the Castorp, the Welser, the Veckinchusen, employed factors specialising on the contrary in a particular merchandise; furs with one, wheat with another, and timber with yet another. Although basically separate companies, they were controlled by the Lübeck or Hamburg establishments which paid their employees. This system was more flexible than the former because it spread the risks, but both systems were exposed to the effects of a sudden failure of one of their counters.

This is precisely what brought about the collapse of the Italian companies in the fourteenth century. Once they had learned their lesson, the Italian associations adopted a much more flexible and informed system. The case of the Medicis is the most well known. To begin with, in the Salvestro period, and even the Cosimo period around 1430–5, the business was a bit like the Függer's in that it was concentrated between a few hands. However Salvestro's ambiguous role during the Florentine insurrections of 1378 revealed a dimension unknown outside Italy; the merchant as man of the city. In order to play a determining role Cosimo needed two trumps: that of affecting a liberal mien without pushing himself to the forefront; and that of collecting many debtors, both clients who could be controlled, and dependant relations who would influence the people and fill positions – after which he would occasionally and modestly accept to be elected *Gonfalonnier* for a year or two before dying in 1464 as an admired Maecenas, a 'Father of the nation', having in passing invented the alum of Tolfa, and triumphed over Milan and Venice. Cosimo managed to amass a capital of two and a half million florins, but he was careful to distribute both the sources of his revenues and their collection points with skill; **435** draperies, banks, lands, corn and the profits drawn from them represented his principal assets. The organisation was based on a dozen branches, whose directors were nominated by Cosimo. He started off by funding them but then left them to make their businesses pay on their own. This meant that he could cut off a profitless branch without affecting the general equilibrium of the company. In general, Cosimo limited himself to setting up his branches in safe and many-faceted places; London, Bruges, Cologne, Geneva, Lyon, Avignon, Milan, Venice and Rome. On one occasion he threw himself into a cartel aimed at removing competitors, but which also dragged him and his docile city into armed conflict; this was for the alum of Tolfa, by agreement with the Pope, against the King of Naples and Venice. He had to be both flexible and energetic to control this hydra-headed business empire. His son Piero died soon after him and was succeeded by the two brothers Lorenzo and Giuliano, who exposed the limits of the company's power. Giuliano died trying to stifle insubordination in the city in 1478 and Lorenzo threw himself into an expensive and dangerous policy of erecting buildings and waging war. His artistic and literary achievements and the brilliance of Florence certainly won him the title of 'Prince of Florence', which he pretended to refuse, as well as the more deserved one of 'the Magnificent'. He still needed to succeed in business: in 1477 the London branch collapsed, as did the Bruges and Milan branches in the following year, and that of Avignon in 1479. Lorenzo was as indifferent to this discomfiture as he was to the fate of his bankrupt directors (the Bruges one, Portinari, died in the hospice in 1501) caring only for poetry and municipal intrigue. By his death in 1492 the company had no purpose other than politics.

A profile of the rich

If these names are among the best known of medieval men of business, I have chosen them because they illustrate certain forms of behaviour in the field of commerce. This is perhaps to neglect other figures, but rather than draw up elaborate lists, let us try to identify the principal means by which they became rich.

One of the centuries-old restrictions on commerce is obvious; the inability of merchants to predict events and the risks inherent to moving goods around, as is adequately demonstrated by the many precautions taken. On top of this, the merchant could not be sure of disposing of his goods, given the near impossibility of storing the greater part of his merchandise, especially foodstuffs. At Prato the Datini firm calculated its profits from most of its sea operations at not more than 7 to 12 per cent. Of course opportunities for cashing in successfully did occur; over their first three years of working the mines of Tolfa, the Medici won a net profit of 48 per cent (25,000 ducats), and in 1494–1500 the Függer found that their profits from the Slovak copper mines, which the Thurzos were in charge of, were in the range of 33 per cent. Money was perhaps the only more profitable business; placements and loans were consented to at very variable rates of interest according to the importance or the length of the loan, but short loans were more often charged 15 to 20 per cent interest; just below the 'usurious' level prohibited, if not always very sincerely, by the Church, because her allies, the Florentines, tendered loans at 33 per cent interest. Credit was only important if the borrower, solvent or otherwise, was a great personage. If he wasn't, he would only rarely be able to raise funds via such transactions. The money changers, the Lombards, the Piedmontese of the Savoy *casane*, and the Jews lent money against sureties, but the flight of a debtor could ruin more than one of these creditors, as was seen at Bruges when a sudden monetary conversion was effected. As for loans granted to the great, the risks were similar to those of the fourteenth century. When Portinari, the director of the Medici branch in Bruges, went bankrupt it was for lending far too much money to Charles *le Téméraire* right up to the moment when the Duke fell under the blows of the Swiss and Lorraine soldiery.

The two other ways of making money should be mentioned. One of them was of course ownership of land. As we have already seen, burghers had their own gardens and little farms; merchants also went in for stock-raising contracts, the *gasailles* or the *soccida* of the Mediterranean countries, or else they invested in manors. Examples can be found in all countries: the Medicis drew a quarter of their income from the land and Francesco Sassetti, their director general, invested as much as 32 per cent of his in 1462. Even in Venice, the Barberigo, who had lands in Treviso or Verona, did not invest more than 10 per cent of their total income in trade. Their compatriot, Caterina Cornaro, drew an annual income of 67,000 ducats from her estates in Cyprus. Across the Alps it was the same story; for every Függer owning only town houses, there were all the Welser, the Humpys, the Hülpüchel, the Imhof, all those in Lübeck, Ravensburg, Nuremberg, and the Heim of Augsburg, not forgetting Kaspar Popplau, the richest man in Germany in 1457, who were all lords of lands and communities and owners of woods and fields. The French were even less keen on taking risks, so the picture there is identical: the Pelletier in Normandy, the Jossard at Lyon, the d'Heu at Metz. As for the Ysalguier of Toulouse, they drew as much as 1,000 livres annual revenues from their 1,000 hectares, their four lordships, their castle in Beauvoir and their baronial rights at Hauterive (around 1458).

It was also in France, more than elsewhere, that another way of becoming rich and powerful widened; access to public office. The king soon appreciated the profits he could draw from the sale of offices. He started off by conceding a few of them when he was in debt, sometimes together with the very places – tolls, castles, forests and provostships – where they were situated. The practice of farming out revenues proved just as useful. Those who thus found themselves in charge of the mint, of levying aids or rounding up sailors, began by enriching themselves before tackling the highest ranks of society; in René of Anjou's time, for instance, one of the Forbin of Marseille rose to be Viceroy of Provence in 1474. We could end with no better example of all these ambitions and disappointments than that of Jacques Cœur, the leading businessman of France, whose extravagant life-style more than matched that of all his predecessors. The son of a Bourges tanner, he raised himself up from trading in wool in the little local markets to advancing loans to the officers in Charles VII's entourage. He then won entry to the royal clientele, becoming master of the Mint in 1436, farmer of the aids and the Gabelle in 1437, and Treasurer and adviser to the King in 1442. He subsequently became the ruler's creditor, providing him with the artillery which won back Normandy. He was sent on missions to Naples and Rome. Cœur managed to exploit all these journeys and functions so efficiently that he was able to launch enterprises of all kinds with astonishing dynamism; opening up mines in the Cévennes, the wine trade in Avignon and Limoges, brokerage and money-changing in London and Bruges, building galleys in Marseille. More than three hundred servants furthered his concerns from Italy to England. His personal estate and his buildings were valued at 600,000 livres, and a few sumptuous traces of his wealth can still be seen in Bruges. This was too much for France then, and what was more, he was without connections, purpose or guarantees. He was arrested for embezzlement in 1453, just after the death of his protectress Agnès Sorel, the king's mistress, but he managed to escape and flee to Rome where he started up again, equipped a few ships and sailed to the Aegean where he died before Chios in 1456. Although his is not at all an exemplary story, it provides a brilliant example of the ascendancy and treachery of money.

A fractured society

If, after surveying the new economic structures, we now inspect the bases of society we find enormous changes. The old framework, already out of date in the thirteenth century, of an ordered society had burst asunder. Some clerics – theoreticians or the implicated agents of authority – still claimed that there were three orders, the 'estates', and indeed this went on being said until 1789, and can still be read in works which reek with nostalgia for sabre and incense; all demented notions which do not stand up to the impartial glance. What gave this sort of social harmony its *raison d'être* was the awareness of belonging to a predetermined group charged by God and the *respublica* with accomplishing a precise task for the greater good of all. Apart from the fact that this Arcadia had never existed, what was left of it by 1500? There were only promotions, forfeitures, excesses, conflicts, redistributions, in short an eminently mobile and new society, founded or about to found itself on the already ancient idea of social classes. To deny this is dishonest or just blind. Worse, the principal pillar of the relationship, at least in theory, between the parties in this 'feudal system', was a tacit agreement between the producer, who was asked to give no more than was necessary, and the master, who used this surplus, these '*rentes*', to ensure the rights and favours of the State; justice, protection and security. This arrangement did not come into question in the fifteenth century, and it can even be said that it was the establishment of new relationships, which were hostile on principle, which marked the end of the medieval age.

New lines of strength

Long-standing phenomena such as the redistribution of wealth or the establishment of new social relationships rarely struck contemporaries as such, being much more sensitive to immediate events – bankruptcies, debts, revolts, and trials – which they failed to interpret fully. By the fifteenth century, however, as in the twentieth, the psychological shifts, the new relations between the generations, the changes within the familiar framework were

Jacques Cœur's luxurious dwelling in Bourges: the Royal Treasurer's principal residence, with its splendid stone tracery, is a masterpiece of the Flamboyant style of civic architecture.

The service of the Lady; 'offering his heart'. This tapestry illustrates the International Gothic style of the 1400s, and is one of its last manifestations. (Paris, Musée de Cluny.)

all more clearly perceived. The moralists invariably stigmatised the decay of morals and the indolence of the young, while the sceptics spoke of passing fashions and fortuitous circumstances. The historian has got to find some continuity to this mass of minor details. In the next chapter we will examine the profound moral and spiritual mutation which distressed a world one hesitates to call Christian, so meaningless this concept seemed to have become between 1450 and 1520. For the moment, a few fundamental features of society should be identified, without which the above would be hard to understand.

To start off with, there were striking innovations in human behaviour. Whether cause or effect of the demographic revival evoked at the beginning of this chapter, the structure of the family, relations between husband and wife, between father and son, changed. The basic catalyst seems to have been the progressive liberation of the individual in relation to his social or family group. Formerly seen as 'solitude' and rejected, individual destinies

440

were now exemplified in the lives of Jacques Cœur, Francisco Sforza or Christopher Columbus. The mingling of peoples had contributed too by tearing so many men away from their roots that a 'letter of naturalisation' could change them, by public consent, into inhabitants equal to the other inhabitants in a country they had newly settled in. This did not mean that relatives and associates ceased to form groups; they continued to play a leading role in municipal affairs or in commerce, estate management or providing support in court. We have seen plenty of examples of this and more are to come. Maybe too, here and there, individuals formed new groupings out of fear or mistrust of the government. Around 1480 or 1490 in the Low Countries, the Cotswolds, and the Pays de Caux, compact groups of several dozen individuals living under one roof have been observed, not to mention the isolated, essentially mountainous, areas in the Basque country, Queyras or Savoy, and in the Apennines, where these arrangements were the rule, if only for reasons dictated by the economy. This was certainly an old trait which faded slowly. But it did not conceal the increasing role of the individual, which entailed the rapid breakdown of the family cell, the new importance of bastards, the sudden generation gap between fathers and sons, the absence of solidarity with collateral relatives. The growing role of money has sometimes been seen as the germ of the dissolution of greater entities; it became the object of all desire, the instrument of freedom, the source of all dissent. All social classes were seized by a profit psychosis which set them one against another; service was effaced by salaries.

Another element harder to distinguish deserves a brief mention. Among the human groups, given that personal destiny was the object of their greatest concern, two developments occurred which seem at first glance to be unconnected but which have the same important origin. On the one hand, the cult of the individual, whether man or woman, external or internal, led to astonishing practices: egoistical and brutal behaviour, self-indulgent pity, as well as that extravagant funerary pomp which was due as much to concern for immortality as to fear of the awful Last Judgement. One recalls the Captal de Buch Jean de Grailly, who had not kept his hands over-clean, ordering and paying for forty thousand masses to be said on the anniversary of his *obit* in the hope of saving his soul. Philip II of Spain himself only went up to twenty thousand. It has been suggested that these practices contributed largely to ruining the nobility, who were more obsessed by these rites than the rest of society. The other evolution affected fifteenth-century women. We saw that, due either to natural selection or to the fall in perinatal mortality and in secret 'infanticides' of female babies, there were from then on more women than men. Their moral prestige must have suffered; signs of this can be found in the archaic 'orders of chivalry' which entertained the nobility by insisting heavily on the service of the Lady, showing how unreal this 'service' must have been in everyday life. On the contrary, an important new female workforce had broken into the urban manufacturing class, a fact of major economic significance. It certainly had a very efficient braking effect on the rise in wages, since women were generally paid less than half what men earned. No canon lawyers or philosophers seem to have found this upsetting, which comes as no surprise to us, even in the twentieth century.

In the country, the triumph of the great

In spite of the urban tentacles which gradually closed around it, the countryside retained its vital importance. It is there that social changes should be first examined. The agricultural revival had created a gulf which grew steadily larger both in lordly as well as peasant society. Not everyone had been able to benefit from the change to pasture. Firstly because grain prices rose only very slowly, kept down by the higher prices demanded for speculative agricultural products; taking the price of wheat around 1350 as a base line of 100, wheat prices by the middle of the fifteenth century were still only 35 in France, 60 in England, 65 in Germany, and they did not return to the 1350 level until 1510 or 1515, at least in the first and last of these countries and in Spain, while in England prices still stagnated. Small farmers could not dream of changing to another crop; only proprietors or farmers of considerable means could profit from so doing, even more since agricultural wages had stopped rising. Besides urban competition, both the rise in population and the influx of a female workforce contributed to this deflationary factor. The 1340–50 level was recovered at different times in different regions, sometimes as a result of authoritarian intervention by the ruling power. The highest figures were reached in 1345–40 in England and Catalonia, in 1452 in eastern Germany, 1460 in Saxony, in 1465–70 in northern and eastern France and in 1482 in Languedoc. Under these conditions the most destitute of the rural workforce were driven to take on piece-work for their neighbouring towns. This does not mean that the situation before 1340 or 1350 was returning, when circumstances favoured high wages. These were not recovered before 1520, except in Germany where they became one of the main detonators of the explosion in 1525, and prices too did not rise until 1550, introducing a new 'classic' type of crisis, with high prices and low wages, which does not concern us here.

Phenomena as closely related as those which led to the redistribution of land in favour of the *coqs*, of enterprising burghers and wealthy lords, should not be disregarded. Some of them were circumstantial; deserted areas, left *en herm* such as Quercy, the Entre deux Mers and in Champagne, were seized and let out on advantageous terms to the first-comers, according to the very ancient principles of *complant*, by which part, or a third or even half of the property reverted to the tenant after the lease had run out. Further, in France in 1447, the State allowed derelict land to be taken in hand by a neighbouring proprietor, if the theoretical proprietor could not present his titles to it. This happened only too frequently with improvident lay persons, who had anyway been more harshly affected by the crisis than churchmen (who thus managed to repair its ravages fairly quickly). In 1489, the King authorised the destruction of unoccupied buildings on plots smaller than 10 hectares, a sure way of scotching all attempts at reconstituting small peasant freeholds. Other methods, this time without intervention by the authorities, permitted the most audacious seizures of land; apart from shifting boundaries and limits in open-field country, a corollary of the desertions, the occasional reassessment of rent quotas, which had fallen to rock bottom, should be taken into account. The lord took every opportunity, for instance over inheritance and the subdivision of plots of land, to introduce a rent increase, or else, when the coinage was debased, he demanded to be paid in the strong 'old' coinage. In many regions of the French kingdom, the Lyonnais, Poitou, Hainaut and the Toulousain, such proceedings benefited the master and even his tenant farmers. They explain the apparently contradictory fact that village communities were growing stronger in their struggle against the lord; in reality, these communities now consisted of big farmers holding fifty, a hundred or more hectares of land.

These new concentrations of land were becoming a feature of the countryside all over Europe. Those who benefited could only be the farmers and the tenant farmers; into their hands fell their disappeared neighbours' portions and those of their childless relatives. They were provided with allotments by landlords with inadequate work forces. They even established themselves in the Cistercians' *bouverots* (as in Ouges in Burgundy) or (as in the Île-de-France and the Cambresis) they founded real farming dynasties lasting a hundred years. The *censes* of Hainaut, the *bordes* of the Toulousain, the *collques* of Quercy, were all units of up to 200 hectares of farmland. In England, we know from a few county records that between 1450 and 1480 the proportion of farms in the 50–200 hectare group increased from 40 to 55 per cent, with a 100 per cent increase in the biggest ones. Newcomers mingled with this core of authentic rustics. As we have seen, some of them were merchants, and lawyers too, who (beginning in 1440–75, and increasingly so after 1490) settled in the country, where nobody dared to deny them contacts, which they then used to raise themselves into the nobility. In the Île-de-France alone, the Bureau, the Montaigu, the Braque, the Budé, the Dormans, the Boulainvilliers were newcomers of this type. They often managed their estates in an exemplary, not to say niggling manner: the mass of estate documents which began to swell our archives is due to a great extent to them.

Apart from the Church, the biggest estates belonged to landlords, *Junkers*, the *grands seigneurs* of ancient lineage or more often to newly created nobles from the great social upheaval at the end of the thirteenth century. These people held firmly on to their lands, even though they were less in evidence because of their military or court duties. They had sometimes spent considerable sums, generally obtained by exercising fiscal pressure, in order to acquire lands. William Sheppart in England paid 7,000 pounds sterling for eight villages; in 1489 the Percys raised 2,000 pounds from imposing indirect taxation on their property as against their 'ordinary' revenue of 600 pounds. Estates also grew as a corollary of political success; the Warwicks dominated five villages in 1400 and twenty-five in 1550; Elizabeth de Burgh acquired manors in ten different counties. Germany was not behindhand, especially after 1470 or 1480: Frederick von der Pfalz, Eberhard von Wurtemberg, Frederick von Hohenzollern owned more than 20,000 hectares; in Castile the Alvarez, the Carillo, the Haro, the Guzman and some Mendoza owned even more. In France and Italy though, this concentration was less strong – perhaps because their population was denser or their peasantry was able to resist it more vigorously.

The ruin of the small folk

Not all lords were in the same league as the Duke of Norfolk or the Margrave of Brandenburg. Those who had not been able or had not known how to grasp fortune by the

Reallocating land benefited the biggest farmers.
A territory is being measured and boundaries set up.
(Arnaud de Villeneuve's *Treatise on Surveying*,
fifteenth century, Ms. 327; Carpentras, Bibliothèque
Inguinibertine.)

forelock slid gently into obscurity. Many formerly illustrious and respected families had to make this descent of the social ladder; infamous marriages had to be consented to (a Montmorency marrying a Poilevilain); honourable dignities, bishoprics, bailiwicks had to be given up, and they had to resign themselves to being mere provosts or salaried castellans. The next step involved withdrawing from the by now outrageous expense of being knighted or of entering the orders of Chivalry. They were no more than squire, *damoiseau* or *hidalgo*; even the word *Ritter* lost its legal content in the Empire. Their genealogies sometimes ended obscurely – when someone became a notary, a vicar or an attorney. The petty squires who clung to their strongholds were effectively powerless to dominate the vigorous labouring communities. We know from the many farming accounts of the fifteenth century that most of the minor nobility's revenues were dwindling. In England this is better documented than in other countries; in Sussex, for instance, the weight of expenditure grew between 1436 and 1456 from 1/7 to 2/5 of the sum of the annual receipts. In the county of Leicester the global value of the gentry's direct or indirect income from their estates fell from a base line of 100 in 1408, which was already pretty low, to 80 in 1477, in the middle of the supposed economic revival. The weaker the lords were, the less willing the peasantry were to pay their capitation taxes or fines. In the Île-de-France, around Josas, delays in payment amounted to 20 per cent of potential returns and increased to 45 per cent in 1508. This list could be extended; the points to be stressed are: the weight of the royal *taille*, the new practice of selling hunting rights for money, the introduction creation in 1480 of very high death duties on the lands of nobles ('quint' and 'requint' = 40 per cent of revenues) and lastly, taxing the registration of coats of arms, which the old nobility held onto all the more tenaciously as they found themselves inundated by bumpkins.

All this money being extracted so assiduously by the ruler reappeared in newly created public offices, in pensions, in military functions, in court duties. The landed nobility was tempted to recuperate part of what was being taken from them, by insinuating themselves into the clientele of dukes or better still of the king. In 1480 the creation of the *Filles d'honneur de la reine* in France, a position reserved for destitute noblewomen, and the creation of corps of cadets in the army, provided a means of taming the nobility. The use which all European monarchs were to make of these institutions is well known, even if it is doubtful whether they really intended, in these first stages, to destroy by these means a too-unwieldy aristocracy. Those who did not want to tear themselves away from their ruinous towers, out of love for their lands or from the feeling that they had a role to play among their villagers, flirted with violence. Certain circumstances, like the English Civil War, served them well. Where violence was resorted to, as with the *Praguerie* of northern France (1440–4) which no ruler interfered with, and the League of the 'Public good' which opposed Louis XI at the beginning of his reign, only the great nobles benefited from it. From then on, they had to live like the average peasant, with no privileges beyond their church pews and the swords they were entitled to wear.

Of course things were much worse for the peasants, who had not been able to participate in the reconstruction of the economy and whose progressive eviction from the community and its advantages threw them gradually within the infamous margins of servitude. I have alluded to this 'new serfdom', which was to persist in central France and in Catalonia, not to mention England, until the end of the eighteenth century. Although we have few means of measuring the volume of this trend, we do have a few insights for England. In Leicestershire, the percentage of cottagers, who were definitely alienated as to their persons and their property, and of villeins, who enjoyed various freedoms, increased from 67 to 72 per cent between 1400 and 1455. Cottagers and squatters, who were lodged on tiny plots on the edges of manors, were stripped of their rights to attend courts of justice. The conditions of tenure worsened all round, both because landlords were able to increase their requirements from the land and because the tenants were severely bound by the Book of Copyholders, which listed their obligations, their rights of inheritance and here and there their labour dues.

Although he might remain free, which on the continent was the essential thing, the peasant found it very difficult to pay his taxes. Royal pretensions were growing and the peasants were made to pay for them through their lords, and worse still, their liability for taxation was determined by the village notables. The *taille* grew prodigiously in France: it was raised from 1,200,000 livres on the death of Charles VII to 4,600,000 livres by Louis XI, to 5,300,000 by Louis XII and reached 6,800,000 livres in 1540. Since neither the pattern of work nor the methods of production nor even their tools had really changed for the most dispossessed people, they remained in a miserable situation, with three serious and almost inevitable consequences.

445

The first was the rush to earn wages, which only the towns could supply. This trend can be traced in the rural cloth manufactures of Sologne, of Brabant, around the *sayetterie* centres which sprang up from Armentières to Audenarde and in the 'serge and ascot' production of Champagne or the Severn valley. It could also be seen in the glass works of the Veneto, the paper mills in the Toulousain, the timber mills in the Jura. Burghers sometimes needed to supplement their workforce; around Lyon *affaneurs* turned up on half wages to help with the citizens' wine harvest, as also happened around Bordeaux. When Louis XI tried to plant mulberries near to Tours and Lyon around 1470, the *soyeux* of the surrounding countryside were appealed to, as had been done in Genoa for ages. In Bohemia miners were sometimes employed by the week, in winter. This sort of employment was risky and it forced countrymen to bow to the townsmens' will.

When there was no work for them to do, the second predictable consequence was the need to borrow money. And from whom? From the same people, whether clothiers or woolmen who came to assess the sheep shearing; *nourriguiers* or *gasailleurs*, who came to buy the flocks; *halliers* or *poorters*, who came to lend money with their tools as surety or to buy their standing wheat in spite of royal ordinances (1476). As for the final effect, it was only a repetition of what had gone before; at the top of the agrarian pyramid, bigger agglomerations of land, at the bottom, increasingly divided plots. This process had been halted by the crises but was now resumed and its lamentable effects are well known; around 1500, 70 per cent of the farming-plots in the Neubourg countryside were smaller than 4 hectares; in the Île-de-France it was 94 per cent.

Defeat

In excessively hard times, when the harvests failed and the king was too extortionate, people revolted. By this time, however, it was no longer an uprising by persons heavily in debt who wanted to secure their acquisitions, but it came from the despair of empty stomachs, the first of those revolts driven on by hunger and poverty which accompanied the Renaissance and the age of greatness.

Since these movements were associated with the Tuchins or a concealed opposition party, they are less well known and they may have impressed chroniclers of the time less than they do present-day historians. However, when one looks at them through the repression which overtook them, one has the feeling of having pierced their depths. Immediately striking is how general and diffuse these movements were; apart from Italy, where a great many of these demonstrations must have been lost in the midst of the general destruction at the beginning of the sixteenth century, every region in Europe was affected. In England the Lollard movement was still simmering around 1430; in 1450 Kent and Essex rose up, as in 1381, at the call of Jack Cade; but the royal army exterminated these 'rebels'. In Scandinavia, between 1411 and 1454, there were constant uprisings, with more or less authentic peasant leaders; 'King David', Engelbrekt, Reventlow. In France the movements were assimilated to banditry and were punished as such, as were the *écoucheurs*, on the rampage between Paris and the Rhône delta from 1411–65, and the

Hard times and bad harvests. The disturbing figure of a vagabond in the Flemish countryside. (*The Prodigal Son* by Hieronymus Bosch, beginning of the sixteenth century, Rotterdam, Boymans-Van Beuningen Museum.)

Coquillards in Burgundy from 1435–45, or even the 'colleagues' of Forez, who were perhaps runaway apprentices. Kings by then had their own armies, and they used them. In Spain, the movement of the *remensas* had not been extinguished: in spite of Alfonso V of Aragon's promises of around 1445 to see that the *malos usos* were abolished, they continued to thrive and the rebellion flared up again between 1462 and 1471, and again between 1484 and 1487, surreptitiously kept alight by runaway slaves and ruined lords.

Germany was a special case; there the religious aspect was fairly closely involved with the claims of the very poor, possibly because spiritual demands and the scandal of a Church associated with the forces of repression were stronger there. The bands of itinerant *béghards*

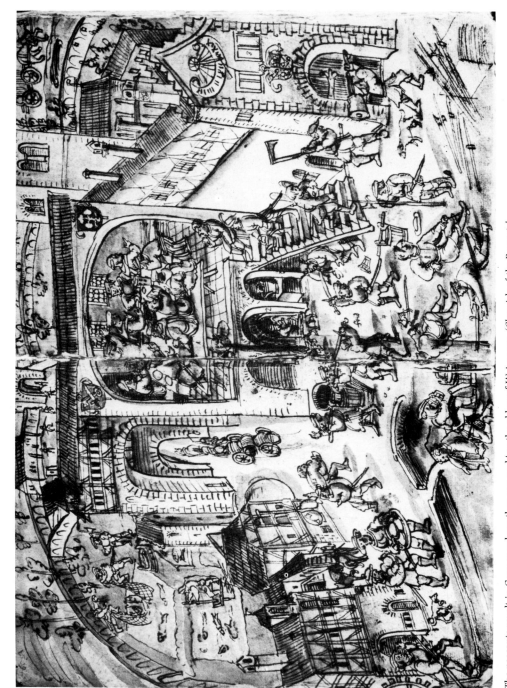

The peasants revolt in Germany; here they are sacking the abbey of Weissenau. (*Chronicle of the Peasants' War*, by the Abbot Murer, 1525; Schloss Zeil archives.)

448

in Thuringia and Alsace, the 1476 movement of the 'Virgin of Nicklaushausen' are difficult to classify. What is not, is the extraordinary violence with which the lords suppressed them. Well might one say that Frederick III's and Maximilian's Germany was built on the Függer's copper and on gallow-trees. This crushing defeat is all the more worthy of notice since most of the features of the social disintegration which I have stressed were present in the Empire, and with a rare acuity. So what ensued will come as no surprise to us, unlike to people then: in June 1524, a rising broke out between the Black Forest and Lake Constance at the exhortation of a certain Münzer, who quite simply called for the overthrow of noble and ecclesiastical society by the sword. In three months, he won over Alsace, the Palatinate, Hesse, Thuringia, Saxony, and in the south, Tyrol, Bavaria and Styria. The whole of peasant Germany seemed to have caught fire, and the towns too, where harshly treated apprentices opened the city gates to peasant bands: Zabern, Ulm, Freiburg surrendered to them; Mainz, Trier and Frankfurt were forced to negotiate with them. Bands of several thousand famished peasants ransacked the public granaries and massacred the knights and the churchmen; they called for liberation from all their shackles and for distribution of all the nobility's possessions. In 1525 the rulers of Hesse, Saxony and Brunswick managed to form mobile army units which tracked down the bands. The whole affair finished in the same way as the *Jacquerie*; as before, the burghers grew tired of the peasants' excesses, and refused to help them. The movement broke up into easily isolated groups; Münzer was taken and strung up in May and Alsace was subdued; the rest of the peasant troops were defeated one by one. The repression was atrocious, in the order of 100,000 executions, and it did not stop there, but was still going on when the wars of religion broke out twenty or thirty years later. But rural Germany had been crushed utterly.

A question of the workers

At the price of annihilating their most impoverished rustics with the sword, the State felt that the peasant issue had been removed, or at any rate adjourned; this held good for the next two centuries both in the Empire and elsewhere. In the towns, however, the problem was quite different. Firstly because the cities were growing increasingly powerful and because the rulers needed them, they were forced to treat them with greater circumspection and concern; the villein might be only an animal, but the goldsmith and the mason were more.

The movements which took place in the cities of the West in the middle of the last quarter of the fourteenth century had shown a good many clear-headed observers and chroniclers, such as Villani, Alain Chartier and Gerson, that urban populations, with their particular crowded and promiscuous living conditions, the strength of their professional or neighbourhood ties and the material difficulties of daily life, could not be treated like the inhabitants of a large village. The growing role of the town as a market, as a royal residence, as a stronghold, as a manufacturing centre, gave a harsh dimension seldom found in the countryside to every form of social relationship. The rhythm of rapid production gave rise to aggressive labour relations, which, together with the reciprocal

A fifteenth-century drawing of a street scene in a German town. Many details illustrate the architecture of the period.

disdain social categories felt towards one another, and which they all felt towards the countryside, are features of urban society which date from the fourteenth century.

These features grew still stronger in the fifteenth century at the same time as the internal structure of the towns was profoundly modified at the end of the 'crises'. Firstly, the newcomers, as is often the case with neophytes, were a great deal more arrogant than those they replaced; they were sometimes extremely numerous: in France, among the cases that have been studied for the period 1470–1510, they made up 9 per cent of the population at Lyon, 47 per cent at Valence, 66 per cent at Périgueux and 75 per cent at Chalon; these recent immigrants soon proved intractable towards other 'foreigners'; the Béarnais were thrown out of Toulouse and the Flemings from Lyon.

Secondly, properly civic activities, the great delight of Mediterranean peoples, which made the history of the Italian cities between 1100 to 1400 so extraordinary, largely faded out. In a time when kings or merchant clans had taken charge of affairs, the problems of urban administration interested only the experts; lawyers, notaries and officials now sat in the consuls' and mayors' seats and executed the orders of their rulers or of the merchant interest. That was enough, as far as the more prudent kings were concerned, like Louis XI, who smiled on his 'good towns'. Even in the Low Countries, the Dukes of Burgundy eventually subdued Ghent and Liège, and Italy just fell into her rulers' arms.

450   This political apathy is very restful for the historian, but it did a great deal of harm.

A group of workmen. (Detail of a miniature illustrating the *Deeds and Sayings of the Romans and other people* by Valerius Maximus, Ms. Harl. 4375, London, British Museum.)

Formerly, the town council had reflected or, on the contrary, had refused to reflect the society it represented. It was inevitably interested in it, and its regulations, whether good or bad, were inspired by it. Once in the hands of experts, the towns allowed a climate of economic tension to develop freely, which aggravated existing problems. One of the most curious signs of this was the progressive stratification of the urban body itself; apart from those large and magnificent structures with their internal gardens on the model of the Hôtel Saint-Paul in Paris, which were being built on undeveloped urban sites, quarters within the very body of the town were subjected to social distinctions, according to the particular trade practised in them or to the presence of a particular guild or palace. As well as this, within the housing blocks themselves, certain parts were considered more 'bourgeois' at the others' expense; it was smarter to look out on the road than the courtyard, or to live on the first floor. It was also in this period, particularly after the pogroms of 1390–2, that the process was completed whereby Jews were systematically segregated in a special quarter, which was closed at night time, but was invariably invaded and pillaged if not worse at each onset of panic: in 1424–30, 1460, 1473, 1486 and 1493 in the case of Languedoc alone.

Once the merchants had been set apart, this left masters and apprentices on their own.

For the former, for those at least who were not rich enough to try for public office or to invest in landed estates, the situation after 1470–80 was only partly satisfactory. Their expenses were certainly reduced as the rise in wages fell off, more perceptibly so after 1464–8, but the falling price of manufactured goods nullified any additional profit margin they might have hoped for. Their attitude betrays their disquiet; the revival of the trades was inadequate and their customers stayed away. As good disciples of the 'classical' medieval doctrines, the masters were determined to eliminate the causes of weakness by concentrating on high-quality produce and on eliminating competition. Supervisors were appointed; the *eswardeurs* of Flanders and the Lombard *gastaldos*, to ensure observance of the norms of work and working hours. After 1480, apprentices were practically forbidden to produce their master-works, and heredity became general; before the end of the fifteenth century showers of regulations hemmed in production and atrophied it. Not content with blocking the quality and volume of production at a given level, at a time when the merchants exemplified the spirit of enterprise, the masters formed understandings, cartels, among themselves in order to reduce wages still further, as in the case of the master-forgers of the Rhineland.

But this was not the countryside. The apprentices were far from lacking in support and energy; to start off with, they were able to make use of the troubles gradually to strengthen their own associations, which, being outside the official guilds where the masters ruled, allowed them to air their views and to engage in those *colloquia* which were already worrying Beaumanoir in the thirteenth century. As they were by definition clandestine reunions, they are hard to spot, but they seem to have been held in Munich before 1440 by the apprentice bakers, ironsmiths and hatters, and in Bavaria and along the Rhône in 1442 by the furriers; by 1500, there were forty such organisations in Bordeaux. These associations were made a great deal easier to organise because, due to the social differentiation mentioned above, masters no longer shared their houses with their apprentices, and could no longer supervise them. Once the workers had united, what was to stop them from forming coalitions, deciding for the *takehan*, stopping work and demanding pay rises?

They certainly had enough motives. They had to bear very heavy taxes; the royal *taille* was supposed to bear more on the peasants (up to 85 per cent) but many other impositions were almost entirely urban; the *taille* for lodging soldiers (1451), and especially the upkeep of their walls, that architectural feature symbolic of the city (it has been calculated that in Paris and Avignon, the upkeep of the walls for 15 to 20 years cost the towns half their civic budget; at Reims, it was 160,000 *livres*). To this must be added the *gabelle*, unavoidable in towns where *greniers à sel* were set up, tolls, and of course fines, rents, death duties, etc., all of which added up to the equivalent of eighty working days around 1480–5. The relative slowing down of business from 1490–1500, and more particularly, the English and French ordinances which demanded that wages be brought down to their 1410 level, only added to the problems of the common people.

There were two ways in which urban discontent was manifested; there were violent riots, sometimes for reasons of personal revenge, and there was mutiny. We can find out about the first only through the law court registers, and these show that individual violence did indeed make up 80 per cent of the cases heard. These were generally cases of wilful destruction or pillage rather than physical assault; the assassination of a Paris master in 1455 caused a sensation. Since truants and beggars were sometimes included in these bands, this form of crime has not been attributed with the social significance it undoubtedly contains. Sedition came in two chronological phases, between 1442 and 1451, when the Low Countries, the Rhineland and the Danube region were especially affected, and between 1516 and 1527, when, as we have just seen, Germany was chiefly involved. Apart from this last instance, which owed its extreme violence to its rural origins, the diverse worker protests of the outgoing fifteenth or the sixteenth century pale beside their forerunners. Apart from the difficulty of isolating the sociological dimension in the religious movements of the following period, the phenomenon of 'hard' opposition was taking shape in the towns. Two forces confronted one another there, both structured and coherent with their essential place in society; it was not a cleavage between strong and weak elements, which many analysts believe to be indispensible, but between two adversaries of comparable standing. In other words, the Middle Ages bequeathed a labour problem to modern times.

9 From Europe to the world

The pilgrims and merchants who travelled to Jerusalem, Alexandria and even Peking had absolutely no global perception of their journey, and they placed sufficient trust in their immediate horizon and their European vision. It was the economic recovery of the fifteenth century which pushed these limited perspectives aside. Western man felt that his field of action had been too reduced to allow him to deploy his energies or to satisfy his appetites: he needed to enlarge it, to test his new vigour, to leave home, and the means of so doing were finally available.

Towards the 'modern' State

I am using the word 'modern' to mean the period so designated by historical tradition, which runs from the sixteenth to the end of the eighteenth century. Although an absurd convention, it does at least serve to reduce confusion. The idea of State has also been given many meanings and lawyers have laboured over this many-sided and arduous question. There was a feudal state like there were city states or tribal states. The 'modern' State is conventionally described as one in which the totality of powers, at least the material ones, is concentrated in one person, or, at the worst, one family which makes full and free use of it. In any case, this 'absolute' power must emanate from the whole social body; it should include tradition, the public good, the honour of a whole people. Whoever did not dispose of this consent was a mere 'tyrant', as Jean Petit pointed out when Louis d'Orléans was assassinated. He could be killed as Pedro the Cruel was, or deposed like Richard II of England. This meant that the ruler who carried out his ministry without dissent, even if his 'subjects' (as they were henceforth to be called) had not really been consulted on the matter, was a sacred depository of the *respublica*, even if he was mad like Charles VI or a certified idiot like Henry VI of Castile.

Until the beginning of the fifteenth century, no responsible ruler in the West could claim to dispose of this power. The family clans, the great territorial lineages, the assemblies of representatives from the orders, all were active in eroding his initiatives. Bodies like the Church and the towns mediated between the ruler and his men and it was only seldom that he was really in control of the essential elements of power; the administration, justice, money and the armed forces. But once they were united in one person, absolute monarchy emerged to create one of the darkest periods in the history of Europe. The economic and social upheavals I have just mentioned served as a base onto which this process was grafted.

First the organisation of brute strength

This was a highly sensible, if also immoral tenet. No authority, with due regard to Montesquieu, could impose its views, however legitimate, without being able to ensure their observance by threats or force; men being so disposed, that they can, as a group, be convinced only by coercion. The Church was alone in refusing to admit this, although she too made use of force under all its forms, and indeed the success or failure of the other medieval 'States' depended on their capacity for coercion. By the middle of the fifteenth century and at the end of the incredible disorder created in Europe by so many armed forces tearing each other apart, all the rulers had understood this, but not all had achieved it.

The French example was the clearest and most enduring. Charles V had assessed the inadequacy of the 'feudal' system, the unreliability of mercenaries, the cost of paying soldiers and of renting artillery. Although one hundred thousand men could be relied on in principle, never more than twenty or thirty thousand ever actually turned up. So he began by looking at the problem of defence, introducing fortresses with reliable captains, militias of footsoldiers and archers who trained in their villages, and a new shipyard at Rouen, the *clos des galées*. Otherwise he relied on the old recipes. Charles VII made a decisive move, when he took advantage of the treaties concluded at Tours with the English in 1444, to turn three wings of the 'royal forces' into the basis of what was to be the French army. Since some of the mercenaries had died on various expeditions into Switzerland, he took the bold step of enrolling all the others, of providing them with pay, lodgings and a cadre. Twenty *compagnies d'ordonnance* of men at arms were created in 1445, thirty-five in 1450, giving the King an army of around three thousand *lances*, consisting each of six men, two of whom were on horseback. In 1448 companies of *francs-archers* (free archers) were formed by calling up one man out of every fifty peasant or town households. They were obliged to turn up for archery practice every week and were supposed to provide eighteen to twenty thousand infantrymen. In 1449 he entrusted Bureau de la Rivière with the task of forming an artillery corps of one hundred and fifty 'flying culverins' who secured his definitive triumph over the English a few years later. The ban of the nobility and of the urban militias was preserved in case their help was needed, as was that of a few *condottiere* and their mercenaries, who though deemed loyal were submitted to very strict reviews, or *montres*. Elsewhere, fortresses and warships continued to be built and launched. The achievement of Charles VII, which Louis XI continued, was much criticised. The populace was annoyed at having troops quartered on them, or by having to pay a *taille* to cover the cost of their accommodation. The nobility despised their new companions in arms. As well as this many other princes maintained their own armies. Finally, the *francs-archers* performed pitiably in combat on several occasions and the new ships did not succeed in controlling the Channel.   **455**

a) Artillery takes to the road. (*Vigils of Charles VII*, 1484; Paris, Bibliothèque nationale.)
b) On the right, a lansquenet, a sixteenth-century statue from the Château de Barrois. (Paris, Louvre.)

None the less the French artillery remained the first in Europe until the eighteenth century and the infantry, by amalgamating with mercenaries or professional *arquebusiers*, gradually managed to show up well in battle.

Other countries did not achieve this degree of perfection in their control over the public forces. In England, however, the rulers had in the Anglo-Saxon *fyrd*, the general levy of free men, the inestimable advantage of an army experienced in foot combat, using pikes or bows; although the English population was never big enough to allow their kings to assemble more than five to six thousand men out of the thirty thousand they were entitled to call up. On the other hand the difficulty of transporting artillery to the Continent led them to neglect this side of their armoury, which they considered too unwieldy. By the time of the Tudors, levies were enforced to a certain extent, but by then the bulk of the money was being spent on the sea forces. The English involvement with maritime trade has been discussed: the construction of an English fleet was broached at the same time. Edward IV must be credited with the initiative, even though Henry VII promulgated a new 'Navigation Act' in 1485 and opened the dock yards of Hull and Bristol. By a curious reversal of history, it was the France of Louis XI which contributed indirectly to this birth, since the greater part of the funds came from the annual pension of fifty thousand pounds paid by the Valois to Edward IV, according to the terms settled at Picquigny in 1475. By Henry VIII's accession in 1509, fifteen ships crewed by 'nationals' could take to the sea.

The Iberian monarchies appear all the more curiously backward, in that the expeditions by sea and on land, which were conducted in their names against the Moors or the Ocean, ought to have incited them to form their own armed forces. It was only slowly, but with devastating strength that the Spaniards supplied their kings with an exceptional army. Since the 'Catholic Monarchs' were unable to pay mercenaries, as they had done up to the capture of Granada in 1492, Isabella and especially Ferdinand, both experts in military matters, resorted to recruitment in the manner of the Valois. Here though, it was not a matter of levying *francs-archers* from the villages; the kings based their army on the long fighting experience of the *hidalgos* and the *caballeria villana*, who had fought for centuries against Islam. All *señors* were *soldado*, all *peones* knew how to use a sword. Added to this, many of them were driven by the poverty of the land to adopt a career in arms. This, together with the harsh climate, which disciplined their bodies and accustomed them to excessive efforts, contributed to the formation of what was to become an exceptional instrument of war. In 1496 the kings decided to make military service obligatory for one man out of every twelve, and these were then given a strict training by Gonzalvo de Cordoba and Gonzalo de Ayala. When a campaign took place the men – pikemen, knights with swords, arquebusiers – were formed into homogeneous units called *coronelia*, whose resistance, courage and cruelty made them famous from the beginning of the sixteenth century, when Spain undertook expeditions of conquest and repression. Once the Swiss had been eliminated, the *tercios* dominated the battle fields until the Thirty Years' War.

. . . Or the opposite

Elsewhere there was almost nothing to compare. The urban militias in Italy had gone up in smoke; the armed burghers of the sixteenth century were decidedly not worthy of their ancestors of Legnano; Duke Francesco Sforza, who knew his warriors, was the first to get rid of them. In Rome Julius II and other warrior Popes preferred their Lansquenets (*Landsknechten*) from Germany; in Venice Slavs and Turks were enrolled. Florence was alone in holding out – Lorenzo the Magnificent paid little attention to these problems. When Charles VIII's Frenchmen poured into Italy they caused great anxiety. Instead of engaging in ingenious manoeuvres at the end of which the vanquished could surrender with very little bloodshed – tactics perfected by the Italian *condottiere* who were careful of their men's health – the French charged, fired canons and killed. Since the Spaniards began to do likewise, it was better to give up; after they were crushed at Prato in 1512 the Florentines too resorted to hiring soldiers from the Empire.

Germany was effectively the reservoir from which the bulk of the professional soldiery was traditionally recruited. As in Spain, poverty drove the *Ritter* to enrol and to pillage. Here there were no Americans to exterminate or Italian kingdoms to conquer; nor were there fleets to man or rulers to serve. Though the Infidel Turks were not far away and were threatening the Danube, it was for the moment, the Hungarians, Czechs and Poles who had the task of restraining them. The incredible disorder and political anarchy which reigned in Germany can perhaps only be explained by the surplus of unemployed warriors. They tended to enter into the service of a local dynasty or a neighbouring ruler, and thus formed

457

very big bands; a reputable captain like Franz von Sickingen commanded fifteen thousand for a time – half the number Charles VIII led into Italy. As well as this, there was no ruler in Germany capable of organising coherent armies.

The only exception to this disorder was provided by the Swiss mountain dwellers, who had snatched their independence from the Habsburgs at the end of the fourteenth century and formed corps of infantrymen – for lack of horses – whose extraordinary fighting ability soon made them the envy of those of their neighbours who were looking for vigorous and honest soldiers. In effect, after having successfully defended their liberty in Alsace and Baden between 1440 and 1444, and then pulverising the proud Burgundian army on the shores of Lake Neuchâtel, the Swiss proved that the reign of heavy cavalry was well and truly over and that the 'queen of battles' was the infantry, in squares of two hundred men, bristling with pikes, slowly sweeping the field, impervious to arrow fire because of their heavy armour. The revival of the Macedonian phalange! Francis I was alone in being able to break them – by directing his cannon against men rather than walls. In spite of reforming, the squares of Swiss infantry had to surrender at Marignano in 1515, but not at Pavia ten years later because the Valois, distrait as usual, made his knights charge in front of his own cannon! The seventeenth century was already to hand, with Swiss fighting *tercios*, almost all on foot, a French artillery, an English fleet and with Germany and Italy as their battlefields.

And then money

The State needed money if only to pay its troops or to equip its ships. The volume of money and its quality were indeed an essential aspect of this problem, but one which was managed by merchant associations rather than by the concerted will of kings. Within this vitally important domain the union between private and public interest is startlingly evident. The King acted as a merchant or as the merchants' hostage; the initiatives he undertook – opening mines, monetary revaluations, conferences on gold and silver rates – were all suggested to him. The poverty of economic thinking among the circles around monarchs of all ranks is remarkable; even a merchant turned prince like Lorenzo de Medici seemed to have completely lost any feeling for financial affairs. Before Jean Bodin, who comes well outside our time limit, the French king had no theoretician close to him, not even one of the calibre of Nicholas Oresme. Gresham was not yet born, and such counsellors as there were (like Charles *le Téméraire*'s Dino Rapondi, Louis XII's Briçonnet or Henry VIII's Wolsey) were not experts and their economic vision was limited to wondering how to get the goose to lay its golden eggs without killing it.

We may ignore their attempts at manipulating money. What matters here is the way kings and rulers progressively secured all the possible sources of revenue. There was nothing revolutionary about this; the detainers of power had long ago started to work towards royal taxation and financial administration, but although the direction was the same, the stages and sometimes the means employed could vary. The ruler generally tried to achieve three basic props; in the first place, he needed to secure a large domain of his own, to provide him with his personal income. Not that it was expected to contribute enormously towards funding public expenses – even the King of France drew no more than 15 per cent of his total income from his private estates by 1480 and the English King's 'forest' was even less profitable – but it allowed the monarch to move about from palace to castle within his own lands and accompanied by his entire entourage. So he would try to increase his domain, by purchase, like any good landowner, sometimes by seizing land from a rebel subject who could be legally robbed. I have also mentioned the incorporation of the military Orders' estates with the Crown Lands in Spain after 1523, which was effected with the authorisation of the Pope, but had actually been going on since 1495. Italy under its harlequin costume presented exactly the same face; the property of the Medicis, that of Venetian Senators, the Sforzas' sequestrations, the Este possessions around Ferrara, were all obtained in the same way. And, as usual, the Emperor was the only ruler to be condemned to a niggardly existence.

All this led towards the imposition of general taxation, but as the French King's treasury was chary of basing this on commercial transactions for fear of annoying the merchants, it was left with hitting the nobility or the peasantry. I have explained how the defeat of Poitiers played a beneficial part in this respect: by forcing the populace, the gentry and the Church to pay annuities towards the ransom, the Valois implanted the idea of regular taxation. They did not cease from increasing this pressure and we have already got some idea of the crushing weight of the *taille*. The sale of hunting rights, the *taille* of men-at-arms, the indirect *aides* at a rate of one *sou* per *livre* of merchandise (5 per cent) all contributed towards the French King's very superior financial position compared to any of his neighbours. A happy ruler indeed, whose prestige was greatly enhanced by his brilliant court and by his châteaux rising up on the banks of the Loire. Unhappy his subjects, who were crushed by the restoration of a good coinage and by the 'financial orthodoxy' which Keynesian monetarists are so keen on. It is difficult for us to extirpate the ideas inculcated by the triumphant bourgeoisie of the nineteenth century from our minds: the 'good kings' who introduced good finance, Charles V and Louis XI; the 'galant' and 'sun' kings who stunned the world, Francis I, Henry IV, and the others. Elsewhere things did not go so far or so fast; the Tudors pushed taxes on trade hard, at a time when English commerce was taking off, so that the more woollens and lead pigs were produced the more they were taxed. There was a lot of resistance to this in the staple towns around 1450 and especially between 1487 and 1490. The same difficulties occurred in Spain, in spite of a violent campaign against seigneurial taxation; here it was the *Mesta*, that all-powerful association of sheep breeders, which fiercely defended its privileges and exemptions. Ferdinand was eventually forced to fall back on the towns where *corregidores* were appointed to supervise and tax commercial activities.

Although taxation in the Valois Kingdom was unquestionably more advanced than that of other ones, even at a high cost, this was not the case with the way tax collection was administered. The attention paid to improving the methods of tax collection will come as no surprise when we remember that the rulers' advisors were mostly lawyers and that they, much more than others, leant towards formalism. In this domain it is clear that officialdom

459

Two tax collectors. A painting by Marinus van Romerswael. This Zeeland painter (1493–1567) was fascinated by money and painted repellent portraits of bankers, usurers and tax collectors.

contributed greatly towards creating its duties. French financial administration dates from Charles V, from the moment when the level of the royal *fouage* was fixed, giving birth to the 'élections', which were in principle derived from the good will of the 'Estates' of the lands of Oïl and Oc. These subdivisions were taken up again and generalised in the fifteenth century, with the fundamental difference that the 'elected' tax collectors were nominated and salaried. A few regions, Languedoc and Provence, retained the privilege of assessing and collecting the *taille* after 1481. They were called *pays d'État* (State territories). The General Treasurers, who had appeared with the accounts and the *tailles* since the end of the thirteenth or the fourteenth centuries, were posts strictly controlled by the king, who nominated his faithful servants and his creditors to them. It is curious in this context that the Valois did not strive for a more clear-cut form of centralisation. In fact it seems that Louis XII and Francis I understood how inconvenient a superior and general agent of the finances could have been. The rather suspect case of Jacques Cœur, who was responsible for the king's personal finances and was finally condemned, was not encouraging. Among the four or five 'secretaries' who surrounded the king, one of them might well be given the job of Intendant of the Finances, but the one to whom Francis I entrusted the task, Jacques de Semblançay, died at Montfaucon like Marigny before him: the age of Fouquet had not yet come.

The Dukes of Burgundy on the contrary tried to achieve this ultimate stage. It is quite clear why: their lands were so dispersed that they were forced to provide different organs and types of taxation for the main parts of their principality. There was no question of applying a uniform taxation: the Chamber of Accounts of Beaune which passed to Dijon in 1477, that of Flanders and that of Brabant, were created in the time of Philip the Good and each one dealt separately with the taxes in each of their jurisdictions. Duke Charles wanted to go a step further: he abolished all urban privileges including those of the most venerable Flemish towns, a measure which did not fail to provoke revolts and repressions in Ghent, Bruges and elsewhere. He also created a Receiver General in 1455, who was told to coordinate all the receipts, amounting in all to 900,000 ducats, it is said. Charles *le Téméraire*'s excessive projects were unfortunately too much for a flexible but adequate organisation. He contracted loans, notably with Tommaso Portinari, director of the Medici branch in Bruges, but these scarcely covered the expenses of his expeditions to Switzerland. The Valois Kings also borrowed from Lyon bankers, but they were in principle solvent and in any case secure on their throne. The same could not be said of the Burgundian. His death brought all his projects to an end.

England's position was somewhere in between these two poles. Since the thirteenth century the English King like the Valois disposed of his Exchequer and his Wardrobe, even though his income was inevitably limited by the modesty of his estates. The eventual control of Parliament as well as the strength of the high aristocracy (the number of earls had dwindled from twenty-five to sixteen between 1412 and 1480 leading to greater concentrations of land) limited the King's freedom to raise taxes. This was why the Tudors gave up the attempt to impose a general organisation, and the long struggle against particular taxes, and made systematic use of the services of their privy seal. This meant the ability to advance the sums they needed by issuing cash receipts against direct or indirect revenues. As for Spain, where the towns were made the centres of taxation, the creation in 1495 of a Chamber of Accounts on the French model, the *Hacienda*, allowed Charles V to launch the whole system of extraordinary taxation, which ended by ruining the country.

The economy of the State

In spite of the unequal achievements, something had begun firmly enough for its outcome to be certain. Nevertheless, it may well have been Spain's and England's backwardness, compared with France, which explains why these countries were keener to profit from the conquest of the seas and new lands. After all, the French King did not need America or the Indies, and these places did not arouse the least spirit of enterprise in the businessmen or the gentlemen of the Valois kingdom; as far as they were concerned, the age of set-backs had yet to come. Instead all these States shared a very new and important phenomenon; they were increasingly perceived as homogeneous economic areas with common interests, which benefited from being properly managed. The merchants certainly played a leading part in this process, by asserting that both control of the coinage and implementing a 'political economy' on which to base the royal army were inevitable. The rulers were encouraged to supervise and to exploit the productive potential of their lands. This attitude developed into 'modern' mercantilism and was strongly opposed both to the traditional indifference of the ruling power towards trade and to the concept of a Christian world whose frontier, where it did exist, was never economic. There was however an increasing tendency towards regulating economic activity by, for instance, limiting production to

461

towns, taxing all transactions, discriminating against foreigners, all of which explain why policies veered between regulated liberalism and production monopolies, and between the vested interest of private groups and establishing 'national' institutions. There are many examples of innovation or adaptation; I have chosen three aspects, which definitely applied to the period before 1500. In the first place the ruler supported economic initiatives, not only when he was himself a merchant (for instance the Medici) or when he was influenced by an interested counsellor (Charles VII listening to Jacques Cœur), but also because he was convinced of the benefits of a grand design. This was why Edward IV and Henry VII supported (for what their help was worth) the efforts of the Merchant Venturers and why Louis XI encouraged the development of the silk industry at Lyon and Rouen in 1470 as well as issuing letters of naturalisation in favour of many foreigners, German miners, Italian glass blowers, Flemish drapers. By an unhappy irony of history those monarchs who lacked any business sense were the ones who drew the greatest profits; the Portuguese, who were fascinated by geography and the Spaniards, who resisted ventures of any kind. In the second place, the State was induced to intervene in affairs which were in principle political but in practice had an economic dimension. Such were, among other examples, the Iberian *Mesta*, which started off as an agreement between the great Spanish landowners and ended by supporting the Castilian treasury; the alum affair at Tolfa, which linked Florence and Rome against Genoa and Naples; Hungarian and Austrian copper and gold, which led the Függer to incite their Habsburg rulers against the Turks; the English wool staple, which wandered from Calais to Bruges to Antwerp at the whim of royal politics. The effects of these examples and a hundred other less glaring ones were as wide ranging as they were lasting and they demonstrated that State politics were largely dictated by merchants. This will come as no surprise to us of the twentieth century.

The final aspect was even more 'modern' in that economic war was now possible. Charles VII's depreciated coinage had already seriously inconvenienced Bedford by affecting his good money, but it cannot be claimed that the 'King of Bourges' was aware of this. After 1470 however, this could no longer be doubted; Commynes has told us that Louis XI used this weapon to 'destabilise' the circulation of money in Charles the Bold's neighbouring lands. Florence, for her part, tried to starve Milan by blockading its ports and preventing wheat or salt from getting through. The Count of Savoy had no financial reason for suspending his annual payments to the Duke of Burgundy. Rome corrupted Venice's mercenaries by offering them double wages and, to a certain extent, the English 'Navigation Acts' of 1485 to 1489 were similarly inspired, not to mention Henry VII's Ordinances of 1495, which threatened the Hanse with an embargo on its wheat imports if it did not allow the English access to Gdansk. What was good for the merchants was good for England, and especially for the Tudors.

Old kings and new

The attitudes of kings in the sixteenth century were still strongly influenced by the past. The pomp which surrounded the monarch was of this sort; although it had not yet turned into the *étiquette* of the seventeenth century, the sovereign's *entrées*, his coronation, his

Ambassadors were appointed by the sovereign and acted as his personal representatives on missions to foreign heads of State. Firmly established States would adopt diplomacy as part of their general development. Holbein the Younger's *The Ambassadors*, 1533, in the National Gallery, London.

obsequies, the archaic costume and emblems which he paraded on essential occasions (crown, mantle, sceptre, globe) were not the attributes of a cult of personality but of a cult of the function, regardless of the merits of its particular representative. All the great lawyers of the fourteenth and fifteenth centuries; Accurso, Ableiges, Revigny, Petit, well understood the medieval inheritance; the King was the incarnation of the *respublica*; he exercised a ministry and was of the Church. Of course this did not stop the Valois from supervising and reducing appeals to Rome; from abusing their regalian rights (the 'Pragmatic Sanction' of Bourges in 1438) and then from rejecting pontifical taxes by means of 'Concordats' in 1472 and 1502, from taxing the 'Gallican' Church, just as the very pious Catholic Monarchs despoiled the religious orders, and as the Tudors soon confiscated the Church's property. These gestures were not 'modern': Rome was a terrestrial power and was treated as such and kings had controlled their local Churches for a long time. As well as the Carolingians and the Emperors of the eleventh and twelfth centuries, both Saint Louis, Edward I and Philip the Fair had acted no differently. This did not entail the 'laicisation' of royalty in any way. The fact that the Church was no longer the pillar of the throne was due to her own weakness.

Old and new too, the intrinsic nature of concrete power was personal and relied

463

Jan Van Eyck's *Madonna of Chancellor Rolin*, 1425, Paris, Louvre. Nicholas Rolin was nominated chancellor of the duchy of Burgundy by Philip the Good and acted as prime minister.

increasingly on powerful personalities. But what a disreputable crowd they were; power was definitely no longer 'feudal', firstly because the territorial rulers gradually took over, secondly because the king did not consult his vassals, whether great or small, in any way. Nonetheless, his power remained family bound and domestic; the princes of the blood conducted intrigues, which hardly ever succeeded, but which continued until well into the seventeenth century. As for the Hôtel, where all decisions were made, it swarmed with coteries. It was no longer staffed by a handful of loyal men, but by a cohort of clients; there were two hundred persons around Ferdinand of Aragon, four hundred around the Pope, eight hundred at the court of Charles VI, a thousand close to Francis I: these people were derived from all social origins and callings and could be promoted or disgraced at will.

The awareness of how unwieldy such a staff was, when prompt or even secret decisions were required, resulted in the gradual supression of the notion that consultation with relations and vassals was an indispensible part of governing. This gave birth finally to the main organ of government, variously known as the Privy Council, the King's Council, the Cabinet, the Secret, which included a dozen officials, 'secretaries of state', 'ministers' who performed this function at the king's behest. Such a body might include a member of the ruling dynasty, a soldier of renown or Church dignitaries, but more often men who had

464

been trained in the legal or financial institutions of the State. One of them might tower over the others as a 'Privy Secretary' in the case of Thomas Beckington and Cranmer, or as *Chancelier d'État* like Nicholas Rolin and after him Granvelle in the Burgundian States, or straight-forward favourites in France such as Etienne Chevalier and Pierre D'Oriole in the time of Charles VII, and Olivier le Daim and Briçonnet who were close to Louis XI. A 'modern' detail was provided by the ruler's private life, which overflowed into his public life through the influence exercised by a lover or a mistress over promotions and disgraces. Among such were Bertrand de la Cueva around 1460 in Castile and Agnès Sorel in France, not to mention some of Henry VIII's wives. Of course, as at each stage in the history of the State, this was no absolute novelty; Philip the Fair and even Saint Louis had been influenced by their intimates. Later on though, such persons were to become a whole team.

Finally, the ruler's justice was one of the last determining attributes of his power. There too the old system gave rise to the new. Since the achievement of French *légistes* and English lawyers like Bracton, the very conception of this justice had evolved. The principle of non-delegation to individuals, a pillar of the seigneurial system, had been assimilated. Even in the fourteenth century when the Estates, the Cortes or the Parliament in France, Castile and England strongly criticised royal 'tyranny', they did not contest the ruler's monopoly of justice. The old adage 'the King is the Law' won increasing weight as Roman Law became more generally taught. But they were aware too that, although the King did not delegate justice, he could not administer it on his own either, and that public justice had fallen into disrepute because it was badly organised. There were of course until the 'war of the public good' petty nobles and even princes in France, who maintained the illusion of their ancient rights, though appeals to the royal *bailli* were in fact in order. From then on the idea that the King alone was able to designate, dismiss and instruct those who administered justice in his name, was gradually adopted. Since the executive was not distinguished from the judiciary in any way, contemporaries were not aware of the risks of abuse.

This time England must serve as our model: the 'popular' justice of the manorial courts and the public assizes conducted by the sheriff indicated a very real familiarity with a legal system, which was both royal and common, and free from pressure by private interests; the royal Justices in Eyre had the job of dealing with appeals or defaults. From the thirteenth century on, however, this very old system, which was apparently the most 'democratic' known to Europe (before the *Habeas corpus* was introduced much later in England), was capped by Parliament. In principle this collaboration, which gradually became very regular, had two objects: that of approving or not approving the ruler's financial demands and then controlling his use of the money, and that of surveying royal behaviour, which led in Edward II's reign to this body setting itself between the ruler and his subjects, particularly for taking cognisance of law cases settled by the sheriffs. Since the participants in these parliaments, who represented the landowners, the gentry and the trading towns, were appointed under irregular conditions and as a result of intrigues, there was the risk that this instrument of government might turn into a political and legal pressure chamber, as indeed happened during the minority of Richard II. This is why one of Lancaster's main achievements was that of profoundly reorganising the Parliamentary body between 1406

465

and 1463, firstly by instituting elections by the sheriffs and the County Courts, so as to appoint sixty-four lords or squires and 250 'burghers' to represent 112 principal localities, whose number could not be altered (a surprising miscalculation in an era of deserted villages and enclosures). Then, in 1453, the King decided to designate the Speaker himself, the president of a Parliament which was beginning to be split somewhat unevenly into two distinct parts; the 'lords' and the 'commons'. Finally in 1463, the ruler reserved the right to introduce Bills, thus depriving the Chambers of the possibility of ruling. Edward IV was subsequently responsible for removing from Parliament all its powers of judicial surveillance; he placed a representative of the Crown, a coroner, beside each sheriff, who was charged with supplementing and then replacing the old county agent. In 1478, both to assist the repression, which followed his resumption of the throne, and to cut short all attempts at avoiding royal control, he created a 'Star Chamber' to deal with political cases and then with many others qualified as such for the occasion. It would not be possible to explain how Henry VIII subsequently managed to get his religious politics, his maritime ambitions or his marital projects validated, without stressing that the English King, in spite of being militarily and financially worse off than his neighbour across the Channel, commanded instead an absolute weapon within his island; complete control over the legal system.

The situation in France is harder to define. Firstly the size of the kingdom, the survival until the end of the sixteenth century especially in the Land of Oc, of great fiefs and *apanages* which controlled their own law courts, sometimes even of lordships which, in return for paying a tax, could still exercise the right to judge middling and lesser cases; all these factors made it harder to achieve rapid success. The *baillis* did not have nearly as much power as sheriffs, which meant that the Valois' efforts could only be effective (apart from whittling away at surviving rights of justice, whenever possible, by defeating a feudatory, or by granting the right of appeal to numerous groups or individuals) in establishing a certain uniformity in the legal 'styles' and procedures employed here and there, and in controlling the *parlements*. In 1454 Louis XI insisted by means of the ordinance of Montils-lès-Tours on drawing up a new Common Law. This turned out to be a very long task. When the 1535 ordinance was promulgated which renewed this obligation, it was far from being achieved. He got better results on the level of the *parlements*; there were several of them, in fact, because the single legal institution of Appeal to emerge from the Court in the thirteenth century was soon incapable, in spite of increasing its viability, of dealing with all the cases which streamed to it. Apart from venality – called the 'spices' – which many of its members succumbed to, hastening or blocking particular cases, it was feared that baillis and seneschals too could interpose themselves between the plaintiff and the King, while simultaneously designating him the sole authentic depository of the law; after all this was precisely what the *états* of the fourteenth century had asked for. This meant that royal justice had to become more accessible to the plaintiff. The division of *parlement* into two on the occasion of the Treaty of Troyes in 1420, when one half was installed at Poitiers, the other remaining in Paris, and the *jours*, *grands jours*, *assises* and *états* which had been held in different places in the Land of Oc since 1355, were all behind a process of reform, which

Charles VII presides over a law suit. The king is exercising his right in the presence of magistrates, to whom he normally delegated it, and of princes of the blood, seated on his right. This picture by Jean Fouquet shows the law court held at Vendôme in 1458. (Codex Gallicus 369, Munich Bayerische Staatsbibliothek.)

finally produced a legal system appropriate to what was to become an absolute monarchy. One *parlement* was created at Toulouse in 1444, another in Grenoble in 1457, another in Bordeaux in 1462, in Dijon (1477), Rouen (1499), Aix (1501), not counting the Courts of the Aids, which could prepare financial reports at Montpellier or at Rouen. The rulers tried to abolish customs such as that of the 'spices' at the same time, and were very careful to supervise the nominations of magistrates. The kingdom was also divided into four huge *généralités*: the Lands of Oïl and Oc, Normandy and Outre-Seine with Yonne, which were in principle supposed to assist financial control, but whose intendants in charge – they were not yet called this – were supposed to report to the King on all kinds of affairs. This process was not yet achieved before the age of the Bourbons, who pushed it to its completion, but the complexity of the problems involved is enough to excuse the last Valois; they laid the foundations on which the future was to build.

The Empire is a case in point, because it was indeed an entity where those in charge were by definition justiciaries. The sovereigns were sometimes aware of this, but the gathering of the Diet of the Empire, the *Reichstag*, never managed to get any sort of organisation started. The princes, many of whose power and wealth rested on their rights of justice, had no intention of relinquishing them, and the Emperor had no way of forcing them to do so. A sort of itinerant tribunal functioned semi-clandestinely until around 1460, when it was encouraged by Sigismund, who himself took part in it. The *Vehmgericht* was born in Westfalia, and its members dispensed sentences against pillagers, heretics and assassins, which they then carried out themselves in a strange form of private justice, which was illegal but completely effective. The movement died out following the abuses of the Bohemian wars. Frederick III secured the creation of an Imperial Tribunal in 1495, a sort of supreme Court of Appeal, but no one answered its summonses after 1500. The Emperor himself was obsessed by his Austrian worries, and of his forty-one years as Emperor (1452–93) he spent twenty-nine outside his Empire – how could he have directed an efficient judicial organisation? This time too, many subsequent events are explained by such complete inadequacy, including the Reformation movement and the 1525 Peasants' Revolt.

One king, one nation

Of course a rich and powerful ruler was the cynosure of all eyes and reverence. To glimpse him as he passed by in his glory, to recognise his features on the coinage (a new practice) was to invest him, in the minds of those who were no longer his 'men' but his 'subjects' with the allure of a demi-god. Surrounded by flatterers, who were also terrified of falling into disgrace, he was overwhelmed with incense. This propaganda was served by the art of printing which enabled little pamphlets to be distributed; Lorenzo the Magnificent, Louis XI himself, Francis I, Charles V, Henry VIII especially, were the objects of panegyrics imitating those of Antiquity. Huge portraits of the rulers were paraded around and were made to appear in the mystery plays enacted in front of the people, who paid for it all. In their portraits of the Ideal Sovereign, around 1515, Erasmus and Machiavelli added a taste for glory and personal prestige to his attributes of peace and justice. Contrariwise, no one found fault with the characteristics which made a ruler different from other men and in any case superior to them: Charles *le Téméraire* because he drank for twenty, Louis XI because he never touched drink, Lorenzo or René of Anjou because they versified and painted, Henry VIII because he was an athlete, Charles V because he was ill and Francis I because the French are indulgent towards dandies in search of thrills. We are only a step away from a religion of the ruler, a cult of royalty.

But not quite there yet. First of all, the King could still be approached; Louis XI could be met visiting a market; people ran to see Francis I and Henry VIII wrestling with bare hands; Charles V could be mistaken for a cloth merchant and Frederick III on his flight from Trèves had to bargain at night for a horse. The deadly incense of the Escorial had not yet wafted from Spain to the rest of Europe. Added to this, the idea of popular consent, however fictional, had not yet dissipated; if the King was endowed with a holy office, a 'civic humanism' as Salutati described it, he held it by right of blood, of course, but also by the will of his subjects. They had to be consulted, especially when he wanted them to pay up. The monarchs of the fifteenth century could not have failed to do this, without ending up as penniless as the Emperor. But we have just seen how the English Parliament gradually turned into a complacent mask, preserving its representative image in principle, but dominated by the King. The case of France might have been more delicate, because the Valois' financial problems had forced them during the fourteenth century to hold frequent if not regular assemblies of the Estates, where hard words were heard, but those who spoke them generally gave in and were at least given the feeling of having intervened in the government of the *respublica*. This was an intolerable practice for a monarchy on the way to becoming absolute, but almost three-quarters of a century had to pass before the French kings got rid of them. They proceeded skilfully; on the one hand by convoking only the regional Estates, which flattered the region concerned and did not involve the others, and then by reducing the object of the convocation to a particular problem. This is what Charles VII and Louis XI did in 1439, 1444, 1454, 1468 and 1470. In the intervening times, they either did without, as in the case of the hunting rights and the *taille du gîte* (accommodation tallage), or else they leant on the advice of a *parlement*. It was only in 1484 that the Regents Anne and Pierre de Beaujeu felt obliged to call a general convocation at Tours, on account of the problems involved in the delicate process of dealing with the defunct Louis XI's affairs. Here they heard such vehement recriminations, which were partly unjustified because the situation was improving, that, after having registered the reprimand, they dissolved the assembly of the Estates. There were two more 'technical' reunions in 1493 and 1500, followed by a general reunion of the Land of Oïl in 1506, at which Louis XII, having carefully selected the representatives, reaped the title of 'Father of the People'. Then silence fell; Francis I was too busy, and the numerous and innovatory ordinances which mark his reign seem to demonstrate that the ruler was quite capable of hearing the request, at least the moderate ones, of his loyal subjects, without their having to shout them in his ears. He felt himself at one with the nation.

Indeed the word 'nation' had only just come to mean what we understand by it today; it **469** is profoundly anti-medieval, and represents the awareness which a collection of men and women have of belonging to a defined territorial entity, to one ethnic group, with one language; and which, at this particular point, acknowledged one ruler, one single head, and one common interest in which their particular interests were merged. Had this stage really been reached by 1520? Nothing is less certain, but they were getting there. Maybe the English and the French did not really identify with the activities of their rulers, or feel that they were involved, any more than they were consulted about them. But without thinking too much about it, they did claim just that, and they do still, in spite of their indifference to Agincourt and even more to Bouvines. It was at the end of these emergent dynastic imperialisms that a Europe of nations would appear, when the Middle Ages were well and truly over.

Imperialism on the march

If the purpose of this book were to provide a recital of dynastic and military events, my task would have become insurmountable by now, and it would be rather boring to read. Nonetheless, these events must be touched on, albeit briefly. They were no longer simply a matter of cities and potentates settling their accounts between themselves, but were dragged out in a series of recurring conflicts, which are inherent to modern history, and indeed (when one thinks of Italy, for instance), to much of subsequent history, especially if one adds the eastern events we discussed earlier. The fact is that behind these conflicts, which had begun fairly traditionally – as a result of disputed successions, of family pretensions, over ownership of a stronghold – princely and economic antagonisms were emerging, which were to develop into national enmities later on. I hope that the preceding pages have shown how very important these were becoming. However, we can see our way through this tumult fairly clearly: the conflicts and preoccupations of the western monarchies tended to be phased out in their traditional stamping grounds, and their rivalries were moving elsewhere. This was a vital development, because the Atlantic-facing monarchies were involved: England, France, Spain and Portugal, and it explains the role which all four were preparing to play overseas. The whole of middle, central and eastern Europe became the theatre of the most lasting confrontations; eastern Europe's confrontations with Islam have been discussed in another chapter. There the Russians, Poles and Hungarians played the role of guardians of the eastern confines of Christendom, which first of all put them out of reach of the confusion in Central Europe and then turned them into docile sentinels extending the European world towards the East. This left the Empire and Italy to be preyed on by their neighbours to the West and North – for many years to come.

Winding up old concerns

When, earlier on in this volume, I suspended my brief account of the Hundred Years' War, its lowest point had been reached, when Joan of Arc was burned at the stake and when

470

France had two crowned and annointed kings; the Valois Charles VII and the Lancastrian Henry VI, the one pusillanimous and ill advised, and the other a ten year old boy controlled by his old uncle, John of Bedford. There was also a third 'King of France', Duke Philip the Good. He was, in his own interest, to undo what he had engineered in order to avenge his father, namely, delivering France over to the English. The English cause was in fact untenable; he was himself harried on his own lands and was especially hard driven in the Low Countries, where the fine edifice he had dreamt of making independent failed to materialise. Further, the death of his brother-in-law, the regent Bedford, freed him from his moral obligations. He was well advised by Nicholas Rolin in initiating conferences at Arras in 1435. Charles VII was ready to pay a very high price which included a due apology, handing back all the land north of the Somme, and dispensing the Duke from paying him homage. The English raged in vain, for Philip withdrew his support. Charles VII paid highly for it; as did Brittany, which rallied to the fold (1435), Paris, which he conquered (1436), and then, after pausing for breath, Normandy (1451) and finally Bordeaux (after two sieges in 1453) were secured. The English were left just with Calais, for a further century. The Hundred Years' War was practically over. In fact bands of mercenaries and *écorcheurs* were still marauding and the English never gave in on principle. It was only during a raid on Picardy in 1475 that Edward IV, in return for a lot of money, consented at Piquigny to salute Louis XI by his title of King of France. This old quarrel of a former age was really ended because the two kingdoms were both engaged in the personal task of clearing their territories of local powers capable of impeding royal authority from establishing itself more strongly.

In France this is generally called the destruction of the feudal class. Louis XI is usually credited with this, but it is fair to remember that Charles VII, by creating a permanent salaried army, was able to eliminate the noble leagues of the *Praguerie*, which were perhaps more dangerous in the long run than the isolated or concerted feudal risings which his son had to face. Between 1465, when he very cunningly got rid of the 'League of the Public Good', and the death of Charles, Duke of Maine, the last member of the House of Anjou in 1481, the Valois succeeded in regulating nearly all the effects of the feudal explosion centuries beforehand. It is important to concentrate on the proceedures he employed, in that they cut through older practices. The King employed legal proceedings, followed by executions against real or supposed rebels, such as the Count of Saint-Pol, the Duke of Alençon, the Duke of Nemours; or else he acted as the secular arm of the Church in striking down the Count of Armagnac, who was accused of incest. He also promised money to the King of Aragon to help him defeat the *remensas*, receiving Roussillon in pledge (1462), and having only partly paid up, he kept the province (1473). His acts sometimes relied on simple external family alliances; his sister Madeleine became regent of Navarre, another sister, Yolande, was made Duchess of Savoy. Better still, he gave one of his daughters, Anne, to the Duke of Bourbon whom he thus recruited to his side, and another, Jeanne, who was said to be infertile, to Louis Duke of Orléans, hoping thus to put an end to his line. He threatened the old 'King René' of Anjou with foreclosure on his debts and got him to promise and then to actually cede Provence and Anjou (1481) to him. As for Brittany,

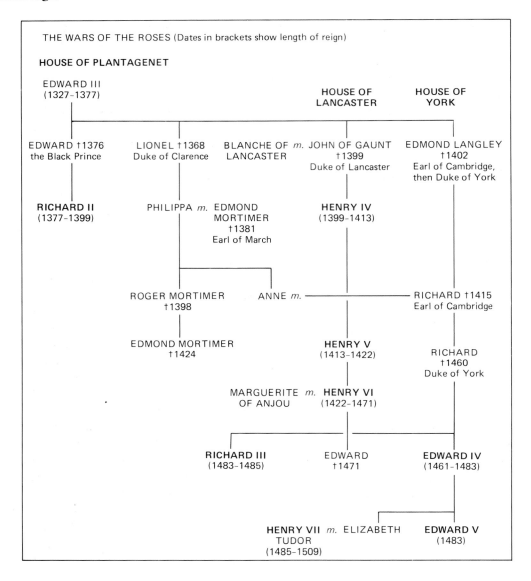

THE WARS OF THE ROSES (Dates in brackets show length of reign)

HOUSE OF PLANTAGENET

EDWARD III
(1327–1377)

HOUSE OF
LANCASTER

HOUSE OF
YORK

EDWARD †1376
the Black Prince

LIONEL †1368
Duke of Clarence

BLANCHE OF _m._
LANCASTER

JOHN OF GAUNT
†1399
Duke of Lancaster

EDMOND LANGLEY
†1402
Earl of Cambridge,
then Duke of York

RICHARD II
(1377–1399)

PHILIPPA _m._ EDMOND
MORTIMER
†1381
Earl of March

HENRY IV
(1399–1413)

ROGER MORTIMER
†1398

ANNE _m._

RICHARD †1415
Earl of Cambridge

EDMOND MORTIMER
†1424

HENRY V
(1413–1422)

RICHARD
†1460
Duke of York

MARGUERITE _m._ HENRY VI
OF ANJOU   (1422–1471)

RICHARD III
(1483–1485)

EDWARD
†1471

EDWARD IV
(1461–1483)

HENRY VII _m._ ELIZABETH
TUDOR
(1485–1509)

EDWARD V
(1483)

although he had counted on recovering it, this was effected only after his death when his successor Charles VIII married its Duchess Anne, and so surrendered a part of the lands his father had acquired from the House of Burgundy to his former fiancée, Marguerite of Austria-Burgundy, in compensation. By 1500 there were no fiefs left in the kingdom except those of Albret-Navarre, Angoulême, Orléans and Bourbon. Events could of course have turned out differently; the House of Orléans might not have produced King Louis XII, that of Angoulême King Francis I and that of Bourbon-Albret King Henry IV. By the accession of

Henry IV these factors had ended by annihilating the principalities. In spite of everything, Louis XI had accomplished the task of cleaning up the kingdom. He has been accused of dishonesty, slyness, and also of having intrigued against Spain in Navarre and Roussillon, and of having allowed the Habsburgs to settle on the frontiers of France. These are facile reproaches and all the more unjust when one looks at England.

Here the problem was not to the same extent due to autonomous princes, because there were not many of these in England, where they tended to be Marcher Lords – the Percys and Nevilles on the Scottish borders and the Lancasters and Tudors in Wales – who were much more closely related by blood to their Kings. The drama was provided by dynastic rivalries, which lasted for twenty years, between the partisans of the red rose grouped around Henry VI of Lancaster, and those of the white rose, the emblem of the House of York, youngest branch of the ruling family, which was descended not from Edward III's second son, as were the Lancasters, but from his third. The interminable War of the Roses lasted throughout Henry VI's reign, the son of the winner of Agincourt, who went mad like his grandfather Charles VI – History's ironic revenge for the Treaty of Troyes. Since the King was incapable, his uncle John of Beaufort and cousin John of Somerset, and a distant cousin, William of Suffolk, claimed the right to rule as 'protectors' in the name of the King and his wife, Marguerite of Anjou. The Duke of York recalled the former revolt of the Lancasters against Richard Plantagenet and took up arms. The two main protagonists were the Queen, who was supported by Louis XI, and a Neville, the Earl of Warwick – 'the Kingmaker'. After the death of Richard of York, his son Edward pursued the contest and, depending on whose side Warwick was at any one time, the Yorkists were beaten (1459), were victorious (1460), were defeated (1461) and finally reestablished when Edward of York was crowned King. The war continued: Warwick dethroned Edward in 1470 and then was himself defeated and killed in 1471. The extremely opportune disappearance of Henry VI ensured Edward a rather more stable second reign. On his death in 1483, his brother Richard III had the 'babes in the Tower' killed and grabbed the crown. But the Tudors who had until then been allied with the Lancasters, attacked him with help from Louis XI and eliminated him (1485). Power thus devolved on Henry VII Tudor, heir to the Lancasters by his father's marriage, and to the Yorks by his own. The Nevilles and Percys had been compromised in these interminable disputes and were reduced to obedience; the Somersets and Suffolks were no more, and the Tudors had become the ruling house. This solution ex nihilo had however bled England dry and, all things being equal, history has judged Louis XI's intrigues more kindly.

In Spain, there was rather less confusion. After fairly fierce family rivalries in the fourteenth and the beginning of the fifteenth centuries, the three Iberian kingdoms experienced a period of relative tranquillity. Castile, the principal Spanish kingdom, was however faced with a succession problem due to Henry IV's notorious imbecility (1454–74), who, to make things worse, was known as 'the Impotent' and his heiress considered, perhaps justly, a bastard. This left Alfonso V, King of Portugal and John II of Aragon to dispute the succession. The latter won it by marrying his son Ferdinand to Henry IV's sister Isabella in 1476. When John died, the two spouses reigned in concert as 'Catholic

THE HOUSE OF BURGUNDY

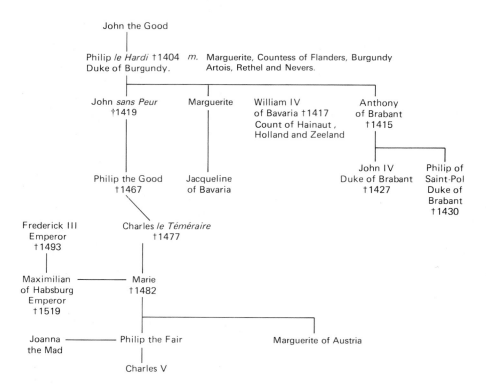

Monarchs' with Portugal renouncing his rights. They completed the *Reconquistà* by annexing Granada and appeared to have inaugurated a common destiny for the peninsula. No one however can control fate: the Catholic King's daughter, Joanna, was mad – a fitting niece for the imbecile Henry IV. She was married to *le Téméraire*'s grandson, Philip the Fair, heir to the Burgundian part of the Habsburg territory. As it was, Ferdinand survived his son-in-law, who died in 1505, by a very long time, so that when the old King of Aragon died in 1516, it was Philip and Joanna's son Charles, known as Charles of Ghent, who inherited both Spain and the Burgundian lands.

The adventure of the Grand Duke of the West

The attempt by the Valois Dukes of Burgundy inaugurated a series of repercussions, which lasted until the end of the Ancien Régime. It was the finest example of how a territorial entity could be formed from nothing, or from absolutely disparate elements. There were, in the new climate of the fifteenth century, few attempts and even few fates more personal than this one. The Burgundian 'State' was also that of Van Eyck and Memling, Sluter and Marville, of the Hospices of Beaune and the Grand' Place in Brussels, of the Orders of the

474

Louis XI, painted by Jean Fouquet (New York, Brooklyn Museum), facing Philip *le Hardi*, Duke of Burgundy. The son of John the Good, he married Marguerite of Flanders, the richest heiress of Europe, and founded the dynasty of the 'Grand Dukes of the West'. (Anonymous, fifteenth century; Château de Versailles.)

Pheasant and the Golden Fleece, and lastly, there was something poignant about this eccentric attempt to return to the past, when another territory had existed between France and the Empire.

Its reconstruction was almost entirely artificial and dynastic. From 1369 to 1470, almost none of the pieces of the puzzle had been joined together by force, but by devolution, inheritance, purchase and marriage, which implied a prodigious continuity of attitudes, although the first three Dukes had completely different characters. All three of them – Philip *le Hardi*, a level-headed and calculating schemer; John *sans Peur*, impetuous and unscrupulous but uncommonly tenacious and lucid; Philip *le Bon* (the Good), spontaneous, unpredictable and immoderately proud as well as extremely prudent – called themselves and felt themselves to be French princes 'of the *Fleur de Lys*' (even the last, who had, after all, delivered France over to the Lancasters), just as French was their only language. The outline had been sketched in by 1369, when the young Valois Duke of Burgundy, brother of King Charles V, married Marguerite of Flanders, heiress to that fabulous and turbulent county and to Burgundy beyond the Saône. The way was clear: between the Burgundian block, which was close to Lyon, Basle, Geneva and Avignon, through which passed one of Europe's great trade routes carrying cloths, salt and wine, and the Flemish block, filled with towns, ports, manufacturers and soldiers, there was a huge space, crossed by the Meuse and the Mosel. This consisted of the Walloon lands, Champagne and Lorraine. Joining these two blocks so as to reach the Rhine in the east and the Marne in the west meant

475

holding the whole of ninth-century *Lotharingia* and also holding the principal European isthmus. Pushing north towards Holland and south to the Alpine passes, meant becoming master of Europe.

The Dukes threw themselves into this task, which historically raised enormous obstacles in their way. The formation of the block consisting of Brabant, Limburg and Luxemburg, where the Imperial family came from, was opposed by Emperors Wenceslaus and Sigismund. Alliances had to be arranged and successions foreseen, not to mention Louis of Orléans coveting Luxemburg. Philip the Good reaped these fruits between 1430 and 1443. Hainaut, Holland, Zeeland, Frisia came with Bavaria and the heiress, Jacqueline, was subjected to every influence. England invoked agreements from the time of Edward III and proposed one of her princes as a husband for Jacqueline. This certainly contributed to Duke Philip's displeasure with the English and to the *lâchage* of Arras I mentioned earlier. He was finally obliged to get rid of Jacqueline in order to take her lands from her in 1433. As well as this, the Gelderland was occupied without brutality in 1432, and he inherited Auxerrois, bought the County of Boulogne (1419), which encircled English Calais, and Namur in 1421. Liège was alone in refusing to be absorbed and, since she was now surrounded, John performed the task of crushing the Liégeois at Othée in 1408, leaving his son to pluck the Bishopric in 1433. After which the Artois and the 'towns of the Somme' were ceded by Charles VII in 1435.

A great deal had been achieved. Around 1440 or 1445, Philip the Good was able, with the help of Nicholas Rolin, to set up the great work of administrative unification which I alluded to. The courts at Dijon, Lille and Ghent reached their apogee with magnificent banquets and the Grand Duke of Ponant's crusading vow. However the plateaux and plains, where the Meuse and Moselle begin, were still lacking. The Lancastrian had been expected to hand over Champagne, but since 1429 this land had belonged to Charles VII. By signing a peace treaty at Arras with his royal cousin, Philip had shown that he would concentrate on lands to the east in Lorraine and Alsace, regions which were in disorder and very fragmented. The Habsburgs had a few lands along the Rhine and the House of Anjou was pushing into the duchy of Lorraine. It was not going to be difficult.

Unfortunately the Valois king finally surmounted his problems and took stock of the danger. He stepped up interference in judicial proceedings, supported René of Anjou at Nancy and warned the Habsburg Emperor Frederick III. The scene changed with the death of Charles VII in 1463 and the retreat of Philip the Good, followed three years later by his death (1468). On one side there was Louis XI, subtle, anxious and muddled but for all that level headed and on the other Charles, soon known as *le Téméraire* (the Rash), a rapt visionary and an imprudent, haughty and furiously dynamic man. The Duke attacked Louis XI and made problems of every kind – family, feudal and economic – for him. He profited from his daring and even forced him to watch the rebellious Liégeois being crushed, a mortal insult concealed by a smile. He then purchased Upper Alsace in 1469 and obtained from Duke René II, who was at bay, a free passage through Lorraine, before setting up a garrison at Nancy. In 1473 he thought he had reached his goal when he secured the Emperor's promise of the succession, or at least a crown, at Trèves. But Frederick stole away by night and simultaneously the English King Edward, *le Téméraire*'s brother-in-law, who was supposed to distract Louis XI, was bought. Lorraine was agitated and Savoy rose up – the hand of the Valois was everywhere to be seen. Charles lost his head; in 1476 he marched into Switzerland in an attempt to extricate himself: his splendid army was crushed at Granson and Morat in the autumn of 1476 under the blows of the Swiss Cantons' uncouth troops, which he had hoped to defeat cheaply. He then resorted to an act of folly by trying to retake Nancy in mid winter from René II, who was reinstalled in the town. On 5 January 1477 his last troops were drawn up in front of the town and two days later *le Téméraire*'s naked and slashed body was found in a frozen ditch. According to Commynes the news was brought in haste to Louis, who was indecently delighted by it.

His joy was certainly both indecent and unwise, although the opposition crumbled immediately. The Flemings imposed a *grand privilège* on Charles' only daughter, Marie, which restored their self confidence, and Louis occupied Burgundy, Picardy and Artois. But this time he was moving too fast – or rather, the Dukes' achievement of a hundred years was not an empty one. In the north the Valois were fiercely resisted. Marie's own resort lay in marrying Maximilian of Habsburg, the Emperor's son, who himself became Emperor in 1493. The danger was growing out of all proportion; in France it was hoped that Marie's daughter Marguerite might marry King Charles VII but instead Marguerite's brother, Philip the Fair, married the heiress of Spain. In 1500 their son Charles was born in Ghent.

The Burgundian menace had indeed been averted, but in its place rose up the Spanish peril: Flanders was lost to France for ever. The French hoped at least to prevent the Habsburgs, who were installed in the Comté, at the mouths of the Rhine and the Meuse and presently in Spain, Sicily and Naples, from getting hold of the Empire now occupied by Maximilian, Charles of Ghent's old grandfather. So when the Emperor died in 1519 the most improbable haggling took place. Charles won, by means of shameless bribery, over Francis I, who had not offered enough; he became Charles V at the age of nineteen. A new Europe was born, the unexpected offspring of the Burgundian Dukes' dream and the Valois Kings' ineptitude.

The birth of 'the two Germanies'

Neither the dishonourable bargaining of 1519, nor even the earlier attempt of the Dukes of Burgundy, would have been possible without the total decomposition of the Empire, which would last four centuries. Of course the Germanic peoples of the past were not interchangeable; no more than they are today were the Bavarians the same people as the Rhinelanders or Saxons, or indeed the Prussians. In the time of the Ottonians, of the Salic Kings and of Barbarossa, many duchies and marquisates (*Stämme* as they were called) claimed to belong to a distinct ethnic and customary group. Taken together, however, with the help of Imperial prestige, there was one *Germania*, one *Reich*, almost one Germany, to a far greater extent than there was one Spain or one France. A common language, often identical reactions, gave some unity to the whole: obviously the francophonic western part had been influenced by the Capetians, and the Slav eastern part was influenced by Poland, but in the middle, from the Rhine to the Oder and from the Baltic to the Brenner, it formed an entity.

It was this entity which exploded during the fourteenth century and especially the fifteenth. The weakness of the rulers is easily blamed for this, but in reality, given the impossibility of establishing a dynasty, the opposite is true. The Emperors were pale figures because they were chosen as such. On top of this they belonged to Houses based at a distance from the Empire; Luxemburg, Bohemia and Austria. These rulers were far from being ridiculous and inadequate; they sometimes had an elevated concept of their function and tried to implement this, as when Sigismund convoked the Council of Constance. But they had no means of action, since they could not rely on the princes nor even on the Church. They were often kept busy with their own marginal, eastern patrimonies, and I recalled how Frederick III spent more time in Austria than in his Empire. This meant that the fiasco was total, encouraging the dislocation of power.

A dislocation, which was to an equal extent due to Germany's economic expansion of the fifteenth century. Mines, fustian, wheat and credit maintained their initial ascendancy, so that, for lack of general regulations and impediments, each sphere of commercial or manufacturing activity overflowed into a corresponding territorial or political sphere. The 350 *Landsherrschaften*, or autonomous 'territories', which shredded the body of the Empire, irrespective of their sizes, which could be tiny, had one specific feature in common; their ruler had his own clergy, his own Diet, his capital, his justice, his mercenaries, his knights, his markets, and even his own coinage. This situation should not be interpreted as an obvious sign of decadence, but all the same, there was plenty of room in this fragmented Germany and along its margins for imperialist ambitions.

The Empire was thus one of the main parts of Europe where unifying projects were formed, where the ambitions of a group or a neighbour could be implemented. The first striking feature was that after Frederick II's reign, German towns had enjoyed almost complete freedom; the Hanse towns on the Baltic and the towns of the Rhine League, followed by those of the Swabian League, which appeared around 1380 to combat Charles IV's modest tax demands – all enjoyed a *de facto* independence. This state of affairs ceased at the end of the fifteenth century when the Leagues were dissolved and the Hanse itself, threatened by the progress of the English and even of the Castilians and the Scandinavian Kingdoms' desire for independence, was on the defensive. After 1472 the Dutch entered commercial history by securing the Danes' permission to set up customs duties on the Sund again, in order to restrict the Hanseatic advance into the North Sea. In 1478 the Grand Duke of Moscow closed the market at Novgorod to the Germans. These blows to the towns came at a time when fairs and industrial production, not to mention the money market, were in full swing in Augsburg, Nuremberg, Frankfurt and Leipzig and must no doubt be ascribed, rather as in neighbouring Italy, to the merchants' and businessmens' growing disinclination for urban administration. They preferred to advise and influence rulers than manage their towns' accounts.

Both the weakness of the sovereign and the listlessness of the towns allowed the princes' demands free rein. The 'Burgundian' case, which became Spanish and then Austrian, was undoubtedly the major fact of the fifteenth century and the beginning of the sixteenth. The accession of Charles V in 1519 introduced a new element into German politics, even

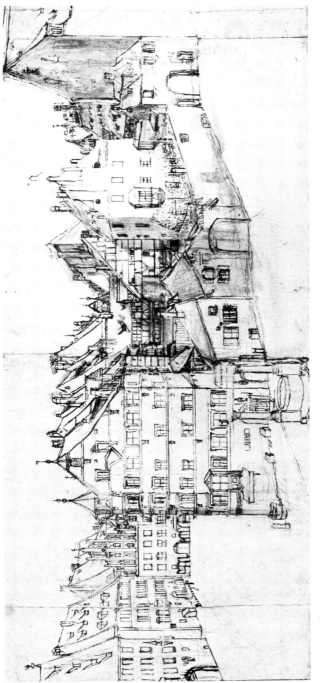

An ink drawing by Dürer of a square in Nuremberg. (Nuremberg, Altstadtmuseum.)

10 Germany at the end of the XIVth century

though Italian affairs, which the Emperors had abandoned for over a century, reappeared in the foreground. Other powers were also getting ready; France had her own claims, not really to the Imperial Crown, because Francis I's candidature had been more of a dissuasive than a sincere nature, but to the whole boundary west of the Rhine, which was to remain the objective of the monarchies of the Ancien Régime, and after them, of the Empire. The first steps were taken at the end of the Middle Ages, but with all the skill and cunning that the Capetians handed on to the Valois, who were normally more impetuous. They aimed at Lorraine, where the King of France had put his own men in the three Bishoprics of Metz, Toul and Verdun, and his Angevin relations on the Ducal throne; he had established garrisons in the Barrois, and his coinage and his agents were everywhere. This was one of the areas where, starting with Francis I, they came into direct confrontation with the Habsburgs.

The Scandinavian awakening was just as cautious. The Dutch tried to stir up Denmark, which worried the Hanse. But the danger lay elsewhere, unseen by the Germans, in Sweden, a country of unexplored resources, but with a large proportion of woodcutters and hunters. As yet no one could know that they were to be to Europe in the seventeenth century what the Swiss had been in the fifteenth. Starting in 1490, they concentrated for the moment on throwing off Danish control, which involved Kings Christian I and II in expensive punitive expeditions, that of 1520 being remembered by its sinister name of *Blodbad*, Bloodbath. The Hanseatics were definitely eliminated in the process, and in 1494 they were driven out of the Sund and from the towns of Sweden and Denmark; in 1512 they were forced at the Peace of Malmo to give up their privileges. Although the Danes and the Russians were the first to profit from the disappearance of the Hanse, the Swedes' turn was to come.

Furthermore, within the very body of the Empire, realignments were taking place, which were to be especially important in determining the extent of the Reformation; positions assumed then by a powerful ruler could have consequences which still mark Germany. Such rulers included the Habsburgs, the Wittelsbachs of Bavaria, the House of Saxony, and the Hohenzollern, newcomers from Swabia, to whom Sigismund entrusted the March of Brandenburg in 1415 and who took control of Lusace and of the Teutonic Knights' possessions in Prussia (who, having been thrashed by the Poles were very happy to be taken charge of in 1455).

Italy, a land held in common

Italy was the place were avid greed really was given a free rein. There was nothing new about this, and it could even be called traditional. Italy offered too many great memories, too much merchandise, too many brilliant towns, too many seductive courts and too much art and wit. Byzantium was gone, the Emperors had retired from the scene, the two- or three-headed Papacy wandered about in distress and without prestige. In spite of all this, the *Quattrocento* was a high point in the history of humanity. It was the age of the Medicis, of Genoese *caraques*, of the triumphant florin. There was however no authority to be found in the whole peninsula capable of directing all this potential and richness of its own advantage. The *mezzogiorno* was divided in two, with Queen Joanna II, a ruthless madwoman, perpetuating the distorted memory of the Angevins in Naples, and with the King of Aragon in Sicily. This dual situation was regulated to the Spaniard's advantage. In spite of opposition from 'King René' and others, he took control of Naples in 1443. But this was the soft part of Italy. The only lasting and damaging consequence was that the expelled Angevins preserved their claims and handed them on to the Valois when their family died out in 1481. As for the Pope, he had since 1438 at last been reinstalled in Rome on the debris of the Latin nobility and was now a ruler like any other. His prestige was strong enough locally to let him convince most of the city states and rulers in Central and

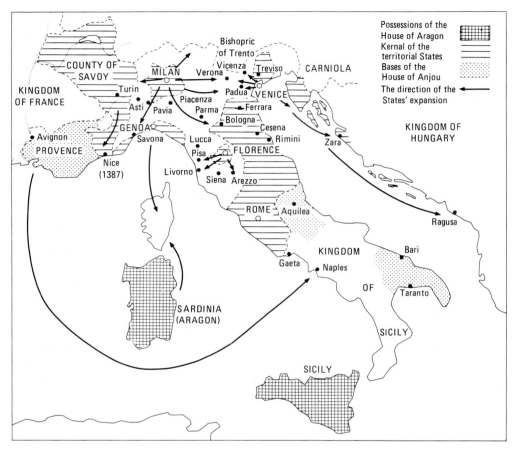

11 The beginnings of the Italian States in the XIVth century

Northern Italy – the Este in Ferrara, the Gonzaga of Mantua, the Medici in Florence, Francesco Sforza in Milan and even egoistical Venice – to agree at Lodi in 1454 to twenty-five years of peace.

A moving harmony which should not deceive us, because its principal motive was the general feeling of impotence and danger. The towns no longer had effective militias or dedicated consuls; the merchants couldn't care less about the *respublica* and the Maecenes among them felt themselves to be international. So all sorts of ambitions were able to flourish at the extremities of the peninsula and within its very body. It was precisely because the Aragonese of Naples were pushing towards Rome, because Charles VII was trying to recover Genoa, because the Dauphin Louis was sending troops against Milan, and René of Anjou was crossing the Alps, that the Italians closed ranks. Only the Turks were absent – and they attacked Otranto, and the Germans – and Frederick III descended on Rome to get himself crowned (1452). Once these perils had faded, the Italians resumed their quarrels, in which foreigners were also involved. There was a new and ineffectual

Angevin attempt on Naples in 1462. A quarrel broke out between the Pope and Florence during which one of Cosimo's grandsons, Giuliano, died (1478), Louis XI formed a close alliance with Savoy, and then with Milan (1475). Charles *le Téméraire* threatened the Alpine passes, and Venetian policies were as variable as weathervanes. This fruitless kaleidoscope of events, devoid of any determining feature or interest, is not worth examining. They are the fumes of Italy's past through which we dimly perceive helmeted Popes, venal *condottiere*, stabbed rulers, blood and celebrations.

But these events had whetted peoples' appetites, and by the very end of the century they had developed into serious affairs. This was when Pope Innocent VIII himself summoned King Charles VIII of France, as the theoretical heir to the Angevin crown of Naples, to Italy to install some order there and to get rid of the Aragonese, much as his successor Louis XII would claim to succeed the Visconti in Milan. The Valois crossed the Alps in 1494, inaugurating the modern history of war and diplomacy. Ferdinand of Aragon had conquered Granada two years ago and was no longer able to leave his cousin, King Ferrante, to hold Naples without his help. In Rome a discredited Pope, Alexander VI, could not reconcile the Italians; in Florence the Medici had gone bankrupt; in Milan Ludovico Sforza had lost his grip, and Venice remained Venice. Henceforth Italy was no more than a magnificent prey over which French, Germans and Spaniards were to quarrel during three centuries. This is why I will not broach the story of where these neophyte imperialist forces clashed, because I would be no more justified in stopping my recital at Marignan than at Pavia and the Sack of Rome. Italy had always been more advanced than the others and was even more so in this respect. While in France, Spain, and within Germany, the features of modern Europe were emerging fairly clearly, if rather less so in England, along the Rhine and the Baltic, Italy was already in the modern world by 1500.

Doors opened onto the world

The 'great discoveries' were by no means exclusively a feature of 'modern' history. One runs the risk of not understanding anything about the medieval achievement if one separates the Middle Ages from Henry the Navigator or Vasco da Gama; or if one chooses to see them as madmen or at best visionaries, which is anyway how Columbus is still considered. Of course, the 'leap into the unknown' which the Genoese sailor made when he sailed due west was in its way a symbolic gesture dividing two periods – are we not all aware of its vital consequences? Columbus' venture only followed closely on a century of a thousand other attempts and itself was not an unforseen act of daring. While we must stop here at Europe's penetration beyond her boundaries, at the colonies, the slave trade and the blood, all that came before belongs to and can be explained only by the Middle Ages.

Why discover new lands?

The phenomenon, whose essential features we will attempt to trace, was indeed 'exotic' in spite of the pages we have been able to devote to Africa or Asia. It was precisely the irruption of the unusual on to the European horizon which characterised the last medieval age. The

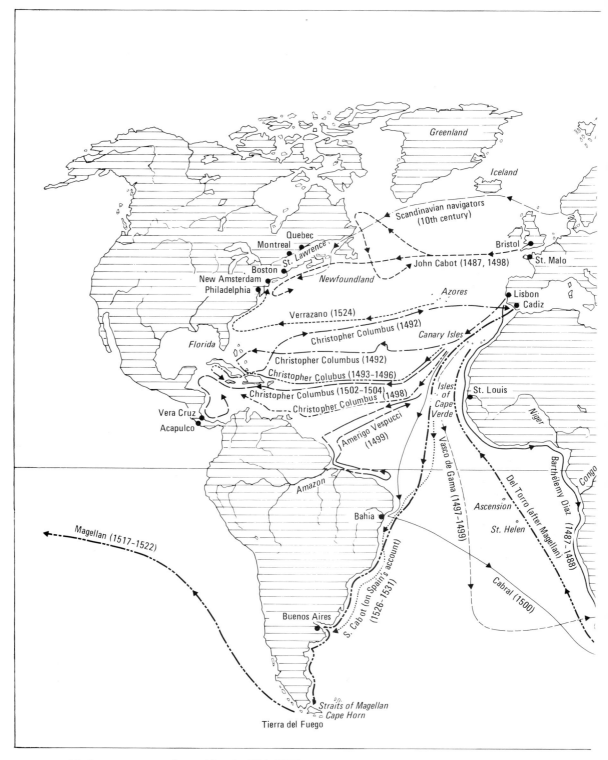

12 Circumnavigating the world in the XVth–XVIth centuries

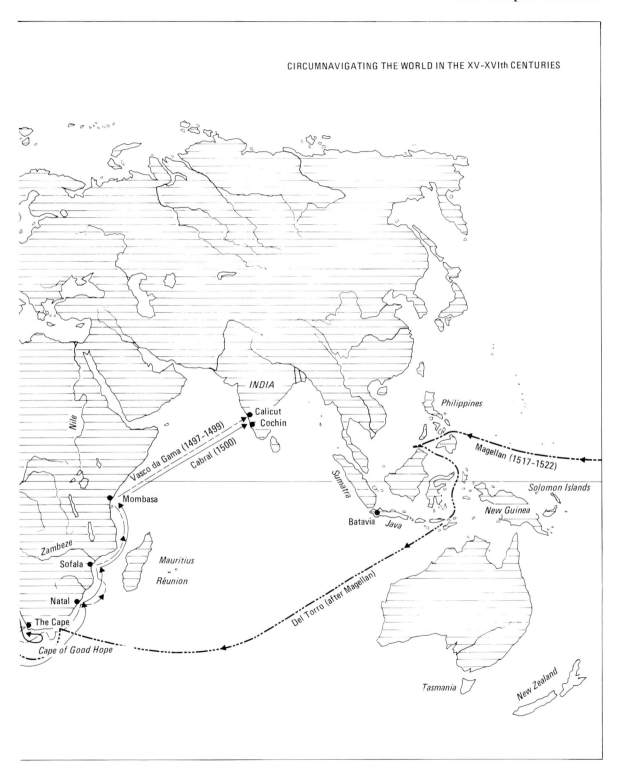

CIRCUMNAVIGATING THE WORLD IN THE XV–XVIth CENTURIES

INDIA

Philippines

Calicut
Cochin

Vasco da Gama (1497-1499)

Cabral (1500)

Magellan (1517-1522)

Solomon Islands

Sumatra

New Guinea

Mombasa

Nile

Batavia   Java

Zambeze

Mauritius

Sofala

Réunion

Natal

Del Torro (after Magellan)

The Cape

Cape of Good Hope

Tasmania

New Zealand

men of Italy, France or Spain felt this and seem to have been gripped by vertigo and maybe fear before the world which opened out to them. For historians scrutinising these first steps and especially for us who have seen the end, this conquest of the continents by the smallest of them over a period of four centuries fits in perfectly with more familiar and 'natural' events such as the domestication of the Slav world, the marginalisation of Islam or the end of the Greeks. Here too, peripheral worlds and riches were put at the disposal of the Western Europeans.

A few qualifications are necessary. With the exception of probable Scandinavian contacts in the early Middle Ages, America was *terra incognita*. As we know, she is to be found on no Christian or Islamic map before Columbus; the Arab geographers calculated the distance between Cathay (China) and the Maghrib at some 16,000 kilometres, which was a fair assessment, but they believed that this route had to go via Cipango (Japan). As for Christian geographers, who were making great advances in knowledge with the advent of merchant atlases, or portulans, and planispheres, whether they were Italians like Toscanelli or Germans like Martin Behaim, they relied on the calculations of Ptolomy and the Ancients, and came up with a distance of not more than 4,000 kilometres. This difference was to be vitally important, but for the moment it was irrelevant. America was still unknown and Asia had been entwined with the past of Europe and Islam for centuries. Very little was known about her, but at least since the Hellenistic age she had been well identified. She represented precious stones, spices, silks and an extraordinary world, which Arab travellers well before the fourteenth century had visited and described; Suleyman, Abu Zayd, Ibn Kordadbeh, Mas'udi. Through them, as Marco Polo has witnessed, Europe did know a few things, even such essential information as the pattern of Monsoon winds or distances between oases. Christian penetration did not get so far; the 'Parisienne' and the 'Marseillais' who were met in the middle of the Mongolian steppe by Fransiscans sent by Saint Louis to the Khan were marginals, as were the tiny Nestorian communities in China, themselves orientals. At Peking, Canton and in the Indies, Polo saw only Arabs and a few Jews. Further, when he returned to Venice in 1295 and dictated his memoirs, nobody believed him. For all that, Asia remained a sort of lost Eden, where possibly 'Prester John' ruled, the ally Christianity hoped would attack Islam in the rear. The ways of getting there were known; by caravan from Asia Minor or the Levant, by sea convoy from Ormuz or Aden. By the end of the thirteenth century the idea was spreading that Asia had to be reached if the stranglehold of the Muslim customs, which raised the prices of all those products beloved of princes' courts, was to be circumvented. Africa was a different case. The periplus of Hanno and other ancient recitals survived only as memories. She was the land of gold and slaves, but Christendom had little to do with the latter and had long been content with the gold supplied by the Berbers, Egyptians and Jews of the Maghrib and Alexandria. Obviously they sought for Prester John in Ethiopia and magical accounts circulated along the Nile or in the Holy Land about the kingdoms of Mozambique, Zanzibar, Madagascar, the lands of Zimbabwe and Monomotapa. But penetrating the Muslim buffer, which separated the lands of Bambuk and Senegal and even the Coptic leaders of Egyptian Sudan from the Mediterranean, seemed purely hypothetical. Even Charles of Anjou did not consider it.

So by the beginning of the fourteenth century geographical curiosity was not alive enough nor were the concrete advantages clear enough to enable the isolation of these separate worlds to be shattered. We should however not forget how the allure of Asia and the mysterious African darkness affected the Christian subconcious.

Were there savages to save?

Another point of view could be adopted. Were Ibn Battuta's writings known in Europe, that tireless pilgrim who crossed and described all these countries between 1325 and 1354? Did they inspire the incredible hoax of John of Mandeville (obit 1372), who, without leaving Paris, produced a description of Asia so detailed that he was taken at his word until the middle of this century? In any case, Europe was aware that these worlds were teeming with unredeemed souls. The preaching orders were encouraged by the Nestorians of Karakorum and then by eastern monks like Rabban Çauma, who came to Europe in 1287, to take pity on them. It was their duty to convert the pagans and at the very least to succour the Christians of the East. The Catalan Ramon Llull's great project was to replace the crusade with the mission. Attempts were organised; *c.* 1291 a Franciscan, Odorico of Pordenone, left to challenge the Brahmins and John of Montecorvino was nominated 'Bishop of Peking'. Monks were able to travel to the Far East until 1320 or 1325 thanks to the 'Mongol Peace'. They were less interested in Africa: Saint Francis was the first to consider the continent, sending two friars sworn to martyrdom to the Maghrib in 1219. Around 1220 a Christian militia led by a Portuguese called Pedro was arrested at Marrakesh, but they had probably not been proselytising.

The missionary work came to an abrupt end after 1340–55, when the routes to Asia were closed. In the Ukraine the Mongols now arrested missionaries; in China the Ming seized religious power; in Delhi Islam triumphed. In 1402, a Spaniard Clavijo did manage to reach Tamerlane, who had defeated the Ottomans, to find out what his intentions were. He found a Muslim settling his accounts, not a 'scourge of God'; and the story of how, at the same time, Ysalguier of Toulouse brought a converted black princess from Gao to the banks of the Garonne is of course a legend. The moment for baptising black or yellow people had decidedly not yet come.

Were there goods to grab?

Instead, without dispensing with the possibility of later conversions, the Europeans probably wanted first of all to control the arrival of those exotic and ruinous products; sugar, pepper, and especially gold, which Europe was beginning to feel the lack of. In Spain, minting gold coins had been suspended in 1384 and in Portugal a year later. In Italy the gold–silver ratio climbed to 1:12; further north the 'famine' was stilled by the new mines of Bohemia and Silesia, but even this adjustment had an unhealthy effect on Christendom. The development of public expenditure drove rulers to war, and war devoured all that it won. Even if the nobility at the end of the fourteenth century had not been obsessed with chivalrous and pious entertainments, or, more prosaically, if they had curbed their appetite for new foods, which swelled the expenses of their table and worried their retailers whose supplies were being exhausted, they would still have hoped to restore their failing fortunes far afield. Geographical curiosity, the hope of conversions, the search for gold, the desire to surmount the rents crisis and maybe already an interest in free labour, were all reasons which served to whet men's courage.

As always on the threshold of decisive events, it is hard to isolate the determining factor; was the interest – and for Prince Henry right up to his death in 1460, the passion – for discovery, which grew up in Lisbon and then in Lagos around the Aviz dynasty, cause or effect of Portugal's essential part in these matters? Was it rather a headlong flight by a near bankrupt country, devoid of gold or artisans? Was it a slowly nurtured plan or a series of accidents? On the other hand, did the Genoese, Pisans and Catalans, who supplied sailors and captains, launch themselves into the adventure out of greed or because they alone could supply experienced crews? Did they dare the adventure when the caravel, a ship half way between the slow *kogge* of the Baltic and the fragile Mediterranean galley, allowed them to confront the ocean blast? Or did this new vessel come into use after 1440 or 1445 as a result of these initial failures?

The one thing we are certain of is just how dogged these Iberians and Italians were in their attempts to reach Asia less expensively by avoiding the route through Mameluke Egypt, which meant braving black Africa. The north–south journey across the continent appears to have been soon abandoned. As Ibn Battuta and Ibn Khaldun tell us, the black empires were then at the height of their medieval brilliance. The art of Benin, in the Nupé country, and of Timbuktu or Cangor is evidence of a civilisation mistress of herself. The Arab travellers praised the public order, the sumptuous courts, the richness of the fairs of Mali, Kano and Gao, even though they deplored the poor progress of Islam and a standard of living inferior to that of the Maghrib. Ibn Battuta waxed enthusiastic about the quality of the ironwork, the beauty of the carved wood, the abundance of glass or copper work which, alongside slaves and gold, supplied the trans-Saharan trade along the south–north or east–west axes since the route via Agades and Chad to Aswan had been reopened. The Italians could not ignore these facts; around 1320 a Genoese was in Tafilalet; *c.* 1350 another is supposed to have reached Timbuktu. By the end of the century the Songhay had developed a shorter Chad–Fezzan itinerary which was less dangerous than the real Sahara crossing. The Catalans, Marseillais and Pisans who trafficked at Tripoli, Tunis, Bougie and Ceuta were able to warn their rulers and other adventurers that it was no longer possible to cross the great desert in order to reach the Empire of the Congo and from there on to Mozambique and the Indies (which they thought quite near).

The attack on Africa

So they had to sail round. In the first place they had a navigation problem because, although the trade winds coming from high up off the Moroccan shore blew the ships in a south-westerly direction, the gulf stream on the return lap required exceptional manoeuvering and patience. The beginning was inauspicious; in 1291 the Vivaldi

An Ife bronze head (tenth to twelfth centuries) The Kingdom of Benin entered its greatest period in the fourteenth century and gave rise to a brilliant civilisation which astonished the first European travellers. (Dpt. of Antiquities, Lagos, Nigeria.)

brothers, two Genoese, left and were never seen again. In 1339 the Canaries were reconnoitred as a future Atlantic port of call, but the Portuguese Jaime Ferrer foundered while trying to land on what was to be Rio de Oro. It seemed advisable to make sure of Petrarch's 'fortunate islands' – Madeira and the Canaries. Various attempts were made between 1350–1402 by Spaniards, Portuguese, Florentines and the Genoese Malocello, who found indolent and friendly peasants there, but no gold. A Norman, John of Béthencourt, took possession of the Canaries archipelago in 1402 and paid homage for it to the King of Castile, whereas Madeira was occupied by Portugal c. 1423. By then this country had already attempted an official operation; the royal army took Ceuta in 1415, allowing them to control Gharb, an outlet for Moroccan wheat, which was sorely needed. Did they consider occupying Morocco? Events such as the set back before Tangiers in 1437 and new attempts in 1471 and 1515 make this plausible, but nothing came of it.

By sea, however, there was some progress due to the caravel, to growing familiarity with the gulf stream, to using the Canaries and the Azores as stop-overs as well as to the constant support of the Portuguese rulers. The Italians had been replaced by hardy crews made up of Basques, Galicians and the people of the Algarve who took their caravels South. In 1434 Gil Eanes doubled the dangerous Cape of Bojador; in 1444 Dinis-Diaz sailed round Cap Verde; in 1446 Gambia was reached; in 1460, Sierra Leone; in 1471, Soeiro da Costa reconnoitred the Gold Coast, the Ivory Coast and passed the Equator, beyond which the **489** winds turned around and caused consternation. From then on the sailors measured their progress by setting up markers along the coast. In 1486 Diego Cao left his, not daring to go beyond the south point, leaving the honour of entering the Indian Ocean to Bartolomeo Diaz in the following year, who gave the Cape of Storms its propitiatory name of 'Good Hope'. Beyond it the Monsoon was waiting for the sailors; in 1497 Vasco da Gama sailed around Africa, called in at Sofala, Mozambique's port, and dropped anchor in May 1498 at Calcutta, in the Indies, where he was welcomed to his dismay by a Tunisian who spoke Castilian.

If this had been just a circumnavigation, a sporting exploit, it would already have been splendid. But it had far greater consequences. However, none of the attempts brought very great results to begin with: the trading post at Arguin on the Senegal estuary just managed to bring in 25 kilos of gold per annum, whereas Ibn Khaldun reckoned that one ton of gold crossed the Sahara every year. It also proved impossible to reach the gold panners by following the coastal rivers of the Gambia or Guinea, because of mountains barring the way. Those who did risk it, like Diego Gomez in 1456, did not bring back much and, on top of that, they even had the shock of meeting an Englishman there! The gold of Sofala and Zimbabwe, where Vasco de Gama set up a trading post in 1502, was certainly more accessible, but the distances were enormous and the gold had to be transported through Aden and so be subjected to Muslim control. To make up for this, the trade in spices, pepper and 'grains of Paradise' which clutter up the recipes of the age, and cola-nuts, the first stimulant with which Europeans began ruining their health, was a complete success. After 1485, Fernando Pó secured the monopoly of this trade all along the Gulf of Guinea, In 1505 Lisbon dethroned Venice and became the capital of the spice and drug trade. Buying or even taking pepper from black men was only a fairly minor phenomenon. But worse was to follow; the slave markets were visited and the slave trade, which was to martyr Africa until the nineteenth century, began. Already in 1444, Henry the Navigator was watching the first 263 slaves of both sexes being disembarked at Lagos, disgorged from the caravels, and he presided over the ensuing auction. It was calculated around 1480 that between 800 and 1,000 slaves were sold through the trading post at Arguin. These figures are so high that it seems clear that the slave traders were selling not only to Europe and Islam: we only have evidence of black men arriving in San-Domingo in 1510 and at Cuba in 1521, but sadly it is probable that the vile trade began earlier.

So contact between conquering Europe and nearby black Africa was financed from the beginning by exploitation. This is surprising, given the initial distinterested motives; the essential objective of the expeditions had not been to know and exploit Africa, but especially to find another route to Asia. Obviously the riches of Africa – gold, slaves, spices, ivory, teak – were a powerful attraction and their discovery was immediately accompanied by raids, followed rapidly by the first transactions. Trading posts were set up in Senegal – Bezeguiche, Portudal, Joal – and others along the Gold Coast – Axim, Shama, Saint-George-of-the-Mine – which, together with the caravels' coastal trade, established a regular trade between West Africa and Europe. This trade disloged new territories and complemented the traditional trans-Saharan trade without interrupting it; it could have served to enrich Africa. With the exception of a few monarchs and States – Mali from the end of the fifteenth

490

to the sixteenth century for instance – we know that this did not happen; Africa was neither really enriched nor encouraged to develop. She was nonetheless the seat of a rich, coherent, complex and remarkable civilisation. Her stagnation, decline and partial destruction has been explained by stigmatising European greed, symbolised in the first place by the Atlantic slave trade, and with good reason. But, when contrasted with Renaissance Europe and its prodigiously brutal dynamism, the black world presented dangerously fragile points inherent to its very structure. Technical backwardness made competition on every level with Europe a risky business; in agriculture, in spite of a considerable experience of soils and plants, there was no harnessed traction and only rudimentary improvements and fertilisers were made use of. There were excellent artisans but no real developments on the technical level nor on the industrial level. There was an administration, which was often competent and careful, but was also handicapped by the weak diffusion of the written word and the summary nature of specific laws. Further, it was still a disunited society – in spite of brilliant political endeavours – and one much more divided even than Europe. This was due to the multitude of dialects (without the help of a common learned language like Latin) and to an ill-realised fusion of animalism and Islam which gave rise, for instance, to incertitude about the rules of succession in certain kingdoms (Mali). Above all, Islamic believers despised pagans and this resulted in the debilitating oriental slave trade which was directed mostly towards white Islam, and was already well established when the Europeans turned up, supplying them with the material for the Atlantic slave trade. On top of this, settlement was still precarious and displaced populations (such as the Peul) could create chaos.

America: a catastrophic surprise

If the world is round, as everyone knew it to be, including the Church who pretended not to, one could expect to reach India by sailing west. The dangers were tripled, but were not all well understood. First the distance; almost five months without being at all sure of replenishing, which meant allowing for huge reserves of food, cluttering up the ship and reducing the number of men. The scale of the problem was not really appreciated in Europe, because the estimated distance was much too small. Both the Nuremberg globe and Behaim's globe of around 1480 allowed for only 2,500 miles from the Azores to Japan. Next came navigational difficulties, which had already been revealed by the Portuguese ventures along the coastline of Africa. These included inverted winds, the hopeless muddle about the Equator and gigantic swells which even caravels of 300 tonnes could not brave without the risk of being overwhelmed. As yet, the Sargassos and the intertropical currents of the Carribean were completely unknown. All the same, the navigators were probably restrained most of all by fear. They had to plunge straight ahead, without any landmarks, guided solely by their compass and such stars as they recognised, across a terrible and unknown immensity. It was a crazy enterprise which was encouraged only by ignorance of the real dangers and by the shameless lies of fantasy travellers like Mandeville. They also needed to be uncommonly forceful and arrogant men.

We all know about this great feat in the history of mankind. Christopher Columbus was a

The Catholic Queen Isabella (1451–1504), dressed very simply. She was then in her thirties and had had four children. A portrait by Bermago, 1403. (Madrid, Royal Palace.)

Genoese, an excellent sailor, well informed in geography and skilled in business. When he set up in his mid twenties in Lisbon in 1477, maybe in the pay of the Lomellini, he was no doubt already considering this project. While working there, he got to know the Ocean, and then went to Madeira and obtained an audience with King John II. He was shown the door, not because they considered his project insane, but because in 1485 or 1487 the Portuguese had passed the Cape of Good Hope and reckoned they had found the route to the East – so why look for another one? Columbus went elsewhere, to England where he was not listened to, to France where the Court was beginning to think only in terms of Italy. From 1488, he began laying siege to Isabella of Castile and was supported by the Franciscans in his attempt to win over the pious and acquisitive Queen. Ferdinand was busy conquering Granada and he found these dreams expensive and superfluous. Finally in April 1492, just as the last Moorish king of Spain was taking his last look at the Alhambra as it faded into the distance, the Queen, in the interval between two masses, granted the Genoese the extraordinary privileges he demanded in the case of succeeding; the titles of Admiral and Viceroy and a share in the gold and spices. In August 1492 three ships, crewed by less than one hundred men, sailed into favourable trade winds. They became discouraged later, by the infinite distance, the quarrels, the thirst, until finally, on 12 October 1492 at 2 o'clock in the morning, a cry came from the *Pinta*'s lookout man: 'land!'.

The land in question was one of the Bahamas peopled by a few amiable and completely naked Arawaks, *sans* gold and *sans* spices. After reconnoitring the Carib world, Columbus returned in March 1493 with seven natives and a little gold. Three other voyages followed which landed on all the Antibes, on the mid-American isthmus and even in Orinoco and Trinité in 1504. By this time, Columbus had long been discredited; since 1494, Hispaniola (San-Domingo) had become a trading centre for sugar, copper and slaves where Catalan, Castilian and other 'colonialists' were sent, and who began to exercise their particular forms of cupidity and brutality. Other pioneers had emerged; in 1498–9 Vespucci gave the new lands his first name Amerigo and started up a pearl trade; in 1500 Bobadilla was nominated Governor of New-Spain and had Cuba prospected, which was occupied before 1512. Columbus had died six years beforehand, forgotten and partly ruined, alone in his belief that he had reached Japan.

John II had missed his chance with Columbus but in 1494 he did at least manage to establish the Treaty of Tordesillas between himself and the Catholic Monarchs, under the aegis of the Pope, which divided the Atlantic in two along the meridian which passes 170 leagues West of the Azores, with Spain's part on the near side, Portugal's on the far side. This division was guided by ignorance and audacity, and when Alvarez Cabral with nearly a thousand men followed in Vasco da Gama's footsteps in 1500, he found that, when he turned around in the southern hemisphere to catch the return winds, he remained in Portuguese waters and fell unexpectedly on a coastland where coloured trees, *ó brazil*, grew along the shore. He returned in 1503 and in 1508, as some Frenchmen may also have done, to reconnoitre the coast as far as Santos; it definitely was not China. Nor was it the isthmus of Panama; Núñez de Balboa crossed it in 1513 and discovered an immense sea which looked exceptionally 'pacific' to him. There seemed no point in striving after the Orient when the Caribbeans, Brazil and Africa contained enough to enrich all the adventurers in a changing Europe, and to satisfy its merchants and rulers. Although both kings and Church said at Burgos in 1512 that it was shameful to make men slaves and that it was better to convert them, the one did not preclude the other and the Cross enfolded the slaves as well. The indignation of Las Casas was near at hand, just enough to give the *conquistadores*, nobles looking for people to dominate, marginals avid for land and gold, or truants who wanted everything, a clear conscience. In April 1519, Hernán Cortés landed with horses and cannon in the Mexican bay which he named Vera Cruz. In September Magellan set sail around the world – the systematic exploitation of the new world had begun, entailing miseries and benefits which we have not nearly finished counting.

10 The reconquest of man

The stranglehold of disasters which had gripped Christianity by the throat for more than a century seems to have slackened after the mid fifteenth century. Society was growing stronger and was moving towards reconstruction and consolidation. However, this was only a respite and not everyone felt its effects. The problems of daily life, of war, of destitution, of taxation and hunger still had many days ahead of them – practically the whole of modern times. But suffering is supposed to ennoble men; it matures their minds and opens up new ways for hope and improvement. In the midst of their material agony, while the old ship of the Christian Church seemed about to founder, signs of a powerful new emotionalism, of intellectual dynamism and of fertile invention were rising up all around. Michelet was prompted to call the fifteenth century the greatest of them all; Poggio was combing through libraries, Bruni was translating Greek authors, Parentucelli (alias Pope Nicholas V) founded the Vatican, Gerson was admonishing kings and Wycliff was meditating on what Huss dared speak out, Sluter, Van Eyck, Ghiberti . . . need I add more? All these men, as well as those who paid them and who read, heard, or saw their works are closely bound to the Middle Ages; they had only opened the windows, picking here and there a flower from Antiquity, especially in Italy. It is to be feared that the bulk of the Christian faithful did not appreciate the change and went on feeling anguish over a salvation compromised by the omnipresence of sin and death by violence. Most people went on sheltering snugly under the wing of centuries-old truths. What does divide the two halves of the fifteenth century from one another, to the extent that the end of the Middle Ages has often been set there – prematurely to say the very least – was precisely the penetration of modern thought into the mass of humanity; the progressive conquest of their souls.

New paths

The old history books tell us that the Middle Ages ended because the Turks took Constantinople and Gutenberg invented the printing press. The Turks had only been waiting for a chance to carry out a formality, but printing was a more serious business.

The diffusion of knowledge

Everyone knows that printing was invented in China even before paper money and cannon powder. Not that this evidence of Chinese genius mattered much to Europe, because no prescription for its use reached the West. It is simply astonishing that it took so long – until the end of the fourteenth century – for someone to realise that a group of monks copying the Bible in unison could only supply a tiny proportion of the total readership. Even the 250 manuscripts of the *Roman de la Rose* which have come down to us were not very many, given the thousands of potential subscribers which the clerks and the burghers of around 1350 doubtless represented. This justifies the suggestion that demand was responsible for increasing the supply of books and that printing was born of an existing need.

The first steps are known; first cut in wood and then inked, little figures or 'markers' were pressed onto parchment to avoid paying a miniaturist and to help *condottiere* conceal their illiteracy. Woodblocks were used rather sporadically between 1380–90 and 1418–20 for printing anything from playing cards to books, but the process proved unsatisfactory both because the wood tended to soften with successive inkings and because of the inevitably 'wooden' nature of the drawings. The first obstacle was overcome by using metal, but it was technically impracticable to engrave a whole page onto copper or iron. Utrecht, Strasbourg, and Avignon all claim – with no evidence whatsoever – the credit of having first thought of the solution. Traditionally, the palm is awarded to the Mainz-born Gutenberg who was inspired to contrive a platen-press with a screw mechanism, to invent movable type and to use an alloy of lead, steel and antimony in order to achieve durability. The Bible he printed using these techniques and the Psalter of 1456 are both landmarks in the history of mankind.

Unlike many 'inventions' which are developed slowly or obscurely, printing had immediate success. Before 1485, printing presses were operating in Strasbourg, Basle, Nuremberg, Rotterdam, Paris, Seville, Saragossa, Lyon, Venice, Milan, Florence and Rome. For once, the Italians had been overtaken, but they were to catch up; from 1476 Greek texts were printed in Lombardy and by 1500 Aldus Manutius in Venice was popularising his 'Roman' and 'Italic' lettering as rivals to the Rhineland 'Gothic', and which gradually superseded it.

The theoretical effects of these means of popularisation do not need to be discussed at length; uncut texts, unalloyed by the inevitable academic or canonic glosses, were now available to individuals, who now had the Scriptures to meditate on – with that margin of erroneous interpretation due to ignorance (one of the follies illustrated by Brandt in his 'Ship of Fools' from 1494). It also had the effect of killing off the delicate art of miniatures, which were priced out of the market because of their one-off quality. Texts also tended to be frozen once and for all, as customs had been when they were first written down. Of course, this did not happen all at once; it was calculated that there must have been about 25,000 printed Bibles in circulation in western Europe around 1515, one third of them in German, for about fifty million inhabitants; i.e. one Bible for every 2,000 souls. Editions were generally in the order of between 300 and 1,500 copies. All the same, this was a hundred times more than the most popular romances of former times.

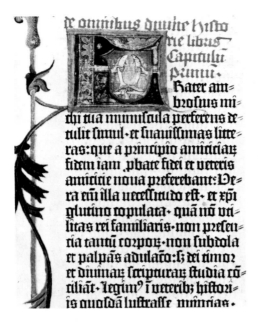

GVILLERMVS Fichetus parisiensis theologus doctor, Ioanni Lapidano Sorbonensis scholæ priori salutem ; Misisti nuper ad me suauissimas Gaspa/rini pergamensis epistolas, nō a te modo diligent emēdatas: sed a tuis quoq̃ ger/manis impressoribus nitide & terse trā/scriptas. Magnam tibi gratiā gasparinus debeat · quem pluribus tuis uigiliis ex corrupto integr̃ fecisti. Maiore uero cæ/tus doctor̃ hoīm: q̃ nō tm sacris litteris (quæ tua prouicia est)magnopere studes: sed redintegrādis etiā latinis scptoribus insegnem operam nauas. Res sane te uiro doctissimo & optimo digna · ut q̃ cū lau/de & gloria sorbonico certamini dux p̃ fuisti: tum latinis quoq̃ lris(quas ætatis nostræ ignoratio tenebris obumbrauit) tua lumen effundas industria · Nam præt alias complures lrā̃ grauiores iacturas, hanc etiā acceperūt · ut libratior̃ uitiis, effectæ pene barbaræ uideant̃ · At uero

Improvements to printing over twenty years. On the left, the first folio of the Bible (the 'thirty-six-line Bible') with painted decoration, probably printed by Gutenberg in Bamberg around 1458–9. On the right, the *Letters* of Gasparino of Pergamo, a book published in 1470 by the Sorbonne printing press.

It is vital to remember that before 1520 three-quarters of this production was religious; 60 editions of the *Imitation of Jesus Christ* and 16 in Paris alone of the Vulgate and 22 in Germany. On top of this, these editions were translations – in response to the general demand: the Bible was edited in German in 1466, in Italian in 1471, in Dutch in 1477, in Castilian in 1485 and in French in 1487. The *illiteratus* of the Middle Ages would henceforth be able to drink at the very fountain of knowledge.

The tainted milk of the Alma Mater

In 1470 Guillaume Fichet installed, not without difficulty, a printing press in the Sorbon college at Paris. The old universities were of course ill-disposed towards this innovation which destroyed the impact of their lectures. Were they anyway still capable of supplying their students with adequate mental nourishment? Villon's sarcasms are only those of a drop-out student, but once the most illustrious masters had been deprived of their political clout in the assemblies of the Council, the University was able to save its status only by changing its methods and the content of its instruction. With regard to the latter, the colleges remained jealously loyal to Ockham and even to Saint Thomas; as former simple residences which had become centres of learning, they now specialised in branches of knowledge, without trying to maintain a plurality of disciplines, which would have been

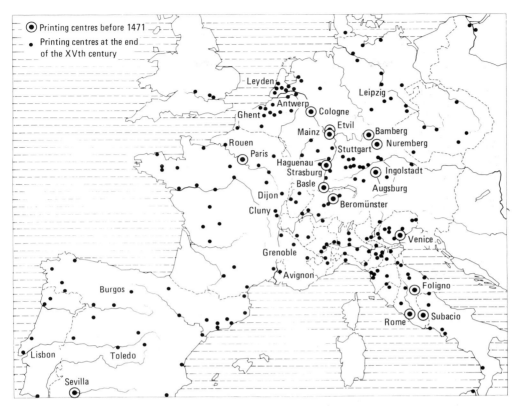

Printing centres before 1471
Printing centres at the end
of the XVth century

Leyden
Leipzig
Antwerp
Ghent
Cologne
Etvil
Mainz
Bamberg
Rouen
Nuremberg
Paris
Stuttgart
Haguenau
Ingolstadt
Strasburg
Augsburg
Basle
Dijon
Cluny
Beromünster

Grenoble
Venice

Avignon
Foligno
Burgos
Subacio
Rome

Lisbon
Toledo

Sevilla

13 The distribution of printing at the end of the XVth century

more in conformity with the spirit of the times. Thus each college became a Temple of the Law, with the Sorbonne representing traditional theology. We recalled above the progressive lowering of standards in the recruitment of masters and scholars. As for the scholastic method, it withdrew as the ancient framework of the *lectio*, the *quaestio* and the *disputatio* were abandoned, ill-adapted as they were to the petulance of now much more sophisticated audiences. This was when scholasticism fell into the disrepute which still tars it; so much argumentation to reach the right answer led to ratiocination; truth was pursued along authoritarian lines, glosses became pretentious and, as the tools of dialectic were sharpened, learning was increasingly systematised.

Plenty of universities were prepared, since Gerson and Salutati, to denounce the danger and to call for reform. This was all the more urgent because the State, conscious of the weakness of the Masters, was attacking their privileges. At Paris, Charles VII limited the professors' fiscal privileges in 1437 to punish them for compromising with the English, and in 1445 this was extended to their legal privileges at the request of the Holy See, whom the Masters had exasperated at the Council of Basle. Attempts at reorganisation were made: in Paris, in 1452, Cardinal d'Estouteville envisaged an oath of allegiance for the Masters, a **497**

A splendid representation of Lorenzo the Magnificent, the greatest of the new Italian lords. (Detail from the Gozzoli fresco, *The Procession of the Magi* (1459–60); Florence, Palazzo Medici-Riccardi.)

boarding house for the students and fixed remuneration. The project came to nothing because the role of this sort of association was in fact outdated. Although all the University professors were made into 'knights' in 1533, they in fact formed only a residual part of the intelligence the universities had represented.

This was because their audience was no longer composed of poor and ardent young clerics; it was henceforth made up of more distinguished minds, of an aristocracy of initiates or would-be initiates. It was often a princely court which prided itself on its *bel esprit* – a logical spin-off of the wealthy patronage which had blossomed since 1390 or 1400. In Florence the austere Cosimo de' Medici fully realised, after 1434, that therein lay one of the attributes of power; he summoned Poggio and Alberti to him. Lorenzo the Magnificent, who was himself a talented writer, founded an Academy in the Greek manner around 1470 where instruction was given in poetry, astronomy and eloquence. Lionel d'Este at Ferrara, Federigo of Montefeltro at Urbino and even Francesco Sforza at Milan, that uneducated *condottiere*, surrounded themselves with Italians, Flemings and Spaniards. In Rome the now decidedly latinised Bessarion presided over *Sapienza* after 1465. In order not to be behindhand, and in spite of all his celebrations, balls and traditional drinking sessions, Francis I created his College of the Royal Lecturers of France to which he drew talent from all over.

In these new schools, which prided themselves above all on their appreciation of man, many much less pure currents also mingled. Without lingering over the interest the rich patrons took in everything that enhanced their glory, and in the case of a ruler, his power, less admissable resurgences can also be discerned. In Rome, shortly before his death in 1472, Bessarion deplored the mishmash of 'Antique' memories dating from Cola di Rienzo, which all tended towards a form of narrow nationalism. In Paris and in many small Italian towns, it was often a case of dispelling boredom by introducing into debates about ideas a little of that faded *courtoisie*, that impudent sensuality which titillated the Courts. In Florence and Milan, a return to nature and the countryside was mooted – laudable in intention but giving rise only to the artificial and empty exercises of neo-Latin poetastry or worse still, to empty verbiage. Certainly Cicero and Strabo were annotated, Livy explained, and the classics were taught; Gemistus Plethon (who had fled to Italy after 1439) could be heard comparing Plato with Aristotle, and Filelfo vituperating all who did not think like him – but were any of these new-style masters more in touch with the masses than the others?

The founding fathers

Humanism is a state of mind, not a school of thought. By putting *homo faber* at the centre of its ideology, the classical Middle Ages of the thirteenth century was 'humanist'. The great thrust of individuality which marks the fourteenth century (even the garrulous circles around educated rulers) was part of the same move towards appreciating creation, either through the medium of artistic expression or through metaphysics. This makes it difficult to discern what is seen specifically as humanism by historiographical tradition, when both the search for the lost world of Antiquity, in which it was easy to believe that man was all in all, and the Christian tradition of God's handiwork, were closely intertwined. The incompatibility of these two notions was not immediately apparent to thinkers and artists; over the next hundred years they veered from one to the other in their quest for the free man in the mould of Diogenes. Some tracked him down in the works of Antiquity, others tried to recapture his gestures and way of seeing, a third group wanted to recreate an environment worthy of him. This desperate attempt to relate the beauty of material things to the beauty of ideas is typically medieval. It is an aberration to see anything 'modern' in this 'humanism', which was the natural consequence of man's victory over himself, precisely at a time when the argument for the authority and the magistrature of the Church was growing weaker.

Without trying to set up obviously subjective value judgements, a little order should be introduced to this abundance of invention, which enabled so many people to be master, poet, artist, philosopher and academic all at once. If Italy is mentioned more often than other countries, this is because the political and intellectual conditions there were most favourable to this fertile state of mind. One has but to think of the ferocious and constant ambitions that were played out in the theatre of Italy between 1480 and 1530. To start with, light should be brought to bear on the first two generations, the one of the mid fifteenth century, and the one that died out at the end of the century.

The first place goes to Laurentio Valla. He was a Roman who wandered from court to court, including that of the Aragonese Alfonso V, before returning to Rome in 1448 to die there nine years later, having well earned the title of 'father of the humanists' (of the fifteenth century of course). Firstly on account of his dedication in restoring to texts their authentic and original form – as he did for the Vulgate in 1456, which was riddled with translation errors, and in discovering fakes, such as the famous Donation of Constantine to Pope Sylvester on which the Papacy had based its temporal pretensions for the last seven hundred years. Secondly on account of his clear-cut independence in regard both to Petrarchian stoicism or epicurianism, which he considered convenient and rather empty attitudes, and to a scholasticism floundering in Ockham's interminable glosses. Valla summoned a new culture to support a renewed faith; he did not believe that a serious synthesis of the pagan philosophies with the Christian Faith was possible, but he was careful not to break with the Church. He went however much further, both in denying the authenticity of a document which had been considered fundamental to the Faith, and in annihilating the reality of Rome's concrete authority.

Nicholas of Cues was a German who responded to the mysticism of Master Eckhart as well as to the Platonic message. Made a cardinal in 1449, he was hard as nails, an energetic thinker and possessed of immense erudition – a fervent supporter of the Church. He did not dream of sapping her strength and revealed an iron fist as Papal legate in Germany. But he suffered from the ignorance, the immorality and the formalism of God's ministers. Valla wanted something else – a reform within the body of the Church herself. Nurtured on Thomism and familiar with the intellectual illuminations of Saint Bernard, he was a man of the past (*Of learned ignorance*, 1440), but he believed that science and experimentation were indispensible to the advance of knowledge, which made him a man of the present. As for the future (*The Summit of Contemplation*, 1463), he envisaged it within the framework of a Judaeo-Christian Church (he had studied the Kabbala at length), enlightened by grace so as to attain the heights of mysticism, but solidly founded on mathematics, the road to infinity. This was almost Neoplatonism, even the beginnings of Pantheism. His death in 1464 put a stop to the development of a philosophy which would scarcely have allowed him to remain within the bosom of the Church.

The generation which came after him was already rich in inheritance, but it was Florentine rather than Roman and gravitated around *Il Magnifico*. Marsilius Ficinus (obit 1499), the eminent translator of Plato, Plotinus and Porphyry, and in fact the real introductor of Platonism to the Laurentian Academy, inclined towards a natural religion from which original sin had been effaced. As for the young Count Pico della Mirandola, whose superhuman scientific reputation has floated down to us to present us with nine hundred propositions on every imaginable subject, his brilliant and brief career (he died aged thirty in 1493) brought him to the extreme limits of scriptural interpretation; he too would not have escaped the condemnation which his rebuttal of the Trinity and his pantheistic vision of Creation undoubtedly earned him.

Expression: a journey into nothingness

It will surely come as a shock and surprise to hear the age of Memling and Mantegna so described. Nonetheless, in the longer term, this really is the impression produced by the

Painting takes on a new look, inspired by love of Antiquity and by rediscovered perspective. (A detail of Mantegna's *Saint Sebastian*, 1467; Paris, Louvre.)

second half of the fifteenth century, when one thinks of all the fertile invention which preceded it. There is a feeling of restraint or of repetition in the literary and artistic works; just when the roots of 'humanism' had been planted at the price of mental agony, pens and paintbrushes seem to have hung suspended in the air, waiting for it to blossom. In this respect, the literature provides the clearest evidence of restraint. Mystery plays, farces, French *stances* and Italian *canzoni* predominated; they borrowed from the past by resorting to a spurious chivalry, *la gentilezza*; in spite of their reputations, Boiardo's *Orlando innamorato* and its sequel, Ariosto's *Orlando furioso*, were only literary anecdotes and moral recitals. The explosive growth of the reading public seemed to have robbed literary expression of its vitality; in the courts it was limited to sweet nothings, in the academies, to serious thought and in the towns, to popular drama. The writing of history, the history of the rulers that is, was reduced to a form of memoir, penned for such as paid for it, or composed by themselves; a Pleiad of historians clustered around the Dukes of Burgundy – but Philip of Commynes' memoirs stand on their own. Written before 1498 or 1500, they bear little relation to those of Froissard or even Villani; as a soldier and diplomat and a man of intrigues, he saw clearly and far. His descriptions of political wheels within wheels and intrigues contain a lesson which anticipates Machiavelli.

It is commonly said that, starting with their first campaigns in Italy, the French rulers were thrilled by the 'Renaissance' and wanted to copy it. The question is what and where, exactly? North of the Alps, on the contrary, tradition held sway; Saint-Maclou, Brou at the beginning of the sixteenth century, did not adopt the ways of Tuscany – just a few loggias or colonnades at Blois or elsewhere was all there was to see. Indeed, when construction on the Milan *duomo* was resumed in 1490, this time it produced a theatrical and Germanic structure, completely foreign to the little Florentine circle. For all that it was the age of Alberti (obit 1472) who codified the architecture of Antiquity, this had yet to come into its own. Once Van Eyck and Masaccio were dead (1411 and 1428 respectively), further disappointments lay in store. Sculpture gave way to painting as the leading art form, or rather to a gigantic miniaturism which was still so close to the 'Gothic' style. In the north there were of course Memling (obit 1494), who painted mystical scenes in Bruges tinted with a few realist details in the Flemish manner, and Fouquet (obit *c.* 1481), the titled royal painter, who was drawn to ingenious virtuosity using the grey tints suggested by Alberti; but in Italy herself there were Uccello (obit 1475), a pupil of Ghiberti, obsessed with colour, movement and tiny details; Filippo Lippi (obit 1469), his pupil Ghirlandaio and his son Filippino who had a taste for dramatic attitudes, naturalism and sensuality; Mantegna (obit 1506), the champion of perspective, counterposed volumes and chiaroscuro; Guido di Pietro and his brother Giovanni at San Marco in Florence; the *Angelico* (obit 1455), the painter of grey tints and inner light, and even Sandro Botticelli (obit 1510) whose lightness of touch, graceful lines and transparent nudities have assured him, as well as Fra Angelico, a leading place in a history of art in which they represent only a modest link between the initiators of 1400 and the giants of 1500. In compensation, it is the dispersed character of this Italian art which strikes one, much more so than in the field of literature. These men worked in Padua, Orvieto, Mantua, Urbino, Ferrara, Rimini, Florence, Fiesole, Pisa, Prato,

The Three Graces, a detail of the Florentine Sandro Botticelli's allegory of *Spring* (1478). The graceful gestures of these dancing figures suggest the slow rhythm of a ritual choreography, which serves to accentuate the imaginative and symbolic quality of the picture.

and in the Sistine Chapel and the various oratories and chambers each Pope felt it incumbent on himself to add to his predecessor's apartments in the Vatican.

Acceleration and explosion

Such history textbooks as do not choose 1453 for the closing date of the Middle Ages suggest instead 1492, when Columbus discovered America and the Spanish kings destroyed the Kingdom of Granada, the last Muslim bastion in Europe. These are useful and striking symbols, but there is even less of a case for 1492 than there is for 1453. Firstly because Columbus never thought he had discovered America and some time was needed before this chance act became a necessity, and secondly because the Muslims, in spite of

503

losing Ceuta and elsewhere since the beginning of the century, in fact did very well after 1492, if the Serbs and the Hungarians are to be believed. So the date must be pushed further forward. Especially in the field through which we have just been wandering, because there was still no sign of really new structures being set up, just as the arts and literature were still treading water. Why stop at the Council of Basle, which finished in an uproar, or at Savonarola's scream, or at Fra Angelico's languor? Ockham or Wycliffe would have been better choices. After 1400, the historian is caught up in the increasingly rapid rhythm of movement, which sweeps him on at full pace into the sixteenth century.

The discomfiture of Rome

When the conciliar crisis and the schism came to an end in the middle of the fifteenth century, the Roman Pontiff felt that he had emerged as the victor of a rough joust against the intellectuals who had wanted to limit his power, and against the international coteries which had manipulated his predecessors at the whim of their dynastic and other interests. Martin V and Eugenius IV even believed themselves entitled to consider as naught their promises of regular consultation with the conciliar fathers. They brandished Papal Supremacy before the ragged Empire, and the Union of Churches, that flyblown pudding that had been served up to the faithful in every century, and they meant the ship of the Church to sail as buoyantly as in the time of Innocent IV, or at the very least, of Avignon.

They did not see that she was slowly sinking. Firstly, the behaviour of individual Pontiffs gave rise to criticism; it is easy for us to get hot about the collar about a 'pornocracy' worthy of the tenth century, and to denounce the venality, the greed and even the impiety of certain Popes, and the constant recourse to intrigue and violence of them all. It is clear at first glance that intoxication with power in an Italy given over to fire and blood, or that an unbridled appetite for luxury and sensation are not pastoral qualities; the assassination of Galeazzo Maria Sforza in 1476 was plotted at Rome, as was the Pazzi conspiracy, which cost Guliano de' Medici his life in 1478; obscure negotiations with the Turks about Otranto, where the Sultan had dared to disembark, were carried out in Rome. Cardinal Cibo, who became Innocent VIII, had sons to provide for; Cardinal della Rovere, once he was Julius II, wore a helmet and entered La Mirandola through the breach his guns had blasted in her walls. The culminating point was reached with the Spanish clan of the Borgia after 1492; Rodrigo became Alexander VI and kept three mistresses; Caesare wore himself to death carving an Italian kingdom out for himself with his sword and his dagger, and his sister Lucretia is still a symbol of luxury and evildoing. All this is true and deplorable, but contemporaries do not seem to have been so sensitive; poison, adultery and drunken words were current money; Alexander VI put the tiara he had bought up for auction only shortly before the incredible auction of Charlemagne's crown took place. Francis I allied with the Turks and reneged on his promises; Henry VIII changed his subjects' religion in order to change his wife, and so on. It would be simplistic to see the awakening of 1517 as a reaction against the private lives of the Popes, even against the infamous traffic in Indulgences. After all, art and philosophy ruled at Rome and the Indulgences were only transactions similar to those which any Italian bank of the time would have agreed to.

A view of Rome by Pol de Limbourg. (Miniature of the beginning of the fifteenth century; Chantilly, Musée Condé.)

The real evil lay elsewhere. It came firstly from above, from the very circle around the Apostolic See, from all those people, university men, humanists and cardinals, who thought, translated and taught. Even those whose lives had been spent in the service of the established hierarchy, for whom the God-given order was not to be questioned, men like Gerson and Nicholas of Cues were induced, Council or no Council, to question the nature of Papal authority. Even prior to 1430, Nicholas of Clamanges and Gerson reckoned that an unworthy Pope should be deposed by the body of the Church and its authorised representatives. The critical achievement of philosophers and exegetists like Valla and Pico devalued the Scriptures, denounced the abuses in their interpretation and placed the Kabbala and Plato on the same level as the Evangelists. Anyway, these 'humanists' were not gnawed by despair or mysticism, they reasoned over the Faith within their own minds. This made them despise all intermediaries and consider all hierarchies superfluous and all ritual ceremonies empty formalism. The Greek exiles also played an active role in this desanctification of the terrestrial Church; Gemistus Plethon, an intractable Spartan, sketched a sort of Christian or deist republic in his *Laws* of *c.* 1440, in which it would be hard to find mention of the Pope. Did not Erasmus and Machiavelli also strike deadly blows against the Bible?

The attack also came from the rulers; their hostility was a by-product of political competition and of the general resentment against a Rome embroiled in its Italian wars. When Louis XI forbade the Inquisition from operating in the Dauphiné in 1478, he was not protecting the Vaudois nor protesting against the bloody abuses of the Holy Office, neither of which he cared about, but the Dauphiné was his land. When Francis I concluded a Concordat with Pope Leo X, who handed over control of the Church's possessions in his territory to him, as the 'reformed' princes of Germany were soon to do for themselves, it was not in order to avoid the excesses of Roman taxation and to save the 'Gallicans', but in order to fill his own coffers and to bully his bishops.

Thus the accelerating decline of the dignity and power of Rome meant that the situation could not be redeemed even by being taken in hand by a secular ruler, as had been done in the tenth and eleventh centuries. Emperor Maximilian, *Max ohne Geld*, was just a drop in the ocean and the kings were too busy. The Church would have to draw new strength from herself. Could she do this without help from the faithful? The clergy was certainly not as depraved and ignorant after the Reformation, as people had been wont to call it before, but it was weak, disarmed and little heeded. Numerous Popes had been vividly aware of the imminent disaster. In this respect, the election of Aeneas Silvius Piccolomini to the Throne of Saint Peter in 1458, when he took the name of Pius II in memory of one of the very first cultured Popes in the second century, gave rise to hope. This learned man, a historian and humanist, albeit hostile to the conciliar idea, was capable of gathering men of good will to him; but his pontificate was a total failure because Pius II attempted to revive the Crusade. He died, despairing for the Church, in 1464. Here and there active legates were at least attempting to brush the dust off slumbering clerics; Nicholas of Cues in Germany and Cardinal Ximenez de Cisneros in Spain (before 1517) could do little more. The vitality of the reforming urge could not be denied; it affected ancient monastic orders like Cluny, gave rise to new creations, such as the Minimal Brothers of Francesco di Paula in southern Italy, and upheld pious sermons and examples. Rome canonised ninety such persons between 1400 and 1520, mostly intellectuals and clerics. The idea of a reforming council advanced slowly to the fore and even Julius II was won over to it. He convoked a preparatory oecumenical council in 1512, but other worries beset him; he had to get the Sistine Chapel painted, contain the French and deal with Venice. The assembly dragged on for five years engaged in drawing up a list of urgent questions without coming to any decisions. By March 1517 it was ready, but too late! Within six months, Luther had pinned his ninety-five theses to the door of the *Schlosskirche* in Wittenberg.

The age of the Italian giants

Now at last, the tree was bearing fruit and the long journey through the Middle Ages had reached its end. It stopped at the extraordinary generation which lived and worked during the first two decades of the sixteenth century; those Portuguese and Spaniards on the seas, those Italians, Frenchmen, Dutchmen, Germans and Englishmen who attained the summits of thought, art and science.

506 Few minds were as influential as that of Leonardo da Vinci (1452–1519) in marking, if

not their own times, at least those of all the subsequent centuries. He has been attributed with having foreseen the machines and technologies realised in the nineteenth century, and his innumerable experimental manuscripts do indeed show that he imagined the hydraulic jack as concisely as he did the armoured tank, the aeroplane and the submarine; that he considered the raking impact of cannon fire and the system of defence which Vauban was to demonstrate; conceived the notion of geological eras; explained the role of water tables; foretold the gravitation and propagation of waves; practised dissection. As a reader and translator of Euclid, Vitruvius, Pliny, Ptolomy, Celsius, as well as of Arab authors, he amassed, as did Pico della Mirandola, whom he met, a range of scientific knowledge apparently unequalled in his age. The practice of experimental induction, root of all scientific reasoning, owes its first real advances to him, as do those 'absolute paradigms of knowledge', mathematics and mechanics. That which Bacon and Alexander of Hales had envisaged in the thirteenth century, he tried to apply. This is why he eventually neglected painting for speculative thought; he was drawn towards the problems of dynamics and of equilibrium, he researched into the interaction of muscular, architectural and chromatic elements which drew him towards architecture and the plastic arts. But all this part of his work, for all that it is the most well known, bore the marks of a very profound empiricism: his human bodies demonstrate his perfect observation of anatomy, his plants a sure botanical competence, his landscapes an acute awareness of geography. In order to create the most exact optical impressions, Leonardo made use of the *sfumato* process, which drowned many of his pictures in a nowadays often degraded cloud of mist. His predominantly mathematical mind led him to invent geometrical compositions (often pyramidical), many of which have posed specialists in parapsychology difficult problems of interpretation. Leonardo seems to have had difficulty concentrating on one thing, among all the urgent inspirations which bubbled up in his mind. He worked first as a painter in Florence, and then in 1483 aged thirty, he went to Milan where he served Ludovico *il Moro*, then he returned to Tuscancy, went back to Milan, and thence to Rome, before being welcomed by Francis I at Amboise in 1515, who kept him there until his death. From the *Virgin of the Rocks* (1481), to the *Last Supper* (1497), the *Holy Family* (1503), and the portrait of the *Mona Lisa*, or the *Joconda* (1507), Da Vinci ceaselessly pursued both the visible form and the symbol which reveal the invisible and the cosmos, as for instance with his blue backgrounds, which recall the role of water in the universe, or with the vaporous aureole he traced around his portraits, especially the female ones. Da Vinci described himself as a 'universal man' and his vanity was indeed justified by the variety of his talents. But, as often happens in these cases, his compatriots did not understand him. He endured deception and criticism and suffered much from the harshness with which Michaelangelo judged him.

Michaelangelo Buonarroti (1475–1564) was twenty years younger than Da Vinci, but this young Tuscan was much closer than Leonardo to the Neoplatonic spirit which had been revived in mid fifteenth-century Florence. For him, the salvation of the soul was central to the artist's activity; Da Vinci's mathematical theories of knowledge and his geometrical rules seemed to offend against the Ideal. It was, on the contrary, necessary to   **507**

a) Michaelangelo's *Rebellious slave* on the left (Paris, Louvre.)
b) On the right, a portrait of Balthazar Castiglione by Raphael (Paris, Louvre). This Italian gentleman was a brilliant soldier, diplomat, artist and writer, who expounded on a new manner of living for an aristocratic and humanist society in *The Courtier*, written in 1506–16 and printed in Venice in 1528. It had considerable influence in Europe.

wrest from brute material the forms which would enable the Ideal to be visualised. This was why he turned from painting to sculpture, since this medium allowed him to express the dramatic, 'Promethean' and Titanic struggle of humanity striving to return to God, the source and the essence, in the power of his statues' violent gestures and forceful expressions. From then on, even architecture was to him, indifferent to geometry as he was, no more than the outward form of higher aspirations. Even more so than Da Vinci, Michaelangelo did not cease throughout his long and tormented life (which came to an end after a pious retreat lasting ten years) from changing his masters and projects, which his irascible nature often left unsatisfied and unfinished. He worked successively in Rome, Florence, Venice, Bologna, Florence again, and Rome. With the creation of his *Pietà* in 1498, his bent for suffering and splendour came to the fore and triumphed in the famous *Moses* he carved for Julius II's tomb (1514). His frescoes covering 500 square metres of the Sistine Chapel ceiling and studded with references to Antiquity demanded four years of prodigious labour from him (1508–12). He was unable to force himself to finish Saint Peter's, which Bramante had begun fairly inadequately in 1506. The melancholic temperament befitting a 'Dante-esque artist' gave rise to poignant poems, in which he breathed his disgust with his time, and which form an astonishing link between the tormented fourteenth century and the Baroque age.

Although Raphael and Machiavelli have their undoubted merits, they cannot be ranked as highly. Raphaello Sanzio (1483–1520) profited from the success of 'Academism' which was prolonged until the nineteenth century and which attached vital importance to symmetry, shades of colour and narrative. Of course, the painter was far more original than this implies, but his preoccupation with 'classical' harmony and his skill with light as well as the official favour of the Roman Pontiffs, which he basked in for fifteen years, won him greater consideration than any other artist of his age. He was entrusted with the decoration of the pontifical apartments where he worked from 1509 until his death. Niccolo Machiavelli (1469–1527) shares with Dante the dubious distinction of being accredited with mental attitudes which their works refute. His life as a Florentine diplomat, who ended up an exile, is not particularly interesting, but his major work, *The Prince*, written in 1513, is one of the most remarkable political treatises of all time. His work was indeed formed by historical circumstances; the destruction of the power of the clerics, and the appeal to a sort of virtuous superman, smack of the pre-Reformation and of Caesare Borgia; but his picture of the ideal State is the model of enlightened despotism. Machiavelli detested the Empire and pleaded for a non-religious society in which the Gospels would no longer soften men; he believed in the virtue of a handful of men, or perhaps just in an appearance of virtue sufficient to lull public opinion. He has been accused of cynicism, but the word should be used in the sense given it by the Ancients; the rule of the wise, of realists, of those who possess *virtus*, or moral strength.

Contagion

Although Leonardo da Vinci died at the Clos-Lucé, and Pico della Mirandola visited Paris in 1485, the Italians generally stayed at home, where they were only too liable to see the lovers of riches, if not of the arts, hurrying to their towns, sword in hand. This was so much the case, that once the Alps had been crossed, the whole physiognomy of the spiritual world changed. Nearly all those of whom we will speak went to Italy, not as servile imitators but as disciples keen on testing their own knowledge before launching into flight. This meant that many of them soon soared above the intellectual attainments of their native lands and, once they had left Italy, they formed a nexus of humanists and universalists. Understanding them is perhaps essential to understanding the progress of the Christian Reformation.

Erasmus of Rotterdam (1469–1536) still represents the spirit of humanism; a gentle, circumspect and cultured scholar, he was an eloquent lecturer and talented stylist who knew Greek and Hebrew. This modest man, who was ordained priest in 1493, found that these attainments protected him nicely from the rigours of a harsh century. Like a sixteenth-century Petrarch, he went from court to court, protected by kings and princes,

509

teaching in London, Paris and Basle and visiting Italy and the Empire. The most striking thing about this personality, to whom everyone deferred, was his extraordinary ability to capture the reverberations of every spiritual horizon. He had studied and assimilated the mysticism of Ruysbroek, the textual stringency of Valla, the Neoplatonism of Nicholas of Cues; he was to approve of Luther, to admire Machiavelli and to make friends with Budé. This synthesis gave rise to his *Annotations to the New Testament* in 1505 and his *De Libero Arbitro* in 1511, both works a sort of cold breviary. Erasmus was careful not to leave the bosom of the Church even after Julius II had released him from his vows, but he did not believe in Divine Grace, he considered the Sacraments no more than symbols and he pleaded for a Faith tempered by reason. His was an admirable equilibrium, but an impossible one.

His English friends did not achieve it. John Colet (obit 1519) whose lectures he attended in London, and Thomas More (obit 1535) who dedicated his *Utopia* to him in 1516, clashed either with Ockhamism or the State, which reduced the one to destitution and led the other to the block. In France, there was a surprising lack of contact with Italy or even Erasmus; it is possible that the University stifled the birth of a new way of thinking for longer there than anywhere else. This meant that the France of Charles VIII and Louis XII was the homeland of philology and history; the former was zealously developed by Guillaume Fichet (obit 1486) and later by Guillaume Budé (obit 1540), and one has the impression of a strong Italian or Dutch influence; as for the latter, without neglecting Commynes who has already been mentioned, the name of Robert Gaguin (obit 1501), as much a canon lawyer as he was a historian, is worthy of a brief salute as a compiler rather than as a thinker. Altogether, it was only much later that a 'founding father' of humanism emerged in France; this was Jacques Lefèvre d'Étaples (obit 1536), the editor of Aristotle who was also tempted by Ficino's Neoplatonism, which he had heard in Italy. He was one of the first Frenchmen to distance himself from scholasticism, but his attempts were pretty timid. Neither his commentaries on the Gospels nor his translation of the Bible reveal the least break with orthodox thinking; it was only in 1519 that as curate of the Bishopric of Meaux, he formed a 'circle' of reflection on the reform of the Church.

Germany remained dumb. Between her grasping merchants and her warriors, her ruined Emperor and her princes (who collected Indulgences), the ulcer-ridden Nicholas of Cues met only peasants crushed by poverty and bad priests. In Italy, the Empire was considered a land of barbarians. Nonetheless, the German soul was seeking to express itself and Albrecht Dürer (1471–1528) emerged from among this pioneering generation as an engraver. The main body of his famous œuvre was created between 1495 and 1519; before then, Dürer had been an engraver in wood in Nuremberg and then in Alsace. He then went to Italy for a long period to study the work of Mantegna, and to the Low Countries to study Van Eyck and Memling; these journeys gave rise to his first copper engravings, which started off very 'Gothic' and then became more aware of naturalism and perspective. Dürer was sustained by a deep sense of religion which enabled him later on to arrive at a very full understanding of the Reformation. His contemporaries may have found his well-defined landscapes and the originality of his shading more seductive but, in terms of the search for a renewed spirituality, his *Apocalypse* of 1498 and his *Saint Jerome* portray the mounting

Florence, the Piazza della Signoria, where Savonarola is led to the stake. The picture shows the condemnation being read to the kneeling prisoners, who are then led along a ramp to the stake, and are finally hanged and burnt. (*The Martyrdom of Savonarola*, fifteenth century; Florence, San Marco Museum.)

anguish of the Christian people. We have now reached the stage at which this anguish exploded.

The final explosion

The crimes which covered the world reopened the wounds of Christ; since war and the plague had started up again around 1420 and 1430, not a single soul had entered Paradise. The faithful were tormented not by the Schism, nor even by the unworthiness of their pontiffs or the inadequacy of their priests, but by their fear of the Turks, the well-deserved punishment sent by God, and of dying unshriven. In former times the poor had been consoled by the belief that their hunger and pains would earn them salvation, but this no longer applied in a world where the enormity of the risks affected all social classes from every side. It was on the contrary in the most backward parts of Europe, those most affected by disasters, by the silver famine or simply by famine, that the fear was at its strongest. Their anguish echoes through their songs (the *dies irae* dates from the mid thirteenth century) and through their art: Dürer's *Apocalypse*, Grünewald's bloody *Crucifixion*. No artist rendered this madness and hideous fear better than Jerome Bosch (obit 1516); his *Last Judgement* mingles prehistoric fantasms, pagan myths and witchcraft in a hallucina-

511

This portrait of Luther was painted by his friend Cranach in 1533, when Luther was fifty. The painter however has shown him as a young monk, inspired by the liberating truth he found in the Bible. (Nuremberg, Germanisches National Museum.)

tory swarm of monsters, of hybrid shapes, or delirious half-macabre and half-erotic scenes of tortured, grimacing, infirm beings – sinister caricatures of all human anguish.

What could be expected of the learned and civil humanists who lectured in front of *Il Magnifico* or meditated in their studies? Consolation could only come from cooperation, the union of the most threatened elements, and this did indeed provide a proletarian dimension to the spirit of the Reformation. Or else each person would have to look inwards for strength to justify his faith by his works and, in order to perform these better, to study those Scriptures, purer versions of which had been produced by the scholars, and translations of which by the printers. This being the case, did not the body of the faithful consider itself capable of exercising its own priesthood without intermediaries? It could be replied that these were clerkish or learned reasonings, but why should the anguished people not understand from the many signs that they had to take their fate into their own hands?

Exalted pious figures invited them to do so; at Notre Dame in Paris 1484 and 1491, *illuminati* interrupted the Mass and broke the chalices and trod the hosts underfoot; in 1499 at Toulouse and in 1510 in Berry, lay militias beat up unworthy priests and hooted at their bishops. A rabble-raiser emerged in Florence after Lorenzo's death called Girolamo Savonarola, an eloquent Dominican who proclaimed Christ the King there in 1494. For the next three years the town was terrorised by a dictatorship of virtue, which failed to relieve poverty. Nonetheless the Friar's apocalyptic vision presaging the fall of the Antichrist Borgia and the end of the Church seduced the crowds and many scholars, until the excommunicated, attacked and abandoned Savonarola was burnt in Florence in 1498. Luther was fifteen at the time.

A drawing of a stag's head by Albrecht Dürer.

Dürer gave Germany a means of self-expression. It was not enough; the ills afflicting Christendom there assumed that roughness and straightforwardness which has always characterised German spirituality. The recourse to humanism was scarce and here, more than elsewhere, the estrangement of the Church was felt, which, by breaking with scholasticism, had lost touch with the religious experiences and the aspirations of faith, which were so intensely felt in the Low Countries and the Rhineland. The abuses of contemporary practices crystallised a deeper discontent; even a ruler of commendable merit like Frederick Elector of Saxony collected 17,143 relics, thanks to which he secured many years of Indulgence for himself. The townsfolk who talked and the peasants who didn't were all exhausted by sieges, alarms and epidemics. Something had to be done.

Martin Luther was brought up in a modest social milieu; he was lucky to be given a place in an Augustinian monastery in Saxony in 1505, but this severely moral man with his horror of sensuality was shattered by what he saw on a business journey to Rome. He threw himself into the study of the Epistles of Saint Paul and the Bible. His brutal ardour and burning instinct convinced him that salvation was justified by faith alone and that the priesthood belonged to all believers, and that the material goods of the Church hierarchy were the works of the Devil. A turbulent and stubborn spirit, he ignored all counsels of prudence. The failure of the synod of 1517 decided him; In October of that year he presented his ninety-five theses at Wittenberg, which brutally exposed the slow accumulation of sediment from over a hundred years in Italy and elsewhere. Cardinal Cajetan rejected his pretensions, which were on the whole familiar to him as a humanist, but whose expression had been restricted to an elite. Luther persisted. He was summoned to appear in Rome in August 1518 but a compromise appeared possible. Luther held out. In June 1519, Charles of Spain was elected Emperor of the Holy Roman Empire under conditions which dishonoured the whole of Christendom; Brother Martin could step out freely. He broke with Rome that very month, denying the Pope all temporal power; he appealed to the General Council, calling on all Christians to revolt.

This time, a decisive turning point had been reached; this was no Savonarola or Huss to be swept aside. In less than six or seven years, the whole of Europe had exploded, bringing down with her the shadow of the Middle Ages.

General conclusion

When did the Middle Ages end? There was no clean break. Could anyone tell at a glance the difference between a Parisian worker in Louis XI's time and his grandson in Francis I's, or between the Pragmatic Sanction and the Concordat of 1516, between Uccello and Da Vinci, between the Constable of Saint-Pol and that of Bourbon, between Jacques Cœur's businesses and those of Jakob Függer? It was at the very most a matter of size. Worse still, much later on, for instance when nobody would suggest that the Middle Ages were still extant, around say 1580 or 1600, one can see in the clear light of day structural elements and motives which historical laziness does not fail to call 'Renascent': a systematic rationalism, an exaggerated individualism, an ardent cult of inwardness. But alongside all these 'Gothic' after-effects, there were also formal social practices, a cult of royalty and a mysticism scornful of all things new. What about two-faced problems such as the 'democratic' leanings of the general convocations, and the birth of nationalism; were they medieval or modern? As for the sempiternal and irresistible rise of the bourgeoisie, a real Jacob's ladder, it probably climbed the first rungs in Hammurabi's time, thousands of years ago.

Let us take the long-term view. The Europe of the cathedrals, whose weaknesses and shadows are known to us, began to cast its slough in the second half of the thirteenth century. The first signs could already be seen in the 'good time of Monseigneur Saint Louis'; of the collapse of the seigneurial structure here, of a technological levelling-off there, and elsewhere, of relative over-population, of spiritual distress, of social differentiation among the propertied members of society, and of growing poverty among the humblest. We tried to sort out the premises of the crisis of feudalism in the preceding pages. If 1230–60 was the high point of the medieval world, it would be logical to stop there. That is one solution, like stopping Roman history at the death of Marcus Aurelius, since all the rest is mere decline and fall, autumnal and dark. But in the same way as late Antiquity managed to make something new out of old materials, so was the fourteenth century medieval. We have discussed its intellectual brilliance, its affective wealth, its powerful hopes, and in spite of its black coinage, the Plague and the wars, its successes and innovations. Radical in its behaviour and its solutions, and often even revolutionary, Michelet's 'great century' wanted to simplify, unite and decide. It also raised problems which it could not resolve; it

515

moved towards individualism and criticism, it repulsed and even destroyed the limitations of tradition; it established the plurality of truths while anticipating that of worlds and it gave the authorities' arguments a good shaking. But when it came to its end around 1410–20 nothing had been solved. The period which came after indulged more in daydreams than actions, amassing information rather than inventing. There is nothing in the fifteenth century which can provide us with a satisfactory break; all the factors which might have served extend beyond this century. Neither Huss, nor Gutenberg, nor Columbus can stop us, since they are but links, symbols, or at best effects. We have to sweep these chimeras aside and penetrate boldly into the sixteenth century, its first two or three decades at least, because here we can be sure that new energies were released. So here I pause; in 1519 Cortez landed, Magellan set out, Charles V was elected and Luther revolted; in 1525 Eldorado was found, Albuquerque blocked the Red Sea, Rome was sacked, and the Peasants made war – some of these events still belonged to the Middle Ages, and others were modern. Hence our problem.

The most surprising was yet to come; America was the daughter of the Middle Ages, but mother of modernity. Her name was soon to mean power and riches, because she was to support Europe while giving herself up to her. Islam, lost in the splendours of the Golconda (Hyderabad), was gradually subsiding before being preyed on in her turn. Suleyman carried out his campaigns along the Danube, but did they really believe then, and do we now, that he could threaten the fate of a Europe now grown to maturity? Blocked in Europe, repulsed in the Mediterranean, deflected in Asia, thwarted in Africa, Islam was to remain on the defensive for a long time to come. Africa, scarcely penetrated, was put up for sale and depleted person by person. Asia was in a better position in spite of the Portuguese, the Jesuits and especially the Russians, who crossed the Urals every hunting season pursuing ermine and bear across a still inviolate Siberia. In fact, China seemed just as capable of expansion as Europe but all her attempts were cut short or else were not properly exploited; she remained a world apart. Under these conditions, once 1520 was past, the world had but one centre capable of absorbing the wealth of the nations. Europe had taken four centuries to achieve this level and was to maintain it for the next four.

The end of an ordered world

Historians in search of 'periods' run into a danger: words, which can mean something different to the sense in which they are used in relation to the past. What is the point of refusing to attribute the birth of Capitalism to modern times (because the economic mechanisms of that mode of production were present among the Italian merchants from the thirteenth century onwards) when one does not take the trouble to spell out the power relationships, as opposed to just the economic structures, implicit in the term? In the same way, I have been careful to voice my reservations – to say the least – about using the term 'feudalism' to describe the Middle Ages.

I want to apply the same remarks to the notion of the ordered hierarchical society. Since the tenth and eleventh centuries, when this doctrine was formulated, until the fifteenth,

The three great representatives of absolute monarchy; Henry VIII (1491–1547) by Holbein the Younger (Windsor, Royal Gallery); Francis I (1494–1547) by Jean Clouet (Paris, Louvre); Charles V (1500–58) by Titian, (Munich, Alte Pinakothek.)

when its demolition was apparent to all, the Middle Ages – certainly the clergy and the dominant element and perhaps the rest of them (by force of hearing it constantly promulgated) – voluntarily erased the idea of classes in favour of that of God-given social orders. Theirs was of course an imaginary society, which could not prevent collisions, rivalries and conflict, but one which assigned to each member his role in a harmony, which was presumed to exist by general consent. Can it seriously be maintained that men still adhered to such an arrangement by the time of the Counter-Reformation, of absolute monarchy, or the Enlightenment? It was quite natural that the handful of men of letters and men of the Church who had dominated the rest of society, should have continued to claim and maybe to believe (though I doubt it) that this was still the case. But not to see that the peasant rebellions, the religious outbreaks, the parliamentary demands, the exploita-

517

tions of the 'colonial pact', were signs of class struggle and negated the concept of the ordered society is to recoil from particular words.

To return to the moment when the Middle Ages of the 'orders' was moving on. The fine construction in which everyone was supposed to find his place was in ruins, and in the towns the growth of wage-labour, of closed guilds, together with the risks of stagnation and the rocketing prices, had caused the relationship between masters and apprentices to deteriorate from grumbling to rioting. The problem of the workforce, backed by the marginals who were prompt to make trouble, preoccupied the employers whose systematic search for profit, formerly reserved for only a handful of merchants, had become their golden rule. 'Good merchandise' disappeared along with the common profit. In the countryside the crisis which had shaken the seigneurial world was only surmounted, and not everywhere, at the price of abandoning the reciprocal relationships of the past. The guarantees which the lord had implemented had collapsed along with his military and judicial roles. Brute force was revealed divested of its trappings. Although one can describe the explosions which shook the peasant strata after the flare-up of 1525 as mere *fureurs*, fleeting rages, the order of the *laboratores* was no less negated.

As for the warrior order, devoid of its function as defender of the Christian people and as depository of power and justice – where was it? At one end of the chain, a few rulers who were no more than small-time monarchs; the Electors of the Empire, the Dukes of Milan and Anjou, the English Marcher Lords, the Grandees of Castile and Aragon, and at the other were the half-starved *hobereaux* and petty squires, hanging onto a few external symbols of prestige which ensured that caps were still doffed to them, but whose chief and nagging worry was storing up enough to get them through the winter. Between the two came the tame nobility which the kings filled with new men who smacked of goose quills and mutton fat, who had no contact with those who had been 'their men' beyond that supplied by their intendant, or a farmer's accounts, or by a brief visit between two court sessions or two royal journeys, journeys which they followed in search of pensions, offices or intrigues. On the surface of this clientele in the style of Antiquity – and for once the word 'Renaissance' applies – a few 'Gothic' trimmings still floated: the Orders of Chivalry, late avatars of the *miles christi*; *gentilezza*, bastard daughter of *courtoisie* and civic virtue; the refusal to work as an ignoble derogation – because for a long time now, pretensions like drinking wine, riding a horse, wearing a beribboned costume and despising clod-hoppers had not been the attributes just of the nobility.

Anyway, let's bury the ordered society before 1500 without further argument, since it was then that the monster was born which took over from the Divine Plan and arranged the social classes as it liked. This was the State, that of Kings, princes and the free German and Italian towns and even of the Holy See. I hear those nostalgic for Antiquity protesting, and rightly so, since a Roman reflection did play on the face of this medieval child. I also hear those who extol Charlemagne complaining that such a notion was still confined to the dozen clerics who mulled over it among themselves, and even the commentators of John of Salisbury, Pierre Dubois, Philip of Mézières and Marsilius of Padua, are cavilling, but did they not strive to emulate these pioneers in the sixteenth century? The idea of the State

The political and administrative machinery of the modern State is already there; these are the king's notaries and secretaries. (Ms. 5169; Paris, Bibliothèque de l'Arsenal.)

belongs to all ages, but it only matters when it takes over the armed forces, taxation, justice, gets involved with the guilds, controls the finances and the regulations of groups in which men thought they were safe; the communes, guilds, and fraternities. The emergence of this single ruling body necessarily annuls all the functions, which have devolved on one or another order in society. Of course, any student of politics could demonstrate that there is no State prototype and that between the Theocratic Empire and the Parliamentary

519

Republic all stages of political development are possible. As it was, the fifteenth century did hesitate between two different ways, as it did in all fields. The Conciliar principle at Constance and Basle, the Provincial Councils in the Burgundian States, the Cortes in Spain and the English Parliament, and the autonomous German *Stände* disputed the Kings', the Emperor's and the Pope's power. But after 1460 or 1470, the reaction set in. The privileged bodies were no longer more than bodies of privileged persons; the hierarchy hardened and absolute power in the Roman manner gradually took over from the 'Gothic' power of the intermediaries. The way chosen was definitely that of absolute monarchy: Charles V, Henry VIII and Francis I all three broached it simultaneously, almost in the same year.

The age of despotism and nations

The Europe of the Pope-Emperor had never been able to control her money or her armed forces and her economy even less. She had found her only remedy in a religion of the ruler, which extended the jurisdiction of the Church, and in a Christian universalist vision; the rest was superfluous. This religious vision was conserved by the people for a long time, well beyond the moment when the Kings had exchanged it for a political vision. This fundamental discordance is one of the mainsprings of modern social history; it was completely lacking in medieval times when the ruler absorbed and represented his subjects. Many humanists tried to bring these two poles closer; Erasmus advised Charles V, More Henry VIII and Budé Francis I. They wanted to enlighten these princes like the *Philosophes* of the eighteenth century would enlighten the despots of their age. Too late! From then on, Latin had been replaced by artillery.

These rulers really were potentates; they controlled the roads, the coinage, the army, the post, and soon the fleet. On them alone depended colonial expeditions, rewards and punishments. Their effigies covered the coinage and monuments and were inscribed on their people's hearts; they were linked with businessmen, bankers and slavers, both as their hostages and their partners. Though the State was King, the King was the Law, and his law was profit. War was no longer a matter of honour – even a King of France would be seen to betray his word to his people's acclaim – and became the monetary, commercial and insidious instrument of ruin for the neighbouring country, a war of tariffs and influence. The economy was no longer the basis of survival but of power: speculation on mulberry trees, the English enclosures, the Iberian *Mesta* and salt monopolies. The Kings were all for it but were the people?

One of the traditional attributes of nineteenth-century historiography, if not of ours, is that of praising these Kings' 'iron fist'. Imbued with Jacobinism or nostalgic for a centralising power which fails to materialise, the historians of France, Germany, Austria, Italy and Spain have long admired those men, around whom fiery furnaces and executioners' blocks put paid to those who dared to think, while the fisc filled its coffers half with coin, half with sweat. These were Kings worthy of the name, restorers of the finances (at what a price), unifiers of the regions (in the service of a mono-culture) founders of empires (too bad for black Africans and red Indians) and finally *ouvriers de la nation*, forgers of the nation. That is the word: the word that the Middle Ages had wanted to contain at the level of university groups or to raise with a capital N to the level of Christendom. Now however, it had spread out over the whole field of the economy dominated by the ruler, because, to start off with at least, the nation had been synonymous with mercantilism and dynastic egoism. When in the nineteenth century factors of language, race and culture were also confused with it, things got much worse. For the moment these nations, our fathers' pride and joy, were in the hands of skilful, calculating and greedy potentates. They got the people to believe that it was forging its own destiny in the defence of its independence, but they did not worry too much about the hatred they were sowing in those first modern furrows.

Thus was medieval Christendom succeeded by the Europe of Kings, preluding that of nations. The collapse was not complete, it is true. Europe's economic and for a while her demographic revival continued to maintain her superiority over other worlds, and these revivals occurred all over. It has even been suggested that, economically speaking, sixteenth-century Europe was more homogeneous and united than in the thirteenth century. The extreme disparity between the price of corn in Poland and Sicily, or between the gold-silver ratio in Lisbon and Bohemia, was slowly reduced. When the silver and gold of America invaded the continent, the global price-rises affected all Europe, the Europe of Kings, even though natural conditions and the level of technology favoured north and north-west Europe, Protestant Europe, while middle and southern Europe, Catholic Europe, was the first to benefit from the fruits of colonisation.

From hope to sorrow

At the dawn of the sixteenth century, and over the next few decades, the Middle Ages, whose reasons for existing died one after another, produced an extraordinary flare of intelligence. First Italy, and then the rest of Europe was filled with new truths; a multitude of brilliant, extravagant, creative minds fermented, driven by an ardent thirst for pleasure, an immense desire to create, a pressing need to push back the limits of knowledge. We have mentioned a hundred of them but they were in their thousands. Everywhere, people spoke of Universal Peace, of Reform, of plurality. The compass of human understanding stretched from Calvin to Lippi, from Cortez to Las Casas. Everything was possible to a Europe freed from her last shackles, about to 'take off': profit, enterprise and individualism replaced good merchandise, custom and the common weal.

A brief moment of extasy and hope, the culminating point of the Middle Ages. After which, no more than two generations passed before catechisms, intolerance, worldly values and elitism were adopted. Religious suspicion rose up from its ashes, fed by civic suspicion, and the mainspring of thought was deviated towards the dreary search for the infinite. Europe was capable of conquering the world but she had missed her entry, just as she is about to miss her exit. After the great surge which had carried the Middle Ages forward and which reached its peak at the beginning of the sixteenth century, followed the obscurantism of modern times. This was the age of the Jesuits, of the Courts, of the slave

General conclusion

The moral prestige of women was weakened in the fourteenth and fifteenth centuries, possibly because they were in the majority. This gave rise to anti-feminist feeling over and above traditional jokes about the deceit and inconstancy of women. This Burgundian water-pourer of the 1400s recalls the misfortunes of the illustrious Aristotle, the master of Medieval thought. The philosopher had scolded Alexander for having neglected his reputation for a woman, and she took her revenge by seducing him in his turn and forcing him to carry her on his back. (New York, The Metropolitan Museum of Art.)

522

trade and of mercantilism, the age of Classicism, as it is called so aberrantly as to leave Medievalists speechless, and indeed anyone who loves or loved the Greek city, the Roman Republic, the 'Enlightenment' or the age of Revolutions. At least the historian of the Middle Ages can console himself in his sorrow with the spectacle, not of our cathedrals or the skeletons of our castles, but that of our villages, our paths; of parcels of land and fields; of the names on our boundaries and of the married couples all around us, and of a popular culture which the progress of the twentieth century has not yet dislodged. The Middle Ages have been on so many levels neither betrayed nor forgotten, nor lost: we are still in them.

Select bibliography

This list does not repeat the titles to be supplied in Volumes I and II unless they are works particularly relevant to the period in question. I refer the reader to the other bibliographies for works of a general nature. On the other hand, given the growing number of books published every year which deal with this final period, I have tried to limit the bibliography to books available in French or English.

WESTERN EUROPE

GENERAL SURVEYS

1. Works dealing with the whole of Western Europe:

Allmand, *The new Cambridge medieval history: volume 7, c. 1415–c. 1500*, Cambridge, 1997.

Allmand, *The hundred years war: England and France at war, c. 1300–c. 1450*, Cambridge, 1988.

Bautier, R. H., *The economic development of medieval Europe*, New York, 1971.

Delumeau, J., *La civilisation de la Renaissance*, Paris, 1967.

Ferguson, W. K., *Europe in transition, 1300–1500*, Boston, 1962.

Hilton, R. H. (ed.), *The transition from feudalism to capitalism*, London, 1976.

Huizinga, J. *The waning of the Middle Ages*, Engl. transl., Harmondsworth, 1976.

Lewis, A. A., 'The closing of the medieval frontier, 1250–1350', in *Speculum*, 1958.

Lopez, R., *The commercial revolution of the Middle Ages 950–1350*, Cambridge, 1971.

Miskimin, H. A., *The economy of early Renaissance Europe, 1300–1460*, Cambridge, 1975.

Wolff, P., *The awakening of Europe*, Engl. trans., Harmondsworth, 1968.

2. Works of a general nature dealing with one country in particular:

Chrimes, S. B., *Fifteenth-century England 1399–1509*. Manchester, 1972.

Gieysztor, A. (et al.), *Histoire de la Pologne*, French transl., Warsaw, 1971.

Jacob, E. F., *The fifteenth century 1399–1485*, Oxford, 1961.

Lewis, P. S., *The recovery of France in the fifteenth century*, Engl. transl., London, 1976.

Luzzatto, G., *Storia economica d'Italia*, London, 1961.

Mackisak, M., *The fourteenth century: 1307–1399*, Oxford, 1961.

Runciman, S., *The Sicilian Vespers: A history of the Mediterranean world in the late thirteenth century*, Cambridge, 1958.

Strayer, J. R., *The reign of Philip the Fair*, Princeton, 1980.
Valdeavellano, L. de., *Historia de España*, Madrid, 3rd. edn, 1964.
Vicens Vives, J., *Historia social y economica de España*, Barcelona, 1957.
Vilar, P., *A brief history of Spain*, Engl. transl., Oxford, 1977.

THE HUMAN AND MATERIAL ENVIRONMENT; THE FAMILY AND EVERYDAY LIFE

1. Man and the natural world:
Alexandre, P., *Le climat au Moyen Age en Belgique*, Louvain, 1976.
Baratier, E., *La démographie provençale du XIIIe au XVIe s.*, Paris, 1961.
Biraben, N., and Le Goff, J., *L'homme et al peste*, 2 vols, Paris, 1976–9.
Klapisch-Zuber, C. and Herlihy, D. *Les Toscans et leurs familles; une étude du Catasto Florentin de 1427*, Paris, 1978.
Leroy-Ladurie, E., *Times of feast, times of famine; a history of climate since the year 1000*, Engl. transl., London, 1982.
Mols, R., *Introduction à la démographie des villes d'Europe du XIVe au XVIIIe s.*, 3 vols, Louvain, 1954–6.
Russell, J. G., *British medieval population*, Albuquerque, 1948.
Titow, J. Z., 'Some evidence of the thirteenth-century population increase', in *Economic History Review*, 1961–2.
Ziegler, P., *The Black Death*, London, 1969.

2. Village houses:
Beresford, M. W., *The lost villages of England*, New York, 1954.
Beresford, M. W. (and St Joseph, J. K. S.), *Medieval England: an aerial survey*, 2nd. edn, Cambridge, 1979.
Chapelot, J. and Fossier, R., *Le village et la maison au Moyen Age*, Paris, 1980.
Demians d'Archimbaud, G., *Les fouilles de Rougiers*, 1980.
Géographie historique du village et de la maison rurale, (Coll. Basas, 1978), 1979.

3. The family group and everyday life:
Ariès, P., *Centuries of childhood*, Engl. transl., New York, 1969.
Boulay, F. R. H. du, *An age of ambition: English society in the late Middle Ages*, London, 1970.
Contamine, P., *War in the Middle Ages*, Engl. transl., Blackwell, 1984.
Contamine, P., *France in the 14th and 15th centuries; people, concepts, war and peace*. Variorum Reprints 1981.
Faral, E., *La vie quotidienne pendant la guerre de Cent Ans en France et en Angleterre*, Paris, 1976.
Heers, J. *Family clans in the Middle Ages; a study of political and social structures in urban areas*, 1978.
Lagarde, G. de, *La naissance de l'esprit laïc au déclin du Moyen Age*, 5 vols, Paris, 1953–62.
Singer, C., *The history of technology*, vol. 1, Oxford, 1954.
White, L., *Medieval technology and social change*, Oxford, 1962.

POWER, STATES AND INSTITUTIONS

1. Power, its nature and exercise:
Autrand, F., *Pouvoir et société en France XIVe–XVe s.*, Paris, 1974.
David, M., *La souveraineté et les limites juridiques du pouvoir monarchique, du IXe au XVe s.*, Paris, 1954.

525

Select bibliography

Folz, R., *L'idée d'Empire en Ocident, Ve–XIVe s.*, Paris, 1953.

Font-Rius, J. M., *Instituciones medievales españolas*, Madrid, 1949.

Guenée, B., 'Etat et nation en France au Moyen Age', in *Revue historique*, 1967.

Lot, F. and Fawtier, R., *Histoire des institutions françaises au Moyen Age*, 3 vols, Paris, 1957–1962.

Marongiu, A., *Storia del diritto publico*, Milan, 1956.

Martinez, L., *City states in Renaissance Italy: power and imagination*, London, 1980.

Mitteis, H., *Der Staat des hohen Mittelalters*, 8th edn, Darmstadt, 1968.

Rubinstein, N., *The government of Florence under the Medicis*, Oxford, 1966.

Strayer, J. R., *Medieval statecraft and the perspective of history*, Princeton, 1971.

Strayer, J. R., *On the medieval origins of the modern state*, Princeton, 1970.

Ullmann, W., *Law and Politics in the Middle Ages*, Cambridge, 1975.

Vaughan, P., *Valois Burgundy*, London, 1975.

2. States and Parliaments:

Favier, J., 'Les légistes et le gouvernement de Philippe le Bel', in *Journal des savants*, 1969.

Fawtier, R., 'Parlement d'Angleterre et Etates généraux de France au Moyen Age', in *comptes rendus de l'Académie des Inscriptions et Belles-Lettres*, 1953.

Marongiu, R., *Medieval parliaments*, London, 1968.

Richardson, H. G., *The English Parliament in the Middle Ages*, London, 1981.

Strayer, J. R., *The reign of Philip the Fair*, Princeton, 1980.

Viala, A., *Le Parlement de Toulouse et l'administration royale laïque, 1420–1525*, 2 vols. Albi, 1953.

3. Financial and economic problems:

Aston, T. H. and Philpin, C. H. E. (eds.), *The Brenner debate: agrarian class structure and economic development in pre-industrial Europe*, Cambridge, 1985.

Braudel, F., 'Economies: precious metals, money and prices', in *The Mediterranean and the Mediterranean World in the Age of Philip II*, vol. I, Engl. transl., London, 1972.

The Cambridge economic history of Europe, vol. 3: Economic organisation and policies in the Middle Ages, Cambridge, 1965.

Favier, J., *Finances et Fiscalité au bas Moyen Age*, Paris, 1970.

Finances et comptabilité urbaines du XIIIe au XVIe s., (Colloquium Blankenberg, 1962), Brussels, 1964.

Fournial, E., *Histoire monétaire de L'Occident mediéval*, Paris, 1970.

Gandilhon, R., *Politique économique de Louis XI*, Rennes, 1941.

L'Impôt dans le cadre de la ville et de l'Etat, (Colloquium Spa, 1964), Brussels, 1966.

Ladero-Quesada, M. A., 'Les finances royales de Castille à la veille des temps modernes', in *Annales ESC*, 1970.

Mate, M., 'High prices in early fourteenth-century England: causes and consequences', *Economic History Review*, xxviii, 1975.

Rey, M., *Les finances royales sous Charles VI*, Paris, 1965.

Roover, R. de, *The Bruges money market around 1400*, Brussels, 1968.

Spufford, P., *Monetary problems and policies in the Burgundian Netherlands, 1433–1496*, Leyden, 1970.

Spufford, P., *Money and its use in medieval Europe*, Cambridge, 1986.

Steel, A., *The receipt of the Exchequer, 1377–1485*. Cambridge, 1954.

THE WORLD OF THE COUNTRYSIDE

1. General works:

Abel, W., *Agrarkrisen und Agrarkonjunktur*, Hamburg, 1966.

Ambrosoli, M., *The wild and the sown: Botany and agriculture in western Europe, 1350–1850*, Cambridge, 1996.

Bader, K. S., *Studien zur Rechtsgeschichte des mittelalterlichen Dorfes*, 2 vols., Cologne, 1957–62.

Bean, J. M. W., *The decline of English feudalism, 1215–1540*, Manchester, 1968.

Duby, G., *Rural economy and country life in the medieval West*, Engl. transl., London, 1968.

Duby, G., *Medieval agriculture 900–1500*, Engl. transl., London, 1969.

Hilton, R. H., *The English peasantry in the later Middle Ages*, Oxford, 1980.

Kosminsky, E. A., 'The evolution of feudal rents in England from the XIIth to the XVth Century', in *Past and Present*, 1955.

Slicher van Bath, B. H., *The agrarian history of Western Europe*, 1963.

Smith, R., *Land, kinship and life-cycle*, Cambridge, 1985.

2. A few aspects of agriculture:

Devèze, M., *La vie de la forêt française au XVIe s.*, Paris, 1961.

Dion, R., *Histoire de la vigne et du vin en France*, Doullens, 1959.

Donkin, R. A. 'Cattle on the estates of medieval Cistercian monasteries', in *Economic History Review*, 1962–3.

Flatrès, P., 'La structure agraire du Devon . . . et les enclôsures des XIIIe et XIVe s.', in *Annales de Bretagne*, 1949.

Fourquin, G., 'Les débuts du fermage: l'exemple de Saint-Denis', in *Etudes Rurales*, 1966.

Hilton, R. H., *The decline of serfdom in medieval England*, Oxford, 1976.

Jones, P. J., 'Per la storia agraria italiana nel Medioevo' in *Rivista storica italiana*, 1964.

Klein, J., *The Mesta*, Cambridge (Mass.), 1920.

Recueil de la société Jean Bodin: La tenure, vols 3 and 4, Brussels, 1938, 1949.

3. Studies of particular regions:

Bean, J. M. W., *The estates of the Percy family, 1416–1537*, London, 1958.

Bois, G., *The crisis of feudalism: economy and society in eastern Normandy c. 1300–1550*, Engl. transl., Cambridge, 1984.

Boutrouche, R., *Seigneurs et paysans du Bordelais pendant la guerre de Cent Ans*, 2nd edn, Paris, 1965.

Charbonnier, P., *La seigneurie en Auvergne*, 2 vols, Clermont-Ferrand, 1980.

Fourquin, G., *Les campagnes de la région parisienne à la fin du Moyen Age*, Paris, 1964.

Génicot, L., *L'économie rurale namuroise au bas Moyen Age*, 3 vols, Louvain, 1943, 1960, 1982.

Hilton, R. H., *The economic development of some Leicestershire estates in the 14th and 15th centuries*, Oxford, 1947.

Le Mené, M., *Campagnes angevines; étude économique 1350–1530*, 2 vols, Paris, 1982.

Le Roy-Ladurie, E., *Montaillou*, Engl. transl., Harmondsworth, 1980.

Miller, R., *The Abbey and bishopric of Ely*, 2nd edn, Cambridge, 1969.

Neveux, H., *Vie et déclin d'une structure agraire; les grains du Cambrésis*, Paris, 1980.

Raftis, J. A., *The economy of the estates of Ramsey Abbey*, Toronto, 1957.

Sivery, G., *Structures agraires et vie rurale dans le Hainaut*, 2 vols, Lille, 1978–80.

Select bibliography

4. Popular movements:

Aston, T. H. and Hilton, R. H., (eds), *The English rising of 1381*, Cambridge, 1984.

Fourquin, G., *The anatomy of popular rebellion in the Middle Ages*, Engl. transl., 1978.

Hilton, R. H., *Bondmen made free*, Oxford, 1977.

Mollat, M. and Wolff, P., *Popular revolutions of the late Middle Ages*, Engl. transl., London, 1973.

TRADE AND THE URBAN WORLD

1. General works:

Braudel, F., *The wheels of commerce*, vol. 2 of *Civilisation and capitalism, XVth–XVIIIth century*, Engl. transl., London, 1983.

Brezzi, G., *I communi medioevale nella storia d'Italia*, 2nd edn, Turin, 1965.

Brezzi, G., *Histoire de la France urbaine*, vol. 1, Paris, 1980.

Recueil de la société de Jean Bodin; la ville, vols. 6 and 7, Brussels, 1954–55.

Roerig, F., *The medieval town*, Engl. transl., New York, 1970.

2. Urban society:

Geremek, B., *Le salariat dans l'artisanat parisien aux XIIIe–XVe s.*, Paris, 1969.

Geremek, B., *The margins of society in late medieval Paris*, Engl. transl., Cambridge, 1987.

Gouron, A., *La réglementation des métiers au Languedoc au Moyen Age*, Geneva, 1958.

Graus, F., 'Au bas Moyen Age: pauvres des villes et pauvres des campagnes', in *Annales ESC*, 1960.

Heers, J., *Parties and political life in the medieval West*, Montreal, 1978.

Le Goff, J., *The town as an agent of civilisation 1200–1500*, Engl. transl., London, 1971.

Maschke, R., 'Continuité sociale et histoire urbaine médiévale', in *Annales ESC*, 1960.

Mollat, M. and Wolff P., *Popular revolutions of the late Middle Ages*, Engl. transl., London, 1973.

Roslanowski, T., *Recherches sur la vie urbaine dans les villes de la moyenne Rhénanie septentrionale, XIe–XVe s.*, Warsaw, 1964.

Verlinden, C., *L'esclavage dans l'Europe méditerranéenne*, 2 vols, Bruges, 1955, 1970.

3. Commerce and merchants:

Abulafia, D., *A Mediterranean emporium: the Catalan kingdom of Majorca*, Cambridge, 1994.

Baratier, E. and Raynaud, R., *Histoire du commerce de Marseille, 1291–1480*, vol. 3, Paris, 1951.

Bautier, R. H., 'Recherches sur les routes de l'Europe médiévale', in *Bulletin philologique et historique*, 1960–1.

Constable, O. R., *Trade and traders in Muslim Spain, the commercial realignment of the Iberian peninsula, 900–1500*, Cambridge, 1994.

De Roover, R., *The Bruges market around 1400*, Brussels, 1968.

De Roover, R., *L'évolution de la lettre de change, XIVe–XVIIIe s.*, 1952.

De Roover, R., *The rise and decline of the Medici bank*, Cambridge (Mass.), 1963.

Dollinger, P., *The German Hansa*, Engl. transl., London, 1970.

Dubois, H., *Les foires de Chalon-sur-Saône et le commerce de la vallée de la Saône*, Paris, 1967.

Hubert, J., *Les routes du Moyen Age (France)*, Paris, 1959.

Le Goff, J., *Marchands et banquiers du Moyen Age*, Paris, 1956.

Power, E., *The wooltrade in English medieval history*, London, 1941.

Renouard, Y., *Les hommes d'affaires italiens au Moyen Age*, 2nd edn, Paris, 1968.

Sapori, A., *The Italian merchant in the Middle Ages*, Engl. transl., New York, 1970.

528

Schulte, A., *Geschichte der grossen Ravensburger Handelsgesellschaft 1380–1530*, Stuttgart and Berlin, 1923.

Stromer, W. von, *Oberdeutsche Hochfinanz 1350–1450, Vierteljahresschrift für Sozial- und Wirtschaffsgeschichte*, Beiheft LV–LVII, 1970.

Wolff, P., *Commerce et marchands de Toulouse (vers 1350–vers 1450)*, Paris, 1952.

4. Studies of towns:

Becker, M. B., *Florence in transition*, 2 vols, Baltimore, 1967–8.

Carrère, C., *Barcelone, centre économique à l'époque des difficultés, 1382–1462*, 2 vols, Paris, 1967.

Favreau, R., *La ville de Poitiers à la fin du Moyen Age*, 2 vols, Paris, 1978.

Hale, J. R., *Florence and the Medici*, 1977.

Heers, J., *Gênes au XVe s.*, Paris, 1961.

Herlihy, D., *Pisa in the early Renaissance; a study of urban growth*, New York, 1973.

Herlihy, D., *Medieval and Renaissance Pistoia*, New Haven, 1967.

Hilton, R., *English and French towns in feudal society: a comparative study*, Cambridge, 1992.

Lane, F. C., *Venice, a maritime Republic*, Baltimore, 1973.

Van Houtte, J. A., *Bruges, essai d'histoire urbaine*, Bruxelles, 1967.

SPIRITUAL AND SCIENTIFIC LIFE

1. The Church and heresy:

Biller, P. and Hudson, A., *Heresy and literacy, 1000–1500*, Cambridge, 1994.

Cohn, N., *The pursuit of the millennium*, London, 1970.

Delaruelle, E., Labande, E. R., Ourliac, P., *L'Eglise au temps du Grand Schisme et la crise conciliaire, 1378–1449 (Histoire de l'Eglise, vol. 14)* Paris, 1962.

De Vooght, P., *L'hérésie de Jean Hus*, 2 vols, 2nd edn, Louvain, 1975.

Gill, G., *Constance et Bâle-Florence*, Paris, 1965.

Leff, G., *Heresy in the later Middle Ages*, Manchester, 2 vols, 1967.

Le Roy-Ladurie, E., *Montaillou*, Engl. transl., Harmondsworth, 1980.

Logan, F. D., *Runaway religious in medieval England, c. 1240–1540*, Cambridge, 1996.

Macek, J., *The Hussite movement in Bohemia*, London and Prague, 1965.

MacFarlane, K. B., *John Wycliffe and the beginning of English nonconformity*, London, 1966.

Mollat, G., *The popes at Avignon 1305–1378*, Engl. transl., London, 1963.

Ourliac, P., *Etudes d'histoire de droit médiéval*, Paris, 1979.

Rapp, F., *L'Eglise et la vie religieuse à la fin du Mohen Age*, (Nouvelle Clio no. 25), 2nd edn, 1981.

Renouard, Y., *The Avignon Papacy 1305–1403*, Engl. transl., London, 1970.

Rubin, M., *Corpus Christi: the eucharist in late medieval culture*, Cambridge, 1991.

Swanson, R., *Religion and devotion in Europe, c. 1215–c. 1515*, Cambridge, 1995.

Waugh, S. and Diehl, P., *Christendom and its discontents: exclusion, persecution and rebellion, 1000–1500*, Cambridge, 1996.

2. Mentalities and practices:

Ariès, P., *Western attitudes towards death; from the Middle Ages to the present*, Baltimore, 1974.

Boase, T., *Death in the Middle Ages*, New York, 1972.

Chiffoleau, J., *La comptabilité de l'Au-delà. Les hommes, la mort et la religion (vers 1320–vers 1480)*. Rome, 1980.

529

Select bibliography

Delaruelle, E., *La piété populaire au Moyen Age*, Turin, 1975.

La Mort au Moyen Age (Congress of 1976), Strasbourg, 1977.

Sykes, N., *The crisis of the Reformation*, London, 1946.

3. Teaching and doctrines:

Baldwin, M. W., *Christianity through the thirteenth century*, New York, 1970.

Beaujouan, G., *Ancient and medieval science from prehistory to AD 1450*, Engl. transl., London, 1964.

Bec, C., *Les marchands écrivains: affaires et humanisme à Florence, 1375–1434*, Geneva, 1966.

Black, A., *Political thought in Europe, 1250–1450*, Cambridge, 1992.

Cobban, A. B., *The medieval universities, their development and organisation*, London, 1974.

Crombie, A. C., *Augustine to Galileo; science in the V–XVIII centuries*, 2nd edn, Harmondsworth, 1980.

Dales, R., *The scientific achievement of the Middle Ages*, Philadelphia, 1973.

Daly, L. J., *The medieval university, 1200–1400*, New York, 1961.

Febvre, L. and Martin, H. J., *The coming of the book; the impact of printing*, Engl. transl., London, 1976.

Garin, E., *Italian humanism, philosophy and civic life in the Renaissance*, Engl. transl., Oxford, 1965.

Gille, B., *The Renaissance engineers*, Engl. transl., London, 1966.

Grant, E., *Planets, stars and orbs: the medieval cosmology, 1200–1687*, Cambridge, 1993.

Kieckhefer, R., *Magic in the middle ages*, Cambridge, 1989.

Knowles, D., *The evolution of medieval thought*, London, 1964.

Lagarde, G. de, *La naissance de l'ésprit laïc au déclin du Moyen Age*, 5 vols, Paris, 1956–63.

Leader, D. R., *A history of the University of Cambridge: the University to 1546*, Cambridge, 1989.

Leff, G., *The dissolution of the medieval outlook*, New York, 1976.

Leff, G., *William of Ockham. The metamorphosis of Scholastic discourse*, Manchester, 1975.

Le Goff, J., *Les intellectuels au Moyen Age*, Paris, 1962.

ART AND EXPRESSION

Alazard, J., *The Florentine portrait*, Engl. transl., London, 1948.

Chastel, A., *Italian Art*, Engl. transl., London, 1972.

Chastel, A., *The age of humanism; Europe 1480–1530*, Engl. transl., London, 1966.

Evans, J., *English Art, 1307–1461*, Oxford, 1961.

Mâle, E., *Religious art in France of the thirteenth century: a study in medieval iconography and its sources of inspiration*, Engl. transl., London, 1913. Published as *The Gothic Image*, New York and London, 1972.

Meiss, M., *French painting in the time of Jean de Berry*, 3 vols, London, 1968–74.

Meiss, M., *Painting in Florence and Siena after the Black Death*, Princeton, 1951.

Monnier, P., *Le quattrocento*, Paris, 1901.

Strohm, R., *The rise of European music, 1380–1500*, Cambridge, 1993.

White, T. H., *The birth and rebirth of pictorial space*, London, 1957.

OTHER WORLDS

BYZANTIUM AND THE SLAVS

1. The problems of the Empire in the East:

Ahrweiler, H., *L'idéologie politique de l'empire byzantin*, (Variorum reprints), London, 1974.

Barker, J., *Manuel II Palaeologus, 1391–1426. A study in late Byzantine statesmanship*, New Brunswick, 1969.

Cambridge medieval history, vol. 4, 1996.

Charanis, P., *Social, economic and political life in the Byzantine Empire*, (Variorum reprints), London, 1973.

Diehl, C., *Byzantium, greatness and decline*, New Brunswick, 1957.

Geanakoplos, D., *The Emperor Michael Palaeologus and the West, 1258–82*, Cambridge (Mass.), 1959.

Hendy, M., *Studies in the Byzantine monetary economy c. 300–1450*, Cambridge, 1985.

Kirsten, E., 'Die Byzantinische Stadt', in *Berichte zum XI. internationalen byzantinischen Kongress*, 1958.

Laïou-Thomadakis, A., *Peasant society in the late Byzantine Empire*, Princeton, 1977.

Lemerle, P., 'Recherches sur les institutions judiciaires a l'époque des Paléologues', in *Le Monde de Byzance*, (Variorum reprints), London, 1978.

Nicol, D., *Church and society in the last centuries of Byzantium*, London, 1979.

Nicol, D., *The last centuries of Byzantium, 1261–1453*, 2nd edn, Cambridge 1993.

Nicol, D., *The Byzantine lady: ten portraits, 1250–1500*, Cambridge, 1994.

Ostrogorsky, G., *Agrarian conditions in the Byzantine Empire in the Middle Ages*, (*Cambridge Economic History of Europe*, vol. 1), 1941.

Rodley, L., *Byzantine art and architecture: an introduction*, Cambridge, 1994.

Runciman, S., *The fall of Constantinople, 1453*, Cambridge, 1965.

Tafrali, A., *Thessalonique au XIVe s.*, Paris, 1913.

Vryonis, S., *The question of the Byzantine mines*, (Variorum reprints), London, 1971.

Zakythinos, D., *Crise monétaire et crise économique à Byzance du XIIIe au XVe s.* (Variorum reprints), London, 1973.

2. The problems of the successor states

Balard, M., *La Romanie génoise (XIIe–début XVe s.)* Genoa, 2 vols, 1978.

Ducellier, A., *La façade maritime de l'Albanie au Moyen Age*, Thessalonica, 1981.

Hill, G., *A history of Cyprus*, 4 vols, Cambridge, 1940–52.

Nicol, D. M., *The Despotate of Epiros, 1267–1479*, Cambridge, 1984.

Jacoby, D., *La féodalité en Grèce médiévale; les 'assises de Romanie'*, Paris, 1971.

Jirecek, C., *Geschichte der Serben*, 2 vols, Amsterdam, 1967.

Kalic-Mijuskovic, K., *Belgrade au Moyen Age*, (Summary in French), Belgrade, 1967.

Miller, W., *The Latins in the Levant: a history of Frankish Greece, 1204–1566*, London, 1964.

Oikonomidès, N., *Hommes d'affaires grecs et latins à Constantinople (XIIIe–XVe s.)* Montreal, 1979.

Zakythinos, D., *Le despotat grec de Morée*, (Mariorum reprints), London, 1975.

EASTERN ISLAM

1. The Mamelukes:

Ayalon, D., *Gunpowder and firearms in the Mameluk Kingdom; a challenge to medieval society*, 2nd edn, London, 1978.

Darras, A., *L'Egypte sous le règne de Barsbay*, Damascus, 1961.

Garcin, J. C., *Un centre musulman de la Haute Egypte médiévale; Qûs*, Cairo, 1976.

Heyd, W., *Geschichte des Levantehandels im Mittelalter*, Stuttgart, 1879. (Fr. transl., Amsterdam, 1959).

Hitti, P., *History of Syria*, London, 1951.

Labib, S., *Handelsgeschichte Ägyptens im Spätmittelalter*, Wiesbaden, 1965.

Lane Poole, S., *History of Egypt in the Middle Ages*, 4th edn, London, 1968.

Rabie, H., *The financial system of Egypt (714–1341)*, London, 1972.

Russell, D., *Medieval Cairo*, London, 1962.

Setton, K. M., *The later Crusades, 1189–1311*, Philadelphia, 1962.

Wiet, G., *Baghdad: metropolis of the Abbasid Caliphate*, Oklahoma, 1971.

Wiet, G., *L'Egypte arabe (Histoire de la nation égyptienne, IV)*, Paris, 1937.

2. The Ottomans:

Addison, J. et al., *Suleyman and the Ottoman Empire*, London, 1980.

Allen, W. E. A., *The problems of Turkish power in the sixteenth century*, London, 1963.

Babinger, F., *Mahomet II le Conquérant et son temps*, Paris, 1954.

Beldiceanu, N., *Le timar dans l'état Ottoman (debut XIVe–debut XVIe s.)* Wiesbaden, 1980.

Beldiceanu, N., *Le monde Ottoman des Balkans, 1402–1566* (Variorum reprints), 1976.

Bombaci, A., *Storia della letteratura turca*, Milan, 1956.

Cahen, C., *Pre-Ottoman Turkey*, London, 1968.

Inalcick, H., *Ottoman Empire: conquest, organisation and economy* (Variorum reprints), 1983.

Inalcick, H., *The Ottoman Empire; the classical ages, 1300–1600*, London, 1973.

Jansky, H., 'Die Eroberung Syriens durch Sultan Selim I', in *Mitteilungen zur osmanischen Geschichte*, 1923.

Koprolu, M. F., *Les origines de l'empire ottoman; Studies in Islamic history*, no. 8, reprint, London, 1979.

Merriman, F. B., *Suleiman the Magnificent*, Cambridge (Mass.), 1944.

Minorsjy, V., *La Perse au XVe s., entre la Turquie et Venise*, Paris, 1933.

Pipes, D., *Slave Soldiers and Islam; the Genesis of a Medieval System*, Yale, 1981.

Shaw, S. J., *History of the Ottoman Empire and modern Turkey*, vol. 1, Cambridge, 1976.

Vogt-Göknil, U., *Les mosquées turques*, Zurich, 1953.

Vryonis, S., *The decline of medieval Hellenism in Asia Minor and the process of Islamisation*, Los Angeles, 1976.

Wittek, P., *The rise of the Ottoman Empire*, 2nd edn, London, 1971.

3. The Mongols:

Boyle, J. A., *History of Iran, vol. 5: the Saljuq and Mongol periods*, Cambridge, 1968.

Boyle, J. A., *The Mongol world empire 1206–1379* (Variorum reprints), 1980.

Lemercier-Quelquejay, C., *La paix mongole*, Paris, 1970.

Olschki, L. *Marco Polo's Asia: An introduction to his 'Description of the world' called 'Il milione'*, University of California, 1960.

Saunders, J. J., *The history of the Mongol conquests*, London, 1971.

Spuler, B., *Die Mongolen in Russland; die Goldene Horde*, Wiesbaden, 1958.

Spuler, B., ed., *The Muslim world: a historical survey; vol. 2, The Mongol period*, 2nd edn, Leyden, 1960.

Vladimirtsov, B., *Le régime social des Mongols; le féodalisme nomade*, Paris, 1948.

WESTERN ISLAM AND AFRICA

1. The Maghrib:

Abun-Nasr, J. N., *A history of the Maghrib*, Cambridge, 1971.

Arié, R., *L'Espagne musulmane au temps des Nasrides (1232–1494)*, Paris, 1973.

Dufourcq, C. E., *L'Espagne catalane et le Maghrib aux XIVe et XVe s.*, Paris, 1966.

Hill, D. and Gohin, L., *Islamic architecture in North Africa*, London, 1976.

Julien, C. A., *History of North Africa; Tunisia, Algeria, Morocco, from the Arab conquest to 1830*, Engl. transl., London, 1970.

Ladero-Quesada, M., *Granada, historia de un pais islamico*, Madrid, 1979.

Laroui, A., *The history of the Maghrib; an interpretive essay*, Engl. transl., Princeton, 1977.

Le Tourneau, R., *Fez in the age of the Marinids*, Oklahoma, 1961.

Mantran, R., *North Africa in the 16th and 17th centuries (Cambridge Medieval History of Islam, vol. V)*, 1970.

Marçais, G., *L'architecture musulmane d'Occident*, Paris, 1964.

Messier, R. A., 'The Almoravids: the West African Gulf . . . and the Mediterranean Basin', in *Journal of Economic and Social History of the Orient*, 1974.

Rosenthal, F. J., *Political thought in medieval Islam*, Cambridge, 1958.

Talbi, M., 'Ibn Khaldun et le sens de l'histoire', in *Studia Islamica*, 1967.

Watt, W. M., *A History of Islamic Spain*, Edinburgh, 1965.

2. Black Africa before Islam and Christianity:

The Cambridge History of Africa, vol. III, 1977.

Cissoko, S. M., *Tombouctou et l'empire Songhay*, Dakar, 1975.

Cornevin, E., *Histoire de l'Afrique*, vol. 1, Paris, 1967.

Devisse, J., Robert, D. and S., Vanacker, C., *Tegdaoust; recherches sur Awdaghost*, 2 vols, Paris, 1970–9.

Diop, C. A., *The African origin of civilisation: myth or reality?*, London, 1974.

Fortes, M. and Evan-Pritchard, E. E. (eds), *African political systems*, Oxford, 1966.

Hama, B., *Histoire des Songhay*, Paris, 1968.

Henige, D. P., *The chronology of oral tradition*, Oxford, 1974.

Hunwick, J. O., *Religion and state in the Songhay Empire, 1464–1591*, London, 1966.

Levtzion, N., *Ancient Ghana and Mali*, London, 1973.

Ly, M., *L'empire du Mali*, Dakar, 1977.

Malowist, M., 'The social and economic stability of the West Sudan', in *Past and Present*, 1966.

Miner, H., *The primitive city of Timbuktoo*, N.Y., 1953.

Niane, D. T., *Recherches sur l'empire du Mali au Moyen Age*, Paris, 1975.

Rouch, J., *La religion et la magie songhay*, Paris, 1980.

Shinnie, M., *Ancient African kingdoms*, London, 1966.

Thilmans, G., Descamps, C., Khayat, B., *La protohistoire du Sénégal*, Dakar, 1981.

Tymowski, M. M. 'Le Niger, voie de communication des grands états du Soudan occidental', in *Africana Bulletin*, 1967.

3. Muslim penetration:

Abitbol, M., 'Juifs maghrébins et commerce transaharien du XIIIe au XVe s.', *Mélanges Mauny*, Paris, 1981.

Bovill, E. W., *The golden trade of the Moors*, 2nd edn, Oxford, 1968.

Cahen, C., 'L'or du Soudan avant les Almoravides: mythe ou realité?', in *Mélanges Mauny*, Paris, 1981.

Devisse, J., 'Routes de commerce et échanges en Afrique occidentale . . . aux XIe–XVIe s.', *Revue d'histoire économique et sociale*, 1962.

Levtzion, N., and Hopkins, J. F., *Corpus of early Arabic sources for West African history*, Cambridge, 1981.

Select bibliography

Lewicki, T., *West African food in the Middle Ages*, Cambridge, 1974.

Lewicki, T., *Arabic external sources for the history of Africa to the south of the Sahara*, London, 1974.

Meillassoux, C., *L'esclavage en Afrique avant la traite atlantique*, Paris, 1980.

Triaud, J. L., *Islam et société soudanaise au Moyen Age*, Wagadugu, 1973.

Trimingham, J. S., *A history of Islam in West Africa*, Oxford, 1962.

Wilks, I., 'The transmission of Islamic learning in the Western Sudan', in *Literature in Traditional Societies*, ed. J. Goody, Cambridge, 1968.

4. The Portuguese:

Blake, J. W., *European beginnings in West Africa*, London, 1937.

Chaunu, P., *European expansion in the later Middle Ages*, Engl. transl., Elsevier, 1979.

Diffie, W. V., *The foundations of the Portuguese Empire*, Minneapolis, 1977.

Godhino, V. M., *L'économie de l'empire portugais aux XIVe–XVe s.; l'or et le poivre*, Paris, 1969.

Ricard, R., *Etudes sur l'histoire des Portugais au Maroc*, Coimbra, 1955.

Subrahmanyam, S., *The career and legend of Vasco da Gama*, Cambridge, 1997.

Index

Note: A page number in italic type indicates a text illustration, and P indicates a colour plate.

Index

Index

539

Index

Index

Index

Index

Index

Index